THE ENGLISH IN PORTUGAL

FERNÃO LOPES

The English in Portugal

1367-87

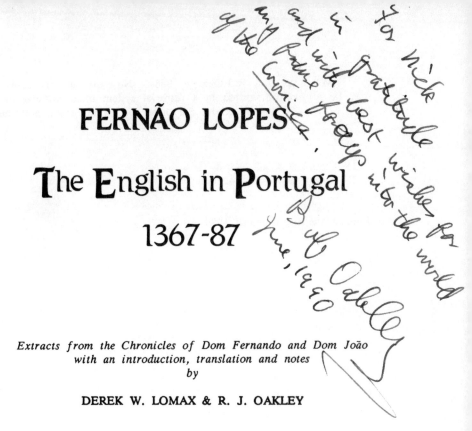

*Extracts from the Chronicles of Dom Fernando and Dom João
with an introduction, translation and notes
by*

DEREK W. LOMAX & R. J. OAKLEY

Aris & Phillips Ltd
Warminster — England

ISBN Cloth   0 85668 341 8
ISBN Limp   0 85668 342 6

Reissued with corrections 1989

The publishers gratefully acknowledge the financial assistance of the Calouste Gulbenkian Foundation with this volume and wish to thank the Imprensa Nacional for the use of the texts of the Crónicas of Fernão Lopes.

Printed and published in England by Aris & Phillips Ltd., Teddington House, Warminster, England.

CONTENTS

FOREWORD

Although Fernão Lopes is one of the greatest chroniclers in medieval Europe, he is relatively little known or read outside his native Portugal, and hardly anything of his writings has been translated into any other language. The present volume contains a selection and translation into English of those chapters of his Chronicle which describe English involvement in Portuguese politics during the late fourteenth century. This subject has already been thoroughly investigated by Professor P.E. Russell in his classic work, *The English Intervention in Spain and Portugal during the Reigns of Edward III and Richard II*; but we hope that those interested will also welcome the opportunity to read the most informative of the primary sources in a convenient form.

This book is not, however, directed solely at lovers of medieval history. We have enjoyed reading Fernão Lopes ourselves, and we think that he will be equally attractive to anyone interested in Portugal and in Anglo—Portuguese relations. The central theme of these chapters is the creation of the longest—lasting alliance in history between any two states, an alliance which the Falklands war showed to be just as vigorous today as ever in the past. This agreement between two states has over the centuries encouraged the growth of a strong friendship between their peoples, which scarcely needs to be described here. If this book contributes to strengthening that friendship, it will not have been written in vain.

That it has been written at all is due in part to the research done by previous scholars, especially Professor Russell, to whose works we owe a significant proportion of the information in this book which is not specifically acknowledged as coming from elsewhere. Otherwise, our thanks are due, and are given most sincerely, to all the friends and colleagues who have helped us, and especially to Patricia Odber de Baubeta, Tom Earle, Laurence Keates, and Lucinda and Adrian Phillips. We alone, of course, are responsible for any errors that may still remain.

INTRODUCTION

1 The Man and his Chronicle

Who is this Portuguese chronicler who relates more closely and vividly than any other both the circumstances in which the Treaty of Windsor came into being and a crucial segment in the life of an important figure in English history of the late fourteenth century — John of Gaunt?

Little is known about the life of Fernão Lopes. Of his private life we know very little indeed, while his date of birth is quite unknown. However, there exist sufficient documents for us to be able to trace the main stages in his career. A royal order of 29 November 1418 refers to him as 'the keeper of our records of the Tombo', indicating that he was the newly appointed keeper of the royal archive, which was housed in the Cartulary Tower (*Torre do Tombo*) of St. George's castle, the citadel of Lisbon. Such a delicate and confidential post would not have been given to a very young man. Therefore, it is reasonable to assume that he was born some time just before or just after 1380. The possibility that he was born slightly earlier than that year has led some readers of Fernão Lopes to the romantic conjecture that he may well have witnessed as a child the dramatic happenings that transpired in Lisbon and Oporto between 1383 and 1387: the Interregnum with its Lisbon rising and the ensuing siege of the city by the armies of Castile; or the celebrations that followed João of Avis's acclamation as King of Portugal and the wedding celebrations two years after that. At the other end of our chronicler's life, a document of 9 August 1458 finds him contesting the claim of a certain Nuno Martins to be his grandson and, therefore, entitled to inherit some of his property; and another document of 3 July 1459 confirms the old man's right to dispose of his goods as he thinks fit, indicating that Fernão Lopes won the dispute, and that he was still alive in that year.

Thus, Fernão Lopes enjoyed both a long life and an extraordinarily successful one. A document issued at his request granting privileges to a relation of his wife informs us that this man was a cobbler. It is conjectured that Fernão Lopes himself may well have come from country stock and that his parents may have been artisans too. The only autograph surviving is the last will and testament of one of João I's younger sons, Prince Fernando, the 'Infante Santo' (Saintly Prince), dated 18 August, 1437. Here, Fernão Lopes signs himself as *tabelião geral* (general notary). Of the office of notary at this time, we know, firstly, that clerics were barred from holding it; and that it was, on the other hand, open to men who had not had a university education. Certainly the evidence of his Chronicle betrays a man of sound but modest education, whose literary and historiographical achievement derives from industry and intelligence, rather than from erudition or vast learning. Fernão

Lopes, then, was almost certainly a man of very humble background who rose to exceptional heights.

This description can be no exaggeration given the surviving documents that relate to his career. In addition to being keeper of the Royal Archive by 1418, in 1422 he is recorded as occupying the post of *escrivão da puridade* (confidential secretary) to Prince Fernando. He was already a royal secretary in 1419 and describes himself as public notary to King João in a document of 1428. In 1434 he is described as royal secretary to the new king, Duarte I. His relationship with Prince Fernando must have been very close indeed, for not only did his son Martinho accompany the saintly prince on his fatal expedition to try and capture Tangier in 1437, but in the Prince's will to which we have referred already, Fernando left to his old retainer the sum of 50,000 *reis* together with a devotional work entitled *Ermo Espiritual* (the Spiritual Desert).

So, Fernão Lopes had reached the top of his profession as well as become a favoured royal secretary and confidant of kings and princes. It is logical that such a man should have bestowed upon him the very special privilege of being made official royal chronicler. We shall never know precisely why he of all people was chosen, although obviously guardianship of the Royal Archive gave him access to many documents that would have been vital to the task; but we do know roughly when he entered upon this task and of what it consisted.

It is certain that the notary and scribe, Fernão Lopes, was commissioned to write a chronicle of all the kings of Portugal from Afonso Henriques (Afonso I), the first king of Portugal, onwards. The precious document informing us of the commission is a letter of 19 March 1434, in which King Duarte, only recently come to the throne, entrusts Fernão Lopes with the task of 'setting down in a chronicle the histories of the kings that had previously reigned in Portugal, right up to, and including, the great and noble deeds of my most able and virtuous father, lord and king; may his soul dwell with God.'

His brief, then, was to carry through the Chronicle right up until his own times in the reign of João I. His royal master, King Duarte, accorded him an annual stipend in order to retain him precisely for this purpose. It is also possible that he was not the first to undertake such a task. As it is, his possible predecessors' writings in the genre have in the main not survived. What have survived are a number of heterogeneous works on some of which he must have drawn. These works, none of which constitutes a substantial part of an enterprise as vast and ambitious as that undertaken by Fernão Lopes, give us some idea of the historiographical precedents for such a chronicle.

The *Chronicon Conimbricense*, dating from around the end of the twelfth century and written in Latin, as its name suggests, was produced in Coimbra, which by then was already an important centre for historical research. Although still influenced by the Roman

tradition of Annals, it gives some account of diverse events in the Reconquest period from Visigothic times up until the reign of Afonso Henriques. Dating from slightly earlier but carrying material that was added in the thirteenth century or even later, the *Chronica Gothorum* and the *Brevis Historia Gothorum* describe in a more chronological fashion details of the Spanish and Portuguese progress in reconquering Iberia from the Muslims. Alongside other brief accounts of the Reconquest, there are extant four *livros de linhagens* (books of noble pedigrees) which narrate in chivalric fashion the deeds of diverse noble families and which the nineteenth—century Portuguese historian, Alexandre Herculano, described as aristocratic registers. Fernão Lopes certainly drew on such literature in order to establish, for example, the genealogy of Dom João's great Constable, Nun'Alvares Pereira, which he tells us (*Dom João*, I, XXXII) he obtained from the *Livro das Linhagens dos Fidalgos* (Book of the Nobles' Pedigrees). The material has certainly been traced to another such work: the *Livro das Linhagens do Conde de Barcelos*. He would certainly have had to hand the great *Crónica Geral de Espanha* (General Chronicle of Spain) of Alfonso the Learned of Castile, which was commissioned by that monarch around 1270, and translated into Portuguese on the orders of King Dinis. Further evidence that Fernão Lopes, although the greatest of Portuguese historians before modern times, is by no means the first, lies in the *Coroniqua de como Dom Payo Corea Mestre de Santiago de Castella tomou este reino do Algarve aos moros*. This dates from the reign of King Dinis and narrates, as the title indicates, the reconquest of the Algarve from the Muslims in the reigns of Sancho II (1223—48) and Afonso III (1248—79); it may perhaps be derived from the lost biography of this heroic Portuguese Master of Santiago. [1]

The total Chronicle of Fernão Lopes would have contained the Lives of ten kings who reigned before King Duarte, beginning with Afonso Henriques, or Afonso I, son of Henri of Burgundy who effectively founded the Burgundian or Alfonsine dynasty in the then County of Portugal when he became Count in 1095. Afonso himself was not recognized as King until 1143. So the reigns Fernão Lopes had to cover were as follows: Afonso I (1143—85); Sancho I (1185—1211); Afonso II (1211—23); Sancho II (1223—48); Afonso III (1248—79); Dinis (1279—1325); Afonso IV (1325—57); Pedro I (1357—67); Fernando I (1367—83); and João I (1385—1433). Although we have accounts dating from the Middle Ages of all these reigns, in the event, what has come down to us as indisputably written by Fernão Lopes is his account of the last three of these reigns: those of Pedro I, Fernando I and João I; and even the last of these is incomplete. Chronicles of the kings of Portugal exist signed by Rui de Pina, one of Fernão Lopes's successors, who was himself the secretary in charge of the Cartulary Tower from 1497, and remained official chronicler until 1522 when he was succeeded by his son. Rui de Pina may or may not have plagiarized the lost

chronicles of Fernão Lopes in order to complete his own cycle of royal Lives. [2]

In the 1940s, two other important manuscripts were discovered which, although they get us no nearer recovering the lost early part of Fernão Lopes's great Chronicle, at least give us a further idea of the historiographical activity of an official or semi—official kind that went on in the late Middle Ages in Portugal. The first of these, discovered in the Municipal Library of Oporto by Artur de Magalhães Basto, is entitled *Crónica dos Cinco Reis* and covers the reigns of the first five kings: Afonso I, Sancho I, Afonso II, Sancho II and Afonso III. The second, called *Crónica dos Sete Reis* (Chronicle of the Seven Kings) was discovered by Father Carlos da Silva Tarouca in the Archive of the Marquess of Cadaval. Both are sixteenth—century manuscripts; and the second, although it contains accounts of the missing two kings, Dinis and Afonso IV, clearly draws on the first as well as on two other chroniclers, Rui de Pina and Duarte Galvão, author of a chronicle of the first of the Portuguese kings, Afonso Henriques. All these fifteenth— or sixteenth—century versions of the royal Chronicle are either dependent upon the lost originals of Fernão Lopes himself, or they draw upon sources which our chronicler may well have used.

As to the principal known sources on which Fernão Lopes drew heavily in order to write the chronicles of the three reigns that we can definitely ascribe to him, one has disappeared and the other two survive. The one that has not survived is the mysterious lost account of events in the reign of João I written in Latin by one Dr. Christopherus, doctor of canon law, and mentioned by Fernão Lopes on several occasions. This is perhaps the most intriguing source of all because it assisted him in writing the *Crónica de Dom João I*, Parts I and II, the longest, and in the opinion of many the greatest, of the three chronicles of Fernão Lopes. The other surviving principal sources are the anonymous *Crónica do Comdestabre* or *Condestável* (Chronicle of the Constable) and the chronicles of the reigns of the Castilian kings Pedro I, Enrique II and Juan I, written in Castilian by King Enrique's Chancellor, Pedro López de Ayala. As the title indicates, the first of these two sources is a Life of Nun'Álvares Pereira, Dom João I's Constable and confidant throughout the troubled times that coincided with and succeeded his rise to power in 1383—5. Its style betrays it to be roughly contemporaneous with the chronicles of Fernão Lopes, and it has even been ascribed to him, although he himself clearly attacks it for unreliability more than once, and on one occasion flatly contradicts it. [3] As for the Chancellor Ayala, he is most important for Fernão Lopes because he lived through the reigns of Pedro I, Enrique II, Juan I and Enrique III (who died in 1406), was very close to the first two of these kings and actually witnessed and took part in the battles of Nájera (1367) and Aljubarrota (1385). [4]

Although the extant Chronicle of Fernão Lopes is a vast work, because he has only been able to bequeath to us his account of the

last three of the ten reigns before the time of writing, while the first of these last three reigns only began in 1357, the span of time that Lopes chronicles is remarkably short. In fact, the period he covers is even shorter than one might suppose, for Fernão Lopes, despite the massive size of his Life of João I (it runs to about a thousand pages), never completed it. The latest historical event he records in the closing chapter of the *Chronicle of Dom João I, Part II* is the peace treaty belatedly signed between Portugal and Castile on 31 October, 1411 (*Dom João*, II, CXCV). The general lack of coherence at the close of Part II of *Dom João* suggests that it was brought to a hurried conclusion; for in fact, he had declared his intention in Part I of relating the Ceuta expedition of 1415. Precisely how and when Fernão Lopes put down his pen for ever, we may never know. Certainly, in 1449, he was still engaged on his great work because in a letter dated 11 January, 1449, Afonso V conceded to the chronicler 'in return for the great labours in which he has engaged as well as those that are to come, to wit, the setting down in a chronicle of the deeds of the kings of Portugal, the sum of 500 *reis* monthly for the rest of his life.' This was, of course, the year in which the civil war between Afonso and his brother Pedro came to an end, to which we shall have occasion to return in our final section. We know that Fernão Lopes was succeeded by Gomes Eanes de Zurara as keeper of the Royal Archive in the Tombo Tower on 6 June 1454, and as royal chronicler some two years earlier. In the document of 1454, Afonso V explains that his faithful servant has been superseded 'por ser ja tam velho e flaco que per ssy nom pode beem servir o dito officio' (on account of the fact that he is now so old and frail that he is no longer equal to the task).

Although Zurara may well have utilized material left by Lopes, it is to his credit that he made no attempt to pass off as his own that part of the Chronicle of the kings of Portugal that Lopes had already written, as appears to have happened in the time of Rui de Pina. Instead, at the opening of his continuation of the *Chronicle of Dom João I*, which constitutes Part III of this royal Life, Zurara generously acknowledged the achievement of his predecessor, explaining that the portion already written was set down by 'Fernão Lopes, homee de comunal ciencia e grande authoridade' (Fernão Lopes, a man of down−to−earth knowledge and considerable authority). He then resumed the *Chronicle of Dom João I* at the point at which Lopes broke off: that is to say, shortly before the expedition to Ceuta (1415). He went on to complete the third part which is appropriately entitled *Crónica da Tomada de Ceuta* (Chronicle of the Capture of Ceuta). As we shall see, the respect accorded to Fernão Lopes by the aristocratic Zurara clashed strikingly with the evident disdain, or at least, indifference, with which the humble notary's writings were treated thereafter; that is, until his name was rescued from virtual oblivion by the admirable humanist and chronicler of the Portuguese Renaissance, Damião de Góis (1502−71). In his chronicle of Manuel

I, the Fortunate, Damião de Góis distinguishes Fernão Lopes's three royal Lives from the rest, separating out that part of the entire Chronicle written by Lopes from the rest, which he felt had been re—written and appropriated by other chroniclers, declaring what a great debt the Portuguese nation owed to our chronicler. By 1799, the poet Francisco Dias Gomes could write that Fernão Lopes was 'pai da prosa portuguesa e o primeiro talvez que na Europa escreveu a história dignamente' (the father of Portuguese prose and perhaps the first person in Europe to write history as it should be written). This is a big claim, but one that several commentators in recent times have sought to sustain. English readers of the *Crónica* can judge for themselves, but clearly, one cannot begin to examine the justice of this claim without some idea of the historical moment to which Fernão Lopes specifically addressed himself.

2   The Historical Context of the Chronicle

To understand the events which Fernão Lopes has chosen to relate in his Chronicle, it is necessary to know something of European history in the century about which he was writing. Although the phrase 'the fourteenth—century crisis' has become rather hackneyed, it remains true that the century of the Black Death (1348—50) was considerably more unstable in almost all of Western Europe than the thirteenth. This was true at all social levels, but especially at the highest, in the Papacy and the great monarchical dynasties. Succession disputes had been almost unknown in the thirteenth century, when eldest sons had always succeeded their fathers on the thrones of France and England, when the normal rules of succession had almost always been accepted in the Iberian kingdoms of Portugal, Castile, Aragon and Navarre, and when no Pope had had to face the challenge of a rival anti—Pope. In the fourteenth century, however, each of these institutions in turn faced a disputed succession, in which determined supporters of rival candidates fought each other in lengthy and savage civil wars.

a)   The French Succession [5]
The first such dispute occurred in France, where King Charles IV died in 1328 leaving no son to succeed him. The throne was claimed by his nephew, Edward, Duke of Gascony and King of England, and by his cousin, Philippe, Count of Valois; and although the latter was recognized by the leading nobles and proceeded to take control of most of France, as King Philippe VI (1328—50), his rival began a war for the French throne which was to last for many decades and be entitled 'The Hundred Years' War'. Indeed, Edward III's descendants would bear the title 'King of France' until 1800.

Naturally the war, although between rival candidates to the French throne, incorporated other quarrels and other motives. As Duke of Gascony, Edward resented his subordination to the French

Crown, and the continual encroachments of its officials within his duchy; it would benefit the English wool interests if Flanders were freed from French control and linked with England; and, most important of all, war in France became very profitable for the English nobility and indeed for all Englishmen who went to fight and plunder there. 'All threw themselves with zest into the business of plundering the French, which, indeed, was one of the major objectives of the war.' Army pay was high, as even a man−at−arms would be paid thirty times as much as a ploughman; and this, plus booty, ransoms of captives and every conceivable sort of valuable taken from prisoners, from rich churches and even from the poorest of non−combatant peasants, all helped to enrich the English marauders, and to make some of them very wealthy indeed. By 1350 the war had turned into a series of plundering expeditions: an English army would land in, say, Bordeaux, ravage through Languedoc and central France and then return to base with few territorial gains but a fortune in booty and, especially, ransom−money. Thus the ransom of King Jean II, captured at Poitiers (1356), was fixed at £500,000, and Du Guesclin, captured at Nájera (1367) was sold for £1483. 6s. 4d.

The war was not, in theory, continuous, and there were numerous truces, some of which lasted for several years. However, English soldiers did not necessarily return home during those periods. Many continued to pillage towns and villages, to fight against anyone daring to resist them and to function as bands of mercenaries, ready to hire themselves to the highest bidder or to operate on their own behalf as little more than well−organized bandits. What distinguished their bands, the so−called 'Free Companies', from those of normal bandits was their size, their military training and organization, and their leaders − often knights who had aspirations to chivalry as well as to profit, and who had learned their often considerable skills under the tuition of Edward III himself or his son, Edward the Black Prince. Of course, not all the Companies were English. Some were French, or Gascon, or Spanish, or a mixture of nationalities. Yet their cumulative effect on France was to complement the devastation caused by the official English expeditions and to turn most of the French provinces into permanent disaster areas.

It was not clear how the Valois kings could solve this problem. England had only a small population of some three millions as against France's twelve, but it was far better organized and its leaders had developed a new tactic and a new weapon. The latter was the long−bow, which constant practice from their youth trained almost all Englishmen to use with devastating effect. The new tactic adopted by Edward III consisted in provoking the enemy into a pitched battle in which he would make a massed cavalry charge, of the sort which had usually won battles in previous centuries; in contrast, the English knights and men−at−arms would send their horses to the rear and form a block of men, ready to fight on foot and to resist the enemy charge, whilst on the English wings their archers, protected by stakes

or wagons, would pour showers of arrows on to the hostile cavalry. The combination of the excellent archery and the steadfastness of the dismounted knights and men—at—arms was to give England victory at Crécy and in many other battles, but it was a surprisingly long time before it was understood by her enemies.

Such victories gave the English a higher morale and a far more united attitude to the war than their enemies. Indeed, profitable warfare in France under a successful warrior—king was the most effective means of unifying English society; without it the English would turn to civil wars as they did under Edward II, Richard II and Henry VI. Above all, along France's Atlantic coast from Calais to Bayonne, England had ports where its marauding armies could land safely and set out on their raids; and if the English king's own ships were few, he could commandeer and arm enough merchant—ships to control the Channel, once the French fleet had been destroyed at the battle of Sluys (1340).

In contrast, the Valois kings had few important Atlantic ports, since Britanny was given over to civil war after 1341, and Normandy was partly in the hands of Carlos the Bad, the treacherous King of Navarre. Attempts were made to rebuild the French fleet, but it was never able to defeat the English by itself, or even to stop them from crossing the Channel whenever they wished. Thus it was vital for France to find an ally with a better fleet than the English, and it looked for this ally in Castile.

b) The Castilian Succession [6]

As Angus MacKay has pointed out, in point of fact, the nine Castilian reigns from 1295 to 1504 were all affected to a greater or lesser extent by power crises produced either by a royal minority or by a disputed succession; [7] but it is also true that the civil war of the mid—fourteenth century in the reign of Pedro I was the longest, the most destructive and also the most important in its consequences for the politics of Castile as well as for the long—term repercussions it had on the neighbouring kingdom of Portugal.

Castile had been totally indifferent to European politics and absorbed by the reconquest of southern Spain from the Moslems until its greatest king, St. Fernando III (1217—52), conquered Córdoba, Murcia, Jaén and Seville, and turned the surviving Moslem kingdom of Granada into a vassal state. His son, Alfonso X, 'the Learned' (1252—84) was the first Castilian monarch to intervene seriously in extra—Peninsular affairs, as he tried, though in vain, to use the wealth and victorious army which he had inherited to make himself Holy Roman Emperor. The concomitant misgovernment and neglect of Castile led to a recapture of beach—heads in southern Spain by the Moors; and in the resistance to the latter his eldest son, Fernando de la Cerda, died, and his second son, Sancho 'the Wild', led the Castilian armies. Though Fernando's eldest son ought theoretically to have succeeded his grandfather, resistance to the new Moorish

invasions needed an adult leader, and Sancho insisted on being recognized as his father's heir, thus depriving his nephew of the throne. Alfonso was reluctant to accept this, and in 1282 Sancho led a revolution of the nobles and cities, who were in any case discontented with Alfonso's erratic government and centralizing policies. Sancho ruled most of Castile as heir—regent until his father died and he was crowned king as Sancho IV (1284—95). He and his immediate successors had to confront four problems: the renewed Moorish invasions; the claims of the Cerda princes to the throne; the encroachments on Castile of the rival Christian kings of Portugal and Aragon, often in nominal support of the Cerda princes and sometimes planning the total partition of the Castilian kingdom created by St. Fernando; and finally the royal minorities of Fernando IV (1295—1312) and Alfonso XI (1312—50), which lasted for six and thirteen years respectively and gave the kingdom over to private warfare and brigandage.

By 1325, when Alfonso XI began to rule on his own behalf, the Cerda claims had been abandoned (though they would be recalled in 1386, as Fernão Lopes relates), and Aragon and Portugal had been bought off with strips of Castilian territory, thus stimulating their appetite for more (as Lopes also shows). Alfonso spent the next twenty—five years suppressing rebellions, building up royal authority and leading his formerly rebellious barons to glorious and profitable victories over Morocco and Granada, rather as Edward III was doing in France, the English Granada. He also built up the Castilian navy, which had been founded by St. Fernando on the basis of his numerous Atlantic ports from Galicia to the Gascon border. Further strength was added later by Seville, a great ship—building centre, and the Mediterranean naval base of Cartagena. Alfonso reinforced all this by importing Genoese sea—captains and by hiring Genoese and other foreign galleys. Thus by 1340, the year of Sluys and also of Alfonso's victory on the River Salado whereby he ended forever the African invasions of the Peninsula, the Castilian navy was probably the strongest in Western Europe, and the only one capable of hampering English crossings of the Channel.

Naturally, the Valois kings tried to make an alliance with Alfonso that would bring his fleet into the war against England and defend France against ever more frequent and more destructive English raids. Naturally, Alfonso refused to take part in a war in which no Castilian interests were involved, and kept Castile neutral until his death. His successor and only surviving legitimate son, Pedro I 'the Cruel' (1350—69) at first seemed to offer France more hope as he agreed to marry a French princess, Blanche de Bourbon, in return for an enormous cash payment; but the foolish King Jean II did not pay the dowry, and Pedro totally abandoned his bride shortly after the wedding. He lived instead with the Castilian noblewoman, María de Padilla, who bore him four children, Beatriz (1353), Constanza (1354), Isabel (1355) and Alfonso (1359—62); and these were accepted as his

legitimate heirs by the Castilian Cortes when Pedro declared in 1362 that he had been secretly married to María de Padilla even before his wedding to Blanche.

The whole affair left Castile further than ever from a French alliance. Indeed, in 1362 Pedro made an alliance with England, whereby he was promised English military assistance against rebels or against the French, without having to offer in return the naval assistance which he could have provided but which England did not need. Castilian neutrality was the policy both of Pedro and of England, and an Anglo — Castilian alliance was merely an extra guarantee for Edward III that the Castilian navy would not be used on France's side.

In contrast, Pedro thought that he might need English help. Although he wished to continue his father's policy of increasing royal power, he had neither the character nor the talents to do so. A homicidal psychopath with a persecution complex, he was incapable of inspiring and leading his barons in, say, a war against Granada, and, too inflexible to deal with them in political terms, he could answer their discontents only by slaughtering them out of hand. The chasm between his personality and the demands of fourteenth — century kingship would be demonstrated by his conversation with the Black Prince (*Dom Fernando*, XI): not only was he incapable of manipulating the rather simple — minded Edward, but he could not even accept his commonsense advice. This situation was the more ominous because he had four ambitious and powerful half — brothers, the illegitimate children of Alfonso XI by his mistress, Leonor de Guzmán: Enrique, Tello, Fadrique and Sancho. The leader was Enrique, Count of Trastámara, who had been born one year before Pedro in 1332, and who would clearly have inherited their father's throne, had his parents been married (as, occasionally, he claimed they were). Enrique led various plots of discontented nobles against Pedro, from the beginning of his reign, and was soon planning to displace him; driven into exile, he served King Pedro IV of Aragon against Castile from 1356 to 1361, and then fled into Languedoc.

Once there, he attached himself to Arnaut d'Audrehem, the Marshal of France, and the great Valois — Trastámara master — plan began to take shape. The Valois had no hope of using the Castilian navy against England so long as Pedro I were king; moreover they wanted to remove as many of the Free Companies from French soil as possible. What better than to finance an expedition of the Companies to Castile, in order to dethrone Pedro and replace him by a grateful Enrique, who would then pay his debt by sending the Castilian navy to fight against England? Pedro IV of Aragon would approve, since it would remove Pedro the Cruel, the chief threat to his own kingdom, and perhaps reward him with some Castilian border — towns. The Papacy would approve, since it wished to end the savage warfare in France; moreover, Pedro the Cruel's rule was harsh and vindictive even by the standards of the day, and certainly by

those of Edward III or Jean II, so that his overthrow would cause no distress in the Papal Court. The only losers would be Pedro himself, his supporters in Castile and, of course, England, though Edward III seemed to have only a hazy comprehension of this fact.

King Jean II approved the plan in principle on 7 July 1362, but the slowness of negotiations with Aragon, Navarre and the Companies, and other obstacles meant that it was not until March 1366 that Enrique led his mercenary army into Castile and had himself proclaimed king in Calahorra. He had no difficulty in conquering the rest of the kingdom, as Pedro fled to Portugal and then to Gascony. Most of the nobility were delighted to see the end of Pedro's tyranny and welcomed Enrique as a liberator; there is no reason to suppose that the majority of the population did otherwise, although there were clearly large groups who remained loyal to Pedro, especially in Andalusia and Galicia.

Meanwhile, in Gascony, Pedro persuaded the Black Prince to restore him to his throne. How the Prince did so, by leading an Anglo−Gascon army and some of the Free Companies to Nájera, defeating Enrique there by using the tactics which Edward III had developed for the Anglo−French wars, and then restoring Pedro to power in Burgos (1367), is told clearly by Fernão Lopes (*Dom Fernando*, I−XIII). It was obviously in England's strategic interest to do this, and to keep Pedro on his throne at almost any cost. However, the Black Prince does not seem to have realized this. He seems to have acted from narrowly chivalrous and mercenary motives, restoring a king whom he considered unjustly dethroned by disloyal subjects, and expecting a large cash reward in return. When Pedro showed himself unchivalrous in dealing with the vanquished and slow to pay for the military assistance, the Prince did not acquiesce and provide further military support, which was what English interests demanded. Instead, he began a plot to remove Pedro entirely, to partition Castile among Portugal, Aragon, Navarre and himself, and to make himself king of the rump Castilian state. This absurd intrigue was of course doomed to failure; and the Prince returned to Gascony in August 1367, effectively washing his hands of Castile and its enormous potential danger for England.

The French were more clear−sighted and single−minded. They helped Enrique to assemble another group of Free Companies with which he returned to Castile in September; and when he proved unable to conquer it alone, Charles V (1364−80) made the Treaty of Toledo with him on 20 November 1368. By this treaty, one of the most important in European history, Charles promised to send enough French troops to make Enrique king of Castile, in return for all Castilian naval strength being used against England, at Castile's own expense, for as long as the Anglo−French war should last. The agreement expresses, as clearly as possible, the reason why France had extended the Hundred Years War to the Iberian Peninsula, and the essential naval link between the two wars of succession, the French

and the Castilian.

French perspicuity and determination reaped their reward. Charles sent Bertrand du Guesclin, Constable of France, with a large army to Castile in the winter of 1368—69, and with their help Enrique was able to defeat Pedro at Montiel and murder him (23 March 1369). [8]

Legitimist resistance continued; Enrique still had to conquer Toledo (June 1369), Zamora (February 1371), Carmona (May 1371) and other towns. Thus it was only in 1372, after a brisk reminder from the French court, that Enrique began to send naval help; but that help was spectacularly successful. [9] An English fleet under the Earl of Pembroke was bringing supplies to English—held La Rochelle, which was under siege by the French; but on 24 June 1372 the fleet was attacked by some dozen Castilian galleys under Ambrosio Boccanegra, who succeeded in sinking fourteen English ships and taking captive many other ships and innumerable prisoners including the Earls of Pembroke and Huntingdon. Shortly afterwards another forty Castilian ships helped the French to capture La Rochelle, which at once became a major base for Castilian and French naval warfare against England. This major victory ended thirty—two years of English naval supremacy in the Narrow Seas and began a period of Castilian dominance which would last until 1588. The Castilian galleys found little difficulty in defeating English ships at sea; and they and their French allies also looted the Isle of Wight (1374), Rye, Rottingdean, Lewes, Folkestone, Dartmouth and Plymouth (1377), the Channel Isles and Gravesend (1380). It was clear that Charles V's investment in the de—stabilizing of Castile was reaping its due reward, that the Black Prince had made a fatal mistake in abandoning Pedro the Cruel, and that Castile would cease to be England's enemy only if the Trastamaran dynasty could be overthrown by a pretender who could reasonably be considered Pedro's legitimate heir.

There were two such men, King Fernando I of Portugal and John of Gaunt, Duke of Lancaster. Shortly after Pedro's murder, his followers offered to accept Fernando as his successor, since Fernando was Pedro's closest male relative about whose legitimate descent there was no shadow of doubt. Fernando agreed. He had the support of the legitimists in Galicia, Zamora, Carmona and other Castilian redoubts, an alliance with the Sultan of Granada, and offers of support from Aragon and Navarre in return for territorial concessions. However, the plan failed: though Enrique's invasion of northern Portugal was unsuccessful, Fernando did not provide effective leadership or hold his disparate allies together, and his fleet was defeated by the Trastamarans off Sanlúcar de Barrameda in the summer of 1370. Papal pressure was brought to bear in favour of peace between the Peninsular kings, a concept which implied the acceptance of Enrique as King of Castile; and by the treaty of Alcoutim (31 March 1371), Fernando I gave up his claim to the Castilian throne and agreed to marry Enrique's daughter, Leonor, in return for four Castilian border—towns and (from the Papacy) the

income of the Portuguese Church for two years.   A few weeks later, Carmona surrendered and Enrique II could feel secure; he now set about paying his debt to France.

The war of the Castilian succession was not, however, concluded. In September 1371 John of Gaunt, Duke of Lancaster, married Princess Constanza, Pedro I's elder surviving daughter and legitimate heiress; and in January 1372 he began to use the title 'King of Castile' and to be recognized as such by the English government and by those Castilians who refused to accept Enrique's usurpation.[10]   It might still be possible, it seemed, to overthrow the Trastámaras and the Castilian naval support for France, as well as providing a crown for a younger son of Edward III; and, lest Gaunt or Constanza should die, his younger brother Edmund was married to her younger sister, Isabel (July 1372).

If Gaunt were to try to overthrow Enrique II, he would need to ally himself with either Fernando I of Portugal or Pedro IV of Aragon.   Gaunt would probably have preferred Aragon, given its proximity to English Gascony; but Fernando proved the more willing, and in July 1372 concluded with Gaunt the Treaty of São Salvador de Tagilde, summarized for us by Fernão Lopes (*Dom Fernando*, LXVII), whereby they would both invade Castile in order to dethrone Enrique II and make Gaunt king.   However, the English government was now reeling under the shock of the La Rochelle disaster, and before it could organize and despatch an army to the Peninsula, Enrique II rushed into Portugal and forced Fernando I once more to make a humiliating peace in the Treaty of Santarém (March 1373). This seemed to tie Fernando's hands for the future, but it left him bitterly resentful and determined to seek English assistance at a later date, for revenge on the Trastámaras; whilst in England the idea gradually became accepted that the way to victory over the Valois might lie through Portugal and Castile rather than through, say, Flanders.

c)   **The Papal Succession** [11]
The third great European institution to suffer a succession—crisis was the Papacy.   Although the Pope was not only the head of the Church but also the Bishop of Rome, central Italian politics had become so intolerable by 1300 that from 1309 to 1377 the Papal Court settled in the safer and more agreeable town of Avignon, just outside the south—eastern frontier of the kingdom of France.   The Avignonese popes were all Frenchmen, and were suspected of favouring the interests of the Valois monarchy, though often unjustifiably.   In France, as in the Iberian Peninsula, their genuine efforts for peace automatically implied leaving royal power in the hands of the Valois and the Trastámaras, rather than allowing the Plantagenets to continue trying to obtain it by violence.   Even if not totally unbiased, however, the Papacy was the one authority above the contending monarchies, and it did have the independence and

self-confidence to deal with them fairly bravely and impartially.

All this changed in 1378, after the death of Pope Gregory XI, who had taken the Papal Court back to Rome. The cardinals elected Archbishop Bartolomeo Prignano as Pope Urban VI (1378-89) on 8 April, under the pressure of the Roman mob; then many of them fled from Rome and elected, instead, Cardinal Robert of Geneva as Clement VII (1378-94) on 20 September. The latter set up his Court in Avignon, so that there was now one Roman and one Avignonese pope, each recognized by different countries. Clement was recognized by France, Scotland and some German principalities, Urban by England, Scandinavia, Hungary, the Emperor and most of Italy. When each pope died, his cardinals elected a successor, and the Schism dragged on until Martin V was elected by a General Council representing all countries, in 1417.

The immediate effect of the Schism was, naturally, to weaken papal authority vis-à-vis all other institutions and especially the national monarchies. Since each pope wanted to canvass the support of as many kings as possible, he had to give them more or less whatever they asked for, revenues, benefices, privileges, powers of appointment, new Church structures, blessings and excommunications and support for all sorts of secular policies. This was equally true in the Iberian Peninsula, where the kings began by adopting a neutral position between the two popes, though under French pressure Castile recognized Clement on 19 May 1381, and Aragon and Navarre did the same in 1387.

Fernando I of Portugal recognized Clement as early as January 1380, perhaps as part of the insincere stance in favour of the Valois and Trastámaran monarchies which he had adopted since his humiliating defeats of 1371 and 1373. Behind the façade, he was reviving his alliance with Gaunt and plotting a new war in which he would invade Castile from Portugal, with some English troops under the Earl of Cambridge, and Gaunt would invade Castile from Gascony with another army. Fernando signed the new Anglo-Portuguese treaty at Estremoz (July 1380); in July 1381 Cambridge landed with his troops at Lisbon; and the next month Fernando declared Urban to be the true Pope. The war, described in some detail by Fernão Lopes (*Dom Fernando*, CXXVIII-CLVI) was not merely in order to give revenge to Fernando for his earlier humiliations, to replace Juan I de Trastámara by Gaunt on the Castilian throne and to stop the Castilian navy fighting against England; it was also, legally, a crusade against the Clementist schismatics aimed at restoring the unity of the Church under Urban VI. The allies moved up to the Castilian frontier in December 1381, and waited, skirmishing, for Gaunt to open a second front in Old Castile. However, despite the moderate enthusiasm of the English Parliament for Gaunt's policy of defeating France through Spain, the London merchants would not supply the necessary finance. Gaunt was unable to mount any expedition, and eventually Fernando was forced to make peace once again with

Castile, in the Treaty of Badajoz (August 1382). He had to recognize Clement once again as the legitimate Pope; he also had to promise that his daughter and heiress, Princess Beatriz, should marry Prince Fernando, the second son of King Juan.

d) The Portuguese Succession [1] [2]

Prince Fernando de Trastámara would one day make a good king of Aragon, and he might have made a good king of Portugal, as Fernando I's son—in—law and successor; but the death of his mother (13 September 1382) led to a new agreement with Portugal, whereby Juan I of Castile married Princess Beatriz on 17 May 1383. The agreement also stipulated that after Fernando's death, Portugal should be ruled by his widow, Queen Leonor, until Beatriz and Juan I should have had a son, and that son have reached his fourteenth year, at which point he would become the next king of Portugal. It was a highly unrealistic proposal, and when Fernando I did die on 22 October 1383, Juan I simply had himself and his new wife proclaimed king and queen of Portugal, crossed the frontier in December and began to occupy the country.

He was not, of course, the only candidate for the Portuguese throne. Pedro I had married the Lady Constanza Manuel of Castile who bore him but one son: the future Fernando I. Constanza died in 1345, but meanwhile Prince Pedro had fallen in love with one of her ladies—in—waiting, Doña Inés de Castro. The story of the love affair between the future Pedro I and Inés de Castro, Portugal's great, semi—legendary, medieval romance, is well known. It inspired poets, playwrights, novelists and historians for centuries to come. It is important to us because it provides another strand in the complex dynastic struggle of the 1380s in which the English will play such an important role. Doña Inés bore Pedro several children including the Princes João and Dinis whom he practically legitimized by claiming to have married their mother. By the time Juan I invaded Portugal, these two princes had long been in his service, and he now had them imprisoned in Castile to avoid either of them becoming his rival for the Portuguese throne. As for the immediate problem of the regency of Portugal, King Juan's mother—in—law, Queen Leonor, should legally have been the Regent, but she was both unpopular and treacherous, so he soon consigned her to imprisonment in Castile. These precautions, Castilian arms and the general acceptance of his rights by the majority of the Portuguese aristocracy seemed to guarantee that Juan I would add Portugal to his other kingdoms.

However, Portugal was unlike Castile in that maritime and commercial expansion over the previous century and a half had given Lisbon (and to a lesser extent Oporto) far more wealth and power vis—a—vis the rest of the kingdom than any city possessed in Castile, even Seville. As Genoa and other Italian cities had spread their trading net—works through the Straits of Gibraltar and up the Narrow

Seas to England and the Low Countries in the twelfth and early thirteenth centuries, Lisbon had become first a staging—post for their ships, and then eventually a centre of commerce in its own right. Lisbon merchants were already trading in London and Dublin by 1200, and soon afterwards could be found all over Western Europe, exporting fruit, salt, wine and other primary products in return for manufactured goods, especially textiles, and, by the late fourteenth century, especially English textiles. By then, Lisbon was at least four times as big as any other city, and unquestionably the centre of the kingdom's economic, social, political and cultural life.

Much of this was due to Fernando I, who provided considerable encouragement to mercantile development with shipbuilding subsidies, compulsory maritime insurance, a stock exchange and a new defensive wall for the city; and although he also tried to keep the peasants on the land through the *Sesmarias* Law of 1375, this did not seriously hinder the steady growth in Lisbon's population, wealth and strength.

Thus whoever was to win the struggle for the Portuguese crown had to carry with him the people of Lisbon. Fernão Lopes, writing sixty years later, clearly understood this; but it is not evident that Juan I did, in 1383, or indeed that many Portuguese did. Yet as soon as King Fernando had died and Queen Leonor had been proclaimed regent, riots broke out in many towns, including Lisbon; Leonor was forced to flee for her life, together with her lover, Andeiro; and a powerful revolutionary movement took over Lisbon, Oporto and many other towns. This movement was directed in the first place against the Regent, who was extremely unpopular in her own right; it had strong social implications of urban lower and middle class hostility to the landed aristocracy (and perhaps of peasant hostility also); and it was nationalistic in the sense of opposing rule by a Castilian dynasty against which Portugal had fought three wars unsuccessfully in the previous fourteen years. Faced with this apparently spontaneous rebellion, and killings such as the mob—lynching of Bishop Martín of Lisbon and the assassination of Count Juan Fernández Andeiro by the Master of Avis, the nobles looked for leadership first to the Regent, Queen Leonor, but she was incapable of providing it. Then most of the nobles turned to Fernando's legal heirs, Juan I and Beatriz, and welcomed the invading (or liberating?) Castilian army. Others, more nationalistic or more anti—Castilian, left Leonor and joined the rising, which by now was acquiring a recognizable leader.

Most of the rebels, or at least of their shadowy leaders, would probably have preferred King Pedro's legitimized son, Prince João, as king, but he was in prison in Castile. As second best, they coalesced around João, Master of Avis, another illegitimate son of King Pedro by a mistress, Teresa Lorenzo; and one of the great merits of Fernão Lopes is the way in which he describes, stage by minute stage, how João of Avis evolved from a puzzled and fearful courtier planning to escape the whole revolutionary chaos by fleeing to England, into the

unquestioned King of all Portugal and founder of a new dynasty.

João of Avis is one hero of Fernão Lopes's Chronicle. The second is Lisbon itself (or, as he often calls it with perhaps unconscious Roman or Byzantine reminiscences, 'The City') which resisted Juan I's siege in 1384 and wore down his forces so that he retired to Castile. The third is Nun'Álvares Pereira, a Hospitaller friar and Constable of João's army, who defeated the Castilians in several battles. His most important victory was at Aljubarrota (14 August 1385) which he won by the Edwardian combination of a dismounted army of knights and men−at−arms fighting on foot in a good defensive position, plus strong wings of crossbowmen and English archers who showered the attacking Castilian cavalry with bolts and arrows. Innumerable Castilian and Portuguese nobles were killed fighting for Juan I, and Castile was left too weak to present a serious threat to Portuguese independence in the near future: but one day, no doubt, it would recover and Juan I might try again to enforce his claims to the Portuguese throne.

If the dispute over the succession to the Portuguese throne were to receive a permanent solution in favour of João of Avis, it might be necessary for the Castilian succession−dispute to be reopened and resolved in Juan I's disfavour. Immediately after Aljubarrota therefore, João sent ambassadors to England to persuade John of Gaunt that this was his best opportunity to conquer Castile (*Dom João*, II, LXXX); Trastamaran Castile was defeated and demoralized, and revolutionary Portugal was prepared to fight to place Pedro the Cruel's legitimate successor on the Castilian throne, on the assumption that he would be a far more friendly neighbour than Juan I, and would even be willing to move the Portuguese frontier eastwards and therefore at a safer distance from Lisbon. It was indeed Gaunt's best opportunity, as changes in English internal politics made Richard II's government willing to pay for the expedition, as it had not done in 1382.

So the Treaty of Windsor was agreed in Windsor Castle on 9 May 1386 (*Dom João*, II, LXXXII). It was the culmination of a series of alliances made in 1372 and 1380. England and Portugal agreed to provide each other with military and naval assistance on request, and to help defend each other's monarchy against Franco−Castilian attacks. On the commercial side, all Portuguese were granted the right to travel freely in England and to trade there on the same terms as Englishmen, as Englishmen were in Portugal.

With solid support thus guaranteed from Richard II and from João I, Gaunt landed with a largish army in Galicia in July 1386 and began to conquer his father−in−law's former kingdom (*Dom João*, II, LXXXIII). Fernão Lopes describes more accurately than any other chronicler the campaign in Galicia (*Dom João*, II, LXXXIX ff.), the formal agreements of Gaunt and João I (*Dom João*, II, XCIII), the latter's wedding to the former's daughter, Philippa (*Dom João*, II, XCIV−XCVI), and the Anglo−Portuguese campaign through the

kingdom of León (*Dom João*, II, XCIX−CXIII). This campaign was unsuccessful because the allies could neither lay effective siege to any city, nor tempt Juan I into a pitched battle. He had learnt the lessons of Nájera and Aljubarrota and of French resistance to English plundering raids: the raiders would cause damage to farms and villages, but would eventually go away, if the king of the country felt confident enough in the loyalty of his subjects not to be tempted into a pitched battle which he might lose. Enrique II had not had this confidence in 1367, had fought at Nájera and had lost; but in nineteen years he and his son had become accepted as king by almost all Castilians, especially when contrasted with obvious foreigners (like Gaunt) willing to concede Castilian towns to Portugal or to Aragon.

Gaunt's expedition was, then, a failure to the extent that it did not dethrone Juan I, nor prevent Castilian galleys from fighting alongside the French against England for the next few decades; but the agreements he made were highly satisfactory to his honour and his purse (*Dom João*, II, CXV−CXIX). One daughter became queen of Portugal, and another queen and then regent of Castile; the Castilian treasury paid him colossal sums of money in compensation for his claim to the throne; Portuguese galleys came to defend the English coast; and if the Castilian−Portuguese wars continued for long after his death, there was no longer any danger that the Avis dynasty would be overthrown or Portugal cease to be England's closest ally.

e) The Succession−Crises in the Military Orders [13]

The succession−crises in the Castilian and Portuguese monarchies seem to have had little direct effect on the secular clergy. Juan Gutiérrez, Dean of Segovia, seems to have been the only Castilian prelate to have gone into exile after the Trastamaran seizure of power; and in Portugal the effects, though more serious, seem not to have extended beyond the lynching of Bishop Martín of Lisbon and the exiling of Bishop Afonso of Guarda. In contrast, the effects on the military orders were much more serious, and since João I, Nun'Álvares Pereira and many other personages in Fernão Lopes's chronicles were members of these institutions, it may be worth explaining their nature and situation in the Peninsula during the late fourteenth century.

A military order was a religious order of friars who took the usual vows of poverty, chastity and obedience, were governed by a Master and lived according to a Rule which included communal prayers and services; but their chief religious function was not prayer, preaching or teaching, but fighting to defend Christian territories against attacks by non−Christians. Many such orders were founded in the twelfth century to defend Christian lands against Moslem attacks and to reconquer lands which Moslems had previously captured from Christians; but by 1300 practically all the military orders in the Iberian Peninsula had been amalgamated into four: the Templars, the Hospitallers of St. John, Santiago and Calatrava.

However, a process of disintegration then set in, so that by the time of our Chronicle eight orders can be distinguished. There is the Hospital, subdivided for administrative reasons under the Castellan of Amposta (for Aragon) and the Grand Priors of Catalonia, Navarre, Castile and Portugal, all of course under the Grand Master of the whole Order in distant Rhodes; the headquarters of the Grand Prior of Portugal was at Crato. The Master of Santiago, based at Uclés in Castile, was assisted by Grand Commanders for León, Castile, Aragon and Gascony. What had formerly been the Portuguese branch of this Order under a Grand Commander based at Alcácer, had declared its independence in the early fourteenth century, and was ruled by its own Master; to distinguish it from its parent body we shall call it the Order of São Tiago. The Order of Calatrava had always had a looser organization. The Master of Calatrava controlled his Order in Castile proper, but the branches elsewhere had much more independence than those of Santiago or the Hospital, even in Aragon under the Grand Commander of Alcañiz. The Order of Alcántara, under the Master of Alcántara, and the Order of Avis, under the Master of Avis, were theoretically the local branches of Calatrava in León and Portugal respectively; but by 1350 they were practically as independent of the Master of Calatrava as the Order of São Tiago was of the Master of Santiago. Lastly, after the Order of the Temple was abolished in 1312, King Dinis (1279—1325) was able to turn its Portuguese branch into a totally new Order, that of Jesus Christ, under a Master owing only the most nominal of obediences to the Master of Calatrava; King Jaime II of Aragon (1291—1327) created the Order of Montesa, in Valencia, in the same way.

The Peninsular monarchs promoted this disintegration, and continued to manipulate and exploit the Orders thereafter, appointing and dismissing masters, priors, commanders and other officials, and using the Orders not only against the Moslems but against other Christian states and even in civil wars. Naturally the Orders, or at least the masters and grand commanders, responded by taking political initiatives of their own, though few were as successful as the Master of Avis. Consequently the succession crises of 1350—88 often produced two or even three rivals for the same Mastership, rebellions within specific Orders, transfers from one Order to another, and, in all, an extremely confused situation which the scanty research so far carried out has done little to clarify.

Very provisionally, however, the following examples may serve to illustrate some of the effects of the Castilian and Portuguese succession—crises on the military Orders. Pedro I was served by Diego García de Padilla (1354—68) and Martín López de Córdoba (1368—71) as Masters of Calatrava, and by García Álvarez de Toledo (1359—66) as Master of Santiago; but they were opposed by followers of Enrique II as rival claimants: Pedro Muñiz de Godoy as Master of Calatrava (1366—84), and Gonzalo Mejía as Master of Santiago (1359—71).

Similarly, when Dom João, Master of Avis, became king of Portugal and was supported by the Master of São Tiago, Fernando Afonso de Albuquerque, Juan I set up Martim Eanes de Barbuda as a rival Master of Avis, and Fernando de Antas as a rival Master of São Tiago.

f) The English Succession [14]

In contrast, the divisions caused in English society by the succession crisis of its own monarchy were extremely short–lived. Richard II (1377–99), though far less cruel than the King Pedros of Castile and Portugal, had few of the gifts for government of an Edward III, João I or Enrique II.   Capricious and erratic, he was constant only in his desire not to make the sort of war on France that was the only guarantee of an English monarch's popularity; and when he had exhausted the patience of the most powerful nobles in the country, they were ready to abandon him in favour of Gaunt's son, the Earl of Derby, who was proclaimed King Henry IV in 1399. Thus the wave of succession crises had at last crossed the Channel; and the Lancastrian dynasty that had already placed daughters on the thrones of Castile and Portugal could now boast also of a king of England.   This did not mean the immediate ending of the wars between the three kingdoms; but the efforts of the three children of Gaunt were now exercised in favour of peace among their states, a peace which was not only desirable in itself, but which might at last (from the English point of view) remove the Castilian navy from the Anglo–French war, and (from the Portuguese) remove the Castilian military threat from the Badajoz–Lisbon highway.

3
The Chronicle: Structure, Purposes and the English.

Beryl Smalley observes of royal biographies in the Middle Ages:

> The writer's purposes and techniques varied, but they all had to find a mould which would contain the unruly facts. [15]

But of course, most medieval chroniclers were, far more than historians of today, prisoners of their caste, upbringing and prejudices; and secondly, controlled and constrained in any case by their allegiance to the rulers of the society within which they moved and operated.   Fernão Lopes was no exception but he is a special case for two reasons: because he came from neither of the two groups that habitually produced the chroniclers of the Middle Ages; and because of his obsessive and peculiar search for historical truth.

W.J. Brandt has divided the chroniclers of the Middle Ages into two main types: the clerical chronicler and the aristocratic chronicler. Bede, John of Salisbury and Matthew Paris can serve as examples of

the former; while the three chroniclers who described events that were to be covered by Fernão Lopes in the following century, Chandos Herald, Jean Froissart and Pedro López de Ayala, represent the latter. Brandt has attempted to define the world view of both types. Neither had grasped the principle of causality. For the clerical chronicler, the 'sequence of action' did not exist. He was 'indifferent to the question of dates and consequently such chroniclers were not concerned about causal processes. They didn't know they existed.'[16]   As for the aristocratic chronicler, although he saw events as a continuous action, this sequence of action emerged with its causal force obscured because the prime function of the aristocratic chronicle is 'to celebrate, not to explain the action with which it is concerned.' An explanation that may 'occur along the way is never the point of the narrative.'[17]

Fernão Lopes, on the other hand, a man of plebeian origins let it be remembered, has been seen almost unanimously by Portuguese and Anglo—American commentators as a singular writer within the world of medieval historiography in that he exhibits so many signs of having broken with the aristocratic tradition of secular history in which great nobles serve princes in chivalric enterprises which are brought to fruition by military victory, or to nothing by military defeat, and in which everyone else serves as a mere backcloth to the spectacular happenings of history. Fernão Lopes, while recording the actions of the great, moves behind the scenes in palace or castle or on the field of battle, in order to flesh out these events and explain the causation that shapes them. He also demonstrates the considerable role played by the common soldier, the petty bourgeoisie, the tradesmen and artisans, the peasantry and the mob.

His narrative of the events that produced a confrontation between King Fernando and the populace of Lisbon angry at his liaison with Leonor Teles gives us a glimpse of the King's understandable fear of an urban populace, temporarily united right across the social spectrum, making its opposition to his projected marriage acutely felt by him and his Court (*Dom Fernando*, LX—LXI). The deputation he receives has as its spokesman a tailor. At the close of *Dom Fernando*, despite her position of power, Queen Leonor is obliged to swear before another deputation of the Lisbon citizenry that she will rule without recourse to foreigners. The final chapters of *Dom Fernando* grant us a panoramic view of the stubborn xenophobia and rising nationalism in the country as a whole and a foretaste of the 'people's power' that will effectively destroy Queen Leonor and her lover, Andeiro, humiliate Juan I of Castile, exalt the Master of Avis, and bring an end to the Interregnum within two years.

Readers of the stirring chapters that open *Dom João, Part I* will observe that the role of the bourgeoisie, the artisans and the mob is portrayed as not only significant but as of crucial importance. On the other hand, the person in whom the people place all their trust for the future and whom they elect as their defender and champion, Dom João, Master of the Order of Avis, is portrayed not as the mighty

paladin who steps forward decisively to save the nation from Castilian tyranny but as the ordinary human being he undoubtedly was: full of fear and uncertainty, driven forward by the rush of events. Even the great hero can be driven on, by ambition, or by ideals; but Fernão Lopes portrays João of Avis as one who had greatness thrust upon him and who subsequently, as Maria Lúcia Perrone de Faro Passos has observed in the course of her study of the concept of the hero figure in the *Crónica*, grew into kingship, so to speak, justifying against all the odds the mantle of hero placed upon his shoulders by the populace of Lisbon.[18] His Constable and right—hand man, Nun'Álvares Pereira, approximates far more closely to the medieval, chivalric ideal of the heroic, bold and victorious general, but even he is frequently portrayed as a chieftain whose destiny depends rather more upon the wholehearted support of the men he leads. *Dom Fernando*, CXXXVII is a good example of this, where finally, his own temerity alone shames his men into returning to the fray; but only then can they collectively carry the day against the Castilian raiding—party. A similar example can be found during Gaunt's campaign in León when an Anglo—Portuguese force is caught unawares by vastly superior forces which it successfully fights off through the courage of a squire and the collective good sense of the rest (*Dom João*, II, CVIII).

The soldiery that can be stout, courageous and disciplined, as in the second of these episodes, not to mention the key victories of Os Atoleiros, Trancoso and Aljubarrota, can also be unruly, and consequently an obstacle rather than an aid to victory. The whole sorry saga of Edmund of Cambridge's sojourn in Portugal as narrated by Fernão Lopes is the most spectacular example of this to be found in the Chronicle. The disputes over booty between Gaunt's men and the Portuguese are another example (*Dom João*, II, CVII). An intriguing aspect of the *Chronicle of Dom Fernando* is its detached depiction of the struggle between Cambridge's marauding soldiers and the Portuguese peasants, the depredations and brutality of the English and the resulting sufferings and eventual vengeance of the peasantry. A.J. Saraiva believes that Lopes stresses these matters in order to undermine the English reputation for chivalry and even the chivalric ideal itself.[19] This may well be. But like most truly great writers, Fernão Lopes's purposes are various and complex almost to the point of contradiction; for he is pointing equally to the premise that without unity, military success is unlikely, and to the foolishness of inviting on to one's territory a foreign army, chivalric or otherwise, in the belief that such a gesture, no matter how bold, will be sufficient in itself to ensure success in the campaign to come. The illusions of King Fernando are what is at stake, and consequently, the futility of his enterprise. This same air of futility will pervade the whole description of Gaunt's campaign in the *Chronicle of Dom João I, Part II*; although here not mere brutality but internecine strife and the seemingly limitless preoccupation with jousting are the features that

express so eloquently the futility and hopelessness of the Duke of Lancaster's cause in Spain. P.E. Russell pointed out this aspect of Gaunt's military tactics in Spain and drew conclusions concerning the personality and the career of the man.[20] Fernão Lopes's thirst for detail and endeavour to give a rounded account pick out this and other negative features of both of the great interventions by the English in Spain and Portugal at this time. The examples we have offered all illustrate what Nicholas Round has called Fernão Lopes's 'greater plenitude of explanation.'[21]

So Fernão Lopes, the man of the people, as Marxist critics like to view him, finds a place for everyone in the shaping of events. At the same time, he shows insatiable curiosity and an eye for detail, for reality in all its facets. He would give his reader historical truth as he declares in startling terms in the extraordinary prologue to *Dom João I, Part I*. João Mendes has discussed at some length this ideal of truth in Fernão Lopes. He sees it as a search for objective truth. *Verdade* is for Mendes a leitmotif of the *Crónica*: Fernão Lopes is a distinctly modern man in that for him there exists a historical truth that may be found by the historian prepared to take sufficient trouble to find it.[22] But how do we reconcile the apparently obsessive search for truth and accuracy in the Chronicle with what J.H. Saraiva has called Fernão Lopes's 'inspired capacity for dramatic composition' and which he ascribes to Lopes's long and broad experience of life at many different levels?'[23] Saraiva goes on to point out that Fernão Lopes devotes as much space to the Interregnum, that is, the whole of Part I of *Dom João*, as he does to either the whole of Fernando I's reign or the career of João I after he becomes king.[24] Furthermore, how do we reconcile this ideal of truth with an equally powerful presence of destiny and providence in the Chronicle? Any attempt to answer the two questions we have just posed leads inevitably to a consideration of both the structure and the purposes of the Chronicle.

Contemporary scholars tend to view the extant three chronicles or royal Lives as a trilogy, given the manifest, official purpose of the Chronicle as it has come down to us. In *Dom Pedro*, XLIII it is announced that the future João of Avis or his brother, Prince João, the elder son of Inés de Castro, will achieve great things. The rest of the Chronicle narrating the Lives of Fernando I and João I is clearly composed with a view to confirming as just and right that João of Avis should found a new dynasty in Portugal. Dom João I is portrayed artfully throughout as the man of destiny. His birth is described briefly but portentously in *Dom Pedro*, XLIII. After these auspicious beginnings, he reappears in *Dom Fernando* as a persecuted victim of the vindictive and ruthless Queen Leonor, suffering his imprisonment fearfully but with stoic nobility (*Dom Fernando*, CXLII−CXLVI). The subtlety of Fernão Lopes in these chapters, as story−teller as well as chronicler, is not apparent until we come to the early chapters of *Chronicle of Dom João I, Part I*, where we see

him triumph over his implacable enemy. Only then does the Queen's failure to have him eliminated in the reign of King Fernando emerge as a crucial turning—point in the careers of these two adversaries. A mysterious providence thus preserves the Master of Avis so that he may fulfil his destiny on the death of Fernando I. This providence is mysterious not because of any obvious intrusion of the supernatural; quite the reverse. Providence is treated in convincingly realistic rather than supernatural terms.

Nicholas Round remarks on the duality in Fernão Lopes's Chronicle whereby one can discern, on the one hand, a providential force, and on the other, realistic chains of causality; and he argues that Fernão Lopes is like a novelist in his creation of a dramatic structure and style, but that, paradoxically, it is precisely this intrusion of art that copes with the complexity of the events Lopes narrates across the three reigns.[25] The art of his narrative enables him to make historiographical sense of human failings as well as of the demands of the historical moment that reveal these failings. The same realistic working out of a providential destiny dependent on human character and motive can be seen in the career of João I's predecessor, King Fernando. The first of the two Anglo—Portuguese campaigns was a fiasco given Dom Fernando's obvious need to avoid alienating either England or his Castilian neghbour. His 'secret' treaty with King Juan, so amusingly described by Fernão Lopes (*Dom Fernando*, CLIV—CLVI) is not so easily explained simply by Fernando's ill—health or plain political folly; rather, these secret dealings with Castile are symptomatic of the diplomatic cleft stick into which he had manoevred himself.

Fernão Lopes fulfils the official purpose of his Chronicle by endowing the career of João of Avis with a frankly messianic quality, nevertheless. This whole aspect of the *Crónica* has been finely studied by Luís de Sousa Rebelo.[26] The messianic process is complete when the new dynasty of Avis has finally disposed of the Castilian threat. Ultimately, of course, this last can only be achieved through treaty. As Rebelo has pointed out, this means that the extant Chronicle spans the entire period that needs to be taken into account in order to explain, even genealogically, the manner in which João of Avis becomes King of Portugal and fulfils his task of defending Portugal from foreign invasion, ensuring its permanent independence. Consequently, the trilogy encompasses, at one end, his birth at the beginning of the reign of Pedro I, and at the other, the date, 31 October, 1411, on which the long—delayed peace treaty with Castile was finally signed.[27]

So on one hand we have in Fernão Lopes the relentless seeker after truth and observer of causality in human affairs; and on the other hand the man invested by his King with the task of writing a chronicle that will legitimize and justify through the written word, through art, the regime he serves. Commentators have faced this seeming contradiction in various ways. For J.H. Saraiva, the vast

amount of space allotted by Fernão Lopes to the Interregnum betrays
him as the populist for whom the greatest hero of the Insurrection of
1383–5 is the common people, the *arraia–miuda* as Lopes calls
them, who are triumphant over the forces of feudal chivalry.[28]   Seen
in this light, *Dom João, Part I* would constitute the apotheosis of the
whole Chronicle.   A.J. Saraiva maintains that although Fernão Lopes
was above all else composing a justification of Dom João I, the
Crónica is an apology for the popular resistance while the great force
in it is collective.   The people no longer accept the role in society
hitherto imposed upon them.   In their revolt they express their love
of country.[29]   According to this view of his Chronicle, Fernão Lopes
sanctifies this love and protest, and later suffers for it in his own
career.   Certainly, on the death of King Duarte, he began to serve
Duarte's brother, Prince Pedro, whose regency (1439–49) was founded
on his popularity with the people; and when Pedro was killed at the
Battle of Alfarrobeira (1449), his regime was replaced by one that was
pro–Castilian, absolutist and dominated by the old feudal aristocracy.
Adams puts it succinctly:

> Fernão Lopes lived on into a period to which he did not belong,
> but he wrote no more.[30]

A.J. Saraiva suggests that Fernão Lopes and his view of history were
out of place in the atmosphere of the Court after 1449.   His
Chronicle appeared, according to Saraiva, to offer too scandalous an
apology for the popular insurrections on which the Regent had
depended.[31]   The anti–Saraiva thesis is supplied by Joaquim
Veríssimo Serrão, for whom Fernão Lopes did not simply use his
position in order to exalt the popular revolution of 1383 swayed by
the fact that he was living through the Prince Pedro regency in which
the aristocracy was again in retreat.   Firstly, according to Serrão,
there is no proof that Pedro encouraged a populist orientation in the
Crónica.   Secondly, there is no proof that Fernão Lopes was replaced
for supporting him.   Moreover, why not then go on to celebrate the
Conquest of Ceuta and record the declining years and death of King
João I?[32]   A. Borges Coelho, in an argument that, in turn, runs
counter to this, seeks to explain Fernão Lopes's failure to chronicle
the capture of Ceuta (1415) by relating it to the Tangier disaster of
1437 in which the Portuguese crusading expedition suffered a terrible
defeat: this catastrophe, swallowing up his own son as well as the
person of his old master Prince Fernando, coloured his vision; it was
not costly foreign adventures that Portugal wanted, but thrift and
justice for all at home.[33]

João Mendes takes up the obvious theme of justice that
dominates the first of Fernão Lopes's three chronicles, *Dom Pedro*,
but which also informs the rest of the *Crónica*.   He approaches the
problem of the conflict, or duality, of history and art in Fernão
Lopes from a different angle altogether, tackling head–on Lopes's
sympathies towards the principal protagonists in the period he
chronicles.   Like Round, Mendes sees the *Crónica* as a vast historical

drama or novel acted out in the Portugal of the 1370s and 80s. Viewed in this fashion, Pedro I is the embodiment of Justice, the fine, upstanding monarch who fails only when he goes against truth. Leonor Teles is the 'treacherous one'. Nun'Álvares is in stark opposition to her. He is the 'winner of battles' and the man without artifice. João das Regras is 'the doctor', also in opposition to Queen Leonor in that his juridical sense corrects and reestablishes what she undermines. The city of Lisbon is 'the martyr', suffering because of its enemies and triumphing despite them.[34]

It is interesting that João I finds no place in this gallery. One can only guess at the reason for his absence. Did he seem too colourless or perhaps too ambiguous a figure? Could it be that, as the ultimate *raison d'être* for the Chronicle, at least in the eyes of King Duarte and Prince Pedro, João of Avis, although actor in the drama, or character in the novel, is, in the final analysis, the beneficiary of its results, the recipient so to speak, through his sons Duarte and Pedro; and therefore, in a way, he lies outside the Chronicle as much as in it, like Christ in the Gospels, with whom Fernão Lopes pointedly compares him (*Dom João*, I, CLXIII)? Does not the Chronicle exist for his sake and for the 'illustrious generation' of princes, as Camões describes them in Canto IV of *The Lusiads*, that he and Queen Philippa generated; and is this not where the English have their most positive role in it? If the Duke of Lancaster and the Earl of Cambridge both failed in the Iberian military arena, it was because destiny and God's providence were against them; while the Duke's daughter and her future husband, João I, by their achievement stand in stark contrast to them.

Man in the Middle Ages was seen as the shaper of his destiny. He had to rise above mere fortune by increasing his reputation and material possessions through prudence and endeavour.[35] Fernando I, Edmund of Cambridge and John of Gaunt all fail to do this in the *Crónica*. The case of Philippa of Lancaster is different; for, as consort of João I, she too lies inside as well as outside the *Crónica*. The trilogy of kings chronicled by Fernão Lopes exemplifies this view of destiny. Not only is Pedro I the father of João I, but also he rises above mere fortune as the Justiciar and the thrifty monarch. Fernando I fails miserably on both these counts, emptying the royal treasury and failing to dispense justice. Fernão Lopes illustrates this throughout his account of the reign. João I makes a fresh start for kingship in Portugal and triumphs with his new wife, Philippa of Lancaster. Now in the Middle Ages the King's authority came from God as did the Pope's. The final two chapters of our longest extract from the Chronicle exemplify, in the papal bulls exonerating and legitimizing the new reign and blessing the marriage of King João and Queen Philippa (*Dom João*, II, CXXV−CXXVI), the vital harmony between Church and State which alone could signal the design of providence in the creation of a new, ideal order.[36] Here, that duality which the commentators have discerned in the Chronicle of

Fernão Lopes is perhaps reconciled. The 'illustrious generation' vindicated the union of João and Philippa on which the Church had smiled; while the Anglo−Portuguese Alliance could be seen to have brought about this providential marriage.

That Fernão Lopes was aware of the importance of this unexpected contribution of the English interventions to political developments in Portugal from 1385 onwards is made obvious, firstly, by his sympathetic depiction of Queen Philippa, future mother of a distinguished generation of princes; and secondly, by the pains he takes to fix in his reader's mind the quality of the relations between Gaunt and João I, especially the latter's treatment of the former: the unwavering respect for and loyalty towards a man whom, according to Fernão Lopes, he treated always as a father and to whom he deferred in all things. To call John of Gaunt Portugal's kingmaker is a gross exaggeration and probably inaccurate in any case;[37] but his intervention in Portuguese affairs nevertheless produced results as real as they were unforeseen. Fernão Lopes also has the merit of having fully appreciated this particular piece of *verdade*.

We have tried to indicate the extent to which Fernão Lopes stands out in the historiography of the Middle Ages through his ability to write history convincingly and truthfully. In point of fact, from Antiquity, of course, as Benoît Lacroix reminds us, historians have, in many disparate ways, professed truth as their principal aim, even if their chronicles have been less convincing than those of Fernão Lopes.[38] If Fernão Lopes sought to do likewise with such exceptional energy, it was because of his zeal to chronicle and exalt the House of Avis to the best of his ability. In adopting this approach to his task, he was doing no more than following the historiographical ideal of the Church Fathers and of his predecessors among medieval chroniclers; for in the Middle Ages, next to praise of God came, in order of priorities, praise of kings.[39]

BIBLIOGRAPHY

Primary Sources

Fernão Lopes, *Crónica de Dom Pedro*, organized by A. Borges Coelho after the edition by Giuliano Macchi (Lisbon, 1977).

Fernão Lopes, *Crónica de Dom Fernando*, edited by Giuliano Macchi (Lisbon, 1975).

Fernão Lopes, *Crónica del Rei Dom Joham I da boa memória, Primeira Parte e Segunda Parte*, 2 vols, edited by A. Braamcamp Freire & W.J. Entwistle (Lisbon, 1977).

Jean Froissart, *Oeuvres*, edited by Kervyn de Lettenhoe, 26 vols (Brussels, 1867–77).

John of Gaunt's Register, 1379–83, edited by E.C. Lodge & R. Somerville, 2 vols., Camden Society, Third Series, Vols. LVI–LVII (London, 1937).

Pedro López de Ayala, *Crónica del Rey Don Pedro*, in *Biblioteca de Autores Españoles*, Vol LXVI (Madrid, 1953), pp. 393–614.

Pedro López de Ayala, *Crónica del rey Don Enrique segundo de Castilla*, in *Biblioteca de Autores Españoles*, Vol. LXVIII (Madrid, 1953), pp. 1–64.

Pedro López de Ayala, *Crónica del rey don Juan, primero de Castilla e de León*, in *Biblioteca de Autores Españoles*, Vol. LXVIII (Madrid, 1953), pp. 65–159.

Life of the Black Prince by the Herald of Sir John Chandos, edited by M.K. Pope & E.C. Lodge (Oxford, 1910).

Secondary Sources

Adams, Nathan, *Fernão Lopes, Late Medieval Portuguese Chronicler* (PhD Thesis, Princeton University, 1955).

Arias y Arias, Ricardo, *El concepto del destino en la literatura española* (Madrid 1970).

Armitage–Smith, Sydney, *John of Gaunt* (London, 1904).

Arnaut, Salvador Dias, 'A crise nacional dos fins do século XIV. A Sucessão de D. Fernando', *Biblos*, 35 (1959), 1–797.

Blair, C, *European Armour* (London, 1958).

Brandt, William J., *The Shape of Medieval History: Studies in Modes of Perception* (New Haven and London, 1966).

Campos, Agostinho, Introduction to *Antologia Portuguesa: Fernão Lopes*, 2 vols (Paris–Lisbon, 1921), I, ix–lxxvi.

Coelho, A. Borges, *A revolução de 1383*, second edition (Lisbon, 1975).

Contamine, Philippe, *War in the Middle Ages* (Oxford, 1984).

Cortesão, Jaime, *Os factores democráticos na formação de Portugal* (Lisbon, 1984).

Costa, A. Domingues de Sousa, 'O célebre conselheiro e chanceler régio Doutor João das Regras, clérigo conjugado e prior da colegiada de Santa Maria de Oliveira de Guimarães', *Itinerarium*, 18

(1972), 232−59.

Costa, A. Domingues de Sousa, *Monumenta Portugaliae Vaticana*, 3 vols so far (Braga, 1968−).

D'Arcy, M.C., *The Meaning and Matter of History.   A Christian View* (New York: Meridian Books, 1961).

Díaz Martín, L.V., *Itinerario de Pedro I de Castilla.   Estudio y regesta* (Valladolid, 1975).

Díaz Martín, L.V., *Los oficiales de Pedro I de Castilla* (Valladolid, 1975).

Goodman, Anthony, 'England and Portugal 1386−1986:   John of Gaunt − Portugal's Kingmaker', *History Today* (June, 1986), pp. 17−21.

Garcia, Michel, *Obra y personalidad del Canciller Ayala* (Madrid, 1983).

Gutiérrez de Velasco, Antonio, 'Los ingleses en España (siglo XIV)', *Estudios de Edad Media de la Corona de Aragón*, 4 (1950), 215−319.

Lacroix, Benoît, *L'Historien au Moyen Âge* (Paris, 1971).

Livermore, H.V., *A New History of Portugal*, second edition (Cambridge, 1976).

MacKay, Angus, *Spain in the Middle Ages: From Frontier to Empire, 1000−1500* (London and Basingstoke, 1977).

Marques, A. H. de Oliveira, *History of Portugal.   Volume I: From Lusitania to Empire* (Columbia, 1972), pp. 108−115.

Martins, Mário, *Estudos de cultura medieval, Volume II (Braga, 1972)*.

Mendes, João, *Literatura Portuguesa*, 4 vols (Lisbon, 1974), I, 73−136.

Menéndez Pidal, R., ed. *Historia de España*, Volume XIV (Madrid, 1966).

Oliveira, M. de, *História eclesiástica de Portugal* (Lisbon, 1958).

Passos, Maria Lúcia Perrone de Faro, *O herói na Crónica de D. João I de Fernão Lopes* (Lisbon, 1974).

Patrides, C.A., *The Grand Design of God: the Literary Form of the Christian View of History* (London, 1972).

Prestage, E., *The Chronicles of Fernão Lopes and Gomes Eannes de Zurara* (Watford, 1928).

Rebelo, Luís de Sousa, *A concepção do poder em Fernão Lopes* (Lisbon, 1983).

Rebelo, Luís de Sousa, 'The Idea of Kingship in the Chronicles of Fernão Lopes', in *Medieval and Renaissance Studies on Spain and Portugal in Honour of P.E. Russell*, edited by F.W. Hodcroft et al. (Oxford)

Round, Nicholas G., 'The Revolution of 1383−84 in the Portuguese Provinces: Causality and Style in Fernão Lopes', *Dispositio*, X, Nr.27, pp. 65−84.

P.E. Russell, *As fontes de Fernão Lopes* (Coimbra, 1941).

P.E. Russell, 'Fernão Lopes e o tratado de Santarém', *Revista*

Portuguesa de História, 5 (1951), 455–73.

P.E. Russell, 'João Fernandes Andeiro at the Court of John of Lancaster, 1371–1381', *Revista da universidade de Coimbra*, 14 (1940), 20–30.

P.E. Russell, *The English Intervention in Spain and Portugal in the Time of Edward III and Richard II* (Oxford, 1955).

A.J. Saraiva, *A cultura em Portugal: Teoria e História*, 2 vols (Lisbon, 1981).

A.J. Saraiva, *Fernão Lopes* (Lisbon, n.d.).

A.J. Saraiva, *História da cultura em Portugal*, 3 vols (Lisbon, 1950–62), I, 470–84.

A.J. Saraiva, *Para a História da Cultura em Portugal* (Lisbon, 1961).

J.H. Saraiva, Introduction to *História de uma Revolução: Primeira Parte da 'Crónica de El–Rei D. João I de Boa Memória'* (Lisbon, 1977).

Sérgio, António, Introduction to *Crónica de D. João* (Oporto, 1945).

Serrão, Joaquim Veríssimo, *A Historiografia Portuguesa*, 3 vols (Lisbon, 1972), I, 35–64.

Serrão, Joel, *O carácter social da revolução de 1383* (Lisbon, 1976).

Sitges, J.B., *Las mujeres del rey Don Pedro I de Castilla* (Madrid, 1910).

Smalley, B., *Historians in the Middle Ages* (London, 1974).

Suárez Fernández, L., *Navegación y comercio en el golfo de Vizcaya* (Madrid, 1959).

Suárez Fernández, L., *Castilla, el Cisma y la crisis conciliar, 1378–1440* (Madrid, 1960).

Suárez Fernández, L., *Historia del reinado de Juan I de Castilla*, 2 vols so far (Madrid, 1977–).

Suárez Fernández, L., 'Política internacional de Enrique II', *Hispania*, 16 (1956), 1–114.

Uría, J., 'El conde Don Alfonso', *Asturiensia Medievalia*, 2 (1975), 177–237.

Valdeón Baruque, J., *Enrique II de Castilla: la guerra civil y la consolidación del régimen* (Valladolid, 1966).

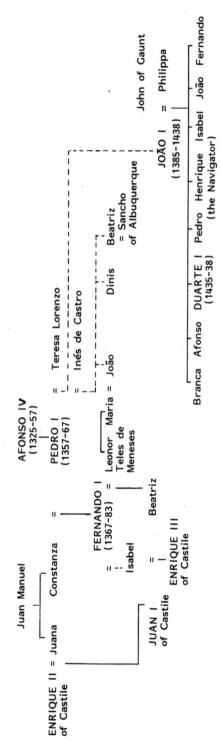

THE ROYAL HOUSE OF PORTUGAL

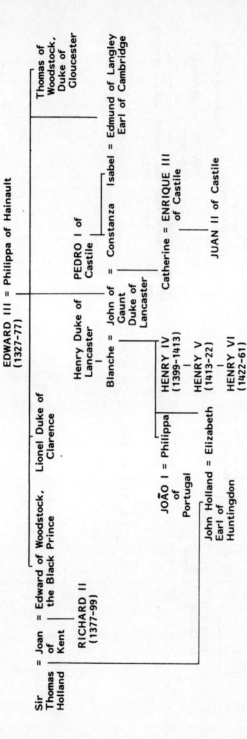

THE ROYAL HOUSE OF ENGLAND

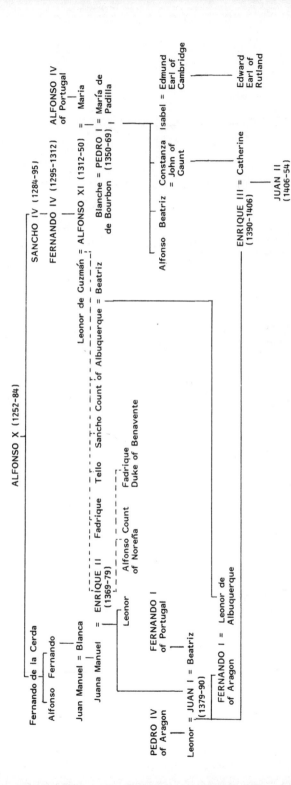

THE ROYAL HOUSE OF CASTILE

Map 1. The Iberian Peninsula in the second half of the fourteenth-century.

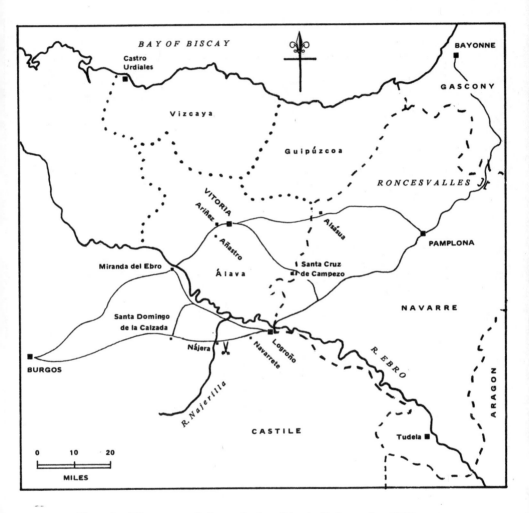

Map 2. The expedition of the Black Prince in 1367

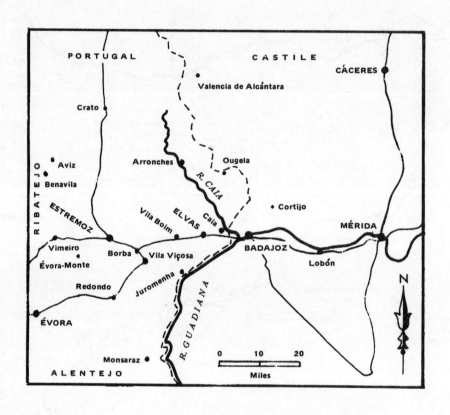

Map 3. The expedition of the Earl of Cambridge 1381-2.

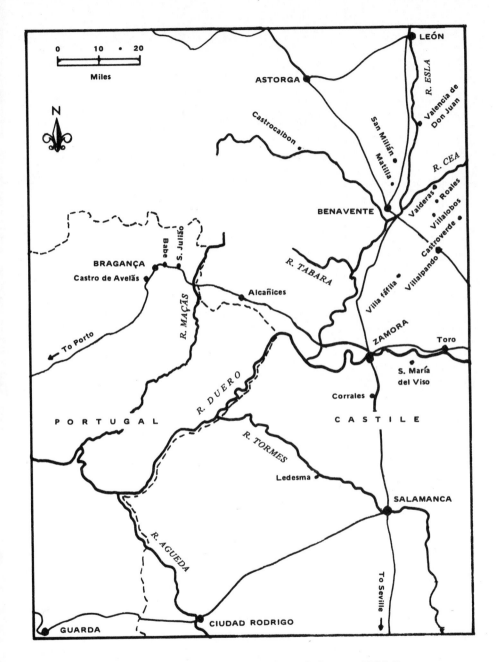

Map 4. The expedition of John of Gaunt 1396-7.

THE CHRONICLE OF DOM FERNANDO
CRÓNICA DE DOM FERNANDO

*As is his custom, Fernão Lopes opens the Chronicle of the life
of Fernando I of Portugal with a prologue containing conventional
praise of the new King's person, character and accomplishments,
although he hints darkly at disasters to come.*

*The opening chapter relates how, as soon as Pedro I has died,
the new King, as though expecting an invasion from the east, reviews
the resources of the country for waging war, and enters into
negotiations with Aragon as well as with Castile. The second chapter
abruptly turns back to the current stage in the civil war between
Pedro I of Castile (Pedro the Cruel) and his rebellious half—brother,
Enrique of Trastámara, taking up the story at the point at which*

III
Como el-rrei dom Pedro se vio com o principe de Guallez, e juntarom suas gentes pera entrar per Castella

Tornando a contar d'el-rrei dom Pedro, onde ficamos
quando passou per Purtugall, ell chegou a Baiona, segundo
ouvistes, e nom achou em aquella cidade o principe de Galez;
mas a poucos dias se vio com elle, e fallou com o principe
quanto avia mester a ajuda de seu padre e sua. E el lhe respondeo que el-rrei de Ingraterra seu senhor e padre e el
isso meesmo estavom mui prestes de o ajudar, e que ja lhe
escrevera sobr'ello e que era bem certo que lhe prazeria.
El-rrei dom Pedro, mui ledo da rreposta, foi entanto veer
a princesa sua molher em hũua villa que dizem Guchesma,
e deu-lhe muitas joyas d'as que tragia. Em esto veherom
cartas d'el-rrei de Ingraterra a el-rrei dom Pedro, em que lhe
fez saber como escrevia ao principe seu filho e ao duque
d'Allancastro seu irmão que per seus corpos, com as mais
gentes que aver podessem, o ajudassem a poer em posse de
seu rreino. E isso meesmo veherom outras cartas ao principe,
em que lhe el-rrei fez saber quanto lhe prazeria de toda ajuda
que lhe fosse feita per ell e pellos seus, aos quaaes escrevia
que sse juntassem todos com elle: e d'alli adeante começou
o principe de mandar por gentes, e juntarom-sse muitas pera
esta cavallgada. E acordarom el-rrei dom Pedro e o principe
o que aviam d'aver suas gentes de solldo: e fazia-lhe el-rrei
pago em ouro e joyas, assi das dobras que levava come
d'ouro amoedado que lhe o principe emprestava sobre pedras
de gram vallor. E foi ı. ·tado em estas aveenças que el-rrei
dom Pedro desse ao principe terra de Bizcaya e a villa de

2

our chronicler broke off in the Chronicle of Pedro I of Portugal. Fernão Lopes explains that Enrique of Trastámara, being aware that his brother has enlisted the assistance of the English army in Gascony, meets with King Carlos II of Navarre at the frontier town of Santa Cruz de Campezo and prevails upon him to close the Pyrenean passes to the Black Prince's troops and to fight them in person on the Trastamaran side if, despite this, they do succeed in crossing the mountains (I—II).

It is now that Fernão Lopes relates the circumstances in which was fought the battle of Nájera as well as the aftermath of the battle.

III
How King Pedro met with the Prince of Wales and how they joined forces in order to enter Castile.

Let us resume our narrative of the doings of King Pedro whom we left travelling through Portugal. He reached Bayonne,[1] as you have heard, but did not find the Prince of Wales in that city. However, a few days later he met up with him and informed him of how much he was in need of help from him and his father. The Prince replied that both the King of England, his lord and father, and he himself were most ready to assist him. Indeed, he had written to his father on the matter and it was certain that the King would be agreeable. Pleased with this response, King Pedro meanwhile went to see the Prince's wife,[2] in a town called Angoulême, and gave her many jewels that he had brought with him. At this time, letters arrived for King Pedro from the King of England in which he informed him that he had written to his son the Prince, and to the Duke of Lancaster, the Prince's brother, instructing them to go in person, with as large a force as possible, and assist him in recovering his kingdom. Moreover, other letters came for the Prince in which his father the King informed him how pleased he would be at any assistance the Prince and his men might give to King Pedro. He also wrote to all the Prince's men ordering them to join up with him; and from then on the Prince began to summon his men, and many came together for this expedition.

King Pedro and the Prince agreed on the pay to be given to the troops, and King Pedro made payment in jewels and gold coins, the latter being *doblas* he had with him as well as some minted gold coins which the Prince loaned him against some jewels of great price. It was stipulated in these agreements that King Pedro would give Vizcaya and the town of Castro Urdiales to the Prince, and the city of Soria to Sir John Chandos, Constable of Aquitaine, who was a

3

Castro d'Ordialles, e a monssé Joham Chantos, condeestabre de Guiana, que era hũu boom e grande cavalleiro muito privado do principe, a cidade de Ssoria; e acordarom mais que ataa que o principe e todollos seus ouvessem pagamento d'o que aviam d'aver do tempo que servissem e estevessem em Castella, que ficassem entanto em Baiona, em maneira d'arrefẽes, as suas tres filhas d'el-rrei. E juntas as companhas pera entrarem em Castella, fezerom saber a el-rrei de Navarra que lhe desse passagem pellos portos de Rroçavalles e que fosse com elles per corpo na batalha; e que lhe daria el-rrei dom Pedro por esto as villas do Gronho e de Bitoria. E el-rrei de Navarra, sabendo como as gentes do principe erom muitas mais que as d'el-rrei dom Henrrique, outrogou de os leixar passar e de seer com elles na batalha per corpo.

IV
Como el-rrei de Navarra hordenou de nom seer na batalha em ajuda d'el-rrei dom Pedro

El-rrei de Navarra, posto em gram cuidado por a promessa que feita avia a el-rrei dom Henrrique e depois a el-rrei dom Pedro, que era seu contrairo, pensou como se escusaria de nom seer em ajuda de nẽhũu d'elles e feze-o de feito, porém feamente. E foi assi que depois que deu logar às gentes d'el-rrei dom Pedro e do principe que passassem pellos portos de Rroçavalles, aveendo rreceo de seer na batalha, nom quis atender em Pampollona, mas leixou hi Martim Anrriquez seu alferez com trezentas lanças que sse fosse com elles, e foi-sse a hũa sua villa que chamam Tudella, que he acerca do rreino d'Aragom, e alli trautou com hũu cavalleiro, primo de monssé Beltram de Claquim, que diziam monssé Oliver de Manar, que estava na villa de Borja que era sua, que fezesse d'esta guisa: que el-rrei de Navarra andaria aa caça antre Borja e Tudella, que eram quatro legoas d'hũa aa outra, e que monssé Oliver sahisse a elle e o prendesse e levasse preso ao castello; e que o tevesse alli preso em Borja ataa que a batalha antre el-rrei dom Pedro e el-rrei dom Henrrique fosse passada, e d'esta maneira teeria boa escusa que nom podera per seu corpo seer com elle na batalha; e que por esto lhe daria el-rrei de Navarra em moradia hũua sua villa que chamam Gabrai, com tres mil francos de rrenda. Hordenado esto e feitas suas juras e prometimentos, foi-sse el-rrei hũu dia aa caça, e saio a elle monssé Oliver e prendeo-o e teve-o preso ataa que a batalha foi feita; e estonce cuidou

4

great and good knight and a close friend of the Prince.[3] Furthermore, it was agreed that the King's three daughters[4] would remain as pledges in Bayonne until the Prince and his forces had received payment for the period during which they were to serve and stay in Castile. Once the Companies had assembled in order to enter Castile, they communicated to the King of Navarre their wish that he should allow them safe passage through the pass of Roncesvalles and that he should join the campaign in person, whilst in return King Pedro would give him the towns of Logroño and Vitoria. Aware that the Prince's forces were much more numerous than those of King Enrique, the King of Navarre agreed to let them pass through and to fight alongside them in person.[5]

IV
How the King of Navarre
arranged not to join the campaign in aid of King Pedro.

Very mindful of the promises he had made first to King Enrique and subsequently to the latter's enemy, King Pedro, the King of Navarre considered how he might avoid helping either of them; and he managed to do so, but in an unseemly manner. Thus, having granted safe passage through the passes of Roncesvalles to the forces of King Pedro and the Prince, but not at all relishing participation in the campaign, he chose not to welcome them at Pamplona, but left Martín Enríquez,[1] his Constable, there to accompany them with three hundred lances. Meanwhile, he himself went to another of his towns, called Tudela, close to Aragonese territory. There he made an agreement with a knight called Sir Olivier de Mauny,[2] a cousin of Sir Bertrand du Guesclin[3] and lord of the town of Borja where he was then living. The agreement was that the King of Navarre would go hunting between Borja and Tudela, which were four leagues apart, and that Sir Olivier would meet him, capture him and carry him off as prisoner to his castle, where he would hold him until the war between King Pedro and King Enrique was over. In this way, the King of Navarre would have a good excuse for not participating in person in the campaign, and in return, would give Sir Olivier one of his villages called Gavray, worth three thousand francs a year in rents.[4]

When this had been arranged, promised and sworn to, the King went out hunting one day, and Sir Olivier came out to meet him, captured him, and held him prisoner until the campaign was over; but

el-rrei outra arte per que saisse de seu poder sem lhe dar nẽhũua cousa, e trautou com ell que lhe leixaria alli em arrefẽes o iffante dom Pedro seu filho, e que monssé Oliver o levasse aa sua villa de Tudella, e que alli lhe daria rrecado de todo o que com el posera. Monssé Oliver disse que lhe prazia, e trouverom o iffante, e elle foi-sse com el-rrei; e elles em Tudella, mandou el-rrei prender monssé Oliver e hũu seu irmaão, e o irmaão fogindo per hũus telhados foi morto; e preso monssé Oliver, derom o iffante dom Pedro por elle. Assi que n'eesta preitesia el perdeo o irmaão e nẽhũa cousa ouve d'o que prometido fora.

V

Das gentes que el-rrei dom Henrrique tiinha pera pellejar, e como hordenou de poer sua batalha

Quando el-rrei dom Henrrique soube como o principe com suas gentes passarom os portos de Rroçavalles per grado d'el-rrei de Navarra, e como sse partira da cidade de Pampollona e se fezera prender per arte, ajuntou suas companhas e foi-sse apousentar acerca de Sam Domingos da Calçada, em hũu azinhall mui grande que hi está; e alli fez allardo e partio e passou o Ebro e pôs seu arreall acerca da aldea de Anastro; e alli lhe disserom como hũus seiscentos de cavallo dos seus, antre castellaãos e genetes, que el mandara por cobrar a villa d'Agreda que estava contra elle, eram passados pera el-rrei dom Pedro; e el-rrei dom Henrrique nom curou d'aquello, mas cada dia hordenava suas gentes pera a batalha. E os estrangeiros que com el estavom d'Aragom eram estes: dom Afonso, filho do Iffante dom Pedro, neto d'el-rrei dom James; dom Filipe de Castro, rric'homem, cunhado d'el-rrei dom Henrrique, casado com sua irmãa dona Johana; dom Joham de Luna, dom Pedro Boil, dom Pero Fernandez d'Ixar, dom Pero Jordam d'Urres e outros; e de França eram hi estes cavalleiros: monssé Beltram de Claquim e o mariscall de França e o begue de Vilhenes e outros; e de Castella e de Leom erom hi todollos senhores e fidallgos, salvo dom Gonçallo Mexia e dom Joham Affonso de Gozmam. E porque soube que seus inmiigos viinham a pee, hordenou sua batalha per esta guisa: na deanteira pôs a pee monssé Beltram e os outros cavalleiros franceses, e com o seu pendom da banda, que levava Pero Lopez d'Ayalla, dom Sancho seu irmaão e Pero Manrrique adean-

6

then the King thought of another trick to free himself from Sir Olivier's power without giving him any reward. He agreed with him that he would leave his son Prince Pedro[5] there as a hostage, and he himself would be taken by Sir Olivier to his town of Tudela where he would pay him all he had agreed. Sir Olivier consented, the Prince was brought, and Sir Olivier went with the King. Once they were in Tudela, the King ordered Sir Olivier and his brother to be arrested. The brother tried to escape across some rooftops, but was killed; and since Sir Olivier was now a prisoner, Prince Pedro was exchanged for him. So in honouring this agreement he lost his brother and yet received nothing of what he had been promised.

V

King Enrique's armed forces, and how he arranged them for battle.

When King Enrique knew that the Prince and his men had crossed the pass at Roncesvalles with the goodwill of the King of Navarre, and that the latter monarch had left the city of Pamplona and had cunningly arranged for himself to be captured, he assembled his troops and went to establish himself in a great oak—forest near Santo Domingo de la Calzada. There he reviewed his forces, led them across the River Ebro and camped near the village of Añastro. He then learned that some six hundred of his mounted troops, whom he had sent to subdue the hostile town of Agreda, had gone over to King Pedro's side; but he did not worry about this, and spent every day preparing his men for battle.

The foreigners who were with him included the following from Aragon: Don Alfonso,[1] son of Prince Pedro and grandson of King Jaime; Don Felipe de Castro, a great nobleman who was King Enrique's brother—in—law as the husband of his sister Doña Juana; Don Juan de Luna,[2] Don Pedro Boil, Don Pedro Fernández de Urriés,[3] and others. The knights from France included: Sir Bertrand du Guesclin, the Marshal of France;[4] the "Stutterer" from Vilaines;[5] and others. And all the great lords and noblemen came from Castile and Leon, except Don Gonzalo Mejía[6] and Don Juan Alfonso de Guzmán.

Because King Enrique knew that his enemies were coming on foot, he arranged his order of battle in the following way. In the vanguard he placed Sir Bertrand and the other French knights, to fight on foot, and with them the banner of the Order of the Sash,[7] carried by Pedro López de Ayala,[8] and followed by Don Sancho, King Enrique's own brother,[9] and by Pedro Manrique,[10] *adelantado*

tado-moor de Castella e Pero Fernandez de Vallasco e Gomez
Gonçaillvez de Castanheda e Joham Rrodriiguez e Pero Rrodriguez Sarmento e Rrui Diaz de Rrojas e d'outros cavalleiros
ataa mill homẽes d'armas pee terra. Aa mão ezquerda da
batalha, honde estavom os que hiam de pee, pôs el-rrei em
hũa alla que fossem a cavallo o conde dom Tello seu irmaão
e dom Gomez Pirez de Porras prior de Sam Joham e outros
fidallgos ataa mill de cavallo, em que hiam muitos cavalllos
armados. Na outra alla da mão direita d'os que hiam
tambem de pee, pôs el-rrei a cavallo dom Affonso neto
d'el-rrei dom James e dom Pero Moniz meestre de Calllatrava
e dom Fernam Osorèz e dom Pedro Rrodriguez do Sandovall,
e eram em esta batalha outros mill de cavallo e muitos
cavallos armados. Na batalha de meo d'estas duas batalhas
hiia el-rrei dom Henrrique e o conde dom Affonsso seu filho
e o conde dom Pedro seu sobrinho, filho do meestre dom
Fradarique, e Inhego Lopez de Orosco e Pero Gonçaillvez
de Mendonça e dom Fernam Perez d'Ayalla e micer Ambrosio almirante e outros que dizer nom curamos ataa mill
e quinhentos de cavallo: e assi eram per todos quatro mill
e quinhentos de cavallo, afora muitos escudeiros de pee
das Esturas e de Bizcaia, que pouco aproveitarom, porque
toda a pelleja foi dos homẽes d'armas. Em esto enviou
el-rrei de França suas cartas a el-rrei dom Henrrique, em
que lhe enviava dizer e rrogar que escusasse aquella batalha
e fezese guerra per outra guisa; ca fosse certo que com
o principe viinha a froll da cavallaria do mundo, e que o
principe e aquellas gentes nom eram de condiçom pera muito
durarem no rreino de Castella, e d'hi a pouco se tornariam;
e que porém desviasse aquella pelleja a todo seu poder que
sse nom fezesse. E escreveo aaquelles cavalleiros franceses
que assi lh'o conselhassem: os quaaes fallando a el-rrei
sobr'esto, rrespondeo ell que o fallaria em segredo com os
seus; e todos lhe conselharom que todavia posese a batalha,
ca sse soomente fezesse mostrança e posese duvida em nom
querer pellejar, que os mais do rreino se partiriam d'elle
e se hiriam pera el-rrei dom Pedro, e isso meesmo fariam
as villas e cidades, pollo gram medo que d'el aviam; e sse
vissem que ell quiria pellejar, que todos esperavom a ventuira
da batalha, a qual fiavom na merce de Deus que el venceria.
E esta rreposta deu el-rrei a monssé Beltram e aos outros,
e determinou de poer batalha.

mayor of Castile, Pedro Fernández de Velasco, Gómez González de Castañeda, Juan Rodríguez[11] and Pedro Rodríguez Sarmiento, Ruy Díaz de Rojas, and up to a thousand other fighting men on foot. On the left flank of these infantrymen, the King placed his brother Count Tello,[12] and the Prior of Saint John, Gómez Pérez de Porras,[13] with up to a thousand mounted knights, many on horses which themselves wore armour. On the right flank of the infantrymen, the King placed Don Alfonso, the grandson of King James, with Don Pedro Muñiz, Master of Calatrava,[14] Don Fernando Osórez,[15] Don Pedro Rodríguez de Sandoval[16] and another thousand mounted knights, many of whom also rode armoured horses. Between these two mounted wings was King Enrique in the centre, with his son Count Alfonso,[17] and his nephew Count Pedro, son of Don Fadrique Master of Santiago, as well as Iñigo López de Orozco,[18] Pedro González de Mendoza, Don Fernán Pérez de Ayala, Master Ambrosio the Admiral,[19] and others whom we shall not bother to name, numbering some fifteen hundred knights. So the total force came to four thousand five hundred knights, as well as many foot — soldiers from Asturias and Vizcaya, who were of little use since all the fighting was done by the knights.

At this moment the King of France sent letters to King Enrique urging him to avoid fighting a pitched battle but to carry on the war in other ways, since he could be certain that the Prince came accompanied by the flower of the world's chivalry, but they were not the sort of men to stay for long in the kingdom of Castile and would soon go away again; so King Enrique should do everything he could to avoid any pitched battle taking place. The King of France also wrote to those French knights that they should give him the same advice; but when they spoke to King Enrique about this, he answered that he would discuss it secretly with his own men. However, all the latter advised him to dispose his forces for a pitched battle, because if he only made a show of doing so and hesitated as to whether he really wished to fight, then his more important subjects would leave him and support King Pedro, and so would the towns and cities because of the great fear that they had of the latter, whereas if they saw that he wanted to fight, then everyone would await the outcome of the battle, and hope that in God's mercy he would be victorious. The King gave this reply to Sir Bertand and the others, and decided to fight the battle.

VI

Como el-rrei dom Pedro e o principe hordenarom sua
batalha, e foi el-rrei dom Pedro armado cavalleiro

Da parte d'el-rrei dom Pedro foi hordenada a batalha
em esta maneira: elles todos viinham pee terra, e na avanguarda viinha o duque d'Allancastro, irmaão do prîncipe, a
que diziam dom Joham, e monssé Joham de Chantos, condeestabre por o prîncipe em Guiana, e monssé Rrubente Caullos
e monssé Hugo Carvaloi e monssé Oliver senhor de Abssom
e muitos outros cavalleiros de Ingraterra, que eram tres
mill homées d'armas, asaz de bõos e husados em guerra.
E na alla da maão dereita viinham o conde d'Arminhaque
e o senhor de Leberte e seus parentes e o senhor de Rrosam
e outros cavalleiros de Guiana do bando do conde de Foix
e muitos capitaães de companhias ataa dous mill homées
d'armas. Na batalha pustumeira viinha el-rrei dom Pedro
e el-rrei de Neapoll e o prîncipe de Guallez e o pendom
d'el-rrei de Navarra com trezentos homées d'armas e muitos
cavalleiros de Ingraterra ataa mill lanças, assi que eram per
todos dez mill homées d'armas e outros tantos frecheiros:
e estes homées d'armas eram estonce a froll da cavallaria
do mundo, ca era paz antre França e Ingraterra, e todo o
ducado de Guiana [estava por o prîncipe de Guallez e assi
viinham com ell todollos bõos do ducado de Guiana] e
Arminhaques e do condado de Foix e todollos cavalleiros
e rricos-homées de Bretanha e toda a cavallaria de Ingraterra;
e viinham com el-rrei dom Pedro dos seus ataa oitocentos
homées d'armas de castellaãos e genetes. E d'esta maneira
forom hordenadas as batalhas de cada hũua parte pera o dia
que sse ouvesse de fazer. E partio el-rrei dom Henrrique
d'aquel logar hu estava e foi-sse contra aquella comarca
d'onde el-rrei dom Pedro era, e pôs seu arreall em hũa serra
alta que está sobre Alava, onde as gentes d'el-rrei dom Pedro
nom podiam pellejar com elles polla fortelleza do aseenta-
mento; e cobrarom os ingreses esforço por esto, porquanto
virom que el-rrei dom Henrrique se posera em aquella serra
e nom decia ao campo, onde elles estavom prestes pera lhe
dar batalha. E alli soube el-rrei dom Henrrique como muitos
do prîncipe se estendiam pella terra a buscar viandas, e
mandou lá algũus capitaães com gentes, e acharom-nos
derramados buscando viandas, e tomaram-nos todos; e duzentos homées d'armas e outros tantos frecheiros colherom-
-sse a hũu outeiro; e pero se bem defendessem, aacima forom

VI

How King Pedro and the Prince arranged their battle—lines, and how King Pedro was dubbed a knight.

On King Pedro's side the troops were arranged for battle in the following way, all of them on foot. In the vanguard was John, Duke of Lancaster, the Prince's brother, and with him Sir John Chandos, the Prince's Constable in Gascony, Sir Robert Knollys,[1] Sir Hugh Calveley,[2] Sir Oliver, lord of Clisson[3] and many other English knights, totalling three thousand warriors, very good and experienced in war. On the right wing were the Count of Armagnac[4] and the Lord of Albret[5] and his relatives, together with the Lord of Rauzan[6] and other Gascon knights who were followers of the Count of Foix, and many captains of companies, totalling in all some two thousand men—at—arms. In the rearguard were King Pedro, the King of Naples,[7] the Prince of Wales, the banner of the King of Navarre with three hundred of his warriors, and many English knights totalling some thousand warriors, so that altogether they numbered ten thousand men—at—arms, and the same number of archers. These men—at—arms were then the flower of chivalry in the world, for there was peace between France and England, and all the duchy of Gascony was on the side of the Prince of Wales and so all the good men of the duchy of Gascony came with him. So too did the Armagnacs, and the men of the County of Foix, and all the knights and great nobles of Britanny and all the chivalry of England; and with King Pedro there came some eight hundred Castilian men—at—arms and lightly—armed horsemen. And in this way were each side's battle—lines laid out ready for the day which was dawning.

Then King Enrique left the place where he had been and went towards the area where King Pedro was, and fixed his camp on high ground above Alava, where King Pedro's troops could not engage him in battle because of the strength of his position.[8] The English were encouraged by this, because they saw that King Enrique had pitched his camp on that height and was not coming down into the plain, where they were ready to give him battle. There King Enrique learned that many of the Prince's men were spreading out over the countryside to forage, and he sent some of his captains there with troops, who found them all scattered and foraging, and captured them all. Two hundred English men—at—arms and the same number of archers took refuge on a hill[9], but although they put up a stout defence, some of them were killed and the rest captured. When King

mortos d'elles e os outros tomados. El-rrei dom Pedro e o
princüpe, que estavom aalem da villa de Bitoria, quando
souberom que as gentes d'el-rrei dom Henrrique alli eram,
cuidarom que era elle que lhe viinha poer a batalha; e
poserom-sse todos em hũu outeiro aalem de Bitoria que
dizem Sam Romam e ali rreglarom sua batalha; e foi el-rrei
dom Pedro armado cavalleiro de mão do principe, e outros
muitos aaquella ora, e tornarom-sse os d'el-rrei dom Henrrique pera seu arreall, e nom sse fez mais aquell dia.

VII

Como o principe de Gallez enviou a el-rrei dom Henrrique
hũua carta, e das rrazoões contheudas em ella

Sabendo el-rrei dom Henrrique como el-rrei dom Pedro
e o principe de Galllez hiam caminho do Gronho por passar o
rrio d'Ebro, partio d'onde estava e foi-sse pera Najara; e pôs
seu arreall aaquem da villa, em guisa que o rrio de Najara
estava antre o seu arreall e o caminho per hu el-rrei dom
Pedro avia d'hir. El-rrei dom Pedro e o principe com sas
gentes partirom do Gronho e veheron pera Navarrete; e
d'alli enviou o principe a el-rrei dom Henrrique hũu seu
arauto com hũua carta que dizia assi: «Eduarte, filho primogenito d'el-rrei de Ingraterra, principe de Gallez e de Guiana
e duque de Cornoalha e conde de Cestre, ao nobre e poderoso
principe dom Henrrique, conde de Trastamara. Sabee que
n'estes dias passados o mui alto e mui poderoso principe
dom Pedro, rrei de Castella e de Leom, nosso mui caro e
mui amado parente, chegou aas partes de Guiana, onde
nós estavamos, e fez-nos entender que quando el-rrei dom
Affonsso seu padre morreo, que todollos poboos dos rreinos
de Castella e de Leom pacificamente ho tomarom por seu
rrei e senhor; antre os quaaes vós fostes hũu d'os que assi
lhe obedecerom, e estevestes gram tempo em sua obediencia.
E diz que depois d'esto, pode ora aver hũu ano, vós com
gentes estranhas entrastes em seu rreino e lh'o teendes
ocupado per força, chamando-vos rrei de Castella, tomando-
-lhe seus tesouros e rrendas, dizendo vós que o deffenderees
d'ell, e d'aquelles que o ajudar quiserem; da quall cousa
somos mui maravilhado, que hũu tão nobre homem como
vós, e demais filho de rrei, fezessees cousa vergonçosa contra
vosso rrei e senhor. E dito rrei dom Pedro enviou mostrar
estas cousas a el-rrei de Ingraterra, meu senhor e padre,

Pedro and the Prince, who were the other side of the town of Vitoria, learned that King Enrique's men were there, they thought that it was Enrique himself who was coming to start the battle; and they all assembled on a hill beyond Vitoria, called San Román[10], and set out their battle—lines there. King Pedro was dubbed a knight there by the Prince himself, along with many others at the same time; but King Enrique's men went back to his camp, and nothing more was done that day.

VII
How the Prince of Wales sent a letter to King Enrique, and what it contained.

When King Enrique learned that King Pedro and the Prince of Wales were heading for Logroño to cross the River Ebro, he left the place where he had encamped and went to Nájera; and he fixed his camp on this side of the town, so that the River Najerilla was between his camp and the road by which King Pedro had to come. King Pedro and the Prince left Logroño with their men and came to Navarrete, and from there the Prince sent King Enrique. a herald with the following letter:

Edward, eldest son of the King of England, Prince of Wales and Gascony, Duke of Cornwall and Count of Chester, to the noble and powerful prince, Enrique, Count of Trastámara. You should know that the most high and most powerful prince, Don Pedro, King of Castile and Leon, our dearest and beloved cousin, came recently into Gascony, where we were, and gave us to understand that when his father King Alfonso died, all the peoples of the kingdoms of Castile and Leon peacefully accepted him as their king and overlord; and among the others, you were one of those who thus obeyed him, and spent a long time as his obedient subject. He said that after this, about a year ago, you entered his kingdom with foreign troops and now occupy it by force, entitling yourself King of Castile, taking his treasures and revenues, and saying that you will defend it against him and anyone who wishes to support him. We are astonished at this: that so noble a man as yourself, and a king's son to boot, should act so shamefully towards your king and overlord. King Pedro sent information about all this to the King of England, my lord and father, and begged him to help him to recover his

e lhe rrequerio que pollo gram divedo de linhagem que antre as casas d'Ingraterra e de Castella ouverom em hũu, desi pollas ligas e amizades que com o dito rrei meu senhor e comigo tiinha feitas, o quisesse ajudar a cobrar seu rreino e senhorio. El-rrei meu senhor e padre, veendo que el-rrei dom Pedro seu parente lhe enviava pedir cousa justa e rrazoada, a que todo rrei deve d'ajudar, prougue-lhe faze-llo assi, e mandou-nos que com todos seus vassallos e amigos ho veessemos ajudar, segundo a sua honrra perteence; polla quall rrazom somos aqui chegados, e estamos em este logar de Navarrete, que he nos termos de Castella. E porque, sse voontade de Deus fosse de sse escusar tam grande espargimento de sangue de christãos, como he per força de hi aver, se a batalha se fezer, de que Deus sabe que a nós pesa muito, vos rrogamos e rrequirimos da parte de Deus e do martir Sam Jorge que sse vos praz que nós sejamos boom medianeiro antre o dito rrei dom Pedro e vós, que no-llo façaaes saber, e nós trabalharemos como vós ajaaes em seus rreinos e em sua boa graça e mercee tam gram parte per que mui abastadamente possaaes manteer vosso boom e honrrado estado: e sse algũas outras cousas entendees de livrar com elle, com a mercee de Deus entendemos de poer hi tal meo como vós sejaaes de todo bem contento. E sse vos d'isto nom praz e querees que sse livre per batalha, sabe Deus que nos despraz d'ello muito; pero nom podemos escusar de hir com el-rrei dom Pedro nosso parente e amigo per seu rreino; e sse nos algũus quiserem embargar o caminho, nós faremos muito pollo ajudar com a ajuda e graça de Deus. Scripta em Navarrete, villa de Castella, primeiro dia d'abrill».

VIII

Da rreposta que el-rrei dom Henrrique enviou ao principe per sua carta

El-rrei dom Henrrique, veendo esta carta, rrecebeo bem o arauto e deu-lhe panos d'ouro e dobras; e ouve conselho como rresponderia ao principe, porque algũus diziam que pois lhe nom chamara rrei, que lhe escrevesse per outra maneira; desi acordarom que lhe escrevessem cortesmente, e foi a carta em esta forma: «Dom Henrrique, pella graça de Deus rrei de Castella e de Leom, ao mui alto e mui poderoso principe dom Eduarte, filho primogenito d'el-rrei de Ingraterra, principe de Gailez e de Guiana e duque de Cornoalha

kingdom and lordship, because of the great family links between the dynasties of England and Castile, and the treaties and agreements which he had made with the King my lord and myself. The King, my lord and father, seeing that his cousin King Pedro was asking him for what was just and reasonable, something which any king ought to support, was pleased to do so; and he ordered us to come with all his vassals and friends to help him, as befits his honour; and so we have come here, and we are in this place called Navarrete, which is inside the boundaries of Castile. And because it may be God's will to avoid such a great shedding of Christian blood as there necessarily will be, if we fight a battle, though God knows that it will distress us greatly, we beg and plead with you in the names of God and of Saint George the Martyr that if you want us to be a good mediator between King Pedro and you, you should tell us so, and we shall strive to get you such a great share in his kingdoms, and in his grace and favour, that you may very fully maintain yourself in a good and honourable estate. If you have any other disputes to settle with him, with God's mercy we intend to mediate in such a way as to make you totally contented. But if you do not want this and prefer to settle your disputes by a battle, God knows that we do not desire this, but we cannot avoid supporting King Pedro, our cousin and friend, in his own kingdom, and if anyone wishes to block our way, we shall do our best to support him with God's help and favour. Written in Navarrete, a town of Castile, on the first day of April.

VIII

Of the reply which King Enrique sent to the Prince's letter.

When King Enrique saw this letter he welcomed the herald and gave him cloths—of—gold and *doblas*; and he took advice as to how to answer the Prince, for some said that since the Prince had not addressed him as a king, he should retort to him in kind; but then they agreed to send him a courteous answer, which eventually took the following form:

Don Enrique, by the grace of God King of Castile and Leon, to the most high and mighty Prince Edward, first—born son of the King of England, Prince of Wales and of Gascony, Duke of Cornwall and

15

e conde de Cestre. Rrecebemos per hũu arauto vossa carta, na quall sse contiinham muitas rrazoões que vos forom ditas por esse nosso aversairo que hi he; e nom nos parece que fostes bem enformado, como assi seja que nos tempos passados elle rregeo estes rreinos de tall maneira que todollos que o sabem e ouvem se podem maravilhar de tanto tempo seer sofrido no senhorio que teve. E todollos dos rreinos de Castella e de Leom, com gram damno e trabalho e mortes e perigos e mazellas que seeriam longas de contar, soportarom atá aqui seus feitos, os quaaes nom poderam mais encobrir nem sofrer; e Deus por sua mercee avendo piedade de todollos d'estes rreinos, por tam grande mall nom hir mais adeante, sem lhe fazendo nẽhũu de sua terra salvo obediencia quall devia, e estando todos com elle em Burgos pera o servir e ajudar a deffender seus rreinos, deu Deus sentença contra elle, e de sua voontade propia os desemparou e sse foi; e todollos de seu senhorio ouverom mui grande prazer, teendo que Deus enviara sobr'elles a sua misericordia, pera os livrar de tam duro e tam periigoso senhorio quall tiinham: e todollos dos ditos rreinos, assi prellados come cavalleiros e fidallgos e cidadaãos, de sua voontade veherom a nós e nos rreceberom por seu rrei e senhor: assi que entendemos per estas cousas sobreditas que esto foi obra de Deus. E portanto, pois per voontade de Deus e de todollos do rreino nos foi dado, vós nom teendes rrazom por que nos ajaaes d'estorvar; e se batalha ouver de seer, sabe Deus que nos despraz d'ello, pero nom podemos escusar de poer nosso corpo por defender estes rreinos, a que tam teudos somos, aaquell que contra elles quer seer; e porende vos rrogamos e rrequirimos da parte de Deus e do apostollo Santiago que vós nom queiraaes tremeter assi poderosamente de em nossos rreinos fazerdes damno, ca, fazendo-o, nom podemos escusar de os deffender. Scripta no nosso arreall acerca de Najara, segundo dia d'abril». Mostrou o principe esta carta a el-rrei dom Pedro, e disserom que estas rrazoões nom eram abastantes pera se escusar de nom poer logo a batalha; e pois todo era na voontade de Deus, que como sua mercee fosse, que assi o livrasse.

16

Count of Chester. By the hand of your herald we have received your letter, which contains many arguments which have been proposed to you by our adversary who is there. We do not think you have been well informed, for in times past he ruled these kingdoms in such a way that everyone who knows or hears about it can be astonished at the length of time that his domination was endured. All the inhabitants of the kingdoms of Castile and Leon, have endured his deeds until now, with great harm, travail, deaths, dangers and humiliation which are too numerous to recount; but eventually they could conceal them and suffer them no more. God in His goodness had mercy on all the people of these kingdoms, that this great evil should no longer continue, since nobody of his land did anything but give him due obedience and were all with him in Burgos ready to serve him and help him to defend his kingdoms. So God gave His sentence against him, and of His own free will withdrew His protection from him, and he went away. All the inhabitants of these kingdoms, prelates, nobles, knights and citizens, came to us of their own free will and accepted us as their lord and king; so that we understand from these events that this was the work of God. So, since this kingdom has been given to us by the will of God and of all its inhabitants, you have no reason to interfere; and if there has to be a battle, God knows we do not want it but we cannot avoid fighting in person to defend these kingdoms, to which we are in duty bound, against the man who wishes to attack them. So we beg and plead with you in the names of God and of St James the Apostle not to try to enter our kingdoms by force in this way to do them harm, for if you do we cannot avoid defending them. Written in our camp near Nájera, on the second day of April.[1]

The Prince showed this letter to King Pedro, and they said that these arguments were insufficient to avoid fighting a pitched battle; and since everything was in God's hands, that He should decide the issue according to His will.

Como se fez a batalha antre os rreis ambos, e foi vencido el-rrei dom Henrrique

Ja ouvistes como el-rrei dom Henrrique tiinha seu arreall posto per honde avia de viir el-rrei dom Pedro, de guisa que o rrio de Najara estava antre hũus e os outros; e ouve estonce seu conselho de passar o rrio e poer a batalha em hũua grande praça que he contra Navarrete, per honde os emmiigos aviam de viir; e d'esto pesou a muitos dos seus, porque tiinham aa primeira seu arreall posto com moor avantagem d'o que o depois teverom; mas el-rrei dom Henrrique era homem de gram coraçom e esforço, e disse que nom quiria poer a batalha salvo em-na praça chãa sem avantagem nẽhũa. E el-rrei dom Pedro e o principe com todas suas companhas partirom de Navarrete sabado pella manhãa, e poserom-sse todos pee terra ante hũua gram peça que chegassem aos d'el-rrei dom Henrrique, hordenados em batalha segundo avemos contado. El-rrei dom Henrrique isso meesmo hordenou sua batalha na maneira que dissemos; e ante que as batalhas juntassem, algũus genetes e o pendom de Sant'Estevam com homẽes d'esse logar, que estavom com el-rrei dom Henrrique, passarom-sse pera el-rrei dom Pedro. Em esto moverom as batalhas, e chegarom hũus aos outros; e o conde dom Sancho irmaão d'el-rrei dom Henrrique e monssé Beltram e todollos cavalleiros que estavom com o pendom da banda forom ferir na avanguarda honde viinha o duque d'Alancastro e o condeestabre; e os da parte d'el-rrei dom Pedro e do principe tragiam todos cruzes vermelhas em campo branco, e os d'el-rrei dom Henrrique levavam esse dia bandas: e assi de voontade juntarom hũus com os outros que cahirom as lanças a todos, e começarom de sse ferir aas espadas e achas e porras, chamando os da parte d'el-rrei dom Pedro, Guiana Sam Jorge, e os d'el-rrei dom Henrrique, Castella Santiago; e tam rrijamente se ferirom que os da avanguarda do principe se começarom de rretraer quanto seeria hũua passada, e forom algũus d'elles derribados, em guisa que os d'el-rrei dom Henrrique cuidarom que venciam, e chegarom-sse mais a elles, e começarom-sse outra vez a ferir. Dom Tello, irmaão d'el-rrei dom Henrrique, que estava de cavallo da maão ezquerda da avanguarda d'el--rrei dom Henrrique, nom movia pera pellejar, que foi hũu grande aazo de sse perder a batalha, e por que lhe el-rrei dom Henrrique depois sempre quis mall; e os d'alla dereita

IX

How the battle was fought between the two kings and how King Enrique was defeated.

You have already heard how King Enrique had placed his camp where King Pedro was due to come, and in such a way that the River Najerilla was between the two sides. He then took counsel as to whether to cross the river and draw up his forces on a large piece of flat terrain opposite Navarrete and in the path of the enemy. Many of his followers were unhappy at this, because their first camp—site was more advantageous than their later one; but King Enrique was a man of great courage and determination, and he said that he did not want to draw up his forces anywhere except in a flat plain offering no advantage.

King Pedro and the Prince left Navarrete with all their forces on Saturday morning, drawn up in the manner we have described, and dismounted a long way before they reached King Enrique's men. King Enrique also drew up his forces in the way we have said; and before the two sides joined battle, some lightly—armed horsemen, and the men with the banner of Santisteban[1] changed sides and joined King Pedro. Thereupon the two sides began to move against each other, and Count Sancho, King Enrique's brother, and Sir Bertrand and all the knights following the banner of the Sash attacked the enemy vanguard under the Duke of Lancaster and the Constable. Those on the side of King Pedro and the Prince all bore red crosses on white fields, and those of King Enrique bore sashes that day. They clashed together so fiercely that all their lances fell, and they began to strike each other with swords, axes and clubs. King Pedro's men shouted their war—cry, "Gascony, Saint George!" and King Enrique's, "Castile, Santiago!" They struck each other with such force that the Prince's vanguard began to give way about a pace, and some of them were knocked down, so that King Enrique's men thought that they were winning, and they closed in on the enemy and began to strike them again. Don Tello, King Enrique's brother, who was riding on the left wing of King Enrique's vanguard, made no move to fight, and this was a main reason why the battle was lost, and why King Enrique always disliked him afterwards. The right wing of the Prince's vanguard charged straight for Don Tello, and he and his companions did not dare wait for them but fled from the field at full

da avanguarda do principe aderençarom contra dom Tello, e el e os que com ell estavom nom os ousaram d'atender e moverom do campo a todo rromper, seguindo-os os d'aquella alla que hiiam a dom Tello; e veendo que lhe nom podiam empeencer, tornarom sobre as espaldas d'os que estavom de pee na avanguarda d'el-rrei dom Henrrique, com o pendom da banda, que pellejavom com a avanguarda do principe, e ferindo-os pellas espalldas começarom de matar d'elles; e isso meesmo fez a outra alla da mão seestra da avanguarda do principe, depois que nom achou gentes de cavallo que pellejassem com elles: assi que alli era toda a pressa da batalha, seendo dom Sancho e os outros todos cercados de cada parte dos emmiigos; porém o pendom da banda ainda nom era derribado. E el-rrei dom Henrrique, come ardido cavalleiro, chegou per vezes em cima de seu cavallo, armado de loriga, alli hu era a pressa tam grande, por acorrer aos seus, teendo que assi o fariam os outros que estavom com ell de cavallo: e quando vio que os seus nom pellejavom, nom pode sofrer os emmiigos, e ouve de volver costas e todollos de cavallo que com ell eram, e d'esta guisa se perdeo a batalha. E afirma-sse, se he verdade, que seendo a batalha da sua parte bem pellejada, era gram duvida nom seer el-rrei dom Pedro desbaratado; e assi mall como o ella foi, se nom fora o grande esforço e ardideza do principe e do duque d'Alancastro, que eram estremados homées d'armas, ainda o vencimento d'ella esteve em grande aventuira; e forom mortos d'os de pee que aguardavom o pendom da banda, e antre cavalleiros e homées d'armas ataa quatrocentos, e presos outros muitos, assi como dom Sancho e monssé Beltram e o mariscall e dom Filipe de Castro e outros, cujos nomes leixamos por nom alongar. E d'os de cavallo forom isso meesmo presos o conde de Denia e o conde dom Affonsso, o conde dom Pedro e o meestre de Callatrava e outros que dizer nom curamos: e forom mortos no encalço atá a villa de Najara muitos d'el-rrei dom Henrrique, e matou el-rrei dom Pedro depois per sa mão, teendo-o preso hũu cavalleiro do principe, Inhego Lopez de Orozco; e fez matar Gomez Carrilho de Quintana camareiro-moor d'el-rrei dom Henrrique e Sancho Sanchez de Orozco e Garcia Jofre Tenoiro, que forom presos na batalha, e teverom-no todos a mall; e foi esta batalha vencida sabado de Lazaro, seis dias d'abrill da era de Cesar de mill e quatrocentos e cinquo annos.

speed. Their pursuers chased after them, but could not catch them, so they returned to the rear of the foot—soldiers of King Enrique's vanguard, who, under the banner of the Sash, were fighting the Prince's vanguard; and, attacking them from behind, began to kill some of them. The left wing of the Prince's vanguard then began to do the same, once they found no mounted troops to oppose them. So all the press of battle was there, and Don Sancho and the others were totally surrounded on all sides by their enemies, although the banner of the Sash was not yet overthrown. King Enrique, being a bold knight, and armed with a breast—plate, charged up on his horse several times to where the press was greatest, in order to support his men, thinking that his companions, who were also mounted, would do the same; but when he saw that his men were not fighting, he could no longer stand against the enemy and had to retreat with all his mounted companions, and so the battle was lost.

It is said, and it is true, that if the battle had been well fought on King Enrique's side, it is far from certain that King Pedro would have avoided defeat; and even though it was badly fought on King Enrique's side, if it had not been for the great efforts and boldness of the Prince and of the Duke of Lancaster, who were excellent soldiers, the result of the battle would still have been in considerable doubt. Those who followed the banner of the Sash, fighting on foot, were killed, and some four hundred knights and men—at—arms, as well; and many others were captured, including Don Sancho, Sir Bertrand, the Marshal, Don Felipe de Castro and others whose names are too numerous to mention. Of those who fought on horseback there were captured the Count of Denia, Count Alfonso, Count Pedro, the Master of Calatrava, and others whom we shall not bother to list; and many of King Enrique's men were killed whilst being pursued towards the town of Nájera. Afterwards, King Pedro killed with his own hand Iñigo López de Orozco, who had been captured by one of the Prince's knights. He had Gómez Carrillo de Quintana, King Enrique's Grand Chamberlain, killed, and also Sancho Sánchez de Moscoso[2] and García Jofre Tenorio, who had all been captured in the battle. Everyone considered this to be wrong. The battle was won on the Saturday before Passion Sunday, on the sixth of April, 1367.[3]

X

Como o principe disse contra o mariscall de França que merecia morte, e como sse livrou per juizo de cavalleiros

No dia seguinte, que era domingo, trouverom ante o principe todollos presuneiros que na batalha forom tomados, porque dizia el-rrei dom Pedro que algũus, contra que el passara per sentença, lhe deviam seer entregues, pera d'elles fazer justiça; antre os quaaes veho o mariscall de França, homem de saseenta anos e mais, e o principe, quando o vio, chamou-lhe treedor e fementido que merecia morte; e o mariscall rrespondeo dizendo: «Senhor, vós sooes filho de rrei, e nom vos rrespondo como poderia em este caso, mais eu nom ssom treedor nem ffementido». E o principe disse que quiria estar a juizo de cavalleiros, e que lh'o provaria, e ell disse que ssi: e forom juizes doze cavalleiros de desvairadas nações. E disse o principe contra elle que na batalha de Piteus, que ell vencera, hu fora preso el-rrei de França, fora elle seu prisoneiro e posto a rrendiçom, e lhe fezera preito e menagem, so pena de traiçom e ffementido, que sse nom fosse em companha d'el-rrei de França ou com algũu de seu linhagem da froll de lis, que sse nom armasse contra el-rrei de Ingraterra nem contra o principe ataa que sũa rrendiçom fosse paguada, o que ainda nom era. «E ora nom foi n'eesta batalha el-rrei de França nem homem de seu linhagem, e vejo-vos armado contra mim, nom teendo paguado o por que ficastes, e portanto avees cahido em maao caso». Muitos cuidarom, ouviindo aquisto, que o mariscall tiinha muito maao feito e que sse nom escusava de morte por ello; e disse o principe ao mariscall que seguramente dissesse todo o que entendesse por deffender sua fama e honrra, ca esto era feito de guerra antre cavalleiros. E ell rrespondeo dizendo que verdade era todo o que dizia. «Mas eu, senhor, disse elle, nom me armei contra vós come capitam d'esta batalha, ca el-rrei dom Pedro o he, a cujas gajas, come soldadeiro, vós aqui viindes: e pois vós nam sooes o capitam e viindes asoldadado, eu nom errei em me armar contra vós, salvo contra el-rrei dom Pedro, cuja he a rrequesta d'esta batalha». Os juizes disserom ao principe que o mariscall rrespondia mui bem com dereito, e derom-no por quite da acusaçom que lhe fazia; e foi bem notada esta rreposta, de guisa que per tall sentença se livravom depois semelhantes casos quando aconteciam na guerra.

X

*How the Prince said that the Marshal of France deserved to die,
and how the Marshal was acquitted by a court of knights.*

On the next day, Sunday, they brought before the Prince all the
prisoners who had been captured in the battle, because King Pedro
said that some of them, whom he had already sentenced, should be
handed over to him to be punished. Among them was the Marshal
of France, a man more than sixty years old. When the Prince saw
him he called him a perfidious traitor who deserved to be killed.
The Marshal answered: "My lord, you are the son of a king, and I
shall not give you the answer which I could give in this matter, but I
am not a traitor nor perfidious." The Prince said that he wanted this
to go before a court of knights, and that he would prove his
accusation; and the Marshal agreed, so that twelve knights of different
nationalites were appointed to judge the question.

The Prince testified against him that in the battle of Poitiers,
which he had won, and in which the King of France had been
captured, the Marshal had been his prisoner and held for ransom, and
had sworn and guaranteed, on pain of being a perfidious traitor, that
unless it were in the company of the King of France or some other
member of the dynasty of the fleur—de—lis, he would never bear
arms against the King of England or against the Prince until his
ransom were paid, which it never had been. "And the King of
France was not in this battle just now, nor any member of his
dynasty, and yet I see you armed against me, though you have not
paid the price of your ransom, and so you have come to a bad end."
Hearing this, many thought that the Marshal had behaved very badly
and could not avoid being executed for this; and the Prince told the
Marshal to say, in all safety, everything he could think of to defend
his fame and honour, since this was a matter of warfare between
knights. The Marshal answered that all he had said was true. "But
I, my lord", he said, "did not take up arms against you as the leader
in this battle, for King Pedro holds that position, and you have come
here paid by him as his mercenary; and since you are not the leader
and are being paid wages, I did not commit the wrong of taking up
arms against you, but took them up against King Pedro, in whose
cause this battle has been fought." The judges said to the Prince
that the Marshal had replied well and in accordance with law, and
they acquitted him of the accusation brought against him; and his
answer was carefully noted down, so that when similar cases occurred
later in the war, they were decided according to this precedent.

XI

*Das rrazoões que el-rrei dom Pedro ouve com o principe
sobre a tomada dos prisoneiros*

Aa segunda-feira partio el-rrei e o principe do campo
pera a cidade de Burgos, nom bem contentos por duas
rrazoões: a primeira, porque o dia da batalha matara el-rrei
per sa mãao Inhego Lopez de Orosco, teendo-o preso hũu
cavalleiro gascom, o quall se queixou ao principe como lhe
fezera perder seu prisoneiro e da desonrra que lhe havia
feita; e o principe disse a el-rrei que bem parecia que nom
avia voomtade de lhe guardar o que com el posera, pois
este, que era hũu dos principaaes capitollos, que nom matasse
nēhũu homem de conta sem primeiro seendo julgado, el
começava de quebrantar; e el-rrei se escusou o melhor que
pôde. A outra rrazom, porque o domingo depois da batalha
pedio el-rrei dom Pedro ao principe que todollos cavalleiros
e escudeiros castellaãos que de conta eram lhe fossem entregues por rrazoados preços, pollos quaaes ficasse o principe
aaquelles que os tiinham, e que el lhe faria hũua obrigaçom
por o que hi montasse; e que, avendo taaes homēes, que
fallaria com elles em tall maneira que fiquassem da sua parte;
e por esta cousa se aficou muito el-rrei dom Pedro, dizendo
que sse d'outra guisa se livrassem, que sempre seeríam em
seu desserviço. O principe disse que nom pedia rrazom, ca
os prisoneiros eram d'aquelles que os tiinham; e que eram
taaes homēes que por mill tanto d'o que valliam nom lhe
daria nēhũu o que tevesse, ca logo cuidariam que os com-
prava pera os matar; e que d'isto nom se trabalhasse, ca nom
era cousa pera viir a fim. El-rrei dom Pedro disse que sse
estas cousas assi aviam de passar, que fazia conta que o
principe ho nom ajudara, e que mais perdido tiinha estonce
seu rreino que da primeira, e que despendera seus tesouros
debalde. O principe ouve menencoria e disse a el-rrei: «Parente senhor, a mim parece que vós teendes agora mais forte
maneira pera perder o rreino d'o que tevestes quando o
rregiades; e governaste-llo de tall guisa que o ouvestes de
perder: porém vos conselho que tenhaães tall geito com
todos que cobrees os coraçoões dos grandes e fidallgos de
vossa terra; e sse o fezerdes como da primeira, estaaes em
ponto de perder o rreino e vossa pessoa; e el-rrei meu senhor
nem eu nom vos poderemos mais acorrer».

XI

*Of the discussions which King Pedro had with the Prince
about the capture of the prisoners.*

On the Monday the King and the Prince left the battle—field for
the city of Burgos, rather discontented for two reasons. The first was
because on the day of the battle the King had killed Iñigo de Orozco
with his own hand, although he was the captive of a Gascon knight
who complained to the Prince of the loss of his prisoner and of the
dishonour which had been done to him. The Prince told the King
that it seemed he was unwilling to keep the agreement they had
made, since he was beginning to break one of its chief clauses which
was that he should not kill any important man without first putting
him on trial; and the King gave such excuses as he could. The other
reason was that on the Sunday after the battle King Pedro asked the
Prince to have all the important Castilian knights and squires handed
over to him for appropriate prices, with the Prince to pay the total
amount. King Pedro said that if he had such men in his power he
would talk to them in such a way that they would join his side, and
he insisted strongly on this request, saying that if the captives were
set free in any other way, they would always try to oppose him.
The Prince said that he should not make this request, for the captives
belonged to those who held them prisoner, and those were men of
such a type as would not hand any of their captives over for even a
thousand times their value, because they would think that he was
buying them in order to kill them; so the King should not insist any
further, since his purpose could never be achieved. King Pedro said
that if things were going to go like this, he realized that the Prince
would not help him, that he had lost his kingdom more surely now
than the first time, and that he had spent all his wealth in vain.
The Prince was angry and said to the King: "My lord and cousin, I
think that you have now an attitude which is more likely to lose you
the kingdom than you had when you ruled it, and governed it in such
a way that you lost it. So I advise you to deal with everyone in
such a way that you win the hearts of the grandees and noblemen of
your country; for if you act now as you did previously, you are on
the point of losing both your kingdom and your life, in which case
neither my lord the King nor I will be able to help you anymore."

XII

Das aveenças que forom feitas antre o principe e el-rrei
dom Pedro sobre as cousas que lhe prometidas tiinha

Passadas estas cousas, fez o principe rrequerir per algũus
dos seus a el-rrei dom Pedro como bem sabia que fora hordenado antr'elles que assi a ell como aos outros senhores e
gentes d'armas que alli eram fossem pagadas suas gajas e
estados e solldo a cada hũu sem nẽhũua fauta que em ello
ouvessem. E como quer que el-rrei avia pagado em Bayona
a ell e aos outros parte d'o que aviam d'aver, que porém
ell ficava em diveda de grandes contias a todos elles, pollas
quaaes elle fezera juramentos e menagẽes aos seus com
acordo d'el-rrei, segundo bem sabia; e portanto fosse sua
mercee, pois ja estava em posse de seu rreino, de hordenar
como ouvessem pagamento, e ell fosse fora das obrigaçoões
que lhe feitas avia; allem d'esto, pois lhe de seu grado
prometera, sem lh'o el rrequerir, que em todas guisas quiria
que ouvesse algũua terra e rrenda no rreino de Castella,
e lhe outorgara o senhorio de Bizcaya e a villa de Castro
d'Ordialles, segundo per suas cartas tiinha outorgado, que
lhe prouguesse de o comprir assi, pera sse tornar cedo pera
sua terra; ca nom era proveito, mas perda grande, estar
muito tempo com tantas jentes em seus rreinos, acrecen-
tando despesa. El-rrei ouvio esto que lhe disserom, e mandou-lhe rresponder por outros que verdade era o que dito
aviam, e que lhe prazia de comprir todo o que prometera;
porém que sobre a paga da diveda quisera el-rrei poer rrevolta,
dizendo que pagara grandes solldos e gajas em joyas e pedras,
avendo-as d'elle por mais pouco preço d'aquello que valliam;
e o principe dizendo que os seus forom agravados em tall
paga, dando-lhe pedras e joias que lhe nom compriam, e nom
moeda que mester aviam pera comprar cavallos e armas
pera o servirem, assi que de tall cousa nom devia de fazer
pallavra; e disse mais o principe que ao que el-rrei dizia
que lhe leixasse mill lanças dos seus a sua despeza e gajas
e solldo, ataa que fosse bem assessegado no rreino, que bem
lhe prazia; mas que os seus quiriam veer primeiro como
pagavom os homẽes d'armas do tempo todo que aviam
servido. Sobr'esto passarom muitas fallas e rrazoões antre
el-rrei dom Pedro e o principe; na fim acordarom fazer conta
das gentes que veherom, e que ouverom de solldo, e quanto
lhe deviam; e acharom que montava em todo mui grande
conthia, polla quall o principe pedio que lhe desse viinte

26

XII

*Of the agreements made between the Prince and King Pedro
about the things which the latter had promised the former.*

After this, the Prince sent some of his men to make a formal
request to King Pedro, reminding him how they had agreed that the
Prince and the other lords and men—at—arms who were there should
be paid their wages, expenses and property, scrupulously, and without
fail. Although in Bayonne the King had paid him and the others a
part of what was due to them, however the Prince was still very
heavily in debt to all of them, because he had provided guarantees on
his sworn oath that the King would pay them, and the King had
authorized this as he well knew. He therefore begged the King, now
that he was in possession of his kingdom, to arrange the form of
payment and so release the Prince from the obligations he had
incurred. Moreover, since the King, without being asked, had
spontaneously promised to give him some land and income in the
kingdom of Castile and to grant him the lordship of Vizcaya and the
town of Castro Urdiales, and had in fact granted them by his
charters, he begged the King that he might see fit to fulfil his
promise so that he, the Prince, might go quickly back home; for to
stay for a long time in his kingdoms with so many men was
unprofitable and very expensive.

The King heard what the Prince's men said to him, and sent
others to reply that all this was true and he intended to fulfil all his
promises. However, the King wanted to review payment of the debt,
saying that he had made great payments of wages in the form of
jewels and precious stones, but received far less for them than they
were really worth. The Prince replied that his own men had lost by
those payments, since they had received precious stones and jewels
which they did not really need instead of the money they did need in
order to buy horses and arms with which to serve him, so that he
ought not to raise that question. Moreover, in answer to the King's
request to leave him a thousand of his own soldiers, to be paid their
pay and expenses by the King until he was quite in control of his
kingdom, the Prince agreed, but said that his men first wanted to see
how the men—at—arms were paid for all the time they had served so
far.

There were many discussions and arguments between King Pedro
and the Prince concerning these matters. In the end they agreed to
draw up accounts of the troops who had come and what they had
been paid and how much was still owing to them; and they found
that it came to a huge sum. So the Prince asked to be given twenty

castellos, quaaes ell nomeasse, em arrefẽes, por segurança
da paga; e que a cidade de Soria, que pormetiida avia a
monssé Joham condeestabre per suas cartas, que lh'a fezesse
entregar. El-rrei disse que per nẽhũua guisa nom podia taaes
castellos poer em fielldade, ca diriam os do rreino que quiria
dar a terra a gentes estranhas, nem as mill lanças que lhe
rrequiria, que nom avia por bem de ficarem em seu rreino,
mas que o senhorio de Bizcaya e Crasto d'Ordialles e Soria
a monssé Joham, que bem lhe prazia de o outorgar. E sobre
estas cousas ouve muitos debates, fallando-sse todo per
aquelles de que fiavom, dizendo o principe que quiria saber
como aviam de seer pagados os seus, e ell seer fora de sua
obrigaçom. El-rrei lhe enviou dizer que loguo mandava per
todo seu rreino a pedir ajuda pera pagua d'estas divedas,
e que a hũu dia certo lhe faria paga da meatade; e pollo
mais tevesse em arrefẽes as suas tres filhas que em Bayona
ficarom, ataa que fosse pagado de todo. E deu-lhe cartas
per que entregassem ao principe terra de Bizcaya e a monssé
Joham a cidade de Soria; e ao principe nom se quiserom
dar os moradores da terra, pero lá mandou seu rrecado,
porque lhe escreveo el-rrei calladamente d'outra guisa que
sse lhe nom dessem; e ao condeestabre pedirom dez mill
dobras de chancellaria da carta, e el nom a quiz tomar,
dizendo que lhe nom pediam tanto salvo por lhe nom darem
a dita cidade. O principe, veendo como estas cousas hiam,
por dar logar que el-rrei nom se tevesse por mall contente
d'elle, disse que lhe prazia atender algũus dias em Castella,
e que lhe fezesse el-rrei juramento de lhe comprir todo o que
lhe avia prometido, e el-rrei disse que lhe prazia; e acordarom que veesse o principe das olgas de Burgos, onde pousava,
dentro aa cidade aa egreja de Santa Maria, e que ally jurasse
el-rrei pubricamente perante todos a lhe comprir todallas
cousas que antr'elles eram devisadas. O principe disse que
nom hiria dentro salvo que lhe dessem hũua porta da cidade
com sua torre, em que posesse jente d'armas por sua segurança, e el-rrei lh'a mandou dar; e forom postos na torre homẽes d'armas e frecheiros; e a fundo da porta, em hũua gram
praça que sse fazia dentro, contra a cidade, pôs o principe
mill homẽes d'armas, e fora da cidade, arredor do moesteiro
onde ell pousava, as mais das gentes que com el veherom,
todos armados. Entrou o principe dentro na cidade per
aquella porta que era guardada, e hiam de bestas el e seu
hirmão, pero nom armados, e arredor d'elle algũus capitaães
e d'outros homẽes d'armas ataa quinhentos, e assi chegou
aa egreja mayor hu aviam de seer os juramentos. El-rrei

28

castles chosen by himself as pledges for the security of payment, and he also asked that the city of Soria should be handed over to Sir John the Constable, to whom the King had promised it in formal charters. The King replied that he could not possibly hand over such castles as a pledge, for his subjects would say that he wanted to give the land to foreigners. As for the thousand soldiers he had asked for, he no longer wanted them to stay in his kingdom; but he was happy to grant Vizcaya and Castro Urdiales, and also Soria to Sir John. There were many debates about these matters, through trusted intermediaries, with the Prince saying that he wanted to know how his men were going to be paid and he himself released from his obligations as guarantor. The King sent to tell him that he was sending through all his kingdom to ask for an aid to pay these debts, and that on a specific day he would have half the payment made; for the rest, the Prince should keep as pledges the King's three daughters who were in Bayonne, until the whole debt was paid; and the King issued writs ordering the land of Vizcaya to be handed over to the Prince and the city of Soria to Sir John. However, although the Prince sent his messenger to Vizcaya, the inhabitants did not want to accept him as their lord, because the King wrote secretly to them that they should not do so; and the Constable was asked for ten thousand *doblas* in chancery fees for the issue of the privilege granting him Soria, and he refused, saying that they were only asking him for so much in order to avoid giving him the city.

Seeing how things were going, and in order to provide no excuse for the King to be discontented with him, the Prince said that he wanted to spend some days in Old Castile and asked the King to swear an oath to fulfil all that he had promised him; and the King agreed. They decided that the Prince should come from Las Huelgas de Burgos,[1] where he was lodging, to the church of Santa María[2] inside the city, and that there the King should publicly swear before everyone to fulfil all the agreements made between them. The Prince said that he would not go into the city unless he were given a gate of the city, with its tower, in which to place men—at—arms for his own security; and the King ordered him to be given it. Men—at—arms and archers were placed in the tower; and at the bottom of the tower, in a great square on the city side, the Prince placed a thousand men—at—arms, whilst outside the city he left all the rest of his troops, all armed, around the convent where he was staying. The Prince entered the city by that gate which was guarded, and he and his brother went on horseback, but unarmed, surrounded by captains and about five hundred other men—at—arms, and so they came to the cathedral where they had to swear the oaths. King

dom Pedro veo aʼlli, e pubricamente leerom as escripturas d'o que el-rrei dom Pedro era theudo de dar ao principe e aos seus, e como sse obrigava de dar a ell ou a seus thesoureiros a meatade da contia d'aquell dia a quatro meses dentro em Castella e a outra meatade em Baiona d'hi a hũu ano, por a quall tevesse em arrefẽes suas filhas que lá ficarom quando d'hi partira. Outrossi jurou el-rrei aquell dia que faria entregar o senhorio de Bizcaya e Crasto d'Ordialles ao principe, e a monssé Chantos condeestabre de Guiana a cidade de Soria que lhe prometido avia: feito esto, foi-sse el-rrei pera seu paaço, e o principe pera o moesteiro onde pousava. El-rrei dom Pedro o foi depois veer, e disse como avia enviado muitos per seu rreino por juntar dinheiros pera a primeira paga; e por dar aguça muito moor em ello, que el meesmo quiria hir pella terra, por poer em ello melhor rrecado. O principe disse que fazia bem e lh'o gradecia, por manteer sua verdade e juramentos que fezera; e disse-lhe mais que a eʼl era dito que elle mandava suas cartas aos de terra de Bizcaya que o nom tomassem por senhor, e que isto nom podia creer, e que lhe rrogava que lh'a fezesse entregar como lhe avia prometido, e a cidade de Soria aʼ condeestabre. E el-rrei disse que nunca taaes cartas mandara, e que de a aver e lhe seer entregue lhe prazia muito, e que em todo lhe poeria bõo rremedio nʼeeste espaço dos quatro meses, e assi se espidio d'elle.

XIII

Quaaes pessoas matou el-rrei dom Pedro depois que partio
de Burgos, e como trautou paz com el-rrei
dom Fernando de Portugall

Partio el-rrei dom Pedro de Burgos e o principe pera hũu logar que dizem Arrusto; e hindo el-rrei pera Tolledo, ante que chegasse aa cidade, mandou matar Rrui Ponce Palomeque cavalleiro e Fernam Martinz homem honrrado do logar, porque andarom com eʼl-rrei dom Henrrique depois que entrara em-no rreino, e levou arrefẽes d'os da cidade, por seer d'elles seguro; e d'alli partio, e chegou a Cordova, e d'hi a dous dias armou-sse de noite e com outros andou pella cidade per casas certas, e fez matar dezeseis homẽes dos honrrados que em ella avia, dizendo que estes forom os primeiros que forom rreceber el-rrei dom Henrrique quando alli chegara. D'alli se partio e foi a Sevilha, e ante

Pedro arrived there, and they read in public the documents stating what King Pedro was bound to give to the Prince and his men, and how he promised to give him or his treasurers in Castile half of the amount within four months, and the other half in Bayonne within one year, for all of which the Prince would keep as pledges the King's daughters who had stayed in Bayonne when he left it. Moreover on that day the King swore that he would have the lordship of Vizcaya and Castro Urdiales handed over to the Prince, and the city of Soria to Sir John Chandos the Constable of Gascony, as he had promised him. After this the King went to his palace, and the Prince to the convent where he was lodging.

Later, King Pedro went to see him and said that he had sent many collectors through his kingdom to collect money for the first payment, and that he himself wanted to travel through his land in order to stimulate the collecting and ensure that it was done thoroughly. The Prince said that he was grateful to him for this good action, because it would maintain his integrity and fulfil the oaths which he had sworn; and he also said that he had been told that the King had sent letters telling the inhabitants of Vizcaya not to accept him as their lord, but he could not believe this. He asked him to have that territory handed over to him as he had promised, and also the city of Soria to the Constable. The King said that he had never sent such letters, and that he wanted the Prince to have that land and to be put in possession of it. He promised to make good all these matters within the space of four months, and so he said farewell.

XIII

The persons whom King Pedro killed after leaving Burgos, and how he negotiated a peace—treaty with King Fernando of Portugal.

King Pedro left Burgos, and the Prince went away to a place called Amusco. On his way to Toledo and before arriving there, the King ordered the killing of Ruy Ponce Palomeque and Fernán Martínez, a knight and an honourable citizen of that city respectively, because they had taken King Enrique's side after he entered the kingdom. King Pedro took hostages from among the citizens of Toledo in order to be more sure of them, and went on to Córdoba.

There, two days after his arrival, he armed himself at night and went with others to certain houses in the city. He had sixteen of the most honourable men in the city killed, saying that they were the first in accepting King Enrique when he came there.

Then he went on to Seville, but even before getting there he

que chegasse fez matar micer Gill Bocanegra almirante de Castella e dom Joham filho de dom Pedro Ponce de Leom e Affonso Airas de Quadros e Affonsso Fernandez e outros: E mandou a Martim Lopez de Cordova meestre de Callatrava, que estava em essa cidade, que matasse dom Gonçallo Fernandez de Cordova e dom Afonsso Fernandez senhor de Montemayor e Diego Fernandez alguazill-moor da cidade, e elle nom o quis fazer, entendendo que faria mall; e el-rrei dom Pedro ouve d'elle queixume por esto e hordenou que o prendessem por traiçom; e a rrogo d'el-rrei de Graada, por rreceo que el-rrei d'elle ouve, soltou dom Martim Lopez, e assi escapou de morte. E por queixume que el-rrei avia de dom Joham Affonsso de Gozmam, que depois foi conde de Nebra, porque sse nom fora nem chegara a elle quando outra vez foi o alvoroço de Sevilha, que el-rrei dom Pedro fugira pera Portugall, e o nom achou na cidade pera o prender, mandou tomar dona Branca sa madre e feze-a matar de cruell morte, e tomou todollos bẽes que ambos aviam; e mandou matar Martinh'Anes seu thesoureiro-moor, a que fora tomada a galee do aver, segundo avees ouvido. Estando el-rrei assi em Sevilha, mandou a Portugall a el-rrei dom Fernando Mateus Fernandez, seu chanceller-moor e do seu conselho, pera trautar com elle paz e amizade; o quall chegou a Coimbra, onde el-rrei dom Fernando era estonce, e trautou com elle e disse que el-rrei dom Pedro queria com elle paz e amizade e seer seu verdadeiro amigo por sempre em todallas cousas que comprisse; entom firmarom suas amizades o mais firmemente que poderom, fazendo sobr'ello suas escripturas quaaes pera tall feito compriam; e partido o embaxador de Castella, mandou el-rrei dom Fernando a Sevilha Joham Gonçallvez, do seu conselho, pera confirmar este amor e paz que o procurador d'el-rrei dom Pedro com elle trautara; e Joham Gonçallvez chegou a Sevilha, e el-rrei confirmou todo o que Mateus Fernandez avia trautado, e veo-sse Joham Gonçallvez; e el-rrei dom Pedro mandou outra vez Joham de Cayom seu alcaide-moor que chegasse a el-rrei dom Fernando e lhe rrequerisse que rratificasse outra vez a amizade que feita aviam; e ell chegou a Tentugall, onde el-rrei entom estava, e rrequirido per elle outorgou el-rrei dom Fernando a paz e amor que ante d'esto feito avia, e rrecebeo d'elle o messegeiro preito e menagem por aquellas aveenças, e espedio-sse d'el-rrei e foi-sse caminho de Sevilha: honde leixemos estar el-rrei dom Pedro, e tornemos a contar d'el-rrei dom Henrrique, que sse fez d'elle

had various men killed, including Master Egidio Boccanegra, the Admiral of Castile,[1] Don Juan,[2] the son of Pedro Ponce de León, Alfonso Arias de Cuadros and Alfonso Fernández. He also ordered Martín López de Córdoba, the Master of Calatrava who had stayed in Córdoba, to kill Gonzalo Fernández de Córdoba, Alfonso Fernández the lord of Montemayor and Diego Fernández, the Chief Constable of the city; but he did not wish to kill them, thinking it wrong. King Pedro was annoyed with him over this and ordered him to be arrested for treason; but, at the request of the King of Granada[3] of whom King Pedro was afraid, he released Martín López who thus escaped execution.

Juan Alfonso de Guzmán, later Count of Niebla, had also aroused the King's resentment because he had not gone to support him on the occasion of the earlier riot in Seville when King Pedro had fled to Portugal. Now, however, the King could not find him in Seville, so he ordered his mother, Doña Blanca,[4] to be arrested and put to death most cruelly, and confiscated all the property of both of them. He also ordered the execution of his Grand Treasurer, Martín Yáñez,[5] who had been captured with his treasure—ship, as you have heard.

Whilst in Seville, the King sent Mateo Fernández,[6] his counsellor and Grand Chancellor, to Portugal to negotiate a treaty of peace and friendship with King Fernando. This ambassador came to Coimbra, where King Fernando then was, and negotiated with him and said that King Pedro wanted peace and friendship with him and to be his true friend forever in all matters. Then they signed as firm a treaty of friendship as they could, with the appropriate documentation; and the Castilian ambassador left. Afterwards, King Fernando sent his counsellor João Gonçalves to confirm this peace and friendship which King Pedro's representative had negotiated with him; and when João Gonçalves arrived in Seville, King Pedro confirmed everything that Mateo Fernández had arranged, and João Gonçalves went home again.[7] Then King Pedro sent another envoy, his *alcaide mayor*, Juan de Cayom, to King Fernando to ask him to ratify yet again the treaty of friendship which they had made; and this envoy came to Tentugal, where King Fernando then was, and at his request the King agreed to the treaty of peace and friendship which he had already made, and confirmed it with oaths and guarantees; and the envoy took his leave of the King and set out for Seville.

Here we shall leave King Pedro, and go back to telling the story of King Enrique and what happened to him between fleeing from the

depois que fugio da batalha ataa que tornou outra vez a
Castella, e isso meesmo de sua molher e filhos; ca, posto
que ante queriamos dizer da paga que el-rrei dom Pedro
fez ao principe, e como lhe entregou as terras que lhe de
dar avia, e se espedio d'el e foi pera sa terra, que era rrazom
de dizermos primeiro, nós isto fazer nom podemos, porque
nas obras dos antiigos que ante de nós fezerom estorias
taaes cousas nom achamos nas escripturas a nós per elles
comunicadas; ante entendemos que foi pollo contrairo e que
nunca lhe mais fez pagamento, segundo adeante ouvirees,
e que ho principe se partio sem lhe mais fallar, por novas
que avia dos franceses que começavam guerra no ducado
de Guiana per maneira de companhias; e porém tornaremos
aos feitos d'el-rrei dom Henrrique, de que, muitos leixando,
algũus diremos por abreviar.

The next few chapters of the Chronicle of Dom Fernando relate
what befell Enrique of Trastámara and his wife after he fled the
battle—field. They repair to France where they are generously
received. After making a treaty with the Duke of Anjou, the
usurper returns to Spain with his wife and is well received in Burgos
(XIV—XVII). Enrique now besieges and captures León, and then
descends into New Castile where he besieges Toledo (XVIII).

At this juncture, the Chronicle switches attention back to Pedro
the Cruel, who in alliance with the King of Granada, makes two
attempts to take Córdoba (XIX).

The ensuing chapters up to and including chapter XXIV narrate
how Pedro is outmanoeuvred, captured and finally killed by his
half—brother.

In chapter XXV, Fernão Lopes reaches the moment in the
Castilian power struggle in which young Fernando I of Portugal
emerges as rival to the Castilian usurper, and effectively is offered
the throne by those Castilian barons who have remained faithful to
the memory of the legitimate King of Castile, Pedro I. Our
chronicler opens this fresh section of his account of this reign by
emphasizing that initially at least Fernando was strongly tempted by
these Castilian legitimists who came to him arguing persuasively that
it would take but little effort on his part to make himself King of
Castile, or the better part of it; and that even if he did not want
this, he could make one of Don Pedro's sons King of Castile, thus
winning much honour and avenging his cousin.

Fernando yields to temptation and embarks on a series of
diplomatic and military manoeuvres designed to isolate the usurper.
He profits by the enmity between Enrique of Trastámara and the
King of Granada to make an alliance with the latter (XXVI); he
names himself King of Zamora and other towns in the West of

battle and returning once again to Castile, and also what happened to his wife and children. We would have preferred to tell how King Pedro paid the Prince, and handed over to him the lands which he had promised him, and how the Prince said farewell and went home, all of which logically ought to come first. However, we cannot do this, because in the works of earlier historians we do not find such things written, at least in the texts which they have left us. We think it more likely that the opposite happened and that the Prince never received further payment, as you will hear later on, and that he went away without speaking further with King Pedro, because he had news that the French were beginning to use the Free Companies to make war again in the Duchy of Gascony. So we shall turn to the deeds of King Enrique, and provide a summary of them, though leaving many untold.

Spain; he embarks on a mission to poach from Enrique's son his betrothed, Leonor of Aragon, and to obtain a military alliance with her father, Pedro IV; and finally, he endeavours to put Galicia on a war footing (XXVII—XXXI).

The stage is now set for the first of King Fernando's three wars with Trastamaran Castile. Enrique II decides to invade Northern Portugal, laying waste the countryside as he goes. He takes several places but fails to in his attempts to capture either Braga or Guimarães. While he is doing this, according to Fernão Lopes, Fernando is losing popularity for his lack of military initiative (XXXII—XXXVI). The chief theatre of conflict between the Portuguese and the Castilian usurper now shifts to the Eastern frontier where the Portuguese skirmish with some success but Fernando loses some ships in the port of Lisbon because of a storm (XXXVII—XXXIX). Enrique besieges Badajoz, then held by the Portuguese, but is beaten off and retreats to Medina del Campo where he pays off his French allies. He then besieges other towns in Spain that had declared against him, including Zamora, which he fails to take (XL—XLI).

Fernando now blockades the mouth of the Guadalquivir, but to little effect, whereas his adversary, arriving in Seville and finding it blockaded, has seven galleys armed in Vizcaya, which return south to catch the Portuguese unawares in the river. These escape only by the use of fire—ships (XLII—XLIV). In the process, the Portuguese lose a pay—ship containing £100,000. Fernão Lopes censures King Fernando for losing money and men in exchange for scant material gain and for loss of honour. Meanwhile, Enrique of Trastámara pursues his campaign in Andalusia with some success (XLV—XLVI).

The next six chapters tell of Fernando's half—hearted and complicated negotiations with King Pedro IV of Aragon for a

marriage with Pedro's daughter Leonor, principally, according to Fernão Lopes, in order to strengthen Fernando's hand in the struggle with Enrique II (XLVII—LII).

Fernando now abandons the agreement with Aragon and signs a peace with King Enrique in Silves whereby he will marry Enrique's daughter, also called Leonor, and receive into the bargain the towns of Ciudad Rodrigo and Valencia de Alcántara. Enrique and Fernando each pardon all towns which declared against them, except for Carmona (LIII).

Hearing of this peace, Pedro IV of Aragon promptly claims all the monies deposited by Fernando in his kingdom as surety for his impending marriage with Leonor of Aragon (LIV).

Looking back on the wars between King Fernando and King Enrique, our chronicler roundly condemns the Portuguese King for the financial losses he incurred thereby and for the inflation that occurred in this period (LV—LVI).

Fernão Lopes now gives his version of how Fernando comes to fall under the spell of a married woman, Dona Leonor Teles de Meneses, lady—in—waiting to his sister, Dona Beatriz, and how eventually her marriage is dissolved so that she may marry the King (LVII).

Despite his annoyance and disappointment on learning that Fernando has broken his promise to marry his daughter, Enrique of Trastámara nevertheless reaches agreement with him over certain territories and places claimed by them both.

Fernão Lopes now turns to the internal political effects of Fernando's marriage to Leonor Teles, describing the shock and displeasure of nobles and commoners alike at Fernando's liaison with a woman they claimed to have been his mistress before their marriage. They grumble that the King prefers to marry a vassal's

---

LXVII

Como el-rrei dom Fernando e o duque d'Allancastro fezerom liança contra el-rrei de Castella e el-rrei d'Aragom

Asi era certo, como contarom a el-rrei de Castella, que el-rrei dom Fernando fazia liança com os ingreses contra elle, nom embargando os trautos e pazes que antr'elles avia, segundo ouvistes; ca o duque d'Allancastro, segundo filho d'el-rrei de Ingraterra, que sse chamava rrei de Castella, por aazo da iffante dona Costança sua molher, filha d'el-rrei dom Pedro, segundo contamos, enviara pouco avia seus embaxadores a el-rrei dom Fernando, *scilicet,* Joham Fernandez Andeiro cavalleiro e Roger Hoor escudeiro outrossi do duque;

wife rather than marry a Castilian princess who would surely have brought him both lands and honour. The common people blame his advisors for allowing it to happen and, through their spokesman, a tailor called Fernão Vasques, they threaten to abduct Leonor Teles if Fernando does not cast her off. The King protests that he has no intention of marrying Leonor Teles, and promises to meet representatives of the people the following day, but in the event fails to appear. Meanwhile, according to Fernão Lopes, Dona Leonor herself seeks out the ringleaders of the protest who are arrested and beheaded and have their goods confiscated (LX—LXI).

The chronicler notes the people's sorrow when Fernando does marry Leonor Teles, but also that many kissed her hand. These include the eldest of the bastard sons of Pedro I, Prince João (LXII).

There is still confusion as to whether or not Fernando has married Leonor Teles, while many courtiers accept the fait accompli in any case. Meanwhile, Dona Leonor, aware of her unpopularity, seeks to secure a power base by obtaining preferment at court for numerous members of her family (LXIII—LXV).

The King of Castile hears of military aggression in Galicia on the part of Fernando who has also contracted for military assistance in England. So Enrique II sends Diego López Pacheco to Portugal to persuade the bastard sons of Pedro I, Dom João and Dom Dinis, that their lives are now threatened by the ambitions of Leonor Teles, and that they would be well advised to flee to Castile. Pacheco then returns to Castile, informing Enrique II that such is the disaffection among the Portuguese nobles and the people, that an invasion would be opportune (LXVI). Meanwhile, Fernando has initiated negotiations with the English.

LXVII
How King Fernando and the Duke of Lancaster made an alliance against the King of Castile and the King of Aragon.

It was indeed true, as had been reported to the King of Castile, that King Fernando was making an alliance with the English against him, notwithstanding all the agreements and treaties which existed between these two kings, as you have already heard. For the Duke of Lancaster, the second son of the King of England, called himself King of Castile on account of his wife, Princess Constanza, who was King Pedro's daughter, as we said above; and he had sent his ambassadors a short while previously to King Fernando. These were the knight Juan Fernández Andeiro[1] and the Duke's squire Roger Hore.[2] These two arrived in July near Braga, where King Fernando

os quaaes chegarom no mes de julho acerca de Bragaa, onde el-rrei de Portugall estonce era. E mostrado abastante poder que pera ello tragiam, firmarom suas aveenças em esta guisa: que el-rrei e o duque fossem verdadeiros amigos por sempre hũu do outro, e que sse ajudassem per mar e per terra contra dom Henrrique, rrei que sse chamava de Castella, e contra el-rrei dom Pedro d'Aragom, *scilicet,* que viindo o duque fazer guerra a el-rrei dom Henrrique ou a el-rrei d'Aragon;, e estando no rreino de Navarra começando de fazer guerra a cada hũu d'elles com as gentes que consiguo trouvesse, que el-rrei dom Fernando fosse theudo de lhe fazer logo guerra; e sse o duque entrasse per seu corpo em cada hũu dos ditos rreinos, que el-rrei de Portugall fosse theudo de entrar com seu corpo per outra parte; e que estas ajudas e guerra que cada hũu fezesse fosse aas suas proprias despesas; e que toda cousa que el-rrei dom Fernando tomasse do rreino de Castella, que nom fosse villa ou castello ou terra, que fosse sua sem outra contenda; e que toda cousa que fosse tomada do rreino d'Aragom, que fosse d'aquell que a tomasse. Estes e outros capitullos que por nom alongar leixamos d'escrever forom entom firmados antre el-rrei e o duque d'Alancastro sobre esta guerra e ajudas que sse aviam de fazer; e o ditado do duque, como sse entom chamava, era este: «Dom Joham, pella graça de Deus rrei de Castella e de Leom e de Tolledo e de Galliza e de Sevilha e de Cordova e de Mollina e de Geem e do Algarve e d'Aljazira, duque d'Allancastro e senhor de Mollina»; e em algũas escripturas emhadiam mais em elle, dizendo: «Rreinante nos ditos rreinos em hũu com a rrainha dona Costança nossa molher, filha primeira e herdeira do mui alto rrei dom Pedro que Deus perdoe». Depois d'estes trautos assi firmados, enviou el-rrei dom Fernando Vaasco Dominguez chantre de Bragaa a Ingraterra pera os o duque firmar e jurar; e forom firmados per elle nos paaços de Saboya, terra de Londres, ficando d'esta vez el-rrei e o duque postos em grande amizade.

LXVIII

Como el-rrei dom Henrrique enviou rrequerir a el-rrei
dom Fernando que ouvesse com elle paz; e das
rrazoões que o embaxador disse

El-rrei dom Henrrique, nom embargando o que lhe Diego Lopez dissera e as outras novas que de Portugall ouvera, como dissemos, nom lhe prazia porém aver guerra com el-rrei

then was, and, having shown the documents which they brought with them authorizing them to negotiate, they made an agreement on the following terms:

The King and the Duke would henceforth always be true friends with each other and help each other on land and sea against Don Enrique, who called himself King of Castile, as well as against King Pedro of Aragon; that is to say that if the Duke came to make war on King Enrique or on the King of Aragon, and having entered the kingdom of Navarre, began to make war on each of them with the men he brought with him, then the King of Portugal would be bound to lead his armies in person into the war from the west; and each of them would pay his own expenses in these wars. Anything that King Fernando captured in the kingdom of Castile, except for castles, towns and land, he might keep for himself without question; and everything that was taken from the kingdom of Aragon would belong to him that took it.

These clauses about the war and their mutual assistance, and other clauses which we shall omit for brevity's sake, were then signed by the King and the Duke of Lancaster. The full title which the Duke then used was: "Don Juan, by the grace of God King of Castile, Leon, Toledo, Galicia, Seville, Córdoba, Murcia, Jaén, the Algarve and Algeciras, Duke of Lancaster and Lord of Molina"; and in some documents the following was added: "Reigning in the aforesaid kingdoms together with our wife, Queen Constanza, eldest daughter and heiress of the most high King Pedro, whom God forgive." [3] When these treaties were signed in this way, King Fernando sent Vasco Domingues, Precentor of Braga, [4] to England so that the Duke could sign and swear to them; and they were signed by him in the Savoy Palace, near London, leaving the King and the Duke as the best of friends.

LXVIII

How King Enrique sent word to King Fernando asking for peace;
and of the arguments put forward by the ambassador.

Despite what Diego López[1] had told him and the other news which he had received from Portugal, as we have said before, King Enrique was reluctant, nevertheless, to have war with King Fernando;

dom Fernando, ante lhe pesava muito de lhe assi quebrantar os trautos e amizade que com el avia posta: e por moor avondança, ante que sse demovesse a entrar em Portugall, enviou por embaxador a el-rrei dom Fernando hũu bispo, o quall dizem algũus que era dom Joham Manrrique, bispo de Segonça; e veo a Portugall e achou el-rrei em hũu logar quatro legoas de Santarem, que chamom Salvaterra de Magos. O bispo era homem entendido e bem rrazoado, e depois que deu a el-rrei as suas encomendaçoões, presente o conde dom Joham Affonsso Tello e outros que com ell estavom, lhe disse em esta guisa: «Senhor, el-rrei dom Henrrique meu senhor, veendo os grandes divedos que antre vós e elle há, e desejando aver paz e amorio convosco, assi por proveito dos poboos que cada hũu de vós ha de rreger como por espiciall amor e boa voontade que vos tem, quis que fosses ambos em tal acordo que antre vós e elle nom podesse vĩir nem rrecrecer depois nẽhũua contenda; e esto o demoveo a fazer paz convosco, a quall foi firmada com certas condiçoões e juras, segundo bem sabem quantos aqui estam. E por moor firmeza d'ellas e vossos bõos divedos seerem acrecentados, foi posto de vos dar sua filha por molher, com algũuas villas e logares de seu rreino: e vós, senhor, nom sei por quall rrazom, o capitulo que mais deverees de guardar, que era casar com sua lidema filha, por seer a vós honrroso casamento e acrecentardes em vosso rreino os logares que vos com ella dava, e vós quebrantaste-llo d'hi a poucos dias, leixando-a de rreceber e casando-vos com outrem, da quall cousa vos mandastes escusar a el-rrei meu senhor, como aa vossa mercee prougue; e posto que ell hi podera tornar com aguisada rrazom e dereito, sofreo-sse de o fazer, por dar logar aa paz que deseja d'aver convosco. E hora, depois d'esto, mandastes aos do seu rreino tomar certas naaos, assi na costa do mar como ante o porto de Lixboa; e pero vos enviou rrequerer que lhe mandassees de todo fazer entrega, nom foi vossa mercee de o poer em obra, ante destes tall rreposta aaquelles que aca enviou, per que mostrastes que de guardar a paz que antre vós e elle foi firmada aviees mui pouca voontade; aalem d'esto lhe fezerom algũus entender que vós faziees liga com os ingreses, pera viinrem a vosso rreino e seerem em vossa ajuda contra elle. E porque todas estas cousas mostram claramente que vós nom teendes voontade de lhe guardar a paz que antre vós e elle foi firmada, vos envia dizer per mim e vos rrequere da parte de Deus que vós lhe guardees compridamente as pazes que antre vós ambos som

and indeed it weighed heavily on him that King Fernando would be breaking the treaties and friendship that he had made with him. Moreover, before he made any move to enter Portugal, he sent as ambassador to King Fernando a bishop whom some say was Don Juan Manrique, Bishop of Sigüenza,[2] and who came to Portugal and met the King in a place called Salvaterra de Magos, four leagues from Santarém. The Bishop was a knowledgeable and well—spoken man, and after presenting his credentials to the King in the presence of Count João Afonso Telo[3] and others who were with him, he spoke in this wise:

"Sire, my lord King Enrique, in view of the great commitments that exist between you both and desiring to have peace and friendship with you, as much for the sake of the two peoples that you and he have to govern as for the particular love and good—will that he feels for you, wanted there to be such accord between you and him that no dispute could ever again arise. This consideration moved him to make a peace with you, which was signed with certain conditions and oaths, as is well known to all here present.[4] In order to reinforce these commitments and to further strengthen your mutual links, it was agreed that his daughter would be given to you in marriage, together with certain towns and other places in his kingdom. Then within a few days, you, my lord, for what reason I know not, broke the article of the treaty which you ought most particularly to have kept: that is, to marry his legitimate daughter, since it was a marriage that would have given you much honour and also increased your kingdom with the places which he was giving you with her. Yet you abandoned her and married another, and sent your excuses for this to my lord the King, as your majesty saw fit; and although he could have punished this with good reason and with right on his side, he refrained from doing so in order to give a chance for the peace which he desires to have with you. Now, after this, you ordered certain ships of his subjects to be captured, off the sea—coast and in front of the port of Lisbon; and although he sent to request you to order everything to be handed over to him, you did not deign to do so. Instead, you answered his envoys in such a way as to show that you had scant interest in keeping the peace that had been signed between you. Moreover, some people have informed him that you have been making an alliance with the English, so that they may come to your kingdom and help you against him. Because all these things make it evident that you set no store by the peace signed between you, my lord sends me to request in God's name that you should observe fully the treaties signed with him, and that you should order reparation to be made to his subjects for all the damage that they have suffered. If you do this, you will be doing what is reasonable and just, as you are bound to do, and he will be most grateful and consider it an act of great friendship. On the other hand, if you wish to break the treaties which you have between you, and he is obliged to defend himself against you, then he will show God and the world that he no

firmadas e mandees fazer entrega aos seus de todo o dano que am rrecebido; e fazendo-o assi, farees em ello rrazom e dereito que sooes theudo de fazer, e ell gradecer-vo-llo-á muito, e teerá em grande amizade: d'outra guisa, se vossa mercee he britardes as pazes que assi avees em hũu, a el he forçado que sse defenda de vós, e entom mostrará a Deus e ao mundo que nom he mais teudo que vo-llo rrequerer, e que Deus, que he justo juiz, teerá justa rrazom de o ajudar contra vós».

LXIX

Da rreposta que el-rrei dom Fernando deu ao bispo, e como se espedio d'ele e se foi

El-rrei dom Fernando, que bem sospeitava as rrazoões que lhe o bispo avia de dizer e as cousas em que o avia de culpar, como aquell que d'ellas era bem sabedor, tiinha ja a rreposta prestes pera sse escusar, e nom pedio espaço pera aver sobr'ello consselho, mas rrespondeo logo dizendo assi: «Eu, todo o que fize, tiinha rrazom de o fazer; e que mais fezera, nẽhũu m'o deve teer a mall, porque eu nom lhe quebrei as pazes, mas elle as quebrantou a mim primeiro; e assi lh'o enviei dizer per Martim Perez, doutor em degredos, chanceller do iffante dom Joham seu filho, quando a mim sobr'esto veo da sua parte: porque, depois das pazes feitas a cabo d'hũus seis meses, chegou a mim a Tentugall, onde eu estonce estava, aquell doutor, e disse-me e rrequirio que bem sabia os trautos e aveenças que por bem de paz antre mim e el-rrei dom Henrrique forom firmadas, e como sse depois perlongarom aalem do tempo, por certas rrazoões da sua proll e minha, as quaaes eram entrega de certos logares e prisoneiros d'hũua parte aa outra, e mais o casamento da iffante dona Lionor comigo. E eu lhe rrespondi que bem sabia el-rrei de Castella que o que eu ficara por fazer ja era da minha parte comprido, leixando-lhe as villas e logares que tiinha, e entregues todollos prisoneiros que em meu rreino eram rreteudos; e que el nunca me quisera entregar a villa de Bragança nem o castello de Miranda e outros logares: e porém que me entregasse ell primeiro os logares todos, como eu fezera a elle, e que bem me prazia casar com sua filha e lhe comprir mais ainda outra cousa, se teudo era de a comprir; assi que eu fiz todo o que devia, e el nom me teve aquello que me pôs: e porém casei com quem me prougue e fize o que entendi por meu serviço». «Senhor, disse o bispo,

longer needs to request anything of you and that God, Who is a just judge, will have every reason to help him against you."

LXIX

Of the reply which King Fernando gave to the Bishop, and how the latter took his leave and departed.

King Fernando, who had a shrewd idea of the points which the Bishop was going to raise with him and of the offences of which he would accuse him, since he was well aware of these, had already prepared a reply to excuse himself; so he did not ask for time to seek advice on the matter, but replied at once in the following manner:

"I had good reason to do all that I have done; and no one could hold it against me, even if I had done more than I did, for it was not I who broke the treaties against King Enrique, but he who first broke them against me. I sent word to tell him so, through Martín Pérez, doctor in canon law and chancellor of his son, Prince Juan, when he came to see me on his behalf; for, six months after the peace was made, that doctor came to see me at Tentugal, where I then was, and he questioned me formally as to whether I knew the treaties and agreements which had been signed between King Enrique and me in the cause of peace, and how they had been prolonged beyond their time — limit, for certain reasons, to his advantage and mine: that is, the mutual exchange by both sides of certain places and prisoners, and in addition my marriage to Princess Leonor. I replied that the King of Castile well knew that I had fulfilled what it was incumbent on me to do, leaving the towns and villages which I held and surrendering up all the prisoners that were still held in my kingdom; yet he had never wanted to surrender to me the town of Bragança or the castle of Miranda or other places. So he should first give up to me all these places, just as I had done to him; and I was ready to marry his daughter and fulfil any other obligation, if it was right for me to do so. Thus I have done all I should, while he has not done what he agreed with me. In view of this, I married the woman I wished and did what I thought best for myself."

"My Lord", said the Bishop, "I have spoken of the marriage

no casamento vos nom fallei se nom por o trazer a meu proposito; e se el-rrei meu senhor algũas cousas por comprir tem d'as que antre vós e elle forom firmadas, he mui bem que seja rrequirido que as compra, e som certo que o fará de boom tallante; d'outra guisa nom me parece que he bem hordenardes per hu antre vós e elle aja guerra e discordia, ca sse os de sua terra furtarom em vosso rreino o castello de Miranda, primeiro sairom os de vossa terra a rroubar na sua e lhe fazer guerra, tomando per força em Galliza o logar de Viana, e d'alli faziam guerra a toda a comarca d'arredor, consentindo-o vós e nom tornando a ello; em guisa que ouve ell hi de mandar o conde dom Affonsso seu filho com gentes a poer cobro em esto; mas antre vós e elle tam pequenas cousas como essas ligeiras ssom de concordar, por seerdes em paz e amorio. Porém, senhor, por mercee esguardaae bem primeiro o que querees fazer, e conhecee que aquella he nobre e bem aventurada paz que he na voontade e nom nas pallavras, e que hũum dos cuidados melhores que aver podees assi he d'aver paz com vossos vizinhos; nem pode nẽhũua cousa mais doce seer antre os rreis e os poboos que viverem em paz e assessego, de guisa que onde he hũu dom de ffe, haja hũua concordia de vida». El-rrei dom Fernando tiinha mandado Vaasco Dominguez chantre de Bragaa a Ingraterra, como ouvistes, por firmar o trauto antr'elle e o duque d'Alancastro, desi por fazer vĩir gentes d'armas; e ouvera ja rrecado d'elle que tiinha oitocentas lanças e outros tantos archeiros prestes; e quando lhe o bispo dizia estas e outras muitas rrazoões, que toda via ouvesse paz, e el-rrei rrespondia per taaes pallavras e com tall doairo que bem mostrava que avia d'ello pouca voontade. E d'essa meesma guisa o dezia o conde dom Joham Affonsso Tello, em tanto que o bispo lhe veo a dizer: «Conde, vós podees consselhar el-rrei que aqui está como vos prouguer; mas se o vós conselhaaes que ell aja guerra ante que paz, vós podees dizer o que quiserdes, mas porém sei que nom avees vós de seer o primeiro que avees de jugar as lançadas ant'elle; e se eu fosse de seu conselho, como vós sooes, eu lhe conselharia ante que escolhesse a certa paz com el-rrei meu senhor que esperar a duvidosa vitoria». Sobr'esto se seguirom outras muitas rrazoões, pellas quaaes o bispo entendeo que el-rrei nom avia voontade d'aver paz; e espedio-sse d'elle e foi-sse seu caminho.

only insofar as it was relevant to my present concern. If the King, my lord, still has some obligations to fulfil of the ones which were formally agreed between him and you, it is only right and proper that he should be required to fulfil them, and I am sure that he will do so most willingly. On the other hand, it does not seem right to me for you to be acting in such a way as to create discord and war between you and him, for if his men seized Miranda castle in your kingdom, your men had previously sallied forth to rob and pillage in his land and make war on him, taking the village of Viana in Galicia by force.[1] From there they waged war in all the region thereabout, with your consent and without your punishing them, so that he was obliged to send his son Count Alfonso there with men in order to restore order. However, such trivial matters are easy to resolve between you and him, for the sake of peace and love. So, my lord, I beseech you, first consider what you want to do, and realize that the truly noble and blessed peace is that which is founded on good—will and not on the words in which it is expressed, and that one of your prior concerns should be to have peace with your neighbours. There can exist no sweeter thing between kings and peoples than to live in peace and tranquillity, so that where there is a single gift of faith there should be a single harmony of life."

As you have already heard, King Fernando had sent Vasco Domingues, the Precentor of Braga, to England to sign the treaty between the King and the Duke of Lancaster, with a view to bringing troops to Portugal; and he had already received word from him that he had eight hundred lances and the same number of archers ready and waiting to come. When the Bishop had said these things and many others to him, urging that there should still be peace, the King replied in such a way that by his language and his flippant manner he made abundantly clear his lack of interest in peace. Count João Afonso Telo spoke in a similar vein so that the Bishop came up to him and said, "Count, you may advise the King in whatever manner you please, but if your advice is for war rather than for peace, you can say what you like, but yet I know you will not be the first one to wield a lance in front of him. If I had his ear, as you do, I would rather advise him to opt for a peace that is certain with my lord the King, than to gamble on a victory that is decidedly uncertain." After this, many more things were said which led the Bishop to understand that the King had no interest in peace; and so he took his leave and went on his way.

Como o bispo chegou a Castella, e como sse el-rrei dom Hen~rique demoveo a fazer guerra a Portugall

Tornou-sse o bispo pera Castella e achou el-rrei dom Henrrique em Çamora; e posto el-rrei adeparte com os de seu conselho pera ouvir a rreposta que o bispo trazia, e elle as primeiras novas que lhe deu disse-lhe que sse percebesse de guerra, e contou-lhe todo o que lhe avehera com el-rrei dom Fernando, e como entendia n'eelle que nom avia voontade de seer seu amigo nem lhe guardar a paz que com el posera, e que assi lhe parecia que o consselhavom algũus senhores d'os que com elle eram. El-rrei dom Henrrique, ouviindo isto, disse entom perante todos: «Deus sabe, que he sabedor de todallas cousas, que eu nom ei voontade d'aver com ell guerra, ante quiria de mui boa mente aver com ell paz e seer seu amigo; mas pois que assi he que eu ei d'aver guerra, eu nom a quero guardar pera mais longe, mas logo em ponto a quero começar; e diga cada hũu de vós o que lhe parece e como sse pode melhor fazer». Os do conselho, vista a rreposta que o bispo tragia e o desejo que el-rrei em esto mostrava, acordavom todos de sse fazer guerra e que el-rrei entrasse per Portugall com todo seu poder, mas que esto nom fosse logo, por certas rrazoões: a hũua, por el-rrei nom teer as suas gentes prestes, e isso meesmo dinheiros pera paga dos solldos e corregimentos que lhe eram necessarios, desi por o inverno que sse seguia: assi que por esto e por outras cousas que cada hũu mostrava a sse nom fazer, eram todos em acordo que el-rrei espaçasse esta guerra ataa o veraão que havia de vĩir, e que entanto faria elle prestes todo o que pera ello era compridoiro, e assi a poderia acabar com mais sua honrra e serviço. El-rrei, quando vio que todos eram d'aquelle acordo e nẽhũu desviava d'elle, deu-lhes em rreposta dizendo: «Ou vós todos estaaes bevedos ou sandeus, ou sooes treedores». «Nom ja eu, senhor, disse o bispo, ca nom som rruivo». «Aa, bispo, disse el-rrei, por mim dizees vos isso?», porque el-rrei era branco e rruivo. «Nom senhor, disse elle, mas por este que aqui está», *scilicet*, Pero Fernandez de Vallasco, que estava junto com elle, que era hũu pouco come rruivo. E rriindo d'estas e d'outras rrazoões que antremetiam por tomar sabor, tornou el-rrei a dizer contra elles: «Aqui nom compre mais perlongas nem outro consselho quando se fará; mas ante que sse nunca el-rrei dom Fernando perceba nem lhe venha ajuda d'ingreses, nem d'outro nẽhũu de fora

LXX
How the Bishop arrived in Castile,
and how King Enrique decided to wage war on Portugal.

The Bishop returned to Castile and found King Enrique in Zamora; and when the King retired with his council to hear the reply brought by the Bishop, the first piece of news they heard was that he should be thinking of war. The Bishop narrated all that had befallen him with King Fernando, and how he understood that the latter had no desire to be King Enrique's friend nor to respect the peace he had made with him. It seemed to the Bishop that King Fernando was being advised in this sense by some of the lords who were with him. On hearing this, King Enrique said, in the presence of them all: "God, Who knows all things, knows that I have no desire to have a war with him, but that I would much rather have peace and be his friend; but given that it seems I must go to war, I do not wish to postpone it any longer but wish to begin forthwith. So, each of you, say what you think and how it can best be done." Considering the reply brought back by the Bishop and the frame of mind shown by the King, all the councillors agreed that they should go to war and that the King should invade Portugal with all his might, but that this should not be done immediately, for the following reasons: firstly, because the King did not have his men ready, nor the money needed to pay their wages and for the provisioning of the army; and secondly, because winter was coming on. Because of these and other reasons which each councillor adduced for not starting the campaign yet, they were all agreed that the King should postpone this war until the following summer, and that meanwhile he should prepare everything that was necessary, so that he might conclude the war with more honour and benefit. When he saw that they were of one accord with no one dissenting, the King gave his reply as follows: "You are all either drunk or mad or traitors!"

"Not I, my lord", said the Bishop, "I am not red—haired."[1]

"Ah, Bishop", said the King, "Are you saying that on my account?" For the King's own face was pale, but his hair was red.

"No, my lord", he said, "but because of this man here", meaning Pedro Fernández de Velasco, who was next to him and had reddish hair.

Laughing at these and other things which people said to lighten the atmosphere, the King again challenged them: "It is not fitting that there should be more delay or any further counsel about when to begin. Before ever King Fernando can realize it, and before any assistance can arrive for him from the English or any other outsiders,

do rreino, ante eu quero que me elle ache consigo; e ou lhe eu destruirei toda a terra, ou nós vïiremos a tall aveença per que sempre sejamos d'acordo: e esta entendo que he bem justa guerra, pois que a faço por aver paz. E logo d'este logar entendo d'encaminhar pera Portugall sem mais tornar atrás; e quem voontade tever de me fazer serviço, ell me seguirá per hu quer que eu for». E n'este conselho dizem que sse firmou muito Diego Lopez Pacheco, dizendo que entrasse logo supitamente per Portugall e que sse fosse logo lançar sobre Lixboa, nom curando d'outro logar nẽhũu, a quall podia tomar ligeiramente; e que cobrando esta cidade entendesse que tiinha todo o rreino cobrado e fiinda sua guerra. Mandou el-rrei logo cartas a todos seus vassallos que sse juntassem a pressa hu quer que elle fosse, ca sua intençom era partir sem mais tardança e entrar em Portugall, e que elle os esperaria aa entrada do rreino. Outrossi escreveo a micer Ambrosio Bocanegra seu almirante que armasse logo em Sevilha doze gallees e que tanto que fossem armadas, que partissem logo em ellas pera a cidade de Lixboa.

Fernão Lopes describes how Enrique of Trastámara now invades Portugal, taking numerous towns during his initial thrust into the north of the country. At the same time, a papal envoy, Guy de Boulogne, enters Portugal to try and bring about a reconciliation between the two kings (LXXI). Dom Fernando, on advice from his council, decides to await the Castilian advance at Santarém. The Castilian usurper passes through Coimbra where Leonor Teles is giving birth to the possible future Queen of Castile, Beatriz. He passes by Santarém and makes for Lisbon (LXXII).

No one thought Enrique would have entered Portugal the way he did nor that Fernando would have tolerated his presence for so long. Aware now of Enrique's power, the inhabitants of Lisbon panic as they crowd into the part of the city that alone has any protective wall about it. Meanwhile, the Portuguese Admiral makes preparations to repel the sea—borne attack of Enrique's ships but when the time comes, he panics, leaving his galleys badly guarded, so that some of these are captured by the Castilians (LXXIII—LXXIV).

I want to be at him; and either I shall lay waste all his country, or we shall come to such an understanding that we may be forever in accord. I believe that this is a very just war because I am waging it in order to have peace. So I mean to proceed immediately from here to Portugal without turning back; and anyone who wishes to serve me will follow me wheresoever I go."

It is said that Diego López Pacheco supported this policy, saying that he should enter Portugal suddenly and at once, and not bother about any other place but make straight for Lisbon, which he could take easily, and once he had captured this city, he would realize that he had conquered the whole kingdom and ended the war. The King at once ordered letters to be sent to all his vassals, ordering them to assemble swiftly wherever he himself might be, for it was his intention to depart without further delay and to invade Portugal, and he would await them on the border of the kingdom. Also he wrote to Master Ambrosio Boccanegra, his Admiral, telling him to equip twelve galleys in Seville and, as soon as they were put into commission, to leave in them straightaway for the city of Lisbon.

It is common knowledge that Diego López Pacheco has encouraged King Enrique to take Lisbon, saying that there is a fifth column in the city. Certain prominent citizens are therefore locked up, tortured, or killed (LXXV).

The next seven chapters describe sundry events that take place during the siege, in the course of which Cascais is sacked and much of Lisbon destroyed and burnt. Despite all this, the Castilian King fails to reduce the city and berates Pacheco for advising him that taking it would be an easy matter. Fernão Lopes describes briefly the career of this man, erstwhile favourite of King Fernando, who went over to the Castilian side because he claimed that Fernando's family had persecuted him.

It is now that our chronicler relates in some detail in the long chapter LXXXII, the manner in which King Fernando and Enrique II made peace.

LXXXII

Como forom feitas pazes antre el-rrei dom Henrrique
e el-rrei dom Fernando, e com que condiçoões

Dom Guido, cardeall de Bollonha, bispo do Porto e dellegado da See apostolica, o quall o papa mandara em Espanha
pera poer paz antre estes rreis ambos, segundo ante avemos
contado, partira de Cidade Rrodriguo por vĩir fallar a el-rrei
dom Henrrique, e porquanto elle ja estava sobre Lixboa,
nom pôde o bispo entrar per aquella comarca que primeiro
nom achasse el-rrei de Portugall; e chegou a Santarem hũua
terça-feira dia d'entruido, primeiro dia de março, nom avendo
mais de nove dias que el-rrei dom Henrrique per alli passara;
e fallou com el-rrei dom Fernando, dizendo como o Padre
Santo, teendo gram sentido da guerra e discordia que o
emmiigo da humanall linhagem a meude se trabalhava de
poer antre os rreis filhos da Egreja, moormente antre aquelles
acerca dos quaaes as barbaras naçoões dos infiees, por aazo
de tall odio e mall-querença podessem aver entrada a destroir
a relegiom christãa, que porém vigiando sobr'esto com gram
cuidado lhe conviinha trabalhar de poer paz antre aquelles
em que o maligno spirito semeava tall departimento. E pois
elle e el-rrei dom Henrrique eram na Espanha dous fiees
defenssores da ffe, que nom quisessem tam a meude arder
em guerra, por seguimento de nom justas voontades, mas
hordenassem antre ssi bem-querença e paz, por amor d'aquell
que a tam aficadamente encomendara, ante que d'este mundo
partisse; desi por seus rreinos e gentes nom seerem gastados
per espargimento de sangue. E ditas estas e outras amoes-
taçoões, que sagesmente ant'elle propôs, rrespondeo el-rrei
que averia seu consselho; e avudo sobr'esto acordo, porquanto
tiinha perduda esperança das gentes que aviam de vĩir de
Ingraterra, por que fora Vaasco Dominguez, segundo ouvistes,
as quaaes avia bem cinquo meses que eram prestes e per
mingua de tempo nom viinham, desi seu rreino nom bem
encaminhado pera aver de proseguir a guerra, outrogou
por sua parte conssentir na paz, como ell visse que era
rrazom, sem desfallecimento de sua honrra. O cardeall,
ouviindo aquesto, foi muito ledo de sua rreposta, e partio
em outro dia pera Lixboa, e fallou a el-rrei dom Henrrique
semelhantes rrazoões d'as que dissera a el-rrei dom Fernando,
e achou em ell voontade d'aver paz, seendo acordados em
certas condiçoões que lhe pello meudo feze declarar. Tornou-sse estonce o cardeall a Santarem e fallou a el-rrei dom

LXXXII
How peace was made between King Enrique and King Fernando, and on what conditions.

Guy de Boulogne, Cardinal—Bishop of Porto and papal legate,[1] whom the Pope had sent to Spain to make peace between these two kings, as we have already explained, left Ciudad Rodrigo to come and speak to King Enrique; and since the latter was already besieging Lisbon, the Bishop could not reach that area without first meeting up with the King of Portugal. He arrived in Santarém on Shrove Tuesday, the first of March,[2] a mere nine days after King Enrique had passed through. He spoke to King Fernando, explaining how distressed the Holy Father was at the war and the discord which the enemy of mankind frequently contrived to sow between the royal sons of the Church, and especially between these two, for, given their proximity to the barbarous nations of the infidels, discord and bad blood between them afforded opportunity for the latter to come in and destroy the Christian religion. So, watching over this with great care, it was only right that the Pope should strive to make peace between those rulers in whom the evil spirit was sowing such discord. Moreover, since Kings Fernando and Enrique were two faithful defenders of the faith in Spain, he asked them to refrain from waging wars so often in pursuit of unjust aims, and to create love and peace between themselves, for the love of Him Who had so earnestly urged this, before He departed from this world; and thus their kingdoms and peoples would not in future be ravaged by bloodshed.

When Cardinal Guy had finished making these and other wise exhortations, King Fernando replied that he would discuss them with his counsellors, and he did so. The King had lost all hope of the men who were supposed to come from England and whom Vasco Domingues had gone to fetch, as you have heard; for these men had been ready and waiting there for five months, but had not come because of the bad weather. Because of this and also since his kingdom was not in a fit state to carry on the war, King Fernando agreed to a truce, seeing that this was a reasonable solution with no loss of his honour. Hearing this, the Cardinal gave a joyful reply, and departed the next day for Lisbon where he spoke to King Enrique in terms similar to those he had used in speaking to King Fernando. He found Enrique desirous of peace provided that the agreement contained certain conditions which he listed in some detail; and he returned to Santarém and acquainted King Fernando with the reply he

Fernando a rreposta que em el-rrei dom Henrrique achara: entom hordenou el-rrei por seus procuradores dom Affonsso bispo da Guarda e Airas Gomez da Sillva cavalleiro, os quaaes partirom pera Lixboa com o cardeall; e de tall guisa andou trautando antre os rreis ambos que prougue ao mui alto Deus, amador e autor de paz, que aos dezenove dias de março, no castello de Santarem, presente el-rrei dom Fernando, com acordo d'os de seu conselho, forom trautadas pazes e aveenças antr'elle e el-rrei de Castella em esta seguinte maneira. Primeiramente que antr'elles e seus filhos e decendentes fosse sempre boa e verdadeira paz, sem nēhũua malicia em ella tocada, e per essa meesma guisa o fosse com el-rrei de França e seus socessores. E que el-rrei dom Fernando e todos seus herdeiros fossem sempre em hũua liança com os rreis de França e de Castella contra el-rrei de Ingraterra e contra o duque d'Alancastro e suas gentes. E que el-rrei dom Fernando fosse theudo de o ajudar per tres anos com duas gallees armadas, porém aa custa d'el-rrei de Castella; e esto quantas vezes elle armasse seis gallees ou mais contra os ingreses; e passados os ditos tres anos, que sse aviam de começar no mes de mayo seguinte, que d'hi em deante el-rrei dom Fernando nom fosse mais theudo de lh'as fazer prestes. E quem escreve que esta ajuda avia de seer cinquo gallees aa custa d'el-rrei dom Fernando erra muito em seu rrazoar, ca nom foi posta tall cousa em seus trautos. E acontecendo que gentes d'hingreses vehessem aos portos dos rreinos de Portugall, que el-rrei dom Fernando nem os seus lhe nom ministrassem viandas nem armas, nem lhe dessem favor nem consselho, mas que os lançassem de seus rreinos e terras come seus capitaes emmiigos, e quando o com seu poderio fazer nom podessem, que estonce fosse rrequirido el-rrei de Castella a viir per pessoa ou mandar seu poder pera os deitar fora. Outrossi que do dia d'esta paz firmada ataa trinta dias seguintes el-rrei dom Fernando lançasse fora de seu rreino, das pessoas que sse pera elle veherom de Castella, estas aqui nomeadas, *scilicet:* dom Fernando de Castro, Sueir'Eanes de Parada, Fernand'Afonso de Çamora, os filhos d'Alvoro Rrodriguez Daça, *scilicet,* Fernam Rrodriguez e Alvoro Rrodriguez e Lopo Rrodriguez, Fernam Goterrez Tello, Diego Affonsso do Carvalhal, Diego Sanchez de Torres, Pedr'Afonso Girom, Joham Affonsso de Beeça, Gonçallo Martïiz, e Alvoro Meendez de Caceres, Garcia Perez do Campo, Garcia Mallfeito, Gregorio e Fillipote ingreses, Paay de Meira dayam de Cordova, Martim Garcia

had had from King Enrique. Then King Fernando appointed as his proctors Don Afonso, Bishop of Guarda,[3] and a knight, Airas Gomes da Silva. These went to Lisbon with the Cardinal, who continued negotiating between the two kings in such a way that it pleased Almighty God, the Lover and Maker of peace, that on the nineteenth of March peace—agreements should be drawn up in Santarém castle, in the presence of King Fernando and with the consent of his Council. These peace—agreements between King Fernando and the King of Castile were as follows:[4]

Firstly, that between them and their children and descendants there would always be a good and true peace, without any deceit; and that the same would apply to the King of France and his successors; and that King Fernando and all his heirs would forever be the allies of the Kings of France and Castile against the King of England and the Duke of Lancaster and their people. King Fernando would be bound to help King Enrique for three years with two armed galleys, although their cost would be borne by the King of Castile. This would happen every time that the latter equipped six galleys or more against the English; but after the end of these three years, which would commence in the following May, King Fernando would no longer be bound to provide these galleys. Whoever wrote that this assistance was to consist of five galleys paid for by King Fernando was well wide of the mark, for no such thing was put into the agreement.[5] In the event of Englishmen coming to the ports of the realms of Portugal, neither King Fernando nor any of his people were to provide them with food, arms, help or advice, but were to expel them from his realms and territories as mortal enemies. If this were beyond their power, then the King of Castile would be enjoined to come in person or send his forces to expel the English. Likewise, within thirty days of peace being signed, King Fernando should expel from his kingdom certain of the people that had come into it from Castile, that is to say, the ones in the following list: Don Fernando de Castro; Suero Yáñez de Parada; Fernando Alfonso de Zamora; the sons of Alvaro Rodríguez de Aza, that is, Fernán Rodríguez, Alvaro Rodríguez and Lope Rodríguez; Fernán Gutiérrez Tello; Diego Alfonso de Carvajal; Diego Sánchez de Torres; Pedro Alfonso Girón; Juan Alfonso de Baeza; Gonzalo Martínez; Alvar Menéndez de Cáceres; García Pérez de Campo; García Malfeito; Gregory and Philpot, Englishmen; Pelayo de Meira, Dean of Córdoba; Martín

d'Aljazira, Martim Lopes de Cidade, Nuno Garcia seu irmaão, Gomez de Foyos, Joham do Campo, Bernalld'Eanes
seu irmaão, Joham Fernandez d'Andeiro, Joham Focim, Fernam Perez e Afonso Gomez Churrichaãos. Estas viinte e
oito pessoas, e mais nom, nomeou el-rrei de Castella que
fossem lançados fora de Portugall, segurando-os per mar e
per terra, ataa seerem postos em salvo; e sse o d'outra guisa
algũus em seus livros escrevem, nom dees fe a tall escriptura.
Foi mais outorgado que el-rrei dom Fernando perdoasse ao
iffante dom Denis seu irmaão e a Diego Lopez Pacheco e a
quaaesquer outros que em graça e favor d'el-rrei dom Henrrique eram toda sanha e pena e sentenças per quallquer
modo contra elles passadas, e lhe tornasse seus bẽes e he-
ranças; e isso meesmo perdoasse a todallas villas e logares
que o por senhor rreceberom. Trautarom mais estas aveenças,
que dona Beatriz, irmãa d'el-rrei dom Fernando, filha d'el-rrei
dom Pedro e de dona Enes de Castro, casasce com dom
Sancho d'Alboquerque, irmaão d'el-rrei dom Henrrique, filho
d'el-rrei dom Affonsso seu padre e de dona Lionor Nunez
de Gozmam sa madre: e quem mais casamentos em estes
trautos assiina, erra em seu estoriar. Outros capitullos que
d'escrever nom curamos forom devisados antre os rreis, os
quaaes forom per elles jurados e firmados e per todollos
senhores e fidallgos e prellados e per viinte cidades e villas
quaaes os rreis quiserom nomear. E que quallquer d'elles
per que estas pazes fossem quebrantadas pagasse trinta mill
marcos d'ouro, e mais que elle e todos seus cavalleiros e
escudeiros caissem em taaes penas assi ecclesiasticas come
seculares que mayores nom podiam ser postas em escriptura
a vista de leterados. E poserom e consentirom que quallquer
que fosse rrequerido pera jurar e fazer as menagẽes que
sobr'esto forom devisadas, e o fazer nom quisesse, que per-
desse a mercee do rrei cujo vassallo fosse, e que o deitasse
do rreino come seu emmiigo capitall. E porque el-rrei dom
Henrrique, nom embargando as juras e menagẽes que el-rrei
dom Fernando e os seus por estas pazes faziam, ainda dovidava que lh'as nom guardaria compridamente como antr'elles
eram firmadas, e esto por o que lhe avehera com ell nas
outras pazes d'Alcoutim, pedio em arrefẽes certas pessoas
e logares por tres anos, *scilicet,* Viseu e Miranda, Pinhel e
Almeida e Cellorico e Linhares e Segura; e as pessoas forom
Joham Affonsso Tello irmaão da rrainha e dom Joham
conde de Viana, filho de dom Joham Affonsso conde d'Ourem, Nuno Freire, Rrodrig'Alvarez filho do prior do Crato,

García de Algeciras; Martín López de Ciudad; his brother Nuño García; Gómez de Hoyos; Juan del Campo; Bernardo Yáñez his brother; Juan Fernández Andeiro; João Focim; Fernão Peres and Afonso Gomes Churrichãos.

These twenty—eight persons, and no more, were named by the King of Castile to be expelled from Portugal, but under safe—conduct by sea and by land, until they could reach somewhere safe. If any have written otherwise in their books, give no credence to such writings. [6] It was also agreed that King Fernando should grant pardon to his brother, Prince Dinis, together with Diego López Pacheco and any others who enjoyed the support and favour of King Enrique, for all the anger, penalties and sentences passed against them in any way, and that his goods and property should be restored to him; and that all those towns and villages which had accepted Enrique as their lord should similarly be pardoned.

The agreements also stated that Dona Beatriz, King Fernando's sister, and the daughter of King Pedro by Doña Inés de Castro, should marry Don Sancho de Albuquerque, who, like his brother, King Enrique, was the son of King Alfonso by Doña Leonor Núñez de Guzmán. Anyone who claims that there were other marriages mentioned in this agreement is writing false history. [7] Other clauses which we are not taking the trouble to set down here were agreed between the two kings, and signed and sworn to by them and by all the lords, nobles, and prelates as well as by twenty cities and towns that the kings nominated. It was agreed that if either king were to break the treaty, he would pay thirty thousand gold marks, and moreover he and all his knights and squires would incur the greatest ecclesiastical and secular penalties that educated men could express in writing.

They agreed, and included a clause, that anyone who was required to swear and guarantee by an act of homage specially devised for this purpose and who refused to do so, should lose the favour of the king whose vassal he was, and should be expelled from the kingdom as his mortal enemy. And because, in spite of the oaths and acts of homage which King Fernando and his subjects performed over this peace—treaty, King Enrique still doubted that he would keep it as completely as had been agreed between them (and this on account of what had happened to him over the other peace—treaty of Alcoutim), he asked to be given, as hostages for a period of three years, certain persons and places, that is, Viseu, Miranda, Pinhel, Almeida, Celorico, Linares and Segura, and the persons of João Afonso Telo the Queen's brother, and Dom João, Count of Viana and son of Dom João Afonso Count of Ourique, Nuno Freire and Rodrigo Alvares son of the Prior of Crato, and the Admiral, Master Lançarote; [8] but it is said that the last—named begged King Enrique

o almirante micé Lançarote: mas este dizem que pedio por mercee a el-rrei dom Henrrique que o pedisse em arrefẽes com os outros, por ho gram queixume que el-rrei° dom Fernando d'elle avia da mingua que mostrara na pelleja das gallees de Castella, segundo ante dissemos. Estas e outras pessoas rrequereo el-rrei de Castella que lhe dessem, e mais seis filhos de cidadaãos de Lixboa quaaes ell demandou e escolheo, e quatro do Porto e de Santarem outros quatro, os quaaes levou consigo; como quer que Joham Affonsso Tello ficou em Portugall per seu prazimento, e foi fora do conto das arrefẽes; e forom postas em fielldade em maão do dellegado as ditas villas, e as pessoas entregues a el-rrei com certas condiçoões que dizer nom curamos, ante que partisse do cerco de Lixboa; no quall jouve trinta dias compridos e mais nom, contados do dia que chegou ataa que as pazes forom apregoadas em Santarem, quinta-feira viinte e quatro dias do mes de março.

After signing the treaty that included Count Sancho's marriage to Princess Beatriz, the King also arranged a marriage between Enrique II's illegitimate son, Count Alfonso de Noreña and Fernando I's illegitimate daughter, Isabel. After informing the King of Navarre that he has no intention of buying off the English by renouncing his French alliance, Enrique II refits his galleys for war. Meanwhile Fernando does likewise, his preparations including the crucial decision to complete the enclosure of Lisbon by walls (LXXXIII—LXXXVIII). He also takes measures to improve agriculture and build up a merchant fleet (LXXXIX—XCI).

The next few chapters describe Enrique's complicated attempts to make a military alliance with Portugal while promoting a marriage between his son, Don Juan, and Doña Leonor of Aragon; as well as the extreme reluctance of Don Alfonso to marry Isabel of Portugal. Eventually the young Count is forced to do so but the couple are later divorced (XCII—XCV).

The following year, the betrothal takes place of Enrique's son, Duke Fadrique of Benavente, to Fernando's first—born daughter, Princess Beatriz. Fernando's half—brothers, Prince João and Dom João, Master of the Order of Avis, are both present at the ceremony. It is agreed that unless Queen Leonor is pregnant with a male heir when King Fernando dies, Princess Beatriz and Prince Fadrique shall be monarchs of Portugal (CXVI). In the meantime, King Fernando treats with the Duke of Anjou with a view to war against Aragon (XCVII).

At this stage in his chronicle of the reign of Fernando I, Fernão Lopes turns to the characters and doings of Prince João and

as a favour to ask for him as a hostage along with the others, because of the great resentment which King Fernando bore him on account of the inadequacy he had shown in the battle with the Castilian galleys. The King of Castile required these and other persons to be handed over to him, and, in addition, six sons of Lisbon citizens whom he demanded and selected personally as well as four from Oporto and four more from Santarém. He took these with him, although João Afonso Telo remained in Portugal as a favour and was not included in the list of hostages. The aforementioned towns were entrusted to the papal legate, and the persons were handed over to the King on certain conditions which we shall not bother to enumerate, before he raised the siege of Lisbon. Just thirty days passed between the day of his arrival and the proclamation of the peace—treaty in Santarém on Thursday, 24 March.

---

his half brother, João of Avis. He emphasizes the friendship between them before going on to relate the sorry tale of the Prince's love affair and secret marriage with Dona Maria, sister to Leonor Teles. Queen Leonor shows her great displeasure at her sister's marriage to Prince João. According to Fernão Lopes, this is because the Queen is aware both of the Prince's popularity with nobles and commoners alike and of her sister's popularity; and consequently she fears that the pair may come to reign in Portugal after the death of King Fernando. So the Queen holds out to the Prince the possibility of marrying her own daughter Beatriz, persuading him that the way to the throne lies more surely by this path. Fernão Lopes narrates with some feeling how the Prince smothers his love out of political expediency and ends by murdering his wife in a brutal fashion. Although he receives a pardon for stabbing Dona Maria, motivated by remorse and fear of vengeance for the murder, he flees into Castile where he is well received by his sister, Beatriz (XCVIII—CVI).

Fernão Lopes now departs from his narrative of events in Portugal in order to explain the Papal Schism, which will have considerable bearing on Portuguese politics at the close of Fernando's reign (CVII—CIX). He then describes the war between Castile and Navarre (1378—79) as well as the death of Enrique II. He also describes the crowning in Burgos of the usurper's son, Juan I, and how ambassadors from Portugal come to Cáceres in order to discuss with him a marriage between his son, Prince Enrique, and King Fernando's daughter, Beatriz. In order to achieve this, they suggest that Beatriz's betrothal to Fadrique of Benavente might be annulled.

Castilian ambassadors are sent to Lisbon where it is finally agreed
that when Prince Enrique reaches the age of seven, he and Beatriz
will be betrothed, and when he is fourteen, they will be wed. Thus,
they would eventually become King and Queen of Castile. Since they
are first cousins, moreover, they may inherit one another's kingdoms
(CX—CXII).

Reverting to the Papal Schism, Lopes explains that Fernando I
declared for the Avignonese pope Clement VII more out of a sense
of solidarity with France and Castile, than out of good sense or
good reason, for had no princes declared for either Pope, some say

---

CXV

Como Joham Fernandez Andeiro veo fallar a el-rrei sobre
a viinda dos ingreses e da maneira que el-rrei
com elle teve

Quando el-rrei firmou em sua voontade de mover guerra
contra el-rrei de Castella, ante per tempo que demandasse
este fingido consselho que teendes ouvido, logo concebeo
em seu entendimento que a maneira como sse esto melhor
podia fazer e com mais sua honrra e avantagem assi era aver
gentes de ingreses em sua ajuda. Hora assi aveo que nos
trautos das pazes que el-rrei dom Henrrique fez seendo vivo
com el-rrei dom Fernando, quando veo cercar Lixboa, foi
posto hũu capitollo que el-rrei de Portugall lançasse fora de
seu rreino, dos senhores fidallgos que sse per'eelle veherom
depós da morte d'el-rrei dom Pedro, viinte e oito pessoas,
quaaes elle quis nomear, como largamente ja teemos contado;
e d'estes nomeados que el-rrei lançou fora, foi hũu d'elles
Joham Fernandez d'Andeiro, naturall da Crunha, que sse
vehera pera elle quando el-rrei dom Fernando fora a Galliza;
e hindo-sse assi do rreino, foi pella Crunha e rroubou-a e
meteo-sse em naves e foi-sse pera Ingraterra; e andando
allá, soube el-rrei como el era mui entrado em casa d'el-rrei
e de seus filhos, o duque d'Allancastro e o conde de Cambrig,
e bem-quisto d'elles todos. E entom lhe escreveo suas cartas
secretamente que trautasse com o duque as aveenças que ja
teendes ouvidas, como quer que nom achamos nẽhũua cousa
que d'ellas vehesse a feito; e quando entendeo outra vez
de mover esta guerra, lhe escreveo que fallasse com o duque
e com seu irmaão, em tall guisa que sse lhe comprisse sua
ajuda, aveendo guerra com Castella, que o vehesse ajudar
per seu corpo e gentes, com certas condiçoões antr'elles

that the Schism would soon have been over (CXIII).

Next we are told how Dom Fernando prepares to betray Castilian trust by seeking a military alliance with the English, out of a thirst for vengeance against the deceased Enrique of Trastámara; yet his counsellors endeavour to dissuade him from seeking a fresh war with Castile, pointing out how much harm was done to the realm when Enrique invaded Portugal. Fernando brushes aside their remonstrances saying that he had asked them for advice not about whether to make war or not, but rather how to do so (CXIV).

CXV

How Juan Fernández Andeiro came to speak to the King about the coming of the English, and of the way in which the King dealt with him.

When the King hardened his resolve to wage war against the King of Castile he decided there and then that he could do this in the best way and with most honour and profit for himself by getting the English to help him. Now it happened that the agreements that King Enrique had made with King Fernando at the time he was besieging Lisbon included a clause stipulating that the King of Portugal should expel from his kingdom twenty—eight persons named by King Enrique from among the nobles that had come to Portugal after the death of King Pedro, as we have already related at some length. Among these named persons whom the King expelled was a certain Juan Fernández Andeiro, who had been born in Corunna and had joined King Fernando when the latter had gone to Galicia; and, leaving Portugal in this way, he went to Corunna, looted it, took ship and fled to England. King Fernando got to know that whilst in England Andeiro had become an intimate of the King of England and of his sons, the Duke of Lancaster and the Earl of Cambridge, [1] and was much loved by them all. So he secretly wrote to him, telling him to negotiate the agreement with the Duke which you have already heard about, although we have discovered nothing to indicate that anything came of this. Now when King Fernando decided to start the war again, he wrote to Andeiro telling him to speak again with the Duke and his brother to the effect that since there was war with Castile, they should honour this commitment and come in person with their men, on certain conditions to be agreed between them. Juan

devisadas. Joham Fernandez foi mui ledo de lhe seer rrequerido per el-rrei que tomasse tall encarrego, assi da primeira vez como d'esta; e fallou com o duque e conde o melhor que sobr'esto pôde, de guisa que acertou taaes aveenças de que el-rrei e o conde forom contentes: e hordenada a maneira como aviia de viinr e com quaaes gentes, partio-sse Joham Fernandez de Ingraterra e chegou ao Porto, e desembarcou o mais encubertamente que pôde, por nom seer visto e descuberto e seerem per tall aazo quebrados os trautos que antre Portugall e Castella avia, e d'alli se foi a Estremoz, honde el-rrei dom Fernando estava; e chegou per tall guisa e assi calladamente que nēhũu por estonce soube parte de sua viinda. E el-rrei foi mui ledo com elle e muito mais das novas que lhe trazia; e por rrazom dos trautos que com Castella tiinha firmados, nom ousava el-rrei que sua viinda fosse descuberta, nem que Joham Fernandez fosse visto; e teve-o escondido em hũua camara d'hũua grande torre que há no castello d'aquelle logar, honde el-rrei costumava de teer com a rrainha a sesta, pera quando allá fosse de dia poder com el mais encubertamente fallar todo o que lhe prouguesse; e depois que sse todos hiam, viinha Joham Fernandez d'outra casa que há na torre e fallava com ell, presente a rrainha, quaaesquer cousas que lhe compriam: e algũas vezes se sahia el-rrei depois que dormia, e ficava a rrainha soo, e viinha-sse Joham Fernandez per'eella depois que sse el-rrei partia, e fallavom n'o que lhe mais era prazivell, sabendo-o porém el-rrei e nom avendo nēhũua sospeita, como homem de saão coraçom: e per taaes fallas e estadas amehude, ouve Joham Fernandez com ella tall afeiçom que algũus que d'ello parte sabiam cuidavom d'elles nom boa sospeita, e cada hũu se callava d'o que prosumia, veendo que de taaes pessoas e em tall cousa nom compria a nēhũu de fallar; e foi esta afeiçom d'ambos tam grande que todo o que sse depois seguio, que adeante ouvirees, d'aqui ouve seu primeiro começo. Depois que el-rrei teve fallado com Joham Fernandez todo o que lhe compria, porque sse temeo de lhe seer sabudo que vehera a seu rreino d'esta guisa que dissemos, feze-o tornar encubertamente assi como vehera ataa acerca de Leirea, e fallou com elle que alli se descobrisse e se mostrasse como que viinha de caminho; e que elle, como lhe taaes novas dissessem, sanhudamente o mandaria prender, por todo mais encubertamente seer feito; e el feze-o assi. E como el-rrei fez que o novamente sabia, mandou logo a gram pressa Gonçallo Vaasquez d'Azevedo, grande seu privado, que o fosse prender, fallando com ell a maneira que tevesse; e el chegou a Leirea

Fernández was overjoyed to be singled out by the King to undertake such a mission, just as on the previous occasion; and he spoke to the Duke and the Earl as best he could, to such effect that he contrived agreements which satisfied both the King and the Earl. Once they had settled the manner in which the Earl was to come and with what men, Juan Fernández left England[2] and came to Oporto, disembarking as discreetly as he could so as not to be seen or identified, as this would have broken the treaties between Portugal and Castile. He went to Estremoz where King Fernando was, and arrived there so secretly and in such a way that no one at that time knew anything about his arrival. The King was delighted with him, and even more with the tidings he brought with him; but because of the treaties signed with Castile, the King did not dare to make Juan Fernández's arrival public nor allow him to be seen. He kept him hidden in a room in a big tower of the castle of that place, where the King and Queen were wont to take their siesta, so that when the King went there in the daytime, he could converse in secret with him to his heart's content. When everyone had gone away, Juan Fernández would come from another section of the tower and talk with the King in the Queen's presence about whatever was profitable to him. Sometimes the King would come out after taking his siesta, and the Queen would remain alone. Juan Fernández would come to her after the King had left, and they would talk of things that amused her; yet although the King knew of this, he had no suspicions, as he was an artless and trusting man. Through such conversations, which occurred frequently, Juan Fernández won so much of the Queen's affections that those who knew of it became quite suspicious but kept their thoughts to themselves, realizing that it was not fitting that anyone should utter a word about such a matter as this, given the individuals involved. The mutual affection was so great that it proved, as you shall hear later, to be the start of all that transpired subsequently.[3]

After the King had discussed with Juan Fernández all that he needed to, because he feared that it would become known that he had entered Portugal in the way we have described, he made him return secretly as he had come until he was near to Leiria, where he instructed him to show himself publicly and act as if he was lately arrived from his travels; then King Fernando would angrily have Juan Fernández arrested, as soon as he was informed of his arrival, so that everything should be kept more secret. Juan Fernández did as he was told; and the King, affecting to have just received the news, hastily ordered Gonçalo Vasques de Azevedo, his great favourite, to arrest Juan Fernández, discussing with him how it was to be done. Gonçalo Vasques de Azevedo arrived in Leiria so early that he found

a horas que o achou na cama, e tomou-ho preso e levou-ho
ao castello d'esse logar e alli o leixou e tornou-sse; e quando
sse d'ell ouve de partir, deu-lhe Joham Fernandez hũu agumill
de cristal obrado d'ouro que desse aa rrainha sua senhora,
e que o encomendasse muito em sua mercee. A poucos dias
fingeo el-rrei que o mandava soltar, e que logo se fosse fora
de seu rreino so pena de morrer porém, e el partio-sse e
foi-sse a pressa, mostrando que sse tornava por aquella rrazom. E porquanto el-rrei dom Fernando tiinha ja acertado
de aquell conde de Cambrig com certos fidallgos e gentes
de ingreses viirem em sua ajuda pera a guerra que contra
el-rrei dom Joham queria cometer, portanto fallou assi fouto
contra os do seu consselho, nom rrecebendo nẽhũuas rrazoões
boas que lhes per elles sobr'esto fossem dadas; ca ell nom
lhe propôs o que fazer quiria pera aver per elles consselho,
mas por lhe nom dizerem depois que cometera tall guerra
sem lh'o fazendo saber primeiro.

---

*King Juan soon hears of the Portuguese preparations. There is
some skirmishing in the frontier region near Badajoz (CXVI—CXIX).*

*At this stage Nun'Álvares Pereira, future Constable of Portugal
and principal aid and champion of João of Avis, enters the
Chronicle. He is posted to guard the frontier between the Tagus and
the Guadiana (CXX).*

*The next three chapters describe how Nun'Álvares, frustrated by
the lack of action against the Castilians, decides to challenge Juan
Osórez, son of the Master of Santiago, to a combat with ten men
on either side. He is forbidden by King Fernando to carry through*

CXXVIII
*Do rrecado que el-rrei ouve da frota dos ingreses,
e como chegou a Lixboa*

El-rrei dom Fernando, depois da partida de Joham Fernandez Andeiro, quando veo a Estremoz com rrecado dos
ingreses, segundo contamos em seu logar, mandou a Ingraterra Lourenç'Eannes Fogaça, homem avisado e de boa autoridade, seu chanceller-moor e do seu consselho, e esto pera
encaminhar e firmar seus trautos segundo o acordo que per
Joham Fernandez enviara; o quall era que o conde vehesse
em sua ajuda com as mais gentes que podesse juntar e que

Juan Fernández still in bed, arrested him and carried him off to the castle there, where he left him and returned. When he was leaving, Juan Fernández gave him a carafe made of crystal worked with gold, asking him to give it to the Queen and to commend him to her. A few days later the King pretended to order him to be released, but to leave the kingdom at once on pain of death; and he departed in haste, making a show of returning the way he had come for that reason alone. Since King Fernando had arranged for the Earl of Cambridge with certain nobles and English troops to come to assist him in the war that he intended to wage against King Juan, he spoke forcefully against the men of his own council, rejecting the good arguments which they they put to him. [4] For he did not make his intentions known in order to have their advice, but rather so that later they could not say that he had begun this war without first giving them due notice of it.

---

the challenge (CXXI—CXXIII).
A Portuguese fleet sails to the Algarve coast under the command of Queen Leonor's brother, Count João Afonso Telo. His impetuosity and foolish arrogance, according to Fernão Lopes, are responsible for the Portuguese suffering a catastrophic defeat, despite some initial advantage near the island of Saltes. All the Portuguese galleys except one are captured (CXXIV—CXXVI). Encouraged by this victory, Juan I attacks Lisbon with his fleet but is repulsed (CXXVII).

CXXVIII
Of the message which the King received from the English fleet, and how it arrived at Lisbon.

After Juan Fernández Andeiro had come to Estremoz with the message from the English and then gone away again, as we related at the appropriate time, King Fernando sent off to England Lourenço Eanes Fogaça, an astute and reliable man, the King's Grand Chancellor and a member of his council. He did this to as to confirm and activate his treaties according to the proposal which he had sent to England with Juan Fernández. This proposal was that the Earl should come to his aid with as many men as he could

trouvésse conssigo hũu filho que tiinha de sua molher, neto d'el-rrei dom Pedro de Castella, o que matarom em Montell, pera casar sua filha dona Beatriz com elle, pera seerem ambos herdeiros e senhores do rregno depois de sua morte. E estando el-rrei assi anojado por a gram perda da frota que avia rrecebida, hũu escudeiro que chamavom Rrui Cravo, que fora em companha de Lourenç'Eannes a Ingraterra, chegou a Buarcos em hũua barcha, e sahiu em terra por levar novas a el-rrei de como os ingreses viinham em sua ajuda: porque tam grande era o prazer que elles entendiam que el-rrei averia de sua viinda, que nom viiam o dia que lh'o fezessem saber, por aver d'elle grande alvissera e lhe dar boas novas. E foi assi de feito que chegou Rrui Cravo a Santarem e deu a el-rrei novas como a frota dos ingreses partíra de Preamua e viinha pello mar, e que mui cedo seeria em Lixboa, contando-lhe que gentes eram e quaaes senhores e de que guisa e como viinham corregidos e com que voontade. El-rrei ouve gram prazer com estas novas, nom embargando o nojo que de presente tiinha por a perda da frota, em guisa que tanto e muito moor foi o prazer que estonce tomou que o nojo que ante ouvera, quando lhe primeiro veherom novas d'ella; e nom soomente el-rrei e os de sua casa mas todollos do rreino foram ledos de sua viinda, nom embargando o nojo que tiinham, sperando per elles de cobrar emenda do dano que dos castellaãos aviiam rrecebido. Estando el-rrei em esta ledice, chegou-lhe em outro dia rrecado de Buarcos que ja a frota parecia no mar, e el-rrei foi com isto muito mais ledo. Estonce hordenou de sse partir pera Lixboa; e ante que partisse, como lhe chegou rrecado dos moradores do logar que os ingreses pousarom ante a cidade, partio logo a pressa em hũu batell e veo-sse a Lixboa. E depois que hordenou as cousas que compriam, foi-sse aa naao do conde, que estava mui nobremente apostada, e fallarom ambos n'o que lhes prougue, mostrando-lhe el-rrei de ssi boa graça e isso meesmo aa condessa e aos senhores e fidallgos que com elle viinham, os quaaes eram estes: primeiramente nomeemos este mossé Heimom conde de Cambrig, filho lidemo d'el-rrei Eduarte d'Hingraterra o velho, o quall tragia sua molher dona Isabell, filha d'el-rrei dom Pedro, rrei que fora de Castella, bem acompanhada de donas e donzellas, e hũu seu filho pequeno que avia nome Eduarte come seu avoo, moço de hidade ataa seis annos; e viinha hi hũu filho d'el-rrei de Ingraterra bastardo e mossé Guilhem Beocap condeestabre de toda a frota e o senhor de Botareeos e mossé Mau de Gornai, que era marichall, e o so-duque de Latram e Tomas Simom alferez do

64

muster, and should bring with him a son [1] that he had by his wife who was the grandson of King Pedro of Castile, whom they killed in Montiel, so that he could be married to King Fernando's daughter Dona Beatriz, and so they would both be heirs and lords of the kingdom after King Fernando's own death. While the King was still much troubled by the loss of the fleet that he had recently suffered, [2] there arrived at Buarcos [3] in a boat a squire called Rui Cravo who had gone to England in the company of Lourenço Eanes; and he came ashore to bring the King news of how the English were coming to his aid. They understood that the King would be so gratified at their coming that, to bring him the good news and be rewarded for it, they did not arrive on the day that they had told him. So it was that Rui Cravo arrived in Santarém and gave the King news of how the English fleet had left Plymouth and was crossing the sea and would be very soon in Lisbon. He also told him what nobles and what commoners were coming, and how and in what manner they were organized and how enthusiastic. The King was very pleased with this news, notwithstanding his present displeasure at the loss of the fleet, so that his joy now equalled and even surpassed the sorrow he had felt when he heard the news of that loss. Not only the King and all his household but the whole kingdom was joyful at their coming, despite their present mood of sorrow, for they hoped that the English would help them to obtain recompense for the harm done them by the Castilians.

While the King was in this happy mood, he received word from Buarcos the following day that the fleet had appeared out at sea, and this made him even happier. Straightaway he ordered the departure for Lisbon; and as before leaving, he was informed by the local people that the English had anchored before the city, he left in a hurry and came by barge to Lisbon. After he had commanded that everything necessary should be done, he made his way to the Earl's ship, which was very nobly appointed. They conversed of whatever they pleased, and the King showed much favour to the Earl and also to the Countess, lords and nobles who accompanied him. These were as follows:

First let us name Sir Edmund, Earl of Cambridge, legitimate son of the old King Edward of England. He brought with him his wife, Isabel, daughter of King Pedro, formerly King of Castile, who was well attended by her ladies and damsels, and also a little son of his, six years old, named Edward like his grandfather. There also came a bastard son of the King of England, [4] and Sir William Beauchamp, [5] Constable of the whole fleet; the lord of Botareos and Sir Matthew Gournay [6] who was the Marshal; and the Sultan of Latrau; [7] and Sir Thomas Symond, [8] the Duke of Lancaster's standard-bearer who

duque d'Alancastro que trazia sua bandeira e o bispo d'Acres e mossé Canom hordenador das batalhas e mossé Tomas Frechete e o Garro e mossé Joham Destingues e Chico Novell e Maao Borni e o senhor de Castelnovo que era gascom e outros capitaães que dizer nom curamos; e traziam consigo de gentes d'armas e frecheiros ataa tres mill, bem prestes pera pellejar, assaz de fremosa gente e bem corregidos. E viinham hi mais algũus cavalleiros d'os que se partirom de Portugall quando el-rrei dom Fernando trautou as pazes com el-rrei dom Henrrique, assi como Joham Fernandez Andeiro e Joham Affonsso de Beeça e Fernam Rrodriguez Daça e Martim Paulo e Bernaldom e Joham Sanchez cavalleiro de Santa Caterina e outros. E chegarom estas gentes todas a Lixboa em quarenta e oito vellas antre naaos e barchas aos dezenove dias de julho da era ja em cima escripta de quatrocentos e dezenove annos.

CXXIX

Como o conde e os outros capitaães forom apousentados na cidade, e da maneira que el-rrei com elles teve

Depois que el-rrei acabou de fallar com o conde, disse que era bem que sahissem em terra: e entrarom nos batees o conde e sua molher e esses senhores e fidallgos e donas e donzellas e muita d'outra gente que com elles viinham; e como forom na rribeira, os da cidade os rreceberom mui honrradamente, segundo el-rrei leixara hordenado. E tomou el-rrei a condessa de braço, e forom todos a pee atá a egreja cathedrall, honde jaz o corpo de Sam Vicente; e como fezerom sua oraçom e sairom da See, estavom ja prestes pera o conde e sua molher e pera as outras honrradas pessoas bestas bem corregidas como compria. E levou el-rrei de rredea a condessa ataa o moesteiro de Sam Domingos, onde hordenou que pousassem, e o condeestabre e o marichall em Sam Francisco e o senhor de Botareeos em Santo Agostinho e os outros senhores e fidallgos pella cidade, cada hũu segundo compria, salvo na cerca velha. E dizem que fallando el-rrei ao conde na perda da sua frota e da guisa que avehera, que rrespondeo ell e disse que par Deus nom forçasse por aquella perda, que quem ouvesse a terra averia as gallees e o mar. A rrainha dona Lionor a mui poucos dias partio de Santarem com a iffante sua filha, e os d'el-rrei e todollos da cidade a sahirom a rreceber; e ella, ante que fosse ao paaço, foi fazer oraçom a Santa Maria de Escada, que he no moesteiro honde pousava

carried his banner; and the Bishop of Dax;[9] and Sir Canon,[10] the organizer of the battle—lines; and Sir Thomas Fychet;[11] and Garro; and Sir John Hastings;[12] and Chico Novell;[13] and Sir John Mauburney[14] and the lord of Castelnau,[15] who was a Gascon; and other captains whom we shall not bother to mention. They brought with them three thousand men—at—arms and archers all ready for the campaign, fine—looking men and well equipped. There came there as well some knights from among those who had left Portugal when King Fernando made the peace—treaty with King Enrique, such as Juan Fernández Andeiro, Juan Alfonso de Baeza, Fernán Rodríguez de Aza, Martín Paulo, Bernaldon, Juan Sánchez the knight of Santa Caterina and others. These people all arrived at Lisbon in forty—eight ships, warships and barges, on July 19, 1381.

CXXIX

How the Earl and other captains were lodged in the city, and how the King treated them.

When the King had finished talking with the Earl, he said that they had better go ashore. So the Earl and his wife and the lords, nobles, ladies and damsels and many other people who had come with them boarded the barges, and when they reached the river—bank, the citizens welcomed them very honourably, just as the King had ordered. The King took the Countess's arm and they all walked to the Cathedral where the body of St. Vincent lies. When they had prayed and left the Cathedral, mounts were ready and waiting, suitably decked out for the Earl and his wife and others of high rank. The King led the Countess by the rein to the monastery of São Domingos, where he arranged that they should lodge; and the Constable and Marshal were accommodated in São Francisco, the lord of Botareos in Santo Agostinho and the other lords and nobles elsewhere in the city, according to their rank, but none of them within the Old Walls. They say that when the King spoke to the Earl about the loss of his fleet and of how it had happened, he replied that in Heaven's name he should not be too worried at that loss, for whoever possessed the land would hold the galleys and the sea.

A few days later, Queen Leonor left Santarém with her daughter the Princess, and the King's men and the whole city turned out to welcome her; and before she went to the palace, she went to pray to Santa Maria de Escada, which is in the monastery, where the Earl

o conde; e a condessa de Cambrig lhe veo fallar, e abraça-rom-sse ambas; e espedio-sse a rrainha e foi-sse pera seus paaços, e a condessa ficou no moesteiro hu pousava. Em esto convidou el-rrei o conde e todollos capitaães que com ell viinham, e a rrainha a condessa·e as donas e donzellas de sua companha: e este convite foi nos paaços d'el-rrei do castello, honde a todos foi feita salla mui honrradamente; e em fim da mesa foi apresentado ao conde e aos outros senhores muitos panos de širgo com ouro. de desvairadas maneiras, segundo por el-rrei era hordenado; e isso meesmo deu a rrai-nha aa condessa e molhéres de sua casa panos e joyas de que forom contentes. E per outras vezes convidava el-rrei o conde e os outros capitaães, e ho hiia veer onde pousava el e a rrainha sua molher, partindo com o conde mui graadamente e com cada hũu dos outros segundo seus estados. E por-quanto nos capitollos antre el-rrei e o conde devisados hũu d'elles era que el-rrei desse encavallgaduras a todos, seendo a cada hũu descontado do solldo que avia d'aver o preço da besta que ouvesse, mandou el-rrei chamar os fidallgos e concelhos de seu rregno e fez cortes com elles, e acabadas as cortes mandou el-rrei por todollos cavallos dos aconthiados de seu rreino e por quaaesquer outras bestas que fossem achadas, assi muares come cavallares, pera dar aos ingreses; e per esta guisa forom todos encavallgados, e tomadas a seus donos as melhores que hi avia, sob esperança de seerem pagadas, a quall paga nunca depois ouverom. Ao conde mandou el-rrei hũu dia doze mullas pera a condessa, as melhores que sse escolher poderom, selladas e enfreadas assaz nobremente, e doze cavallos pera elle per essa meesma guisa, antre os quaaes hia hũu grande e fremoso cavallo que el-rrei dom Henrrique, seendo vivo, mandara em presente a el-rrei dom Fernando, que era o milhor que estonce deziam que avia na Espanha. E estas bestas escolheitas que derom aos ingreses, muitas d'ellas avia taaes que aadur podia hũu ingres levar hũua d'ellas à auga; e como forom em seu poder, trautavom-nas de tall guisa que hũu levava depois viinte e trinta ante ssi, como manada de mansso gaado.

CXXX

Como el-rrei declarou por o papa de Rroma e esposou sua filha com·o conde de Cambrig

Segundo ouvistes em seu logar, el-rrei dom Fernando tiinha declarado por aquell que sse chamava Clemente sep-

was lodged.[1]   The Countess of Cambridge came to talk with her and they embraced each other.   Then the Queen took her leave and went to her palace while the Countess stayed in the monastery where she was lodging.   Afterwards the King invited the Earl and all the captains who had come with him, and the Queen invited the Countess and ladies and damsels in her train, to the King's state—rooms in the castle, where a hall was laid out for all of them in a fitting manner. At the head of the table many cloths of silk, adorned with gold in different ways, were presented to the Earl and other lords, all as ordered by the King; and in the same way the Queen gave to the Countess and the ladies of her household cloths and jewels with which they were delighted.   The King invited the Earl and the other captains on other occasions, and went with the Queen to see him at his lodgings, treating him in the most agreeable manner and treating everyone else according to his rank.   Because one of the clauses agreed between the King and the Earl stipulated that the King should provide a mount for every Englishman but discount its value from his pay, the King summoned the nobles and town—councils of his kingdom to a meeting of the Cortes.   When the Cortes had been dissolved, the King demanded all the horses of the tax—payers of the realm and any other mounts that could be found, mules as well as horses, to give them to the English, who in this way were all provided with mounts.   The former owners lost their best mounts on the understanding that they would be paid, but in the event they never received any payment.   One day, the King sent a dozen mules, the best that could be found, with noble saddles and harness, to the Earl for the Countess, and he similarly sent him for himself a dozen horses, including one big beautiful horse which King Enrique, when he was alive, had sent to King Fernando as a present, and which they said was the best horse in Spain.   Many of these selected animals which they gave to the English were so wild that an Englishman could hardly lead them to water; yet as soon as they got hold of them, they handled them in such a way that later on just one Englishman could drive twenty or thirty of them before him like a herd of gentle cattle.

CXXX
How the King declared for the Pope of Rome
and married his daughter to the Earl of Cambridge.

As you have heard above, King Fernando had declared in favour of the man who entitled himself Clement VII[1] and who was supported

timo, cuja parte favorizava el-rrei de França e el-rrei de Castella e algũus outros senhores. E quando os ingreses veherom, porquanto tiinham com o papa de Rroma Urbano sexto, nom ouviam missa de nẽhũu frade nem clerigo portuguees. Estonce disse o conde a el-rrei que ell viinha pera o servir e ajudar em sua guerra contra el-rrei de Castella, que era cismatico, teendo com hũu papa que estava em Avinhom; e que sse ell quiria que o Deus ajudasse em sua guerra, que desse a obediencia ao padre santo de Rroma, e que d'esta guisa lh'o enviava el-rrei seu senhor e padre dizer e todo o consselho de Ingraterra, porquanto eram certos que aquel era verdadeiro papa e outro nom; e ell disse que lhe prazia e outorgou de o fazer assi. E quando veo aos dezenove dias do mes d'agosto, na festa da degollaçom de Sam Joham Baptista, el-rrei dom Fernando, avendo maduro consselho com o arcebispo de Bragaa e outros leterados homẽes de seu rreino juramentados sobre hũua ostia sagrada na see cathedrall da dita cidade, pubricamente presente todo o poboo declarou Urbano sexto seer verdadeiro papa e outro nom; e isto presente os ingreses e muito outro poboo. E logo em esse dia a hora de terça esposou el-rrei sua filha a iffante dona Beatriz, per pallavras de presente, com Eduarte, filho do conde de Cambrig, moços muito pequenos; e forom ambos lançados em hũua grande cama e bem corregida, na camara nova dos paaços d'el-rrei; e o bispo d'Acres e o de Lixboa e outros prellados rrezarom sobre elles, segundo costume de Hingraterra, e os beenzerom. A cama era bem emparamentada, e a cubricama d'hũu tapete preto com duas grandes figuras de rrei e de rrainha na meatade, todas d'aljofar graado e meaão, segundo rrequeria honde era posto; a bordadura d'arredor era toda d'archetes d'aljofar, e dentro iguaaes feguras d'aljofar brolladas das linhagẽes de todollos fidallgos de Portugall, com suas armas acerca de ssi: e este corregimento de cama foi depois dado a el-rrei dom Joham de Castella quando casou com esta iffante dona Beatriz, segundo adeante ouvirees, e era avuda em Castella por mui rrica obra, quall outra hi nom aviia. E forom estes esposoiros feitos com esta condiçom, que morrendo el-rrei dom Fernando sem aveendo filho de sua molher, que este Duarte e sua esposa sobcedessem o rregno depós sua morte, outorgando isto todollos fidallgos e fazendo-lhe menagem por todallas villas e cidades e fortellezas do rregno. E depois d'esto, no mes de setembro, aos oito dias d'elle, foi pubricada, presente el-rrei e o conde e muitos senhores e prellados, hũua letera do papa Urbano em que privava de todo bem e honrra ecclesiastica Rroberte, que sse

by the King of France and the King of Castile and some other lords. When the English came, because they were on the side of the Pope of Rome, Urban VI, they would not hear mass said by any Portuguese friar or priest.   So the Earl said to the King that he had come to serve him and help him in his war against the King of Castile, who was a schismatic, supporting as he did a Pope who was in Avignon; that if King Fernando wanted God's help in his war, he should give obedience to the Holy Father in Rome; and that this was what his lord and father the King and the whole Council of England had sent him to say, for they were sure that Urban was the real Pope, whilst the other was not.   Dom Fernando agreed to this and promised to act accordingly.   On August 19, the feast of the Decapitation of St. John the Baptist,[2] having taken careful counsel with the Archbishop of Braga[3] and other learned men of his realm, all of them swearing upon a sacred host in the cathedral of the aforementioned city, King Fernando declared Urban VI to be the true Pope and the other not; and the English were present along with many more people.

Immediately afterwards, on the same day at the third hour, King Fernando betrothed his daughter Princess Beatriz to Edward, son of the Earl of Cambridge.   Both children were very small and were put in a great bed, grandly decked out, in the new chamber of the King's palace.   The Bishops of Dax and Lisbon[4] and other prelates prayed over them, according to the custom of England, and blessed them. The bed was well adorned and the coverlet was made of a black tapestry with two great figures of a King and a Queen in the middle, worked in large and middle—sized pearls according as their position required.   The edging all around it was of loops of pearls and inside these were woven figures in mother—of—pearl depicting the lineages of all the nobles of Portugal, each with its coat—of—arms next to it. This bed coverlet was afterwards given to King Juan of Castile when he married Princess Beatriz, as you will later hear; and it was considered in Castile to be a very costly piece of work, such that there was not another one like it anywhere.

This betrothal was made on this condition: that if King Fernando should die without having a son by his wife, this Edward and his wife would inherit the kingdom after his death; and all the nobles agreed to this and did him homage for all cities, towns and fortresses of the kingdom.   After this, on September 8, in the presence of the King, the Earl and many lords and prelates,. a letter of Pope Urban was published whereby he deprived of all property and ecclesiastical honour both Robert, who called himself Clement VII, and

chamava Clemente septimo, e isso meesmo todollos cardeaaes
e pessoas leigas que lhe davom consselho e favor e ajuda,
assi pubricamente come em ascondido, scomungando-os que
nom podessem seer asolltos se nom pello papa, salvo se fosse
em artiigo de morte, dando seus bẽes e elles por servos
aaquelles que os tomassem, outorgando-lhe ainda aquelles
privillegios que dam aaquelles que vaão em ajuda da terra
santa.

CXXXI
Como el-rrei de Castella ouve novas da viinda dos ingreses
e da maneira que em esto teve

O conde dom Alvoro Perez de Castro estava em Elvas por
fronteiro, segundo ja teendes ouvido: e o iffante dom Joham
seu sobrinho, que andava em Castella, com o meestre de
Santiago dom Fernand'Azores e o meestre d'Alcantara com
muitas companhas tiinham cerco sobr'elle aviia ja dias.
E quando os ingreses chegarom a Lixboa escreveo logo el-rrei
dom Fernando ao conde toda sua viinda, e que gentes eram.
O conde, mui ledo com estas novas, mandou dizer ao iffante
que o tiinha cercado que sse lhe comprissem algũas mercadarias ou outras cousas de Ingraterra, que mandasse a Lixboa,
honde estavom hũuas poucas de naaos de ingreses que estonce
veherom, e que alli acharia todo o que mester ouvesse.
E quando isto foi assi dito escusamente ao iffante, come-
çou-sse a rrogir pollo arreall parte d'estas novas encubertamente. Algũus cavalleiros, ouviindo-o dizer, preguntarom a
Pero Fernandez de Vallasco, que era na companhia, que
novas eram aquellas que sse assi rrugiam. «Que novas ham
de seer? disse el. Som novas que el-rrei dom Fernando há
mais de nove meses que era prenhe dos ingreses e pariu-hos
agora em Lixboa, e tem-nos consigo». Estonce hordenarom
de nom estar alli mais, e partirom d'Elvas hũua terça-feira
no mes d'agosto, aveendo viinte e cinquo dias que tiinham o
logar cercado. E esta partida dizem que foi per mandado
d'el-rrei de Castella, que tiinha cercada Almeida, como dissemos; e quando foi certo da viinda dos ingreses, mandou
chamar estas gentes que se vehessem per'eelle: e chegou o
iffante dom Joham e o conde de Mayorgas dom Pedro Nunez
de Lara, filho bastardo do dito Joham Nunez de Lara senhor
de Bizcaya, e outros cavalleiros, e acharom el-rrei nom bem
saão por estonce. Hora algũus screvem aqui que seendo el-rrei

all those cardinals and lay—people who gave him advice, favour and help, publicly or secretly; he excommunicated them so that they could be absolved only by the Pope (unless at the point of death); and he decreed that anyone who captured them might enslave them and take their property, and would moreover enjoy the same privileges as a crusader to the Holy Land.

CXXXI
How the King of Castile had news of the coming of the English, and the way in which he reacted to this.

Count Álvaro Peres de Castro was in Elvas, defending the frontier, as you have already heard; and his nephew, Prince João,[1] who was in exile in Castile, had been besieging the town for several days, together with the Master of Santiago, Don Fernando Osórez, the Master of Alcántara,[2] and a considerable force. When the English arrived in Lisbon, King Fernando wrote there and then to the Count telling him of their coming and of what manner of people they were. The Count was delighted at the news and sent word to the Prince, who was besieging him, that if he needed any merchandise or other things from England, he should send to Lisbon where several English ships had lately arrived and where he would find all that he might need. When the Prince was told this discreetly, a version of the news began to circulate in whispers through the camp of the besiegers. On hearing it, some knights asked Pedro Fernández de Velasco, a member of the company, what were these tidings that were being noised abroad.

"What tidings do you expect?", he replied. "The news is that King Fernando has been pregnant with the English for more than nine months, and has at last given birth to them in Lisbon, and has them with him there."

So the order went out for them to stay no more; and they left Elvas one Tuesday in the month of August, having besieged the place for some twenty—five days. They say that this departure was effected on the orders of the King of Castile, who was besieging Almeida, as we have said. Once he knew for certain that the English had come, he ordered these men to come to him; and Prince João and the Count of Mayorga, Don Pedro Núñez de Lara (the bastard son of the abovementioned Juan Núñez de Lara, lord of Vizcaya) and other knights all arrived, to find the King unwell. Now some have written[3]

73

de Castella certo da viinda dos ingreses e que gentes e capitaães eram, e como nom embargando que viinham em ajuda d'el-rrei dom Fernando contra seu rregno, que aalem d'esto tragiam voz e titullo do duque d'Alencastro, por aazo de dona Constança sua molher, filha que fora d'el-rrei dom Pedro, que el screveo suas cartas ao conde de Cambrig, dizendo que sabia per certas novas como el e muitos bõos cavalleiros e homẽes d'armas aviam chegado a Lixboa por fazer guerra e dano em seu rreino, em ajuda d'el-rrei dom Fernando; e que sse o elles fezessem certo de batalha, que el partiria d'aquell logar, o quall tiinha ja cobrado per preitesia, e entraria pello rreino duas ou tres jornadas e os esperaria em logar aazado pera lhe poer a praça. E que porquanto em esta sazom os ingreses nom eram ainda encavallgados, que nom derom rreposta a isto, ante fezerom maao gasalhado ao que lhe levou as cartas. El-rrei de Castella hordenou estonce de poer suas gentes acerca do estremo de Portugall, e mandava por todollos seus percebendo-sse de batalha, a quall viia que sse nom podia escusar, querendo os ingreses entrar em seu rreino.

CXXXII
Das maas maneiras que os ingreses tiinham com os moradores do rregno, e como el-rrei nom tornava a ello porque os avia mester

Estas gentes dos ingreses que dissemos, como forom apousentados em Lixboa, nom como homẽes que viinham pera ajudar a defender a terra, mas come se fossem chamados pera a destruir e buscar todo mall e desonrra aos moradores d'ella, começarom de sse estender pella cidade e termo matando e rroubando e forçando molheres, mostrando tall senhorio e desprezamento contra todos come se fossem seus mortaaes emmiigos de que sse novamente ouvessem d'asenhorar. E nẽhũu no começo ousava de tornar a ello, por grande rreceo que aviam d'el-rrei, que tiinha mandado que nẽhũu lhes fezesse nojo, polla gram necessidade em que era posto de os aver mester, cuidando ell aa primeira mui pouco que homẽes que viinham pera o ajudar, e a que esperava de fazer graadas mercees, tevessem tall geito em sua terra; e porém quando lhe algũus faziam queixume das grandes sem-rrazoões que d'elles rrecebiam, fallava el-rrei ao conde sobr'ello, mas em todo sse fazia pouco corregimento. Que compre dizer mais? Em tanta pressa e sojeiçom forom postos os da cidade e seu

74

that the King of Castile knew that the English had arrived and which captains and troops were in their force, and that notwithstanding the fact that they were coming to help King Fernando against Castile, they also came in the name of, and with the authority of, the Duke of Lancaster, husband of Doña Constanza, the daughter of the late King Pedro; so that King Juan wrote letters to the Earl of Cambridge saying that he knew for certain that the Earl and many good knights and men—at—arms had arrived at Lisbon to make war on and ravage his kingdom in support of King Fernando, and that if they were to agree formally to meet him in open battle, he would leave that place,[4] which had already capitulated to him, and would come some two or three days journey into the kingdom of Portugal and await them in some site agreed on for battle. Since the English were at that time still horseless, they made no reply to this but maltreated the messenger who had brought the letters. The King of Castile then ordered his troops to be positioned close to the Portuguese border and all his men to prepare for battle, seeing that fighting was inevitable since the English wished to enter his kingdom.

CXXXII

Of the bad behaviour of the Englishmen towards the inhabitants of the kingdom, and how the King did not punish it because he needed them.

We have explained how the English troops were lodged in Lisbon, but they began to behave not as men who had come to defend the country but as if they had been called in to destroy it and to visit upon its inhabitants as much suffering and dishonour as possible. They started to stray out and around the city and its district, killing, robbing and raping, and treating everyone with such haughtiness and contempt as if they were their mortal enemies whom it was necessary to dominate. At first, no one dared to punish this because of their great fear of the King, who had ordered that no one should annoy the English on account of the fact that they were so necessary to him. He seemed not to care at first that men who had come to help him and of whom he expected much should behave in this way in his country. Yet when some complained to him of the outrages they had suffered at the hands of the English, he spoke to the Earl about it; but little was done to put the matter right. Need one say more? The inhabitants of the city and district found

termo, avendo d'elles medo come de seus grandes emmiigos, que o conde hordenou por guarda das quintãas e casaaes que cada hũu tevesse senhos pendoões de sua devisa, que era hũu falcom branco em campo vermelho; e a quintãa e casall honde os ingreses nom achavom aquell pendom logo era rroubada de quanto hi avia; e quantas bestas viinham pera a cidade, assi das quintãas come dos casaaes e montes d'arredor, pera venderem suas cousas, cada hũu avia de trazer hũu pendom d'aquelles, que custava certa cousa, por lhe nom fazerem mall. Veede se era bõo jogo d'elles: levando à agua as bestas d'el-rrei, lançarom mãao d'ellas, e tomarom--nas per força, dizendo que el-rrei lhe devia solldo e que o queriam penhorar em ellas; e foi assi de feito que as tomarom, e per mandado do conde forom tornadas. Hũua vez chegarom algũus d'elles a casa d'hũu homem que chamavom Joham Vicente, jazendo de noite na cama com sua molher e hũu seu filho pequeno que ainda era de mama, e baterom aa porta que lhe abrisse; e ell com temor nom ousou de o fazer, e elles britarom a porta e entrarom dentro e começarom de ferir o marido; a madre com temor d'elles pôs a criança ante ssi polla nom ferirem, e nos braços d'ella a cortarom per meyo com hũua espada, que era cruell cousa de veer a todos; e tomarom aquell menino assi morto e levarom-no a el-rrei aos paaços em hũu tavolleiro, mostrando-lhe tall cruelldade como aquella; e ell nom ousou de tornar a ello, e mandou que o mostrassem ao conde, que fezesse dereito d'aquelles que tall cousa feze-rom; e o conde o mandou fazer. E d'esta guisa lhe mandava el-rrei rrogar muitas vezes, pollos grandes queixumes que lhe viinham fazer, que posesse castiigo em suas gentes, que nom destruissem assi a terra; e ell dezia que bem lhe prazia, mas cada vez faziam peor. Outros chegarom acima de Loures por rroubar hũua aldea que he hi acerca; e em-na rroubando, matarom tres homẽes; e assi rroubavom e matavom e des-truhiam mantiimentos que muitas vezes mais era o dano que faziam que aquello que gastavom em comer; que tall aviia hi, se aviia voontade de comer hũua lingua de vaca, matava a vaca e tirava-lhe a lingua e leixava a vaca perder; e assi faziam ao vinho e a outras cousas. E el-rrei por esta rrazom, como os encavallgava, mandava-os a rriba d'Odiana pera a frontaria; e elles, em vez de entrarem por Castella a forrejar, davom volta sobre Rribatejo a rroubar quanto achavom, e as gentes nom os queriam colher nas villas e cerravom-lhe as portas, por o gram dano que faziam; assi como fezerom em Villa Viçosa, quando hi chegou Maao Borni com outros

76

themselves in a state of such danger and subjection, being as afraid of the English as of their worst enemies, that the Earl ordered each one of them to display his emblem in the form of a pennant as a protection for his garden and house, the emblem being a white falcon on a red field. The garden and house where the English found no such pennant were immediately robbed of everything there; and every pack—animal coming into the city from the neighbouring gardens, farms and pasture—lands for the purpose of trading, had to carry one of these pennants, which cost a certain amount, in order not to be harmed. Judge for yourselves if they played fair: when the King's horses were being led to the water, they seized them and took them by force, saying that the King owed them pay and that they would take the horses as surety; and they did in fact take them, and they were only returned at the Earl's command.

Once a group of them came to the house of a man called João Vicente, as he lay in bed one night with his wife and his little son who was not yet weaned. They banged on the door for him to open it, and he was too afraid to do so; so they broke down the door, came straight in, and began to strike the husband. The terrified mother held the child close to her breast so that they might not hurt it, but they cut it in two with a sword, in her very arms, which was a cruel thing for anyone to see. They took the child, dead as it was, and carried it on a plank to the palace of the King, showing him just what cruelty this was; but he did not dare to punish it and merely ordered them to show the corpse to the Earl so that he might do justice on the culprits; and the Earl did.

In the same way, because of the great complaints which came to him, the King frequently sent to the Earl begging him to punish his men and stop them destroying the country; and the Earl agreed, but every time they behaved worse and worse. Some other Englishmen went to Loures to rob a village nearby, and in the robbery they killed three men. They robbed, killed and destroyed provisions in such a way that the damage done was often far greater than what they merely ate; as for example when such—and—such a man felt like eating a cow's tongue, he killed the cow, cut out its tongue and left the cow to rot. They did the same sort of thing with wine and other things.

For this reason, once the King had given them horses, he sent them off to the frontier along the River Guadiana;[1] but instead of entering Castile to plunder, they came back into the Ribatejo to pillage whatever they found, so that people would not receive them in the towns and closed the gates to them on account of the great damage they were doing. They did this in Vila Viçosa when Mauburney arrived there with other Englishmen who created a

ingreses que alçarom volta com os do logar e matarom Gonçall'Eannes Santos e ferirom outros da villa; e isso meesmo matarom os da villa dos ingreses, e forom feridos algũus; elles combaterom Borva e Monssaraz, e escallarom o Rredondo e combaterom Avis, e quiserom escallar Evora--Monte e nom poderom. Nos lugares honde pousavom, ao termo d'elles hiam aa forragem, fazendo gram dano em paães e vinhos e gaados, e atormentavom os homẽes, ataa que lhe deziam honde tiinham os mantiimentos e rroubavom-lhe quanto achavom; e se lh'o queriam defender, matavam-nos. As gentes começarom de tornar a esto o mais escusamente que podiam, e em fojos de pam e per outras maneiras matavom muitos d'elles escusamente, de guisa que per sua maa hordenança perecerom tantos que nom tornarom depois pera sua terra as duas partes d'elles.

CXXXIII

Como as gallees de Castella chegarom a Lixboa, e nom podendo fazer nojo aas naaos dos ingreses se tornarom pera Sevilha

A frota das naaos e barchas em que veherom os ingreses jaziam todas ante a cidade; e veherom novas a el-rrei dom Fernando como a frota das gallees de Castella viinham por fazer nojo e dano na cidade e especiallmente aas naaos dos ingreses; e el-rrei acordou que era bem que aquella frota e outros navios que hi jaziam, que sse fossem todos a Sacavem, que som duas legoas da cidade, e alli se lançassem todos por jazerem seguros; e as mayores naaos estavom deante todas com as alcacevas contra o mar, armadas e apavesadas, percebidas de trõos e outros arteficios pera sse defender; e mais aviiam duas grossas cadeas, que estavom deante tendidas d'hũua parte aa outra, que lhe nom podessem fazer nẽhũu nojo quaaesquer navios que contrairos fossem. Em terra aviia trõos e engenhos pera ajuda de sua defensom, com gentes assaz, se lhe tall cousa avehesse. Jazendo assi a frota d'esta guisa, veo Fernam Sanchez de Thoar almirante de Castella com a armada das gallees com que desbaratara as de Portugall, quando fora a de Saltes, cuidando d'achar as barchas e naaos dos ingreses ante Lixboa, por lhe empeecer em todo o que podesse; e quando chegarom ante a cidade, acharom o mar desembargado de navios, e souberom como todos jaziam em Sacavem; e quando allá forom e virom o rrio guardado

commotion with the locals and killed Gonçalo Eanes Santos and wounded other townspeople. Similarly, the townsmen killed some Englishmen and wounded others. The English attacked Borba and Monsaraz, and climbed the walls of Redondo and attacked Avis; and they tried to climb the walls of Évora—Monte, but could not. They went foraging all round about the places in which they were billeted, doing great damage to wheat, vines and cattle. They tortured men until they revealed where they kept their food—stores and then they stole whatever they found; and they killed anyone who tried to stop them. People began to punish this as discreetly as they could, and killed many of them with poisoned bread and in other unobtrusive ways, so that through their own indiscipline so many English soldiers died that two—thirds of them never returned to their native land.

CXXXIII
How the galleys of Castile arrived at Lisbon and, not being able to damage the galleys of the English, returned to Seville.

The fleet of ships and barges in which the English came was lying before the city; and news came to King Fernando that the fleet of galleys of Castile were coming to cause trouble and damage in the city and especially to the English ships. The King decided that it would be prudent for that fleet and other vessels lying there to go to Sacavém, some two leagues from the city, and stay there to be safe. The biggest ships were lying in front of the rest with their poops facing the sea, fully equipped and decked out with pennants, and provided with guns and other engines of war with which to defend themselves. Moreover they had two big chains which were hung across from one side to the other, so that no ships, however hostile, could do them any harm. On the land there were guns and war engines, with enough men, to help in their defence if need be. As the fleet lay in this fashion, the Admiral of Castile, Fernán Sánchez de Tovar[1] came with the fleet of galleys with which he had routed the Portuguese fleet in the battle of Saltes. He expected to find the barges and ships of the English before Lisbon and hoped to harm them in any way he could; but when the Castilians arrived in front of the city, they found the sea devoid of ships, and learnt that they were docked at Sacavém. When they went there and saw the river

e as naaos estar d'aquella guisa, tornarom-sse, e nom acharom em que fazer damno segundo seu desejo, e forom-sse pera Sevilha. As naaos dos ingreses, avendo certas novas que as gallees de Castella nom aviam tam cedo de tornar, e que lhe nom podiam fazer nojo, fezerom-sse prestes e partirom da cidade, ellas e outros navios, aos treze dias de dezembro da dita era, e d'elles carregarom de mercadarias, e forom-sse suas viagães.

CXXXIV

Como el-rrei e os ingreses partirom de Lixboa e chegarom aa cidade d'Evora

Esteve el-rrei em Lixboa, em dar cavallgaduras aos ingreses e hordenar as cousas que compriam pera a guerra, todo aquell inverno ataa ho veraão seguinte; e tanto que a frota dos ingreses partio de Lixboa, logo el-rrei partio acerca caminho de Santarem com suas gentes, e partio com ell o conde de Cambrig e muitos dos seus com elle, leixando na cidade e termos d'ella muitos malles e rroubos feitos; em tanto que deziam algüus que el-rrei era mui arreprehendido porque os mandara vĩir, por o grande estrago que faziam na terra. E nom entendaaes que el-rrei foi detehudo nem partio tam tarde de Lixboa por aazo da frota dos ingreses, mas foi assi per aqueecimento que n'aquella somana que as naaos partirom d'ante a cidade, partio el-rrei e a rrainha e as gentes todas que hi eram, e chegarom a Santarem; e mandou el-rrei fazer hũua ponte de barcas, pera poderem passar mais toste, que atravessava todo o rrio; e esteve hi o Natall e depois algüus dias; e ante que d'hi partisse, morreo o conde d'Ourem dom Joham Affonsso Tello, e foi per aazo da rrainha dado o condado a Joham Fernandez d'Andeiro, e d'alli em deante foi chamado o conde d'Ourem dom Joham Fernandez. Porém, leixando de fallar hũu pouco d'esta storia que seguinte trazemos, vejamos algũua cousa de sua fazenda, pois ainda d'o que dizer queremos em outro logar nom ouvestes conhecimento. Onde sabee que Joham Fernandez vivendo na Crunha, morreo Fernam Bezerra, hũu cavalleiro muito honrrado de Galliza; e sua molher, a que ficara hũu filho que chamavom Joham Bezerra, casou com este Joham Fernandez que chamavom d'Andeiro, posto que nom fosse iguall pera casar com ella; e houve Joham Fernandez d'ella quatro filhas e hũu filho: hũa chamavom, depois que ell foi conde, dona

well guarded and the ships in the situation already described, they turned back, and finding no opportunity of causing damage as they wanted, they returned to Seville. The English ships, having received information that the galleys of Castille were unlikely to return in the near future and consequently would give no trouble, made ready and departed the city, along with some other ships, on December 13, 1381, some of them loaded with merchandise, and so they put out to sea.

CXXXIV
How the King and the English left Lisbon and arrived at the city of Évora.

All that winter until the following summer the King was in Lisbon, providing horses for the English and making the necessary preparations for war. As soon as the English fleet set sail from Lisbon, the King left in the direction of Santarém with his men. The Earl of Cambridge and many of his men went too, leaving behind in the city and its environs a trail of destruction and theft, so much so that some say the King bitterly regretted having asked them to come, seeing the manner in which they were laying waste the country.

But do not imagine that the King lingered overlong nor departed so late from Lisbon on account of the English fleet; but it so fell out that in that very week the ships left the city, the King and Queen and all their people left as well, and came to Santarém; and the King ordered a pontoon bridge to be built all across the river so that they could arrive all the quicker. He stayed there for Christmas and a few days afterwards, and before he left the Count of Ourém, Dom João Afonso Telo, died. On the Queen's recommendation, his county was given to Juan Fernández Andeiro, who henceforth was entitled Dom Juan Fernández, Count of Ourém. But now, laying aside for the moment the story we have been telling, let us examine the circumstances of this man, since you have heard nothing of him so far except for what we said in one other place.

You must understand that Fernando Becerra, a most honourable knight of Galicia, died while Juan Fernández was living in Corunna; and his wife, who already had a son called Juan Becerra, then married this Juan Fernández who was known as Andeiro, even though he was too inferior to her in social rank. Juan Fernández had four daughters and one son by her. One daughter was called, after he was made a count, Doña Sancha Andeiro, who later was married to

Sancha d'Andeiro, que foi depois casada com Alvoro Gonçallvez, filho de Gonçallo Vaasquez d'Azevedo; outra dona Tareyja, que foi molher de dom Pedro da Guerra, filho do iffante dom Joham de Portugall, e casou com ella per amores, muito contra voontade do iffante; a terceira, dona Isabell, esta casou depois el-rrei dom Joham de Castella com hũu filho d'Alvoro Perez d'Osoyro, que chamavom Fernand'Allvarez d'Osoyro; outra, que chamavom dona Enes, morreo em Galliza nom seendo casada; o filho ouve nome Rrui d'Andeiro, que foi page-moor d'el-rrei de Castella. Sua molher do conde avia nome dona Mayor, molher de proll e de boom corpo. A rrainha, depois que sentio sua nom boa fama com Joham Fernandez em algũua guisa seer descuberta, ouve com elle que mandasse por a molher, penssando cessar o que d'ella deziam, pois que ell tiinha sua molher na terra. Feze-o el assi, e mandou por ella, e tinha-a per a moor parte no castello d'Ourem, depois que foi conde; e quando ella viinha aa corte, ante que fosse condessa e depois, fazia-lhe a rrainha grande gasalhado, dando-lhe joyas d'ouro e de prata e grandes dadivas de dinheiros. A gallega era sisuda, e tiinha-lh-o em grandes mercees, louvando-a muito per deante; e depois que d'alli partia, apregoava-a com louvores quaaes hũua combooça tem costume de dizer da outra. El-rrei partio de Santarem, e foy-sse caminho d'Evora, andando ja a era em mill e quatrocentos e viinte; e alli mandou fazer engenhos e carros e bombardas e outros percebimentos de guerra. E d'alli hordenou os lugares honde ouvessem d'estar os ingreses e cavalleiros certos que lhe fezessem dar todallas cousas por seus dinheiros; e pousava o conde em Villa Viçosa no moesteiro de Santo Agustinho e os outros nos arravalldes de Borva e Estremoz e d'Evora-Monte e pellas comarcas d'arredor.

CXXXV
Como a frota de Castella chegou a Lixboa, e do mall e dano que fez em algũus logares

Quando el-rrei dom Fernando partio de Lixboa, avendo novas como sse em Castella armava grande frota pera viir sobre a cidade, leixou por fronteiro em ella Gonçallo Meendez de Vaasconcellos e seus filhos e outros algũus com elles. E estando ell assi por fronteiro em Lixboa, chegarom sobr'ella, aos sete dias de março da era sobre dita, oiteenta vellas antre naaos e barchas que forom armadas em Bizcaya

Álvaro Gonçalves, a son of Gonçalo Vasques de Azevedo. Another was Doña Teresa, who was the wife of Dom Pedro da Guerra, son of Prince João of Portugal, who married her for love, quite against the wishes of the Prince. The third was Doña Isabel, whom King Juan of Castile later married to a son of Alvaro Pérez de Osorio, called Fernando Alvárez de Osorio. The fourth was called Doña Inés, who died in Galicia without marrying. The son was called Rui Andeiro, who was the principal page of the King of Castile. The Count's wife was called Doña Mayor, a woman of good character and fine appearance. When the Queen felt that the dubious reputation acquired by her relationship with Juan Fernández was somehow being discovered, she made him send for his wife, thinking that the fact that the latter was now with him would put a stop to all the talk about herself. He did send for his wife and kept her for the most part in Ourém castle after he was made a count. When she came to Court, both before she became countess and afterwards, she was most honourably treated by the Queen who gave her jewelry in gold and silver and generous gifts of money. The Galician lady was prudent and very grateful, greatly praising the Queen to her face; and after she left the Court, she praised her with the sort of praises that a woman usually applies to her rival in love.

The King left Santarém and set out in early 1382 for Évora, where he ordered war—machines, carts, bombards and other provisions for war to be prepared. He ordered that the places where the English and other knights were to stay should provide them with everything, but only in exchange for money. The Earl settled in Vila Viçosa in the monastery of Santo Agostinho, and the others in the suburbs of Borba, Estremoz and Évora—Monte, and in other districts nearby.

CXXXV

How the Castilian fleet arrived at Lisbon and of the damage and destruction which it wrought in some places.

When King Fernando set out from Lisbon, he had already received the news that in Castile a huge fleet was being prepared to attack the city, so he left Gonçalo Mendes de Vasconcelos there as commander—in—chief, together with his sons and some others; and whilst Vasconcelos was commander in Lisbon, there appeared on 7 March eighty sailing—ships and barges, which had been fitted out in Vizcaya and other seaports. In them were good knights, squires and

e em outros logares dos portos do mar, nas quaaes viinham bõos cavalleiros e escudeiros e hom̃ees d'armas e muita gente de pee escudados a que chamavom allacayos; e chamavam--lhe assi porque eram das montanhas de Bizcaya e viinham todos descallços e mall corregidos. A frota como pousou ante a cidade, lançarom todos os batees fora armados e pavesados, e forom juntamente assi sahir ante o moesteiro de Santa Clara, que será hũu tiro de beesta aalem da cidade. As gentes de dentro quiserom sahir pera lhe embargar o tomar da terra; e Gonçallo Meendez, que era fronteiro, deffendia que nom sahisse nẽhũu fora, ca el-rrei nom lhe mandara outra cousa se nom que guardasse mui bem a cidade; pero, nom embargando isto, sahirom algũus poucos contra sa voontade, e forom d'elles feridos, e morto Gomez Lourenço Fariseu, que por estonce era juiz da cidade; e os castellaãos tomarom entom a terra sem achando mais quem lh'a deffendesse. E logo a poucos dias, veendo os da frota como os da cidade nom sahiam a elles, armarom todollos batees outra vez de gente d'armas e beestaria e sahirom todos em terra antre Santos e a cidade, que he d'outra parte contra a entrada do rrio quanto pode seer dous tiros de beesta; e Gonçallo Meendez embargava todavia os da cidade, dizendo que nom sahissem fora, que el-rrei nom lhe mandara salvo guardar a cidade, e que elles assi o fezessem. Os bizcainhos, quando virom que nẽhũu nom sahia a elles, tornarom-sse a seus batees, e desi aa frota; e d'alli em deante tomarom fouteza de sahirem fora, assi da parte da cidade come da parte de Rribatejo, honde queimarom muitas quintãas e fezerom muito damno; e da parte da terra queimarom hũus graciosos paaços d'el-rrei acerca da cidade junto com o mar, hu chamom Exobregas, no começo de hũu valle de muitas e prazivees ortas; e queimarom outros paaços d'el-rrei acerca d'hũu solaçoso rrio, que ssom duas legoas da cidade, honde chamam Freellas; e forom pollo rrio de Tejo acima, e queimarom outros paaços d'el-rrei hu chamam Villa Nova da Rrainha, que ssom oito legoas da cidade; e chegarom muito mais acima aas leziras d'Aalbaçotim e d'Alcoelha, e alli matavom muitos gaados e faziam carnagem e tragiam pera a frota. E tanto sse atreverom, sem achando quem lh'o contradizer, que forom em batees pello rrio de Couna acima, que som atraves tres legoas da cidade, e alli sahirom em terra e forom queimar o arravallde de Palmella, que som d'ali grandes duas legoas; e mais queimarom o arravallde d'Almadãa e muitas casas e quintãas per aquella comarqua.

men—at—arms together with many foot—soldiers with shields whom they called lackeys because they were from the Basque mountains and came all barefoot and ill—armed.

When the fleet arrived before the city, they lowered into the water all their small boats, all equipped and decked out with flags, and they all went to land in front of the Convent of Santa Clara, which must be about one crossbow shot beyond the city. The people within the walls wanted to go out to stop them getting a foothold on land; but Gonçalo Mendes, the commander—in—chief, forbade anyone to go out, for the King had not ordered him to do anything other than to guard the city very well. Despite this, nevertheless, a few went out against his orders, and some of these were wounded; and Gomes Lourenço Fariseu, who was at that time the city judge, was killed. So the Castilians captured a beachhead without any further resistance.

In a few days, seeing that no one was coming out of the city against them, the men from the fleet fitted out all the longboats once again with men—at—arms and mounts; and landed between Santos and the city in the direction of the river's mouth at a distance of two crossbow shots. Gonçalo Mendes still maintained a prohibition on anyone going out because the King had only ordered them to guard the city and they ought to obey. When they saw that no one was coming out again, the Basques returned to their boats, and thence to the fleet. Thereafter they became bolder, sallying forth, both on the city side and on the Ribatejo side, where they burned many farms and did much damage. On the landward side they burned a fine palace belonging to the King on the shore near the city at a spot called Ábregas at the entrance to a valley containing many pleasant fruit and vegetable farms. They burned another royal palace near an attractive river, two leagues from the city at a place called Frielas; and they went up the Tagus and burned another palace of the King at a spot called Vila Nova da Rainha, some eight leagues from the city. They went on well above the meadows of Alboçatim and Alcoelha, and there they killed many cattle, butchered them and brought them back to the fleet. Not meeting any resistance, they became so bold that they even went in their boats up the River Couna, about three leagues from the city. There they disembarked and went some two leagues on land and burned the outskirts of Palmela, and they also burned the outskirts of Almada and many houses and farms in the area.

CXXXVI

Por que rrazom tirarom de fronteiro Gonçallo Meendez de Vaasconcellos, e foi posto o prior do Crato em Lixboa

Fazendo-sse assi muito mall pella terra, sem avendo nẽhũu que lh'o embargasse, forom novas a el-rrei dom Fernando do grande damno que os da frota faziam per termo de Lixboa mui soltamente, e como Gonçallo Meendez nom tornava a ello com algũu rremedio nem leixava sahir as gentes da cidade, dizendo que de guardar o logar aviam de teer cuidado e d'outra cousa nom. El-rrei ouve d'ello grande menencoria e disse que lhe parecia que Gonçallo Meendez era em esto tall como o servo que diz no Evangelho, a que o senhor deu hũu marco d'ouro com que trabalhasse por seu serviço e proveito, e el escondeu-ho sob terra sem fazendo com el nẽhũua proll, por a quall rrazom foi jullgado do senhor por servo maao e priguiçoso. «E Gonçallo Meendez, disse el-rrei, por tall deve seer jullgado: queria guardar a cidade honde estava seguro dos emmiigos e leixar destroir o termo e logares d'arredor d'ella». Entom hordenou el-rrei de o tirar de fronteiro e mandar aa cidade por guarda e deffenssom da terra ho prioll do Espitall dom Pedr'Allvarez e seus irmaãos com elle, scilicet, Rrodrig'Alvarez que chamavom Olhinhos e Nun'Allvarez e Dieg'Allvarez e Fernam Pereira e Joham Alvarez e Rrui Pereira e Alvoro Pereira, parentes do prioll e de seus irmaãos, e Gonçall'Eannes de Castell da Vide e outros bõos que viinham com elle, que seeriam per todos ataa duzentas lanças bem encavallgados. Hora aveo que no dia que o prioll aviia de chegar aa cidade, viindo caminho de Santarem, ouve novas como parte das gentes da frota eram a termo de Sintra rroubar e tomar gaados pera trazerem aos naviios. D'estas novas foi o prioll mui ledo e todollos que viinham com elle, e encaminharom pera aquella parte per hu ouverom rrecado que os castellaãos viinham; e como era muita gente de pee sahindo afouto por o acustumado huso que tiinham, hordenou o prioll de lhe lançar hũa cellada; e elles, que viinham muito desegurados a seu prazer, ledos com gram rroubo, sem algũu temor, deu o prioll com suas gentes em elles, e como gente despercebida nom se poderom deffender de guisa que lhe prestasse e começarom de fogir, leixando o que tragiam: mas seu triigoso fogir a mui poucos deu vida, ca os da cellada derom em elles, e forom presos e mortos muitos e tomado

CXXXVI

The reason why Gonçalo Mendes de Vasconcelos was relieved of the command of Lisbon and replaced by the Prior of Crato.

While the countryside was being ravaged in this way without let or hindrance, news reached King Fernando of the great harm the men of the fleet were doing freely in the district of Lisbon, and of how Gonçalo Mendes de Vasconcelos was not reacting to this in any way, nor even allowing people to go out of the city, but saying they had to take care to guard the place and nothing else. The King was sorely vexed at this, and said that Gonçalo Mendes reminded him of the servant in the Gospels [1] who was given a gold mark by his master so that he might serve the latter by making a profit from it, but who hid it in the earth, thus achieving nothing with it, so that his master considered him to be a wicked and lazy servant. "And so", said the King, "Gonçalo Mendes must be considered the same. He wanted to guard the city where he was safe from the enemy, leaving the surrounding district and places to be destroyed by them." Then the King ordered him to be dismissed from his post as defender of the city, and the Prior of the Hospital, Dom Pedro Álvares [2], to be sent to the city to guard it and defend the land together with his brothers, that is to say, Rodrigo Álvares who was nicknamed 'Little—eyes', Nun'Álvares [3], Diogo Álvares, Fernão Pereira, João Álvares, and Rui Pereira, and Álvaro Pereira, who were relatives of the Prior and his brothers, as well as Gonçalo Eanes of Castelo de Vide and other worthy men who came with him, numbering some two hundred lances riding good horses.

Now, it so fell out that on the day the Prior was due to arrive in the city from Santarém news came that some of the forces from the fleet had gone to the district of Sintra to pillage and to rob cattle to take to the ships. The Prior was delighted to hear this news, as were all his companions, and they made their way to the area where the Castilians were said to be. As these were mainly foot—soldiers and out on their customary foraging, and therefore quite off their guard, the Prior decided to ambush them. As they came along quite unsuspecting and at their ease, full of rejoicing at their booty and without any fear, the Prior and his men fell upon them. Like anyone caught off guard, they were unable to defend themselves effectively and so started to flee, leaving their spoils behind. But their desperate flight availed most of them little, for they were caught in the ambush, many were captured and many killed, and their booty was taken from

ho rroubo que traziam. O prioll veho entom pera a cidade, honde foi rrecebido com gram prazer, e pousou no moesteiro de Sam Francisco, e seus irmaãos e outros d'arredor d'elle. Quando os da frota virom como aquellas gentes de cavallo veherom por guarda da cidade, nom ousarom d'alli em deante sahir tam soltamente como ante faziam; ca o prioll tiinha atallaya com elles, que como algũu batell queria sahir fora, logo os seus cavallgavom e lhe embargavom a sahida, e sse algũus sahiom fora que eram vistos logo os da cidade eram alli prestes; de guisa que ao rrecolher dos batees, com a pressa grande se lançavom muitos das barrocas a fundo: e des entom começarom os da frota d'aver d'os da cidade maa vezinhança.

CXXXVII

Como Nun'Allvarez lançou hũua cellada aos da frota,
e d'o que lhe aveo com elles

A frota era grande e de muitas gentes, e nom lhe podiam os da cidade per tall guisa embargar a sahida da terra que elles per muitas vezes nom sahissem aa sua voontade em logares nom vistos e outros arredados da cidade, per cujo aazo se faziam antre elles muitas escaramuças, das quaaes, por a Deus assi prazer, sempre os portugueses levavom a melhor d'elles. Hora assi aveo em esta sazom que Nun'Allvarez, amando muito serviço d'el-rrei, desi por seer conhecido por boom, hordenou de fazer hũua escaramuça per ssi, sem o fazendo saber ao prioll nem a algũu dos outros seus irmaãos; e veendo como os das naaos sahiam ameude a colher huvas e fruita, porque era estonce tempo d'ellas, fallou com hũu boom cavaleiro, casado com hũua sua irmãa, que chamavom Pedr'Affonso do Casal, como era sua voontade de em outro dia lançar hũua cellada aos da frota, pera sse ajudar d'elles se sahissem fora como sohiam; e se lhe prazeria a elle de sse hir em sua companha: o quall outorgou que de boa voontade; e per esta guisa ajuntou Nun'Allvarez dos seus e d'outros ataa viinte e quatro de bõos homẽes de cavallo, e seeriam hũus trinta antre beesteiros e homẽes de pee. E esto assi acertado, cavallgou Nun'Allvarez em outro dia bem cedo pella manhãa e foi-sse lançar em cellada aa ponte d'Alcantara, asso o moesteiro de Santos contra Rrestello, cobrindo-sse ell e os seus o melhor que podiam antre as vinhas e barrocaaes que hi avia muitos, por nom seerem vistos da frota. Estando

88

them. The Prior then came to the city where he was welcomed with great rejoicing, and lodged at the monastery of São Francisco, with his brothers and the rest lodged nearby. When the men of the fleet saw that these horsemen had arrived to guard the city, they did not dare henceforward to sally forth as freely as had been their custom, for the Prior kept such an intense watch on them that whenever a boat set out from the fleet, straightaway his men would gallop out and prevent it from coming ashore; and if some of them did get ashore, they were spotted at once and the men from the city were ready for them; so that in trying to regain their boats, many of them, in the panic, fell overboard into the depths of the sea. From then on the men of the fleet began to be harassed by those that were defending the city.

CXXXVII
How Nun'Álvares ambushed the men from the fleet, and what befell him in the process.

The fleet was big and carried very many men. For this reason the defenders of the city were often unable to prevent them from getting ashore at will at points that could not be watched and some other points that were far from the city. Consequently, there were many skirmishes between the two sides, in which it pleased God that the Portuguese should always be victorious. Now it happened at that time that Nun'Álvares, being eager to serve the King so that he might be held in high regard, decided to skirmish on his own account, without letting the Prior or any of his other brothers know. Noticing that the men from the fleet would often come ashore to gather grapes and fruit, for these were in season, he spoke with a good knight who was married to his sister, named Pedro Afonso do Casal. He told him that on the following day he intended to ambush these men and capture them if they came ashore as they usually did; and he asked him if he was disposed to join him in this ambush, to which Pedro happily agreed. In this way, Nun'Álvares assembled from his own men and others a force of twenty—four good horsemen, and some thirty crossbowmen and foot—soldiers. With everything ready, early next morning Nun'Álvares rode to lay an ambush at the Alcántara bridge, below the convent of Santos[1] opposite Restelo. He concealed himself and his men as best he could among the vines and gullies which were numerous there, in order not to be seen from the fleet.

assi Nun'Allvarez fallando com os seus a maneira que ouvessem de teer em topar com os castellaãos se sahissem fora, e elles virom viir hũu batell da frota, e em elle ataa viinte homẽes que viinham aas vinhas por colher huvas. Nun'Allvarez e os seus, como os virom, esguardarom bem honde sahiam e hu aviam de rrecudir aa tornada; e cavallgarom logo os de cavallo e os beesteiros e homẽes de pee com elles e forom--sse aaquel logar per honde elles sobiam, que era hũu barranco grande contra as vinhas; e como alli chegarom, Nun'Allvarez se deceo do cavallo, e outros algũus com elle, e aderençarom rrijo contra os castellaãos: e elles, quando os virom consigo, mais rrijo d'o que sobirom decerom a fundo contra a praya, e Nun'Allvarez e outros de volta com elles; e veendo-sse os castellaãos muito aficados e por guarecer de morte que a seus olhos viiam muito prestes, lançarom-sse todos na agua; e d'elles nadando sem armas nẽhũuas, outros amergulhando so aagua, cobrarom seu batell sem mais empeecimento e forom-sse pera seus navios.

CXXXVIII

Das rrazoões que Nun'Allvarez disse aos seus por os esforçar
que pellejassem, e d'o que lhe a ell aconteceo soo
em pellejando com os castellaãos

Veendo Nun'Allvarez que por entom lhe nom podia fazer mais damno, rrecolheo ante ssi os que hiam com elle e foi-sse poer em hũu teso ante a porta do moesteiro de Santos, logar onde os bem viiam os da frota; e como correrom em pós os seus e os fezerom lançar na agua, e com despeito cobrarom coraçom e sahirom das naaos ataa duzentos e cinquoenta homẽes d'armas com lanças compridas e muitos beesteiros e peoões, desejosos pera pellejar, segundo depois pareceo. Nun'Allvarez, como vio sahir os batees, foi mui ledo com sua viinda, como aquell que de tall jogo nom aviia menos voontade que elles, e começou d'avivar seu cavallo, e disse assi contra os seus. esforçando-os: «Amigos irmaãos, bem sabees a teençom com que sahistes da cidade, que nom compre de vos seer mais declarado: hora me parece que teendes prestes o que vehestes buscar, d'o que devees seer mui ledos, ca de mim vos digo que da minha parte ho som assaz; e rrogovos que pois nos aas maãos vem o que desejamos, que vos praza de todos seer nembrados de vossas hon-

As Nun'Álvares and his men were discussing how to proceed in order to engage with the Castilians if they came ashore, they saw a boat coming shorewards from the fleet, and in it some twenty men who were coming to the vines to pick grapes. As they saw them coming, Nun'Álvares and his men took careful note of just where they were coming ashore and where they would have to come back in order to return to the boat. Then his horsemen galloped along, with the crossbowmen and foot—soldiers, to the place where the Castilians were coming up, which was a deep gully opposite the vines. When they got there, Nun'Álvares dismounted and some others with him; and they charged the Castilians, who, on seeing the Portuguese so close, went down to the beach much faster than they had come up, with Nun'Álvares and the others hot on their heels. The Castilians saw that they were hard pressed, and in order to cheat death, which seemed very near, they all threw themselves into the water. Some of them, without weapons, could swim, and others floundered in the water, but they reached their boat without further mishap and went back to their ships.

CXXXVIII
The speech which Nun'Álvares made to his men in order to encourage them to fight, and what happened to him while fighting the Castilians.

Seeing that he could do the Castilians no more harm for the time being, Nun'Álvares assembled his men in front of him and stood on a mound before the door of the convent of Santos, a place where they could clearly be seen by the men in the fleet. Because his men had been so hot on their heels that they forced them to throw themselves into the water, now they were driven by their disgrace to take courage, and two hundred and fifty men—at—arms with good lances and many crossbowmen and foot—soldiers left the ships keen to fight, as afterwards it appeared. When he saw the boats lowered, Nun'Álvares was delighted by their coming, for he had quite as much thirst for action as they did. He livened up his horse, and he encouraged his men with the following words: "Friends and brothers, you well know with what purpose you came out of the city, and there is no need for me to remind you. Now I think that what you came for lies near at hand, and therefore you should be very joyful. For my part, I tell you that I certainly am; and I beg you, now that we are coming to blows as we desired, all please to remember your

rras, aperfiando em pellejar sem tornando costas por cousa que avenha; e pera isto, com a ajuda de Deus, eu serei o primeiro que toparei em elles, e vós segui-me fazendo como eu fezer; e seede certos que elles vos nom sofrerám se em vós sentirem esforço, mas logo volveróm as costas, porque d'acorro nom têm esperança e assi vos ajudarees d'elles». Estas e outras boas rrazoões que Nuno Alvarez disse aos seus por os esforçar nēhūua cousa aaquella hora prestarom, ca elles viiam ja muita gente da frota em terra a quall viinha pera elles e era muito acerca, e cada vez mais crecendo temiam de os esperar. Nun'Allvarez, conhecendo em elles medo, trabalhava de os esforçar quanto podia, mas suas doces pallavras mesturadas com asperos braados nom os podia a esto demover, mas mostrando que o nom ouviam nem tiinham d'el conhecimento arredavom-sse afora nom querendo atender, outros fugirom logo de todo nom podendo sofrer a vista dos castellaãos. Hora aqui he de saber que posto que os alheos louvores sejam ouvidos com iguaaes orelhas, muito he grave conssentir o que impossivel parece de seer; e porque o seguinte rrazoado mais parece millagre que naturall aqueecimento, dizemos primeiro, rrespondendo a taaes, que ssem duvida verdade screvemos, mas que o poderoso Deus, que soo aaquella hora o quis livrar d'antre tantos contrairos, teendo-o guardado pera mayores cousas, nom outorgou n'aquella pelleja que seus emmiigos lhe podessem dar morte. Nun'Allvarez, veendo que os seus nom davom volta e que os castellaãos chegavom acerca d'onde ell estava, aderençou contra elles com gram virtude cavalleirosa, a algūus impossivell de creer, e soo sem parceiro se lançou na moor espessura dos emmiigos, honde eram aquelles duzentos e cinquoenta homēes d'armas. E como sse assi lançou antre elles e fez de lança o primeiro encontro, perdida a lança tornou aa espada; e nom ho seguindo nēhūu dos seus dava tam assiinados golpes a toda parte que pero os castellaãos fossem muitos assaz avia de logar antr'elles; mas em todo esto foi elle servido de lanças e pedras e viratoões que era maravilha pode-llo sofrer; e prougue a Deus que nēhūua lhe deu em logar que lhe fazer podesse nojo, ca o corpo era bem armado de hūuas assaz fortes solhas, de guisa que os golpes maçavom o corpo e nēhūu damno faziam na carne: pero ell penssava que era chagado de morte, por os muitos golpes que em ssi sentia. Mas seu cavallo com as muitas lançadas pose as ancas e cahiu em terra, e Nuno Alvarez isso meesmo; e em cahindo assi ambos, começou o cavalo bullir rrijamente com as mãos

92

honour and to remain steadfast in combat without turning your back on the enemy, no matter what happens. For this reason, with God's help I shall be the first to attack them, and you must follow me and do as I do. Be assured that they will not be able to resist you if they sense your strength, but rather will show us their heels at once, for they can expect no help from anyone, and so you will win the victory over them." These and other good arguments which Nun'Álvares addressed to his men in order to encourage them had no effect at that moment, for they could see many men from the fleet already ashore. These were advancing fast, already close and in ever—increasing numbers, so that they were afraid to wait for them. Sensing his men's fear, Nun'Álvares strove with all his might to encourage them, but his speech, a mixture of gentle words and rough cries, was unable to sway them. Showing that they could not hear or understand him, they ignored him, rushed away and fled there and then at the sight of the Castilians.

Now here one must recognize that although one can listen to other people's praises unmoved, it is very difficult to accept something which seems to be impossible; and because what follows seems more like a miracle than a natural event, we shall answer such an objection by saying straightaway that we are certainly writing the truth, but that God Almighty at that moment simply chose to deliver Nun'Álvares from so many enemies because He wished to preserve him for greater things and so would not permit his enemies to kill him in that skirmish.

Seeing that his men were not turning to face the enemy and that the Castilians were now very near at hand, Nun'Álvares rode against them with a knightly courage so great that some find it impossible to credit. Quite alone, without any companion, he hurled himself into the very thick of the enemy where those two hundred and fifty men—at—arms were waiting for him. Since he charged in amongst them and used his lance in the first blow, he lost it and drew his sword; and as none of his men had followed him, he dealt out such spectacular blows in all directions that, although the Castilians were so numerous, he made quite a space in their midst. Yet he was assailed by lances, stones and arrows so that it was a marvel that he was able to withstand it; but it pleased God that none of these objects should hit him in a dangerous place, for his body was well protected by some quite strong pieces of plate—armour, so that the blows pounded his body but did not injure his flesh. Nevertheless, he thought that he had received fatal wounds, from the many blows he felt. With the many spear—wounds it had received, his horse fell down on its haunches, and Nun'Álvares came down with it. As they both fell, the horse's four legs began to flail desperately; and as they did so, the

e com os pees; e perneando assi rrijamente, acertou o canello da ferradura da mão ho tecido d'hũua fivella das solhas de Nun'Allvarez, de guisa que ell nom sse podia desaprender do cavallo, e alli cuidou de seer logo morto. Os seus, que estavom a longe oolhando, veendo o gram periigo em que Nuno Allvarez era, costrangidos de doo e vergonha, correrom rrijamente cobrando coraçõões, e acorrerom-lhe mais toste que poderom: e hũu dos primeiros que a ell chegou foi hũu clerigo em cuja casa Nun'Allvarez pousava, que hia em sua companha com hũua besta, e cortou-lhe a pressa o tecido per que estava preso. Nun'Allvarez, desatado, se levantou rrijo e tomou hũua lança de muitas que jaziam arredor d'elle; e com esforço e ajuda d'os que ja com elle estavom, começou de seguir os castellaãos. E em esto chegarom a pressa Dieg'Allvarez e Fernam Pereira seus irmaãos, que d'isto souberom parte, que lhe forom assaz bõos companheiros; e todos seguirom os emmiigos, de guisa que prendiam e matavom muitos. Aacima, nom podendo ja mais sofrer tall dano, tornarom costas por se acolher aos batees; e aa entrada perecerom muitos por entrar mais a pressa d'o que aviam em custume. Nun'Allvarez se tornou com os seus pera a cidade sem morrer nẽhũu da sua parte, mas forom d'elles mall feridos, e nove cavallos mortos; e quando o prioll ho vio viir com os prisoneiros que consigo tragia, ouve gram prazer com ell e com os outros, e forom todos d'elle mui bem rrecebidos.

CXXXIX

Como sse começou o aazo da prisom do meestre d'Avis e de Gonçallo Vaasquez d'Azevedo

Leixando estar Lixboa cercada e tornando a fallar d'el-rrei dom Fernando, que estava em Evora fazendo-sse prestes pera a guerra de Castella, convem que digamos ante que d'hi parta como mandou prender o meestre d'Avis dom Joham seu irmaão e Gonçallo Vaasquez d'Azevedo, hũu bom fidallgo e muito seu privado: e pois esta estoria avemos de trager à praça, nom como algũus que fezerom livrezinhos que pubricados em algũuas maãos as cousas como passarom nom [se] comprehendem per elles perfeitamente, mas guardando a rregra do Fillosofo que diz que nam podemos saber as cousas como ssom se da causa do seu primeiro começo carecemos de todo ponto, nós o nacimento da sua prisom d'elles vaamos

iron shoe on a front hoof caught on one of the buckle — straps of the armour plating, so that Nun'Álvares could not release himself from his horse and expected to be killed there and then.

Then his own men, who were watching from a distance, saw his great danger and, full of sorrow and shame, regained their courage, leapt into action and hastened to his aid with all possible speed. One of the first to reach him was a cleric in whose house Nun'Álvares was lodging; he rode up to him and swiftly cut through the strap which held him fast. Once freed, Nun'Álvares leapt up and snatched a lance from among the many that lay about him. Then, with the support and help of his companions, he began to follow the Castilians. At this point, his brothers Diogo Álvares and Fernão Pereira, who were his good companions and had just heard the news, galloped up; and they all chased after the enemy, to such good effect that they captured and killed a great number. Moreover, unable to withstand this assault, the Castilians turned their backs and retreated to their boats, where, in their extraordinary rush to get aboard, many perished. Nun'Álvares and his men returned to the city without any loss of life, although some of them had been seriously wounded, and nine of their horses had been killed. When the Prior saw him coming with the prisoners he brought with him, he was delighted with him and his men and gave them a fine welcome.

CXXXIX
Of how the Master of Avis and Gonçalo Vasques de Azevedo came to be imprisoned in the first place.

Leaving Lisbon under siege, let us speak again of King Fernando who was in Évora preparing for war with Castile. It is necessary to tell how, before he left there, he ordered the arrest of his brother, Dom João,[1] the Master of Avis, and of Gonçalo Vasques de Azevedo, a fine nobleman and close confidant.[2] For we must bring this story into the full light of day, but not in the manner of some who have written booklets of reduced circulation from which it is difficult to understand how these things really happened. Rather would we observe the rule of the Philosopher who states that we can never know the true nature of things if we lack all knowledge of the cause that first brought those things about.[3] We therefore intend to delve deep into the original causes of their imprisonment so we may know how this came about.

95

buscar longe d'onde veo. Assi foi, segundo ouvistes, que quando Joham Fernandez d'Andeiro veo fallar a el-rrei dom Fernando em Estremoz sobre a viinda dos ingreses e que o el-rrei teve ascondido per algũus dias na torre d'esse logar, sohou nom onesta fama antr'elle e a rrainha; e posto que aa primeira fosse escura e nom teendo certos autores, depois per firme opinion fallavom em ello mui largamente, por a quall rrazom eram ambos avudos em grande odio das gentes, espiciallmente dos grandes e bõos que sse dohiam da desonrra d'el-rrei. Hora assi aveo que estando el-rrei em Evora, como dissemos, chegarom hũu dia pella sesta aa camara da rrainha ho conde dom Gonçallo seu irmaão e Joham Fernandez d'Andeiro com elle; e por a calma que fazia grande hiam elles suando muito; e ella quando os assi vio viir, preguntou-lhe se tragiam sudairos com que sse alimpar d'aquella suor, e elles disserom que nom; entom tomou a rrainha hũu veeo e parti-ho per meo e deu a cada hũu sua parte pera sse alimparem. E andando-sse Joham Fernandez passeando pella camara com aquell veeo na maão, ficou-sse em joelhos ante ella, e disse com voz baixa mui manssamente: «Senhora, mais chegado e mais husado queria eu de vós o pano, quando m'o vós ouvessees de dar, que este que me vós daaes»; e a rrainha começou de rriir d'esto. E pero lhe dissesse estas pallavras mui mansso, nom as disse porém tam passamente que as nom ouvio hũua dona que siia acerqua d'ella, que chamavom Enes Affonso, molher d'hũu grande privado d'el-rrei e de seu consselho, que avia nome Gonçallo Vaasquez d'Azevedo, de que el muito fiava; e porque lhe parecerom mui mall ditas, callou-sse estonce por aquella hora, e disse-o depois a seu marido. A cabo de dias, seendo a rrainha fallando em cousas de sabor, louvando muito o costume dos ingreses e d'aquelles que com elles husavom, rrespondeo aquell privado d'el-rrei e disse: «Certamente, senhora, quanto a mim, seus costumes em algũuas cousas nom me parecem tanto de bõos como os vós louvaaes». «E quaaes?» disse ella. «Senhora, disse ell, nom he boom costume nem de louvar a nẽhũu o que muitos d'elles husam, que sse algũua dona ou donzella por sua mesura lhe dá algũu veeo ou joya, elles se chegam a ellas aa orelha e dizem-lhe que mais chegadas e mais husadas queriam elles as joyas d'ellas que nom aquellas que lhe ellas dam». A rrainha, quando esto ouvio, sospeitou logo por que ell aquello dezia, e callou-sse por entom e nom disse nada, dando a entender que nom parava em aquello mentes; e depois chamou-ho adeparte e disse: «Gonçallo Vaasquez, eu bem ssei que vossa molher vos disse aquelo que vós ora ante dissestes;

So it was, as you already heard, that when Juan Fernández Andeiro came to talk with King Fernando in Estremoz about the coming of the English and the King kept him hidden for some days in the fortress of that place, rumours of dishonourable conduct between him and the Queen began to circulate. Although at first the rumours were vague and their sources unreliable, later the affair was talked about much more widely and with greater conviction. For this reason, both of them began to be detested by the people, especially the great and the good, who lamented the dishonour done to the King. Now it so happened that whilst the King was in Évora, as we have said, Count Gonçalo, the Queen's brother, arrived one day in the Queen's chamber at siesta time with Juan Fernández Andeiro and because of the extreme sultriness of the weather, they were sweating profusely. When the Queen saw them arrive in this state, she asked if they had any kerchiefs with them with which to wipe away the sweat; and they said they had not. So she took a veil and tore it down the middle, giving each of them a piece with which to wipe himself. As he walked about the chamber, with that veil in his hand, suddenly Juan Fernández knelt down before her, and very gently and quietly said to her, "My lady, rather than this cloth which you have just given me, I would prefer another one which you have used more and kept more about your person, when you have it to give to me." Although he spoke these words very quietly, he did not say them too softly to be heard by a lady standing close by, called Inês Afonso, who was the wife of one of the King's favourite counsellors, Gonçalo Vasques de Azevedo by name, a man he greatly trusted. Because these words seemed to her to be in bad taste, for the time being she kept silent, but spoke of them later to her husband.

Some days later, when the Queen was talking about pleasant things and praising highly the customs of the English and those who followed them, that counsellor of the King answered thus:

"Certainly, my lady, from my own point of view, in some respects their customs do not merit the praise you have given them."

"Which ones are you referring to?" she enquired.

"My lady, he said, "one custom that many of them have is not good or praiseworthy, for if some lady or damsel out of courtesy gives a man a veil or a jewel, he comes close to her and whispers in her ear that rather than the jewel which she has given him, he would prefer another one which she has used more and kept more about her person."

On hearing this, the Queen immediately suspected the reason why he was saying this, so she remained silent, making no comment and affecting to pay no attention. Later, she drew him on one side and said, "Gonçalo Vasques, I know perfectly well that your wife told you what you said just now. You can both be sure that your words have

mas seede certo que vós e ella nom ho lançastes em poço vazio, e prometo-vos que ambos m'o paguees mui bem». E el escusando-sse que nom sabia d'ello parte, e ella dizendo que era assi, leixarom aquello e fallarom em all. Honde sabee que este Gonçallo Vaasquez era segundo com-irmaão da rrainha dona Lionor, e per ella fora feito e posto em grande estado: porque dona Aldonça de Vasconcellos, molher de Martim Affonsso Tello, madre da rrainha dona Lionor, era prima com-irmãa de Tareija Vaasquez d'Azevedo, filha de Vaasco Gomez d'Azevedo, irmaão de Gonçallo Gomez d'Azevedo, alferez d'el-rrei dom Affonso, o que foi aos mouros; assi que a iffante dona Beatriz, molher que depois foi d'el-rrei de Castella, era sobrinha d'este Gonçallo Vaasquez, filha de sua segunda com-irmãa: e por este divedo que ell avia com a rrainha e o acrecentamento que n'eelle avia feito teve ella gram sentido das rrazoões que d'ella dissera e aazou como depois fosse preso.

CXL

Como Vaasco Gomez d'Aavreu fallou aa rrainha, e das rrazoões que ambos ouverom

Depois d'esto a poucos dias hũu fidallgo que avia nome Vaasco Gomez d'Aavreu, que sse chamava parente da rrainha, veendo como ja tempo avia que lhe nom mostrava boa voontade como d'ante avia em costume, desi porque deziam algũus que lhes parecia que a rrainha lhe nom tiinha boom desejo, chegou hũu dia a ella e disse: «Senhora, vós me fezestes muito bem e posestes em honrra, de guisa que eu nom som mais que quanto a vossa mercee em mim fez; por a quall rrazom eu som mui tehudo de vos servir e amar enquanto viver, e assi o entendo de fazer sempre; e ora nom sei porque dias há vós mostraaes que me avees hodio, como sse vos eu ouvesse feito algũu grande erro e deserviço: porém vos peço por mercee que me digaaes esto porque he, ou sse vos disserom algũa cousa que eu contra vosso serviço fezesse; e sse for verdade o que vos de mim disserom, eu vos faço preito e menagem que d'este logar me nom parta ataa esperar aqui a morte». Rrespondeo a rrainha e disse: «Nom sem gram rrazom eu ei de vós mui grande queixume, e nom sei pèra que ssom essas pallavras e essa avondança de rrazoar, ca bem sabees vós que vós me teendes feito hũu erro tam grande per que vós mereciees de vos eu mandar cortar a cabeça

not been wasted, and I promise you that you will both pay me for it." He protested that he knew nothing of the matter and she said that he did; but they dropped the subject and spoke of other things. You must know that this Gonçalo Vasques was a second cousin to Queen Leonor, and it was through her that he had been raised to high estate. For Dona Aldonça de Vasconcelos, the wife of Martim Afonso Telo and Queen Leonor's mother, was first cousin to Teresa Vasques de Azevedo, daughter of Vasco Gomes de Azevedo, brother of Gonçalo Gomes de Azevedo, the standard—bearer of that King Afonso who had fought against the Moors.[4] So Princess Beatriz, who later married the King of Castile, was the niece of this Gonçalo Vasques, as the daughter of his second cousin; and because he was deeply in the Queen's debt and had been so exalted by her, she was deeply hurt at what he had said about her and she planned to have him put into prison.

CXL
How Vasco Gomes de Abreu spoke to the Queen and of the words that passed between them.

A few days later, a nobleman called Vasco Gomes de Abreu, who claimed to be related to the Queen, seeing that for some time she had not shown herself to be so well disposed towards him as formerly she was wont to be, and because some said that they thought that the Queen had something against him, came to her one day and said, "My lady, you were good to me and gave me honour, to such an extent that everything I now am I owe to you. For this reason, I feel obliged to serve you and love you while I live, and so I intend to go on doing forever. Now I do not know why it is that for many days you have shown signs of hating me, as if I had done something very wrong and failed to serve you. Therefore I beseech you to tell me why this is, or if someone has informed you of something that I may have done to wrong you. If what others may have told you about me is true, I swear to you on my oath of vassalage that I will not stir from this spot, but await my death here."

The Queen answered him in this way: "I have considerable cause to complain of you, and indeed I am astonished at your words and that you should protest so much, for you know only too well that you have done me such a great wrong that you fully deserve that I should have your head cut off and even have you put to death in a more dreadful manner."

e ainda matar de peor morte que esta». «Senhora, disse ell, vós podees dizer o que vossa mercee for, mas outro nēhũu nom me dirá com verdade que vos eu nunca aja feito nēhũu erro per que eu esso mereça; e se vos algũua cousa vos alguem de mim disse, pesso-vos por mercee que m'o digaaes». «Onde me podiees vós moor erro fazer, disse ella, que hirdes vós dizer ao conde dom Joham Affonsso meu tio que eu dormia com Joham Fernandez d'Andeiro?» «Senhora, disse ell, Deus me guarde de mall que eu tall cousa dissesse, e quem vos esso disse mentio-vos falssamente; e nom há nēhũu que m'o diga a que eu nom ponha o corpo, ainda que seja de muito moor estado que eu». «Para que negaaes vós esto, disse a rrainha, e o desdizees? Ca eu vos darei pessoa a que o vós dissestes». «Senhora, disse ell, eu nom o desdigo, ca pois o eu nom dixe nom o posso desdizer; mas nego e digo que nunca foi nēhũu que me tall cousa ouvisse». «Certo he, disse ella, que vós o dissestes, ca Gonçallo Vaasquez d'Azevedo me disse que vós lh'o disserees». «Nom vos disse verdade, disse elle, nem Deus nunca quisesse que eu tall cousa dissesse de vós; mas pois vós dizees que vo-llo elle disse, a verdade he que eu lh'o ouvi dizer a ell, estando presentes o conde dom Joham Affonsso vosso tio e outros; e vós mandaae-o chamar e eu lh'o direi presente vós, e se m'o el negar eu lhe quero poer o corpo sobr'esto ou lh'o provarei pellos que hi estavom, quall ante vossa mercee for». Quando a rrainha esto ouvio disse-lhe que nom curasse mais d'aquello nem o dissesse a nēhũu, e que ella mandaria hũa carta a seu tio que lhe enviasse dizer a verdade d'esto como sse passara.

CXLI

Como el-rrei pôs em sua voontade de mandar prender
o meestre seu irmaão e Gonçallo Vaasquez d'Azevedo,
e por que rrazom

A rrainha, depois que ouve estas pallavras com Vaasco Gomez, cuidou em esto que lhe ell disse e n'o que ante ouvira dizer a Gonçallo Vaasquez, e pesou-lhe muito de coraçom, e entendeo que per aquell privado d'el-rrei avia de seer pubricada sua fama e descuberto todo seu feito, e que seendo esto sabudo era a ella mui grande vergonça e periigo e isso meesmo d'aquell cavalleiro com que ella era culpada, cuja morte ella nom desejava de veer. E penssou como no rreino nom avia outro nēhũu do linhagem d'el-rrei que esto quisesse

"My lady", he said, "you may say whatever you please, but no one else can truly tell me that I ever did you any wrong that might merit this. If anyone has said anything to you about me, I beseech you to tell me what it is."

"What greater wrong could you do me", she replied, "than to go to my uncle, Count João Afonso, and tell him that I slept with Count Juan Fernández Andeiro?"

"My lady", he said, "God preserve me from ever saying such a thing, and whoever told you this lied to you shamelessly. There is no man living who can say this to me without my challenging him to single combat, even if he be of much higher rank than I."

"Why do you deny", asked the Queen, "and gainsay this? For I shall produce the person to whom you said it."

"My lady", he answered, "I do not gainsay it, for the simple reason that I cannot gainsay what I did not say in the first place; but I do deny it and maintain that no one has ever heard me say such a thing."

"It is certain that you did say it", she said, "for Gonçalo Vasques de Azevedo told me that you had said it to him."

"He did not tell you the truth", he said, "and God forbid that I should ever have said such a thing of you; but since you say he said this to you, the truth of the matter is that I heard him say it in the presence of Count João Afonso, your uncle, and others. Summon him and I will say as much to him in your presence. If he denies it, I intend to challenge him to single combat over the matter, or else I shall prove it by means of those that were with us, whichever of these two you choose."

When the Queen heard this, she told him not to worry anymore nor say anything to anyone about it, and that she would send a letter to her uncle requesting him to send to her a true statement of what had happened.

CXLI

How the King decided to order the arrest of the Master his brother and Gonçalo Vasques de Azevedo, and for what reason.

After this conversation with Vasco Gomes, the Queen was concerned about what he said to her and what he had previously heard Gonçalo Vasques say. It worried her deeply. She realized that through this counsellor of the King her dishonour would be made public and all her actions revealed; and that if all this were made known she would suffer great shame and danger, as also would that knight with whom she had sinned. His death was something she certainly did not want. It occurred to her that if there was in all the kingdom one man of the King's line who would wish to avenge this

vingar se nom aquell seu irmaão bastardo que era meestre d'Avis, segundo ja dissemos, e entendeo que seendo aquell privado d'el-rrei e este seu irmaão mortos, que ella seeria de todo segura, porquanto todollos outros moores do rreino eram seus divedos ou postos em honrra per ella. Entom cuidou de os fazer culpar em algũua tall cousa per que el-rrei ouvesse aazo de os mandar matar; e dizem algũus que fez fazer cartas falssas em nome do irmaão d'el-rrei e d'aquell seu privado, as quaaes pareciam seer enviadas per elles a Castella em deserviço d'el-rrei e de todo o rreino, e fingerom estas cartas seer enviadas e tomadas no estremo caladamente, segundo a maneira que sobr'ello foi hordenada. E hũus dizem que foram tragidas a el-rrei, outros contam que aa rrainha e que ella as mostrou a elle, e que el-rrei, quando as vio, foi d'esto muito espantado, porque nom avia d'elles tall sospeita nem sabia cousa por que sse a esto demovessem. Nós porém como ella isto hordenou por satisfazer a seu desejo nom somos em certo conhecimento, salvo que el-rrei e a rrainha, e ainda presumem que aquell com que ella era culpada, virom taaes cartas; e fallando que sse devia em esto de fazer, foi per elles acordado que era bem de seerem presos, e nom leixar passar tam maa cousa como aquella sem grande vingança, por seer escarmento a todollos outros que nunca sse nẽhũu atrevesse a fazer semelhavel cousa; e que a prisom fosse logo, e que depois averia el-rrei acordo sobre a pena que deviam d'aver. A el-rrei pareceo este boom consselho, e pôs em voontade de o fazer assi, e cuidou de os mandar prender, de guisa que elles nom podessem fugir nem seer tomados a aquell a que os entregasse.

CXLII

Como el-rrei mandou prender o meestre seu irmaão
e Gonçallo Vaasquez d'Azevedo

Estando el-rrei em outro dia em hũu eirado de seus paaços, e com elle ho meestre seu irmaão e Gonçallo Vaasquez d'Azevedo e algũus outros senhores e cavalleiros, chegou aa porta do paaço hũu scudeiro que avia nome Gonçallo Vaasquez Coutinho com suas gentes e outros, em guisa que seeriam ataa duzentas lanças, todos armados sem mingua de nẽhũua cousa; e ho logar honde el-rrei com elles estava era tall que sse viiam d'alli; e posto que o meestre e Gonçallo Vaasquez as vissem assi estar d'aquella guisa, nom cuidarom nẽhũua

affront, it was his bastard brother the Master of Avis, as we have already said. She calculated that if both the King's counsellor and his brother were dead, she would be quite safe, since all the other powerful men in the kingdom owed their status to her or were otherwise obliged to her. So she tried to have them blamed for some offence so that the King might have a reason for having them executed. Some say that she had counterfeit letters written in the names of the King's brother and of his counsellor which appeared to have been sent by them to Castile against the interests of the King and of all the realm. They pretended these letters were sent and intercepted at the frontier under cover, according to some prearranged plan. Some say these letters were brought directly to the King, while others say they were brought to the Queen who then showed them to him, and that when the King saw them, he was aghast, for he had no suspicions about either man and could imagine no motive for their doing this. We do not know for certain how the Queen arranged this to achieve her aim but only that the King and Queen (and even, presumably, her alleged lover) saw these letters. After discussing what to do, they decided it was best that the two be arrested, and that such a serious matter should not be passed over without condign punishment as a warning to everyone else, so that no one should ever dare to do anything similar. The King thought that this was a good plan, and decided to carry it out. He took care to order them to be arrested in such a way that they could not flee nor be rescued from their captor.

CXLII

How the King ordered the arrest of his brother the Master and of Gonçalo Vasques de Azevedo.

On another day when the King was in a courtyard of his palace with his brother the Master and Gonçalo Vasques de Azevedo, and some other lords and knights, a squire called Gonçalo Vasques Coutinho together with his men and other people arrived at the palace door. They numbered some two hundred lances and were well armed. From the spot where the King and his train were standing, these men were quite visible. Although the Master and Gonçalo Vasques de Azevedo could see them in that manner, they took no notice, for they were fearless men, especially the Master. Besides,

cousa sobr'ello, como hom̃ees que sse nom temiam, special-
mente o meestre; desi, porque era tempo de guerra, nom lhes
pareceo aquello cousa nova. E el-rrei, depois que vio alli
estar aquellas gentes, disse a todollos que com ell estavom
que sse fossem pera as pousadas; e ell foi-sse logo pera sua
camara e os outros começarom de sse hir; e estando ainda
alli o meestre e Gonçallo Vaasquez, tornou a elles Vaasco
Martĩiz de Mello que sse fora com el-rrei e disse contra ho
meestre: «Senhor, e vós Gonçallo Vaasquez, eu vos trago
novas de que me muito pesa. El-rrei meu senhor vos manda
que sejaaes presos». «Porque?» disserom elles «Nom ssei
mays, disse ell, se nom quanto me mandou que vos guardasse
bem e lhe desse de vós boom conto e rrecado». «Há nos de
veer el-rrei?» disse o meestre. «Nom, disse ell, mas viinde-vos
comigo e vaamo-nos pera a pousada». Entom sse decerom e
cavallgarom em cima de senhas muas, e com cada hũu d'elles
hũu dos escudeiros de Vaasco Martinz de trás, e aquellas
gentes todas com elles. E hindo assi pello caminho, chegou-
-sse Gonçallo Vaasquez Coutinho a aquell privado d'el-rrei
que era seu sogro, e disse-lhe mui mansso, em guisa que o
nom ouvio ho escudeiro que com ell hia: «Parece que vós
e o meestre hiis ambos presos; esto porque he?». «Nom ssei
mais, disse ell, que quanto vós veedes». «Esto, disse el, nom
pode seer se nom por grande cousa; e pois assi he, parece-me
que he bem que eu trabalhe em toda guisa por vós nom hirdes
aa prisom, ca muito me temo de esta cousa vĩir a mall».
«E como poderees vós esso fazer?» disse Gonçallo Vaasquez.
«Eu darei volta com todollos meus, disse ell, que aqui vaão;
e entendo com a ajuda de Deus de vos poer em salvo, e depois
el-rrei me perdoará; e posto que me nam perdooe, eu nom
dou nada de perder quanto tenho por vós todavia serdes livre
d'este periigo». «Filho amigo, disse ell, vós dizees mui bem e
eu vo-llo gradeço muito; mas porém nom vos curees de
trabalhar d'esto, porque aqui vaão muitas gentes, como vós
veedes; moormente seer dentro da cidade, esto era cousa mui
grave de fazer, e nom sse acabando, vós seeriees preso e
morto e eu logo morto convosco; e moor pesar e nojo averia
eu veendo como vos matavom por me vós quererdes livrar
que da morte que eu morresse, ainda que fosse sem meu
merecimento: e porém nom vos trabalhees de nẽhũua cousa,
que Deus que sabe que eu nom fige per que eu esto mereça,
elle me livrará por sua mercee». E pero lhe el disse que nom
tomasse d'aquello cuidado, que ell em toda guisa o livraria,
nunca em ello quis conssentir, rreceando-sse do grande pe-

104

since it was a time of war, there seemed to them to be nothing unusual about it. When the King saw that those men had arrived, he told everyone in his train to retire to their lodgings. He repaired straightaway to his own rooms while the others began to disappear too. The Master and Gonçalo Vasques de Azevedo were still there when Vasco Martins de Melo, who had gone off with the King, returned and said to the Master, "My lord, I bring you, and you Gonçalo Vasques, news that grieves me. My lord the King has ordered your arrest."

"Why?" they asked.

"I do not know why", he said, "only that he ordered me to guard you well and to be answerable to him for you."

"Will the King see us?" asked the Master.

"No", he said, "but come with me and we shall go to the lodging."

Then they went down and rode out on two mules, each followed by one of Vasco Martins' squires and accompanied by the entire armed band.

As they were going along, Gonçalo Vasques Coutinho went up to Gonçalo Vasques de Azevedo who was his father—in—law and spoke to him in a low voice so as not to be heard by the squire who was close by.

"It appears that you and the Master have been arrested. Why is this?"

"I know no more than you can see", he replied.

"There must be some important reason for this", responded Gonçalo Vasques Coutinho, "and therefore I think that I had better do everything I can to prevent your going to prison, for I am very much afraid that the affair would come to a bad end."

"And how can you do that?" asked Gonçalo Vasques.

"I shall turn round with all my men who are here with me", he answered, "and with God's help I intend to set you free. Afterwards, the King will pardon me, and even if he doesn't, I don't mind losing all I have, to set you free from this danger."

"My son and my friend", Gonçalo Vasques de Azevedo replied, "you have spoken very well and I am very grateful to you for it. But do not make any attempt of the kind, because there are many men with us, as you can see. Moreover, seeing we are inside the town, this makes it a much more desperate thing to do. If you fail, you will be arrested and killed and I with you. I should suffer more grief and misery seeing them kill you for having tried to free me than I would through dying myself, even though my death were undeserved. Therefore, I beg of you, do not make any such attempt. Since God knows that I have done nothing to deserve this, He will deliver me of His own accord."

And although his son—in—law told him not to worry and promised to free him in any case, Gonçalo Vasques de Azevedo would in no way consent to it, fearing that both of them would be in grave

riigo que sse poderia seguir a ambos; e assi chegarom ao castello da cidade, onde aviam de jazer presos. E depois que forom dentro e descavallgarom, enquanto as gentes andavom d'hũua parte pera a outra, estando ainda as portas abertas, chegou-sse ao meestre hũu escudeiro que avia nome Affonsso Furtado, que era anadall-moor do rreino, e disse-lhe se sabia porque era preso, e ell disse que nom. «Senhor, disse ell, o grande e boom quando he preso nom o he se nom por grande cousa; e posto que vós nom saibaaes porque sooes preso e entendaaes que o sooes sem porque, parece-me que nom he bem que vós aguardees a ffim d'este feito. E vós sabees bem como el-rrei dom Pedro vosso padre me criou e pôs em estado e me deu quanto eu ei; e ainda que eu d'el-rrei dom Fernando vosso irmaão rrecebesse muitas mercees, muito mais theudo ssom a amar as cousas d'el-rrei vosso padre e poer o corpo e quanto eu tenho por ellas, moormente por vós que sooes seu filho. E porém enquanto estas gentes assi andam e a porta está aberta, sayamo-nos logo ambos, e como nós formos fora eu vos entendo de poer em salvo, ainda que perca quanto tenho». E o meestre disse que lhe gradecia muito e lhe prazia. Entom se tomarom pellas maãos indo fallando, e elles que chegavom acerca da porta e o porteiro que a acabava de fechar: e elles tornarom-sse entom sem dando a entender nada d'o que fazer quiserom. Em esto penssarom cada hũus d'os que hi estavom de sse hir pera as pousadas e Vaasco Martïiz de poer boa guarda em elles; e forom ambos bem aprisoados com senhas grossas adovas e cadea pellas pernas e postos em hũua tall casa d'onde nom podessem fogir. E por o gram temor que ouverom de em outro dia seer mortos, enviarom logo a pressa hũu escudeiro ao conde de Cambrig que estava em Villa Viçosa, que erom d'ali oito legoas, e mandarom-lhe dizer como os el-rrei mandara prender nom sabiam porque, e que lhe enviavom pedir por mercee que os enviasse pedir a el-rrei, e sse lh'os dar nom quisesse que lhe dissesse porque eram presos. O conde, quando esto ouvio, rrespondeo que com aquello nom tiinha que fazer, e que sse elles algũua cousa fezerom contra serviço d'el-rrei, que era mui bem de o pagarem; e que sobre aquello nom entendia de fazer nẽhũua cousa. Quando o escudeiro que allá foi tornou a elles com este rrecado, pesou-lhes muito, e nom souberom mais que fazer. E tanto que elles forom presos, logo el-rrei mandou prender hũu veedor do meestre que chamavom Lourenço Martïiz, que estava d'alli oito legoas em hũua villa que chamam Veiros, e tomar-lhe quanto

danger as a result. So they arrived at the citadel where they were to be imprisoned. After they had entered and dismounted, and while people were still going backwards and forwards with the gates still open, there came up to the Master a squire named Afonso Furtado who was commander of crossbowmen in the kingdom. He asked the Master if he knew why he had been arrested, and the Master replied that he did not. "My lord", said the squire, "when a great and good man is arrested, there is always an important reason for it; and since you have no idea at all why you have been arrested and you feel that this has been done without due cause, it seems to me unwise to await the outcome. You know well how your father King Pedro brought me up and established me in a high rank and gave me everything I have. Even though I have received many favours from your brother King Fernando, I have even greater cause for loving gratitude towards your royal father and for risking my life and all my worldly goods for his sake, and for yours even more so, since you are his son. So while there are still people coming and going through the gate, let us go out together, and if we do get outside, I mean to save you, even though I may lose everything I have as a result." The Master replied that he was grateful and pleased at this. Then they walked towards the gate, holding hands and talking; but the porter had just closed it; so they turned back without showing anything of their intentions.

By this time everyone there was thinking of retiring for the night, and Vasco Martins of putting a good guard on his prisoners. The Master and Gonçalo Vasques de Azevedo were both chained up with heavy rings and fetters on their legs and put into a building from which they could not possibly escape. Given their great fear of being killed next day, they sent a squire in great haste to the Earl of Cambridge, who was in Vila Viçosa, some eight leagues away, to tell him how the King had had them arrested for reasons unknown and to beg him as a favour to ask the King to release them, or, if the King refused this, at least to get him to tell the Earl why they had been arrested. When he heard this, the Earl said that it had nothing to do with him, and that if they had done some disservice to the King it was only just that they should pay the penalty, so that he himself had no intention of interfering in the matter. When the squire returned to them with this message, they were saddened by the news, and could think of nothing else to do. As soon as they were arrested, the King straightaway ordered the arrest of one of the Master's stewards, one Lourenço Martins who lived eight leagues away in a village called Veiros; and he ordered that all the man's goods be

tiinha, entendendo que quanto o meestre fezera em mandar aquellas cartas que elles cuidavom que ell enviara, que todo fora per seu consselho.

CXLIII
Do rrecado que Vaasco Martiiz ouve per que matasse o meestre e Gonçallo Vaasquez, e como ho nom quis fazer

Logo como foi sabudo que o meestre e Gonçallo Vaasquez d'Azevedo eram presos, forom todos maravilhados d'esta cousa; e foi logo soado per todo o rreino como o forom per aazo da rrainha e a maneira que tevera pera os fazer prender e porque rrazom fizera esto; e nēhũu nom podia d'elles sospeitar nēhũua maa cousa, ante lhe pesava a todos muito de sua prisom e maravilhavom-sse de o nom entender el-rrei; e bem cuidavom que taaes cousas se aviiam de dar a mall, e eram os entendimentos dos homēes cheos de desvairados penssamentos. Onde em este logar departem algũuas estorias, e dizem que logo aquella noite que elles forom presos a rrainha fez fazer hũu alvara falsso, que parecia siinado per mão d'el-rrei, em-no quall mandava aaquel cavalleiro que os tiinha em seu poder que tanto que o visse, sem outra deteença os fezesse logo degollar; e sse o alvara hia mui afficado, que muito mais afficadamente lh'o disse o messegeiro em nome d'el-rrei. Quando Vaasco Martiiz vio aquel alvara maravilhou-sse muito que podia seer tall cousa; e porquanto ell entendia que elles eram presos per aazo da rrainha, dovidou muito no alvara, porque elle sabia que muitos alvaraaes passavom pera outras cousas em nome d'el-rrei, feitos per aquella guisa; pero disse aaquell que lh'o trouxe que elle o compriria como em ell era contheudo; e que logo a cabo de pouco veo saber outro messegeiro em nome d'el-rrei se era ja feito o que lhe mandara fazer, e el disse que nom; e entom se foi aquell e veo outro com outro alvara muito mais afficado que o primeiro, em que lhe mandava el-rrei que logo lhe fezesse cortar as cabeças, dizendo que el-rrei era mui queixoso porque ja nom era feito. E porque sse aficava muito aquell que o tragia, e Vaasco Martinz viia a cousa mui dovidosa, disse-lhe assi: «Amigo, vós veedes como ja he alta noite e oras em que sse nom costuma de fazer justiça; e parece que el-rrei com gram sanha que agora há d'estes homēes manda fazer esto, e pode seer que depois se arrependeria

108

confiscated for he believed that it was through Lourenço Martins' advice that the Master had sent those letters which he was believed to have sent.

CXLIII
Of the order received by Vasco Martins to kill the Master and Gonçalo Vasques, and how he did not want to carry it out.

As soon as it was known that the Master and Gonçalo Vasques de Azevedo were in prison, everyone was astonished at the news. The rumour quickly spread throughout the whole kingdom of how they were there because of the Queen, the way in which she had had them arrested, and her reason for doing so. No one could suspect anything wrong in the conduct of either the Master or Gonçalo Vasques de Azevedo; and everyone was distressed at their imprisonment, astonished at the King's lack of comprehension of the matter, and convinced that such an affair would have a harmful outcome. The result was that men's minds were in turmoil over this.

At this point, accounts diverge. It is said that the very night they were arrested, the Queen had a writ forged, apparently signed by the King's own hand, ordering that as soon as he read the order, the knight who had them in his charge was to have their heads cut off without further ado; and if the writ was most insistent, the messenger who brought it in the King's name was even more so. When Vasco Martins saw that writ, he was astonished that such a thing could be; and because he knew that they were imprisoned because of the Queen, he had grave doubts about the writ, for he knew that many writs were issued in the King's name that were of the same type, treating of other matters. However, he told the man who brought it that he would obey it to the letter. In a very short while, another messenger came in the King's name to enquire if what he had ordered him to do had been done. He replied that it had not. Then that messenger departed and another one came with another writ, much more peremptory than the first, by which the King ordered that he should have their heads cut off at once, and informed him that the King was most displeased because this had not been done already. Because the second messenger was so insistent, Vasco Martins was very suspicious and spoke to him in this manner: "Friend, you appreciate that it is now very late at night and a time of day when it is not customary to carry out a sentence. It is clear that it is because the King feels great anger towards these men that he is ordering their execution, and it is possible that later he may repent of it, as has happened before in the case of certain other

109

muito, como ja aconteceo a algũus senhores; e sse fossem homẽes d'outro estado, ainda nom era tanto d'arrecear: mas matar eu hũu irmaão d'el-rrei e hũu dos grandes privados que elle tem per esta maneira, digo-vos que o nom cuido de fazer per nẽhũua guisa ataa de manhãa que eu com elle falle e saiba como he sua mercee de sse fazer; e sse os elle mandar matar, elles bem guardados estom e será feito seu mandado: e esto entendo por mais seu serviço ca sse fazer perda a quall depois nom podia seer cobrada». Foi-sse o messegeiro com este rrecado e nom tornou depois mais a ell: e elle levantou--sse em outro dia pella manhãa bem cedo e foi-sse a el-rrei e mostrou-lhe os alvaraaes e contou-lhe todo o que sse passara aquella noite; e el-rrei ficou espantado, dizendo que de tall cousa nom sabia parte, e que lhe gradecia muito o que fezera; e disse-lhe que sse callasse e que nom dissesse a nenguem nemhũua cousa.

CXLIV

Do gram temor em que o meestre e Gonçallo Vaasquez d'Azevedo estavom, e como a rrainha buscava aazo pera matar Gonçallo Vaasquez

Com gram temor e cuidado passarom aquella noite o meestre e Gonçallo Vaasquez, cuidando que o dia seguinte era o postumeiro de sua vida; e muito mayor fora o medo se elles souberom parte d'o que sse entanto acontecia; e quando veo a manhãa e o dia começou a crecer, tam grande era o temor que aviiam que como alguem batia aa porta do castello logo elles cuidavom que era algũu messegeiro que tragia rrecado per que os matassem. E fallavom antre ssi ambos que era aquello por que eram presos; e o meestre dezia que nom achava em ssi cousa per que merecesse de o seer, e Gonçallo Vaasquez dezia que bem sabia porque o era, ainda que dessem a entender que por all o prendiam; e que moor pesar averia quando o levassem a justiçar por nom ousar a dizer o por que o matavom que da morte que lhe dessem sem porque. E forom-nos veer em aquell dia todollos senhores da corte, dizendo que lhe pesava muito de sua prisom, a quall nom sabiam por que era, e que toda cousa que por elles podessem fazer, que o fariam mui de grado, nom seendo contra serviço d'el-rrei seu senhor: mas nom foi allá Joham Fernandez Andeiro. Grande guarda poinha Vaasco Martĩiz em elles, nom embargando o que lhe el-rrei dissera.

lords. If they had been men of another rank, there would be less cause for hesitation; but for me to kill in this manner the King's own brother and one of his own great favourites, I tell you that I am not at all disposed to do it until tomorrow when I can first speak to him and know what is his will. If he commands they be executed, they are under secure guard, and his command shall be obeyed. I believe that this is a better way of serving him than to cause a loss that later cannot be restored."

The messenger then went with this answer and did not come back to him anymore. Vasco Martins rose very early next morning, went to the King, showed him the writ and related the happenings of the previous night. The King was appalled, saying he knew nothing of it, and was very grateful to him for what he had done; and he told him to remain silent and to say nothing to anyone.

<h2 style="text-align:center">CXLIV</h2>

*Of the great fear of the Master and Gonçalo Vasques de Azevedo,
and how the Queen sought a reason for killing Gonçalo Vasques.*

The Master and Gonçalo Vasques spent that night in terror and affliction, afraid that the following day would be their last; and their fear would have been much greater had they known what was happening at the same time. When morning came and daylight grew stronger, so great was their terror that when someone knocked at the castle gate, they feared that it was a messenger bringing the order for their execution. They talked together about the reason for their arrest, and the Master said that he could see no cause why he should have deserved this. Gonçalo Vasques said that he knew the cause perfectly well even though they might pretend that he was imprisoned for other reasons; and that it would grieve him far more if they took him off for execution without daring to say why they were killing him than if they were to execute him for no reason at all. All the lords of the Court visited them that day saying that they were most sorry to see them in prison, and would most gladly do anything they could for them, provided it were no disservice to their lord the King. However, Juan Fernández Andeiro did not go there. Vasco Martins put a heavy guard on them despite what the King had said to him;

ca ell comia e dormia sempre com elles, e eram guardados de dia e vellados de noite de viinte scudeiros que dormiam sempre armados aa porta da casa honde elles jaziam. Em esto partio-sse el-rrei d'aquella cidade onde estava e foi-sse a hũu logar que chamam o Viimeiro, e a rrainha ficou alli. Quando elles virom que sse el-rrei partia e a rrainha ficava, teverom que era por seu mall, ca muito se temiam d'ella, e que nom avia em elles se nom morte. E em este temor stavom cada dia, sem avendo sperança de poder fugir nem seer livres per nẽhũua outra guisa, em tanto que o meestre fez voto e prometeo a Deus que sse o livrasse d'aquella prisom a seu salvo, que fosse a Jerusalem visitar o Santo Sepulcro. A rrainha, quando vio que seu desejo nom fora acabado sobre a morte d'elles, assi como avees ouvido, cuidou que o poderia seer per outra guisa, e escreveo hũua carta ao conde dom Joham Affonsso seu tio que estava em Santarem, rrecontando--lhe em ella todo o que lhe avehera com Vaasco Gomez d'Aavreu e como lhe dissera que ell estava presente quando Gonçallo Vaasquez d'Azevedo dissera d'ella as pallavras que dissemos; e que lhe rrogava que lhe enviasse dizer per sua carta a verdade d'aquell feito como sse passara. O conde dom Joham Affonsso, quando vio a carta, como era homem sisudo entendeo a voontade d'ella quegenda era, e trabalhou de buscar taaes rrazoões per que os desculpasse ambos; e hũus dizem que lhe nom screveo rreposta, mas que chegou aaquella cidade onde ella estava e que lhe contou quanto d'aquello sabia, per guisa que nẽhũu d'elles nom ficou em culpa, e que sse tornou pera Santarém; outros dizem que lh'o screveo per carta per esta meesma guisa. Entom cuidou ella que era bem de trabalhar que elles fossem soltos, por dar a entender que ella nom fora em culpa de sua prisom; e ouve com o conde de Cambrig que os pedisse a el-rrei: mas de que guisa esto foi, nós nom ho sabemos em certo, salvo tanto que avendo ja viinte dias que elles eram presos, enviou a rrainha chamar aquell cavaleiro que os tiinha em seu poder e mandou que lhe tirasse os ferros; e ell feze-o assi. E o meestre, quando isto vio, preguntou a Gonçallo Vaasquez que lhe parecia d'aquello. «Senhor, disse ell, parece-me boom sinal, e ey-o por boom começo de meu feito, e entendo, mercees a Deus, que som seguro de morte. Mas de vós me pesa muito, porque quando tal homem come vós he preso nom ho he por pequeno feito; pero pois vos tirarom os ferros devee-llo aaver por começo de bem». «E a mim, disse o meestre, muito me praz de vós seerdes livre; e Deus que sabe que eu som sem culpa d'esta prisom, elle encaminhe meus

112

for he ate and slept with them always, and they were guarded during the day and watched over at night by twenty squires who slept with their arms about them at the very door of the building where the prisoners lay.

At this time the King left the town in which he was staying and went to a place called Vimeiro while the Queen stayed where she was. When they saw that the King was leaving but the Queen was staying on, they felt this was a great threat to them, and that they were as good as dead, for they were very afraid of her. Day by day they were in constant fear of their lives, without any hope of escaping or of being freed in any other way, so that the Master vowed to God that if He would but deliver him from that prison safe and sound, he would go to Jerusalem to visit the Holy Sepulchre.

When she saw that she had been frustrated in her desire to have them killed, as you have heard, the Queen thought of trying another way. So she wrote a letter to her uncle, Count João Afonso, who was in Santarém, recounting to him all that had passed between her and Vasco Gomes de Abreu, and of how he had told her he was present when Gonçalo Vasques de Azevedo uttered those words that we have quoted already. She asked him to send her a letter telling her truthfully what had really happened. When he saw the letter, Count João Afonso, who was an intelligent man, well understood just what she wanted, and so he strove to find such words as might excuse them both. Some say that he did not send a written reply to her but went to that city where she was staying and there recounted to her all he knew in such a way that no blame could be attached to either of them, after which he returned to Santarém. Others say that he put all this into a letter to the Queen. Then she decided that it was better to work for their release so as to give the impression that she had not been the cause of their arrest. She agreed with the Earl of Cambridge that he would intercede with the King; but in what manner this came about, we do not know for certain, except that after they had been in prison for twenty days, the Queen sent for the knight who had charge of them and ordered him to remove their fetters, which he did.

When the Master saw this, he asked Gonçalo Vasques what he thought of it.

"My lord", he answered, "it seems to me a good sign, and I consider that, God be thanked, I am saved from death; but I grieve on your account for when a man such as you is arrested it is for some important reason. However, since they removed your fetters the outlook is encouraging."

"As for me", said the Master, "I am most pleased to see you free. May God, who knows that I have not deserved this imprisonment, guide my future actions according to His mercy. As

feitos como sua mercee for; e vós, depois que fordes livre
e solto e fordes no vosso rregno, rrogo-vos que vos nembrees
de mim».

CXLV

Como o meestre teve hordenado pera fugir, e da guisa
que ouvera de seer

Depois que o meestre e Gonçallo Vaasquez forom solltos
dos ferros em que jaziam, tirarom-nos d'aquella casa onde
jouverom presos todo aquell tempo, e derom-lhe logar que
andassem follgando pello currall do castello, e homẽes com
elles que os guardassem sempre. E o meestre depois que sse
vio sem ferros, pero que o teve a boom sinall, cuidou em
aquello que lhe Gonçallo Vaasquez dissera, e penssou em
como podesse fugir. E hũu dia pella manhãa que fazia frio,
disse o meestre a hũu filho d'aquell cavalleiro que o tiinha em
seu poder: «Martinho, subamos aaquell muro, e aqueentar-
-nos-emos aaquell soll que alli faz»; e o moço se foi com
elle, e os scudeiros que o guardavom. E andando follgando
pello muro do castello, oolhava ell com gram femença se
veeria algũu logar aazado per que depois podesse fugir, e vio
hũu que lhe pareceo geitoso pera sse poer per elle em salvo,
mais baixo da terra que nẽhũu dos outros, e pôs logo em sua
voontade de fugir per'alli o mais cedo que ouvesse geito de
o poder fazer; e depois que os a claridade do soll ouve es-
queentados a seu prazer, decerom-sse do muro sem avendo
nẽhũu d'elle tall sospeita. Em outro dia foi o meestre follgar
aaquel logar meesmo honde ante fora e levou consigo hũu
seu page a que era dada lecença com que fallasse apartado,
e mostrou-lhe aquell logar per que entendia de fugir, e disse
assi: «Johanne, trager-me-ás o meu arco dos pellouros com
hũua corda bem rrija e outras duas cordas no seo; e depois
que me isto deres, hirás sellar o meu cavallo e trazer-m'o-ás
alli prestes, fazendo que vaas pera a agua, e hũua vara na
mãao, e hũu par d'esporas no seo, que sse m'as tam aginha
nom poderes poer, que com a vara as escuse; e eu andarei
per'aqui tirando aas poombas, e chegar-me-hei aaquell logar,
e atarei as cordas no arco, e decer-m'ei per ellas». Entom
lhe divisou o dia e hora a que esto fezesse, e que o tevesse
em grande segredo; e ell disse qu assi ho faria, e espedio-sse
d'ell e foi-sse; entom se deceo do muro com aquelles que o
guardavom, sem descobrindo sua puridade a outro nẽhũu.

for you, when you are released and free and back in your own home, pray remember me."

CXLV
How the Master had decided they would escape, and of the manner in which it was to be done.

After the Master and Gonçalo Vasques were released from their chains, they were removed from that building in which they had been held prisoner all that time and were allowed to exercise in the castle—yard, but there were always men on hand to guard them at all times.

When the Master saw himself without chains, he took this to be a good sign but was mindful of what Gonçalo Vasques had said to him, and thought hard about how he might escape. One morning when it was cold, the Master said to a son of that knight who held him prisoner: "Martinho, let us climb that wall, and warm ourselves, for there we shall be in the sunlight." The boy went with him, and so did the squires who guarded him. As he wandered along the castle wall, he looked very carefully to see if there was a suitable point across which he might escape in the future. He saw one that seemed to him a possibility. At that place, the top of the wall was closer to the ground than elsewhere, and so he decided there and then to effect his escape at that point at the earliest opportunity. When the sunlight had warmed them to his satisfaction, they descended from the wall without anyone being suspicious of his motives.

Another day, the Master went walking to that selfsame spot taking with him one of his pages with whom he was allowed to converse in private. He showed him the place where he intended to escape and said, "João, you shall bring me my sling together with a very strong bowline and two more beneath your shirt. When you have given them to me you are to saddle my horse and bring it here straightaway, making out that you are taking him to the water. Bring a staff in your hand and a pair of spurs beneath your shirt. If you cannot provide the latter at short notice, make do with just the staff. I'll walk about here, shooting at doves, and you, approach the same spot. I'll tie the ropes to the sling and descend by those." Then he set the day and the hour when he would do this and told him to keep it totally secret; and the page said that he would do it, said good—bye and left. Then the Master came down from the wall with those who were guarding him without revealing his secret to anyone.

Como o meestre foi solto e comeo aquell dia com a rrainha, e das rrazoões que com ella ouve

Teendo ho meestre hordenado pera fugir da guisa que avees ouvido a hũu dia certo, chegou a elle Vaasco Martīiz, ante d'aquell dia que a fugida avia de seer, e disse a ell e a Gonçallo Vaasquez: «Senhor, eu vos trago mui boas novas». «Quegendas?» disserom elles. «A rrainha minha senhora, disse ell, vem de manhãa ouvir missa aa See, e manda-vos soltar e que vaades ouvir missa com ella». E elles forom muito ledos com esto e disserom que lh'o tiinham em grande mercee. Em outro dia veo a rrainha ouvir missa aa See, e estando aa missa chegou Vaasco Martīiz com elles ambos honde a rrainha estava, e elles beijarom-lhe as mãaos e fallarom aos outros senhores que hi estavom e ao conde Joham Fernandez com elles. E depois que sahirom de missa, tomou o conde Joham Fernandez a rrainha pollo braço e o meestre a iffante dona Beatriz sua filha e veherom assi atá a porta da See; entom entrou a rrainha em-nas andes em que fora, porque andava prenhe, e o conde hia a par das andes fallando com ella, e o meestre levava a iffante de rredea. E quando chegarom aa porta do paaço, quisera-sse o meestre e Gonçallo Vaasquez espedir d'ella pera sse hirem pera as pousadas; e ella lhe disse que sse nom fossem, mas que vehessem comer com ella; e o meestre foi mui sospeitoso d'este convite, cuidando que o queriam matar com peçonha, e bem o leixara por aquella hora, sse sse podera scusar d'ello. Entom se assentarom a comer na camara da rrainha, e ella siia aa sua mesa, e o meestre em cabeceira d'outra mesa, e o conde Joham Fernandez junto com elle, e Gonçallo Vaasquez a fundo d'elles ambos; e o meestre comia com grande medo, rreceando o que ja dissemos. Acabado o jantar, trouverom a fruita; e a rrainha começou de fallar nas joyas que tiinha e quanto lhe custarom, gabando-as muito; e o conde alçou-sse da mesa ficando os outros asseentados, e chegou-sse a par da cama honde a rrainha estava aa mesa, e ella tirou hũu anell que tiinha no dedo, d'hũu rrubi que dezia que era de gram preço, e tendeo a mão com elle e disse ao conde, em guisa que o ouvirom todos: «Johane, toma este anell». «Nom tomarei» disse ell. «Porque?» disse ella. «Senhora, disse ell, porque ei medo que digam d'ambos». «Toma tu o que te eu dou, disse ella, e diga cada hũu o que quiser»; e elle tomou-ho e pose-o no dedo; e ao meestre e aos outros que hi estavom nom lhes pareceo bem esta cousa, e teverom aquellas por mui maas

CXLVI
How the Master was released and ate that very same day with the Queen, and of the conversation that he had with her.

The Master having organized his escape on a set day in the manner you have heard, Vasco Martins came to see him before the day fixed for the escape and said to him and to Gonçalo Vasques, "My lord, I bring you very good news."

"What manner of good news?" they asked.

"My lady the Queen", he replied, "is coming in the morning to hear Mass at the cathedral, and she orders that you be released and go to hear Mass with her."

They were greatly cheered at this news and said that they thanked him warmly for the message. The next day the Queen came to hear Mass at the cathedral, and during Mass Vasco Martins arrived with them, taking them to the Queen. They both kissed her hand and spoke to the other lords who were there, including Count Juan Fernández. When they came out from Mass, Count Juan Fernández gave the Queen his arm while the Master gave his to her daughter, Dona Beatriz; and in this fashion they came to the cathedral door. Then the Queen mounted the litter by which she had come, for she was pregnant, and the Count travelled alongside it conversing with her as they went, whilst the Master led the Princess's rein.

When they reached the palace gate, the Master and Gonçalo Vasques would have preferred to take their leave so as to repair to their lodgings; but she told them not to go but to enter and eat with her. The Master was very suspicious about this invitation, fearing that they intended to poison him, and he would have avoided going at this particular juncture, if he could have found an excuse for so doing. So they sat down to eat in the Queen's chamber. She sat at her own table, while the Master sat at the head of another with Count Juan Fernández beside him and Gonçalo Vasques at the far end of the same table. The Master ate fearfully, dreading the possibility we have just described. When the meal was over, fruit was brought in. The Queen began to talk about her jewels and how much they cost, and praised them greatly. The Count rose from the table while the others remained seated, and came to the divan on which the Queen reclined at table. She pulled from her finger a ring set with a ruby that she said was a stone of great price. She held it towards him and spoke to him so that all could hear her: "João, take this ring."

"I cannot", he replied.

"Why?" she asked.

"Madam", he answered, "because I am afraid of what the others will say."

"Take what I give you", she said, "and let the rest say what they like." So he took it and put it on his finger. The Master and everyone present disapproved of this, finding this exchange most unseemly.

117

rrazoões. Entom se levantarom de comer, e o meestre ficou-
-sse em joelhos ante a rrainha e disse: «Senhora, bem vistes
como el-rrei meu senhor me mandou prender e o desejo
que contra mim teve enquanto fui preso; e pero eu per
muitas vezes cuidasse em minha voontade, enquanto jouve
na prisom, que o demoveria a me assi mandar prender, nunca
pude achar em mim cousa nem deserviço que lhe eu fezesse
per que merecesse de o seer; pero, nom embargando esto,
eu tenho a ell e a vós em grande mercee por me mandardes
soltar. Mas porque eu entendo que vós saberees o por que o
eu fui, porém vos peço por mercee que m'o diguaaes, pera
me eu avisar de outra hora nom fazer ou dizer cousa per
que anoje el-rrei meu senhor e aja de mim outra tall sanha
como esta». «Irmaão amigo, disse ella, bem sabees que aos
mall-dizentes nunca lhes mingua que digam; e algũus cava-
leiros de vossa hordem que convosco andam, espiciallmente
o comendador-moor Vaasco Porcalho, fez entender a el-rrei
meu senhor que vós vos quiriees hir pera Castella pera o
iffante dom Joham em deserviço d'este rreino, dizendo certamente que era assi, porque vós tomarees gaados de duas
albergarias que há em Avis e os mandarees vender». «Senhora,
disse ell, esse era mui maao cuido que elles cuidavom, que
por dezesete cabeças de gaado que eu mandei tomar pera
algũuas cousas que me compriam nom deveram elles a dizer
de mim tam maa cousa; mas Deus dará a elles seu gallardom
e a mim ajuda e graça como serva el-rrei meu senhor, segundo meu desejo foi sempre de o bem servir». E nom podendo d'ella mais saber, alçou-sse e pedio-lhe lecença pera
hir veer el-rrei.

CXLVII

Como o meestre foi veer el-rrei, e das pallavras que com
el ouve; e das rrazoões que o meestre disse em casa
do conde de Cambrig

Quando o meestre vio que mais nom podia saber da rrainha em feito de sua prisom, espedio-sse d'ella e foi-sse logo
ao Viimeiro onde el-rrei estava; e chegou ante a cama onde
ell jazia doente e beijou-lhe as maãos e disse: «Senhor, vós
me mandastes prender, e eu vos tenho em grande mercee por
me mandardes soltar, se eu algũua cousa fige per que merecesse de o seer e ainda que o nom fezesse; e vós, senhor,
sabees bem como me creastes e a honrra em que vossa mercee

118

Then they rose from table, but the Master knelt before the Queen and said: "Madam, you have seen the way in which my lord the King ordered my arrest and his ill—will towards me during my imprisonment. Yet, for all that I have racked my brains while lying in prison, to ascertain precisely what might have caused him to have me detained in this way, I have been unable to find any cause in me or any disservice I might have done him that would have justified my imprisonment. Yet, notwithstanding this, I am most grateful to you both for having ordered my release. However, since I am aware that you will know why I was arrested, I beseech you to tell me why, so that on another occasion I may be able to avoid doing or saying anything that might anger my lord the King or provoke him again to such wrath."

"My dear brother", she replied, "you know all too well that slanderers are never lacking in something to say. Some knights of your own order who are often in your train, especially the Grand Commander Vasco Porcalho,[1] gave my lord the King to understand that you had the intention of going to Castile to join Prince João against the interests of this kingdom. They said this was certain because you had taken cattle from two hospices in Avis and had ordered them to be sold."

"Madam", he replied, "this is a mischievous thing that they have thought of me: just because I ordered seventeen head of cattle to be taken out for certain reasons, they had no cause to speak ill of me in this way; but God will give them their just reward and to me he will give me assistance and grace sufficient to serve my lord the King, for it has always been my desire to serve him well." As he was unable to learn anything more from her, he rose to his feet and asked leave to go to see the King.

CXLVII

How the Master went to see the King and of the conversation they had together; and of the things said by the Master in the Earl of Cambridge's house.

When the Master saw he would learn no more from the Queen concerning his imprisonment, he took his leave and went straightaway to Vimeiro where the King was staying. He came to the King's sickbed and kissed his hands saying: "My lord, you ordered my arrest, and I thank you very much for having me freed, if I did anything to deserve imprisonment, and even if I did not. My lord, you know well that you raised me up and gave me what honour I

foi de me poer; e antre as outras muitas mercees que eu de vós rrecebi ataa o dia d'oje agora vos peço por mercee que me façaaes hũua, a quall he esta: que me digaaes quall foi a rrazão por que me mandastes prender. Ca ainda que vos eu com boom desejo servisse e tenha em voontade de vos servir, pero pode seer que algũuas d'aquellas cousas em que eu cuido que vos faço serviço e voontade serám a vós nojo e desprazer, e nom seendo eu percebido d'esto servir-vos-hia como atá aqui fige; e sperando de vós bem e mercee por gallardom de meu serviço, seguir-sse-hia o contrairo d'esto: e porém vos peço por mercee que me queiraaes dizer que-genda he vossa voontade». Rrespondeo el-rrei e disse: «Vós dizees mui bem, e eu entendo vosso boom desejo; mas vós seede certo que eu nom vos mandei prender se nom por vos mostrar quanto o meu poderio era de grande sobre vós e nom por outra cousa». «Senhor, disse o meestre, des aquell tempo que me Deus chegou a hidade de vos eu conhecer por meu rrei e senhor, sempre eu soube e ssei o gram poderio que vós sobre mim avees e sobre todos os outros de vosso rreino: e sse por all nom foi se nom por esso, parece-me que per outra guisa poderees saber se avia em mim tall conhecimento como esse; e se per outra rrazom he em que vos eu nom serva a vosso prazer, como ja dixe, peço-vos por mercee que m'o digaaes». E el-rrei disse que nom fora por outra cousa se nom por aquello; entom lhe beijou as maãos e espedio-sse d'elle. E porque ao meestre era dito que o conde de Cambrig fora em ajuda de el seer solto, porém se foi aos paaços honde o conde pousava, e fez-lhe sua rreverença e disse: «Senhor, bem sabees como el-rrei meu senhor me mandou prender e hora por sua mercee me mandou soltar; e perc eu em toda minha prisom nunca puide saber porque fui preso, nem o ssei ainda agora, eu vos tenho em grande mercee o que por mim fezestes em trabalhardes por eu ser solto. Aallem d'esto, senhor, porquanto a mim he dito que algũus disserom de mim cousas quaaes nom deviam, eu digo aqui perante vós que sse hi há algũu que me diga que eu errei ou fiz algũua cousa contra serviço d'el-rrei meu senhor, que eu lhe farei conhecer que nom disse nem diz verdade, mas que sempre me trabalhei de o servir o melhor que eu puide, sem lhe fazendo nẽhũu erro por que me esto devesse seer feito»; e esto disse o meestre porque hi estavom com o conde muitos cavalleiros e escudeiros d'os que andavom com el-rrei; mas nom ouve hi nẽhũu que lhe a esto rrespondesse. Entom disse ao conde Vaasco Martinz da Cunha o moço que hia com o meestre: «Ainda, senhor, que o meestre dissesse o que era

have. May I ask one more boon to be added to the many that until now I have received from you: pray tell me the reason why you ordered my arrest. For although I served you and desired to serve you with the best of intentions, nevertheless, it may well be that some of the deeds whereby I imagine to be doing you service and doing your will may vex and displease you; and without my realizing it, I would serve you as I have done so far. So I could expect to be well treated by you and receive some reward for my service, and yet the opposite would be the result. So I beg you to have the goodness to tell me just what it is you hold against me?"

The King replied, "You speak truly, and I appreciate your good will; but let it be clear that I only ordered your arrest so as to demonstrate the extent of my power over you and for no other reason."

"Lord," said the Master, "since that time when God brought me to the age at which I recognized you as my king and lord, I have always known and I still know just how great your power is over me and over all others in your kingdom. If my arrest were for no other reason than this, it seems to me that you could have found out by some other way whether or not I realized your power; but if there is any other way in which I am not serving you to your satisfaction, as I have already said, I beg you to inform me of it." The King said that it was for no other reason than the one he had given. Then he kissed the King's hands and took his leave.

Because the Master had been told that the Earl of Cambridge had played a part in his release, he therefore went to the house where the Earl was staying and bowed down before him saying: "My lord, you well know that the King ordered my arrest and has now seen fit to have me released; yet in all the time I was in prison I was unable to discover why I was arrested, nor do I know even now. I am, nevertheless, deeply in your debt for all that you have done in working for my release.[1] Moreover, my lord, since I am informed that some people say unjust things about me, I declare in your presence that if there is any man who says I have behaved badly or done my King any disservice whatever, I shall say to his face that he has lied and still lies, and that I have always striven to serve the King to the best of my ability, and have never done him any wrong whatever that should have given him cause to do this to me." The Master said this because the Earl had with him many knights and squires of the King's retinue; but not one of these made any response. At this point, the young man who accompanied the Master said to Count Vasco Martins da Cunha, "Although, my lord, the

121

theudo de dizer por sua honrra, pero porque pode seer que porque elle he tam grande homem nẽhũu queira rresponder a esto, porém eu que soom cavalleiro de mais pequeno estado, a que de melhor mente rresponderam, digo que eu som prestes pera fazer conhecer que nom he verdade a quallquer que disser que o meestre fez nem disse nẽhũua cousa contra serviço d'el-rrei per que merecesse de seer preso»; e esta meesma rrazom disserom algũus outros d'os que hi estavam, e o conde disse que bem criia que assi era. Entom sse foi o conde pera honde el-rrei pousava e o meestre com elle ataa os paaços; e espedio-sse d'elle e tornou-sse a Evora.

CXLVIII

Como Lourenço Martĩiz quizera matar Vaasco Porcalho
e lhe o meestre disse que o nom matasse

Tanto que o meestre chegou a Evora, espedio-sse logo da rrainha pera sse hir aa terra da ordem, e foi-sse de pee em rromaria a Santa Maria de Benavilla que prometera quando fora preso; e d'hi se partio e foi a Veiros e achou hi ja solto Lourenço Martĩiz, aquell seu veedor que d'ante disse-mos, mas nom lhe foi entregue o que lhe tomaram. E con-tou-lhe o meestre todo o que lhe avehera em sua prisom e as rrazoões que ouvera com a rrainha depois que fora sollto e o que lhe dissera de Vaasco Porcalho. «Senhor, disse elle, e vós bem sabees como eu fui preso quando o vós fostes e como me foi tomado quanto me acharom: e segundo parece todo o que a vós e a mim foi feito veo per aazo das cousas que este treedor andou dizendo: e porém he bem que ell aja galardom de sua malldade e nom escape de morte por tam maa cousa como esta que disse; e vós leixaae a mim o encar-rego d'este feito, e sem vós em ello poer mão eu o entendo de matar mui cedo». E o meestre disse que lh'o gradecia muito e lh'o tiinha em grande serviço. Aquella noite seguinte cuidou o meestre em esta cousa, e em outro dia chamou-ho adeparte e disse: «Lourenço Martĩiz, cuidei em aquello que ontem fallamos, e nom me parece que he bem que matees este homem, por duas rrazoões. A primeira, vós sabees bem como esta molher he sages em muito mall e sabedor de grandes artes; e porque vio que nom pôde acabar seu maao desejo contra mim enquanto fui preso, pode seer que cuidou de me dizer esta cousa por tall que eu com menencoria, penssando que a ssem-rrazom que me foi feita foi per seu aazo d'este homem, me demovesse ao matar; e matando-o elle

122

Master has said what his honour obliged him to say, nevertheless, since he is a man of such high rank, it may be that no one dares to gainsay him. Therefore I, who am a knight of lower rank and more easily to be answered, declare that I am ready to show that it is untrue, if any man says that the Master did or said anything against the King's interest that would have warranted imprisonment." Some others among those present spoke in a similar way and the Earl said he believed that it was so. Then the Earl went to the King's quarters, and the Master accompanied him as far as the palace. There he took his leave of him and returned to Évora.

CXLVIII
How Lourenço Martins had wanted to kill Vasco Porcalho and how the Master told him not to do so.

As soon as the Master arrived at Évora, he took leave of the Queen so that he could go to the territory of his Order. He made a pilgrimage on foot to Santa Maria de Benavila [1] — something he had promised to do when he was in prison. After leaving there he went to Veiros and there he found Lourenço Martins, his chief steward whom we have already mentioned, and who had been set free though the property which had been taken from him had not been restored. The Master told him all that had befallen him in prison and his conversation with the Queen after his release and what she had said to him about Vasco Porcalho.

"My lord", said Lourenço Martins, "you know perfectly well that I was arrested when you were, and that all I had was taken from me. It seems that everything that has been done to you and me has been done by reason of the things that traitor went around saying about us. This being so, it is only right that he should receive the appropriate reward for his wickedness, and wrong that he should escape death for such an evil deed. Leave this to me for I have it in mind to kill him at the earliest opportunity without your having to soil your hands in the matter." The Master told him he was grateful to him for this and much in his debt because of it.

That night the Master pondered the affair, and the next day he took him on one side and said: "Lourenço Martins, I have thought over our conversation of yesterday, and I do not think it a good idea for you to kill this man for two reasons. Firstly, you know all too well that this woman is full of cunning and knows all sorts of evil tricks. Now, knowing that she was unable to achieve her wicked ends while I was in prison, it is quite possible that she thought of saying what she did to me in order that I, convinced that the outrage committed against me was due to this man, might be provoked out of anger into killing him. So he would die without good reason, while

morreria sem porque, com gram pecado de minha alma, e eu era per força leixar o rreino e me hiria fora d'elle, e per esta guisa seeria ella desempachada de mim. A segunda, posto que assi fosse que o elle dissesse, a mim nom vem grande honrra de eu matar hũu homem tall como este; e ainda que o vós matees, dando a entender que eu nom sei d'esto parte, logo a rrainha cuidaria que eu vo-llo mandara matar por o que me disse; e poderia seer que averia el-rrei de mim tam grande queixume per que eu poderia vĩir a prisom e periigo de morte ou perderia a terra de todo ponto, o que a mim nom compria, moormente em tempo de guerra como ora estamos: porém me parece que he bem que na duvida d'estas cousas escolhamos ho mais seguro e nom curemos d'esto; e elle se mall fez ou disse, Deus lhe dará seu gallardom». «Senhor, disse Lourenço Martĩiz, a mim parecem estas booas rrazoões, e como vossa mercee for eu assi o farei»; e o meestre disse que nom curasse d'elle, e elle assi o fez.

CXLIX
Como os ingreses e o meestre com elles entrarom per Castella e tomarom os castellos de Lobom e do Cortijo

A poucos dias que o meestre foi solto, estando ell em Veiros, como dissemos, ouverom consselho algũus capitaães dos ingreses de fazerem hũua entrada per Castella; e devisarom logo antre ssi o dia a que sse todos juntassem com suas gentes em hũua villa que chamam Arronches, que era duas legoas do rreino de seus immiigos. E os capitaães eram estes: hũu filho bastardo d'el-rrei de Ingraterra que avia nome ... o Canom de Rrabi Sallas, o so-duc de lla Trava, mossé Joham Falconeth e outros; e hindo pera aquell logar hu aviam de seer juntos, hũu cavalleiro ingres que avia nome mossé Rrogel Othiquiniente chegou per honde o meestre estava, e em fallando com elle disse assi: «Sabees vós, senhor, parte d'o que sse faz em esta terra, onde nós estamos?» «Nom» disse o meestre. «Seede certo, disse o cavalleiro ingres, que nós queremos fazer hũua cavallgada e entrar per Castella, em-na qual se vos quiserdes seer podees fazer muito de vossa honrra»; e disse-lhe logo o dia em que todos aviam de seer juntos e quando sse aviam de partir. «Muito me praz, disse o meestre, e soom d'ello mui ledo e gradeço-vos muito esto que me avees dito; e eu me farei logo prestes, em guisa que seja com esses senhores em esse dia que vós dizees». Entom se espedio d'elle; e o meestre nom ho pôs mais em

my soul would be put in danger, and I would be forced to leave the country and would go into exile. Thus she would be rid of me. Secondly, even if it were true that he said those things, killing a man of this type brings little honour to me; and even if you were to kill him, making out that I have no knowledge of it, the Queen would automatically think that I had ordered you to do it because of what she told me. It could well be that the King would be so enraged against me that he might imprison me. My life might be at risk and my lands utterly forfeit, which would be inconvenient, especially in this time of war in which we are living. So it seems to me that since there are grave doubts as to what is the best course to follow, we shall be wise to choose the safest and leave well alone for now. If he did or said anything wrong, then God will give him his just reward."

"My lord", said Lourenço Martins, "these seem wise words to me, and I shall do your bidding, whatever that might be." The Master told him not to worry any further, and he obeyed.

CXLIX
How the English and the Master entered Castile and took the castles of Lobón and Cortijo.

A few days after the Master was released, while he was in Veiros as we said, some English captains held council and decided on an expedition into Castile. They fixed the day between them on which they would assemble with their men at a village called Arronches, which was two leagues from their enemies' kingdom. These were the captains: a bastard son of the English King by the name of Sir John Southeray, [1] Canon Robersart, the Sultan of Latrau, Sir John Falconer [2] and others. While on his way to the place where the others were gathered, an English knight by the name of Sir Roger Othiquiniente came up to the Master and said to him, "Are you acquainted, my lord, with the reasons for our presence in this part of the country?"

"No", said the Master.

"I would have you know", the English knight went on, "that we have it in mind to make a raid into Castile, and if you care to be a part of it, you can gain much honour." He informed him of the day on which they were to assemble, and when they would leave.

"This pleases me", replied the Master. "It makes me happy and I am grateful to you for what you have told me. I'll make myself ready immediately so as to be with these lords on the day you mention." So the knight took his leave.

125

tardança, e juntou suas gentes a pressa e outras da comarça as mais que aver pôde, e com ell Vaasco Perez de Caamoões, e levou consigo antre lanças e corredores duzentos de cavallo e quatro mill homēes de pee. E chegou a Arronches honde os ingreses estavom e foi d'elles bem rrecebido; e fezerom-sse prestes pera entrar, e eram per todos oitocentas lanças e quinhentos archeiros e seis mill homēes de pee. Entom sse partirom d'alli e levarom caminho d'Ouguella, e chegarom aquella noite a hūua rribeira onde está hūua irmida que chamam Sam Salvador da Matança. Alli dormirom algūus em casas que faziam de rramos de arvores e os mais d'elles sobre a erva da terra; o ceeo era cobertura a todos, ca alli nom avia outras tendas que os emparasse de tempo contrairo. O dia seguinte chegarom a hūu castello que chamom Lobom, em que estavom ataa saseenta homēes; e aquell filho bastardo d'el-rrei de Ingraterra que dissemos foi o primeiro que o começou de combater, e desi os outros; e os que eram dentro deffendiam-sse quanto podiam, e deram-lhe de cima hūua gram pedrada, em guisa que cahiu logo em terra e todos cuidarom que era morto: e ell alçou-sse e cobrou sua força e nom com menos esforço que da primeira tornou outra vez a combater. E polla fraqueza do logar e pollo fogo que lhe poserom aas portas forom logo entrados per força, e foi ell o primeiro que entrou dentro; e matarom d'elles e outros fogirom e algūus levarom cativos, e derribarom o logar todo. Partirom-sse entom d'alli e chegarom a hūu castello que chamom ho Cortijo, e alli estavom duzentos homēes de pee e trinta scudeiros, antre os quaaes estavom sete que eram alcaides de senhos castellos, homēes de grande esforço que em sse deffendendo bem mostravom pera quanto eram. E como chegarom ao logar começarom de o combater mui rrijamente, poendo o fogo aas portas e picando o muro per outra parte; e os de dentro, em se deffendendo com toda sa força, matarom dous scudeiros, hūu portugues e outro ingres, escudeiro de mossé Joham Falconet; mas nom lhe prestou nada sua deffenssom, ca a multidom das gentes de fora lhe fez perder toda sua virtude, em guisa que desesperarom de sse poder deffender; e preitejavom-sse que os leixassem a vida e que lhes dariam o logar; e os ingreses cobrarom tam gram sanha pella morte d'aquelle escudeiro ingres que o nom quiserom conssentir, mas cada vez se esforçavam mais pera o entrar. Quando os de dentro virom esto ouverom mui gram medo e bem entenderom que sse os entrassem per força que nom avia em elles se nom morte; e rrevestirom-sse os sacerdotes e sobirom-sse ao muro e mostrarom-lhe o corpo de

The Master lost no time, but hastily summoned his men, together with as many more from the region as he could muster. He took with him Vasco Peres de Camões, and also some two hundred cavalry, including heavy and lightly—armed horsemen, and four thousand foot—soldiers. He arrived in Arronches where the English were already assembled, and was given a warm welcome by them. They made themselves ready to enter Castile. The force numbered in all eight hundred lances and five hundred archers, together with six thousand foot—soldiers.

Then they set out, making towards Ouguela. They arrived that night on the bank of a stream where there was a hermitage called São Salvador da Matança. There some slept in shelters that they made out of foliage from trees, but the majority just slept on the grass. The sky was their coverlet because there were no other tents to shelter them in the event of bad weather. The following day they arrived at a castle called Lobón in which there were up to sixty men. That bastard son of the King of England whom we mentioned was the first into the fray, followed by the others. Those within defended themselves as best they could, hurling down from above a great many stones, so that he was knocked to the ground and everyone believed him dead; but he got up, and summoning up his strength, returned to the battle with the same determination as before. Due to the weakness of the place and the firing of the gates, they soon gained entry, and he was the first to do so. Some they killed, some fled and some were captured. They demolished the whole place before leaving it behind in order to continue to a castle called Cortijo. Inside were two hundred foot—soldiers and thirty squires among whom seven were governors of similar castles, men of great strength and determination who, by their defence, gave good account of themselves. As soon as the raiders arrived at the place, they began to attack it furiously, setting fire to the gates and piercing the wall at the rear. Those within, defending themselves stoutly, killed two squires, a Portuguese and an Englishman who was squire to Sir John Falconer; but their defence proved futile in face of the huge numbers outside. For this reason they despaired of defending themselves successfully and therefore pleaded for their lives in return for giving up the castle; but the English were so enraged at the death of that English squire that they rejected the plea and redoubled their efforts to enter. When the besieged saw this, they were very afraid and realized that if the besiegers got in by force, they could expect certain death. So the priests dressed in their robes and climbed onto the wall, showing them the Host and begging them for the love of God to have mercy on

Deus, rrogando-os que por amor d'aquell senhor se quisessem amercear d'elles; e os ingreses com gram sanha que sse em elles mais acendia nom curavom d'aquello e braadavom-lhe altas vozes que sse deffendessem todavia; e o arroido grande de hũua e da outra parte fazia que aadur suas prezes podiam seer ouvidas; e eram as frechas tantas alli honde o corpo de Deus estava e pellos outros logares d'arredor que temor grande os fazia d'alli partir. Em esto foi o combato tam aficado que pero o muro fosse mui forte, com alta cava e bem deffenssavell, todo nom aproveitou nada; e durarom des a manhãa ataa hora de terça em-no combater; e rroto o muro entrarom dentro per força, e depois pellas portas que forom ardudas, e começarom de matar quantos homẽes acharom, em guisa que outra nẽhũua pessoa nom ficou a vida salvo molheres e moços pequenos; e derribarom todo o logar o mais que poderom e rroubarom-no de quanto em ell acharom e tornarom-sse pera Portugall.

CL
Como el-rrei dom Fernando e os ingreses chegarom a Ellvas e pario a rrainha dona Lionor hii hũu filho

A rrainha, como avees ouvido, depois que aazou que o meestre e Gonçallo Vaasquez fossem soltos, por dar a entender que nom era em culpa, hordenou como casasse hũu filho de Gonçallo Vaasquez que avia nome Alvoro Gonçallvez, com hũua filha de Joham Fernandez d'Andeiro que chamavom dona Sancha d'Andeiro, creendo que por tall casamento cessaria Gonçallo Vaasquez de fallar mais em seus feitos e seeria da parte d'ella. Em esto hordenou el-rrei de todos fazerem mudança, por hir mais adeante; e screveo ao conde que partisse de Villa Viçosa, e ell partio logo hũua segunda-feira postumeiro dia de junho com sua molher e gentes e foi pousar seu arreall em Odiana a par de Jerumenha. E el-rrei e a rrainha partirom d'Estremoz, onde ja estavom, aa quarta-feira seguinte com todas suas gentes e veherom-sse a Borva e aa sesta-feira chegarom a Villa Boim; ao sabado forom pousar a Ellvas, que eram seis dias do mes de julho, onde depois se juntarom todos; e pousava el-rrei em cima na villa velha e o conde em Sam Domingos, e a hoste d'el-rrei pôs seu arreall nas ortas arredor da villa, e os ingreses nos ollivaaes caminho de Badalhouce, e começarom de correr a terra hũus aos outros. A rrainha, que andava prenhe, avendo treze dias que alli estava, pario hũu filho, e mostrou el-rrei

them. The English became even more enraged and, quite unmoved, yelled to them at the tops of their voices to defend themselves. Such was the great din on both sides that the pleas of the besieged could scarcely be heard. The arrows flew so thick and fast at the point where God's body was being displayed as well as all around it, that fear made the priests leave. The battle was so fierce that even though the wall was very strong, with a deep ditch and good defences, it was all useless. They held out from morning through to mid—afternoon. Once the wall was broken, the besiegers forced their way in, and then through the burning gates; and they began killing any men they found so that no one was spared except women and children. They demolished the place entirely as far as they were able and pillaged from it everything of value they found there. Then they returned to Portugal.

CL
How King Fernando and the English arrived at Elvas and how Queen Leonor gave birth to a son there.

As you have heard, once the Queen reached the conclusion that the Master and Gonçalo Vasques should be released, in order to avoid all suspicion of her own involvement in the affair, she ordered the marriage of one of Gonçalo Vasques's sons, Álvaro Gonçalves, with a daughter of Juan Fernández Andeiro, whose name was Doña Sancha de Andeiro. The Queen thought that such a marriage would make Gonçalo Vasques join her side and remain silent about her affairs in future.

At this time, the King ordered everyone to start moving towards the frontier; and wrote to the Earl requesting him to set out from Vila Viçosa. Accordingly, on Monday, the last day of June, the Earl set out with his wife and his followers and set up camp by the River Guadiana, near Juromenha. On the following Wednesday, the King and Queen left Estremoz where they had been staying, with all their followers, and came to Borba; and on the Friday they arrived at Vila Boim. On Saturday, 6 July, they installed themselves in Elvas, where all the others later joined them. The King lodged up in the old town and the Earl in São Domingos. The King's forces set up camp in the fields around the town while the English camped in the olive groves on the road to Badajoz; and both sides began to raid each other.

The Queen, who was pregnant, gave birth to a boy there on the thirteenth day of their stay in Elvas. The King showed great joy at

mui gram prazer e aquelles que da parte da rrainha eram; e acabados quatro dias morreo: e por sua morte tomarom todollos grandes que com el-rrei estavom capas de burell por doo, mais por seguirem voontade d'el-rrei que por entenderem que era seu filho, ca muitos presumiam que era filho do conde Joham Fernandez, dizendo que el-rrei, por seer adoorado, aviia tempos que nom dormia com a rrainha; e outros que sse mais estendiam a murmurar deziam que el-rrei por esta rrazom ho afogara no collo de sua ama. Onde sabee que n'eeste tempo e em esta hida se começarom dous officios em Portugall novamente que ataa estonce em ell nom avia, *scilicet,* condeestabre e marichall; e tomado tall costume dos ingreses que entom veherom, fez el-rrei condeestabre o conde d'Arrayollos dom Alvoro Perez de Castro e marichall Gonçallo Vaasquez d'Azevedo. E sse alguem disser quem husava ante das cousas que a estes cavalleirosos officios perteence, dizee-lhe que fazia todo o alferez-moor; e o officio que agora he do camareiro-moor suhia de seer do rreposteiro-moor.

CLI

Como Nun'Allvarez pedio lecença ao prioll pera seer na batalha com el-rrei, e que maneira teve de sse partir porque lh'a nom deu

Estando assi el-rrei dom Fernando com todo seu ajuntamento em Ellvas, era a todos comũu fama per rrecontamento verdadeiro como el-rrei de Castella juntava suas gentes pera sse viir a Badalhouce e lhe poer a praça a el-rrei dom Fernando, e que sse nom escusava batalha antre os rreis. Nuno Allvarez, que estava com o prioll na frontaria de Lixboa, como dissemos, esperando cada dia que el-rrei mandasse chamar seu irmaão e os outros pera seerem com ell na batalha, e o prioll rrecebeo sua carta que nom sse trabalhasse de hir allá mas que todavia estevesse em Lixboa com os seus como estava, ca assi o entendia por seu serviço. Ao prioll pesou muito de tall rrecado, porque sua voontade era seer todavia na batalha com el-rrei; pero foi-lhe forçado fazer o que lhe mandavom e nom partir da frontaria; e fallou esto com seus irmaãos e com os outros segundo lhe el-rrei screvera. Nun'Allvarez ouve gram tristeza por esto, e por os muitos que estonce hi estavom nom rrespondeo nẽhũa cousa ao prioll; e como sse os outros partirom foi-sse o prioll pera sua camara e Nun'Allvarez com elle, e tanto que ambos forom dentro Nun'Allvarez disse ao irmaão em esta guisa: «Senhor irmaão, por determinado avees vós todavia nom

the event as did the Queen's supporters, but at the end of four days the child died. When this happened, all the grandees in the King's company donned sackcloth capes in mourning, more in order to obey the King's wishes than because they thought the child was his; for many took it for granted that Count Juan Fernández was the father, saying that because of his illness the King had not slept with the Queen for many a day. Meanwhile others who carried their gossip much further were saying that precisely because of this the King had smothered the child in the very arms of its nurse.

Also, you should know that it was at this particular time and on this journey that two offices hitherto unknown in Portugal were created: namely, the Constable and the Marshal. Adopting the custom from the English newcomers, the King appointed Dom Alvaro Peres de Castro, the Count of Arraiolos, to the post of Constable and Gonçalo Vasques de Azevedo to that of Marshal. If anyone asks who fulfilled previously the duties belonging to these knightly offices, tell him that the Grand Standard—bearer used to do them all; and the office now known as the Grand Chamberlain used to be that of the Grand Butler.

CLI

How Nun'Álvares asked the Prior's permission to join the King's forces for the war ahead, and the manner in which he departed in the face of the Prior's refusal.

Whilst King Fernando and all his forces were in Elvas, it was common knowledge and rumoured with complete truth that the King of Castile was gathering his men together to come to Badajoz in order to confront King Fernando, and that war between the two kings was now inevitable. Nun'Álvares, who was with the Prior defending Lisbon, as we have recounted, was expecting every day an order from the King to his brother and the rest to join him in the war. The Prior received his letter instructing him to make no move to go there but to remain with his men in Lisbon, for it suited the King's purposes that they should stay as they were. The Prior was very disappointed with the message for he wanted nothing better than to accompany the King in battle, but he was forced to obey orders and remain at his post; and he explained the King's written instructions to his brothers and his other followers. Nun'Álvares was very distressed indeed at the news but, because of the great number of people present, made no reply to the Prior.

When the others had dispersed, the Prior went to his chamber with Nun'Álvares and, as soon as they were inside, Nun'Álvares spoke to his brother in this manner: "My lord brother, are you really so determined to remain here and not join the King at the war? Please,

partir d'aqui pera seer com el-rrei na batalha? Por mercee, declaraae-me sobr'esto vossa voontade». O prioll, ouvindo esto, começou de rrir e rrespondeo d'esta guisa, dizendo: «Irmaão, bem veedes vós que eu nom posso hi all fazer se nom comprir o que me el-rrei meu senhor manda, e fazendo o contrairo nom m'o contariam por serviço; mas espero em Deus que ell será veencedor da batalha, e a nós encaminhará com as gentes d'esta frota que o serviremos de tam boom serviço como lhe lá podiamos fazer: e porém, irmaão, a vós nom seja esto empacho, nem vos anogees por ello». Nun'All-varez, mui cuidoso por todavia seer na batalha, pareciam-lhe estas rrazoões compridas por que sse o prioll escusava de todo; e como as acabou, muito mesuradamente disse: «Senhor irmaão, a mim semelha que todallas cousas vós avees de leixar esqueecer por todavia seer na batalha com vosso senhor el-rrei, de que vosso padre e vós e toda vossa linhagem tantas mercees avees rrecebidas; pero porque ja per vezes ouvi dizer a algũus que melhor he obediencia que o sacrificio, parece-me que he bem de lhe seerdes obediente e comprirdes seu mandado. Mas porque eu entendo que em esta frontaria, onde há tantos bõos como convosco estam, eu ei de fazer pequena mingua, desi porque me parece que eu faria a moor maldade do mundo se em esta batalha nom fosse, vos peço por mercee que me dees logar pera seer em ella, e eu leixarei aqui todollos meus, que nom quero levar se nom cinquo ou seis companheiros com nossas armas». O prioll rrespondeo es-tonce, ja quanto de sanhudo, que tall logar lhe nom daria, ante lhe rrogava e mandava que de tall cousa se nom traba-lhasse. Nun'Allvarez, ouvindo a rreposta de seu irmaão, par-tio-sse d'ant'elle nom mui ledo e foi-sse pera sua pousada; e logo, mais em segredo que pôde, começou de concertar sua hida, e nom o pôde fazer tam calladamente que o prioll d'ello parte nom soubesse; e tanto que o ouvio, porque lhe conhecia bem a voontade, que pois que o começava que o avia d'acabar, mandou logo perceber as portas da cidade e poer em ellas tall guarda que nom leixassem per ellas sahir nẽhũua gente d'armas, especiallmente aa porta de Sam Vi-cente, per hu ell entendeo que avia d'hir. Nun'Allvarez por aquell dia e noite seguinte ataa mea noite nom sse trabalhou de nẽhũua cousa; e aaquellas horas ell e cinquo escudeiros que levou consigo começarom de sse correger elles e seus pages, sem outras azemellas, e cavallgarom nom muito ma-nhãa e chegarom aaquella porta; e os homẽes d'armas que hi estavom por guardas abriam ja as portas aas gentes serviçaaes

132

tell me what your true desire is." On hearing this, the Prior burst out laughing and replied thus: "Brother, you know perfectly well that I can do absolutely nothing but obey the order of my lord the King, and were I to do otherwise, I would be deemed to have done him a disservice. However, I hope that God will give him victory in the war, and will guide us so to confront the men of this fleet that we shall serve the King as well here as we could have done in that expedition. Therefore, brother, have no fear, and do not fret because of this." Still desirous of taking part in the campaign, Nun'Álvares felt that these arguments perfectly justified the Prior in not going; and as soon as the Prior finished speaking, he replied very calmly: "My lord brother, it seems to me that you have to put everything on one side in order to be at your King's side in the campaign since your father, you and all your family have received so many boons from him. However, I have sometimes heard some people say that obedience is better than sacrifice, so I believe that you ought to obey him and do his will. On the other hand, because in my estimation I shall not be missed in this garrison for you have here with you many good men, and also because in my opinion I would be committing the worst crime in the world if I did not take part in the campaign, I beg of you to give me leave to do so. I shall leave all my men here, and take with me no more than five or six companions with our weapons." The Prior now replied hotly that he would give him no such leave, and begged him and enjoined him to desist forthwith from such an enterprise. On hearing his brother's reply, Nun'Álvares left him and, sad at heart, went to his lodgings. Straightaway, in the greatest secrecy, he began to prepare his departure, although he was unable to do it so unobtrusively that the Prior did not learn of it. As soon as he got wind of these preparations, knowing that Nun'Álvares was a determined man who never failed to finish what he had begun, he ordered the city gates to be watched and a guard to be put on them so that no men—at—arms would be allowed to go out. He put an especially close watch on the São Vicente gate because he expected his brother to attempt an exit by that route.

Nun'Álvares made no move to leave the city on that day and the night following up to midnight; but at that hour, he and five squires who were with him began to equip themselves and their pages, without any pack—animals, and rode in the very early hours to that gate. The soldiers on guard were opening up the gates to allow out those people whose work customarily took them outside the walls every

que sahiam pera fora. E como Nun'Allvarez e os seus chegarom, as guardas os quiserom torvar que nom sahissem, e elles mostrarom que quiriam sahir per força, e derom-lhe logar, e forom-sse seu caminho. Nun'Allvarez quando chegou a Ellvas el-rrei o rrecebeo mui bem, louvando-o muito perante todos, e muito mais o louvou depois, quando soube o que lhe avehera com seu irmaão, e como sse partira da cidade sem sua lecença e contra sa voontade.

CLII
Como el-rrei de Castella juntou suas gentes e sse veo pera Badalhouce com ellas

Tornando a fallar d'el-rrei de Castella, que hordenava em seu rreino enquanto estas cousas todas passarom, he de saber que depois que el-rrei tomou o castello d'Almeida per preitesia e mandou a carta ao conde de Cambrig, de que nom ouve rreposta, segundo ouvistes, tornou-sse pera Castella. E porquanto sabia que tanto que os ingreses fossem encavallgados se trabalhariam todos d'entrar em seu rreino, porém nom quis suas gentes afastar de ssi, mas hordenou de as poer acerca do estremo de Portugall, e alli aviiam pagamento de seu solldo; e ell entanto juntava as mais companhas que podia, estando na cidade d'Avilla e per aquella comarca d'arredor. D'alli partio el-rrei e veo-sse pera Outerdesilhas e esteve hi algũus dias; e desi veo-sse a Simancas e esteve alli hũu mes. E sabendo elle como o conde dom Affonsso estava em Bragança trautando suas aveenças com el-rrei dom Fernando, screveo-lhe suas cartas por o torvar d'ello e trager pera sua mercee; e des que vio que lhe o conde nom rrespondeo como ell queria, partio de Simancas e foi-sse pera Çamora, e alli ajuntou suas gentes, porque o certificarom que el-rrei de Portugall com os ingreses quiriam entrar per Castella; e screveo outra vez ao conde per cartas e messegeiros e a todollos que com ell estavom, que por a natureza que com ell aviam se vehessem logo pera sa mercee, ca sua voontade era partir d'alli a pressa, por hir pellejar com el-rrei dom Fernando. O conde rrespondeo bem a suas cartas, pero demandava arrefées de pessoas e castellos certos que lhe fossem dados; el-rrei nom quis conssentir em ello, ca lhe demandava o iffante dom Fernando seu filho e seis filhos de cavalleiros quaaes elle nomeasse. Aacima, veendo o conde como todollos seus se partiam d'elle e se hiam pera el-rrei, trautou suas preitesias com elle e veo-sse pera sua mercee. Estonce fez

day. When Nun'Álvares and his men reached the gate, the guards wanted to stop them leaving, but when they showed that they were willing to use force in order to leave, the guards let them pass, and so they went on their way. When Nun'Álvares arrived at Elvas, he was welcomed by the King who praised him in front of everyone. He praised him all the more, later, when he learned of what had passed between him and his brother, and of how he had left the city without his brother's leave and against his will.

CLII
How the King of Castile gathered together his forces and came with them to Badajoz.

Returning now to the King of Castile, who was devoting himself to the affairs of his kingdom while all this was happening, you must know that after receiving the capitulation of Almeida castle and sending the Earl of Cambridge the letter to which he received no reply, as you have heard, he returned to Castile. Since he knew that as soon as the English had horses they would lose no time in entering his kingdom, he did not want his men to disperse, but made sure that they were deployed close to the Portuguese frontier, and that that was where they would receive their pay. Meanwhile, he assembled as many companies as he could whilst he was in the city and district of Ávila. From there he went to Tordesillas, where he spent some days, and then to Simancas, where he stayed for a month. Learning that Count Alfonso was in Bragança, negotiating with King Fernando, he wrote him letters to prevent this and to bring him back on his side; but when he realized that the Count had not replied as he would have liked, he left Simancas and went to Zamora. There he gathered his forces, for it was confirmed that the King of Portugal and the English intended to invade Castile. He now wrote again to the Count and sent messengers to him and to all his companions, appealing to him for the sake of family ties to come to him immediately for he wanted to set out in all haste to fight King Fernando. The Count replied favourably but asked to be given certain people and castles as hostages. The King refused, however, for the Count was demanding Prince Fernando, his son, and six sons of knights of his own choosing. Moreover, seeing that all his men were leaving and going over to the King, the Count made an agreement with the King and

135

el-rrei alli em Çamora condeestabre de Castella dom Affonsso
marques de Vilhena e conde de Denia, e fez mariscall da
hoste Fernand'Allvarez de Tolledo, e estes officios nunca
foram dados em Castella atá aquell tempo: e desi partio
el-rrei de Çamora com todas suas gentes, que eram cinquo
mill hom̃ees d'armas e mill e quinhentos genetes e muita
gente de pee e beesteiros, e chegou a Badalhouce hũua
quinta-feira pella manhãa, pustumeiro dia de julho da dita era.

CLIII

Como el-rrei dom Fernando pôs sua batalha e esperou no campo, e el-rrei de Castella nom quis pellejar

Ante hũu dia que el-rrei chegasse a Badalhouce, que eram
trinta dias do mes de julho, sahirom os ingreses de seu arreall
e forom a Caya, contra Badalhouce, veer ho campo hu avia
de seer a batalha. E andando allá em Caya, disserom a el-rrei
dom Fernando que gentes dos castellãaos pellejavom com os
ingreses; e ell, tanto que o ouvio, partio logo d'Ellvas com
toda sa gente e quando lá foi achou nom era nada e tornou-sse
pera a villa. Em outro dia, quando el-rrei de Castella chegou
a Badalhouce, como dissemos, armarom os seus hũua tenda
n'aquell logar de Caya; e veherom dizer a el-rrei dom Fernando como os castellãaos armavom suas tendas e poinham
suas aazes pera pellejar, e nom era assi. El-rrei e o conde
partirom logo com todas suas gentes e forom-sse aaquell
logar de Caya, e os castellãaos, como os virom hir, alçarom
a tenda e tornarom-sse pera Badalhouce. Entom cortarom
os portugueeses as pontas dos çapatos, que husavom em aquell
tempo muito compridas, e deitadas todas em hũu logar, era
sabor de veer tall monte de pontas; ca por judeu ou clerigo
aviam estonce quem nom tragia as pontas compridas. El-rrei
tiinha bem seis mill lanças antre suas e dos ingreses e muitos
beesteiros e hom̃ees de pee, assi que os rreis aviam assaz de
gente cada hũu por sua parte pera pellejar; e hordenarom
logo sua batalha per esta guisa: o conde de Cambrig estava
na avanguarda e el-rrei dom Fernando na reguarda, e postas
suas allas como compria. E teendo suas aazes postas aten-
dendo a batalha, começou el-rrei de fazer cavalleiros assi
ingreses como portugueeses, e tomarom de sua mão honrra
de cavallaria mossé Canom e outros ingreses; e dos portugueses o conde dom Gonçallo e Fernam Gonçallvez de Sousa
e Fernam Gonçalvez de Meira e Gonçallo Veegas d'Ataide

joined him. Then, in Zamora, the King appointed Don Alfonso, the Marquess of Villena and Count of Denia, to be Constable of Castile, and Fernán Álvarez de Toledo to be Marshal of the Army. These offices had never existed previously in Castile. [1] Then, the King left Zamora with all his forces; that is, five thousand men — at — arms, one thousand five hundred lightly — armed horsemen and many foot — soldiers and crossbowmen; and he came to Badajoz on the morning of Thursday, 31 July of the same year.

CLIII
How King Fernando drew up his troops and waited in the field, and how the King of Castile would not fight.

On 30 July, the day before the King arrived at Badajoz, the English left their camp and went to Caia [1] near Badajoz to inspect the proposed field of battle. While they were in Caia, King Fernando was informed that some of the English forces were fighting Castilians there; and as soon as he heard this, he left Elvas immediately with his whole army; but when he got there, he found it was untrue so he returned to the town. The next day, when the King of Castile arrived in Badajoz, as we said before, his men put up a tent in that place of Caia. King Fernando was told the Castilians were setting up their tents and drawing up their battle formation ready to fight, but this was not so. The King and the Earl left immediately with their entire army and came to Caia; but as soon as the Castilians saw them coming, they took down the tent and returned to Badajoz. Then the Portuguese cut the toes from their shoes, which at that time it was the fashion to wear very long; and when these were all thrown down together, it was amusing to see such a pile of toes; for at that time anyone who did not wear long toes was considered a Jew or a cleric. The King had a good six thousand lances including those of the English, as well as many crossbowmen and foot — soldiers. Thus both kings had quite enough men with which to fight. They deployed their men in this fashion: the Earl of Cambridge in the vanguard and King Fernando in the rearguard, with their flanks formed up as was appropriate. With his squadrons formed in battle order, the King began to create knights from among the English as well as the Portuguese. Sir Canon and other Englishmen received the honour of knighthood from his hand, as did Count Gonçalo, Fernão Gonçalves de Sousa, Fernão Gonçalves de Meira, Gonçalo Viegas de Ataide and other noble squires to the number of twenty — four. When however he

e d'outros escudeiros fidallgos ataa hũus viinte e quatro.
E avendo ja el-rrei feitos algũus cavalleiros, disserom a el-rrei
que os nom podia fazer, pois ell ainda nom era cavalleiro;
ca, posto que rrei fosse, nom avia poder d'armar cavalleiros
pois ainda o ell nom era. Estonce o armou cavalleiro o conde
de Cambrig, e feito el-rrei cavalleiro tornou a fazer os que
ante avia feitos e outros algũus. E com os ingreses viinha o
alferez do duque d'Allancastro, que sse chamava rrei de
Castella por aazo de sua molher dona Costança, filha d'el-rrei
dom Pedro, que tragia sua bandeira; a quall tendida na batalha, braadavom os ingreses todos: «Castella e Leom por el-rrei
dom Joham de Castella, filho d'el-rrei Eduarte de Ingraterra!»
E tragiam outro pendom da cruzada contra el-rrei de Castella,
porque eram cismaticos, nom teendo com o papa de Rroma.
E assi com as aazes prestes e suas bandeiras tendidas este-
verom per grande espaço ataa depois de meo dia; e veendo
que el-rrei de Castella nom quiria viir aa batalha, tornarom-
-sse os ingreses pera seu arreall e el-rrei pera Ellvas com toda
sua companha.

CLIV
Como foram pazes trautadas antre el-rrei dom Fernando
e el-rrei dom Joham de Castella, e com
que condiçoões

Som algũuas cousas calladas nas estorias, nom sabemos
por quall rrazom, que muitos que as leem desejam de saber;
outras, acerca de mudas, nom fallom como devem aquello
de que homem queria seer certo; assi como em este capitullo,
fallando da aveença d'estes rreis, quall d'elles foi o primeiro
que a mandou trautar, nẽhũu autor o escreve claramente;
e porque nos parece rrazoado fallar em ello, posto que a
certidom d'isto bem nom saibamos, diremos as openioões
que cada hũus têm. Hũus dizem que vendo-sse el-rrei dom
Fernando eibado de doores, que ja tempo avia, e que suas
guerras sse lhe perlongavom, desi porque os ingreses som
homẽes de forte condiçom e lhe faziam muitos nojos em seu
rreino, como ja ouvistes, avendo tanto tempo que estavom em
elle; aalem d'esto, porquanto el-rrei de Castella non quisera
logo viir aa batalha, teendo-lhe a praça posta tão preto de seu
arreall, que per ventura queria teer outra hordenança de per-
longada guerra, que a ell muito desprazia, que porém lhe
mandou cometer mui escusamente que ouvesse com elle paz,

had already dubbed several knights, the King was informed that he could not do so since he himself was not yet a knight; for, although he was a King, he had no power to knight others since he was not one himself. There and then, the Earl of Cambridge dubbed him knight; and once he had himself been knighted, the King repeated the ceremony with those men he had already knighted, and went on to knight others. [2] In the English host was the standard—bearer [3] of the Duke of Lancaster (he who called himself King of Castile by reason of his wife Constanza, daughter of Don Pedro). This man carried the Duke's banner, and when this was unfurled before the battle, the English all roared: "Castile and León for King John of Castile, son of King Edward of England!" Then they brought forward another banner signifying the crusade against the King of Castile (because he was a schismatic and did not support the Pope of Rome). So they stood in battle order with their banners unfurled for a long time until well after midday; but seeing that the King of Castile did not care to take the field against them, the English returned to their camp and the Portuguese King with all his company to Elvas.

CLIV
Of the Peace negotiated between King Fernando and King Juan of Castile, and what were the conditions.

In some histories, for reasons which we do not know, things go unmentioned that many readers would like to know. Other histories, almost equally unforthcoming, fail to deal adequately with those things of which a man would like some account. Thus it is with this chapter, for no writer gives any clear report about the agreement between these kings and which of them actually initiated the negotiations; and because it seems to us only reasonable to speak of this matter, even though we possess no certain knowledge about it, let us set down the various points of view held by historians.

Some say that King Fernando made the first move because his belly was swollen painfully and had been for some time, because his campaigns were now becoming somewhat prolonged, and also because the English are rough men by nature and had been doing great harm in his kingdom for a long time, as you have already heard. Moreover, although the field of battle had been arranged so near to the camp of the King of Castile, the latter did not wish to fight a pitched battle, perhaps preferring the alternative of prolonged warfare (which King Fernando did not want at all). Because of this, King Fernando sent to propose to him that they should make peace, but

e esto pollo nom saberem os ingreses, de que era certo que lhe nom prazia outra cousa se nom guerra. Outros rrazoam muito pello contrairo, dizendo que el-rrei de Castella, quando soube que ante hũu dia que elle chegasse, que el-rrei dom Fernando chegara ao campo com toda sua gente, cuidando que pellejavom ja os seus com os ingreses, desi no dia que el chegou, que logo sse veherom portugueses e ingreses todos ao campo e hordenarom sua batalha, mostrando grande voontade de pellejar, e que veendo estas foutezas, lembrando--lhe sobre todo como seu padre fora veencido dos ingreses na batalha de Najara, que rreceou muito de lhe poer o campo, e que ell foi o que primeiro rrequereo a paz. Algũus outros autores nom screvem a primeira nem esta segunda rrazom, mas dizem que ouve hi taaes pessoas que desejavom paz e amor antre estes rreis, porquanto eram primos com-irmaãos, e que trautarom antr'elles algũas maneiras de bem e d'asses-sego; e que el-rrei de Castella enviou a elle secretamente seus embaxadores e el-rrei dom Fernando isso meesmo a elle. Mas de qualquer guisa que seja, el-rrei de Castella foi entom mui prasmado por nom pellejar com el-rrei dom Fernando, moormente por a ardideza que ell e os seus mostravom aa viinda quando chegarom, dizendo hũus contra os outros per modo d'escarnho: «E onde vos hiis, compadre?» «Vou-me a pressa, dezia ho outro, defender a minha quintãa de tall logar, que logo em Portugall nomeava, que m'a nom tomem os ingreses». «E eu tambem vou deffender a minha», rres-pondia. E depois que forom no campo nem defenderom a quintãa nem os casaaes mais pequenos, mas enviou el-rrei de Castella trautar suas aveenças a Portugall, hũua vez per Pero Sarmento e outra per Pero Fernandez de Vallasco, grande seu privado; e el-rrei dom Fernando enviava a elle o conde d'Arrayollos dom Alvoro Perez de Castro e Gonçallo Vaas-quez d'Azevedo. E estes hiam sempre de noite encubertamente ao arrayal d'el-rrei de Castella, que estava antre Ellvas e Badalhouce, com senhos escudeiros, nom mais, por nom averem aazo os ingreses de saberem d'isto parte; e forom per tantas vezes os embaxadores d'hũua e da outra parte e vehe-rom que foi antre os rreis posta aveença per esta seguinte maneira. Primeiramente foi posto antre as outras cousas hũu capitullo, de que os ingreses nom souberom parte, *scilicet,* que a iffante dona Beatriz filha d'el-rrei dom Fernando, que fora primeiro esposada com dom Henrrique primogenito filho d'el-rrei de Castella e depois que os ingreses veherom com Eduarte filho do conde de Cambrig, que sse desatassem estes

140

keeping the negotiations a secret from the English, whose only desire was to make war.

Against this, others argue that the King of Castile knew that, on the day before his own arrival there, King Fernando had appeared with all his forces on the battle—field, thinking that his own men and the English were already fighting there, and that on the very day that King Juan arrived, the Portuguese and the English all came to the battle—field and set out their battle—lines with great enthusiasm for a fight. Seeing this warlike attitude, it is argued, King Juan remembered above all how his own father had been defeated by the English at the battle of Nájera, was afraid to meet them in battle and therefore was the first to seek for peace.

Yet other writers say neither the one thing nor the other. They say that there were men there who wanted peace and love between these kings, because they were cousins, and who acted as mediators between them to achieve a harmonious agreement; and that the King of Castile and King Fernando sent messengers secretly to each other.

However this might be, the King of Castile was very much censured for not fighting King Fernando, especially because of the ardour shown by him and his men on their arrival, when they would say to each other in mocking tones, "Where are you going, my friend?", and receive the answer "I am hurrying to defend my estate in such—and—such a place (giving the name of some place in Portugal), so that the English don't take it." "And I am going to defend mine", the first man would reply. Yet when they got to the battle—field they did not defend any estate, or even the tiniest of dwellings; but the King of Castile began to negotiate for an agreement, sending Pedro Sarmiento to Portugal on one occasion, and his favourite, Pedro Fernández de Velasco, on another. King Fernando sent to him Álvaro Peres de Castro, Count of Arraiolos, and Gonçalo Vasques de Azevedo. These two always went by night, and in disguise, to the camp of the Castilian King which was situated between Elvas and Badajoz; and they were each accompanied by only one squire so as to minimize the possibility of discovery by the English. Both sides' envoys came and went so many times that an agreement was eventually made between the two kings on the following terms:[1]

Before anything else it was agreed in one clause, of which the English knew nothing, that Princess Beatriz, King Fernando's daughter, who had been betrothed originally to Don Enrique, the first—born son of the King of Castile, and, after the arrival of the English, to Edward, son of the Earl of Cambridge, should have these betrothals

esposoiros e que casasse com ella o iffante dom Fernando filho segundo d'el-rrei de Castella: e d'isto prazia mais a el-rrei dom Fernando que do casamento do iffante dom Henrrique, porque o iffante dom Fernando, pois era segundo filho, casando com sua filha ficava rrei de Portugall sem sse mesturando o rreino com o de Castella, o que era per força de sse mesturar casando com o iffante dom Henrrique que era herdeiro do rreino. Outrossi que el-rrei de Castella desse e entregasse a el-rrei dom Fernando os loguares d'Almeida e de Miranda e todallas gallees que tomadas forom na pelleja de Saltes, com todas suas armas e esquipaçoões; e que soltasse dom Joham Affonsso Tello, irmaão da rrainha, almirante de Portugall, com todollos outros que forom presos na frota, sem rrendiçom nẽhũuma, salvo aquellas que pagadas fossem. E mais que el-rrei de Castella desse tantos navios da sua frota **que jazia em** Lixboa, em que o conde com todas suas gentes **podessem hir** seguros em paz e em salvo pera sua terra, sem **lhe pagando** nẽhũu frete por sua partida; e que por segurança d'esto se posessem certas arrefẽes da hũa parte aa outra.

CLV
Como o conde e Gonçallo Vaasquez levarom os trautos das pazes, e das rrazoões que ouverom ante que as asiinasse

Esto assi acordado e os trautos escriptos, partirom-sse o conde e Gonçallo Vaasquez muito cedo alta madrugada, hũu domingo dez dias do mes d'agosto, e chegarom ao rreall d'el-rrei de Castella e mostrarom a el-rrei os trautos que levavom assiinados na maneira que avees ouvido, e forom d'elle bem rrecebidos. E el-rrei, ssem mais leer os trautos, ante que os assiinasse, mandou logo tanger hũua trombeta, pera sse juntar a gente e ouvir o pregom, segundo he costume quando apregoam pazes; e começando de as apregoar, as gentes do arreall aviam tam gram prazer que muitos ficavom os joelhos em terra e a beijavom, e taaes avia hi que a comiam. Aquell dia forom convidados o conde dom Alvoro Perez e Gonçallo Vaasquez de dom Fernand'Azores meestre de Santiago, e deu-lhes de comer mui honrradamente e com gram prazer, em tanto que ell nom quise seer por os melhor fazer servir; e preguntava aaquelles escudeiros que hiam com o conde e com Gonçallo Vaasquez, que lhe parecia d'aquella

cancelled and should be married instead to Prince Fernando, the second son of the King of Castile. King Fernando preferred this marriage to the one originally planned with Prince Enrique, because Prince Fernando was a second son and by marrying Beatriz would eventually become King of Portugal without any entanglements with Castile, which was what would have happened had she married Prince Enrique, who was the heir to that kingdom.

It was also agreed that the King of Castile would hand over to King Fernando the places of Almeida and Miranda, and all the galleys captured at the battle of Saltes, together with all their arms and equipment; and that he would free the Queen's brother and Admiral of Portugal, Dom João Afonso Telo, together with all the other prisoners captured with the fleet, without any ransoms being paid other than those which had already been paid. Moreover, the King of Castile would provide, from his fleet now lying off Lisbon, enough ships to take the Earl and all his forces back to their own country, safe and sound, and without paying anything for their voyage. Lastly, hostages were to be exchanged by both sides as a guarantee for this agreement.

CLV
How the Count and Gonçalo Vasques carried the treaty documents with them, and of the conversation that took place before they were signed.

This being agreed and the treaty written down, the Count and Gonçalo Vasques set out in the small hours of Sunday 10 August, and came to the camp of the King of Castile. They showed him the treaty signed in the manner you have heard, and he welcomed them. Before signing the treaty and without even reading it, the King ordered a trumpet to be blown, summoning his men to assemble and hear the proclamation, as is the custom when peace is proclaimed. As the proclamation began, people in the camp were so overjoyed that many knelt on the ground and kissed it, and there were even some who ate bits of earth. That day Count Álvaro Peres and Gonçalo Vasques were the guests of Don Fernando Osórez, the Master of Santiago, who entertained them at table most honourably and with great pleasure, in such a way that it would have been impossible to receive them better. He asked the squires who accompanied the Count and Gonçalo Vasques what they thought of the event; that is to

obra que fora feita em rrazom das pazes antre aquelles rreis, que eram em tão gram desvairo; e elles disserom que lhe parecia que fora feita per Deus: «Nom soomente per Deos, disse elle, mais ainda per todollos anjos do ceeo»; e assi acabarom seu jantar com muita follgança. O comer acabado, folgarom alli hũu pouco, desi partirom-sse com outros cavalleiros pera honde el-rrei estava e o meestre ficou em sua tenda. El-rrei, quando os vio, rrecebeo-os mui bem, e apartarom-sse com ell, pedindo-lhe por mercee que assiinasse os trautos, e el-rrei disse que lhe prazia; e fez chamar o seu scrivam da poridade e mandou-lhe que os leesse: e quando chegou aaquel logar onde era contheudo que ell entregasse todallas gallees com suas esquipaçoões, disse que tall cousa nom outorgara nem o faria por cousa que fosse; que bem lhe prazia dar ho almirante com a gente toda, de quaesquer condiçoões que fossem, mas que dar as gallees que o nom faria per nẽhũua guisa. O conde e Gonçallo Vaasquez, quando isto ouvirom, ficarom espantados e disserom: «Quanto nós, senhor, somos muito maravilhados de tall cousa: mandardes vós apregoar as pazes, sse vós em voontade nom tinhees de assiinar os trautos segundo per vós foi outorgado»; e el-rrei disse que leesse mais adeante, e sobre todo o que duvidasse queria aver seu consselho. O escripvam tornou a leer, e quando chegou aaquell capitollo hu fazia meençom que el-rrei desse de sua frota tanta em que os ingreses fossem, e isto sem frete nẽhũu, disse que esto nom faria por cousa que fosse no mundo, ca nom era rrazom de ell dar suas naaos em poder de seus immiigos pera fazerem d'ellas o que quisessem, e posto que seguras fossem, hirem sem frete nẽhũu. Quando isto ouvirom os embaxadores, entom forom muito mais maravilhados, e disserom que lhe pediam por mercee que quisesse outorgar estas cousas segundo per elle fora acordado, se nom que a paz que apregoada era, que todo sse tornaria em nẽhũua cousa; e el-rrei disse que ante queria aver guerra como quer que fosse que aver d'outorgar taaes cousas. Ouvindo Gonçallo Vaasquez que el-rrei per nẽhũua guisa nom queria assiinar os trautos, por quantas boas rrazoões que lhe dizer podiam, entom disse ao conde que lhe pedia por mercee que disesse a el-rrei de Castella o que lhe seu senhor enviava dizer; e o conde rrespondeo que lhe dava logar que o dissesse e que o escusasse por entom d'aquell trabalho: e esto dezia o conde porque nom tiinha a voz bem clara, por aazo de hũu cerco em que comera rratos e outras taaes cousas. «Pois m'o vós mandaaes, disse Gonçallo Vaasquez, eu o direi da guisa que o el-rrei meu senhor disse». Entom disse a el-rrei em csta

say, the peace made between these two kings whose relationship had been so troubled. They replied that it was as if God himself had made the peace. "Not only God", he replied, "but all the angels in heaven, too." So they ended their luncheon with much rejoicing.

The meal over, they celebrated a little more before going with other knights to the King, leaving the Master of Santiago in his tent. When the King saw them, he welcomed them; and they took him on one side and entreated him to sign the treaty. The King said he would do so willingly, summoned his private secretary and commanded him to read it out. When he got to the point where it was stated that the King should hand over all the galleys with their equipment, he said that he would not do so under any circumstances; that he was quite happy to free the Admiral and all his men, whosoever they might be, but he most certainly would not surrender the galleys. When they heard this, the Count and Gonçalo Vasques were aghast and said: "We are astonished at what you say, my lord: to order the public proclamation of the peace when you had no intention of signing the very treaty that had been agreed by you." The King ordered the reading to continue and said that he would like to have advice about every doubtful point. The secretary resumed reading, and when he got to the clause where it said that the King should give enough of his fleet to transport the English home again, without any payment, he said he would not do this at any price, for it would be absurd of him to give his ships to his enemies to do with as they willed. Moreover, even if the ships were safe, to let them go without payment was unthinkable. When they heard this, the ambassadors were even more astonished and said that they entreated him to make these concessions according to what had been agreed, or else the peace which had been proclaimed would come to nothing. The King replied that he would rather have war in any circumstances than have to make such concessions.

Seeing that the King was refusing point—blank to sign the treaty, no matter what they said to him, Gonçalo Vasques begged the Count to tell the King of Castile what their lord had sent him to say. The Count replied that he gave Gonçalo Vasques leave to say it in his stead, excusing himself from the task. This he did because his voice was not at all clear on account of the fact that during a siege he had eaten rats and other similar things. "Since you order me to do so", said Gonçalo Vasques, "I shall say it as my lord stated it." Then he addressed the King in this manner: "My lord, since you choose not

guisa: «Senhor, pois vossa mercee he de estas cousas nom querer outorgar, segundo bem sabees que foi devisado, el-rrei meu senhor vos manda dizer que vós assiinees hũu logar, quall vos mais prouguer, honde vos ell venha poer a praça; e que aaquell dia que per vós for devisado, ell he mui ledo de vĩir pellejar convosco». «Assi, disse el-rrei em rriindo, e sooes pera tanto?». «Certamente, disse Gonçallo Vaasquez, eu nom digo el-rrei meu senhor, que he assaz de poderoso rrei pera isto fazer, mas o conde de Cambrig soo com as gentes que consigo traz he abastante pera vo-lla poer». Estando el-rrei em estas pallavras, chegou o meestre de Santiago dom Fernand'Osorez, e quando os vio em este desvairo disse contra el-rrei preguntando: «Que he esto, senhor, em que estaaes?». «Em que estamos?» disse Gonçallo Vaasquez. «Estamos na mais vergonhosa cousa que nunca eu vi acontecer antre dous rreis tam nobres como estes, seerem ja as pazes apregoadas, como ouvistes, e hora el-rrei nom quer assiinar os trautos da guisa que em elles he contheudo; por a quall rrazom he per força que a paz se desfaça e isto fique em memoria vergonhosa pera os que depois veherem». «Santa Maria vall, disse o meestre, em que os dovida el-rrei d'assiinar?» E foi-lhe rrespondido quaaes eram, e ell feze-os leer outra vez; e quando vio que el-rrei dovidava n'aquellas cousas e nom em outras, disse contra el-rrei: «E como, senhor, por viinte e duas fustas podres que nom vallem nada e por emprestar quatro ou cinquo naaos sem dinheiro dovidaaes vos d'assiinar os trautos? Certamente tall cousa como esta nom he pera vĩir à praça; e sse o avees por custa e despeza, eu quero que a casa de Santiago pague esto e toda a despesa que sse em ello fezer». Entom rriindo filhou a mão a el-rrei come per força e disse: «Hora, senhor, eu quero todavia que vós que os assiinees e tall mingua como esta nom passe per vós». Entom el-rrei isso meesmo rriindo tomou a pena e assiinou-hos: forom estonce todos mui ledos, e tornarom-sse ho conde e Gonçallo Vaasquez pera a villa d'Ellvas, honde el-rrei dom Fernando estava.

CLVI

Como os ingreses souberom que as pazes eram trautadas
e que as arrefẽes forom postas d'hũua
parte aa outra

Chegarom a Ellvas o conde e Gonçallo Vaasquez e contarom a el-rrei todo o que lhes avehera com el-rrei de Castella;

to make these concessions even though they were set down thus as you well know, my lord the King commands us to tell you to name whatever place you please where he may meet you on the field of battle, and that on the day you have chosen, he will gladly do battle with you."

"Is that so?" laughed the King, "and are you up to it?"

"Most certainly", replied Gonçalo Vasques, "for even without my lord the King, who is quite strong enough to fight you on his own, the Earl of Cambridge alone and the force that he has brought with him, are quite sufficient to face you in the field."

While the King was discussing the matter, the Master of Santiago, Don Fernando Osórez arrived, and when he observed that they were in dispute, he turned to the King and enquired, "What is going on, my lord?"

"What is going on?" said Gonçalo Vasques. "It is the most shameful thing that I have ever seen occur between two kings as noble as these. The peace has already been publicly proclaimed, as you have heard, and now the King refuses to sign the treaty according to the conditions laid down. In view of this, there is nothing for it but to tear up the peace treaty and let the event remain hereafter as a shameful example to posterity."

"Saint Mary help us!" said the Master. "What part is it that the King hesitates to sign?" The clauses in question were pointed out to him and he ordered them to be read out again. When he realized that these particular clauses, and only these, caused the King such difficulties, he turned to the King and said, "And how is it, Sire, that you are hesitating to sign this treaty for the sake of twenty−four, rotten, worthless hulks and a loan of four or five ships without payment? It is certainly not worth fighting a pitched battle for so little; and if you find it all too much to pay, I insist that the House of Santiago should foot the bill, whatever the amount may come to." Then, laughing, he took the King's hand as though by force and said, "Now, Sire, I insist that you sign so as to be rid of this cause of annoyance forthwith." Then the King, laughing even as he did so, took the pen and signed the treaty. Then they were all most glad and the Count and Gonçalo returned to the town of Elvas, where King Fernando was waiting.

CLVI

How the English found out that a peace had been negotiated and that hostages had been exchanged.

The Count and Gonçalo Vasques arrived back in Elvas and told the King all that had befallen them during their visit to the King of Castile. The King laughed, saying that in his opinion all this was a

e el-rrei rriindo disse que entendia que todo aquello fora fingido, por mostrar que outorgava taaes cousas contra sua voontade, porquanto nom eram muito sua honrra; e logo em esse dia mandou apregoar as pazes. Os ingreses, quando as ouvirom apregoar, ouverom tam gram menencoria que mayor nom podia seer, e deitavom os bacinetes em terra e davom-lhe com as fachas, dizendo que el-rrei os traera e enganara, fazendo-os vĩir de sua terra pera pellejar com seus immiigos, e agora fazia paz com elles contra sua voontade; e dezia o conde de Cambrig sanhudamente, quando as vio apregoar, que sse el-rrei trautara paz com os castellaãos, que elle nom a fezera; e que sse elle tevera juntas suas gentes como as tiinha quando chegara a Lixboa, que nom embargando o apregoar das pazes que el-rrei mandava fazer, que ell posera a batalha a el-rrei de Castella. Sobr'esto rrecrecerom tantas rrazoões que algũus se soltarom em desmesuradas pallavras contra el-rrei, a que Pero Lourenço de Tavora rrespondeo como compria. El-rrei disse que nom curasse de suas rrazoões nem ouvessem arroido, dizendo contra elles que elle os contentaria e os mandaria pera sua terra honrradamente como veherom; e assi o fez depois, mas nom a todos, ca mui gram parte d'elles ficarom mortos em este rreino. Entom hordenarom entregar as arrefẽes d'hũua parte aa outra, segundo era devisado nos trautos: e forom entregues a Castella da parte de Portugall seis: hũua filha do conde de Barcellos e hũa filha do conde dom Gonçallo que chamarom dona Enes, que depois foi casada com Joham Fernandez Pacheco, e outra filha do conde dom Hanrrique, que havia nome dona Branca, que depois foi casada com Rrui Vaasquez Coutinho, filho de Beatriz Gonçalivez de Moura e de Vaasco Fernandez Coutinho, e Martinho, filho de Gonçallo Vaasquez d'Azevedo, e Vaasco, filho de Joham Gonçallves Teixeira, e hũu filho d'Alvoro Gonçallvez de Moura que chamavom Lopo. E da parte de Castella forom entregues a Portugall quatro, *scilicet,* hũu filho de Pero Fernandez de Vallasco que chamavom Diego Furtado de Mendonça, que depois foi almirante de Castella, e outro de Pero Rrodriguez Sarmento, e outro de Pero Gonçallvez de Mendonça, e hũu filho do meestre de Santiago dom Fernam Osorez, que chamarom Diego Fernandez d'Aguillar. Forom aallem d'esto feitos preitos e menagẽes, per algũus condes e cavalleiros e fidallgos de Portugall e de Castella, por certas villas e castellos, por guarda e firmeza d'aquestas pazes. Esto acabado, tornou-sse el-rrei dom Fernando pera dentro do rreino, e mandou as gentes cada hũus pera seus logares, e trouve a estrada de Rrio Mayor pera

mere deception just to show that the King of Castile had conceded these things against his will, since they did not redound to his honour. Then, that very day, he ordered the proclamation of the peace. When they heard the peace being proclaimed, the English were as angry as they could possibly be. They threw their bacinets on the ground and hit them with their axes, saying that the King had betrayed and deceived them, making them come from their own country to fight his enemies, and now he was making peace with those same enemies in the teeth of his allies, the English. When he saw the peace treaty being proclaimed, the Earl of Cambridge said wrathfully that even though the King had made peace with the Castilians, he certainly had not; and that if he had had with him his entire army at the strength it had been when he arrived in Lisbon, notwithstanding the proclamation of the peace ordered by the King, he would have done battle with the King of Castile on his own. There was a great outcry in which many heated words were hurled in the King's direction. Pedro Lourenço de Távora replied to these attacks as was only right. The King said that he should pay no attention to them nor should they make such a fuss. He told them that he would compensate them and send them back to their own land as honourably as they had come. And so he did, later, although not all of them, for very many had been killed in this kingdom.

Next, they arranged the exchange of hostages, as had been set down in the treaty. Six hostages were given by Portugal to Castile: a daughter of the Count of Barcelos; a daughter of Count Gonçalo called Dona Inês who later married João Fernandes Pacheco; another daughter of Count Henrique, Dona Branca by name who later married Rui Vasques Coutinho, the son of Beatriz Gonçalves de Moura and Vasco Fernandez Coutinho; Martinho, the son of Gonçalo Vasques de Azevedo; and Vasco, the son of João Gonçalves Teixeira, as well as a son of Álvaro Gonçalves de Moura whose name was Lopo. From Castile came four hostages: that is, a son of Pedro Fernández de Velasco called Diego Hurtado de Mendoza, who was later to become Admiral of Castile; a son of Pedro Rodríguez Sarmiento; another of Pedro González de Mendoza; and a son of the Master of Santiago, Don Fernándo Osórez, whose name was Diego Fernández de Aguilar. Besides this, certain counts, knights and gentlemen of Portugal and Castile were called upon to provide guarantees and oaths with respect to certain towns and castles, as pledges and assurance for this peace treaty.

This business having been concluded, King Fernando came back inside his own kingdom and sent his forces home to their respective regions. He took the Rio Maior road to get to Santarém. On the

vĩir a Santarem; e no caminho se espedio d'ell o conde de Cambrig e chegou a Almadãa com sua molher e filho e gentes primeiro dia de setembro pera embarcar nos navios de Castella. Aos castellaãos pesou muito d'esto, por rreceber os ingreses em suas naaos, que eram seus emmiigos, porém foi-lhe forçado comprir mandado de seu rrei; e ouverom boom tempo e partirom logo; e das outras naaos, que per bem de paz ante a cidade seguras ficarom, d'ellas tomarom carrega e outras nom e forom-sse cada hũuas pera hu lhes prougue. Em esto veo-sse el-rrei a Rrio Mayor, e estando alli per spaço de dias chegou a ell o cardeall dom Pedro de Luna da parte d'aquel que sse chamava Clemente, a pedir que lhe desse a obediencia e tevesse por sua parte assi como ante que vehessem os ingreses. El-rrei mandou chamar a Lixboa algũus leterados, assi como o doutor Gill do Ssem e Rrui Lourenço dayam de Coimbra e outros e o doutor Joham das Rregras com elles, que pouco avia que vehera do estudo de Bollonha: e depois d'algũus dias que el-rrei teve seu consselho, tornou a obediencia aaquel papa Clemente com que ante tevera, muito porém contra voontade d'algũus e especiallmente do doutor Joham das Rregras, o quall dezia a el-rrei que mostraria per dereito que nom era verdadeiro papa. E entom sse partio dom Pedro de Luna pera Avinhom, e mandou el-rrei Joham Gonçallvez seu privado e o bispo de Lixboa dom Martinho em duas gallees dar a obediencia aaquel papa Clemente. Em este comeos, avia el-rrei mandado a Sevilha por suas gallees e gentes que forom tomadas na pelleja de Saltes, segundo nas pazes era outorgado; e fora allá micé Lançarote, com tantos que as podessem trager; as quaaes entregues e as gentes todas que jouverom presas dez e oito meses, veo o conde dom Joham Affonsso Tello, que em ellas fora tomado hindo estonce por almirante; e quando a Lixboa chegou, soube que a nom boa fama que a rrainha sua irmãa aviia com o conde Joham Fernandez era cada vez muito peor e de maa guisa pobricada a todos; em tanto que pôs em sua voontade de o matar, segundo acerca verees adeante, honde fallarmos da morte do conde.

way, the Earl of Cambridge took his leave of him, and arrived at
Almada with his wife, son and followers on the first day of
September, in order to embark in the Castilian ships. The Castilians
were very unhappy to be taking the English, who were their enemies,
on board their ships; but they were forced to obey the commands of
their king. The weather was favourable and so they departed without
more ado. Of the other ships which now profited by the peace
treaty to lie at safety in front of the city, some took cargo on board
and others did not, but they all went away wherever they wished.

At this time, the King arrived in Rio Maior, and while he was
there for a few days, Cardinal Pedro de Luna[1] came to him on
behalf of the self—styled Pope Clement, asking for his obedience and
for him to take his side as he had done before the arrival of the
English. The King summoned certain scholars from Lisbon: men like
Doctor Gil do Sem[2] and Rui Lourenço, the Dean of Coimbra,[3] and
others. With them came Doctor João das Regras,[4] who had recently
arrived from studying in Bologna. After some days of consultation
with these men, the King reverted to a position of obedience to that
Pope Clement as previously, even though this was done very much
against the advice of some of them; especially of Doctor João das
Regras, who told the King that he would demonstrate how, in law,
Clement was not the true Pope. Then Pedro de Luna left for
Avignon, and the King sent his favourite, João Gonçalves, and the
Bishop of Lisbon, Don Martín, in two galleys to give obedience to
that Pope Clement. At the outset the King had sent to Seville for
his galleys and men captured at the battle of Saltes, as had been
agreed in the treaty. Master Lançarote went there, with enough men
to bring them all back, the ships and all the people who had lain in
prison for eighteen months. There came Count João Afonso Telo,
who had been captured amongst them whilst occupying the post of
Admiral. When he arrived in Lisbon, he learnt that the dishonour
that had come upon his sister the Queen through her liaison with
Count Juan Fernández was getting ever greater and was being noised
abroad by everyone; so much so that he decided to kill him, as you
will see hereafter when we describe the death of the Count.

The closing chapters of the Chronicle of Fernando I narrate the events leading up to the eventual marriage between Juan I of Castile and Princess Beatriz of Portugal, the death of Fernando I himself, how Queen Leonor becomes Regent of Portugal, and the mixed reception that greets this news.

After the signing of the peace treaties comes news that the Castilian Queen, Leonor of Navarre, has died in childbirth. When Fernando learns that King Juan is now a widower, he decides to renege on the commitment to wed his daughter Beatriz to the Castilian Prince, Fernando, as had been agreed in the Treaty of Badajoz and instead to seek to marry her to Juan I himself. The latter is agreeable seeing that it affords him the chance of becoming King of Portugal (CLVII).

Juan Fernández Andeiro travels to Castile and there the treaty is ratified in April of 1383. By its provisions, Princess Beatriz will inherit the kingdom if Fernando I dies without a male heir. If Beatriz dies without issue and there is no other heir from the marriage between Fernando and Queen Leonor, the throne will be inherited by Juan I of Castile. While Beatriz lives and until she gives birth and also her child reaches the age of fourteen, Queen Leonor will remain Regent of Portugal (CLVIII).

In these closing chapters, Juan I brings the new agreement to a conclusion by marrying the Princess Beatriz while King Fernando, by now a very sick man, shows his own disapproval of the match by refusing to allow his Chancellor to attend the wedding in Badajoz and by sending an envoy to England to apologize for this new political development and make known to the English that none of this is of his own making. According to Fernão Lopes, as Fernando lies dying, Juan I makes it clear that he has no intention of honouring the treaty but will claim the Portuguese throne as soon as the Portuguese King is dead. In his description of that death, which follows soon after, Fernão Lopes reports that the King considers himself guilty of leaving his country in great peril and weeps openly, asking God's forgiveness for this. Fernando I died on the night of 22 October in the year 1383 (CLIX—CLXXII).

With Fernando's death Leonor Teles assumes the power and position of Regent, styling herself 'Dona Leonor by the grace of God, Queen, Governor and Regent of the kingdoms of Portugal and Algarve'. Before a deputation of citizens of Lisbon, she undertakes to rule Portugal with the aid of a council composed entirely of native Portuguese (CLXXIII—CLXXIV).

After receiving news of Fernando's death, his daughter, Beatriz, and her husband, the King of Castile, write to Queen Leonor asking her to declare in their favour for the succesion. They write in this same manner to many governors of citadels all over Portugal. In Lisbon in particular, there emerges a strong current of opinion in support of the claims of the elder of the bastard sons of Inés de Castro, Dom João, for many fear that otherwise Portugal will simply

152

be absorbed by Castile (CLXXV). The same thing happens in many other towns; notably in Santarém where an attempt is made to lynch the governor of the citadel and in Elvas, where, when the standard is raised in favour of Queen Beatriz, an opposition standard is promptly raised in favour of 'Portugal', and the castle is attacked when the leader of the opposition protest is arrested. However, at the official funeral of King Fernando, Alfonso López de Tejada delivers letters to the Queen and barons of Portugal on behalf of the King of Castile reminding them all that his wife, Queen Beatriz, who is also King Fernando's daughter, is the legitimate heir to the throne, while he, being her husband, is their king and lord. The barons reply that they accept Dona Beatriz as their queen and are disposed to adhere to the treaties concluded between King Juan and King Fernando. López Tejada returns to Castile with this reply (CLXXVI—CLXXVIII).

* * *

THE CHRONICLE OF DOM JOÃO
CRÓNICA DEL REI DOM JOÃO I

*In the prologue to this, the last of his three extant Lives of
Portuguese monarchs, Fernão Lopes departs from his custom of
introducing the physical and moral characteristics and
accomplishments of the new king, in order to present, instead, his
conception of how history should be written. His historiographical*

PROLOGO

G RAMDE licêça deu a afeiçom a muitos, que teverõ carrego dor.
denar estorias, moormente dos senhores em cuja merçee e terra
viviam, e hu forom nados seus antiigos avoos, seemdo lhe
muiito favoravees no rrecomtamento de seus feitos; e tall favoreza
como esta naçe de mumdanall afeiçom, a quall nom he, salvo comformidade dalguũa cousa ao emtemdimento do homẽ. Assi que a terra
em que os homẽes per lomgo costume e tempo forom criados, geera
huũa tall comformidade amtre o seu emtemdimento e ella, que avemdo
de julgar alguũa sua cousa, assi em louvor como per contrairo, numca
per elles he dereitamente rrecomtada; porque louvamdoa, dizem sempre mais daquello que he; e sse doutro modo, nom escprevem suas
perdas, tam mimguadamente como acomteçerom.

Outra cousa geera aimda esta comformidade e naturall inclinaçom,
segundo semtença dalguũs, dizemdo que o pregoeiro da vida, que he
a fame, reçebemdo rrefeiçom pera o corpo, o sangue e spritus geera-
dos de taaes viamdas, tem huũa tall semelhamça amtre ssi, que causa
esta comformidade. Alguũs outros teverom, que esto deçia na semente,
no tempo da geeraçom; a quall despõe per tall guisa aquello que
della he geerado, que lhe fica esta comformidade, tam bẽ açerca da
terra, como de seus dividos.

E assi pareçe que o sentio Tullio, quamdo veo a dizer: *Nos nom
somos nados a nos mesmos, porque huũa parte de nos tem a terra, e outra os paremtes.* E porem ho joizo do homem, açerca de tall terra ou
pessoas, rrecomtamdo seus feitos, sempre çopega.

Esta mundanall afeiçom fez a alguũs estoriadores, que os feitos de
Castella, com os de Portugall escpreverom, posto que homẽs de boa
autoridade fossem, desviar da dereita estrada, e correr per semideiros
escusos, por as mimguas das terras de que eram, em çertos passos
claramente nom seerem vistas; e espiçiallmente no gramde desvairo, que
o mui virtuoso Rei da boa memoria dom Joham, cujo rregimento e rrei-

ideal is of such exceptional interest that, although it has no direct relevance to the English interventions in Portuguese affairs in the fourteenth century, it justifies translating in full this extraordinary prologue.

PROLOGUE

The force of sentiment has caused those whose task has been to write history to take liberties, especially when writing about those great men on whom the historian may depend, and within whose territories they may live, and where their ancestors were also born; so that in relating the deeds of these great men, they show great partiality. This partiality stems from a worldly affection that is no more than the way in which human understanding relates to the real world around it. Thus, so strong a sense of identification is created between the land to which men have been accustomed and in which for so long they have lived, and their own understanding, that when the time comes to take stock of any aspect of that land, whether the aspect is positive or negative, they are incapable of doing so impartially; for if they praise, they exaggerate; while if the reverse, they fail to give as full an account as they should of the failings of their country.

According to some, this conformity and natural inclination is due to the fact that hunger is the sign of life, drawing food into the body, while blood and spirit, being generated through identical sustenance, are therefore so alike, that such conformity is inevitable. Others hold that this conformity stems from the seed at the moment of fecundation, which controls to such an extent that which is generated from it, that it leaves the imprint of country and ancestry upon it.

It seems that this is what Cicero meant when he averred: "We are not born of ourselves but rather a part of us comes from the soil, and another part from our forebears."[1] And so, when it comes to judging the reality of our own land or people of our own nationality, and narrating their actions, a man must always fail.

This natural subjectivity has caused some historians who have written of matters involving Castile and Portugal, although they may have been authoritative writers, to stray from the right path and to take short cuts so that at certain points the failings of their countries would not be seen. This has happened particularly in the case of the most virtuous King João of happy memory, whose regency and reign henceforth concern us, and of the serious conflict he had with the

nado se segue, ouve com ho nobre e poderoso Rei dom Joham de Castella, poemdo parte de seus boõs feitos fora do lovor que mereçiam, e emademdo em alguũs outros, da guisa que nom acomteçerom, atrevemdosse a pubricar esto, em vida de taaes que lhe forom companheiros, bem sabedores de todo o comtrairo. Nos certamente levamdo outro modo, posta adeparte toda afeiçom, que por aazo das ditas rrazoões aver podiamos, nosso desejo foi em esta obra escprever verdade, sem outra mestura, leixamdo nos boõs aqueeçimentos todo fimgido louvor, e nuamente mostrar ao poboo, quaaes quer comtrairas cousas, da guisa que aveherõ.

E sse o Senhor Deos a nos outorgasse o que a allguũs escrevemdo nom negou, convem a saber, em suas obras clara certidom da verdade, sem duvida nom soomente memtir do que sabemos, mas ahimda erramdo, falsso nom quiriamos dizer; como assi seja que outra cousa nom he errar, salvo cuidar que he verdade aquello que he falsso. E nos emgamdo per ignoramçia de velhas scprituras e desvairados autores, bem podiamos ditamdo errar; porque scprevendo homem do que nom he çerto, ou contara mais curto do que foi, ou fallara mais largo do que deve; mas mentira em este volume, he muito afastada da nossa voomtade. Oo! com quamto cuidado e diligemçia vimos gramdes vollumes de livros, de desvairadas limguageẽs e terras; e isso meesmo pubricas escprituras de muitos cartarios e outros logares nas quaaes depois de longas vegilias e gramdes trabalhos, mais çertidom aver nom podemos da contheuda em esta obra.

E seemdo achado em alguũs livros o comtrairo do que ella falla, cuidaae que nom sabedormente, mas erramdo muito, disserom taaes cousas. Se outros per ventuira em esta cronica buscam fremosura e novidade de pallavras, e nom a çertidom das estorias, desprazer lhe ha de nosso rrazoado, muito ligeiro a elles douvir, e nom sem gram trabalho a nos de hordenar.

Mas nos, nom curando de seu juizo, leixados os compostos e afeitados rrazoamentos, que muito deleitom aquelles que ouvem, amte poemos a simprez verdade, que a afremosemtada falssidade. Nem emtemdaaes que certeficamos cousa, salvo de muitos aprovada, e per escprituras vestidas de fe; doutra guisa, ante nos callariamos, que escprever cousas falssas.

Que logar nos ficaria pera a fremosura e afeitamento das pallavras, pois todo nosso cuidado em isto despeso, nom abasta pera hordenar a nua verdade. Porem apegamdonos a ella firme, os claros feitos, dignos de gramde rrenembrança, do mui famoso Rei dom Joham seemdo Meestre, de que guisa matou o Comde Joham Fernamdez, e como o poboo de Lixboa o tomou primeiro por seu rregedor e deffensor, e depois outros alguũs do rregno, e dhi em deamte como rregnou e em que tempo, breve e sãamente comtados, poemos em praça na seguimte hordem.

noble and powerful King Juan of Castile; for these writers omitted to give due praise to certain of his deeds, while they added others inaccurately, daring to publish them within the lifetime of persons who shared with him in these events and who knew perfectly well that the truth was otherwise. We are following a different route and, putting to one side all the affection which we might have by reason of the said causes, we have wanted to write in this work only the unadulterated truth, omitting all feigned praise from the good events and simply showing the people whatever negative things may have happened, just as they did happen. If God were to vouchsafe to us what He did not deny to some others, that is to say, the gift of telling the truth in their writings, we would most certainly refrain not only from lying but also from making false statements through error, for to err is no more nor less than to assume to be true that which is false. Now we too, persuaded by the ignorance of old documents and of various authors, are quite capable of making mistakes; for when a man writes about something of which he is unsure, he will end up saying too little or too much. However, to tell lies is the very last thing that we wish to do. If you could only know with what care and diligence we have consulted an enormous number of books in diverse languages and from many countries, as well as official documents from numerous archives and other places by means of which, after long and arduous study, we are as certain as it is possible to be concerning the content of this work!

If by chance you discover in some other books the contrary of what you find here, be assured that they have said such things through ignorance and much error. If others by chance are looking in this chronicle for beauty and linguistic novelty rather than for the truth of these accounts, they will find no pleasure in our discourse, which is so easy for them to hear but cost us so much effort in the composing.

However, disregarding the attitude of such people, and putting on one side all those affected and pretentious arguments that so delight those that hear them, our intention is to set forth the simple truth, rather than decorated untruth. Neither should you assume that we state anything save that which is confirmed by many people and by documented evidence. If this were not so, we would rather remain silent than write what is untrue.

What place is there for beauty and decoration in what we say, for all our great efforts expended in this history are insufficient to set down the naked truth? So we shall adhere steadfastly to the truth and relate the fine deeds, worthy of remembrance, of the most famous King João, at the time he was Master of Avis; how he killed Count Juan Fernández and how the people of Lisbon and, later, some others in the kingdom, adopted him firstly as their regent and defender, and how and when he became king thereafter. These things we shall make known, briefly and soberly, in the order that ensues.

Fernão Lopes, indeed, honours in the opening chapters of Part I of his chronicle of João I, his promise made at the close of the prologue, to give some account of the circumstances in which Count Juan Fernández was killed, opining moreover that it was God's will that the Count should die by the hand of the man who was to be King of Portugal — Dom João, the Master of the Order of Avis. After some other attempts are made on Andeiro's life, the Master consents to take charge of the assassination, provided that he can be assured of the assistance of the people of Lisbon (I—VI).

The Master and his supporters invade the palace and murder Andeiro in the Queen's presence. Supporters of Queen Leonor and her dead lover flee the palace for their lives while the populace, under the impression that, on the contrary, it is the Master whose

XX

Das rrazoões que os da çidade deziam ao Meestre por que sse nom devia de partir.

A MDAMDO o poboo assi levamtado, posto em trabalho de fallar em tam gramdes duvidas; e veêdo no Meestre tamta autoridade, que pera os deffemder era perteemçemte, ardiam todos com cobiiça de o averem por senhor; e fallamdo huũs com os outros deziam: *Que estamos fazemdo? Tomemos este homem por deffemsor, ca sua discriçom e fortelleza he tamta, que abastara pera empuxar todollos periigoos que nos aviinr podem.*

Estomçe chegarom a elle, pedimdo lhe por merçee que os nom quisesse desemparar leixamdo elles e o rregno todo, que com tamto trabalho fora gaanhado pellos Reis domde elle viinha, em poder de Castellaãos; ca elles bem çertos eram, que elRei de Castella era a pressa chamado da Rainha; e viimdo ao rregno poderosamente era per força de sse asenhorar delle, se nom tevesse quem no defemder, e elles postos em mezquinha e rrefeçe sojeiçom; e que porem lhe pediam por merçee, que sse nom quisesse partir, mas que ficasse na çidade, ca elles o queriam tomar por senhor, que os rregesse e mamdasse em toda cousa.

E sse per vemtuira lʰo Iffamte dom Joham vehesse e lhe o rregno perteençesse per dereito, que o tomariam por rei, doutra guisa nom; e seemdo assi como todos cuidavom, que elles o tomariam por seu rei e senhor; e que sse asenhorasse logo dos tesouros e alfamdega e almazeẽs, e de todollos outros dereitos e cousas que perteeçiam ao Rei; e que elles o poeriam em posse do castello e fortelleza da çidade; e que escprevessem cartas per todo o rregno de como sse esta cousa fazia, e que elles eram çertos que os mais de todollos logares teeriam esta teemçom,

life is threatened, take to the streets and riot in his favour. During the riot the Bishop of Lisbon is killed because he is a Castilian who was appointed by the Avignonese Pope, Clement VII. The Master exonerates himself before the Queen saying that he killed Andeiro because the latter threatened his life. The populace continues to rampage and threatens the Jews, whom the Master is obliged to protect (VII—XIV)

Fernão Lopes describes how the Queen leaves for Alenquer with her train, while the Master himself contemplates flight from Lisbon, for he too fears for his life. Meanwhile, the people seek ways of persuading him to stay to protect them against the Castilians. As he prepares to sail for England, pressure is put upon him (XV—XIX).

XX
Of the arguments put forward to the Master by the citizens of Lisbon to persuade him not to leave

Now the people had risen up in revolt and were in a mood to voice their considerable worries. They recognized in the Master a man of such great authority that they felt him to be up to the task of defending them. Everyone was most eager to have him as their lord. So, in discussing the issue among themselves, they posed the question as follows: "What are we waiting for? Let us adopt this man as our defender, for his discretion and fortitude are such that he would be equal to any dangers that can possible befall us."

Then they came to see him, begging him not to leave them and the whole kingdom, which had been won with much sacrifice by his royal ancestors, at the mercy of the Castilians. For they were convinced that the King of Castile was being hastily summoned by the Queen; and if he came into the kingdom with a large force, he was bound to conquer it if there was no one there to defend it, and then they would be placed in wretched and miserable servitude. This being so, they begged the Master not to leave, but to stay in the city, for they would like to accept him as their lord to rule them and govern them in all matters.

If Prince João were to come back, and the kingdom were to belong to him by right, they would accept him as king; but not otherwise. Since the present circumstances gave them such cause for concern, they would be prepared to accept the Master as their lord and king; and he could take possession, there and then, of the treasury, the customs house and the arsenal, and of all the other royal rights and property; and they would give him possession of the castle and fortress of the city. They would write letters to the whole kingdom informing everyone of what was happening, and they were sure that all the other towns would be of the same mind for fear of

por nom cahirem em poder de Castellaãos. Desi deziam lhe com esto, como por seerem da sua parte na morte do Comde Joham Fernamdez, e cousas que sse estomçe acomteçerom, eram postos em gramde homezio da Rainha, per cujo aazo era forçado, nom teemdo quem sse por elles poer, de rreçeberem gram dano nos corpos e nas fazemdas.

Com taaes ditos e outros semelhamtes se trabalhavom todos de mover o Meestre a sse nom partir da çidade, e ficar no rregno por seu defemssor; mas elle se escusava com boas e doçes rrazoões, esforçamdoos quamto podia com pallavras de comforto, que nehuũs delles rreçeber podiam, nehuũa cousa lhe outorgamdo do que lhe em tall feito hiam rrequerer ; e elles nom embargamdo esto, quamtas vezes o Meestre cavallgava pella villa, era assi acompanhado do comuũ poboo, como sse das maãos delle caissem tesouros que todos ouvesse[m] dapanhar.

E seguindoo as gemtes com gramde prazer, huũs lhe travavam da rredea da besta, outros das falldras da vestidura ; e braadando todos deziam altas vozes, que os nom quisesse desemparar, mas ficasse no rregno por senhor e regedor prometemdolhe cada huũ das rriquezas e averes que tiinham, offereçemdo os corpos aa morte por seu serviço ; e elle olhavoos rriindo do que deziam; e assi chegavom cõ ell ataa homde o Meestre pousava, e desi tornavomsse.

XXI
Da maneira que a Rainha hordenou pera matar ho Meestre quamdo soube que sse queria partir pera Imgraterra.

Nom tem ho odio menos semtido daver vimgamça daquell que desama, que o amor de trigosos pemssamentos, de çedo possuir quem muito deseja ; e assi como homde ha mui grãde amor se geeram desvairados cuidados, por çedo percallçar a fim de seu desejo, assi o que tem rramcor dalguũa pessoa, nom çessa pemssar desvairados caminhos com que apague a sede da sua mortall sanha. E por tamto a Rainha dona Lionor per voomtade femenina que geerallmente he muito desejador de vimgamça, desi husamdo dhuũ gramdioso coraçom de que natureza lhe nom fora escassa, nehuũa cousa por estomçe a seu emtemdimento era mais rrepresemtada, que cuidar ameude todollos modos, per que do Meestre podesse aver comprida ememda. E seemdo çerta como sse ell trigava pera partir ẽ naves que ja tiinha bem abitalhadas e sse hir pera Imgraterra ; e que nehuũs rrogos nem prezes do poboo o podiã fazer rreteer, emtemdeo que a viimda delRei de Castella nom podia tam a pressa seer, que sse ell muito mais çedo per mar nom partisse.

E leixado o modo da viimda delRei que terminado tiinha pera delle seer vimgada, cuidou dordenar per outra maneira, per que de morto

162

falling under Castilian domination. Moreover, they told him that at the moment their lives and their property were bound to be in great danger from the Queen, unless someone defended them, because they had taken the Master's side over the killing of Juan Fernández and the subsequent events.

With these arguments and others besides, they strove to persuade the Master not to leave the city, but to stay in the kingdom as their defender; but he excused himself, politely and affably. He encouraged them as much as he could with words of comfort that none of them would accept, but he would not make any concession at all to their entreaties in this matter. Yet despite this, whenever the Master rode out and about in the city, he was accompanied by the common people as if he were dropping precious treasures for them all to grab. The people enjoyed following him about, some clutching at the reins and others at the sleeves of his tunic, and entreating him incessantly at the tops of their voices not to abandon them but to stay in the kingdom as lord and regent, each one promising him a share of his own wealth and goods, and offering up his life in the Master's service. He, all the while, contemplated them, laughing at what they said; and so they would accompany him all the way to his lodging and only then would they return the way they had come.

XXI
Of the manner in which the Queen ordered the assassination of the Master when she knew that he wanted to leave for England.

Just as love entertains rash thoughts of swift possession of the object of desire, so does hatred experience to an equal degree a lust for vengeance upon the object of hatred. Thus, just as when one feels great love, one can always produce a variety of ideas for achieving one's desired goal, so when one feels a furious rancour towards another, one keeps dreaming up fresh ways of venting one's deadly fury upon that person. The female mind is prone to vengeful desires and so it was with Queen Leonor now. Moreover, as she was by nature proud and courageous, she became at this time obsessed with the Master, turning over constantly in her mind all possible ways imaginable of getting her revenge over him. She knew that he was in some haste to go to England and had had ships already provisioned for the voyage; and she was equally aware that none of the entreaties of the people were able to keep him from the journey and the King of Castile could not possibly arrive before he left. So, laying aside the plan to avenge herself through the invasion of the King of Castile, she decided to achieve her ends in another fashion whereby, whether through death or imprisonment, the Master could not possibly escape.

ou posto em prisom, ho Meestre per nehuũa guisa podesse escapar ; e foi deste geito. Quamdo ella foi çerta que sse o Meestre despoinha pera partir do rregno, pemssou que emtom tiinha muito mais prestes aazo pera o aver aa maão preso ou morto ; e dizem que mamdou fallar em gram segredo com os meestres daquelles navios espeçiallmente com ho meestre daquella naao em que ell avia dhir, prometẽdolhes gramdes e asiinadas merçees se esto quisessem poer em obra, convem a saber : que como as naves fossem atraves da costa da Atouguia que ssam quatorze legoas da çidade, que tevessem geito os meestres e marinheiros de sse todos meter nos batees e hir em terra; e leixadas as naaos desemparadas de mareamtes que era per força de viimrem aa costa, e que estomçe seeria forçado de o Meestre em toda guisa seer preso ou morto ; e tall maginaçom lhe pareçeo mui comvinhavel pera seu preposito seer muito mais çedo acabado.

E presumesse que prougue aaquelles a que foi cometido ; porque nom damdo ella tardamça a tal pemssamento, quamdo soube que sse ho Meestre trigava pera embarcar, e nom queria ficar na çidade, fallou esta cousa com Vaasco Perez de Caamoões.

E tamto aaficou sua trigosa voomtade, que amte que fosse çerta se era partido ou nom, ho mamdou duas vezes dAllamquer a Atouguia com çertos homeẽs, que levava comsigo, pera aguardar que como sse esto posesse em obra, lho trouvesse preso alli homde estava, ou çerto rrecado como era morto. E quamdo a Rainha soube de çerto que o Meestre aimda nom partira, e que os da çidade se aficavom em toda guisa de o tomar por senhor, çessou de mamdar saber novas desto, ataa que soubesse se partiia ou nom.

XXII
Das rrazoões que Alvoro Vaasquez ouve com ho Meestre sobre sua partida pera Imgraterra.

SEEMDO no poboo cuidado notavell por sua seguramça e defenssom da terra da guisa que teemdes ouvido, nom embargamdo que sse o Meestre escusasse per suas rrazoões a nom poder ficar em no rregno; as gemtes porem nom leixavom de o seguir, pedimdolhe cada dia por merçee que os nom quisesse desemparar.

E porque era pubrica voz e fama que sse ell hia pera Imgraterra, veemdo Rui Pereira tamto poboo a rredor delle braadamdo todos que o queriam por Senhor, disse huũa tall rrazom comtra ho Mestre : *Querees que vos diga, Senhor? Vos, dizem que vos hiis pera Imgraterra; mas a mim pareçe que boom Lomdres he este.*

Estomçe huũ escudeiro fidallgo que chamavom Alvoro Vaasquez de Gooes chamou o Meestre adeparte, e disse desta guisa: *Vos, Senhor, dizem que hordenaaes de vos partir daqui, e vos hir pera outra terra? E* o Meestre rrespomdeo que ssi.

164

The plan was as follows. When she was quite sure that the Master was preparing to leave the kingdom, she realized that it was imperative for her to imprison or kill him. It is said that she ordered people to speak very secretly to the captains of those ships, and especially to the captain of the ship that was to transport the Master, promising them spectacular rewards if they would obey her orders; that is, that when the ships reached the coast of Atouguia,[1] some fourteen leagues from the city, the captain and the sailors were to take to the boats and come to land. The ships, deprived of their crews, would inevitably drift inshore, and so the Master must surely be either arrested or killed. This seemed to her to be the plan that could most conveniently and swiftly achieve her goal.

You may imagine that this plan was to the liking of those to whom it was put, for without more ado, as soon as she knew that the Master was hastening to embark and did not wish to linger in the city, she spoke to Vasco Peres de Camões.

Her impatience was such that, even before she knew for certain whether he had embarked or not, she sent certain men of her company twice from Alenquer to Atouguia to wait there so that as soon as the plan had been carried out, they should bring her either the Master as a prisoner or definite news of his death. When the Queen learned for certain that the Master had still not left and that the citizens of Lisbon were obstinately trying every possible way to make him their lord, she stopped asking for news until such time as she could ascertain whether or not he was leaving.

XXII
Of the discussions that Álvaro Vasques had with the Master about his departure for England.

The people were desperately worried about their safety and the defence of the country as you have heard, so that even though the Master made excuses for not staying in the kingdom, the people persisted in following him everywhere, begging him every day not to abandon them.

Now, because it was strongly rumoured that the Master was going to England, seeing so many people around him crying out that they wanted him to be their lord, Rui Pereira spoke to him in this fashion : "Shall I tell you something, my lord? They are saying that you are going to England, but it seems to me that this is as good a place as London." Then a gentleman squire named Álvaro Vasques de Góis called the Master on one side and spoke to him thus: "My lord, they say you are arranging to leave here to go to another country?" The Master confirmed that this was true.

Que rrazom vos move, disse ell, *pera fazerdes tall partida?*

Mooveme, disse ho Meestre, *a viimda delRei de Castella, que he certo que sse vem aqui. Desi os moores do rregno teem todos da parte da Rainha, a quall me quer mui gram mall por a morte do Comde Joham Fernamdez, e som çerto que me aazara todo mall e desomrra per hu quer que poder.*

Pera quall parte, disse o Escudeiro, *vos emtemdees de partir?*

Emtemdo, disse o Meestre, *de me hir pera Imgraterra.*

Que vida emtemdees la de fazer? disse Alvoro Vaasquez.

Emtemdo, disse elle, *servir elRei na guerra que ouver com seus ēmiigos, e gaanhar aquella homrra e fama que todollos boōs desejam percalçar.*

Em verdade, Senhor, disse Alvoro Vaasquez, *eu nom ssei em isto bem vossa voomtade; mas peçovos por merçee que me digaaes, posto que vos la amdees quamto tempo quiserdes, e que sirvaaes mui bem elRei, como eu emtemdo que o vos servirees, quamdo emtemdees vos la de cobrar outra tam boa çidade per força darmas, como a çidade de Lixboa em que vos estaaes, hu sse offereçem os moradores della, a vos servir e dar quamto teem, ataa morrerem por vos ajudar? E sse vos em outra terra emtemdees de servir por alcamçar homrra em feito darmas; hu podees vos moor serviço fazer, e que melhor rrenembramça fique de vos, que a terra que foi gaamçada per os nobres Reis dhu vos desçemdees e domde sooes naturall; moormente com gemtes que tamto de coraçom e de voomtade vos offereçem sua ajuda e serviço?*

Quando ho Meestre ouvio taaes rrazoões, pareçerom lhe boas e começou de cuidar em sua ficada, per que maneira poderia seer com sua homrra e proveito.

The Master of Avis consults a visionary Castilian hermit who puts courage into him, exhorting him not to leave Portugal and prophesying that he and his sons will be kings hereafter (XXIII—XXIV). He takes further counsel and is advised to marry the Queen and thus assure himself of the Regency. Queen Leonor refuses this offer when the ambassadors visit her in Alenquer. In any case, hearing news of the approaching Castilians, the populace turns its back on the Queen and clamours for the Master of Avis to claim the Regency. In the Monastery of São Domingos, he finally accepts the offices of Regent and Defender of the realm (XXV—XXVI).

Fernão Lopes stresses that it is not the Master's intention to reign, despite the prophetic words of the hermit, but he is won over by the enthusiasm of the people. Nevertheless, he makes contact with

"What prompts you to make such a move?" he enquired.

"I am prompted", said the Master, "by the approach of the King of Castile who is certainly coming here. Also, there is the fact that the nobles are all on the Queen's side, and she bears a mortal grudge against me for the death of Count Juan Fernández. I am certain that she will do me as much harm and bring me as much dishonour as she possibly can."

"Where are you bound for when you depart?" asked the squire.

"I intend to go to England", said the Master.

"What manner of life do you intend to live there?" asked Álvaro Vasques.

"I intend to serve the King of England in any war he may have with his enemies", replied the Master, "thereby winning the honour and fame that all good men strive to obtain."

"Truly, my lord", said Álvaro Vasques, "I cannot know your thoughts on this matter, but I entreat you to tell me this. Even though you may spend as long as you like there, and no matter how well you may serve the King (and I am sure that you will serve him well), when do you expect to win by force of arms over there a city as fine as Lisbon, the city in which you now are and the citizens of which have laid at your feet all their worldly goods as well as their lives to be used in your service? You intend to serve in another country to win honour through force of arms and yet, where better to serve and to win the admiration of posterity, than in the land that was won by the noble kings your forebears and in which you were born; all the more alongside people who stoutly and willingly offer you their support and their service?"

When the Master heard these arguments, they seemed to him persuasive, so that he began to ponder on how best to stay whilst protecting his honour and profit.

---

the imprisoned Prince João in Castile, who replies, urging support for João de Avis in his name. Meanwhile, the Queen leaves Alenquer for Santarém on the advice of Gonçalo Vasques de Azevedo, but not before reminding the inhabitants that the town is hers (XXVII—XXX).

At this point, Fernão Lopes chooses to interrupt the chronology of his narrative in order to discuss at length the figure of Nun'Alvares Pereira. After this biographical interlude full of prophecy and portent, the chronicler describes how Nun'Alvares declares in favour of the Master while his followers declare their unanimous support. He arrives in Lisbon to a joyous welcome. Nun'Alvares declares himself free of all ties of vassalage towards the Queen. The section describing his adhesion to the Master's cause concludes with his mother's attempt to dissuade him. In the end, it

is the son who converts the mother to that cause (XXXI–XXXIX).

Turning to the problems of João of Avis who must face the combined power of Queen Leonor and the King of Castile, Fernão Lopes describes how he decides once and for all not to go to England. At the same time, the commander of the fortress of Lisbon surrenders it to him and comes over to the Master's side with

---

XLVII

Por que rraẑom emviou o Meestre Embaixadores a Imgraterra, e da rreposta que lhe de lla veo.

PORQUE toda rrazom naturall outorga, que melhor e mais poderosamente podem os muitos dar fim a huũa gram cousa quamdo a começar querem, que os poucos por mui ardidos que sejam, hordenou o Meestre com os de seu Comsselho, que era bem daver gemtes em sua ajuda. E acordarom de emviar pedir a elRei de Imgraterra, que lhe prouguese dar logar e leçemça aos de seu rregno, que por solldo aa sua voomtade o vehessem ajudar comtra seus emmiigos.

E foi hordenado de hirem la por seus Embaxadores Louremço Martïiz criado do Meestre, que depois foi Alcaide de Leirea, e Tomas Daniell, Imgres; os quaaes partirom em duas naaos dante a çidade em aquell mes de dezembro; e depois foi acordado de mamdarem dom FernamdAffomsso dAlboquerque Meestre da Hordem de Samtiago, e LouremçEanes Fogaça Chamceller moor que fora delRei dom Fernamdo, o quall emtõ na See o Meestre fez cavalleiro amte que partisse.

Omde sabee, que este dõ Fernamdo Affomsso dAlboquerque, estamdo na villa de Pallmella, se veo com todas suas gemtes a Lixboa pera o Meestre, e o rreçebeo por senhor, e ficou por seu vassallo pera o servir. Mas porem nom embargamdo esto, por quamto ell fora feito pella Rainha, rreçeamdosse del que sse poderia deitar com elRei de Castella, e lhe dar as fortellezas do Meestrado, disserom que era bem que fosse por Embaxador, por seer allomgado de tall aazo; desi que era moor homrra do Meestre emviar taaes Embaxadores, que de mais pequena comdiçom, outorgarom todos de o emviar.

E embarcarõ em dous navios, ho Meestre em huũa naao, e Louremce Anes em huũa barcha e forom sua viagem; e chegarom daquel dia a oito dias que era sesta feira, a hũa villa que chamam Preamua, logar de Imgraterra; e dalli ouverom bestas, e emcaminharom pera Lomdres homde elRei estomçe estava, e forom dell bem rreçebidos, e de todollos senhores e fidallgos da corte. E [despois que forão falar ao Duque dAlan-

all his men (XL—XLI).

Fernão Lopes now relates how, despite the fear instilled into some people by the Queen's representatives who still hold many towns and city fortresses, the people rebel, taking several of these including Beja, Portalegre, Estremoz and Évora XLII—XLVI).

XLVII
Of the reasons why the Master sent ambassadors to England, and of the reply that came back to him from that country.

It stands to reason that a large number of people are in a far better position to bring a great enterprise to a successful conclusion than are a small number, no matter how valiant. Mindful of this, the Master and his council decided that it would be advantageous to obtain men from outside to help them. So they resolved to send word to the King of England, asking that he might see fit to give leave to soldiers of his kingdom to come of their own free will as mercenaries to aid the Master against his enemies.

So it was ordained that Lourenço Martins, one of the Master's servants who subsequently became castellan of Leiria, and Thomas Daniel,[1] an Englishman, should go to England as ambassadors. These two men departed from the city in two ships in the month of December. Later, it was agreed to send Dom Fernando Afonso de Albuquerque,[2] Master of the Order of São Tiago and Lourenço Eanes Fogaça,[3] who had been the Grand Chancellor of King Fernando and whom the Master dubbed knight in the cathedral before he left.

You need to know that this Dom Fernando Afonso de Albuquerque, who had been in Palmela, had come to the Master in Lisbon with all his followers, and there recognized him as his lord and became a vassal in his service. However, despite this, since he had been made Master of São Tiago by the Queen, there was the fear that he might throw in his lot with the King of Castile and hand over to him the strongholds of his Mastership, and therefore it was considered prudent that he should go as ambassador for in that way he would be kept from having such an opportunity. In any case, there was more honour for the Master in sending such great men as ambassadors than in sending ones of humbler rank. Therefore, they all agreed he should go.

They embarked in two vessels, the Master of São Tiago in a ship and Lourenço Eanes in a barge; and eight days later they landed in England on a Friday at a town called Plymouth. They obtained mounts there and travelled to London where the King then was. He welcomed them and so did the lords and nobles of his

castro, ordenou elRei de ter conçello em hũa cidade de Sarasbri, despois que o Duque veo, onde os Embaxadores] preposerom sua embaxada, cuja cornclusom em breve era esta: Que seemdo o rreino per seu aazo despachado e livre dos emmiigos, que toda ajuda que os Portugueeses fazer podessem, assi de gallees come de seus corpos, omde ell mais por seu serviço emtemdesse, que eram muito prestes de o fazer [e que se o Duque dAlencastro por seu corpo vir quisesse cobrar o regno de Castella que lhe por azo de sua molher de direito pertençia, que tinhão o tempo muito prestes e todo Portugal em sua ajuda], levamdo o Meestre e LouremçEanes pera firmar esto, e outras cousas, grandes e largos poderios, per procuraçom do Meestre e de Lixboa e do Porto.

 EllRei avudo sobrello acordo, prougue a ell, e a todollos do Comsselho, que quaaes quer gemtes darmas que por seu solldo em ajuda de Portugall lhes prougesse viinr, que livremente o podessem fazer, juramdo elRei e prometemdo, que nom faria menos pera poer em obra toda boa ajuda que neeste feito dar podesse, do que faria por deffemder seu rreino.

E por quamto o Duque dAllamcastro era em Calles, a trautar tregoa com elRei de Framça, e esperavom por elle cedo, pera lhe elRei dar emcarrego como sse esto melhor emcaminhasse, trabalhou emtamto o Meestre e LouremçEanes Fogaça, de emviar alguũas gemtes darmas e archeiros, por a neçessidade em que o rregno estava, porem forom poucos; das quaaes eram capitaães huũ que chamavom Elisabri, e outro Tersimgom, e huũ cavalleiro gascom que avia nome mossem Gavilho de Momferro. E elles prestes pera partir em duas naaos, mamdou ho Meestre Louremço Martïiz ao dito logar de Preamua pera os fazer viinr e embarcarem alli; e ell como hi chegou meteosse com elles nos navios e veosse a Portugall como adeamte diremos; da quall cousa o Meestre e LouremçEanes Fogaça ouverom mui gramde queixume por sse viinr daquella guisa.

E tamto prougue aos Imgreses desta ajuda que lhe os Portugueeses rrequerir emviavom, que muitos hi ouve que lhe emprestarom dinheiros pera paga do solldo das gemtes que logo aviam de emviar. Assi come mosse Nicoll, Mayre de Londres, e Amrrique Bivembra cavalleiro, que lhe emprestarom tres mill e quinhemtos nobres, e assi outros mais e menos como cada huũ podia; de guisa que com esto e com as mercadarias dos Portugueeses que la achavom que tomavom a seus donos per escripto, dizemdo que lhas pagariam depois, comtemtavom as gemtes per tall modo que lhes prazia viinr com leda voomtade.

E a rreposta que elRei de Imgraterra emviou ao Meestre sobresta ajuda que lhe emtom foi demamdada, podees veer per esta seguïte carta:

court. After they had been to speak to the Duke of Lancaster, the King convened his council in the city of Salisbury,[4] once the Duke had arrived. In the course of this council, the ambassadors explained the motive for their embassy, the conclusion of which can be summarized as follows. Once their kingdom had been freed from its enemies by his help, the Portuguese were willing to put at the disposal of the English King both galleys and soldiers for him to use in whatever way he might think best. Secondly, if the Duke of Lancaster were disposed to come personally to claim the kingdom of Castile, which rightfully belonged to him by reason of his wife, the moment was opportune and all Portugal was at his service to this end. The Master of São Tiago and Lourenço Eanes had been given full authority by the Master of Avis and the cities of Lisbon and Oporto to sign this agreement and any other.

Once there was general agreement on the offer the King and his council announced that any men—at—arms who might wish to go to help Portugal for pay should be free to do so; and the King swore that he would strive as hard to give Portugal all the help he could as he would to defend his own kingdom.

Seeing that the Duke of Lancaster was in Calais negotiating a truce with the King of France and was expected home shortly so that the King could place in his hands responsibility for how best to proceed in the enterprise, meanwhile, the Master of São Tiago and Lourenço Eanes Fogaça went to work recruiting men—at—arms and archers, given the urgent need in their own country. However, these were only a small force, of which the captains were Elias Blyth, Cressyngham and Guilhem de Montferrand, a Gascon knight.[5]

Once they were ready to leave in two ships, the Master ordered Lourenço Martins to get them to the aforementioned place, Plymouth, for embarcation. When Lourenço Martins arrived, he too took ship with them and came to Portugal, as we shall explain by and by. The Master and Lourenço Eanes Fogaça were extremely annoyed that he went off in this fashion.

The English were so pleased at the help that the Portuguese were asking of them, that there were many who lent them money in order to pay the wages of the men being sent. Those who loaned money included Sir Nicholas, Mayor of London, and Henry Bivembra,[6] a knight, who loaned them three thousand five hundred nobles, together with others who loaned other amounts, greater or less, according to their means. So from these loans and from Portuguese merchandise, impounded and taken from its owners against a written guarantee that they would be reimbursed later, it was possible to pay the soldiers satisfactorily so that they were quite happy to take part in the expedition.

You may judge from the following letter the reply that the King of England sent the Master concerning the aid requested of him:

«Ricardo, pella graça de Deos Rei dImgraterra, e Senhor dIbernia,
«ao mui nobre e gramde barom Johane, per essa meesma graça Mees-
«tre da Hordem da Cavallaria dAvis, Regedor e Deflemssor dos rreinos
«de Portugall e do Algarve, nosso mui preçado amigo, saude e desejo
«de limpa amizade.

«Pouco ha que rreçebemos ledamente os nobres e exçellemtes ca-
«valleiros, Fernamdo, Meestre da Hordem de Samtiago, e Louremço
«Fogaça, Chamceller moor de Portugall, vossos Embaxadores a nos em-
«viados; e claramente emtemdemos todo o que nos da vossa parte dis-
«serom. E çertamente, mui preçado amigo, de coraçom vos gradeçe-
«mos o boom desejo que vos, e os gentiis homeēs dessa terra, a nos
«por vosso aazo teem, segūdo per obra e conheçimento veemos.

«E quamto he ao que nos per elles foi declarado sobre vossos offe-
«reçimētos, assi de serviço de gallees, come doutras cousas. que nos
«desses rregnos compridoiras fossem, isto vos gradeçemos muito; e am-
«tre elles e os do nosso Comsselho, foi sobrello feito çerto trauto, se⁻
«gumdo esse meesmo Louremço vos mais largamente pode rrecontar.
«E pera ho acorrimento que a vos e vossos alliados desses reinos com-
«pridoiro era, nos outorgamos aos ditos Embaxadores, que de nossa terra
«podessem tirar homeēs darmas e frecheiros por seu solldo, quamtos e
«quaaes lhe prouguesse. O que em verdade comsiiramdo as rrevoltosas
«guerras, em que pollo presemte somos postos, assi de ligeiro a outra
«pessoa nõ outorgariamos. E queremos que em huū trauto, que ora com
«nossos aversairos de Framça e de Castella fezemos em Calles, que sse
«emtemdam hi, vos e vossos alliados.

«E bẽ nos prouguera que vossos Embaxadores derom a ello com-
«ssemtimento, mas escusamdosse disserom, que nom aviã de vos tall
«mamdado. E porque o nom tragiam, aquelles que por nossa parte alli
«eram nos [a]ficarom que vos escprevessemos, e isso meesmo os Françe-
«ses por sua parte ao ocupador de Castella, que as tregoas per nos fei-
«tas ataa primeiro dia de mayo seguimte, com os ditos averssairos, dhuūa
«parte aa outra fossem guardados; a quall cousa se o nosso comū aver-
«ssairo, nom quiser comssemtir, nos vos rreservamos propria liberdade,
«pera averdes guarda e deffemssom de nossas gemtes.

«E esto emtemdemos que era bem de escprever aa Vossa Nobreza,
«por fazerdes rrequerer esse vosso averssairo o mais çedo que poder-
«des; por tall que vista sua rreposta, nos com boom e maduro com-
«sselho, possamos esguardar vossa e primçipallmemte nossa comū def-
«femssom. Vos emtanto seede forte, teemdo booa esperamça em Deos,
«creemdo firme que o Rei dos Reis, que he justo, e nom desempara os
«que por justiça pellejam, nom desemparara vossos feitos, mas fazervos
«ha glorioso veemçedor com gramde e homrrada vitoria. Nobre e Ex-
«cellemte Barom, todas vossas obras guye o Senhor Deos, e vivaaes
«boõs e perlongados dias a vosso prazer. Scripta. (L»

Richard, by the grace of God King of England and Lord of Ireland, to the most noble and illustrious man João, by that same grace Master of the Order of Chivalry of Avis, ruler and defender of the kingdoms of Portugal and the Algarve, our very dear friend, greetings and wishes of sincere friendship.

A short while ago we received most gladly the noble and excellent knights Fernando, Master of the Order of São Tiago, and Lourenço Fogaça, Grand Chancellor of Portugal, your ambassadors, who had been sent to us. We understand clearly all that they have told us on your behalf. Certainly, most dear friend, we thank you most sincerely for the goodwill you and the gentlemen of your land have for us in this matter as we see by your words and deeds.

With respect to what they told us concerning your offers, of galleys as well as of other assistance from your kingdoms that might prove useful to us, we thank you heartily. An agreement has been reached over this matter between your ambassadors and our council, of which the said Lourenço will give you fuller information. As to the aid that you and your allies there in Portugal needed, we gave leave to the aforementioned ambassadors to recruit for pay as many men—at—arms and archers as they wished. It must be said, however, that given the rebellious wars in which we are presently embroiled, we would seriously hesitate to give such permission to anyone else.

We want to include you and your allies in a treaty we are negotiating in Calais right now with our adversaries of France and Castile. We should have liked your ambassadors to give their consent to this treaty but they declined saying that they had no mandate from you to do so. Since they brought no mandate, our own negotiators there have urged us to write to you, and the French have written in the same way on their own behalf to the occupier of Castile, that the truce we made up to the first day of next May with the aforementioned adversaries should be kept on both sides. If our common adversary refuses to do so, we reserve full freedom for you so that you may guard and defend our subjects.

We consider it advisable to write this to your Highness so that you may contact your adversary as soon as possible. Then, depending on his reply, after due consideration of the matter, we may be able to see to your defence and, above all, our common defence.

As for you, meanwhile, stand firm and trust in God, in the belief that the King of Kings, who is just and never deserts those who fight for justice, will not fail to support your enterprise, but rather will make you emerge triumphant with a great and glorious victory.

Noble and excellent man, may the Lord God guide all your actions, and may you live well, long and happily.

Written...

Fernão Lopes now explains the disastrous condition of the royal finances in 1383, since King Fernando had squandered in useless warfare the treasures so painstakingly stored up by King Pedro. In order to finance resistance to the Castilian invasion, João of Avis adopts various expedients: he borrows money from the Jews, the clergy and other groups in Lisbon; he issues a new, debased coinage; and he allows certain private individuals to coin money, acquiring great popularity through this and other acts of liberality. In contrast, Nun'Alvares is depicted by Fernão Lopes as losing popularity in the eyes of the Master's council because of what they see as the excessive attention João of Avis pays to his advice (XLVIII–LI).

Meanwhile, in Castile. King Juan I takes steps to neutralize political danger–points. He imprisons Count Alfonso of Noreña and the Portuguese Prince João, whose flight into Castile was narrated in the Chronicle of Dom Fernando. King Juan now orders a funeral service for King Fernando in Toledo cathedral and holds council to decide whether or not to invade Portugal. Some advise against it because this means breaking the treaties made with Fernando I and because it threatens King Juan's honour. He ignores this because of his desire to be King of Portugal and, encouraged by the Bishop of Guarda, he crosses the frontier and is received in that town, though the commander of its citadel refuses to yield to him. Other Portuguese nobles rally to him but some make it plain that their first loyalty is to Queen Leonor as regent (LII–LIX).

Queen Leonor sends letters all over the kingdom declaring that she intends to remain as regent and to write to King Juan requesting him not to enter Portugal because his regency would threaten Portuguese independence. In reality, she writes to him urging him to come as quickly as possible to Santarém, given the insults she has received from the Master of Avis and the citizens of Lisbon. The common people do not support the Queen but are very afraid of a Castilian invasion; and some claim that the Queen wishes King Juan to be the instrument of her vengeance (LX–LXI).

Like Gonçalo Vasques de Azevedo, Lopo Dias de Sousa, the Master of the Order of Christ, is dissuaded from joining the Castilian camp and therefore refrains from receiving King Juan in Tomar. Nun'Alvares urges the Master of Avis to order the ambush of King Juan's forces before they become too numerous, but he considers this to be dangerous and returns to Lisbon (LXIII).

When King Juan reaches Santarém, the Queen, after some hesitation, goes out to meet him, staying the night at his lodgings. After secret talks, she abdicates in his favour and orders the gates opened to the Castilian forces (LXIV–LXV). The Grand Chancellor, Lourenço Eanes Fogaça, is obliged to hand over the royal seals so that others can be made in which the arms of Portugal and Castile will be mixed. He does so and promptly defects as do many others

(LXVI—LXVII). Fernão Lopes laments the state of civil war into which the country is about to plunge but stresses the common people's hostility towards Queen Leonor and Castile *(LXVIII).*

Lisbon has the good luck to capture in the Tagus estuary some Galician ships laden with food. In February, Nun'Alvares is sent on a foraging expedition in the direction of Sintra with a view to preparing for the coming siege *(LXIX—LXXI).*

News reaches the Master from Santarém of Castilian ill—treatment of its populace but he is powerless to help. However, he is able to force a temporary Castilian retreat *(LXXII—LXXV).*

Relations between King Juan and Queen Leonor deteriorate to such an extent that she even urges her followers to desert to the Master of Avis. Juan I moves against Coimbra but fails to persuade the governor to surrender the city to him. A conspiracy between Don Pedro de Trastámara and Queen Leonor is discovered and Don Pedro flees to Oporto. The Queen is sent to a nunnery in Tordesillas (Castile) and the populace of Alenquer, faithful to her, passes over to the Master's side in protest. King Juan now debates whether he should besiege Lisbon. Despite the beginnings of plague among his troops, he decides to do so *(LXXVI—LXXXVI).*

News reaches the Master of Avis that forces led by the Grand Chancellor of Castile, Fernán Sánchez de Tovar, are laying waste the South. In the teeth of João das Regras's opinion that a man of great experience is needed to defend the south—eastern frontier, the Master chooses Nun'Alvares. On the way south, Nun'Alvares tests the commitment of his men and then invites them to elect the members of his council. They do so and at this time begin to call him lord *(LXXXVII—XCI).*

Well received in Évora, Nun'Alvares moves on to Estremoz where he announces to his men news of the presence of a large force in Crato and his intention to take the field against it. They hesitate because of its size and strength. They also point out that Nun'Alvares's brother, the Prior of Crato, is with the Castilians. Despite these arguments, he stands firm *(XCII—XCIII).* A Castilian squire who once lived with him and his brother comes from the Castilian side bearing a message from the Prior to the effect that the coming battle is foolish and that even though he would spare his brother in the fight, he cannot do so. Nun'Alvares rejects the plea and forms up his small squadron. After praying to God and the Virgin for success in the just struggle on behalf of himself, his country and his lord, he repulses the Castilian attack *(XCIV—XCV).* This is the battle of Os Atoleiros.

The next few chapters describe the largely successful exploits of Nun'Alvares and other Portuguese commanders in the south as well as some of their raids across the Castilian border *(XCVI—CVIII).*

Having failed to capture the fortress of Alenquer, the Master concentrates on preparing a fleet to beat the expected blockade of the port of Lisbon. A nocturnal vision of martyrs in procession is

seen from the walls by the watch. On the following day another propitious portent is the arrival of three Castilian ships blown into the Tagus by contrary winds, while four of the Master's galleys are saved from destruction through God's intervention (CIX—CXI).

Meanwhile, the first Castilian land forces set up camp near Lisbon and there is skirmishing beneath the city walls. On 29 May, forty Castilian ships arrive in the Tagus so that the blockade can begin (CXII—CXIV). Even in the presence of the besiegers, work on the outer walls continues together with other preparations. There is also an exchange of noble prisoners; most notably, Diego López Pacheco is exchanged for the Castilian knight, Juan Ramírez de Arellano (CXVI).

Fernão Lopes now turns his attention to Northern Portugal, which Don Juan Manrique, Archbishop of Santiago, has invaded with an army of Portuguese and Castilians, pillaging and laying waste the Minho region. Portuguese nobles in his army advise him that since Oporto is only guarded by peasants, he need not hesitate to attack it; but he himself is more circumspect, which tallies with the customary historical view of Manrique as a person of considerable intelligence and prudence (CXVII—CXVIII). When the defenders counter—attack, he orders a withdrawal. The Portuguese return in triumph to Oporto. The defenders of Oporto now rig ships and carry the war into Galicia (CXIX—CXXIV).

After hints that some of the Master's chief captains are corrupt, Nun'Álvares is forced to borrow money in Coimbra in order to return to Évora while he himself refuses blandishments that come indirectly from the King of Castile. On his way back to the Alentejo he ambushes a Castilian convoy and thus recovers much booty that was on the way to Castile (CXXV—CXXVIII).

After taking council, King Juan decides on a battle in the Tagus estuary. The two fleets meet indecisively on 17 June 1384 (CXXIX—CXXXIII). King Juan then besieges Almada for two months. Many people die of thirst before the town falls (CXXXIV—CXXXVII).

The famous section of the Chronicle describing the siege of Lisbon is prefaced by two inglorious episodes which tell how some Portuguese nobles attempt to sell the city to the Castilians and how the Master is unhorsed in the water during the naval engagement that precedes the siege (CXXXVIII—CXXXIX).

Plague emerges as a significant protagonist in the drama. King Juan is forced to treat with the Master, but achieves no result. The Master meanwhile, haunted by the spectre of starvation, feels forced to fight with the Castilians. He writes to Nun'Álvares appealing for help, but the latter cannot convince his men to join him in a combined attack on the Castilians (CXL—CXLII).

After some chapters devoted to skirmishing by Nun'Álvares and his forces around Almada, Fernão Lopes describes in graphic detail the extreme sufferings of the besieged city of Lisbon in its battle

against hunger *(CXLIII—CXLVIII)*.

Meanwhile, the Castilian camp is suffering just as acutely from the plague. King Juan's son—in—law, the future Carlos III of Navarre (1387—1425), pleads with him to lift the siege in the face of the pestilence, but he stubbornly refuses until Queen Beatriz shows signs of having contracted the disease. Only then does he order his camp raised and burnt, retreating towards Torres Vedras *(CXLIX—CLI)*.

Nun'Álvares now journeys portentously to Lisbon where he warns the Master that some of his nobles may not be loyal, and persuades him that all his supporters should renew their oath of allegiance to him as regent. They are convened in October 1384 and do so. In return, the Master grants certain privileges to the city of Lisbon and demolishes the castle at the citizens' request *(CLII—CLIV)*.

Meanwhile, King Juan reaches Santarém, tricking Gonçalo Vasques de Azevedo into accompanying him into Castile where he is made adelantado of Old Castile *(CLV—CLVI)*.

Fernão Lopes now pauses to take stock of the careers of Nun'Álvares and of João of Avis, and tries to record the names of their chief supporters. Just as Jesus Christ founded His Church on St. Peter, he explains, and gave him all authority over it, and sent out His disciples to preach His Gospel, in the same way the Master of Avis founded his enterprise on Nun'Álvares, and gave him all authority over it, and sent out his followers to preach the 'Portuguese Gospel' of support for Pope Urban VI, and the defence of Portuguese independence *(CLVII—CLXIII)*.

The Master makes an abortive attempt to take Sintra but is thwarted by a great flood and returns, ingloriously, to Lisbon. The people of Almada show their loyalty to him, despite hostages taken by the King of Castile. The Master besieges Alenquer but does not take the town. He obtains its loyalty but only on its terms *(CLXIV—CLXVIII)*.

He now attacks Torres Vedras. In November of the same year, 1384, the Master of Christ also tries without success and is captured by the Castilians. Meanwhile, Nun'Álvares expels Gil Fernandes and others from Elvas. His brother is killed in an attempt to take Vila Viçosa. The forces holding Gaia oppress the populace of the region who complain to Oporto. The forces of this city reply by destroying Gaia. The Master now fails ignominiously to take Torres Vedras and is most downhearted at the suite of misfortunes assailing his armies *(CLXIX—CLXXIV)*.

Several nobles in the Master's train now hatch a plot to kill him. When he convenes his council on 8 January, 1385, he has two of his captains arrested. The real conspirators take fright and flee. One is caught, confesses all under torture and is burnt at the stake. The people are revolted that the Master's previous kindness to such men should be repaid in such a way. King Juan of Castile receives with satisfaction news of the disasters befalling João of Avis, while

177

Queen Leonor remarks pithily that the Master has but one good tooth left in his head: Nun'Alvares (*CLXXV—CLXVIII*)!

Things seem to be going from bad to worse when Alenquer restates its loyalty to King Juan; and the governor of Leiria, despite favour shown to him by the Master of Avis, refuses to open the gates to his army which is burdened with a considerable number of starving civilians (*CLXXIX—CLXXX*).

At this apparent nadir of his fortunes, the Master arrives in Coimbra where the Cortes, or Parliament, is to be held. He is greeted by the populace shouting 'Portugal! Portugal! Long live King João!' etc. This reaction is taken to be God—inspired. The scene complements that in the previous chapter where Fernão Lopes likens João of Avis to Moses leading the Children of Israel in the desert. All this takes place on Friday, 3 March, 1385.

There follow long summaries of the arguments put forward in the Cortes in support of the various pretenders to the throne: firstly, those arguments put forward in favour of the sons of Inés de Castro, Prince João and Prince Dinis, as well as King Juan of Castile and Queen Beatriz; and then those in favour of Dom João, the Master of Avis. The learned jurist, João das Regras, addresses the Cortes of Coimbra. He attempts to prove by various arguments that neither King Juan, nor his wife, Beatriz, nor either son of Inés de Castro, has a right to inherit the throne. Finally, João das Regras endeavours to show João of Avis as a man with the necessary qualities to be the new king. He finds agreement in his hearers. The Master at first refuses, but finally accedes and is acclaimed king on 6 April, 1385. He names Nun'Alvares Pereira, at the time aged but twenty—four years, nine months and twelve days, his Constable. The new Constable, declares Fernão Lopes, is like the morning star; he is the light of his generation. This, Part I of the Chronicle of Dom João, ends with a panegyric concerning the knightly qualities of Nun'Alvares (*CLXXXI—CXCIII*).

PART II
PARTE SEGUNDA

Fernão Lopes opens the Second Part of his Life of João I with praise of the King. He lays particular stress on two virtues of the new King: Dom João's devotion to the Virgin Mary and reverence towards the Holy Scriptures; and his exemplary behaviour as a husband.

After describing the rewards and privileges conceded by João of Avis to various places that have so stoutly supported him during the Civil War, especially Lisbon, Fernão Lopes reverts to the continuing

threat of renewed Castilian invasion. He informs us that Juan I is engaged in gathering together a fresh army in Southern Spain, while a Castilian fleet appears in the Tagus estuary and, after a fierce engagement, fails to prevent an English sailing—ship and barge from reaching the port of Lisbon. These two vessels carry soldiers and wheat to the city. Lopes tells us that this sea—battle took place on 2 April, 1385 (I—IV).

In order to combat the maritime threat, King João sends Nun'Álvares, his new Constable, northwards to prepare a force and consolidate his position in an area much of which is still loyal to Juan I of Castile. The Constable pushes north taking Neiva and Viana after fierce fighting (V—VII).

King João now moves north and is acclaimed king and warmly welcomed by the populace of Oporto. It is now the month of May. At the beginning of June, he attacks and captures Guimarães while Nun'Álvares captures Braga; and then Dom João and his forces take the stronghold of Ponte de Lima. Fernão Lopes stresses that all these places harbour men who support the cause of the House of Avis. He also notes, in chapter XVII, the presence of English archers among Dom João's force for the assault on Ponte de Lima (VIII—XVIII).

King Juan continues preparing to attack Portugal through Badajoz while a Castilian force led by Juan Rodríguez de Castañeda enters Portugal from the direction of Ciudad Rodrigo, sacking Viseu as it goes. After bringing about a reconciliation between Gonçalo Vasques Coutinho and Martim Vasques da Cunha, in July, João Fernandes, one of Dom João's most trusted captains, combines with them to intercept Castañeda and decisively defeat a vastly superior army at Trancoso (XIX—XXI).

The theatre of war is now moving southwards as the Portuguese face the threat of a Castilian invasion from Extremadura. We are now in the middle of July, 1385. In chapter XXV Fernão Lopes again notes the presence of Englishmen in the army of João of Avis: some twenty—one men among the cavalry (XXII—XXV).

Again following the Castilian chronicle of López de Ayala, Fernão Lopes relates how, in face of the stern challenge of the Portuguese frontier commander, Gil Fernandes, King Juan decides to withdraw from the Badajoz area and move north towards Ciudad Rodrigo. There, he holds council as to what best to do: to invade or not to invade? Among those reasons put forward in favour of an invasion as soon as possible is the argument that João of Avis has sent to England for help and if the English return to Portugal in strength, King Juan's ambition will be completely frustrated (XXVI—XXVII).

Among the arguments put forward in order to persuade King Juan to postpone an invasion until the following year are the King's own bad health, his lack of experienced captains, most of whom had died of plague during and after the siege of Lisbon, and the

determination of the Master of Avis and his forces, including 'some archers who had come from England, even though these were few' (XXVIII).

Juan I, however, is determined to invade and does so, according to Fernão Lopês, with great cruelty, decapitating or cutting off hands or cutting out the tongues of many Portuguese who fall into his hands, out of vengeance for his great losses during the earlier invasion (XXIX).

João of Avis now takes counsel. Some advise a diversionary attack on Andalusia given the huge size of the Castilian army. However, the Constable Nun'Álvares fears that this will not divert King Juan from his purpose of capturing Lisbon, and he argues strongly that the Portuguese have no choice but to face the Castilians in the field. The Master decides in favour of giving battle and joins force with his Constable at Tomar (XXX—XXXI). There they draw up their battle order: the van, the rear, and right and left wings. Fernão Lopes notes that this terminology has been adopted only recently by the Portuguese according to the model provided for them by Edmund of Cambridge's force during the first of the two English interventions in Portugal (XXXII).

The two kings now exchange defiant challenges; and then Dom João and Nun'Álvares leave Tomar and camp five leagues out of Ourém on Saturday, 11 August. On the following Tuesday early in the morning, the Constable sets out in search of 'a convenient spot' in which to do battle with the Castilian army. The enemy is two leagues distant when Juan I parleys with Nun'Álvares (XXXIII—XXXIV).

King Juan again takes counsel. Among those who advise caution is, significantly, a French knight, Sir Jean de Rye, who has fought twice on the losing side against the King of England and the Black Prince in France. Both battles were lost because the French battle—lines were inferior to the English. Finally Juan I ignores this advice and decides to dispose of the Portuguese main army so as to avoid harassment from the rear when he descends on Lisbon XXXV—XXXVI).

Fernão Lopes puts the total army of the Portuguese at some six and a half thousand and that of the Castilians at slightly over thirty thousand (XXXVII). On the Portuguese left flank are some 'English archers and men—at—arms, numbering at the most another two hundred men', and other foreigners including the Gascon knight, Guilhem de Montferrand, who prophesies victory for João I, for in seven battles in which he has fought he has never seen soldiers so cheerful as these (XXXVIII).

After listing the chief captains of both sides, Fernão Lopes describes the arrival of some Portuguese reinforcements just as battle is about to commence, the charge of the Castilians and their unexpected rout, and King Juan's subsequent flight to Santarém (XXXIX—XLIII). From there he sails secretly to Seville but, unable

to bear the lamentations of the people, takes refuge in Carmona. Soon after, in the Cortes of Valladolid, it is decided to send to France for military aid, with all the more urgency because King Juan has learnt that immediately after his defeat at Aljubarrota, the Portuguese sent to ask for the help of the Duke of Lancaster, a pretender to the Castilian throne (XLIV).

The next few chapters recount the joy and thanksgiving in Lisbon over the victory of Aljubarrota. All fortresses occupied by the Castilians, even Santarém, are evacuated (XLV—LI).

In September and October 1385, Nun'Álvares decides to exploit the enemy's disarray in order to make an incursion deep into the region beyond Badajoz and wins the notable victory of Badajoz. One of his captains, Antão Vasques, follows his example (LII—LX).

At the same stage in the new campaign, the remaining Castilian troops are departing by sea from Lisbon while the victorious King João goes on a pilgrimage of thanksgiving in the region of Guimarães and Leiria. He also visits Coimbra and Oporto; and while in the latter city, in October 1385, he receives the glad tidings of his Constable's latest exploits in Castile. In his joy, King João awards him the County of Barcelos. December finds the King besieging Chaves with little success. Being so near to Galicia he is worried lest the Castilians decide to relieve the town and renew their broader campaign against him. In the midst of these worries an English knight disembarks unexpectedly in Oporto and brings Dom João a message from the Duke of Lancaster to the effect that, having heard news of the defeat of King Juan of Castile, the Duke has decided to come to Spain in order to make good his claim to the Castilian throne. The news pleases King João especially because it lessens the Castilian threat now that King Juan will have two armies to contend with (LXI—LXV).

In his turn, Juan I seeks aid abroad, finding a sympathetic response from his allies, the French. King Charles promises him two thousand lances. Meanwhile, King Juan feels obliged to tell the Governor of Chaves, Martim Gonçalves, that he cannot aid him and therefore he should surrender to the Portuguese. King João spends several more months trying to capture various places, some of which surrender without a fight; but in the middle of July 1386 he hears that King Juan is preparing a fresh offensive reinforced by two thousand lances commanded by the Seigneur de Longueville. Fernão Lopes doubts, however, whether the Castilian King really wishes to fight at this time (LXVI—LXXVIII).

Do recado que el-Rey emuyou a seus embaxadores, e como souberam em Imgraterra que el era feyto rey.

Bem seres nembrados que no começo destes feitos, quamdo el Rey semdo Mestre tomou carego de regedor e defemssor do regno, como emuyou per seus embaxadores requerir a el-Rey de Imgraterra que desse logar aas gemtes de seu regno, a que prouguesse de o fazer, que por seus dinhejros o veessem ajudar aaquella guerra em que era posto; e que se o Duque dAllancastro, seu tio, quisesse vijr demandar o regno de Castella que lhe per direito pertemçia, que lhe offereçiam toda ajuda per mar e per terra, da guissa que lhe prouguesse: e como alla forom por esto o Mestre de Santiago dom Fernamdaffonso dAlboquerque e Louremçeannes Fogaça, chançeller moor do regno; os quaaes partirom de Lixboa postumeiro dia de março de iiijᵉ.xxj, posto que ja outros primeiro fossem enuiados: e a reposta que della veeo.

E depois em Cojmbra, quando o Mestre foy alçado por rey, emuiou seu recado e outra procuraçam a estes mesegeiros, que por este negoçio ajmda alla eram detheudos, em que lhe daua poder abastamte pera trautar com el-Rey de Imgraterra e com o Duque dAllamcastro e assy outras pessoas, de quallquer homra e estado que fossem, aquellas liamças e amizades que por proll e seruiço do regno e homra de sua pessoa emtendessem, auemdo por firme todo o que dante tinha feito e quanto dally em diamte fezessem, e outras taaes razoões dabastamça; os quaaes mesegeiros fallarom a el-Rey, comtamdo-lhe toda a hordenamça que o poboo em esto fezera e teuera, e como o Mestre, seu senhor, fora alçado por rey per os fidalgos e gemtes do regno; e como tinham emujados seus embaixadores ao Padre Santo, pedimdo-lhe por merçee que ouuese por firme sua emliçam e aprouase quamto em ello auyam obrado.

E assy era verdade que tamto que el foy alçado por rey, logo os prellados, senhores e fidalgos e todo o poboo das villas e çidades que voz por Portuguall mantinham fezerom saber ao Papa Vrbano per huuma larga supplicatoria que leuarom dom Joham, bispo dEuora, e Gonçallo Gomez da Silua ; cuja comclusom breuemente tal era:

Que por euitar gramdes danos e perigos das almas e corpos e beens, ficamdo os regnos de Portugall per morte del Rey dom Fernamdo sem rey nem gouernador que os defemder ousasse daquel çismatico, a elle reuell, que se chamaua Rey de Castella, emtrando em elles forçosamente por os sujugar e destroir, sem temdo o regno duque nem capitam que açerca de sua guouernamça alguum cuydado teuesse, e por esto serem elles

Of the message that the King sent to his ambassadors and how they knew in England that he been made king.

You will remember that at the beginning of these events, when the Master of Avis and future King accepted the post of ruler and defender of the kingdom, he sent his ambassadors to ask the King of England if he would allow volunteers to come from his kingdom and assist, for payment, in the war in which he was engaged; and to say that if his uncle the Duke of Lancaster were disposed to come and claim the kingdom of Castile which was his by right, they would offer him all possible help by land and sea, in whatever way he might wish. You will recall that the ambassadors charged with this mission were the Master of São Tiago, Dom Fernando Afonso de Albuquerque, and the Grand Chancellor of the kingdom, Lourenço Eanes Fogaça. These men left Lisbon on the last day of March, 1383;[1] for others had gone previously, and you will remember the answer they brought back.

Later in Coimbra, when the Master was made king, he sent a message and another letter of proxy[2] to these messengers, who were still detained there on this business, in which he gave them sufficient authority to treat with the King of England and the Duke of Lancaster and with any other persons of whatever rank and social status they might be, about such alliances and friendly understandings as they might understand to be of profit and service to his kingdom, and to bring honour to his person, and he confirmed all that had been achieved hitherto and whatever they might do in the future, and he granted them authority in other ways, too. These envoys spoke to the King of England, relating to him the whole arrangement which the people had made and held to in this matter, and how their lord, the Master, had been raised up as king by both the nobles and the common people in the realm, and how they had sent ambassadors to the Holy Father, begging him to confirm their election and to give his blessing to all that they had done in the event.

It was true that as soon as he was raised up as king, the prelates, lords and nobles, and all the people of the towns and cities which supported Portugal, informed Pope Urban of it in a long letter of supplication the bearers of which were Dom João, Bishop of Évora,[3] and Gonçalo Gomes da Silva. The conclusion of this letter was as follows:[4]

"On the death of King Fernando, the kingdoms of Portugal were left without a king or ruler to defend them from that schismatic rebel against the Pope who called himself King of Castile, and who invaded them to subjugate and destroy them by force. There was at that time neither duke nor captain in the kingdom who was prepared to assume responsibility for the government of the country, so that men were in great fear and affliction. Therefore, in order to avoid

*em gramdes meedos e trabalhos postos; que por em pedirom por merçee
ao muy nobre Senhor dom Joam, Mestre da Cauallaria da Hordem
dAujs e jrmaão do dito Rey dom Fernamdo, que lhe prouuesse tomar emcarego de sua hordenamça e prouer de taaes remedios per que menos
sentir podesem os jmpetos de seus emmigos, o quall, ajudado da diuinall
deestra, os soportara esclareçidamente com nome de gramde memoria; e
porque pera remediar depois tamanhos malles, assy per mar come per
terra, nom se podia achar mais conueniente modo que per prouidençia de
rey que os ditos regnos sempre ouuerom; que todos juntamente na çidade
de Cojmbra, emqueremdo dalguum magnjfico barom que de reall lijnha-
gem trouuesse seu naçimento pera delles teer cuidado, nom fora visto
semelhante antrelles aaquell que de os³ gouernar tinha regimento; e que
estomçe, com deuida madureza e descriçom, por os gramdes e commuum
poboo a el seer mais obediemte e moor espanto de seus emmigos todos
dhuum desejo e determinado comselho em Rey e Senhor dos ditos Regnos,
com gram festa e allegria a nouo rey pertemçente, fora em real homra
posto; na quall se auya muy sagesmente e com gram deseio prestes. E'
pois com dignos fauores e conuenientes ajudas del mereçesse seer pro-
uehudo, que por em aa Sua Santidade humjldosamente pediam que, es-
guardadas taaes cousas cheas de neçessidade, e nom ley, per comsiraçom
piadosa com elle despemsasse que nom embargando que fosse caualleiro
professo de tal hordem que aa de Çister deuia conformar, que liure e
jssemtamente homra e nome de rey podesse teer e possoir, asoluendo-(o)
per comprimento dapostollico poderio de todo atamento a esto comtrairo.*

LXXX

*Como o Mestre de Santiago e Louremçeannes Fogaça forom fallar ao
Duque, e das razoões que ouueram.*

Estas nouas em Imgraterra sabudas como o Mestre fora alçado por
rey e o modo que se nello teuera, pasados nom muytos meses chegarom
outras muyto melhores dinas de grande prazer, as quaaes os mesegeiros
forom apresa comtar a el-Rey, de como seu Senhor el-Rey de Portugall
vemçera os castellaãos em campo, damdo-lhe desto suas cartas; e jsso
mesmo ao Duque dAllamcastro, a que o logo forom dizer, presemte a
Duquessa sua molher, comtamdo-lhe como se todo pasara segumdo que
o per escprito çertas nouas auyam, dizemdo em suas razoões, fallamdo
em esto, *que pois el auya dereito nos regnos de Castella e se delles chamaua rey, que ora tinha tempo de os cobrar de todo; ca pois el-Rey de
Portugall auya de seus emmjgos cobrada tam booa amdança, e el teria
nelle tal amigo como bem era de cuydar, que nom podia em nenhuum
tempo tomar trabalho de lhe esto tam bem vijr a seu prazer e desejo como
estomçe, e que faria muyto de sua homra e proueito hordenar como pasasse.*

great damage and danger to souls, bodies and property, they entreated the very noble lord, Dom João, Master of the Military Order of Avis, and brother of the aforesaid King Fernando, to assume authority and provide such remedies as would counter the attacks of their enemies. Aided by the right hand of God, he supported them brilliantly and in memorable fashion; and since no more effective way could be found of dealing with such evils in future by land or sea than by providing the kingdoms with a king, for they had always had one, everyone convened in the city of Coimbra to look for some magnificent nobleman of the royal blood to govern the kingdoms. They could find no one who measured up to him who was already governing them; and so, after careful and wise reflection on the matter, as was only right, he was placed on the throne by the magnates and the common people who swore obedience to him, to be king and lord of the aforesaid kingdoms to the consternation of his enemies. This was done by their unanimous desire and decision, with the great celebration and rejoicing which befit the enthronement of a new king. All this while, he carried out his duties most wisely and willingly. Because he deserved to be given worthy favours and appropriate assistance they would humbly beg His Holiness that, since these things had been done out of necessity and not law, he might be so good as to grant him a dispensation so that notwithstanding the fact that he was a professed knight of an order following the Cistercian rule, he might freely and unreservedly assume the honour and title of king, and be absolved by apostolic authority from any impediments to this."

LXXX
How the Master of São Tiago and Lourenço Eanes Fogaça went to speak to the Duke and of what passed between them.

Not many months after the news reached England that the Master had been made king and the way in which this had been done, there arrived news calculated to bring even greater pleasure to the English. The messengers hastened to the King to tell him how their lord the King of Portugal had defeated the Castilians in pitched battle, handing over letters about this to the King.[1] They told the Duke of Lancaster the same, in the presence of his wife, the Duchess, explaining how everything had happened, according to the news—letter they had received. They also told him that "since he had a right to the kingdom of Castile and called himself King thereof, now was the moment to claim it once and for all; for since the King of Portugal had won such a success over his enemies, he would have in him as good a friend as he could ever imagine; and he was unlikely ever again to be in such a good position to help him realize this, his heart's desire. Moreover, it would greatly increase his honour and profit to arrange how best to set the enterprise in train."

O Duque outorgaua com o que elle dezia; mas por os feitos da casa de Imgraterra, em que ataa emtam fora ocupado, se escusaua de o nom poder fazer. E fallamdo em estas razoões, a Duquesa se fincou [2] em giolhos amtelle com a jffante dona Catellina sua filha, e começou a dizer: *Senhor, de quamtas booas amdanças vos Deus deu neste mundo em vossas guerras e trabalhos por os feitos alheos pareçe-me que (mais)[3] raʒom seria trabalhardes uos por vossa homra e de uosa filha, e por cobrar a eramça que he mjnha e de vossa filha, de que estamos deserdadas. Ca o regno de Castella a mym perteņçe de dereito, ca nom aos filhos do treedor bastardo que matou meu padre como nom deuja.* E em dezemdo esto, chorauom ambas, a filha e a madre.

O Mestre de Santiago, vemdo esto, começou a dizer ao Duque: *Em verdade, Senhor, a mym pareçe que estas senhoras vos pedem gramde raʒom. Ca nom digo eu auerem ellas comuosco tam gramde diuado como tem, mas ja ellas seriam huumas donas estrangeiras que de uos nom aueriam conheçimento, e ujmdo-uos pedir por merçee que lhe ajudassees a cobrar o seu que lhe tem forçado, vos por o de Deus e por mostrar que sooes abastante de o poder faʒer, vos trabalharyees de o poer em obra, quanto mais pòr o dereito de vossa molher e por o ditado que ja tomastes de rey uos deues de trabalhar dello com muyto moor vomtade: moormente agora que uos tam boom aaʒo veem aa mão!*

Verdade he, disse o Duque, *todo o que uos diʒees, e eu muyto ha que o trago em cuidado; mas por a guerra dEscorçia de que me escusar nom pude, homde ja fuy per duas veʒes per hordenamça do Conselho de Imgraterra, que me rogarom que lha posesse em fym, pois el-Rey era em tal hidade que o per seu corpo faʒer nom podia, por tamto nom pude esto poer em obra. Mas ora a Deus graças, pois que a guerra ja he em ta. ponto com homra da casa de Imgraterra em que eu posso bem seer escusado, eu uos prometo que eu me trabalhe de muy çedo pasar a Espanha demandar o regno que meu he, de guissa que ellas nem outro nenhuum nom aja raʒom de me em esto fallar.*

Estomçe a Duquesa com sua filha lho teueram em gramde merçee; e jsso mesmo os embaxadores; e foram-sse pera as poussadas.

LXXXI
Como o Duque fallou a el-Rey e aos do Comselho sobre sua vimda pera Espanha, e lhe foy outorgada leçemça.

O Duque depois desto, presente el-Rey e os do Comselho e outros gramdes senhores, que por este aazo aquell dia forom jumtos, fez recom-

The Duke agreed with what the King of Portugal was saying; but because of the affairs of the House of England in which he had hitherto been so occupied, he offered his excuses for not being able to act. Then, whilst they were speaking of these matters, the Duchess fell on her knees in front of him together with her daughter, Princess Catherine, and began to speak:

"My lord, for all the success that God has given you in this world in your wars and struggles on behalf of others, it seems to me that you have even greater reason to struggle for your own honour and for that of your daughter, and to claim the inheritance which is mine and your daughter's, and of which we have been deprived. For the kingdom of Castile belongs to me by right and not to the sons of that bastard traitor who wrongfully killed my father." As she spoke, mother and daughter were both weeping.

When he saw this, the Master of São Tiago turned to the Duke and said, "Truly, my lord, it seems to me that these ladies are appealing to you with good cause. Even if they were not so closely connected to you, but were simply two foreign ladies unknown to you, coming to beg you to help them recover the property of which they have been robbed, I am sure that, for God's sake and in order to show what you can do, you would make an effort to respond to their call. That being so, how much more are you bound to respond, and with an even greater will, in order to enforce the rights of your own wife and the royal title that you have already assumed, especially now, when you can see such a good opportunity at hand."

"Everything you say is true", said the Duke, "and I have been pondering the matter for a long time; but I have been unable to make any move in that direction because I could not extricate myself from the war against Scotland. I have been there twice on the orders of the Council of England, which asked me to bring this war to a conclusion given that the King is not of an age to be able to do so in person; but now, thank God, that the war is at a point where the honour of the House of England is assured, I am in a position to take my leave. I promise you that I shall do all I can to travel to Spain very soon in order to claim the kingdom that is mine, so that henceforth neither these ladies nor anyone else may have cause to reproach me on the matter."

Then the Duchess and her daughter thanked him profusely, and so did the ambassadors before retiring to their lodgings.

LXXXI

How the Duke spoke with the King and Council about his coming to Spain and how he was given leave to do so

After this, in the presence of the King, the Council, and other great lords who had gathered that day for the purpose,[1] the Duke

tamento dos muytos seruiços que ao regno auja feitos, e como sempre amdara em gramdes trabalhos, assy em ujda del-Rey seu padre como depois que seu sobrinho regnara, e esto por leuar adeamte a homra e boom estado da casa de Imgraterra; e posto que el teuesse razom de o fazer por o gram diuedo que em ella auia, desy por el-Rey seer em tal jdade que o per seu corpo nom compria cometer, que el nom erraua porem nenhuuma cousa, posto que taaes seruiços amte a ssua merçee apresemtasse. Dessy disse como todos bem sabyam como el era casado com a mayor filha del-Rey dom Pedro, Rey que fora de Castella, a que o regno de dereito pertemçia e nom aaquell que o tinha per força; e por em tomara ja dias auya titullo del-Rey de Castella, e sua molher nome de rainha, teemdo em uontade, com ajuda de Deus e sua, de o auer dhijr conqujstar; mas por as guerras que ditas auya, em que ataa estomçe fora embargado, o nom podera fazer: e ora, pois que a Deus graças (seus) feitos estauom em boom asessego, que el queria hir demandar seus regnos; o que muy bem podia fazer, pois tinha el-Rey de Portugall em ajuda, que auja guerra com seu aduersairo; e por em pedia a el-Rey por merçee que lhe desse lecemça e o ajudasse pera poder pasar a Espanha e dar fym a este negoçio, que tamto era sua homra e da casa de Imgraterra.

El-Rey, que seria estomçe pouco menos de vimte annos, fallou com aquelles com que esto compria de fallar, e acordarom que era bem de lhe outorgar aquello que pedia; e pera se esto melhor fazer e seus feitos seerem bem (em)caminhados , que compria primeiro trautar booa liamça e amizade com el-Rey de Portugall, em que estaua grande ajuda de sua requesta. Emtom hordenou el-Rey, pera esto trautar por sua parte, dous homrados caualleiros de seu comselho e huum doutor em lex; os quaaes com o Mestre de Santiago e Lourençeannes Fogaça concordasem esta amizade como melhor emtendessem per boo(m) asessego e homra dos reis ambos, e que o Duque se fezesse em tanto prestes de gemtes e nauios pera sua pasagem, e mandasse pedir a Portugall alguumas naaos e gallees pera hirem com elle; e este foy o recado que chegou a el-Rey quamdo jazia sobre Chaues, como ja ouujstes.

LXXXII
*Da liamça e amizade que foy trautada amtre el-Rey de Portugall
e el-Rey de Ingraterra.*

Fazemdo-se o Duque prestes e emcaminhamdo sua passagem, os embaxadores portuguesses trautauom em tamto com aquelles que el-Rey

described his many services to the realm, and how he had always been involved in great enterprises to further the honour and the good estate of the House of England during the lifetime of his royal father and ever since his nephew had come to the throne. Even though it was right that he should do all this out of a sense of duty and because the King was too young to assume personally such responsibilities, he was not therefore doing anything wrong for he had never previously presented this list of his services deserving of reward. After this, he affirmed that all knew perfectly well that he was married to the elder daughter of Don Pedro, who had been King of Castile, and that the kingdom belonged to her by right and not to him who held it by force. Therefore, he, the Duke, had assumed a few days ago the title of King of Castile, and his wife that of Queen, since she was determined, with God's aid and his, to go and conquer the kingdom. However, because of the aforementioned wars in which he had been so embroiled, he had not been able to do anything about it hitherto; but now that his affairs were in good shape, thank God, he wished to go and claim his kingdom. He was in a good position to do this, because he would have the help of the King of Portugal who was at war with the Duke's enemy. Therefore, he begged the King for permission to go and also for help in going to Spain and in bringing the enterprise to a successful conclusion, for this would redound to his honour and to that of the House of England.

The King, who would be at that time a little under twenty years of age, consulted those most appropriate to advise him on the matter, and they agreed that it was quite in order to grant the Duke's petition. They also agreed that in order to put the arrangements on a good footing, it was advisable to make a friendly alliance with the King of Portugal who was offering substantial assistance in the expedition. The King then ordered two honourable knights from his council[2] and a doctor of laws[3] to negotiate such an alliance on his behalf, and together with the Master of São Tiago and Lourenço Eanes Fogaça, to prepare the way for this treaty of friendship in whatever way they thought best with a view to the peace and honour of both kings. In the meantime, the Duke should make ready men and ships for his voyage, and also request as well ships and galleys from Portugal to be added to his own fleet. This was the message that the King of Portugal received when he was besieging Chaves, as you have heard already.[4]

LXXXII
Of the Treaty of Friendship that was negotiated between the King of Portugal and the King of England.

While the Duke was making everything ready for his voyage, the Portuguese ambassadors negotiated with those men that the King

escolhera suas auenças, em que despemderom assaz despaço por se comcordar em boõa amizade. E huum dia, que era noue de mayo da era que entom corya de iiij°.xxiiij°., no castello de Windesore, que som huumas sete legoas de Lomdres, no paaço que tinham costume de fallar, presentes tres homrados bispos e o duque dIorca, tio del-Rey, e outros senhores e nobres baroões pera ouujr esto ally chamados, aquel doutor Richarte Rronhalle em alta e clara voz propos amte todos, dizemdo desta guissa:

Aquell deue ser ofiçio proposito dos que direitamente regnam, e a final emtençam dos que justamente teem senhorios, que o bem comuum dos seus sobditos amem muyto mais que o seu, e que o amteponham aos propios e particulares proueitos; e com taaes defemdimentos a reepublica a elles sogeita deuem de teer guarneçida que, lamçadas fora todallas çegas toruaçoões que a esto comtradiȝem, e fiel poboo, per taaes primçepes e senhores manteudo, nom soo em bemauenturamça seja acreçemtado, mas soo delectauell folgamça de paȝ, que todos desejar deuem, em-nas auersidades seja conseruado e defesso; a quall cousa certamente emtam se espera seer mais çedo posta em obra, quamdo taaes reis e primçepes christaãos em emteira humanjdade e perfeita obediemça da Santa Madre Egreja de Roma em huuma vomtade comcordam per amoor nom departido. E por em o muy alto e esclareçido primçepe, digno de temer e homrar, el-Rey RICHARTE, nosso Senhor, vemdo e esguardamdo bem no exame da sua profunda comsiraçam todallas cousas a esto pertemçentes, desy com acordo dos de seu Comselho, lhe praȝ de trautar e firmar com o muy nobre Rey dom JOHAM de Portugall e do Alguarue, seu paremte e boom amigo, esta seguimte amiȝade:

PRIMEIRAMENTE, que por bem pubrico e folgamça de seus regnos e subditos seja amtrelles e os herdeiros que depois veerem booa e firme paȝ por sempre, per nenhuuma guisa britada, e que huum ao outro dee socoro e ajuda comtra quaaesquer pessoas que seiam, saluo, saluo Vinçeslaao, Rey dos Romaãos, e dom Joham, Rey de Castella, duque dAllamcastro, tio del-Rey nosso Senhor; que comtra estes se nom emtenda. Nem jsso mesmo comtra o Papa Vrbano que ora he, so cuja obediemça (e) de todos seus sobçessores canonicamente emlegidos ambos deuem de uiuer.

OUTROSSY, que todos e cada huum vassallo dos ditos regnos, assy eslesiasticos prellados come duques e baroões e outras quaaesquer pessoas do mayor estado destes ataa o mais pequeno, possam liure e seguramente hijr dhuum regno pera outro, terras, senhorios e partidas delles, assy por comprar e vemder come por estar quanto quiserem e partir se lhe prouuer, semdo reçebidos e honestamente trautados com homra e boom gasalhado segumdo a comdiçam de cada huum; pagamdo taaes pessoas aos reis e senhores das ditas terras seus dereitos e costumes, quall se vssar nos logares hu acomteçer de vijr.

had chosen to make the agreements. They went at a fairly slow pace in order to come to a really amicable agreement. On a particular day, 9 May 1386 to be exact, in Windsor castle,[1] some seven leagues from London, in the hall in which it was the custom to hold council, in the presence of three honourable bishops and the Duke of York,[2] the King's uncle, and other lords and noble barons who had been summoned to hear this, Dr Richard Ronhale read out in a loud, clear voice before everyone, the following:

"It should be the official intention of all who reign by right, and the ultimate goal of all who legitimately hold lordships, to love the common good of their subjects far above their own, and to put this common good before their own private interest. The state over which they rule should be equipped with such defences that, having cast out all obstacles that might militate against good government, the loyal people, protected by such princes and lords, not only may see their fortunes greatly prosper, but also know peace, that exquisite contentment that all men should desire, and be preserved and defended in adversity. Such a thing can certainly be expected to come to pass all the sooner, when such Christian kings and princes, in perfect humanity and utter obedience to the Holy Mother Church of Rome, are of one accord thanks to an indivisible love. Therefore, the most high and illustrious prince, deserving of being feared and honoured, King Richard our lord, having seen and considered fully all aspects of the present matter, after reaching agreement with his council, is pleased to negotiate and sign, along with the most noble King João of Portugal and the Algarve, his relation and good friend, the following Treaty of Friendship:

"Firstly, for the public good and for the peace of their kingdoms and their subjects, let there be, between them and between their heirs who may come after, a true and secure peace forever, never to be broken in any way. Let them succour and assist one another against all other persons except Wenceslas, King of the Romans,[3] and John, King of Castile, Duke of Lancaster, uncle to our lord the King; but not against these, nor against the present Pope Urban, for both men must forever live in obedience to him and his canonically elected successors.

Also, let each and every vassal in the said kingdoms, ecclesiastics, prelates, dukes, barons and any other persons, from those of great estate right down to the humblest, be allowed to travel freely and safely from one kingdom to the other, and in their lands, lordships and regions, in order to buy and sell, and to reside and to depart as they so desire; let them be always received and honestly treated with honour and hospitality according to their rank; and let such people pay to the kings and lords of the said kingdoms such tolls and dues as may be the custom in the places to which they happen to come.

ITEM, que per nenhuum modo nom comuenha aos ditos reis ou aalguum de seus subditos de quallquer graao e dignidade que seia que de comselho, fauor ou ajuda, per maar nem per terra, aalguuma naçam de gemte reuell e comtraira a ca da huum dos ditos regnos; mas que cada huum delles e os que depois veherem seiam theudos e obrigados que os comtrairos de cada huum ajudem a destroir com todas suas forças. E se alguuns sobditos comtra jsto qujser obrar , logo sem outro detimento seja dignamente punido per o senhor cujo for aa vomtade, de quallquer delles a que for feita a ofemssa.

E AIMDA MAIS OUTRA COUSA, que se pellos tempos que ham de vijr cada huum destes reis ou seus herdeiros quiser ajuda do outro per quallquer guissa que seia, que lho faça saber primeiro per seis meses; e a parte requerida seia theuda de a dar aquell tempo o melhor que o bem poder fazer sem emgano e maa tardamça, pedimdo pera os seus rezoado soldo, ou segumdo comcordarem aquelles que pera hordenar esto forem escolhidos.

Estes capitollos e outros de liamça concordauel por sempre forom estomçe ally trautados, que myngua nom fazem de uer.

LXXXIII

Como o Duque partio de Ingraterra, e aportou em Galliza.

Os trautos firmados e tal liança feita, o Duque se fazia em tanto prestes pera passar a Espanha poderosamente. Em esto chegou huum dia Afomsso Furtado, capitam de Purtugall, com as naaos e gallees que de Lixboa partirom quando el-Rey jazia sobre Chaues, a huum logar do Duquado de Cornoalha que he chamado Fauwyc ; e achou hij Lourençeannes Fogaça, que por cousas alguumas de sua embaxada era estomçe ally vimdo, e tor(nou)-se com el nas gallees a Llomdres.

Pera esta vynda do Duque foy jumta em Amtona e em Pream(ua) gram frota de naaos e doutros nauios; e toda a gemte se ueo a estes logares pera auerem em elles de embarcar. E dally partio o Duque, e seguio sua viagem com emtemçam de portar em terra de Galliza, do senhorio de Castella. E ujndo pello mar com vemto contrairo, foy-lhe forçado tornar em Bretanha a huum logar que chamam Brestes , castello bem forte daquel ducado, o quall Ruberte de Clipsso , comdestabre de Framça, com muytas gemtes tinha emtom çercado. E mandara fazer, preto delle o traito de viratom, huum castello de madeira quamto se pode obrar de forte, em que se colhiam daquellas gemtes, e tinham todos seus mantimentos. E quamdo virom vijr aquella frota, bem emtenderom que eram jmgreses por a gram fama que damte soaua; e conheçemdo que vinha ally o Duque, começarom de fugir os mais delles, e muytos se meteram demtro no castello. O Duque sayo em terra com suas gemtes, e começarom de o combater. Os de demtro com temor de morte de-

Also, let neither of the said kings nor any one of their subjects, whatever his rank and dignity, give any counsel, favour or assistance, on land or sea, to any nation that is rebellious or hostile to either of the two kingdoms; but let the kings and their successors be bound and obliged to aid each other with all their might to destroy one another's enemies.   Moreover, if any subjects should seek to act contrary to this, may they be appropriately punished forthwith without delay by whichever lord wishes, no matter against whom the offence may have been committed.

There remains one more thing: that if in times to come one or other of these kings or his heirs should need the assistance of the other in whatever circumstances, he should give him six months notice of the fact; and the one whose assistance is sought shall be bound to give it to the utmost of his power without trickery or undue delay, asking for his men only such pay as is reasonable or as may be agreed by those chosen to arrange the matter."

These clauses for a permanent alliance were there agreed, together with others which there is no need to see.

LXXXIII
How the Duke left England and landed in Galicia.

With the treaties signed and this alliance made, the Duke made ready meanwhile to go to Spain with a considerable force.   At this juncture, one day Afonso Furtado, a Portuguese captain, arrived with the ships and galleys that left Lisbon when the King was besieging Chaves.   He landed at a place in the Duchy of Cornwall called Fowey.   There he found Lourenço Eanes Fogaça, who had come there for reasons to do with his embassy, and he returned with him to London in the galleys.

A great fleet of ships and other vessels was assembled at Southampton and Plymouth for the Duke's voyage; and every man reported to these places in order to embark. [1]   The Duke took ship from there and set sail with the intention of disembarking on the Galician coast which is in Castilian territory.   An unfavourable wind forced him to put in at a place called Brest, a very strong fortress in the duchy of Brittany which Olivier de Clisson, the Constable of France, was then besieging with a considerable force.   He had ordered the building, just a bow—shot away, of a wooden castle as stout as it was possible to make, in which his men could shelter and keep all their necessary supplies.   When they saw the fleet arrive, they knew that it was an English fleet for there had been much talk of its coming.   Realizing that the Duke was coming there, most of the besiegers began to flee; and some of them got into the castle.   The Duke came ashore with his men and started to attack it.   Fearing for their lives, the occupants fought stubbornly;   then, seeing that a

femdiam-se rijamente; e uemdo que nom auya nelles defemssam, pedirom por merçee ao Duque que os leixasse sair a vida, e tomasse o castello com quanto nelle estaua. Ao Duque prougue dello, e feze-o destroir; e cobrarom os jmgreses muytos mantimentos e outras cousas que os emmigos em elle tinham, e ficarom por estomçe seguros.

Dally seguyo o Duque sua viagem com tempo razoado que lhe sempre fez; e chegou aa villa da Crunha, hu desejaua de pousar sua frota; e foy esto em dia de Santiago, aos xxv dias de julho da era que ja dissemos de iiijº.xxiiijº. E eram per todas çemto e trimta vellas bem armadas com muytos mantimentos; amtre os quaaes vinham doze gramdes naaos, que de Portugall forom com as gallees. E a ffama das gemtes que o Duque ally tragia eram duas mjll lamças e tres mjll archeiros, e estes de booa gemte, afora outros muytos que nom comtauom com elles; de que eram capitaães muy homrados senhores e fidalgos: assy como monsire Joham dOllamda, comdestabre desta hoste, jrmaão del-Rey de Ingraterra da parte da madre — aquelle que emtom regnaua, — que vinha esposado com dona Issabell, filha do Duque, e o senhor dEscallas, e o senhor de Ponjns , e o senhor de Astimgues, e o senhor de Ferros e seu jrmaão monsire Thomas Frecho, e monsire Tomas Symom, e monsire Richart Burley, que era mariscall, e monsire Richart Persy e monsire Tomas Persy o moço, e monsire Maabornj , e monsire Joham Falconer, e monsire Baldouym de Freiul, e outros muytos cujos nomes nom fazem myngua.

Omde sabee que seis gallees de Castella, que amdauom coremdo a costa de Imgraterra quamdo o Duque juntaua esta armada, sabemdo como auya de partir, mas nom semdo çertos pera quall porto, veeram-sse vimdo primeiro pera Galliza e jaziam no rio de Betamços, tres legoas da Crunha, nom penssamdo que esta armada tam çedo chegasse, desy pareçeo-lhe segura jazeda; e aquell dia que o Duque chegou, por ser festa de Samtiago e naquella terra de gramde romagem, eram todollos patroões e muytos outros dellas vissitar a sua jgreja, que eram dally dez legoas. As gallees de Portugall e outros nauios pequenos, como dellas ouueram vista, meteram-se pello ryo açima. Os gallyotes que nellas estauom, quamdo se uirom sem patroões e sem gemte darmas, amte que os de Portugall chegassem, desempararam-nas logo, fogimdo todos quem melhor podia; e os portugueses acharom em ellas muytas boõas cousas que estas gallees roubarom amdando pella costa de Ingraterra, e em nauios que no mar tomarom. E o Duque hordenou estomçe que todollos nauios que com el veerom, que se tornassem pera suas terras; e ficarom as naaos e gallees que de Portugall forom.

long—term defence of the castle was hopeless, they begged the Duke to spare their lives, in return for the castle and its contents. The Duke agreed and had the castle destroyed; and the English acquired considerable provisions and other items that the enemy had therein, and so remained safe and sound.

From there the Duke continued his journey, always with reasonable weather, and arrived at the town of Corunna where he planned to dock his fleet. The arrival date was the feast day of St James himself, on 25 July of the year 1386. The fleet comprised some one hundred and thirty vessels, well—armed and well—provisioned. Among these were a dozen great warships that had come from Portugal with the galleys. It is said of the men the Duke brought with him that he had two thousand lances and three thousand archers, and these were very good men; and this does not take into account the many more he also had with him. The captains were very honourable lords and nobles, including Sir John Holland,[2] the Constable of the army, who was a brother of the King of England through his mother (I refer to the King then reigning) and was married to the Duke's daughter, Elizabeth;[3] Lord Scales;[4] Lord Poynings;[5] Sir Hugh Hastings;[6] Lord Ferrers;[7] and his brother Sir Thomas Fychet; Sir Thomas Symond; Sir Richard Burley,[8] who was the Marshal; Sir Richard Percy; Sir Thomas Percy the younger;[9] Sir John Mauburney; Sir John Falconer; Sir Baldwin de Frevill;[10] and many others unnecessary to name here. Now you must know that six Castilian galleys that were occupied in harrying the English coast while the Duke was assembling his fleet, learning that he was soon to set sail but with no sure intelligence concerning the precise port where he would land, had come to Galicia ahead of him and lay in the mouth of the Betanzos river, three leagues from Corunna, oblivious of the fact that this fleet had arrived so soon. Consequently, it seemed to them a secure anchorage.

Now on the day the Duke arrived, since it was the Feast of St James and a day of many pilgrimages in that land, all the captains of these ships and many others who were with them were going to pay a visit to his church ten leagues away. When they saw these vessels, the Portuguese galleys and other smaller craft started up river. Before the Portuguese ships arrived, realizing that they were without captains and men—at—arms, the rowers in these galleys abandoned them forthwith, fleeing as best they could. The Portuguese found in them many useful things that these galleys had pillaged along the English coast as well as from vessels they had captured at sea.

The Duke then ordered all the vessels that had come with him from England to return home, while the ships and galleys that had come from Portugal stayed on.

Das pallauras que o Duque emviou dizer a el-Rey de Castella, e da re-
posta que per seus messegeiros mandou.

Mais lomge conuem que nos leue esta estorea, segundo a hordem que
compre dizer do que aa primeira teuemos temçom; porque comtando
todo o que ao Duque aqueçeo na Espanha, que se deue per meudo
scpreuer, faz mester que digamos logo o que lhe aueo com el-Rey de
Castella, desy as cousas que depois com el-Rey de Portugall trautou, e
como fezerom ambos sua entrada, e quanto tempo em ella durarom, e
emtam poel-lo dacordo com seu aduersairo e tornal-lo pera Ingraterra.
Ca pois que o discpreto emtendimento deseia saber a uerdade de todo,
e nos nom o fazemdo desta gujssa ficaria a estoria jndeterminada, por
em destas quatro cousas a primeira, que uos logo offereçemos, çertamente se passou assy: que, como o Duque foy em Galliza, enuiou recado
a el-Rey de Castella, e nom per seu jrmaão como alguuns dizem, ca o
nom trazia comsigo, mas per outrem lhe fez saber que el era vimdo em
aquella terra, como ja ouuira contar, e que tragia comsigo a Rainha
dona Costamça sua molher, filha del-Rey dom Pedro que fora de Castella e de Leom, por auer aquelles regnos que seus eram de dereito; os
quaaes entemdia de cobrar pois lhe pertemçiam; e que se el dezia que
nom era assy e lhos embargar quisesse, que el o queria liurar per batalha, avemtuirando poder a poder.

El-Rey de Castella reçebeo bem o mesageiro e deu-lhe alguumas
joyas; e emuyou a elle dom Joham Serano, priol de Gadalupe, chamçeller do sello da puridade, e huum caualleiro que chamauom Diogo
Lopez de Mendrano e huum doutor em lex e degredos, que deziam
Aluaro Martjnz de Villa Reall. E auemdo primeiro seguro, chegarom aa
çidade dOuremse, homde o Duque estomçe estaua. E desque forom
amtelle com boom gasalhado e reçebimento diserom que fosse sua merçee de lhes dar dessy huuma audiença. E el disse que lhe prazia, e que
disessem como a queriam, se de praça ou em segredo. E elles respomderom que peramte os do seu comselho, e o Duque ho outorgou.

E huum dia, estamdo com elle os capitaães e mayoraaes de sua companha, fez vijnr amtesy aquelles messageiros, e dise-lhe que propo-
sessem a embaxada que de seu senhor tragiam, que el prestes era de a
ouujr, e que por temor nem reçeo nom leixassem della nenhuuma cousa;
ca seguros eram dizer por sua parte todo o que por seu seruiço emtem-
dessem. E elles teueram-lho em merçee, e o priol começou e disse assy:

Senhor, el-Rey de Castella e de Leom e de Portugall meu Senhor, uos
enuia dizer que a el diserom dias (ha) que uos aportastes em seu regno
nesta terra de Galliza em huum logar que chamam a Crunha, com gramde

Of the message that the Duke sent to the King of Castile and of the reply this King sent by his messengers.

It is necessary to take this story further, if we are to preserve the order in which we originally intended to narrate the events; for in describing all that befell the Duke in Spain, all of which needs to be set down in detail, it is indispensable to relate first of all what happened to him with the King of Castile; then we shall explain his dealings with the King of Portugal, how the two of them entered Spain, and how long they remained there; and finally we must see the Duke coming to a reconciliation with his adversary and returning home to England. For given that the intelligent mind desires to know the whole truth, the story would remain unclear were we not to relate it in this manner. Therefore, the first of these four episodes we offer you certainly happened in the following way.

As the Duke was in Galicia, he sent word to the King of Castile, and not by means of his brother as some have said, for he had not brought him on the expedition, but rather by means of someone else he acquainted the King of his arrival in the country, in the manner you have already heard, and that he had brought his wife Queen Constanza, a daughter of King Pedro who had been King of Castile and León, in order to obtain those kingdoms that were hers by right. She fully intended to recover them because they belonged to her, and if Don Juan maintained that this was not so and chose to put obstacles in their way, the Duke was determined to decide the dispute by fighting a pitched battle.

The King of Castile received the messenger well, giving him a present of jewels, and in reply sent Don Juan Serrano,[1] Prior of Guadalupe and Chancellor of the Privy Seal, a knight called Diego López de Medrano, and a doctor in civil and canon law named Álvaro Martínez de Villa Real. First obtaining a safe—conduct, they came to the city of Orense where the Duke was; and as soon as they were in his presence and had been generously welcomed and entertained, they asked if he would be pleased to grant them an audience. He said he was willing to do so; and he asked them how they wanted it, in public or in private. They replied that they would like it to be before his council, and the Duke consented.

One day, in the presence of the captains and great men of his retinue, he summoned those messengers before him, and told them to explain the message that they had brought from their lord, for he was ready to hear it. He also urged them not to be afraid to state everything the King's message contained; for he guaranteed that they were perfectly safe to say anything they considered necessary in order to do their duty by their lord. They thanked him for this and so the Prior began in this manner:

"My lord, the King of Castile and León and Portugal, my lord, sends us to say that he was told some days ago that you came ashore

197

armada de naaos e doutros nauios e muytas gemtes em elles; e que uos chamaaes Rey de Castella e de Leom, e taaes armas tragees e synaaes, diᶎemdo que estes regnos vos pertemçem de dereito por heramça de vossa molher que com uosco traguees, filha que foy del-Rey dom Pedro. E diᶎem-lhe que uos querees jumtar com o Mestre dAujs, que se chama Rey de Portugall, pera entrardes em seu regno, mostramdo que o auees de comqujstar e auer; e que sobresto lhe emuyastes vosso recado, diᶎemdo que o queriees liurar per batalha, avemtuiramdo poder a poder. E meu Senhor vos respomde assy: que el tem e possuue os regnos de Castella e de Lleom per justo titollo e heramça dereita, e que uos nom fostes bem emformado per quem uos feᶎ entemder que vossa molher tinha nelle melhor dereito; e que se jsto quiserdes demandar peramte aquell que de tall feito pode seer juiᶎ, que el he prestes pera de ssy faᶎer dereito e justiça; e pois el esto quer faᶎer, que el uos requere da parte de Deus que lhe nom emtres em seus regnos, nem lhe danes sua terra. E se o assy nom qujserdes comprir, que emtemde que o faᶎees com argulho e soberua, e nom por dereito que emtemdaaes de teer; e faᶎ disto juiᶎ o Senhor Deus.

LXXXV
Das raᶎooes que diserom mais ao Duque os outros dous embaxadores.

O prior acabou sua razom e calou-sse sem mais dizer. E o Duque, pemsamdo que aquell soo fallara por todos, quisera logo (respomder haaquello. Estomçe disse Diogo) Lopez: *Senhor, seia vossa merçee que pois o doutor e eu somos vimdos em companha do prior per mandado del-Rey nosso senhor que uos diga cada huum de nos aquellas raᶎooes que uos mandarom diᶎer. E depois, se a uossa merçee prouguer, podees respomder sobre todo.*

E o Duque disse que fallassem o que lhe prouguesse, e que os ouuiria de boõa vomtade. E Diogo Lopez disse assy:

Senhor, el-Rey de Castella, meu senhor, vos emuia diᶎer que uos lhe emuiastes recado como uos auyees nos regnos de Castella muyto moor dereito que nom elle, e que se el deᶎia que nom era assy, que uos lho combateryees [3] *poder por poder. Hora a jsto uos diᶎ el-Rey, meu senhor, assy que elle ha nos regnos de Castella mayor dereito que vos; e se uos diᶎees que nom, que el se combatera comvosco corpo por corpo e deᶎ a deᶎ ou çemto por çemto, quall uos mais prouguer, por quamto por seruiço de Deus e escusar spargimento de sangue de christaãos que poder por poder nom o quer sperar.*

E logo o doutor Aluaro Martijnz, como este acabou, começou a dizer assy:

Senhor, e eu por parte del-Rey de Castella, meu senhor, e por guarda

in his kingdom at a place they call Corunna in Galicia, with a huge fleet of warships and other vessels and many men. He also heard that you call yourself King of Castile and León, and bear coats−of−arms and heraldic insignia to that effect; and that you say these kingdoms rightfully belong to you through the inheritance of your wife who was the daughter of King Pedro and whom you have brought with you. He is told that you wish to join with the Master of Avis, who calls himself King of Portugal, in order to enter my lord's kingdom with the manifest intention of conquering and possessing it. To this end, you sent him a message, declaring that you wish to decide the dispute by fighting a pitched battle. My lord replies to you thus: he possesses the kingdoms of Castile and León by just title and rightful inheritance, and you were misinformed by those who gave you to understand that your wife had a better right than his. If you wish to make a claim before one who is competent to give judgment on the matter, my lord is ready to seek a fair and just ruling on the case. Since he wishes to do this, he charges you in God's name not to enter his kingdoms nor to destroy his land. If you do not accede to this request, in his view, you are acting out of arrogance and pride, and not because of any justice you may think you have on your side. May God be the judge of this!"

LXXXV
Of more things said to the Duke by the other two ambassadors.

The Prior brought his speech to a conclusion and was silent. Thinking that this man had spoken on behalf of all the ambassadors, the Duke had been on the point of making his reply to all that, when Diego López spoke up: "My lord, since the doctor and I have accompanied the Prior here on the order of the King, may it please you to allow each of us to say what we were commanded to say. Then you can reply to all of it, as you think fit." The Duke said that they might say whatever they wished and that he would willingly listen. So Diego López spoke thus:

"My lord, the King of Castile, my lord, sends me to say that you have sent a messenger to him claiming that you have more right to the kingdom of Castile than he, and that if he denies this, you will fight him pitting your strength against his. To this my lord the King now replies that he has a stronger claim to the kingdom of Castile, and that if you deny it, he will fight you, in single combat, or ten against ten, or a hundred against a hundred, whichever you choose, because, for God's sake and to avoid the shedding of Christian blood, he does not want a pitched battle."

At the end of this speech, Doctor Álvaro Martínez began to speak in this manner:

"My lord, on behalf of my lord the King of Castile, and out of

199

de todo seu dereito vos digo em esta guissa: que os regnos de Castella e
de Lleom que uos demandaaes por aazo de uossa molher, dizemdo que a
em elles dereito por seer filha del-Rey dom Pedro... *a esto respomdo que,*
salua vossa senhoria, vossa molher a Duquesa dona Costança nom ha em
elles nenhuum dereito; e a razom por que he esta: El-Rey dom Afomsso,
que foy enleito por emperador, era filho del-Rey dom Fernamdo, que
gaanhou Seuilha a mouros. Este dom Afomso ouue dous filhos: ao pri-
meiro diserom dom Fernamdo de la Çerda e ao segumdo dom Sancho.
Este dom Fernamdo, que era o mayor e herdeiro do regno, finou em vida
del-Rey seu padre e leixamdo huum legitimo filho que chamarom dom
Afomsso, assy como seu avoo. E este segundo jffamte dom Sancho, com
reçeo que de seu padre ouue, que quisesse emcamjnhar como herdasse os
regnos de Castella e de Leom este seu neto dom Afomsso, filho do jffamte
dom Fernando, seu primogenito, tomou a amjnistraçam delles, e deserdou
el-Rey dom Afomsso, seu padre; por a quall razom nom lhe deu a sa
bemçam quando moreo, amte o priuou de quallquer heramça que lhe nos
ditos regnos per alguuma gujssa pertemçesse; e assy o leixou em seu tes-
tamento, o quall oge em dia pareçe. E semdo neste passo, moreo el-Rey
dom Afomsso, seu padre, sem mais auemça que amtrelles ouuesse de serem
comcordados. E per esta guissa dom Sancho nom podia herdar, pois que
o padre o deserdaua em seu testamento, como dito he. E mais ajmda, por
outra forçada razom, que he esta: Por quamto os regnos de Castella e de
Leom de dereito pertemçem aos herdeiros do jffamte dom Fernamdo, que
era primogenito filho del-Rey dom Afomsso; assy que dom Sancho nom
podia herdar, nem el-Rey dom Fernando, seu filho, que depois foy rey,
nem dom Afomsso, que era seu neto, e tam pouco el-Rey dom Pedro nem
vossa molher, que foy sa filha. E quamdo tall eramça demandar qui-
sesse, mais razom era demandal-la dona Issabell pera seu filho que he
barom, que dona Costamça vossa molher, ajmda que a nenhuuma nom
pertemça — ffallamdo esto, Senhor, com reueremça presemte a uossa pes-
soa; ca pois que eu ey de dizer e mostrar todo dereito que emtender por
parte del-Rey, meu senhor, conuem que nomee vossa molher, per cujo aazo
entendees auer dereito em estes regnos. Mas herda em elles dereitamente
el-Rey dom Joham, meu senhor, vimdo da linhagem dos de la Çerda; ca
sua madre, a Rainha dona Joana, era bisneta do jffamte dom Fernamdo
de la Çerda, e per dereito he herdeiro destes regnos. E se aquy, Senhor,
ha alguuns leterados que comtra esta razom alguuma cousa dizer queiram,
eu som prestes pera tal desputaçam e prouar per dereito todo esto que
digo.

O Duque ouuio muy bem todo o que os mesegeiros diseram; e acabada sua embaxada, disse que *elles faziam como boons e leaaes seruidores*
em dizer por parte del-Rey, seu senhor, todo o que entemdiam e lhes era

regard for his right, I must speak to you in this way. Concerning the kingdoms of Castile and León to which you lay claim through your wife, saying that she has a right to them because she is the daughter of King Pedro, I have to reply that, saving your grace's presence, your wife the Duchess Doña Constanza has no right to them whatever. The reason is this. King Alfonso, who was elected emperor,[1] was the son of King Fernando who won Seville from the Moors.[2] This Alfonso had two sons, the first called Don Fernando de la Cerda[3] and the second Don Sancho.[4] Don Fernando, the elder and the heir to the kingdom, died before the King his father, leaving behind a legitimate son called Don Alfonso like his grandfather. The second prince, Don Sancho, was afraid that his father might arrange for his grandson Don Alfonso to inherit the kingdoms of Castile and León, as the son of Prince Fernando who was the King's firstborn. So Don Sancho ousted his father, taking the government of the kingdoms into his own hands. For this reason, when his father was dying he refused to give him his blessing, and thus took away from Don Sancho any right to the succession that he might otherwise have claimed; and so he set it down in his last will and testament where it is to be seen to this day. This was the state of affairs when his father King Alfonso died, without any reconciliation between them having been achieved. Because of this, Don Sancho could not succeed to the throne in view of the fact that his father disinherited him in his will, as I have said.

Moreover, there is yet another reason. The kingdoms of Castile and León belong by right to the heirs of Prince Fernando who was King Alfonso's first—born son. Therefore, Don Sancho could not succeed to the throne, nor could his son King Fernando who was king thereafter,[5] nor Don Alfonso his grandson;[6] and neither could King Pedro nor your wife who was his daughter. Now, if she were to wish to claim this inheritance, Doña Isabel would have a stronger case on behalf of her son because he is a male, than would your wife Doña Constanza, although neither has any right — and I say this with all due respect and saving your presence, my lord. For since I am bound to express and demonstrate as best I may the legitimate claim of my lord the King on his behalf, it is fitting, my lord, that I should name your wife by reason of whom you are a pretender to these kingdoms. On the other hand, King Juan my lord has inherited the throne legitimately because he is of the de la Cerda line of succession, for his mother, Queen Juana,[7] was great—granddaughter of Prince Fernando de la Cerda; and so he is the rightful heir to the kingdoms. If there are here any learned men, my lord, who wish to say anything against these arguments, I am prepared to dispute with them and to provide legal proof of everything I have said."

The Duke heard with attention everything the envoys had said. When the embassy was concluded, he said that they were behaving like good, loyal servants of the King in saying what they thought and what they had been ordered to say; and that since it was now time to

mandado; e pois ja era ora de comer, que fossem jamtar, e que el lhe
mandaria depois dar sua reposta.

Emtom se foy asentar, e feze-os comer comsigo, fazemdo-lhes boom gassalhado e toda homra.

LXXXVI
Como o Duque deu sua reposta a estas cousas que os embaxadores diserom.

Logo esse dia, depois que o Duque com(e)o, ouue seu comselho com esses senhores e leterados que com el vinham; e no outro seguimte mandou vijnr perante sy os embaxadores, e disse a huum bispo natural de Castella, criado del-Rey dom Pedro padre de sua molher, que sempre amdara com ella, que ja pera esto era aujssado, que respomde aaquelles mesageiros; o quall respomdeo a cada huum segundo a hordem que leuarom em propoer, e disse desta guissa:

Prioll, vos dires a uosso senhor, teente dos regnos de Castella e de Leom, que meu senhor, el-Rey de Castella e de L(e)om e Duque d'Allamcastro, que aquy estaa e vimdo a esta terra que he sua por causa e razom de sua molher, mjnha senhora, a Rainha dona Costamça, filha legitima del-Rey dom Pedro, e uosso senhor, que se chama rey della, ha gram tempo que a tem per força e assy fez seu padre. E tem meu senhor el-Rey que vosso senhor, que ora possue estes regnos, he theudo de lhos tornar com todallas remdas e proueitos que el e seu padre ataa ora delles ouuerom; e mais os danos que el-Rey, meu senhor, por tall aazo a reçebidos e as despessas que por esto ha feitas e faz em cada huum dia. Empero pello de Deus elle quer fazer assy que vosso senhor lhe desembargue logo sem outra condiçam os ditos regnos que assy detem, e el-Rey meu senhor e a Raynha sua molher lhe querem quitar todo o que ham leuado elle e seu padre, e lhe leixam as despessas que por tall aazo tem feitas e todo dano que por esta razom tem reçebido. E se o assy fazer nom qujser, meu senhor el-Rey ho entemde de liurar per diuinall juizo que julgue estas cousas.

E dada reposta a este, disse depois a Diego Lopez: *Caualleiro, uos dizee assy a uosso senhor que el-Rey meu senhor, que aquy estaa, breuemente lhe diz que el ha dereito nos regnos de Castella e de Leom por parte de sua molher, a Rainha dona Costamça, filha legitima e herdeira del-Rey dom Pedro, seu padre; e quamdo esta razom nom vallesse, que outras muytas e çertas tinha de que se bem ajudar pode quamdo elle emtendese de poer este (feyto) a demanda; o que el nom cuida fazer.*

eat, they should go to lunch, and afterwards he would order a reply to made to what they had said. So he sat down and made them eat with him, making them most welcome at his table and treating them with much honour.

LXXXVI
How the Duke made his reply to the things the ambassadors had said.

That same day, after he had eaten, he held council with the lords and learned men who had come with him. The following day he summoned the ambassadors before him and told a Castilian—born bishop[1] who had served King Pedro, his wife's father, and who always accompanied him and was an authority in the matter, to reply to the envoys. This bishop then responded to each envoy in the order in which they had each spoken, and did so in the following manner:

"Prior, tell your lord who holds the kingdoms of Castile and León that my lord the King of Castile and León and Duke of Lancaster, here present, has come to this land, which belongs to him by reason of his marriage to his wife, my lady Queen Constanza, legitimate daughter of King Pedro. Your lord, who calls himself king of this land, has held it by force for a long time as his father did before him. My lord the King says that your lord, who holds these kingdoms now, is obliged to return them to him, together with all income and profits that your lord and his father have derived from them; and he should also pay for the damages and expenses that my lord the King has incurred and still incurs every day. However, for the love of God, he is willing to accept the following terms: that your lord should immediately and unconditionally restore to him the aforementioned kingdoms that he holds thus, and my lord the King and his wife the Queen will excuse him from repaying all that he and his father have taken, and also the expenses that they have incurred in this matter as well as all the damages that for this reason they have borne. If he refuses to do this, my lord the King intends to leave these matters to the judgement of divine justice."

Having made this reply, he then spoke thus to Diego López: "Knight, tell your lord that my lord the King here present tells him in brief that he has the right to the kingdoms of Castile and León through his wife, Queen Constanza, legitimate daughter and heiress of King Pedro her father. Moreover, if this argument were not enough, there are many other good arguments to which he can have recourse when he decides to take the matter of judgment — something which he does not choose to do.

LXXXVII

Das raҙoões que mais emadeo o que daua a reposta por parte do Duque.

Respomdido aaquèlles dous esto que temdes ouujdo, emadeo o bispo em suas razoões e disse contra o doutor:

Doutor uos [5] diҙees em nome de uoso senhor que el-Rey dom Sancho deserdou seu padre el-Rey dom Afomsso, e que por esta raҙom o padre nom lhe deu a sa bemҫom nem o erdou em seu testamento, e que segundo esto nenhuum seu descendente nom pode herdar os regnos de Castella, pois os nom herdaua el-Rey dom Sancho. A esto respomde el-Rey, meu senhor, que aquy estaa, que segundo el pode ɀeer enformado el-Rey dom Sancho nom feҙ erro comtra seu padre como uos diҙees; ca em vida del-Rey seu padre nunca se el-Rey dom Sancho chamou rrey, mas vemdo os fidalgos de Castella e de Lleom como aquel Rey dom Afomso era prodigo e degastador e mjnjstraua mal os beens do regno e nom se auya bem nos feitos da justiça, tiram-lhe a menjstraçam e prouymento dos ditos regnos, e emcomendarom-no emtom a este jffamte dom Sancho, que depois da morte de seu padre foy rey. E diҙem que o dito Rey dom Afomsso, pero que soube que a emliçam do emperio dAlemanha nom fora feita a elle cm concordia, saluo alguumas poucas voҙes que por sua parte ouuera, desejamdo de seer emperador, lamçou em-no regno gramdes peitas, e foi sse ataa Avinham, homde o Papa estomçe estaua, pedindo-lhe que o coroasse, e esto com muytas companhas e gramdes despessas; e o Papa o nom qujs faҙer, e tornou-se pera o regno, leixamdo-o muy gastado e bem destroido. E mais, que el casou huuma filha bastarda, que diserom dona Briatiҙ, com el-Rey dom Afomsso de Portugall, comde que foy de Bolonha; e por aaҙo deste casamento lhe deu çertos logares que Castella naquell regno auja, e lhe quitou o ffeudo que el-Rey de Portugall era theudo por elles de faҙer. E jsso mesmo falleçeo na justiça, que sem semdo ouuidos de seu dereito, mandou matar dom Fadrique, seu jrmaão legitimo, e a dom Ximom dos Cameiros, que era huum gram rico (o)mem, e assy a outros fidalgos; por a quall raҙom dom Nuno, senhor de Lara, e dom Fernam Ruiҙ de Saldanha e outros senhores e fidalgos que se forom do regno pera el-Rey de Graada. Por esto, quamdo foy dada comtra elle semtença em Valhadollide aa petiçom de todollos do regno que perdese a mjnjstraçam, huuma das raҙoões que forom postas comtra elle foy esta: que lhe deuya seer tirada a espada da maão e a justiça, pois que mal husara della, —e assy se mostra seu regimento quegemdo era! — o quall lhe tirarom, e derom a seu filho o jffamte dom Sancho, que depois regnou. E assy nom erou comtra elle o dito jffante que o padre o quisesse deserdar; amtes foy muy boom rey e manteue o regno em dereito e em justiça, e guereou os mouros, e ganhou

LXXXVII
Of the further arguments added by the Duke's spokesman on his behalf.

Having replied to these two spokesmen as you have just heard, the bishop added these words, saying to the doctor:[1]

"Doctor, you say in your master's name that King Sancho ousted his father King Alfonso, and that for this reason the father did not give him his blessing or leave him anything in his will, so that none of his descendants can inherit the kingdoms of Castile, since King Sancho himself did not inherit them.   My lord the King here present answers this by saying that as far as he is able to judge from information received, King Sancho did not wrong his father as you claim; for Don Sancho never called himself king while the King his father lived.   However, seeing how prodigal and spendthrift King Alfonso was and how poorly he administered the resources of the kingdom, as well as how unjust he was his rule, the nobles of Castile and León took from him the government and administration of the said kingdoms and entrusted them to this Prince Sancho, who became king after his father's death.   It is said that although this King Alfonso knew that he had not been elected Emperor of Germany unanimously but had had only a tiny number of votes in his favour, yet he was still desirous of becoming emperor, and levied heavy taxes in the kingdom; then he went with a great retinue and at heavy expense to Avignon, where the Pope then was, asking him to crown him.   The Pope refused to do this, so he returned to the kingdom which he had left so wasted and dilapidated.   Moreover, he married his bastard daughter Beatriz to King Afonso of Portugal, who had previously been Count of Boulogne; and because of this marriage, he gave him certain places that Castile possessed in that kingdom and relieved him of the feudal service that the King of Portugal was obliged to perform in return for these possessions.

He also acted quite unjustly in ordering Don Fadrique, his legitimate brother, and Don Simón de los Cameros, a great magnate, to be killed, along with other nobles, without letting them be heard in their own defence.   For this reason, Don Nuño, lord of Lara, and Don Fernán Ruiz de Saldaña and other lords and nobles left the kingdom and went into exile at the Court of the King of Granada. Because of this, when sentence was passed against him in Valladolid, at the request of all his subjects, that the government of the kingdom be taken out of his hands, one of the arguments brought against him was this: that the sword of justice should be taken from him, since he had wielded it so badly; and so, from this, the nature of his rule is quite obvious!   They took away his right to rule and gave it to his son Prince Sancho, who reigned after him.   So this prince committed no offence against his father for which the latter should wish to disinherit him.   On the contrary, he was a very good king who ruled the kingdom fairly and justly, fought against the Moors, won from

delles a villa de Tarifa, e nunca em vida de seu padre se chamou rey.

Outrossy el-Rey dom Fernamdo, filho deste Rey dom Sancho, foy muy boom rey, e ganhou aos mouros a uilla de Gibaltar e a villa de Castello dAlcoudete. E seu filho el-Rey dom Afomsso, que muytos dos que som viuos o conheçerom, sabem que foy muy nobre rey; e vemçeo os Reis de Belamarym e de Grada na batalha de Tarifa, de que a chrijstandade cobrou gramde homra. E guanhou-lhe as villas dAljaʒira e Allcalla a Rreall e Teba e outros castellos; e leixou por herdeiro seu filho, el-Rey dom Pedro, em hidade pouca mais de qujmʒe annos. E todollos do regno, assy senhores come prellados e villas e çidades de Castella, todos o reçeberom per seu Rey e senhor paçificamente e sem nenhuuma comtradiçom. E ajmda dom Emrique, padre de uosso senhor teedor que ora he dos regnos de Castella e de Leom, lhe obedeçeo estomçe, e o tomou por seu Rey e senhor. E assy tem el-Rey, meu senhor, que esta raʒom que uos diʒees nom ha logar em tal caso.

Outrossy ao que diʒees que vosso senhor vem de linhagem dos de la Zerda, e que por esta raʒom ha dereito em estes regnos, a esto vos respomdo que bem sabem em Castella como dom Afomsso de la Çerda, filho legitimo desse jffamte dom Fernamdo que vos diʒes, renunçiou alguum dereito, se o no regno auja, por çertos logares que lhe foram dados, de que ouuesse gram remda de dinheiro, e que nunca mais trouuesse taaes armas nem sello como damte tragia; semdo deste feito juiʒ el-Rey dom Denjs de Portugall e el-Rey dom James dAragom, de que sobresto ouuesse feitas muy firmes scprituras. Assy que esta questom que ora moues, ja dias ha que he cessada.

E quamto he ao que tocastes da heramça do filho de dona Issabell, bem he çerto e sabem todos que morto dom Afomsso, filho del-Rey dom Pedro, a que todo o regno tinha feita menagem de o reçeber por senhor, que el-Rey hordenou depois cortes em que declarou por herdeiras suas filhas todas tres como naçerom, huuma depos outra, e que assy herdassem os regnos, e ho feʒ jurar aos poboos: saber, dona Briatiʒ primeiro; e acomteçemdo de morer sem filhos, herdasse dona Costamça. E por emde em desputaçam de leterados el-Rey, meu senhor, e a Rainha dona Costança, sua molher, nom ham porque poer seu dereito, saluo semdo elles primeiro restetuidos aa posissam dos ditos regnos segundo os teue paçificamente el-Rey dom Pedro, que ˀelles foj lidimo posuidor, padre da Rainha dona Costança, minha senhora, que aquy he, e aquelles reis domde ella uem de muy gram tempo aca. E semdo el-Rey, meu senhor, e a Rainha sua molher restituidos em paçifica posissam dos ditos regnos, emtom lhe praʒ de mostrar seu dereito perante quallquer juiʒ que pera esto abastamte for.

them the town of Tarifa, and never called himself king while his father lived.

Furthermore, King Fernando, son of this King Sancho, was a very good king, and won from the Moors the town of Gibraltar and the town and castle of Alcaudete. There are many people still alive who knew his son, King Alfonso, and who know him to have been a very noble king. He defeated the Kings of the Banu Marin and Granada at the battle of Tarifa, which brought great honour to Christendom; and he won for Christendom the towns of Algeciras, Alcalá la Real and Teba as well as other strongholds. He left behind as heir his son, King Pedro, who was at that time but a little over fifteen years of age. The whole kingdom, lords, prelates, towns and cities of Castile, all recognized him as their king and lord, peacefully and without opposition. Even Don Enrique, father of your lord who today holds the kingdoms of Castile and León, obeyed him at that time and recognized him as his lord and king. Therefore, my lord the King maintains that your argument on this point has no foundation.

Furthermore, regarding your argument that your lord is of the line of the de la Cerdas and therefore has a claim to these kingdoms, I have to reply to you that it is well known in Castile that Don Alfonso de la Cerda, legitimate son of that Prince Fernando of whom you speak, renounced any right he might have had to the kingdom, in return for certain lands that were given to him, from which he stood to derive a considerable income, and on the understanding that henceforth he would no longer use the royal coat—of—arms and seal that he had used hitherto. King Dinis of Portugal and King Jaime of Aragon were mediators who saw to it that there should be firm documentary proof of the transaction. So this dispute that you now raise was in fact settled long ago.

Concerning the inheritance of the son of Doña Isabel that you mentioned, it is certain and well known to everyone that on the death of King Pedro's son Alfonso, [2] whom the whole kingdom had sworn to accept as their lord, the King summoned a parliament at which he declared his heirs to be his three daughters in the order in which they were born; and he made the people swear that they should succeed to the kingdoms in this manner, that is: Doña Beatriz would be the first in line; and in the event of her dying without issue, Doña Constanza would succeed to the throne. Because of this, my lord the King and Queen Constanza here present have no need to put their formal case until they have first had restored to them the aforesaid kingdoms in the manner in which they were peacefully held by King Pedro, their legitimate owner, and father of my lady, Queen Constanza here present, and by those kings from whom she is descended going back to the distant past. Once my lord the King and his wife the Queen have had the aforementioned kingdoms peacefully restored to them, then they are pleased to demonstrate their right to them before any judge deemed competent in the matter."

Os embaxadores, desque todo ouuirom, diserom ao Duque que elles auyam bem emtendido quamto por sua parte fora preposto, mas que elles se firmauom no que ja amte tinham dito; e pedirom leçemça ao Duque, e tornaram-sse pera Castella.

Hora neste logar scpreuem alguuns que o prior de Gadalupe, depois que a primeira disse sua embaxada, que fallou ao Duque secretamente, dizemdo que a prinçipall cousa por que o el-Rey a el mandara, assy fora por lhe dizer da sua parte que el nom auja mais dhuuma filha de dona Costamça, sua molher, que era neta del-Rey dom Pedro, e que el tinha huum filho lidimo, que chamauam dom Emrique; e que se a el prouguesse de casarem ambos, que seriam depois herdeiros dos regnos, e çesaria esta questam e comtemda. E enhadem mais que acabada esta reposta de dar aos embaxadores, que o Duque mandou a Castella com elles huum caualleiro chamado Thomas Persy, e que emtom se trautou o casamento do jffante dom Emrique com dona Catellina, filha do Duque, prometendo-lhe el-Rey gram conthia douro por com elle seer dacordo.

A outros despraz de tall razoado, dizemdo que nom foy assy. Ca se o casamento fora emtom trautado e firme, nom se seguirom depois taaes reuoltas e desuairos como adeamte verees. Ca el emtemdia de cobrar o regno, que hera mais homra que tal casamento; nom he de cujdar que logo assy apresa, por lhe esto mouerem sem mais seer açertado, dese fim a sua requesta.

LXXXVIII

Que homem era o Duque dAllamcastro e sua molher dona Costança.

A nos pareçe errarem muyto quantos naquell tempo scpreuerom a vimda deste Duque e casamento del-Rey com sua filha nom poer que homeem era e o linhagem domde vinha. E pois que a preguiça de taaes autores foy madre daquesu eror, e as cousas tostemente passam e se dam a esqueçimento, por se esto de todo nom perder de memoria queremos aqui em breue nembrar, quanto fezer a nosso proposito, quem foy seu padre e madre, pois que os reis de Portugall com el tem tam grande diuedo.

Omde, segumdo tam tarde apanhar podemos, deues de saber que el-Rey de Imgraterra, dom Duarte o quarto, ouue da Rainha dona Issabell sua molher cimquo filhos baroões. Ao primeiro, segumdo costume de nosso fallar que foy o Prinçepe de Gallez, chamarom dom Duarte

When they had heard everything, the ambassadors told the Duke that they had well understood everything that had been expressed on his behalf, but that they firmly stood by all that they had said already. So they asked the Duke for leave to depart and returned to Castile.

Now, at this point, some have written[3] that after he had presented his first embassy, the Prior of Guadalupe spoke secretly to the Duke saying that the main reason the King had sent him had been to tell him on his behalf that the Duke and his wife Doña Constanza had only one daughter, who was King Pedro's granddaughter, while he himself had a legitimate son called Don Enrique. If the Duke were agreeable, these two people could be married, thereby becoming heirs to the throne, and thus the dispute would be at an end. These writers add that when he had made reply to the ambassadors, the Duke ordered a knight called Thomas Percy to accompany them to Castile, and that there he had discussions concerning the marriage of Prince Enrique with Lady Catherine, the Duke's daughter, during which the King promised the Duke a large sum of gold in return for his assent to this marriage.

This theory finds no favour with other writers who say that this did not happen. For if the marriage had been arranged at that time on a firm basis, the violent reactions and disagreements that you shall later see would not have ensued. For the Duke was intent on recovering the kingdom as there was more honour to be gained thereby than through such a marriage; and since they were urging him to accept the arrangement without any real guarantee, it is inconceivable that he would renounce his quest so soon and so quickly.

LXXXVIII
Of what kind of man the Duke of Lancaster was and what kind of woman his wife Doña Constanza was.

It seems to us a mistake on the part of those who wrote in those times of the arrival of this Duke and the marriage of his daughter to our King, not to set down what manner of man the Duke was or to describe his lineage. Since the laziness of those writers was the mother of their error, and since, too, things pass away so quickly and are soon forgotten, in order that some record should be preserved of the matter, we intend at this point to remind you briefly, in so far as is relevant to our purpose, who his father and mother were, seeing that the kings of Portugal are so closely linked with him.

As far as we have been able to gather so long after the events, you should know that the King of England, Edward IV,[1] had five sons by his wife, Queen Isabel. The first of these, whom we customarily refer to as the Prince of Wales, was called Edward like

assy como seu padre; o segundo ouue nome dom Lionel, que foy duque de Claremça; ao terçeiro diserom dom Joham; o quarto dom Edmondo ; o quinto Thomas Hulestoque , duque de Glossestre.

E tornamdo a fallar do terçeiro e quarto filhos, acomteçeo desta gujssa: que semdo aquell jffante dom Joham solteiro, casou com dona Bramca, filha herdeira do muyto homrado e exçellente prinçepe dom Emrique, duque dAllamcastro, huum senhor muy rico e dalto linhagem e em autos de caualaria muy famosso; e per bem deste casamento, semdo o padre della ja finado, cobrou el a homra do sogro, que a filha soçedia; e foy chamado Duque dAllamcastro. Este dom Joham ouue desta sa molher duas filhas e huum filho: a primeira ouue nome dona Issabel, que foy casada com monsire Joham dOlamda, comde de Huntingdon, jrmaão del-Rey Richarte dIngraterra da parte da madre; a segumda ouue nome dona Filipa, que desta vimda ficou casada com el-Rey dom Joham de Portugall de que fallamos. O filho ouue nome dom Emrique, que primeiro foy comde (de) Derby e desy duque de Hereforte, e depois da morte de seu padre foy duque dAllancastro e em fym foy Rey dImgraterra; e assy forom depois delle don Emrique seu filho e jsso mesmo dom Emrique seu neto.

Hora assy foy, como temdes ouujdo, que el-Rey dom Pedro de Castella, estamdo em Seuilha e sabemdo que dom Emrique seu jrmaão se coroara em Burgos e tomara titullo de rey, e lhe deziam que vinha sobrelle, que fogio da çidade, e passou per Portugall e se foy a Galliza e dhij a Bayona, a logar de Ingraterra, leuamdo comsigo suas tres filhas, saber, dona Briatjz e dona Costamça e dona Issabell; e feitas suas auemças com o Prinçepe de Gallez sobre aquella ajuda que lhe de fazer auya, foy posto nos trautos amtrelles concordados que ataa que o Primçepe e suas gemtes ouuessem pagamento de todo o que auiam dauer, ficassem suas filhas per maneira darrefeens em Imgraterra. A batalha feita como comtamos e el-Rey posto em posse do regno, tornou-se o Prinçepe bem mall comtente, sem lhe seer feito pagamento. Foy el-Rey depois vemçido e morto como ouujstes, e ficarom estas jffantes orfaãs de todo, sem terras nem remdas nem outra cousa que teuessem; e falleçemdo dona Briatiz per morte, ficarom as duas em tal desemparo. Em esto, açertou-se de fazer fym de sa vida dona Bramca, molher do Duque dAllamcastro; e o muy poderoso e muy exçellemte senhor dom Eduarte, Rey de Imgraterra, veemdo a orfimdade destas jffamtes, hussamdo dhuuma nobre e façanhosa gramdeza, casou a mayor dellas, chamada dona Costamça, com este dom Joham, Duque dAllancastro, e dona Issabell, a mais pequena, com o seu quarto filho dom Edmondo, comde de Cambrix, que depois foy duque dIorca, o que veo a este regno em tempo del-Rey dom Fernamdo, como em seu logar compridamente possemos.

his father. The second was called Lionel, Duke of Clarence. The third was called John; the fourth, Edmund; and the fifth, Thomas of Woodstock, Duke of Gloucester.

Returning to the third and fourth sons, it happened this way. When Prince John was a batchelor, he married Blanche, daughter and heiress of the most noble honourable and excellent Prince Henry, Duke of Lancaster, who was very wealthy and high−born, and renowned for his deeds of chivalry. As a dowry for this marriage, he acquired the honours of his father−in−law, who was already dead and had been succeeded by his daughter;[2] so he gained the title of Duke of Lancaster. This John of Lancaster had two daughters and a son by this wife. The first−born was called Elizabeth, and was married to Sir John Holland, Earl of Huntingdon and brother to King Richard of England on his mother's side. The second was called Philippa who became the wife of King João of Portugal as a result of the voyage we are describing. The son was called Henry, who was at first Earl of ˙Derby, and then Duke of Hereford, and, after the death of his father, Duke of Lancaster and finally King of England, as were his son Henry and grandson Henry after him.[3]

So it was that, as you have heard, King Pedro of Castile was in Seville and learnt that his brother Don Enrique had had himself crowned in Burgos and assumed the title of king. He was told that Enrique was coming to attack him; so he fled the city and passed by way of Portugal to Galicia and thence to Bayonne, an English possession, taking with him his three daughters, Doña Beatriz, Doña Constanza and Doña Isabel. When coming to an understanding with the Prince of Wales about the assistance he would receive, it was stipulated in the agreements made between them that until the Prince and his men had received payment of all that was due to them, Don Pedro's daughters would remain as hostages in England. After the battle we described and with the King in possession of his kingdom, the Prince was discontented because he had not received payment. Later, the King was defeated and killed as you have heard, so that these princesses were now orphans, without any lands or income or any other property of their own. When Doña Beatriz died, the other two were left without any protection whatever. At this point, the Duke of Lancaster's wife Blanche happened to die; and the most powerful and excellent King Edward of England, seeing these two princesses orphaned, made a most noble and magnanimous gesture, marrying the elder of the two, Doña Constanza, to John, Duke of Lancaster; and the younger, Doña Isabel, to his fourth son Edmund, Earl of Cambridge, who was later to become Duke of York, and who came to Portugal in the time of King Fernando, as we related at length in the proper place.

Como o Duque partio da Crunha e ouue a çidade de Santiago.

Este dom Joham, Duque dAllancastro, era homem de bem feitos membros , comprido e dereito, nom de tantas carnes que requeria a gramdeza de seu corpo, e seria de jdade ataa lx annos, de poucas cãas segundo taaes dias, e de boõa pallaura nom muyto trigosa, mesurado e de booas comdiçoões; e tragia comsigo sua molher e filhos, chamando-se em suas cartas Rey de Castella e de Lleom e dos outros logares que se em tal ditado custumam poer. E tragia nas bamdeiras e sellos castellos e leoões, posto que trouuesse com ellas mizcladas as armas de Framça e de Imgraterra. E sua molher chamauam (a) Rainha dona Costamça e suas filhas jffantes por bem daquelle ditado. E nas cartas e desembargos poinha o Duque por sinall: *Nos elRey;* e sua molher dona Costamça scpreuya: *la Raina.*

O Duque na Crunha como dizemos, estaua no logar por guarda delle huum boom fidalgo gallego, chamado Fernam Perez dAmdrade, com gentes quantas pertemçiam, mas nom pera tall poder. E uemdo que lhe nom prestaua defemssam que prouar quisesse, mandou dizer ao Duque que lhe queria obedeçer e fazer seu mandado; e que nom auya por se ally mais deteer, mas que se fosse logo a Santiago, que era o prinçipall logar daquella comarca; e cobrado aquelle, tomados eram todos, e dessy pello regno adeamte, ca nelle nom tinha nenhuuma referta. O Duque ouue estas por boõas razoões, e partio-sse pera aquella çidade, que eram dally dez legoas, com sua molher e filhos e toda sua gemte. E porque el nom emtrou na Crunha, nem se apoderou do logar leixamdo alcayde de ssa maão como he costume, diserom alguns que o nom tomara; e contauom jsto a Fernam Perez por gramde sageza e ao Duque por simprizidade.

O Duque em Santiago cobrou logo a çidade, e assy pella mayor parte toda (a) terra de Galliza, sem outra pelleja nem combato de logares, vimdo-sse pera elle muytos caualleiros gallegos e castellaãos, prometendo-lhe as villas e logares que tinham, e beixando-le a maão por senhor. Os poboos jsso mesmo em bestas e carros lhe tragiam muytos mantimentos e cauallos a uemder; as quaaes cousas os jmgreses comprauom por acostumados preços aa vomtade dos que lhas vemdiam, sem tomando a seus donos vallor dhuum dinheiro, so pena de perder a cabeça quallquer que o comtrairo fezesse, segumdo a hordenamça do Duque. O quall, vemdo este boom começo, cuidamdo que toda Castella lhe obedeçesse por aazo de sua molher, como dizemos, fez logo na See de Santiago tomar voz do Papa Vrbano e leixar do que chamauom Clemente Septimo; e emlegerom de nouo arçebispo e dayam, que pouco durarom naquella homra;

How the Duke left Corunna and took the city of Santiago de Compostela.

This Dom John, Duke of Lancaster, was a well built—man, tall and upright, carrying less weight than one would expect from the size of his frame. He would be about sixty years old[1] but with fewer white hairs than is normal for one of his age. He spoke well and without haste, being self—controlled and good—humoured. He brought with him his wife and children. In his documents, he always styled himself King of Castile and of León and of other places that are customarily included. He had castles and lions on his banners and seals even though this meant they were mixed up with the arms of France and England. His wife was called Queen Constanza and his daughters princesses in the same way. The Duke always signed his letters and legal documents, "We the King", while his wife Doña Constanza signed: "The Queen".

When the Duke was at Corunna, as we have said, the castellan there was a good Galician noble called Fernán Pérez de Andrade, with the troops assigned to the town's defence, but they were insufficient for the task of resisting such a large invasion. Judging that no defence he might attempt would be successful, he sent word to the Duke that he would obey him and do his bidding. He advised him not to linger there, but to go on straightaway to Santiago, the principal town of the region. Once Santiago was taken, the other towns would all surrender and thereafter the whole kingdom, for there would be no resistance. The Duke found these arguments convincing and so set out, together with his wife, children and all his forces, for that city which was ten leagues distant. Now because he neither entered Corunna nor took formal possession of it by leaving there a castellan of his own choosing, as is customary, some said that he had not captured it; and they considered that this showed the great wisdom of Fernán Pérez and the naivety of the Duke.

The Duke captured Santiago very quickly and, in general, the whole land of Galicia, without any further fighting or besieging of strongholds. Many Galician and Castilian knights came to him promising him the towns and fortresses they held and kissing his hand as a sign that they accepted him as their lord. Similarly, the peasants brought him provisions on pack—animals and in carts; and they also brought horses to sell to him. The English bought these things at their usual prices, according to the vendors' wishes, without stealing a single penny from them, in obedience to the Duke's ordinance, that anyone who did otherwise would lose his head. In view of this good start to the campaign, the Duke felt that all Castile would obey him by reason of his wife, as we have said; so, there and then in the cathedral of Santiago, he had a proclamation made in favour of Pope Urban and rejecting the man called Pope Clement VII. They elected a new archbishop[2] and dean, for Don Juan

ca dom Joham Garçia Manrique, arçebispo desse logar, amdaua estomçe em casa del-Rey de Castella e nom podia esto comtradizer.

XC
Como el-Rey soube parte da ujnda do Duque, e se ueo ao Porto.

El-Rey de Portugall estamdo em Lamego, homde (o) leixamos quando partio de Coyra, trouueram-lhe nouas Joham Gill do Porto e Gomez Eannes , seu moço destrebeira, como o Duque chegara a Galliza da guissa que dissemos. O Duque jsso mesmo, segumdo alguuns afirmaam, emuiou logo a el-Rey suas cartas, em que lhe fez saber como el era vimdo em Galliza e aportara naquel logar da Crunha, trazemdo comsigo sua molher e filhos, por cobrar o regno de Castella que lhe per dereito pertemçia, e (que lhe prazeria)[3] de se veer com elle.

El-Rey, com taaes nouas, foy assaz de ll(ed)o , e veo-sse logo caminho do Porto; e ally teue comselho denuiar seus embaxadores ao Duque, e mandar chamar o Comdestabre e outros do regno, e fazer liures pera quamdo se ouuessem de uer.

Em esto aconteçeo que Martim Rodriguez de Seuilha que fora com as outras gallees corer a costa dlngraterra, e ueeram primeiro trazer nouas a el-Rey de Castella daquella armada que se comtra elle fazia, que amdaua emtom no mar em dereito da çidade do Porto, e tinha ally o caminho a quaeesquer nauios de Portugall e de Imgratera com que sentia sua melhoria. E huuma nom bem clara manhaã seguya aquella gallee huum nauio de Portugall por lhe fazer maa companhia ; e temdo(-o) ja açerca tomado , sobreueo huuma naão de portuguesses, e com vento auomdo chegou-sse a elle e matou-lhe muyta gente, tomando-a per força; e liurou o nauio que tinha tomado, e trouue-a ao Porto com muyta riqueza que em ella amdaua. E Martym Rodriguez veo presso na gallee; o quall depois deu por sy dez mjll dobras. E solto, foy-sse logo a Castella, e emcaualgou-sse e ouue gemtes, e veo-sse a Oliuemça, que tinha po(r) Castella Pero Rodriguez da Fomsseca. E vimdo corer a Portugall, sayram a elle do redomdo, e emcalçarom-no e premderam-no, e foy morto per Estaçinho dEuora.

E logo açerca pasados poucos dias que Martim Rodriguez fora tomado, veeram as naaos e gallees de Portugall que estauom na Crunha, e o Mestre de Santiago e Louremçeannes Fogaça em ellas; os quaaes durarom fora do regno, do dia que partirom de Lixboa ataa que chegarom a Crunha, tres annos e tres messes e vimte e çimquo dias. E em huuma vinha todo o thesouro do Duque, o quall tragia pera fazer moeda de que

García Manrique, Archbishop of Santiago, was away at the·time at the court of the King of Castile and therefore was unable to resist this move; but the new prelates enjoyed their new honours for only a short time.

XC
How the King learnt of the Duke's arrival, and came to Oporto.

Whilst the King of Portugal was in Lamego, where we left him after he had departed from Coria, João Gil de Oporto and Gomes Eanes, his stable—boy, brought him news of how the Duke had landed in Galicia in the way we have described. Some writers assert that in fact the Duke immediately sent letters to the King, informing him of how he had come to Galicia and landed in Corunna, bringing with him his wife and children, in order to win the kingdom of Castile that was his by right, and that he was most anxious to meet him.

The King was most pleased at the news, and travelled immediately to Oporto. There, he was advised to send ambassadors to the Duke, summon the Constable and others, and to make arrangements for when they were to meet.

At this time, it happened that Martín Rodríguez de Sevilla, who had gone with a force of galleys to harass the English coast, and had been the first to bring news to the King of Castile of that fleet that was being prepared to come against him, was sailing towards the city of Oporto. There he encountered some Portuguese and English vessels to which he felt his force to be superior. One morning in poor visibility he was pursuing a Portuguese vessel in order to engage it and, when he had already captured it, suddenly a Portuguese warship with a good following wind came from nowhere and attacked him, killing many of his men and capturing his ship. It freed the ship that he had taken, bringing it to Oporto with all the wealth it contained. Martín Rodríguez was a prisoner in the galley, but he subsequently ransomed himself in exchange for ten thousand *dobras*, and, once released, he went Castile. Then he got himself a horse, collected some troops and went to Olivenza which was held for Castile by Pedro Rodríguez de Fonseca. From there he set out to make marauding raids in Portugal; but people came against him from all around, pursued and captured him, and he was killed by Estacinho de Évora.

Only a few days after Martín Rodríguez was captured, the Portuguese ships and galleys which were in Corunna arrived, together with the Master of São Tiago and Lourenço Eanes Fogaça. From the time they left Lisbon until their arrival in Corunna, they were out of the kingdom three years, three months and twenty—five days. One of the ships transported the whole of the Duke's treasury which he

fezesse pagamento aos seus; assy como a ffez de pois em Galliza e naquella çidade do Porto; ca laurou reaaes de prata de sete dinheiros e de seis e outra moeda semelhante aa de dez soldos que em Portugal corya, e tinha no cunho armas de Castella com outras mesturas; e moeda mais pequena fazia outra pera cambiar.

El-Rey, quamdo soube que o Mestre ally vinha, foi-sse aa ribeira por o reçeber. E ue(o)-sse o Mestre com el pera hu pousaua; e ally fallarom per gramde espaço em sua embaxada e cousas que lhe compriam.

O Mestre vinha muy garnido de roupas e armas e apostamentos de casa, como aquell que o bem fazer podia segumdo o poder que leuaua de tirar emprestado sobre as mercadorias do regno em quamto tempo la esteuesse; e mandou logo aa terra da ordem por gentes e cauallos e bestas de seruemtia; e vinham-lhe assaz dellas e muytos escudeiros e freires de sua hordem. E el emuolto em mundanal gloria e muyto priuado del-Rey, amtre os outros mandou-ho chamar a Morte, que o auya mester, e fez ally fim de seus dias. E ouue el-Rey de seus guarnimentos e cousas quamtas lhe prougue. E ficou delle huuma filha pequena que ouuera dhuuma jngresa, que chamauom Lora, que tragia comsigo; a quall el-Rey criou e a casou depois per tempo com Gomçallo Vaasquez Coutinho, marichall de sua hoste, semdo el emtom vehuuo da sua primeira molher. E foy esta chamada dona Joana da parte do padre que era Mestre.

XCI

Como el-Rey emuyou fallar ao Duque, e omde comcordarom de se veerem ambos.

Hordenou el-Rey demuyar seus embaxadores ao Duque, e mandou la Vaasquo Martjnz de Mello e Louremçeannes Fogaça, com suas cartas e messagem, cuja finall comclusom era que lhe prazia muyto de sua vimda e da temçom que tragia, e que compria de se ueerem ambos por comcordar e auer comselho que maneira auiam de teer no proseguimento da guerra de Castella. Os quaaes leuarom caminho de Galliza, e chegarom ao Duque, homde pousaua, a horas que se leuamtaua de jamtar. E bem reçebidos delle e dos fidalgos que eram presemtes, logo sobre mesa lhe derom as cartas e fallarom todo aquello por que eram emuyados. O Duque, sem mais delomga, teue esse dia comselho; e comcordado com os embaxadores, acharom que era bem de se veerem aa Ponte do Mouro amtre Melgaço e Monçom, que eram dezanoue legoas do Porto, e que o Duque fosse emtom chegamdo aaquell (logar), e el-Rey jsso mesmo

carried with him so as to coin money and pay his men. He did this later, in Galicia and in the city of Oporto itself; for he minted silver coins (*reales*) worth seven pennies each, as well as others worth six, and he also minted another coin like the ten—shilling piece which was current in Portugal then, but its die contained the arms of Castile in combination with others. He also minted another smaller coin to facilitate money—changing.

When he knew that the Master of São Tiago was coming, the King went to the quayside to welcome him. The Master went with the King to his lodging; and there they talked a long time concerning his embassy and other matters relating to it.

The Master had returned well provided with fine clothes, arms, and furniture. He was in an excellent position to acquire these things, thanks to the powers with which he was invested throughout the time he was in England, that enabled him to borrow against the credit accruing there for imported Portuguese goods.

As soon as he landed, he summoned men, horses and pack—animals from his Order's lands. Many came with squires and friars of the Order. There, surrounded by worldly pomp, the King's favourite was himself summoned from among his men by Death, who had need of him; and there he ended his days. The King it was who had the pick of these luxuries and fine purchases. The Master left behind a little daughter whom he had had by an English woman called Laura, and whom he had brought back with him. The King himself raised her and married her in due course to Gonçalo Vasques Coutinho, the Marshal of his army, who was at the time a widower having lost his first wife. She was called Dona Joana because of her father who was the Master of São Tiago.

XCI
How the King sent word to the Duke and
where they agreed to meet each other.

The King ordered ambassadors to be sent to the Duke. He sent Vasco Martins de Melo[1] and Lourenço Eanes Fogaça with letters and a message the conclusion of which was that he was very happy at the Duke's coming and at his purpose. He also said that it was important that they should see one another so as to reach an understanding and take counsel concerning how best to prosecute their Castilian war. These two envoys set out for Galicia and arrived at the Duke's headquarters when he had just finished dinner. They were well received by him and by the nobles present; and without more ado they handed to him at table the letters they carried and imparted to him everything as instructed. Without delay, the Duke held council the same day. With the agreement of the ambassadors, they thought it best that they should meet at Ponte do Mouro between Melgaço and Monção, some nineteen leagues from Oporto. The Duke should

parteria daquella çidade e leuaria aquell camjnho. Estomçe comerom com o Duque aa çea em salla que mandou fazer a elles e aos senhores que com el estauom; e espedidos delle, tornaram-sse com sua reposta.

Hora aquy dizem alguuns que logo nesta embaxada foy fallado sobre casamento del-Rey com huuma filha do Duque; mas quamdo quer que fosse mouido, el-Rey teue comselho sobrello, no quall lhe muytos com-selhauom que casasse com dona Catellina, neta del-Rey dom Pedro, dizemdo que per ally lhe podia vijr aazo de hordenar depois os regnos de Castella; outros deziam com a jffamte dona Felipa ; e a comclusom de todos foy que el (a) que esto mais pertemçia, escolhesse quall sua merçee fosse.

E el-Rey disse que *pois a escolha auya de ficar neelle como era de razom, que sua vomtade nom se outorgaua casar com a jffante dona Ca-tellina, porque lhe pareçia casamento com mestura daroydo de nunca perder guerra quem com ella casasse por aazo da heramça que sua ma-dre emtemdia dauer no regno de Castella; doutra guissa, leixamdo-a de fazer quem a ouuesse por molher, que lho comtariam por myngua e seria sempre prasmado; e que pois, a Deus graças, el estaua com ujtoria de seus emmjgos, que lhe nom entemdia de mouer mais guerra, saluo por cobrar o que lhe tomado tinham e ataa que lhe dessem paz, e estomçe viuer asessegado, gouernamdo seu regno em dereito e em justiça. E ajmda dizia el que esto era muyto melhor pera o Duque; porque amdando elles em guerra, podia seer que falleçeria a el-Rey de Castella sua molher, e casaria com esta jffamte ou casaria com ella seu filho que esperaua de herdar o regno; e esto lhe vinha muyto bem aa maõo pera cessar tall comtenda com homra dhuum e do outro, o que a ell avijr nom podia. E assy ficou determinado, prazemdo a Deus, de casar com a jffamte dona Phillipa.*

XCII
Como el-Rey e o Duque se uirom a primeira vez.

Em passamdo assy estas cousas gastauam-sse os dias, e era ja no mes doutubro. E o Duque chegou aaquell moesteiro de Çellanoua, que he em Galliza, da hordem de Sam Bento, no bispado dOuremsse açerca de Mjlmanda, (dez) legoas de Samtiago, com sua molher e filhos e parte de sua gemte. E el-Rey partio do Porto bem coregido e acompa-nhado. E amtre os apostamentos que assy leuaua, deu a todollos que amdauom com elle de cote, que seriam ataa quinhentas lamças, loudees de fustam bramco com cruzes de Sam Jorge; e el leuaua outro seme-lhante de pano de sirgo bramco. E com as outras gemtes dos fidalgos podiam seer per todos dous mjll; e leuaua amtre cauallos e mullas e

218

make his way to that place, whilst the King would set out from Oporto for the same destination. Then with the Duke in that very hall they ate the supper that he ordered to be served to them and to the lords who were attending him. When they had taken their leave, they returned with his reply.

Now at this juncture, some say that the King's marriage with one of the Duke's daughters was mooted as early as this embassy; but whenever it was, the King took counsel on the matter, during which he was strongly advised to marry Catherine, granddaughter of King Pedro. In this way, they said, he might well find a means to govern the kingdoms of Castile. Others advised him to marry Princess Philippa. The conclusion reached was that it was up to him to choose which of them he preferred.

The King said that since the choice in the matter was his prerogative, as was only right and proper, he was not inclined to marry Princess Catherine because this seemed to him a union that could easily bring upon him who entered into it a state of perpetual war, given her mother's claim to the succession in the kingdom of Castile. On the other hand, anyone who married her but did nothing about this hereditary claim whould always be censured and considered as failing in his duty. Since, God be thanked, he himself was victorious over his enemies, he had no intention of waging further war except in order to recover what had been taken from him, and only until he had secured peace. Then, he would live in peace, ruling his kingdom lawfully and justly. Moreover he said that this would be in the Duke's interest; for in the course of the campaign, it was always possible that the Castilian King's wife might die, in which case, the King could either marry this princess himself or else marry her to his son who expected to succeed to the throne. This would be a most convenient way of bringing the dispute to an honourable close for both sides, which was something that he himself could not achieve. So he had decided, God willing, to marry the Princess Philippa.

XCII
How the King and the Duke first met.

Some days were spent on these matters and by now it was the month of October. The Duke arrived at the Benedictine monastery of Celanova, which is in Galicia, in the bishopric of Orense near Milmanda, ten leagues from Santiago. Here he came with his wife and children and some of his retainers. The King set out from Oporto in some style and with a large escort. Among the trappings he carried with him were surcoats of white fustian with crosses of Saint George which he presented to all those who went daily with him and who numbered some five hundred lances. He himself wore something similar made of white silk. Including the nobles in the escort, the party numbered about two thousand people in all. He

219

facas bem quoremta, todas a destro, cubertas de suas armas e doutros coregimentos o melhor que se fazer pode, como aquell que se auja de uer com huum tam nobre senhor com que se ajmda nunca vira.

O Comdestabre, que dasessego estaua em Riba dOdiana quamdo se estas cousas começarom, quando vio o recado del-Rey como o Duque era em Galliza, e que por quamto compria de se uer com elle lhe mandaua que se fezesse prestes, e se fosse pera aquell logar hu auyam de seer as fallas; e trabalhou logo de se coreger. E com çertos caualleiros e escudeiros bem coregidos e emcaualgados partio peralla. E achou el-Rey na Pomte da Barca; que de sua vimda foy assaz ledo e o reçebeo muy bem.

E himdo assy seu camjnho da parte aaquem da Ponte do Mouro, o Duque pareçeo da outra parte que vinha per a par de Melgaço, que estaua estonçe por Castella. E el-Rey, quamdo vio que o Duque assy uinha, passou da parte aallem, e açertarom-se ambos em huuma ladeira. E el-Rey hia armado de todas armas, que lhe nom mynguaua senom o baçinete; e muytos dos seus daquella gujssa. E os do Duque tragiam cotas e braçaaes com jornees brolladas, e outros farpadas, assaz de vistosos e bem coregidos. E uinham de mestura alguuns gallegos e castellaãos, dos que se pera el veerom e reçeberom por senhor. E ally se reçeberom, abraçamdo-sse e fazemdo suas mesuras com gram prazer e lediçe, e esteuerom huum pouco fallamdo, e desy pasaram-se aaquem do rio, homde el-Rey tinha suas temdas postas. E ally se desarmarom, e asentaram-se a comer ambos dhuuma parte, sem curamdo da parte dereita nem esquerda, ca ajmda nom era entom em vsso; e assy os que vinham com o Duque. E era esto primeiro dia de nouembro em festa de Todollos Santos. E depois que comeram, foi-sse o Duque pera seu alogamento homde pousaua; e el-Rey ficou ally.

Em outro dia armarom contra fumdo do rio huuma gramde temda que fora del-Rey de Castella, tomada na batalha reall; e ally fazia el-Rey depois e o Duque seus comselhos.

XCIII

Das auenças que el-Rey e o Duque trautarom amtresy.

As liamças e conuemças que el-Rey e o Duque ally trautarom contam alguuns per desuairados modos, mas a uerdade, que errar nom pode, nos çertefica que foram desta guissa:

El-Rey e o Duque, com os prellados e baroões de sua falla, avemdo sobresto maduro comselho, hordenarom amtre sy *que por bem e homra de suas pessoas e estados de seus regnos fossem ambos e seus sobçesores e*

took with him a good forty horses, mules and nags, which were used as extra pack—animals and were decked out with their heraldic arms and other accoutrements so that they could not have been better equipped, as was fitting for meeting such a noble lord for the very first time.

The Constable, who was resting in the Guadiana valley when this business began, received the message from the King informing him of the Duke's arrival in Galicia. In it the King instructed him to make ready and go to the place where their discussion would take place; so he set about preparing for the journey straightaway. He set out for that destination together with certain knights and squires, well equipped and well horsed. In Ponte de Barca he found the King who was pleased to see him and welcomed him.

Whilst the King was making his way on this side of Ponte do Mouro, the Duke made his appearance on the other bank near to Melgaço, a place which supported Castile at that time. When he spied the Duke coming in this fashion, the King crossed over the river and the two of them met on the hillside. The King was in full armour except for his helmet, and many of his men were dressed likewise. The Duke's men wore coats of mail, bracers and woven cloaks. Others wore these cloaks cut in slits. They were a fine sight and well accoutred. There came with them some Galicians and Castilians, who had rallied to him and acknowledged him as their lord. There, they greeted and embraced one another with most willing and joyful salutations. They stood there talking a while before passing back to this side of the river[1] where the King had had his tents pitched. There they disarmed and sat down together to eat without any ceremony whatever for it was not felt that there was any necessity for it. The Duke's retinue followed their example. All this took place on the first of November, the Feast of All Saints. After they had eaten, the Duke went to his own camp. The King stayed where he was.

The following day they pitched a great tent on the river bank. It had belonged to the King of Castile and had been captured in the great battle.[2] The King and the Duke used it in order to hold their council.

XCIII
Concerning the agreements which the King and Duke discussed together.

Differing accounts have been offered of the alliances and agreements negotiated there by the King and the Duke; but the truth, which must prevail always, confirms that they were as follows:

The King and the Duke, together with the prelates and barons who were privy to the council, after a thorough discussion, decreed that for the good and the honour of their persons and the welfare of

221

poboos a elles sogeitos boons e leaaes amjgos, sem maliçia nem emgano; e que esta liamça e amizade fosse jumta e hunida de guissa que se ajudem huum a outro, e jsso mesmo seus herdeiros, comtra quaaesquer pessoas que comqujstar quisessem seus regnos ou parte delles, tam çedo e trigosamente como cada huum bem fazer podesse.

E que el-Rey de Portugall, em esta comquista por que o Duque era vimdo, fosse theudo de o ajudar, fazemdo guera claramente comtra o deteedor dos regnos de Castella; e que a teuesse assy aberta comtra elle e os temtes sua voz , e nom çessar della por nenhuuma guissa, nem fazemdo com el paz nem tregoa; e que esto se emtemdesse em quamto o Duque ou seus soçesores esteuesem em esta terra por fazer tal conquista e compril-la: e que per esta guissa o dito senhor Duque e seus herdeiros fezessem comtra quaaesquer pessoas que tomar e ocupar quisessem os regnos de Portugall ao dito Rey dom Joham ou seus deçemdentes, teemdo guera aberta por sua parte, como dito he.

Hordenarom mais e firmarom *que el-Rey de Portugall, com hoste de duas mjll lamças e mjll besteiros e dous mjll homeens de pee, em sua propria pessoa ajudasse o dito Duque comtra o deteedor dos ditos regnos e comtra quaaesquer que da sua parte fossem; e que esta ajuda que lhe el-Rey de Portugall auia de fazer fosse aa ssua custa e despessas,* — e nom que o Duque ouuesse de pagar a el-Rey nem a suas gemtes soldo nem outra cousa, como alguuns mall scpreuemdo diserom; — *o quall fosse presto dencaminhar pera fazer em ella começo des primeiro dia das oitauas de natall seguimte ataa deradeiro dia dagosto, que eram oito meses; e que cada huum partisse dhu melhor emtendesse, e se ajumtassem a emtrada de Castella, hu per elles fosse deuissado, e dally caualgassem juntamente ou apartados como lhes melhor pareçesse;*

E se amte dos oito meses acabados o deteedor dos regnos de Castella se metesse em villa ou çidade ou alguum logar desses regnos, que el-Rey de Portugall esteuesse em tall çerco com o dito Duque ataa que esse deteedor fosse tomado ou morto ou fogido; e se per uentura duramdo os oito meses ouuessem çertas nouas que esse ocupador dos regnos de Castella quisesse poer batalha ao Duque, e o dia assynado pera ella passasse aallem daquel tempo, que em tal casso el-Rey de Portugall fosse theudo atemder per todo o mes de setembro aas suas proprias despessas e seer na batalha em ajuda do dito Duque; e se a batalha fosse feita duramdo o tempo dos oito meses, que el-Rey de Portugall se tornasse pera seus regnos ou hu lhe mais prouuesse; e tornamdo-sse assy e o Duque ouuesse mester de suas gemtes, que el-Rey lhe desse leçemça e comgeito de ficarem, e esto aa custa do Duque; e aqueçemdo tall casso que, depois que el-Rey de Portugall tornasse pera seus regnos, vehessem çertas nouas que o deteedor dos

their kingdoms, both they and their successors and subjects would henceforth be good and loyal friends, without malice or deceit; while this alliance and friendship would be forged and sealed in such a way that, as promptly and swiftly as was humanly possible, they and their successors would always come to one another's assistance against any persons that might seek to conquer the whole or a part of their respective kingdoms.

The King of Portugal would be bound to assist the Duke in the campaign of conquest for which he had come, openly making war against the usurper of Castile and campaigning openly against him and his supporters, and under no circumstances would he cease to do so nor make peace or truce with him. This state of affairs would obtain for so long as the Duke or his successors might remain in the land to attempt and to complete its conquest. By the same token, the said lord Duke and his successors undertook, as is herewith set down, to make open war on behalf of King João and his descendants against any person who might wish to take and to occupy the kingdoms of Portugal.

They further decreed and confirmed in writing that the King of Portugal in person, with a force of two thousand lances, a thousand bowmen and two thousand foot, would assist the said Duke against the usurper of the said kingdoms and his supporters. This assistance that the King of Portugal was bound to offer was to be at his own expense. Moreover, it is untrue that the Duke was to pay wages or anything else to the King or his soldiers, as some have inaccurately written. The King was to be ready to set out to campaign from the day after Christmas Day until the last day of August, a period of eight months. Each army would set out from the point of departure most appropriate to it; they would join forces for the entry into Castile at a prearranged spot; and from there on would travel together or separately, as they thought best.

If before the end of the eight–month period, the usurper of Castile should take refuge inside a town or city or some other fortress in those kingdoms, the King of Portugal would participate in the siege along with the said Duke, until the usurper was either captured or dead or had fled. If by chance, during those eight months, news were received that this usurper of the kingdoms of Castile wished to fight a pitched battle against the Duke and the day of battle occurred after the end of the stipulated period, in these circumstances the King of Portugal would be bound to stay for the whole month of September, at his own expense and fight in the battle at the Duke's side. If the battle had been fought during the eight–month period, the King of Portugal would afterwards be free to return to his kingdoms or wherever it was necessary for him to go. If he returned home in this manner and yet the Duke needed his forces, the King would give them permission and leave to stay, but at the Duke's expense. Should it happen that, after the King of Portugal had returned to his kingdoms, news arrived that the usurper of the

223

regnos de Castella queria poer ao Duque batalha e o Duque mandasse
requerer que veesse a ella, que el fosse theudo dhijr com sua hoste e see(r)
presente per pessoa o mais apresa que o fazer podesse, sem emgano de
detemça; e feita por aquella vez tal batalha ou nom, que el-Rey de Portugall, requerido outra vez, nom fosse theudo dhijr alla.

E por mais liamça damizade e seguramças destas cousas hordenarom
emtom e prometerom que o Duque desse sua filha, a jffante dona Filipa,
a el-Rey de Portugall por molher, e que el-Rey a reçebesse, avuda primeiro despemsaçam per que tal casamento fosse valliosso; e que essa dona
Philipa jurasse de reçeber el-Rey de Portugall por marido, avuda primeiro aquella despemssaçom. E por bem e razom deste matrimonio e
ajuda que del-Rey de Portugall auja dauer aa sua custa, hordenou o
Duque e sua molher por sy e por seus soçessores, per aquell titollo
del-Rey e da Rainha que tragiam, que elles dessem e outorgasem a el-Rey
de Portugall pera sempre pera coroa de seus regnos huuma parte de
Castella e de Leom per villas e logares nomeados desta guisa, saber: a
villa de Ledesma com seus termos e o castello de Matilha, o logar de
Monleom , assy como vay o caminho que se chama de Plato com a
çidade de Prazemça, e dhi himdo dereito ao logar que dizem Grimoaldo,
e assy a outro que se chama Canauerall, e dhi pasando a Alconetra , e
desy a Caçeres e a Alosca ; e emtom a Amenda ᵇ e aa Fomte do Mestre,
e desy a Çafra, e pellas Torres de Medina, e dhi dereito a Freixinall,
e quaaesquer outras villas e logares que antre estes e os regnos de Portugall fossem contheudos, com todos seus termos e logares, saluo o logar
dAlcantara e Vallemça dAlcantara. E porque deziam que estas duas
villas e alguuns logares em çima   nomeados eram de çertas hordens de
cauallaria, ficou o Duque que el desse aas hordeens cujos fossem outros
tam boons por elles; e quamdo se per alguum modo fazer nom podese,
que el daria a el-Rey em recompemsam outros semelhantes em remda e
bomdade açerca de Portugall, os quaaes ouuesse a seu padre por sempre,
quam çedo todos ou cada huum delles veessem aa obediemçia do dito
senhor Duque, sem el Rey seer theudo de nunca a outrem fazer conheçimento.

E este foy o trauto da auemça que amtrelles ally foy firmada; doutra
guissa nom.

XCIV

Como el-Rey partio pera Riba dOdiana, e foy a jffante tragida ao Porto.

Feitas assy estas fallas e concordadas como dizemos, chegarom ally
de sospeita cartas dos embaxadores, que auja mais dhuum anno que eram

kingdoms of Castile was preparing to do battle with the Duke and the Duke sent a call for help, the King of Portugal would be bound to go in person to the battlefield with his army as quickly as possible, and without making any excuses. If however he later received a second summons to another battle, he would not be obliged to go, irrespective of whether the first battle had taken place or no.

As a further proof of friendship and a safeguard for these matters agreed upon, they then decreed and promised that the Duke would give his daughter, the Princess Philippa, to the King of Portugal to be his wife, and the King would take her to wife once he had obtained the dispensation necessary in order that this marriage be valid. The aforesaid Dona Philippa was to swear to receive the King of Portugal as her husband, once that dispensation was obtained.

By reason of this marriage and in return for the assistance that the King of Portugal was to give at his own expense, the Duke and his wife decreed on their own behalf and on behalf of their successors, by virtue of the titles of King and Queen they bore, that they surrendered to the King of Portugal forever a portion of Castile and León, to be incorporated into his kingdom. This portion was to be expressed in terms of towns and fortresses as follows: the town and district of Ledesma; the castle of Matilla; the place of Monleón;[1] and then along the Silver Road, with the city of Plasencia, as far as the place called Grimaldo, and another called Cañaveral, and on to Alconétar and after that, Cáceres and Alcuéscar. The line would then pass through Almendralejo to Fuente del Maestre, Zafra, Medina de las Torres and finally Fregenal. It would contain all other towns and villages lying between these and the kingdoms of Portugal, with all their dependent districts and villages, but excluding the towns of Alcántara and Valencia de Alcántara. Now, because they said that these two towns and some others among the above—mentioned places belonged to particular military orders,[2] the Duke promised that he would give to these orders to which they belonged, others just as good in exchange, and that wherever, for some reason, he was unable to do so, he would recompense the King with other places of equal revenue and excellence close to Portugal, which he could hold forever, and he would do this as soon as each or every one of them declared obedience to the aforesaid Duke without the King ever being obliged to take him to court to achieve this.

This was the nature of the agreement that was signed between them, and not otherwise.

XCIV
How the King left for the Guadiana Valley, and how the Princess was brought to Oporto.

These talks and agreements having being conducted in the manner in which we have described, letters arrived suddenly from the

partidos pera (a) corte, dizemdo como acharom o Padre Santo em Genoa, e que apresentada antelle a suplicaçam que leuauom e dita sua mesagem, que el em todo o que lhe por sua parte pedirom beninamente despemsara, e que o rol era ja assinado e emcaminhariam de tirar as leteras. El-Rey ouue desto muy gramde prazer e o Duque jsso mesmo; e outorgou logo demuiar sua filha ao Porto pera a el-Rey reçeber e casar com ella, quando pera ello fosse prestes e lhe prouguese de o fazer.

Em esto conujdou el-Rey huum dia ao Duque e quamtos caualleiros jngreses hi eram, e gallegos e castellaãos dòs que em sua companha vinham; e fez-lhe huuma muy reall salla naquella temda hu forom os comselhos, e em outras que armarom junto todas ao lomgo huuma ante outra; na quall Nunaluarez Pereira, comdestabre de Portugal, era ally veedor, asseentando cada huum segumdo seu estado aas messas hu aujam de comer, omde gramdes fidalgos seruiam de toalha e copa e das outras cousas a tal conuite pertençemtes. E em fym da mesa fallarom per boom espaço, desy mandaron-se alguumas cousas huum ao outro; e espedio-se o Duque, e foi-sse pera Çellanoua, que eram dhij humas quatro legoas.

El-Rey, como fora comcordado amtrelles, mandou outro dia seus procuradores aaquel moesteiro homde o Duque pousaua, saber: dom Louremço, arcebispo de Bragaa, e Vaasquo Martijnz de Mello o velho, e Joham Rodriguez de Saa com elles. E pasados ja tres dias que hij eram, aos homze de nouembro que dissemos, a senhora Rainha dona Costamça, presente el-Rey seu marido e a jffante dona Philipa sua filha e muitos fidalgos de sua casa, louuarom e aprouarom os trautos que dissemos por sy e por seus soçessores, quanto a cada huum pertençia, fazendo juramento de os guardar e firmes scprituras sobrello.

Em se seguimdo assy esto, mandou el-Rey tornar o Conde a Riba dOdiana pera juntar as mais gemtes que podesse; e el ueo-se caminho do Porto e dessy a Lixboa com muyto poucos dos seus, porque os outros leixara amtre Doiro e Minho, homde o aguardassem ataa Natall. Naquella çidade esteue sete dias, e dhij se passou a Alentejo por dar aguça ao juntar das gentes.

E amdando el em este cujdado e estando emtam em Euora, foy em tanto tragida muy homradamente de mandado de seu padre a jffante dona Philipa aa çidade do Porto, segundo dizemos que fora acordado. Omde foy recebida com gram festa e prazer, vimdo muyto acompanhada de jmgreses e portugueses, assy como monsyre Joham dOlamda, comdestabre do Duque, e Thomas Persy, almirante da frota, e Rricharte Burley, seu mariscall, e aquell dom Joham Goterez, bispo dAcres, e o arçebispo de Bragaa e Vasco Martijnz de Mello e Joham Rodriguez de

ambassadors who had set out for the papal court more than a year previously. These letters explained that having found the Holy Father in Genoa, they had presented to him the petition they brought, and explained its import, and he had graciously acceded to all that was being asked of him. The petition—roll was already signed, and they were well on their way to obtaining the formal letters from the papal chancery. [1]

The King was overjoyed at this news and so was the Duke who agreed to send his daughter to Oporto so that the King could welcome her and marry her once he was ready for it and felt disposed to do so.

At this juncture, one day the King invited the Duke and the English knights who were with him, together with Galicians and Castilians in his retinue. By joining that tent in which they had held council to other tents which were pitched end—to—end, the King transformed it into a magnificent hall. Here, Nun'Álvares Pereira, Constable of Portugal, acted as master of ceremonies, placing each and every man according to his rank at the tables where they were to eat, and where great nobles stood by to hand them napkins, cups and other table—ware. Discussions went on for a considerable length of time after the meal had ended, and after this presents were exchanged. Then the Duke took his leave and went to Celanova, some four leagues from there.

As had been agreed between them, the next day the King sent his proctors to the monastery in which the Duke was staying, that is, Dom Lourenço, Archbishop of Braga, [2] Vasco Martins de Melo the elder, and João Rodrigues de Sá. On 11 November, three days after their arrival, as we have said, Queen Constanza, together with her husband the King and Princess Philippa his daughter and many nobles of his household, approved and agreed to the agreement that we have described on behalf of themselves and their descendants, as far as in each of them lay, and they swore to keep it and the treaty in which it was enshrined.

Following upon this, the King ordered the Count [3] to return to the Guadiana Valley so as to gather together as many men as he could; and he went via Oporto to Lisbon with a very few companions because he had left the rest of his men between the Douro and the Minho where they were to wait for him until Christmas. He stopped seven days in Lisbon, and from there he went into the Alentejo to speed up the assembling of troops.

While he was on this mission and staying in Évora, Princess Philippa was brought to the city of Oporto in a most honourable manner on the orders of her father, and as we said it had been agreed. There she was welcomed with great celebration and joy. Her large escort of Englishmen and Portuguese included Sir John Holland, the Duke's constable; Thomas Percy, Admiral of the fleet; Richard Burley, his marshal; Juan Gutiérrez, Bishop of Dax; and the Archbishop of Braga, Vasco Martins de Melo and João Rodrigues de

Saa e outros que se alla forom; e pousou nos paços do bispo, que som muyto preto da See desse logar. El-Rey partio dEuora e o Comdestabre com elle, e quamdo chegou ao Porto, achou hi a jffante dona Philipa, sua molher que auja de seer, e pousou em Sam Françisco. E em outro dia foy veer a jffante, que ajmda nom vira, e fallou com ella, presente aquell bispo, per huum boom espaço; e espidio-sse e foy jamtar. E depoys que el-Rey comeo, enujou aa jffante suas joyas, e ella a elle; amtre as quaaes lhe emuyou el-Rey huum firmall em que era posto huum gallo, com ricas pedras e aljoffar marauilhosamente feito. E ella enuyou a elle outro em que era huuma aguya bem obrada com pedras de gram vallor. E el-Rey esteue ally poucos dias, e foy-sse caminho de Guimaraaes, leixamdo carego a Gomçallo Perez, que emtom fez veedor de sua fazemda, que lhe fezesse dar todallas cousas que a ella e a ssuas gemtes pertençessem.

XCV

Como el-Rey hordenou de tomar casa e screueo aos comçelhos de seu regno.

El-Rey naquella villa hordenamdo os feitos da guerra, veeram a fallar em seu casamento, e acharom que se no dia seguinte lhe nom fossem as bemçoões feitas, que se nom podia fazer dhij a gram tempo por a Septuagessima que emtraua segumdo costume da egreja, em que se nom deue fazer offiçio, e per acordo de todos scpreueo logo el-Rey ao bispo do Porto que em outro dia teuesse todo prestes pera lhe fazer as bemçoões. O bispo feze-o assy. E el-Rey caualgou esse dia tarde e andou toda a noite, em guissa que, amdadas aquellas oito legoas, amanheçeo el-Rey na çidade. Dom Joham estaua ja prestes, reuestido em pomtificall, e seus benefiçiados coregidos como compria. A jffante foy tragida muy homradamente dos paaços, homde pousaua, aa Ssee; e ally em nome do Senhor Deus a reçebeo el-Rey, presemte todos, por sua espossa e molher lidima, fazendo-lhe tal offiçio o mais sollepne que se fazer pode. E esto foy dous dias de feuereiro em festa da Purificaçom da Bemta Virgem, avemdo estomçe el-Rey vimte e noue annos e a jffante sua espossa vinte e oyto.

Esto acabado, hordenou logo el-Rey de fazer sua voda e tomar casa, da quinta feira seguimte a oito dias, e escreueo aas çidades e villas de seu regno, quanto lhe prouguera seerem em sua festa presentes; e a nota das cartas, que a todos emuiaua, hija em esta forma:

Sá, as well as certain others who went with them. The Princess was lodged in the Bishop's palace which is situated close to the cathedral of that city. The King left Évora accompanied by the Constable, and when he arrived in Oporto, he found his bride—to—be, Princess Philippa, already there. The next day, he went to see the Princess whom he had still not set eyes upon, and talked with her for some considerable time in the presence of the Bishop. Then he took his leave and went off to supper. When the King had eaten, he sent jewels to the Princess and she sent some to him. Among the presents the King gave her was a brooch with a cockerel on it, studded with precious stones and mother—of—pearl, and exquisitely made. She gave him another one on which there was a pin well studded with the costliest gems. The King stayed only a few days before proceeding to Guimarães, but he left Gonçalo Peres, who was at the time overseer of his finances, with instructions to provide anything that she or her attendants might need.

XCV
How the King prepared to set up his matrimonial household and how he wrote to the city councils of his kingdom.

While the King was in that city directing preparations for the campaign, there was some discussion concerning his marriage. It was felt that if it were not to receive the blessing of the Church on the following day, this might not be possible for a long time because it was the beginning of Lent, when Church custom forbids such celebrations.[1] So with everyone's agreement the King then wrote to the Bishop of Oporto asking him to have everything made ready the following day for the blessing; and the Bishop did so. The King rode out on the afternoon of the same day and travelled all night so that he arrived in the city in the early morning, having completed a journey of eight leagues.

Dom João was already prepared, dressed in his episcopal robes, and with his clerics arrayed in the appropriate manner. The Princess was escorted with pomp and ceremony from the palace where she had been staying to the cathedral; and there, in the presence of everyone, in the name of the Lord God, the King received her as his lawfully wedded wife. The ceremony was conducted with the utmost solemnity. This took place on 2 February, the Feast of the Purification of the Blessed Virgin, when the King was twenty—nine years old and the Princess his wife, twenty—eight.

The ceremony of the blessing over, the King ordered the wedding and the establishment of his household eight days after the following Thursday, and wrote letters to the cities and towns throughout his kingdom, declaring it to be his pleasure that they should send representatives to his wedding festivities. The summary of the letters he sent to all of them was in the following form:

229

Comçelho e homeens boons da nossa villa ou çidade de tal logar: Nos el-Rey uos enuiamos muito saudar. Cremos que bem sabees como auemos jurado e prometido de casar com a jffante dona Filipa, filha del-Rey de Castella e Duque d Allancastro. E ora, estamdo nos em Gnimaraaes prestes pera seguir nosso caminho segundo bem sabees, fomos requerido per o dito Rey de Castella, seu padre, que a tomemos por molher, segumdo auemos com el posto ante que desta terra partissemos, diʒemdo que o emtende assy por seruiço de Deus e sua homra e melhor aderemçamento de seus feitos e nossos. E por quanto nosso senhor o Papa ja auya despemsado comnosco que podessemos casar, ouuemos sobrello nosso comselho, e foy acordado que casassemos com ella amte que partissemos desta terra. E nos por esto veemos logo aquy aa çidade do Porto, e feʒemos com ella bemçoões oje que foy dia da Purificaçam de Santa Maria, porque se em este dia nom forom feitas, nom se poderom depois faʒer ataa oyto dias depois de Pascoa, segumdo hordenamça da santa Egreja; e emtendemos, praʒemdo a Deus, de tomar nosa casa segumdo a nosso estado compre, desta quimta feira que vem a oito dias, que seram quatorʒe de feuereiro. E seede çertos que a nos prouguera muyto dalguuns de uos serdes em esto e em toda outra cousa que fosse feito por nossa homra; mas porque a nos compre de seguirmos logo nossa guerra, abreuiamos o tempo em que se esto auia de faʒer; e porque emtendemos que nom podiades a ello vijnr per nenhuuma guissa, por em uos faʒemos saber todo, porque somos çertos que uos praʒera dello. Scprita etcetera.

XCVI

Como el-Rey jeʒ voda com sua molher na çidade do Porto.

Nom embargamdo que os dias fossem breues pera hordenamça de tamanha festa, moormente como naquel tempo tinha em costume de fazer, emcomendou a certos de sua casa e aos offiçiaaes da çidade ho emcarego que cada huum desto teuesse; e com gram diligemçia e sentido tinham todos cuidado do que lhe el-Rey emcomendara, huuns pera fazer praças e desempachar as ruas per hu aujam damdar as gemtes, outros de fazer jogos e trebelhos e matinadas de noite. E fezerom muy apresa huuma muy gram praça amte Sam Domyngos e a rua do Souto, que eram todo ortas, hu justauom e torneauam gramdes fidalgos e caualleiros que o bem sabiam fazer, e outra gemte nom. Assy que toda a çidade era ocupada em desuairados cuidados desta festa.

"To the most noble council and good citizens of our town or city of such and such a place.

We, the King, send you greetings. We believe you are well aware of how we have sworn and promised to wed the Princess Philippa, daughter of the King of Castile and Duke of Lancaster. Now, finding ourselves in Guimarães on the point of departure for a destination with which you are acquainted, her father, the aforesaid King of Castile, requested us to take her as our wife before we left this country, as we had agreed with him. He said that he would have it so for the sake of God, his honour, and the advancement of his and our own interests. In view of the fact that our lord Pope had given us a dispensation to marry, we took counsel on the matter, and it was agreed that we should get married before we left this region. For this reason, we came there and then to the city of Oporto and received together the Church's blessing this very day, the Feast of the Purification of St. Mary. This is because if it were not done on this day, it could not be done until eight days after Easter, according to the ordinances of Holy Church. We intend, God willing, to set up house together in a manner fitting our rank and station eight days after the Thursday of this week, which will be the fourteenth of February. We would have you know that it would please us greatly that some of you should be present at this ceremony and at all others that might be conducted in our honour. However, given the need we have to proceed immediately with our military campaign, we are cutting short the time devoted to this matter. Because we know that you may not be able to come for whatever reason, we are making all this news known to you, because we are certain that it will please you. Written, etc."

XCVI
How the King had his marriage with his wife in the city of Oporto.

Despite the fact that time was short for the making of arrangements, all the more at that period when elaborate celebrations were customary, nevertheless, he issued instructions to certain members of his household and officials in the city concerning their respective duties regarding the celebrations. Whether their job was to clear the squares and streets through which the procession was to pass, or to organize games, toys and night revels, each one endeavoured to dispatch the task assigned to him by the King with diligence and good sense. A great open space was hastily cleared in the area between São Domingos and the Souto Street, which was mostly taken up by gardens. Here, great nobles and knights took part in jousts and tourneys, but only ones expert in the art, and not others. In this way, the whole city was engaged in the many different tasks relating to the celebrations.

E todo prestes pera aquell dia, partio-sse el-Rey aa quarta feira domde pousaua, e foy-sse aos paaços do bispo, homde estaua a jffante.

E a quynta feira forom as gemtes da çidade jumtas em desuairados bamdos de jogos e damças per todallas praças, com muytos trebelhos e prazeres que faziam. As primçipaaes ruas per hu esta festa auya de seer todas eram semeadas de desuairadas verduras e cheiros. El-Rey sayo daquelles paaços emçima dhuum caualo bramco, em panos douro realmente vestido; e a Raynha em outro tal muy nobremente guarnida. Leuauam nas cabeças coroas douro ricamente obradas de pedras e aljofar de gramde preço, nom himdo aredados huum do outro, mas ambos jguall. Os moços dos caualos leuauom as mais honradas pessoas que hij eram, e todos a pee muy bem coregidos. E o arçebispo leuaua a Rainha de redea. Deamte hiam pipas e trombetas e doutros estormentos tanto que se nom podiam ouuir. Donas filhas dalgo e jsso mesmo da çidade cantauom himdo detras, como he costume de uodas. A gemte era tamta que se nom podiam reger nem hordenar, por o espaço que era pequeno dos paaços a egreja. E assy chegarom aa porta da Ssee, que era dally muyto preto, homde dom Rodriguo, bispo da çidade, ja estaua festiualmente em pomtificall reuestido, esperando com a clerezia; o quall os tomou pellas mãos, e demoueo a dizer aquellas pallauras que a Santa Egreja manda que se digam em tal sacramento. Emtom disse mjssa e pregaçam; e acabado seu officio, tornarom el-Rey e a Rainha aos paaços, domde partirom, com semelhante festa, hu auiam de comer. As mesas estauom ja muyto guarnidas de todo o que lhe compria, nom soomente homde os noiuos auyam destar, mas aquellas hu era hordenado de comerem bispos e outras homradas pessoas de fidalgos e burgeses do logar e donas e domzellas do paaço e da çidade.

O mestresalla da uoda era Nunaluarez Pereira, Comdestabre de Portugall. Seruidores de toalha e copa e doutros officios eram gramdes fidalgos e caualleiros, homde ouue assaz de jguarias de desuairadas maneiras de manjares. Em quanto o espaço do comer durou, faziam jogos a vista de todos homeens que o bem sabyam fazer, assy como trepar em cordas e tornos de mesas e salto reall e outras cousas de sabor; as quaaes acabadas, alçarom-sse todos e começarom a damçar, e as donas em seu bamdo cantando arredor com gramde prazer. El-Rey se foy em tanto pera sua camara; e depois da çea ao seraão o arçebispo e outros prellados com muytas tochas açessas lhe bemçeram a cama daquellas bemçoões que a Egreja pera tal auto hordenou. E ficamdo el-Rey com sua molher, foram-sse os outros pera suas pousadas.

O padre da Raynha nem a Duquesa nom veerom a estas vodas, porque todo seu cuydado era em ocupaçom de se chegar com suas gentes aaquell logar homde com el-Rey fallara pera fazer sua emtrada.

Once everything was made ready, on the Wednesday, the King departed from where he was staying and repaired to the Bishop's palace where the Princess was staying. On the Thursday, the citizens came together in various groups for games and dances in all the squares. There they enjoyed many amusements and indulged in other delights. All the main streets through which the procession was to come were strewn with a variety of green and aromatic plants. The King rode out of the palace, mounted on a white horse, royally dressed in gold cloth. The Queen rode on another, dressed in an equally royal fashion. They wore on their heads gold crowns richly studded with costly gems and mother−of−pearl. Neither of them took precedence but rather they rode in complete equality. The grooms, on foot and elaborately dressed, led the steeds of the most high−ranking people that were there; and the Archbishop led the Queen by the rein. Ahead of them went so many pipes, trumpets and other instruments, that nothing else could be heard. As is customary at weddings, noblewomen and citizens' daughters came along at the back, singing.

So great was the crush and so small the space between palace and church that it was impossible to control and marshal the huge crowds.

In these conditions they arrived at the cathedral door which was very near there. Here, Dom Rodrigo, Bishop of Ciudad Rodrigo, [1] was awaiting them in his pontifical vestments, together with the clergy. He took the couple by the hand and instructed them to say the words ordained by Holy Church to be uttered in this sacrament. Then he said mass and preached. When he had performed his task, the King and Queen returned with similar rejoicing to the palace from which they had come and where they were to eat. The tables were already laid out with everything necessary; and not only the table at which the newly−wedded couple were to sit, but also the tables reserved for the bishops and other persons of rank, nobles and local merchants as well as ladies and maidens from the palace and the city.

The master of ceremonies was Nun'Álvares Pereira, Constable of Portugal. The napkin− and cup−bearers and other attendants were high−ranking nobles and knights. There were sufficient dishes of all manner of different foods. For the duration of the meal, men skilful in certain games performed for all to see: balancing on a tightrope, chasing round tables, acrobatic jumping and other enjoyable games. When these were over, everyone rose and began to dance while the ladies stood around in a group, singing joyfully. Meanwhile, the King went to his chamber: and after supper, in the evening, the archbishop and other prelates with many burning torches, blessed his bed with those benedictions that the Church has ordained for such occasions. Then the King remained with his wife, and the others all went to their lodgings.

Neither the Queen's father nor the Duchess witnessed these wedding celebrations because all their attention was taken up with the task of meeting together with their forces in the place where they had agreed with the King to make their incursion into enemy territory.

Como el-Rey deu casa aa Rainha e remda pera sua despessa.

Per quimze dias ante e depois durarom festas e justas reaaes por homra desta voda como dizemos, e nom soomente em aquell logar, mas em todallas villas e çidades do regno, segumdo que cada huum era, forom feitas grandes allegrias e trebelhos, como se emtom custumaua. E hordenou el-Rey casa aa Raynha e çerta remda pera sua despessa, ataa que lhe desse, como prometera, terras pera guouernança de seu estado. E deu-lhe offiçiaaes que a seruissem, fazemdo seu moordomo moor dom Lopo Diaz de Soussa, Mestre de Christus em Portugall, e gouernador de sua fazemda Lourençeannes Fogaça, e ueedor da casa Afomsso Martijnz que depois foy priol de Santa Cruz, copeiro moor Gomçallo Vaasquez Coutinho, e por elle Rodriguiannes, criado del-Rey, reposteiro moor Fernam Lopez dAaureu, e assy mantieiro e jcham e os outros offiçiaaes neçesarios; jsso mesmo capellam moor e comfessor e outros ministros do diuinall offiçio; e scudeiros seus pera (a) acompanharem jngreses e portuguesses, quamtos vio que compria. Molheres pera (a) guardar e seruir: Briatiz Gomçaluez de Moura, molher que fora de Vaasco Fernamdez Coutinho, que lhe foy dada por aya. Domzellas: dona Briatiz de Castro, filha de dom Aluaro Perez; Tareija Vaasquez Coutinha, filha de Briatiz Gonçalluez, camareira moor da Raynha, molher que (ffoy) de dom Martinho, filho do comde dom Gomçallo; Lianor Vaasquez, sua jrmaã, que depois casou com dom Fernamdo, que chamarom de Bragamça; Biringeira Nunez Pereira, filha de Ruy Pereira que moreo na pelleja das naaos amte Lixboa, molher que foy dAfomsso Vaasquez Corea; Briatiz Pereira, filha dAluaro Pereira, marichall, ja finado, molher que foy de Martym Vaasquez de Reesemde; Lianor Pereira, sua jrmaã lidema, que foy casada com Gomez Freire; e assy outras donzellas e molheres da camara, quaaes compria a homra de seu estado. E mandou que ouuesse pera despessa de sua casa, ataa que teuesse terras, as remdas da alfamdega e da portagem, com o Paaço da Madeira, de que largamente podia auer vimte mjll dobras bem prestes, se as todas despemder quisesse.

How the King gave the Queen a household and an income for her expenses.

For the space of fifteen days, before and after, feasts and royal tournaments in honour of the wedding took place as we have been describing; and festivities and revels were held, not only in that place, but in all the towns and cities of the realm, according to the capacity of each, as was normal at that period.

The King established a household for the Queen and a certain income for her expenses until such times as he could give her, as promised, lands for the maintenance of her status. He assigned officials to serve her, appointing Lopo Dias de Sousa, Master of the Order of Christ in Portugal as her chief steward, Lourenço Eanes Fogaça as manager of her finances, Afonso Martins, who later became Prior of Santa Cruz, as overseer of her household, Gonçalo Vasques Coutinho as her head butler and as his deputy Rodrigo Eanes, the King's own servant, and Fernão Lopes de Abreu as head of the stores. Also, there were to be officers to take charge of cutlery and table—linen and the pantry, together with other necessary officials; and also the Grand Chaplain and the Confessor and other ministers of the divine office; and squires, as many as were necessary, to attend upon the Queen.

The women appointed to attend and serve her were Beatriz Gonçalves de Moura, the wife of Vasco Fernandes Coutinho, who was to be her housekeeper. Her maids of honour were Dona Beatriz de Castro, daughter of Dom Álvaro Peres; Teresa Vasques Coutinho, daughter of Beatriz Gonçalves, the Queen's chief lady—in—waiting and wife of Dom Martinho, son of Count Gonçalo; Leonor Vasques, her sister, who later married Dom Fernando whom they called Fernando de Bragança; Berengeira Nunes Pereira, daughter of Rui Pereira who died in the sea—battle in front of Lisbon and wife of Afonso Vasques Correa; Beatriz Pereira, daughter of Álvaro Pereira the Marshal (already deceased) and wife of Martim Vasques de Resende; and Leonor Pereira, her legitimate sister who was married to Gomes Freire. As well as these, there were other maidens and waiting—women to a number appropriate for one of the Queen's rank.

The King ordered that until she had lands of her own, the Queen should receive, in order to meet her expenses, the income from customs—duties and port—duties together with the palace of Madeira, from which the income amounted to easily twenty thousand *dobras* which were all at her disposal if she wanted to spend them all.

Dalguuns costumes e bomdades da Rainha dona Filipa.

Esta Rainha dona Filipa, nada de nobre padre e madre, assy como era louuada em semdo jffamte de todas bomdades que a molher dalto logar pertee(n)çe, assy foy e muyto mais depois que nouamente foy casada e posta em real estado; aa quall Deus outorgou marido comcordauell a sseu deseio, de que ouue fremossa geraçam de bemauentuirados e virtuosos filhos, como adeamte ouuires. E por em nos fora praziuell trabalho, podemdo louuar as virtudes que em ella ouue; mas porque disto nom somos abastamte, compre espedirmos dello muyto breue.

Esta bemauentuirada Rainha, assy como em sua moçidade era deuota e nos diuinaaes offiçios sperta, assy o foy e muyto mais depois que teue casa e os hordenou aa ssua vontade. Ella rezaua sempre as oras canonicas pello costume de Saresbri; e por o el seia nom bem ligeiro dordenar, assy hera em esto atemta, que seus capellaães e outras honestas pessoas reçebiam nelle pera ella emsinamça. Todallas sestas feiras tinha costume rezar o psalteiro, nom fallamdo a nenhuuma pessoa ataa que o acabaua de todo; e quando era embargada per doemça ou constramgida per empedimento de parto, açerca de ssy lhe rezauom todo o que ella auja em husamça, ouuyndo deuotamente sem nenhuuma outra toruaçam. Dos jejuuns nom compre fazer sermom, nem do leer das Santas Scprituras em conuenhauees tempos; ca assy era todo repartido com tam madura discriçom que nunca a oçiosidade em sua maginaçam achaua morada.

Era cuidadossa açerca dos pobres e mynguados, fazendo largas esmollas aas egrejas e moesteiros. Amou bem fielmente o sseu muy nobre marido, teemdo gram semtido de o nunca anojar, e da boa emsinamça e criaçam de seus filhos. Nom fazia cousa alguuma com ramcor nem odio, mas todas suas obras eram feitas com amor de Deus e do proximo.

Em ella auia huuma chaã conuersaçam, proueitosa a muytos sem oufana de seu real estado, com doçes e graçiosas pallauras a todos praziuees douuir. Allegraua-sse alguumas (vezes), por nom pareçer de todo apartada despaçar com suas domzellas em jogos sem sospeita demgano licitos e conuinhaaues a toda onesta pessoa; assy que, semdo seus perfeitos costumes em que muyto floreçeo per meudo postos em scprito, assaz seriam dabastosa emsinança pera quaaesquer molheres, posto que de moor estado fossem.

XCVIII
Of some of the ways and virtues of Queen Philippa.

This Queen Philippa, daughter of a noble father and mother, had been praised when a princess for all the virtues that are appropriate to a high—born woman, and the same was true and indeed even more so after she was married and raised to royal estate. Moreover, God granted her a husband to her taste, and their union produced a fine generation of virtuous and successful sons, as you shall hear later on. For this reason, it would have been for us a most pleasurable task to praise her virtues, if we had been capable of doing so; but because we lack the necessary skill, we must content ourselves with describing these virtues only briefly.

If in her youth this blessed queen was devout and had a good knowledge of the divine liturgy, later she was even more so once she assumed reponsibility for her own household and organized the services as she wished. She always prayed the canonical hours according to the Use of Sarum[1] and although this observance was by no means easy to arrange, she was so keen on this that she taught it to her chaplains and other worthy persons. Every Friday it was her custom to read the Book of Psalms and she would speak to no one until she had quite finished it. When she was prevented from doing so through illness or through giving birth, somebody would read to her all that she was wont to read on that particular day; and she would listen devoutly and without interruption. There is no need to speak at length about fasting or the practice of reading the Holy Scriptures at convenient times; for all this was a regular part of her life and ordered so wisely that idleness could gain no foothold in her imagination.

She cared for the poor and needy, giving alms most liberally to churches and monasteries. She loved the noblest of husbands most faithfully. She made great efforts never to annoy him, and set great store by the education and sound upbringing of her children. Nothing she did was done out of rancour or hatred. On the contrary, all her actions were dictated by love of God and of her neighbour.

Her conversation was plain, and often helpful without showing any pride in her royal rank; and her way of speaking was sweet, gracious and most pleasing to all who heard her. In order not to appear too cut off from others, she delighted sometimes in relaxing with her maidens in those lawful games in which no trickery could be involved and which were seemly for any honest person. So if the perfect manner in which she lived could be recorded in detail, any woman could study it with profit, no matter how high her rank.

Como se el-Rey escusou ante o Duque nom sser prestes ao tempo que de-uera.

Em quamto el-Rey fez sua voda e folgou huuns dias no Porto, passou o tempo que era deuisado pera se juntar com o Duque e fazer sua emtrada per Castella; ca el ouuera de seer prestes depois do Natall no seguimte dia, e esto era ja no mes de março de iiijº.xxv, semdo estomçe o Duque com sua molher em huuma aldea termo de Bragamça. El-Rey partyo do Porto pera se hir aaquell logar, e leuou a Rainha comsigo; e mandou a toda sua gente que se fossem em pos elle. E chegou açerca do moesteiro de Crasto dAuellaans, que (he) huuma pequena legoa de Bragamça. E porque el-Rey, como dizemos, era theudo de se fazer mais çedo prestes, e por çertos jmpedimentos o fazer nom podera, e nom lhe seer comtado que preguiçosa tardança emcorera em quebrantamento do trauto, chegou logo aaquella aldea homde o Duque pousaua, semdo hij dona Costamça presemte e monsse Joham dOlanda e outros fidalgos; e em presemça de todos propos el-Rey, dizemdo assy:

Que bem sabiam como amtrelles era trautado per capitollos e juramento feito liamça e amjzade per sy e per seus sobçessores; amtre os quaaes era contheudo que el com çertas lamças e beesteiros e homeens de pee per sua pessoa o ajudasse aaquella guerra que hordenada tinham; e que por casamento que el com sua filha auya de fazer e por esta ajuda que aa ssua custa auya de see(r) feita, que el ouuesse delles çertas villas e logares de Castella depois que per elles fossem cobradas, quaaes no trauto eram comtheudas; e que guissamdo-sse el com suas gemtes pera começar seu camjnho segumdo prometido auya, que ouuera taaes jmpedimentos, assy do matrimonio que sua filha a sseu requyrimento fezera, come doutras cousas neçesarias, de guissa que nom podera tam aginha fazer nem comprir aquella ajuda que theudo era. Mas que el estaua ally prestes com suas gemtes pera o ajudar e fazer o que prometera; e que esto lhe dezia por seu boom contentamento com tanto que a elles prouguera dello. E que sua ajuda nom emtendesse porem seer começada saluo des o primeiro dia da Coresma, que elle partira do Porto com suas gemtes, e mais nom.

O Duque e sua molher, quamdo esto ouujrom, diserom *que bem çertos eram de seus razoados jmpedimentos e de todo o que proposera; e que lhes prazia e se comtentauom de quanto per el ataaly fora feito, e nom auyam por ello o trauto amtrelles posto em nenhuuma guissa seer quebrado; e que se desto quisesse alguumas scprituras, que mandasse fazer quantas lhe prouguesse.*

How the King made excuses to the Duke for not being ready by the time he should have been.

The time spent by the King on his wedding celebrations and a few days of relaxation in Oporto meant that he exceeded the period within which it had been agreed that he and the Duke would join up in order to enter Castile; for he should have been ready on the day after Christmas Day and yet it was now the month of March 1387, at which time the Duke and his wife were staying in a humble village near Bragança.[1]

The King left Oporto to go to that place, taking the Queen with him and commanding all his men to follow him; and he came to the monastery of Castro de Avelãs, a mere league from Bragança. Now, as we have explained, the King ought to have been ready earlier, but because of certain obstacles he was prevented from arriving in time. However, not wishing to give anyone occasion to say that the agreement had been broken through his own dilatory loitering, he came straightaway to the village where the Duke was staying. In the presence of Doña Constanza, Sir John Holland and other nobles, the King addressed them in the following manner.

They well knew, he said, that an alliance and treaty of friendship between them and their descendants had been drawn up in great detail and confirmed with oaths. Among the clauses was one stipulating that he in person, with a stated number of lances, crossbowmen and foot—soldiers, would assist the Duke in the war that he had declared; and that, because of the marriage he had been bound to make with the Duke's daughter, and in return for this assistance given at his own expense, he was to receive certain towns and places in Castile once they had been captured. All of these places were listed in the treaty. In the course of preparation for the journey with his forces as promised, certain impediments such as the marriage with the Duke's daughter, undertaken at that time and at the Duke's request, together with other necessary matters, had conspired to prevent him from setting out as expeditiously as he might. However, now he was there ready with his forces to help the Duke and to do what he had promised. He was telling him this in the hope that it would give the Duke satisfaction. In the light of this, the Duke could take it that the assistance he offered him would only be reckoned to have begun on the first day of Lent, which was when he had set out from Oporto with his forces.

When they heard this, the Duke and his wife said that they were quite satisfied by his explanations concerning the delay and by everything that he proposed. They were quite happy and contented with everything the King had done so far; they in no way considered their treaty to be broken; and if the King wanted this in writing, he could have it.

Tornou-sse el-Rey estonçe a sseu alojamento, e esteue alguuns dias assy esperamdo gemtes. E dally alçarom seu arreall, e foram-no poer aallem duas legoas de Bragamça, açerca do estremo (muyto junto) , el-Rey em huuma aldea que chamom Babe, (e o Duque em outra, espaaço de mea legoa).

Em esto amte que partissem, foy el-Rey e a Rainha çear huum dia com o Duque a(a) aldea homde el e sua molher estauom, com os quaaes ouuerom gramde prazer. E depois comeo com el-Rey e com a Rainha o Duque e Duquessa e muytos homrados de sua casa; e desque comerom e folgarom, espedio-se a Rainha de seu padre e della. E a cabo de dous dias se tornou pera Cojmbra, bem acompanhada do arcebispo de Bragaa e Gomçallo Mendez de Vaasconçellos e Diogo Lopez Pacheco e Joham Rodriguez de Saa, porque nom era bem saão, e outros fidalgos. E ally mandou el-Rey que esteuessem com ella doutores e prellados e a casa dos desembargadores do regno, homde todos requerisem dereito.

E quamdo se a Rainha ouue despedir, disse Gomçallo Mendez como em sabor a el-Rey: *Senhor, nesie regno sohia dauer huum costume dantigo tempo que o homeem no anno que casaua nom auia dhir em guerra nem seer costrangido pera ella. E uos, que a tam pouco que casastes, o queres agora britar e vos hir fora.* E el respomdeo que assy lhe compria por defemssam de sua terra e fazer dano a seus emmjgos.

Assy que na fym deste capitollo temdes vistas duas cousas, saber o que aueo ao Duque com el-Rey de Castella logo como chegou aa Crunha, e as liamças que com el-Rey de Portugall fez pera seer depois em sua ajuda.

C

Como el-Rey e o Duque partirom e chegarom a Benauente de Campos.

A Rainha partida e seu conselho feito, emcaminharom logo de fazer huuma gram ponte de barcas no Doyro, hu chamam a Barca da Regoa, per hu pasauom as gemtes da Beira, e nom hirem pasar ao Porto. E nom leixo(u) frontaria no regno, saluo amtre Tejo e Odiana, homde ficou Vaasco Martijnz de Mello com Gomçallo Vaasquez e Martym Afomsso, seus filhos, e Martym Gonçalluez, tyo do Comde, e Gomez Garçia de Foyos e outros, per todos duzemtas e çimquoenta lamças. E as gemtes que el-Rey leuaua eram tres mjll lamças e dous mjll beesteiros e mais de quatro mjll peeões, afora outras que se forom logo açerca per aquell geerall mandado como ordenara quamdo foy sobre Coira.

E se alguem posser duujda que el-Rey nom leuaria tanta gemte, por nom seer theudo segundo o trauto, desy por a despessa que se recreçia de pagar mal soldo, rezam tem de esto cuidar; mas el-Rey teue com-

Then the King returned to his lodging and stayed there for some days waiting for reinforcements. Then they struck camp, moving on to a place two leagues beyond Bragança, near the frontier. The King stopped at a village called Babe, and the Duke at another, half a league from there.

At this time, but before they set out, the King and Queen dined one day with the Duke and his wife at the village where they were staying, and enjoyed themselves very much. After this, the Duke and Duchess and many nobles in their train ate with the King and Queen; and after they had eaten and enjoyed themselves, the Queen took leave of her father and step—mother. At the end of two days, she went back to Coimbra well accompanied by the Archbishop of Braga, Gonçalo Mendes de Vasconcelos, Diego López Pacheco, João Rodrigues de Sá, who was unwell, and other nobles. The King ordered learned men and prelates to remain with her in the house of the chief magistrates of the kingdom, where everyone came for justice.

When the Queen was about to take her leave, Gonçalo Mendes said to the King as a joke, "My lord, in this kingdom since olden times there has existed a custom that in the year of his marriage a man need not go off to the wars nor be obliged to do so. Yet you, who have married so recently, intend to break this custom and sally forth." He replied that it was incumbent upon him to do so for the defence of his country, and in order to hurt his enemies.

Thus, at the close of this chapter you have seen two things: what happened to the Duke in his relations with the King of Castile when first he arrived at Corunna; and the alliance that he made with the King of Portugal so that the latter might aid him thereafter.

C
How the King and the Duke set out and arrived at Benavente de Campos.

The Queen having departed and the council having been concluded, they set about the task of constructing a great bridge of boats across the Douro at a place they call Barca da Regua, [1] in order that forces could cross over from Beira without making a detour via Oporto. The King left no garrison anywhere in the kingdom except between the Tagus and Guadiana where Vasco Martins de Melo was stationed with his sons Gonçalo Vasques [2] and Martim Afonso, Martim Gonçalves the Count's uncle, Gomes Garcia de Foios and others, numbering in all two hundred and fifty lances. The King had with him three thousand lances and two thousand crossbowmen, and more than four thousand foot—soldiers, besides others that had come in response to the general summons he had made when at Coria.

If anyone should doubt that the King would take so many men with him, more than he was obliged to by the treaty, for this entailed a rising wage bill, then he would have good reason to do so; but in

selho primeiro; e huuns lhe deziam que nom jumtasse mais gemte daquella que theudo era; outros afirmauom que tall hida sem mais companhas nom era a el segura nem pera fazer; porque, emtramdo desta guissa em terra de seus emmjgos, podia o Duque trautar com el-Rey de Castella alguuma comuemça, com pouca sua homra, e que por em el deuia dhijr perçebido poderosamente, que de todo contrairo que avijr podesse fosse bem seguro; allem desto, por mostrar que era abastamte de o ajudar com as gemtes que ficara, e com outras mais quando mester fezesse. E por tamto leuou aquellas que aquy dizemos.

O Duque leuaua muyto poucas das suas, porque gram parte eram ja mortas, assy dos capitaães de booa comta come darcheiros e outros homeens darmas, e esto naquell jnuerno em quamto esteue em Galiza. Ca segumdo comtam, huuns morryam de pestellença, outros de quoremça; delles er matauom per esses boscos e deuesas os que os achauom andar buscamdo mantimentos pella terra. Porque assy como alguuns² daquella comarca se veerom aa primeira pera elle, assy depoys mudarom temçom e faziam muyto dano ascomdidamente nelles; em tanto que o Duque nom tinha comsiguo ataa seis çemtos homeens darmas e outros tantos archeiros.

E prestes pera fazer sua emtrada, disse el-Rey ao Comdestabre que a el prazia e tinha em tallante que o Duque dAllancastro, seu padre, leuasse a avamguarda daquella hoste, dizemdo muytas razoões sobresto por que lhe pareçia seer bem; comtando-lhe como leuara a avanguarda na batalha de Najara, e como a mais homrada pessoa da hoste afora o rey deuia de leuar a avanguarda; e pois el era rey e tam gramde senhor e a queria leuar amtelle, que a el deuia de prazer; e outras taaes razoões. A esto respomdeo o Comde, e disse: *Senhor, minha vomtade he firme de todo, que em quamto vos Deus leixar teer este poder que vos temdes e eu amdar em vossa companha, de nunca leixar a avamguarda a nenhuuma pessoa, nem ajmda em outro logar homde eu com minhas gemtes for.* E assy o costumaua de feito, que nas batalhas que o Comde per sy mesmo fazia, el era sempre na avanguarda e nom a fiaua de nenhuum outro; dizemdo que nom queria teer cuidado que a avanguarda, desbaratada, ouuesse de sseer acorida da reguarda. El-Rey, veemdo sua leal e fiel vomtade, outorgou no que lhe dezia, e nom o quis mais aficar por esto.

Emtom mouerom com sua hoste, leuamdo o Duque sua molher e filhos, e pasaram o ryo de Maçaãs, que he no estremo damtre Portugall e Castella, semdo emtom xxv dias de março daquella era de iiijᶜ.xxv; e chegarom a terra dAlcanizes, que he a primeira terra de Castella. E dally partirom e forom a huuma ribeira, que chamam Tauora; e porque era Vespera de Ramos, teuerom naquell logar a festa. Em outro dia partirom e foram caminho de Benauemte de Campos; e a terça feira, que eram dous dias dAbrill chegarom ao logar — huuma villa assaz booa e bem

fact, the King took counsel first. Some said he should not assemble more men than the numbers stipulated in the treaty. Others declared on the contrary that to set out without additional forces was unsafe and inadvisable, for if he entered enemy territory in this manner, the Duke might make a dishonourable treaty with the King of Castile; and so he ought to go there in some considerable strength so that he might be well prepared if events took an unpleasant turn. Besides, it showed that he had sufficient forces to assist the Duke, and yet had extra men if they were needed. Therefore, he took with him those forces we have described.

The Duke took very few troops, because many of his men had died whilst spending that winter in Galicia,[3] including good captains, archers and men−at−arms. According to accounts, some died of the plague, and others of homesickness; and some were killed in the woods and on the moors when found wandering about looking for food in the countryside. For although some people in that region were at first in favour of the Duke, later their attitude changed, and covertly they did much harm to him. The result was that the Duke had with him fewer than six hundred men−at−arms and an equal number of archers.

When ready to make his entry into Castile, the King told the Constable it was his wish that the Duke of Lancaster, his father, should take the vanguard of the army, proffering numerous arguments on the matter to explain why he was in favour of this. He explained that the Duke had commanded the vanguard at the battle of Nájera, and that the highest−ranking person in the army after the King should command the vanguard; and that since the Duke was a king and a great noble who wanted to lead, he himself ought to agree; and he gave other such reasons. The Count replied to him, saying, "My lord, it is my most heartfelt wish that so long as God allows you to enjoy the power you wield at present, and me to accompany you, you should never surrender the vanguard to any other person whatever, either here or in any other place where I am present with my forces." And in fact it was always the custom that in the battles in which the Count fought in person, he always commanded the vanguard and never entrusted it to anyone else, for he would say that he did not want to have to worry that the vanguard might be defeated and need to be supported by the rearguard. Appreciating his loyal and faithful wish, the King let him have his way and pressed him no further on this point.

Then they set out with the army, the Duke taking his wife and daughters with him, and they crossed the River Manzanas, which forms the border between Portugal and Castile, on 25 March 1387. They found themselves in the district of Alcañices, the first piece of Castilian territory. They went on to the banks of a river called the Tábara, and because it was now the eve of Palm Sunday,[4] they stayed there to celebrate this feast−day. On the next day, they set out for Benavente de Campos; and on the Tuesday, 2 April, they

çercada, de muyta e gramde poboraçam, huumas quatorze legoas do estremo. E camjnhamdo pera alla, hiam hordenados tódos em batalha a cauallo; saber, Nunaluarez Pereira, comdestabre de Portugall, e Monsire Joham dOlamda, comdestabre do Duque, na avamguarda, e o Priol do Spitall; e em huuma das allas Martym Vaasquez da Cunha e Gill Vaasquez e Lopo Vaasquez, seus jrmaãos, e a gemte do Mestre de Christus com os caualleiros da hordem e gemtes de suas (terras), ca el era doemte e nom podia la hir. E leuauom em uez de bamdeira huum gramde prumam e huuma lamça darmas, porque o Mestre nom tragia bamdeira des que fora preso com o Priol do Crato em Tores Nouas, como ja ouujstes. E mais, na outra alla hija Gomçallo Vaasquez Coutinho e Ruy Mendez de Vasconçellos com outros fidalgos que hiam na sua quadrilha. E na reguarda hija el-Rey e o Duque com muyta gemte darmas, e a cariagem toda em meo; e tomaua gram praça de campo a ordenamça destes gemtes, que era assaz fremossa de uer e espantossa a seus emmjgos. E assy chegarom ao meo dia e assentarom seu areall muyto açerca da villa, homde nojo fazer nom podesse o tirar dos viratoões; ca outro troom nem emgenho nom auya demtro que lhe nojo podesse fazer.

CI

Como a terra estaua perçebida per homde el-Rey e o Duque emtrarom.

El-Rey de Castella, como dissemos, estaua em Çamora quamdo o Duque aportou na Crunha e ouue del o recado que ouujstes; e pesou-lhe muyto de sua vimda, temendo assaz aquesta demanda por a gram myngua de gente darmas que estomçe em seu regno auya, ca as mais e melhores tinha perdidas na guera passada que ata ally fora. E porque soube que el-Rey e o Duque tinham hordenado demtrar per esta comarca, enuiou aaquella parte, assy a Benauemte come a Villalpando e a Vallemça de dom Joham e a Crastoverde e aos outros logares daredor, muytos estrangeiros e de suas companhas pera a defemderem; e mandou deribar alguuns logares chaãos, de(s)çercados, e colher as gemtes e mantimentos aos que se defemder podiam. E aquelles fidalgos e escudeiros que se de França e doutras partes pera o seruir nesta guerra vinham, ell os reçebia bem, fazemdo-lhe merçees e damdo soldo pera as gemtes que tragiam, e emuiaua-os alla. E mandou dom Joham Garçia Manrique, arçebispo de Santiago aa çidade de Leom por aquel logar estar mais seguro. E assy mandou as mais companhas que jumtar pode de pee e de cauallo aos logares hu compria; ca el nom tinha vomtade de uemtuirar este feito per batalha, mas soomente per tal guerra com que se defemder podesse seu regno.

reached it. It is a fine town, securely walled about, with a considerable population, and is at a distance of some fourteen leagues from the frontier. As they approached it, they were drawn up in battle—formation as though for a cavalry charge. That is to say, Nun'Álvares Pereira, Constable of Portugal, and Sir John Holland, the Duke's Constable, were in the vanguard together with the Prior of the Hospital.[5] On one wing was Martim Vasques da Cunha, with his brothers Gil Vasques and Lopo Vasques, together with the forces of the Master of the Order of Christ. The Master himself was ill and could not come there; but his Order's knights and vassals were present and instead of a banner they carried a large feather on a jousting lance bearing the arms of the Order, for the Master had not had a banner since the time he and the Prior of Crato were captured at Torres Novas, as you have heard. In the rearguard came the King with the Duke and many men—at—arms, together with the baggage train. These battle lines meant that the forces were spread out across a broad terrain and consequently made an imposing sight, frightening to their enemies. So they proceeded until midday, when they pitched camp very close to the town at a point where they could receive no harm from anyone firing crossbow bolts; for there was no other kind of sling or engine inside the walls capable of endangering them.

CI
How the country was prepared for the invasion by the King and the Duke.

As we have said, the King of Castile was in Zamora when the Duke had landed at Corunna and received the message of which you have already been informed. The Duke's coming worried him, for he was afraid of the latter's claim, given the great scarcity of fighting men in his kingdom at that time, since he had lost most of them, including the best, in the recent war. Because he knew that the King and Duke had arranged to invade Castile through that district, he sent many foreigners and their Companies there, to Benavente, Villalpando, Valencia de Don Juan and Castroverde and other neighbouring places, in order to defend them.[1] He ordered the demolition of certain places that were either without ramparts or had lost them, as well as the recruitment of men and the gathering of provisions for those places that could be defended. As for those nobles and squires that had come from France and other countries in order to serve him in this war, he welcomed them and sent them into the district with rich rewards and pay for the men they had brought with them. He ordered Don Juan García Manrique, Archbishop of Santiago, to the city of León to make it more secure; and he sent as many companies of cavalry and foot as he could muster to the most appropriate places; for he was not of a mind to tempt fate by fighting a pitched battle, but preferred to wage a defensive war to protect his kingdom if he could.

Em este logar de Benauemte estaua por fromteiro Aluaro Perez dOsoyro, huum caualleiro de terra de Leom, com seisçentas lanças de castellaãos, afora monse Roby de Brocamonte e outros estrangeiros gascoões e doutra lingua que hi eram. E logo esse dia (pelejarom) os da uilla com os do areall. E jsso mesmo depois, em quanto hij jouuerom, sempre forom feitas booas escaramuças amtrelles; mas destas e doutras nom diremos mais, saluo alguumas cousas que de notar sam: assy como quando chegarom, que tanto que o areall foy posto, logo os da uilla sayrom escaramuçar com elles; na quall escaramuça moreo da parte do Duque monse Joham Falconer, aquell caualleiro jmgres que ja nomeamos, ca el nom tragia boa besta e os da ujlla eram bem encaualgados e gramdes caualgadores; e este foy o aazo de sa morte.

El-Rey mandou depois aa foragem Martym Vaasquez e seus jrmaãos e Joham Fernamdez Pacheco, e com elles beesteiros e peoões quantos compria. E leuarom caminho dhuum logar que chamom Crasto Caluom comtra a çidade dEstorga, que seriam dally çimquo legoas. Aquel logar combaterom, damdo fogo aas portas; e foy emtrado per força e roubado de quamto em el auya, e as gemtes espalhauam-se pellas aldeas a buscar mantimentos. E Martym Vaasquez e outros comsigo amdauom pellos altos, olhando se vinham alguuns pera lhe fazer nojo. E depois que ouuerom forrejado naquel logar e muyto mais adeante, tornaran-se ; e chegarom vespera de Pascoa ao arreall. E trouueram gaados e outros mantimentos; nom porem muytos, porque os nom achauom.

CII
Como coreram pomtas Aluaro Gomez e huum castellaão.

No seguimte dia era festa de Pascoa. E açertou que, fallando os de demtro com os de fora como he costume aa salua ffee, veeram-se a dessaffiar pera corer pontas Aluaro Gomez, criado do Comdestabre, com outro escudeiro castellaão; as quaaes auyam de seer coridas a cauallo com baçinetes de camal sem escudos, nom mais de tres careiras. Isso mesmo desaffiarom huum caualleiro gascom do Duque, que chamauom Maaborny, com monse Roby, que estaua na villa. Veo Aluaro Gomez o primeiro (dia) com o seu ao campo, armado em huumas solhas, e nom qujs leuar faldrom pero lho comselharom muytos, e amdaua bem desemvolto e boo(m) caualleiro; e o castellaão muyto per comtrairo. E a primeira careira ho emcomtrou Aluaro Gomez de guissa que deu com elle em terra. E el tornou a caualgar, e coreram outra. E o castellaão, nom leuamdo a lamça bem asessegada, emcontrou-ho baixo per aqueçimento, e ouue huuma ferida de que depois moreo , e nom coreram emtom mais.

The commander at Benavente was one Álvaro Pérez de Osorio, a Leonese knight. He had six hundred Castilian lances, as well as Sir Robert de Bracquemont[2] and other foreigners, Gascons and men speaking a strange language. On that day, the defenders at once fought with the besiegers; and so long as the siege lasted, there were skirmishes between the two sides, but of these and other engagements, we say no more save to point out one or two things worthy of report. As soon as the attacking force arrived, no sooner did they set up camp than the defenders made a sally to skirmish with them. In the course of this skirmish, the Duke's man, Sir John Falconer, an English knight we have already mentioned, was killed, for he was not well horsed, while those from the town had good horses and were good riders. This was the reason for his death.

The King subsequently sent out a foraging—party that included Martim Vasques and his brothers, as well as João Fernandes Pacheco together with as many crossbowmen and foot—soldiers as was necessary. They set out for a place some five leagues away in the direction of Astorga, called Castrocalbón. They attacked it, setting fire to the gates, forcing an entry and robbing all that was there; then they spread out into the neighbouring villages in search of provisions, whilst Martim Vasques and others with him kept to the high ground watching out for possible enemies. After they had foraged in the area and far beyond, they returned to the camp arriving on the evening before Easter Sunday. They brought with them some cattle and other provisions, but not in great quantity however. This was because they simply had not found much.

CII
How Álvaro Gomes and a Castilian jousted together.

The following day was Easter Sunday.[1] Defenders and besiegers were talking together, as is the custom whenever a safe—conduct is issued, and it happened that Álvaro Gomes, a servant of the Constable, and another squire, a Castilian, challenged one another to a joust. They were to joust on horseback with helmets of mail but without shields, and be limited to three charges only. A similar challenge was made and accepted by Mauburney, one of the Duke's Gascon knights, and Sir Robert, who was in the town. Álvaro Gomes arrived first on the field with his retinue. He wore plate armour, but refused to wear a fauld even though many strongly advised him to do so. He cut a fine, knightly figure, whereas the Castilian certainly did not. At the first charge, Alvaro Gomes caught him in such a manner that he brought him down. Thereupon, the other man remounted and they charged again. This time, having failed to couch his lance as he ought to have done, the Castilian caught Álvaro Gomes low, unintentionally, so that he received a wound from which he later died. On that day there was no more jousting.

El-Rey seguraua, corremdo estas pomtas, quantos (d)os da uilla as quisessem veer, e sahyam muytos fora por esta razom; amtre os quaaes vinha huum escudeiro, bem guarnido e homem de proll, e trazia huum collar de prata ao collo. E em olhamdo e fallamdo com alguns portu-guesses, soltaua-sse em desmesuradas pallauras comtra el-Rey, nom lhe chamando senom Meestre, e quamdo muyto vsaua de cortesya, nomeaua-o dizemdo: *o Mestre, vosso senhor,* e outras taaes razoões desapostas. Os que as ouujam pesaua-lhes desto; porem nenhuum ousaua de respomder, porque os (el-)Rei[4] segurara, desy porque estaua açerca olhamdo come os outros. Naquell dia aa noite, pedimdo el-Rey vinho e fruita, nom se poderom alguuns teer que nom fallassem nesta estorya, contando-lhe como se pasara, e que nom ousaram de lho contradizer por o nom anojar, pois os tinha seguros. El-Rey disse que el nom seguraua nenhuum saluo pera vijnr veer e folgar, mas que se alguem dizia razoões que as nom deuia, que de alguum tornar a ello nom o aueria (e)l por mall.

CIII

Como corerom pontas Maabornj com monsse Roby.

Como jsto passou, no seguinte dia veerom ao campo corer suas pontas aquel caualleiro chamado Maaborny e monse Roby, que estaua na villa; e vinham ambos bem guarnidos, assy elles como os cauallos, de coregi-mentos. Maabornj era de boom corpo e corera ja pomtas muytas vezes, e monse Roby era mais pequeno e nom tam sages em aquell feito. E quamdo Maaborny coria, hia armado dessta gujssa: (leuaua ho bacinete sem cara e com a brooca do escudo cobria o rosto de guyssa) que lhe nom paresçia mais que o olho direito; e seu cauallo nom hia mais rijo que quanto podia amdar a galope; e nom emcontraua dereito, mas de trauees em perpassamdo. E a primeira carreira que coreram, encontrou Maaborny o outro no pescoço; e pero trouuesse dous camaaes e huum gorjall, pasou-lhe todo e teue a llamça da outra parte, e posse-o na pomta della fora da sella limpo no chaão, cujdamdo todos que era morto. Caualgou outra vez monsse Roby, e ouue huum emcomtro de que se embellecou; e da terçeira nom se emcontrarom e per aquy çessou aquell jogo.

Hora sabee que se a primeira, quando coreo pomtas Aluaro Gomez, sayrom muytos castellaãos e doutros estrangeiros a veer como as cor-ryam, que muytos mais sayrom veer estas; amtre os quaaes veeo aquell escudeiro, que dissemos que se soltara em villaãs pallauras fora de booa hordenamça. E se damtes husara de pouca mesura, mais pouco husou emtom, e com peor soom. Aluaro Coitado, huum boom caualleiro portu-gues da companha do Condestabre, homeem de boom corpo e pera

At this time, the King gave safe—conduct to all who wished to come from the town to see the jousting, and, in consequence, many did come. Among them was a squire, a worthy man, well dressed and with a silver chain about his neck. While he was watching and talking to some Portuguese, he let slip insulting words against the King. He referred to him merely as *Master* and when he wished to be particularly respectful, he referred to him as *the Master, your lord,* together with further impertinent remarks. Those who heard these remarks were very angered by them. However, nobody dared to reply, because the King had given safe—conduct, and because in any case he was close by, watching like the rest. That night, when the King called for wine and fruit, some people could not refrain from discussing the event and recounting to him what had transpired, and how they had not dared to make a riposte for fear of annoying the King, since he had given the defenders safe—conduct. The King said that he had only given safe—conduct so that they might come to watch and enjoy themselves, but that if someone made remarks that were uncalled for, he would not hold it against anyone who punished him.

CIII
How Mauburney and Sir Robert jousted.

It happened that on the following day that knight called Mauburney and Sir Robert from the town took the field to joust. Both they and their horses were well equipped with protective armour. Mauburney was well built and had jousted many times before; but Sir Robert was smaller and not as expert in this particular accomplishment. When he jousted, Mauburney was armed in the following manner: he wore a helmet without visor, with the rim of his shield held to protect his face in such a way that only the right eye was visible. His horse charged at no faster than a gallop; he did not engage his adversary head on, but at an angle as he passed. The first joust they made, Mauburney caught the other man in the neck; and even though he wore two bacinets one on top of the other, and a throat—piece, the lance passed through and out the other side, hoisting him clean out of the saddle and throwing him to the ground. Everyone feared him dead. Sir Robert remounted and they jousted again, but this time they merely feinted. At the third attempt, they missed each other and the play was terminated.

Now I must emphasize that if, at first, when Álvaro Gomes jousted, many Castilians and other foreigners came out to see how they performed, many more came out to watch the encounters I have just described. Among these spectators was that squire who, as we related, had let slip remarks that were coarse and quite uncalled for. But if his remarks had previously been unseemly, they were now even more so, as well as offensive to the ear. Álvaro Coitado was a fine Portuguese knight from the Constable's company. He was a

muyto, que ouuira o que el-Rey disera quamdo-lhe fezerom queixume
de suas desmesuras, nom deitou sua reposta em esqueçimento, e çinte-
mente estaua açerca por veer se deria alguumas semelhantes cousas. E
quamdo ouuio tam mall razoar como da primeira, semdo ja as pontas
açerca dacabadas, chegou-se a el de besta assy como estaua; e reuatou
pello collar com huuma maão, e deu-lhe com a outra huuma gram pu-
nhada que o atordoou logo. E deu com elle tamanha tirada pello collar,
que o deribou de çima da mulla, e forom ambos a terra. Omde lhe
começou a dar couçes e punhadas, tomando-o pello collar e dizemdo
que fosse perante el-Rey. Ally foy gramde aluoroço de muytos que se
jumtarom a veer, assy dhuuma parte como doutra, dizemdo os castellaãos que aquel era muy maao feito virem seguros pera auer solaz e
reçeberem desomra de nenhuum. El-Rey, que era açerca, chegou ally a
pressa veer que era aquello. E Pero Diaz de Cardoniga, huum caualleiro
castellaão, fallou a el-Rey mais que nenhuum dos outros, dizemdo que
aquello era muy mal feito seerem todos seguros per elle e reçeberem tal
desomra dos seus. El-Rey disse que os segurara todos de jda e vimda e
estada por veer e folgarem com os do areall, mas que os nam segurara
que huum a outro disesse desmesuradas pallauras; e se aquell escudeiro
dezia razoões que nom deuya, que bem empregado era nelle seer feito
aquello e muyto mais. Estomçe se partirom todos, e nom coreram mais
pomtas em aquell logar.

CIV

Como os da villa sayram a escaramuçar amte que el-Rey partisse.

El-Rey, em quanto ally esteue, nom provou de combater a uilla,
porque nom leuaua artefficios taaes que aproueitar podesse seu combato; desy o logar fornecido de muytas boas gemtes, emtendeo que sua
estada ally mais toda seria em vaão e propos de se partir; porem, em
quamto ally durou, se faziam escaramuças como dissemos, saymdo os da
ujlla aos do areall, de que os portugueses sempre leuauom o louuor. E
huum dia sayrom da uilla per huuma pomte per que costumauom vijr aa
escaramuça parte das gemtes que na villa auya. E tinham costume,
quamdo os do areal hiam apos elles, de chegarem açerca da ponte e
mais nom; e ally se tornauom e er uoltauom os castellaãos sobrelles, e
assy se remesauom, himdo e vimdo sem mais (fazer). Gomçallo Vaasquez Coutinho, que amdaua neesta escaramuça, vemdo como os castel-

redoubtable and well—built man; and he had heard what the King had said when people had complained at this lack of courtesy. He had borne the King's reply in mind and therefore was deliberately standing close by to see if the man would say something similar again. When he heard him speaking as impolitely as on the first day, the jousting being almost over, he approached him; and, although the squire was mounted on a mule, Coitado seized him by the necklace with one hand and with the other gave him a heavy punch so that he was momentarily dazed by the blow. Then he pulled so hard on the necklace that he pulled him clean off the mule and the pair of them fell to the ground where Coitado started to rain down kicks and punches upon him, grabbing him by the necklace and telling him to come into the King's presence. There was a general disturbance among the many people from both sides who gathered round to see what was happening. The Castilians said that it was quite unfair that one should come there with safe—conduct for some diversion and yet be dishonoured in this way. The King, who was nearby, hurried up to see what was the matter. Pedro Díaz de Cardoniga, a Castilian knight, acted as spokesman for the rest, saying that it was not right that, given safe—conduct by the King, they should suffer such dishonour at the hands of his men. The King said that he had given them all safe—conduct so that they might come and go freely and stay there to watch and enjoy themselves with the besiegers; but that he had not given them safe—conduct to insult one another. If that squire said things he ought not to have said, then he deserved what had been done to him, and more besides. Then they all dispersed and no more joustings were held in that place.

CIV
How the defenders sallied to skirmish before the King left.

Throughout the time he spent there, the King made no attempt to attack the town because he did not carry with him the equipment that would have made such an attack practicable. Moreover, since the place was garrisoned by very good troops, he realized that it would be useless for him to stay there any longer and so he decided to leave. Nevertheless, for as long as he remained there, as we have said, there was constant skirmishing. The defenders would sally forth from the town to attack the besiegers, but the Portuguese always carried the day.

One day, a contingent from the garrison defending the town made a sortie across a bridge by which they were wont to cross in order to engage in skirmishing. Habitually, when pursued by the besiegers, the Castilians would flee back to the bridge, stop there, turn round and attack their enemies once again, in a confused struggle to and fro without any result. Gonçalo Vasques Coutinho, who was

laãos parauam cada uez aa pomte e que os portugueses voltauom dally sem mais fazer, fallou com elles em esta maneira, dizemdo que quamdo os seguissem e os emmigos deteuessem em aquell logar, que desem com elles de uolta pella ponte demtro, e assy cobrariam delles gramde melhoria. E foy assy de feito que, voltamdo os castellaãos ata a pomte e nom esperamdo que os mais seguissem, derom os portugueses de topo em elles; os quaaes, desperçebidos de tall cousa, nom podiam caber polla pomte, e delles se lamçauom a augua, outros forom presos e mortos. E nom tornarom mais a tal jogo; ca el-Rey partio dally, e nom teuerom aazo de o fazer.

CV
Como foy cobrado Roalles e doutras cousas que se segu(i)rom.

Partio el-Rey daquel logar como dizemos, passados ja oito dias que ally chegarom, e foy a hoste pousar duas legoas, a par huum logar çercado que chamam Matilha. E dally moueo outro dia, passamdo a rybeira de Ricouao , huum rio que naçe nas Esturas, que era daquel Aluaro Perez dOsoyro. E pella ribeira daquel rio açima vaão muytas aldeeas ataa Vallemça de dom Joham. A este iogar forom corer Martym Vaasquez da Cunha e Gill Vaasquez, seu jrmaão, e Gomçallo Vaasquez Coutinho e Ruy Mendez de Vasconçellos e Joham Afomsso Pimentell e outros, e chegarom a huum logar que chamam Santilham, preto de Vallemça e da villa, homde estaua muyta booa gemte pera a defemder. E veerom a escaramuçar, estando o rio amtre huuns e os outros; amtre os quaaes veo Aluaro dOuter de Fumos, aquell famosso homem darmas de que em çima he feita mençam. E saymdo com outros, meteram-se a augua damballas partes; e os portugueses damdo nos castellaãos, nom os poderom sofrer, e uoltarom costas. E foy ally ferido aquel Aluaro dOuter de Fumos de guissa que depois moreo; e tornaram-se os portugueses ao arreall com gados e outras coussas que trouuerom.

Outro dia partio a hoste e pousou sobre Roalles. Ally nom estauom gentes darmas, saluo lauradores, assy do logar come das aldeas daredor; e uemdo que se nom podiam defemder nem auer outro acoro, deu-sse per preitesya que leixassem a villa, e foy o logar roubado de mantimentos e de quanto hij auya.

Estando assy em aquel logar, foy huum dia gemte darmas por guarda daquelles que hiam aa herua; e himdo el-Rey por lhe mandar como fossem ordenados, cayo o cauallo com elle e quebrou-lhe a asylha dhuum braço, e coregeram-lho. E el-Rey tomaua gram nojo por lhe tall cajom aconteçer em tera de seus emmjgos, amdando por lhe fazer guerra. Em

taking part in this particular engagement, noticing how the Castilians would halt each time at the bridge and how the Portuguese would return from there without further success, addressed the men in this manner, saying that when they were in pursuit and the enemy stopped at that point, they were to descend along with them on to the very bridge itself, and in this way could gain an advantage over them. So it proved, for when the Castilians turned at the bridge, not suspecting that they would press them further, the Portuguese charged them suddenly. Caught totally off their guard, there was no room for them all to retreat across the bridge, so some threw themselves in the water while others were captured or killed. They never repeated the manoeuvre, for the King departed and there was no opportunity to do so.

CV
How Roales was captured and of other happenings that followed on from this.

The King left that place, as we have said, just eight days after their arrival. The army camped two leagues on, close by a walled village called Matilla de Arzón. The following day, he moved on across the Esla, a river that rises in Asturias, a territory governed by Álvaro Pérez de Osorio. Upstream from there are a large number of villages along its banks as far as Valencia de Don Juan. Martim Vasques da Cunha, Gil Vasques his brother, Gonçalo Vasques Coutinho, Rui Mendes de Vasconcelos, João Afonso Pimentel and others set out to ride towards Valencia de Don Juan, near to which they came to a place called San Millán,[1] which was strongly defended. The defenders came out to skirmish, although the river divided one force from the other. Among the enemy was Álvaro de Tordehumos, that celebrated warrior whom we have mentioned previously. The Castilians made a sally and both sides plunged into the water. The Portuguese attacked the Castilians who were unable to withstand them and fled. That Álvaro de Tordehumos received a wound there from which he later died; and the Portuguese returned to camp with cattle and other things they found.

The next day, the army moved on and camped outside Roales. There was no garrison there, only peasants from the town and the surrounding countryside. Realizing that they could neither defend the place nor expect assistance, they offered surrender in return for a safe—conduct to leave, so that the place was pillaged of all the stores it contained.

While they were there, some men—at—arms went out one day, to escort those men who went out for hay, and as the King rode to give them their orders, his horse fell down with him and he broke his collar—bone. This was splinted for him, but the King was very annoyed that such an accident should happen in enemy territory when

esto começou-se dizer — e nom era assy — que os moradores de Ualdeiras, que era outra villa daquell Aluaro Perez, fugiam com medo,
leixamdo-a desemparada. E como taaes nouas foram ouujdas, caualgarom
apresa alguuns do areall com homeens de pee, e forom rijos pera alla
por tomar das gemtes que fogiam e roubar a villa dos mantimentos. E
dos que assy caualgarom foy Joham Fernamdez Pacheco e Joham Gomez
da Silua e Antam Vaasquez e outros fidalgos, e chegarom ao logar.
Acharom-no bem perçebido e acompanhado, e fora da ujlla bem iiij°. de
cauallo, amtre os do logar e das outras companhas que eram postas por
guarda daquella comarca; omde era o Almirante e Pero Soarez de Qui-
nhones, adeantado de terra de Leom, e outros boons caualleiros. E como
virom os portugueses que era pouca gente, veerom logo topar em elles.
E (foy) (a)quell juntamento assy pellejado que ouue hij feridos dhuuma
parte e doutra e alguuns mortos. E tornaram-sse os castellaãos pera a
villa e os portugueses pera o arreall. E huum caualleiro de sua companha, quando vio tamta gente da uilla e os portugueses emuorilhados com
elles tomou tam gram medo que fogio pera o arreall, damdo nouas que
todos ficauom mortos. E porque tal cousa sayo mentirosa e lho desde-
ziam todos, tomou tam gram nojo que tresualiou o miollo; e se lhe
deziam: *Esforçar com Deus,* assy dezia elle: *Esforçar com Deus;* e
assy de quaaesquer cousas que lhe fallauom. E durou com aquella maginaçom tres dias, e logo moreo. E este era Gomçallo Garçia de Farya.

CVI
Como el-Rey cobrou Valdeiras.

Cobrado Roalles desta maneira, partyo el-Rey caminho de Valdeiras
com o Duque e suas gemtes.

Em este logar estaua por guarda Sancho de Vallasco, filho bastardo
de Pero Fernandez de Vallasco, com oytemta de cauallo consigo. E
estaua hij mais Gomçallo Fernamdez dAguillar e Gomez Eannes Maldorme e Gonçallo de Paredes, grande beesteiro e muyto çerto com os
da nomina del-Rey, e monse Roby Brocamonte, com framçeses e outros
estrangeiros que por guarda daquella comarca eram postos; assy que a
uilla estaua bem perçebida de quamto compria a sua defemssam.

El-Rey leuaua huuma escalla pequena e huum emgenho, se mester
fezessem pera alguum logar; e porque o muro era astrosso, feito de taipa
e a logares fraco, teuerom comselho el-Rey e o Duque de o combater e
tomar per força, por ser escarmento a outros logares. E armada a escalla
e emgenho e repartidos os combatos a cadahuns, e todos armados, ante
que dessem aas trombetas tomarom tal medo daquella grua que nom
aujam em vsso de ueer, espeçialmente o Sancho de Ualasco que tinha

he was on a military campaign. At this time, they began to say (it was untrue) that the inhabitants of Valderas, another town governed by Álvaro Pérez, had fled in terror, leaving it undefended. As soon as the news arrived, a reconnaissance party composed of cavalry and foot soldiers quickly set out to that place to take prisoner those who were fleeing and to pillage whatever stores were in the town. João Fernandes Pacheco, João Gomes da Silva, Antão Vasques and other nobles were among those who rode to this place. They found it well equipped and well defended, and with some four hundred knights outside the town, including its permanent garrison and other companies which had been sent to defend that district. Among these were the Admiral[2] and Pedro Suárez de Quiñones, governor of the kingdom of León as well as other good knights. When they saw that the Portuguese were a small force, they came at once to attack them, but the fighting became so fierce that men were wounded and a few were killed on both sides. Then the Castilians returned to the town and the Portuguese to the camp. When he saw so many from the town locked in a skirmish with the Portuguese, one knight from the reconnaissance party was so afraid that he fled back to the camp with the news that all had been killed. Because this turned out to be false and because everyone gainsaid him, he was so appalled that he lost his wits. If they said to him, "Strive with God", he would repeat, "Strive with God"; and similarly with whatever else anyone said to him. This delusion lasted three days, at the end of which he died. His name was Gonçalo Garcia de Faria.

CVI
How the King captured Valderas.

Roales having been captured in this way, the King set out in the direction of Valderas with the Duke and his men.

Sancho de Velasco, bastard son of Pedro Fernández de Velasco, was guarding this place with a force of eighty cavalry. Among these there were Gonzalo Fernández de Aguilar, Gómez Yáñez Maldorme, Gonzalo de Paredes, who was a fine marksman and very accurate with the crossbow, and those on the King's pay—roll, as well as Sir Robert de Bracquemont with a force of French and other nationalities that had been assigned to defend the district. So the town was well equipped with everything necessary to its defence.

The King had a small siege—belfry and a siege-engine, in case they should be needed in any place. Because the town—wall was flimsy, built out of mud, and weak at certain points, the King and the Duke were advised to mount an assault and take the town by storm, and in this way panic other strongholds into surrender.

When the belfry and engine were in position and everyone was assigned to his post and armed, but before the trumpets sounded, the defenders were most alarmed at the unfamiliar sight of the crane.

255

carego do logar, que bem emtende(o) que nom auya nelles cobro, saluo serem emtrados per força. E fez sair huum caualleiro da uilla armado, braadamdo se estaua hij Pedrafomsso da Ancora, caualleiro portugues, que lho chamassem por lhe dar o galgo que lhe prometera. El Rey, que o ouuyo, feze-o chamar, e dise-lhe como ho chamaua huum dos da villa, e por que. Pedrafomsso da Ancora disse que se nom acordaua de tal promesa, mas que demtro auya huum jrmaão de sa molher e alguuns seus parentes; e que pemsaua que o chamauom por seer avimdor amtre el e os da uilla.

El-Rey sospeitou que era assy, e mandou-lhe que fosse la, dizemdo que se lhe desem çerto pam e vinho [1], nomeando-lhe logo quanto, fazemdo porem vassallagem ao Duque, que preitejasse o logar; e em tanto mandou que esteuesem todos quedos ataa que el ueesse da ujlla, pera veer que recado tragia.

Pedrafomsso foy honde o chamarom e deram-lhe o galgo, de que parte nom sabya; e falarom-lhe logo em avemça. E depois de mujtas razoões ficarom em tal acordo que sayssem da uilla, e que os mantimentos e o al que achassem fosse seu. O caualleiro tornou a el-Rey e contou-lhe (a) avemça em que ficarom, e el-Rey falou com o Duque, a que prougue de tal preytessya; ca el-Rey em estas auenças nom outorgaua majs, saluo quamto ao Duque prazia, semdo-lhe muito obediente em todallas cousas. E quamdo hordenaua de partir ou asessegar ou semelhamte cousa, sempre lho mandaua dizer per estas pallauras: *Senhor, vosso filho vos enuia dizer tal cousa.*

Emtam foy outrauez demtro Pedrafomsso; e fallado com os do logar, veerom fora em arefeens por elle Sancho de Ualasco e Gonçallo Fernandez e outros dous; e ficou la Pedrafomsso essa noite. Em outro dia foy o Comdestabre aa porta da uilla com suas gemtes; e poseran-se em duas aazes, huuma dhuuma parte e os outros da outra, e elles sayam per meyo, e o Comde ooulhaua que lhe nom fezessem nenhuum nojo. E assy sayram todos hordenadamente, e o Comde foy com elles ataa mea legoa do logar, por nom auerem dano dos da hoste, como fora na auemça. E depois que os pos em saluo, as gemtes darmas castellaãos e framçesses, que veerom por guarda da uilla e hiam com os moradores do logar em companha, depois que se o Comde tornou, roubarom-nos de quamto auer lhe acharom. E assy foy cobrado Valdeiras.

This was particularly the case with Sancho de Velasco who was in command of the garrison; for he knew that there was no way of avoiding the storming of the town. So he sent out from the town an armed knight who shouted that if Pedro Afonso de Ancora, a Portuguese knight, were there, he should be sent for so that he might be given a grey—hound which he had promised him. The King heard this, summoned Ancora himself and told him that one of the defenders was calling for him and why. Pedro Afonso da Ancora said that he had no recollection of such a promise, but that a brother of his mother and certain relatives of his were in the town, and he thought that they had called for him in order that he should act as negotiator between the King and the townspeople.

The King suspected that this was indeed the case. He ordered him to go there, saying that if they gave him a certain specified quantity of bread and wine and became the Duke's vassals, he would accept the town's capitulation. In the meanwhile he ordered the army to remain calm until the knight should return from the town so that they might see what kind of message he brought back with him.

Pedro Afonso went to the place where they had summoned him, and they gave him the grey—hound, but from whom it came he did not know. There they spoke with him about an accord. After much argument, an agreement was reached whereby they would leave the town, and the stores and everything else therein would belong to the Duke. The knight returned to the King and explained to him the accord that had been reached. The King then spoke to the Duke who gave his approval to this understanding. The King in such negotiations would agree to nothing unless the Duke wished it so, for he always deferred to the Duke in everything. Whenever he gave the order to depart or stop or anything like that, he always sent a message to the Duke with these words: "My lord, your son sends you word that such and such..."

Then Pedro Afonso went into the town a second time, and talked with the garrison. Then Sancho de Velasco and Gonzalo Fernández and two more defenders came out as hostages in exchange for him, and Pedro Afonso remained inside for the night. The following day, the Constable came to the town gate with his men. They formed up in two lines, one on one side and the other on the other side, while the defenders came out passing between these while the Count watched to see that they were unmolested. In this fashion all came out in an orderly manner and the Count went with them until they were half a league distant from the town so that they could receive no harm from the army, as had been agreed. Once the Castilian and French soldiers and the inhabitants who were with them had been conducted to safety, the Count returned and the besiegers pillaged everything they could find in the town.[1] In this manner was Valderas captured.

CVII

Como foy roubado Valdeiras.

As gemtes do Duque, pero fossem poucas como dissemos, porque som homeens fora de sa terra de maa gouernança e pouca prouissam açerca dos mantimentos, amdauom muy desbaratados e com gram myngua; e elles (chamando) a toda a terra sua, deziam aas vezes aos portugueses, quando cobrauom alguuma villa, que par Deus! elles faziam mall de lhes roubarem suas fortallezas e villageens, e outras taaes razões de que os portugueses escarneçiam; e tanto que el-Rey era posto em afam e cuidado por sua guarda e booa hordenamça. E depois que o Conde tornou de poer em saluo os de Ualdeiras, ouue el-Rey comselho que maneira se teeria no roubar daquella villa, por quamto o Duque dezia que suas gemtes nom auiam boa companhia dos portugueses. E mandou que os jmgreses roubassem o logar ataa ora de meyo dia e os portugueses ata a noite. E foy assy que o Duque e suas gemtes emtrarom pella menhaã e começarom de roubar; e os portugueses, vemdo-lhe trazer os mantimentos, auiam-no por gramde agrauo, dizemdo muytas razões amtre ssy sobresto, em tanto que se forom aa villa muyto primeiro amte de meyo dia, e começarom de roubar de mestura com elles. Os jmgreses, queixamdo-se desto muyto, avyam aroydo huuns com os outros. Emtom o Duque foy aa temda hu el-Rey estaua, fazemdo lhe gram queixume dos seus, que nom soomente emtrarom ante do meo dia a roubar comtra seu mandado, mas ajmda tomauom aos jngreses o que roubado tinham.

El-Rey, como ouuio esto, caualgou apressa com gram queixume por pasarem seu mandamento, que muyto he destranhar nos feitos da guerra roubamdo daquell geito amte das oras que deuerom. E açesso com gram sanha, leuamdo huuma espada nas maãos, fazia sayr fora, damdo com ella aos que achaua pellas ruas, de guissa que ouue hij feridos e mortos per tall aazo, porem que os mortos nom forom mais que dous, huum que el-Rey degolou per sa mão e outro que fez saltar do muro a fumdo, de que logo moreo. E posta nas ruas tal guarda per aquelles a que el-Rey emcomendou como se fosse menagem de ujlla, tornou-sse pera o areall. E depois forom os portugueses roubar como era hordenado; e foy hij achado muyto pam e vinho, de que todollos do areall forom abastados; e o logar ficou desemparado, que nom curarom mais delle.

CVII
How Valderas was sacked.

Few in numbers as they were in any case, as we have explained, the Duke's forces, who were far from their own land, in disarray, and poorly equipped, were now sorely depleted and the worse for wear. Nevertheless, they claimed a right to the whole country, saying to the Portuguese from time to time, when they captured some town or other, that by God! they did them injury by sacking their strongholds and villages, as well as making other remarks, at which the Portuguese mocked. So much of this sort of thing went on that the King was put to some trouble and concern in order to maintain order and discipline. When the Count returned from taking the garrison of Valderas to safety, the King took his advice about the manner in which the sack of the town should be conducted, given that the Duke was saying that his men and the Portuguese were not on good terms. So the King commanded that the English should pillage the place until midday and the Portuguese thereafter until night. So it was that the Duke and his force entered the town in the morning and began the sack. When they saw him bringing out stores, the Portuguese were most annoyed, protesting vociferously over this; so much so that well before midday, they went into the town and began pillaging alongside the English. The English complained loudly about this and disputes broke out between the two armies. So then the Duke went to the King's tent and complained bitterly about the Portuguese, saying that not only had they entered the town well before midday against the King's orders, but in addition were robbing the English of the booty they had already pillaged.

When he heard this, the King rode quickly thither to call his men to account for contravening his orders, for to pillage before the agreed hour in such a manner is most reprehensible in warfare. The King, in a rage, forced them out, his sword in his hand, striking with it at those he found in the streets. For this reason, there were woundings and deaths, although in fact there were but two deaths. One of these happened when the King himself decapitated a man, and the other when he forced a soldier to jump off the wall, from which fall he died there and then. Having placed a guard in the streets from among those to whom he had enlisted the care of the town, he returned to the camp. Later the Portuguese went in to pillage as had been arranged; and much bread and wine was found, which was sufficient to supply the needs of the whole camp. So the place was sacked and thereafter they lost interest in it.

Como el-Rey çercou Villalobos, e se Martym Vaasquez da Cunha defemdeo aos castellaãos.

Depois de quimze dias que ally esteuerom, el-Rey e o Duque partirom com sua hoste e forom pousar a Villalobos, logar bem çercado, segumdo os outros daquel mesmo Aluaro Perez dOsoyro. E auya dhuuma parte a caua com muyta auguoa, e da outra era de todo seca; e estauam em elle [1] gemtes darmas, assy como das outras companhas; mas nom era hi capitam famosso que de as acaudellar teuesse gouernamça.

E hordenamdo el-Rey de o combater, mandou que pera tapar aquella caua seca, que çerta herua da que veesse pera o arreall fosse lamçada em ella, pera seer de todo chaão e passarem as gemtes per çima. E foy assy lamçada per espaço de tres dias, pera quamdo fosse prestes a ora de o combaterem.

Em esto mandou el-Rey aa herua e por guarda dos que la hiam Martym Vaasquez da Cunha e seus jrmaãos e outros fidalgos com çertas gemtes. E partimdo do areall as azemellas e muytos dos que hiam por guarda dellas, ficarom detras per aqueçimento Martym Vaasquez e Gill Vaasquez e Lopo Vaasquez, seus jrmaãos, e Maaborny e Louremço Martiinz do Avellaar e Joham Portella, e doutros escudeiros e caualleiros ataa dezoyto; e hiam fallamdo muyto de seu vagar, fazemdo aquell dia huum gram neuoeiro e a menhaã nom bem descuberta. E sem paramdo mentes que tera leuauom per aazo daquell espesso aar, erarom o camjnho. E semdo ja huuma gramde legoa do arreal, forom dar comsigo na ribeira que vem de Mayorgas, homde jaziam iiijº. lamças de castellaãos e muytos homeens de pee amtre huuns vlmos que ally avija, homde dormiram essa noite; de que eram capitaães dom Fadrique, duque de Benauemte, jrmaão bastardo del-Rey, e Aluaro Perez dOsoiro e Ruy Pomçe de Leom e outros. E quamdo os virom tam jumto comsigo, conheçemdo que eram portuguesses, começarom bradar: *Mata, Mata! Castilha, Castilha!* E elles, vemdo-sse em tal cajom postos, começarom dizer altas vozes: *Sam Jorge, Sam Jorge! Portugall, Portugall!* E muyto trigos(os) se desuiarom logo a huum pequeno e baixo logar amotado, que era hij preto, que pareçia em outro tempo seer feito aa maão, em que os antigos, segumdo fama, faziam sacrifiçio a seus deoses; ca naquella terra nam ha outras seras a que se acolher podessem. E descaualgarom apressa todos e poseram as bestas aredor de ssy, atadas huumas com as outras; e elles em meo, com as lamças nas maãos e as costas huuns comtra os outros, dizemdo logo amtre ssy como compria que huum delles fosse tostemente dar nouas ao areall, que lhes acoresem. E cada huum se escusaua de tal

CVIII
How the King besieged Villalobos and how Martim Vasques da Cunha defended himself against the Castilians.

After a sojourn of fifteen days in this place, the King and the Duke departed with their army and camped outside Villalobos, a stoutly–walled place, like the others belonging to Álvaro Pérez de Osorio. On one side the moat had a lot of water in it, but on the other it was dry. Inside were soldiers to defend it, assisted by reinforcements from other companies. However, there was no commander of note in the town with sufficient authority to provide effective leadership.

When organizing the attack on the place, the King commanded that some of the hay which was coming into the camp should be thrown into the dry moat so as to fill it up and render the ground flat, for the soldiers to walk across. They threw hay into it for the space of three days so as to make it ready for the moment of attack.

The King sent Martim Vasques da Cunha, his brothers and other nobles with certain soldiers for the hay and to protect those who fetched it. When the pack–animals and many of those assigned to guard them left the camp, Martim Vasques and his brothers Gil Vasques and Lopo Vasques fell behind because of the heat, together with Mauburney, Lourenço Martins do Avelar, João Portela and other squires and knights to the number of eighteen. They talked as they travelled, making slow progress, for the morning was very misty and overcast. Not realizing quite where they were in the hazy atmosphere, they strayed out of their way. When they were already a good league from the camp, they found themselves by the river that runs from Mayorga[1] where there were four hundred Castilian lances and many foot–soldiers among some elms, under which they had camped the previous night. The commanders of this force were Don Fadrique, Duke of Benavente and bastard son of the King, Alvar Pérez de Osorio, Ruy Ponce de León and some others. When these caught sight of them so close, realizing that they were Portuguese, they began to yell: "Kill, kill! Castile, Castile!" Seeing themselves in the midst of a disaster, the Portuguese force began to shout: "St. George, St. George! Portugal, Portugal!" Then they rushed to a small, low mound nearby. It seemed to have been built by men in an earlier age and had the reputation of being a place where men in ancient times made sacrifice to their gods. In fact, in that area there is no other high ground where they could have found any protection whatever.

They all swiftly dismounted, positioning the animals around them, each tied to the next, and themselves in the centre, lance in hand, and back to back. Then they began to say that one of them should hurry to the camp to report the news and ask for assistance. Everyone gave excuses for not going, and excuses which presented

hida, mostramdo que o fazia por melhor.

Emtom disse huum escudeiro, que chamauom Diogo Perez do Auellaar, que viuia com Martim Vaasquez: *Quall era mais homrosa cousa e de comtar por moor façanha, ajudallos a defemder assy como estauom ou passar peramt(r)e tamtos castellãos e hir dar nouas ao areall?* E todos diserom que moor cousa era avemturar-sse a passar peramtre tamtos emmjgos. *Pois,* disse elle, *eu quero seer esse.*

Emtom caualgou peramtre aquelles que o matar desejauom; e pero lhe fossem muytas lamças remesadas, nenhuuma foy que lhe empeçesse. E quamdo vinham a el dhuma parte e dooutra pera o auerem de lleuar demcontro, estemdia-sse ao lomgo da besta; e assy prazia a Deus que lhe escapaua, de guissa que passou em saluo per todos elles e foy dar nouas ao arreall.

Os castellãos çercarom em tanto os dezasete que ficauom, sobimdo pella ladeira daquel cabeço e remesando-lhe muytas lamças, assy das que tragiam come das que tomauom aos homens de pee, de que gramde rumo jazia bem preto delles. Dellas er nom lhe chegauom porque remesauom de fumdo pera çima; outros nom se ousauom tamto de chegar, porque os portugueses, das lamças que lhe emuyauom, tornauom-nas a remesar, e porque era sopee a fumdo e os de cauallo muyto bastos, quantas remesauom nom hiam em vaão, bradamdo altas vozes Martym Vaasquez quamdo os castellãos vinham a elles e os remesauom: *Cunha, Cunha! Quem-na ouuer de leuar, salgada (a) ha de leuar!* E assy se defemdiam, matando seus emmjgos com as lamças que lhe emprestauom, com que os de matar ouuessem. E os cauallos feridos topauom huuns nos outros, matamdo taaes que escaparom se lhe aquello nom fora. E moreram bem quorenta escudeiros castellãos e muytos cauallos. E dos portuguesses nom foy nenhuum ferido nem morto saluo Maaborny, que saymdo fora por tomar das lamças pera remesar e colhemdo-sse demtro, foy-lhe remesada huuma lamça per Martym Gomçalluez dAtayde, que amdaua em Castella como dissemos, e amtresolhou a lamça per huumas solhas que trazia, e ouue huuma ferida de que a poucos dias moreo.

Chegarom as nouas ao arreal e foy dito ao Comdestabre, e ssayo apressa com gemtes por lhe acorer. E jmdo-se ja o neuoeiro alçamdo por o dia que era creçido, ouuerom os castellãos vista do acoro, e começarom de se partir; e hiam dizemdo: *Doge mais nom compre que se leam as proeças de Tristam e de Lamçarote, mas fallemos no esforço de Martym Vaasquez da Cunha, que com dezasete homens darmas se defemdeo a quatroçentas lamças que eramos per tamanho espaaço em tam fraco logar.*

them in the best light. Then up spoke one Diogo Peres do Avelar, a squire who attended Martim Vasques, asking, "What would be the most honourable thing to do and would rate as a greater deed in the telling? To help in the defence of our position? Or to pass through this numerous Castilian force and take news to the camp?" They all said that the greater deed would be to run the danger of passing through the enemy lines. "In that case", he said, "I want to be that man."

So he rode through the lines of those who wished to kill him; and although many lances were thrown at him, none halted his progress. Whenever they approached to challenge him, on the right or on the left, he would lie flat along the horse's back. So, by God's will he escaped and passed safely through their lines and took the news to the camp.

Meanwhile, the Castilians surrounded the seventeen men who remained, climbing the slope of that mound and hurling many lances at them — those that they carried with them as well as those they took from the foot—soldiers, of which a great number lay close by. Some of these lances did not reach the Portuguese because they were being thrown upwards from lower to higher ground. Other attackers did not dare come too close because the Portuguese collected some of the lances thrown at them and then threw them back. Because they were throwing towards the lower ground where the horsemen were thickly bunched, not all of these lances missed their mark, so that Martim Vasques roared at the top of his voice when the Castilians were charging and they were hurling lances at them: "Cunha, Cunha! Whoever takes it must take it salty!" Thus did they defend themselves, killing their enemies with lances lent to them by an enemy who had intended using those lances to kill them. The wounded horses collided with each other, killing those which escaped if the wounding itself did not do so. A good forty Castilian squires and many horses were killed. None of the Portuguese was wounded or killed, only Mauburney, who made a sally to collect lances to be hurled back. As he was returning, a lance was hurled at him by Martim Gonçalves de Ataide [2] who was living in Castile, as we have said. The lance found its way between the scales of the armour Mauburney was wearing, and he received a wound from which he died a few days later.

The news reached the camp and was told to the Constable who set out quickly with help. As the day was now well advanced and the mist was lifting, the Castilians could see the relief force approaching and began to depart. As they went off, they were saying, "From today onwards we should not read of the deeds of Tristan and of Lancelot; rather let us speak of the valour of Martim Vasques da Cunha who, with seventeen armed men, defended himself against our four hundred lances for so long and in such a poor weak position."

A quall cousa nenhuum entemdimento dhomem esqujue crer que foy assy, nem presuma que comtamos esto por louuor dos portugueses e desfazimento de seus comtrairos, mas porque certamente assy acomteçeo de feito.

CIX

Do que el-Rey mandou fazer aos que tomarom a erua, e como foy cobrado Villalobos.

Aquell dia nom veo herua ao arreall como deuera por aazo desto que aconteçeo, e porque aquel neuoeiro fez espalhar huuns dos outros. E por myngua de erua que aquell dia hij ouue, desy porque se rogia que os do logar mouyam a auemça no outro seguynte, semdo oras do meo dia, leuantou sse huuma voz sem mandado del-Rey, dizemdo alto huuns aos outros: *Aa herua, aa herua! Ca preitejada he a villa.* E como esto começarom de dizer, forom alla moços e azemees e homeens de pee, e foy muy asinha leuada quamta ally jazia. El-Rey ouue disto gramde merencoria, e mandaua prender quamtos achassem que a tomarom; e forom presos e leuados amtelle seis moços culpados em esto.

O Comde, ouuyndo como os el-Rey mandaua premder e sospeitamdo mal de tall feito, trigosamente se foy aa temda homde pousaua; e nunca tantas boas razooes pode dizer a el-Rey e lho pedir por merçee, que o demouer podesse que os nam mandasse decepar. O Comde, quamdo jsto vio, say(o)-sse fora nom fallamdo, com vulto triste e chorosso; e foy-sse logo pera sua temda, e deitou-sse de bruços emçima da cama. E posto que suas lagrimas constrangidamente fossem retheudas, nom o pode tamto emcobrir que os que eram daredor o nom ouuyssem chorar muyto e dar gramdes salluços por tall justiça como aquella. Isso mesmo huum escudeiro, criado del-Rey, que o bem auia seruido na guerra, afficadamente lhe pedia por merçee que huum daquelles moços, que era seu jrmaão, que o nom mandasse deçepar; e pero se muyto aficasse por esto, nom pode com el Rey que lho outorgasse. E el desnaturou-sse delle e foy pera Castella, e sempre amdou em seu desseruiço.

Em esto, vemdo os da uilla como el Rey nom tinha artefiços taaes com que gram nojo lhe fazer podesse, desy a herua tirada ja toda e que tarde vimria ally outra tamta, cobrarom esforço de se defemder e nom quiserom mouer preitesia.

Hora assy foy que per çima da caua, que era chea daugua, jaziam deitados huuns paaos compridos que atrauesauom dhuuma parte aa outra a modo de ponte. E daquella parte pousaua Gomçallo Vaasquez

Let no man shrink from believing that it happened in this way, nor presume that we relate this in order to exalt the Portuguese or to demean their adversaries. We are telling the story because it really happened in this way.

CIX
What the King ordered to be done to the men who took the hay, and how Villalobos was captured.

That day no hay reached the camp as it should have done, by reason of that mist that separated the forces and the events that ensued. Because of the shortage of hay that happened on that day, and also because it was being noised abroad that the defenders were preparing to come to terms on the following day, people began shouting to each other about midday and without any orders from the King: "The hay! Let's get at the hay! For the town has agreed to surrender!" No sooner had they started to say this than lads with pack—animals as well as foot—soldiers went there and quickly gathered up all the hay that lay there. The King was furious, and commanded that all who were found there taking the hay should be arrested. So six boys guilty of the deed were arrested and brought before him.

Learning of how the King was ordering arrests and foreseeing that ill would come of it, the Count hurried to the King's tent. It would have been impossible to forward as many good arguments as he did to the King, beseeching him to countermand the order to cut off their heads. When he realized he was unsuccessful, the Count came out tight—lipped and with a sad and tearful expression. He went straight to his tent and threw himself face down on the bed. Although his tears had been held back out of embarrassment, he was unable to hide them sufficiently to prevent those around from hearing him cry copiously, giving out loud sobs in the face of such injustice. Similarly, a squire who was a servant of the King and who had served him well in the war, persistently entreated him to spare one of those boys, his brother, from beheading; but no matter how hard he tried, he could not extract this boon from the King. As a result, he became disaffected and went over to Castile where he continually acted against the King.

At this juncture, the defenders realized that the King had no machinery at his disposal capable of doing them much harm, and that with all the hay removed, it would be some time before as much had been brought to replace it, so they took heart and resolved to go on defending the town and not to discuss surrender.

Now it happened that across that moat which was full of water were lying some long poles which crossed from one side to the other as a kind of bridge. On the far side, Gonçalo Vasques Coutinho and

Coutinho e Ruy Mendez de Vasconçelos, ambos companheiros em armas. Estes eram dous notauees fidalgos que na hoste del-Rey amdauom, ardidos e de boons corpos e gramdes caualgadores e muy esforçados em quallquer boom feito que lhe a maão vijnha; de guissa que em Benauente e nos outros logares, homde se fezerom assaz descaramuças, assy eram nomeados e conheçidos pellas armas que tragiam que muytos reçeauom de sair a elles. E nom soomente eram gabados e temidos dos emmigos, mas os jmgreses os louuauom muyto; em tanto que dezia o Duque que se ouuese dauentuyrar o regno de Castella e poer seu dereito em maão dhuum homeem que o combatesse, que cada huum delles era abastamte pera lhe dar tal emcarego.

Estes e outros jazemdo huuma vez desegurados, folgamdo a sesta pouco mais de meo dia, sayrom da uilla muytos de uolta e passarom a caua per aquelles paaos , por darem no areall e fazer dano em alguuns. Ruy Mendez e Gomçallo Vaasquez, quamdo esto virom, lamçaran-se fora das temdas com alguuns comsigo, sem outras armas nem coregimentos senom os escudos nos braços e remessoões nas maãos, e forom a elles bem trigosamente. E como jumtarom com os castellãos, nom os poderom soffrer; e derom volta pera a villa mais rijo do que sairom. E nom podemdo caber pellos paaos, matarom ally delles, e outros moreram na agua da caua em que cahyam. E tornamdo-sse Ruy Mendez e Gomçallo Vaasquez, hia ja el-Rey pera alla por veer que era aquello a que assy sayrom. E quamdo os vio assy vijr daquella gujssa com lamças nas maãos e escudos nos braaços, pero lho prouguese do que a seus emmjgos fezerom, começou-se de queixar contra elles, dizemdo que tal sayda desarmados nom compria a elles de fazer por serem pessoas a que nom comvinha, por quanto ligeiramente podiam reçeber cajom dhuum vil homem de pee, de que se seguiria gram dano, e assy outras taaes razoões. Ruy Mendez tragia huma pequena ferida da parte dereita e coria-lhe o ssangue per seu aluo braço, daquall nom fazia comta; e disse comtra el-Rey: *Nom curees, senhor, ca a tal tempo nom compria doutra guissa.* E em dizemdo esto, alçou com a lamça o braço ferido, dizemdo: *A lla fee! Eu som Rodrigo, que tam bem las fago como las digo.* El-Rey e os outros rirom daquesto, e assy se veerom pera as temdas.

Os da villa, por a perda das gemtes que ally ouuerom, mouerom logo preitessya ao Duque; e foy que teuessem sua voz e lhe dessem çertas cantaras de uinho e fanegas de trigo e mais mantimento por seus denheiros. E foy o Duque em posse do logar, emtrando demtro e postas suas bamdeiras emçima das portas da uilla; e vemdiam aos do areall os mantimentos que mester auyam.

Em esto mandou el-Rey a herua a huum logar que chamam Villa

Ruy Mendes de Vasconcelos stationed themselves. These two comrades—in—arms were two famous nobles serving in the King's army. They were bold, well—built, great horsemen, and quite equal to any worthwhile adventure that came their way; so much so that in Benavente and elsewhere where much skirmishing went on, they were so famed and well known for the arms they bore that many feared to come against them. Not only were they celebrated and feared by the enemy, but the English also praised them highly, so that the Duke used to say that if he were forced to entrust his claim to the kingdom of Castile to the fighting ability of one champion, either of these would be equal to the task.

Now one day when these two with some others were off their guard and resting during siesta time, a little after midday, a large number of men sallied forth from the town with much hullabaloo and crossed the moat over those poles in order to attack the camp and harm those in it. When they saw what was happening, Ruy Mendes and Gonçalo Vasques sprang out of the tents in the company of some others without any weapons or protection other than the shields on their arms and lances in their hands, and rushed to attack them. When they closed with the Castilians, the latter were unable to stand against them; and they turned tail back towards the town even faster than they had left it. Since they were not all able to cross by the poles at the same time, some were killed, while others died in the water of the moat into which they had fallen. While Ruy Mendes and Gonçalo Vasques were on their way back, the King was already making his way to the spot in order to find out why they had made a sally from the camp in this manner. When he saw them coming in such a state, lances in hand and shields on their arms, although he was pleased at what they had done to the enemy, he began to admonish them, saying that it was wrong for them to make such a sally from the camp without armour, for they could easily receive a wound from a mere foot—soldier which might lead to something far worse. He produced some other arguments as well. Ruy Mendes had a slight wound in the right side and blood was flowing down his white arm, but he made light of it. He said to the King, "Do not worry, my lord, for at the time we really had no alternative." As he said this, he raised the wounded arm holding his lance saying: "By my faith! I am Rodrigo, whose deeds are as good as his words." The King and all the rest laughed at this and so they all returned to the tents.

In view of the men they had lost in the engagement, the defenders asked the Duke for terms. His terms were that they should do him homage, and should sell him for cash a certain number of pitchers of wine and bushels of wheat together with further provisions. The Duke took formal possession of the town, entering it and placing his banners above the main gates; and the besiegers were sold the provisions they required.

At this time, the King sent for hay to a place near Zamora

Fauilla [1] contra Çamora, que he bem sassemta legoas do mar, e fazem em ella sal dhuuma lagoa. E foy estomçe o Comdestabre por guarda da cariagem. E aquel dia que alla forom, tornando as azemellas caregadas pera o areall, veerom gemtes de framçesses dhuum logar que dizem Vilhalpando; e daquellas que ja eram nom muy lomge do areal tomarom alguumas, por quanto o Comdestabre vinha na reguarda de todas, aredado dally per gramde espaço. Os do areall, como souberom que leuauom aquellas azemellas, caualgarom apressa; e jmdo apos elles, emcalçarom-nos no camjnho, e tolheram-lhas e tornarom-sse. O Comde, quamdo veo e soube parte daquell feito, hordenou dhir aaquell logar; e forom com el Gomçallo Vaasquez Coutinho e outros fidalgos. Em este Vilhalpamdo estaua huum capitam framçes que chamauom comde de Lomgavilla, que auya em sua companha bem mjll lamças. E quando vio o Comde e aquelles portuguesses, sayo fora com suas gemtes; e o Comde foy a elles, e nom ousamdo de o atemder, tornaron-se os framçeses pera a villa, e o Comde pera o areall dhu partira.

CX

Como el-Rey hordenou de se tornar pera seu regno, e da morte de Ruy Mendez.

El-Rey de Castella, passamdo estas cousas, andaua açerca daquella comarca, mudando-sse dhuum logar pera outro, assy como em Outerdesilhas e desy em Touro e em Sallamanca e pellos logares per homde entemdia que compridoiro era a seu seruiço; e cada dia lhe chegauom nouas como lhe estragauom a terra. E el fallaua esto com o jffante dom Joham, jrmaão del-Rey de Portugall, e com os comdes e mestres das hordens e Prior de Sam Joham, que hij eram com elle. E avudo sobresto comselho, por quanto el nom tinha vomtade daventuirar este feito per batalha, todos lhe deziam que *a andada del-Rey e do Duque nom podia seer muyta em Castella, por quamto lhes falleçiam os mantimentos que nom podiam achar; assy por as gentes que por guarda dos logares estauom pella comarca, que gastauom gram parte delles, come por o alçamento das viamdas que el aa primeira mandaua fazer, desy er por a destruyçam que os jmgreses e portugueses em elles faziam; e por tanto era per força de se partirem çedo. Moormente, deziam elles, que de uossas gentes e destrangeiras sempre a geito do arreall amdam tres e quatro mjll lamças, que lhe nom leixarom fazer tal dano que vossa terra muyto sinta. E em tanto viram as gentes del-Rey de Framça, por que speramos, muy çedo, e emtom podes hordenar o que mais por vosso seruiço*

called Villafáfila, which is a good sixty leagues from the sea and where they obtain salt from a lake. The Constable accompanied the expedition in order to act as guard for the convoy. The day they went there, as the pack—animals were returning loaded to the camp, French forces from a place called Villalpando appeared on the scene. They captured some of the animals that were by now only a short distance from the camp. This was because the Constable was in the very rearguard and consequently some long way behind. Learning of the capture of these animals, the forces in the camp rode fast to the place. They went after the French and, having caught up with them, took the animals from them and returned. When he learnt of this deed, the Count ordered an expedition to Villalpando, and Gonçalo Vasques Coutinho and other nobles went with him. In this stronghold of Villalpando there was a French captain called the Count of Longueville[1] who had a good thousand lances in his company. When he saw the Count and his Portuguese force, he sallied forth with his own men. The Count prepared to attack, but the French did not dare to await him, and returned to the town; and the Count returned to the camp from where he had set out.

CX
How the King ordered a return to his kingdom, and of the death of Ruy Mendes.

While these things were happening, the King of Castile was in the vicinity. He was moving about from place to place, Tordesillas, and then Toro, and Salamanca, as well as all those places which he deemed it to be in his interests to visit. Every day news reached him of how the invaders were devastating the countryside. So he discussed this with Prince João, brother of the Portuguese king, and with the counts, the masters of the military orders, and the Prior of St. John, all of whom were with him. Because he had no desire to put the war to the test of a pitched battle, he called a council. His counsellors were unanimous in telling him that the Castilian expedition of the King and the Duke could not be a lengthy one because they were short of provisions and could not find more. This was because the forces that defended the strongholds in the district had used up the major part of these provisions, because of the requisitioning of food that he himself had ordered, and because of the subsequent destruction of provisions perpetrated by the English and the Portuguese. Therefore, they would soon be forced to leave the country. "Moreover", they said, "you have Castilian and foreign forces numbering three to four thousand lances continually harassing them and preventing them from doing too much damage to your land. As soon as the forces of the King of France come, which we expect will be very soon, you will be in a position to plan things in whatever way you feel is most in your interests. As for the enemy,

emtenderdes. E elles, pois seu arreal nom he bem saão e morem em elle segumdo afirmam, nom podem aquy fazer gram detemça. El-Rey ouuya suas rezoões, outorgando no que elles deziam, passamdo estas cousas da guissa que comtamos.

El-Rey de Portugall jsso mesmo, vemdo como nenhuuma villa daquellas hu chegauom nom se demouia a reçeber o Duque por senhor, nem outros logares nem gemtes nenhumas, e que aquellas fracas villas que tomauom eram tam demtro no regno e assy mall aazadas pera manter, que nom era cousa pera poer em obra, achou que tal amdada per esta gujssa era pouco homrrosa e de muyto trabalho; e damdo taaes coydados a discreto pemsamento, fallou el-Rey estas cousas com o Duque, dizemdo *quamtos dias auia que em ello tinha maginado, e pois que todo (o) regno era em huum comtra elle, nom o queremdo auer por senhor, desy tamtos estrangeiros em ajuda de seu auersairo, e outros mais por que esperauam, e elle com poucas gemtes alomgado de sa terra, que lhe pareçia tal demanda como esta — se elle esperaua tomar toda Castella villa e villa — cousa pera numca vijnr a ffym. Porem que se el comtinuar quisesse a temçom que começara, que el prestes estaua e era com as gemtes que tragia, e com outras mais se comprisse, de o ajudar, como prometera; mas que os seus eram tam poucos pera aquell negoçio, que era gram myngoa de uer pera huum tal senhor como elle; e que por este aazo os emmjgos creçiam cada uez mais, e tomauom fouteza de se chegar a elles como el bem vya: assy que de duas cousas lhe pareçia fazer huuma, ou hir por gemtes a Ingraterra e emtrar poderosamente com ellas, ou cayr em alguuma homrosa conuemça se lhe per seu auersairo cometida fosse.*

O Duque, ouuimdo todas estas cousas em que largamente ouuerom fallado, disse que *lhe pareçiam suas razoões booas, e que ja alguuns seus lhe cometerom esto da parte daquelles estrangeiros com que auyam conheçimento, dizemdo que el-Rey de Castella cayria em quallquer booa auemça que honra dambos fosse, especialmente daquel casamento do jffamte seu filho com sua filha delle; e que el nom lhe respomdera de ssy nem de nom, saluo quamto dera a emtender que sua vomtade era tornar a Imgraterra por jumtar mais gemtes das que trouuera, e tornar outra vez aa Espanha com moor poderio. Porem se lhe homrosa cousa fosse cometida, que bem se moueria de o fazer, posto que leixase parte de seu dereito ou todo se mester fezesse; e que emtendia por este aazo e por os seus que adoeçiam muyto, que taaes auya hy que ja mandauom pedir a el-Rey de Castella cartas de saluo comduto pera passar per sa terra, emtendendo que se auya com el de conuijr —* da quall cousa se el Rey muyto espantou e de tal maneira de gemtes!

E razoamdo assaz sobresto, acordarom de se tornar, nom damdo

since their camp is unhealthy and it is said that they are dying there, they cannot remain here for very much longer." The King heard their arguments, agreeing with what they were saying, while events transpired in the manner in which we have described.

Similarly the King of Portugal could see that none of the towns which they had approached was disposed to receive the Duke as its lord, that the same applied to other places and people, and that those weak towns that they were taking were situated so deep inside the kingdom and would be so difficult to retain that it was not worth the effort; so he decided that pursuing the expedition in this fashion was winning them little honour and bringing them much touble. Having given careful consideration to these worries, he spoke to the Duke about it, saying that for many days he had been turning the matter over in his mind. The whole kingom was against the Duke, refusing to acknowledge him as lord. Many foreigners were there to assist the enemy while more were expected, whereas he was there with a small force and so far from home. Therefore, if he really hoped to win the whole of Castile town by town, the task seemed to the King endless. Of course, if the Duke wished to persist with the plan with which he had set out, he was ready and willing to assist him with the men he had brought and any more that might be necessary as he had promised, but the Duke's force was now so small for such a task, that it was dishonourable for such a great lord as he was. For this reason the enemy was growing ever stronger and feeling encouraged to attack them, as the Duke himself could see. Therefore, the King saw only two alternatives: to go to England for reinforcements and invade the country more effectively with these; or to come to an honourable agreement, if his adversary would propose one.

On hearing all these things which they discussed for a long time, the Duke said that his arguments seemed to him to be good ones, and that already some of his own men had suggested this to him on behalf of the foreign troops of Castile with which they were acquainted. These had informed them that the Castilian King would be perfectly agreeable to any accommodation that would safeguard the honour of both parties, especially an agreement involving the marriage of the Prince, his son, with the Duke's daughter. The Duke had not answered yes or no to this, but rather had implied that he wished to return to England to recruit more men than he had brought before, and then to come back to Spain in greater strength. However, if an honourable agreement were proposed to him, he would willingly support it, even if this meant relinquishing some of his rights, or even all, if necessary. He was of this mind also on account of his men who were very sick, so that there were some who had already sent to ask the King of Castile for letters of safe—conduct in order to pass through his country, for they felt that an agreement with him was now inevitable. The King was astonished at this statement and at such behaviour.

After much debate over the question, they agreed to retreat,

porem a entemder que se partiam da guerra começada. E por esto el-Rey nom quis vijnr per homde forom, mas trouue outro caminho, por mostrar que mais queriam amdar per Castella. E veeram-sse a Vijlhallpamdo.

E himdo aquell dia Ruy Mendez de Vascomçellos com outros corer a Crastoverde e amdando escaramuçando, deram-lhe com huum viratom huuma pequena ferida per çima do mangote açerca do ombro. Emtrou tam pouco que amdaua o uiratom pemdurado, nom curamdo nenhuuma cousa delle. E como veeo aa temda e foy desarmado, disse aaquelles que eram presentes: *Por çerto eu som ferido dherua.* E os outros dizemdo que nom, e el aperfiamdo que sy, foram-no dizer a el-Rey; ao quall pessou desto muyto, e veo logo ally por lhe tirar tall maginaçam. E esforçando que nom era nada, respondeo el e disse: *Senhor, eu ouuy sempre dizer que aquelles que ferem com herua, que lhe formiguejam os beiços; e a mym pareçe que quantas formjgas no mundo ha, que todallas tenho em elles. — Pois assy he,* disse el-Rey, *bebee logo da ourina, que he muy proueitossa pera esto.* E el disse que a nom beberia por cousa que fosse. E el-Rey afficamdo-o todauya, e el dizemdo que nom, como amauiosso senhor com desejo de sua saude, por lhe mostrar que nom ouuesse nojo, gostou a ourina e disse comtra elle: *E como nom beberes vos do que eu bebo?* E el nunca o quis fazer por quanto lhe dizer poderom. E el-Rey vinha a o veer cada dia duas e tres vezes; e ao terçeiro dia, estamdo com el fallamdo, dizemdo-lhe muytas razoões desforço, el disse comtra el-Rey: *Senhor, eu uos tenho em gramde merçee vossas pallauras e visitaçam. Mas eu emtemdo que em mym nom ha senom morte; porque homde eu deuia de folgar com vosa falla e boom esforço, eu nom me anojo menos que se uos fossees huum homem a que eu bem nom quisesse.*

El-Rey, como ouuyo esto, voltou as costas e sayo da temda com os olhos nadando em lagrimas, dizemdo aos outros como tinha a maao[3] sinal sa vida por aquello que lhe disera. E logo esse dia fez seu acabamento; de cuja morte el-Rey e o Duque e todollos do areal tomarom gram nojo e tristeza, por seer tam boom caualleiro em força e ardimento, e morer assy de ligeira cousa per tam desauentuirado cajom. Gomçallo Vasquez fazia por el tal doo que ajmda que fora seu jrmaão ou filho, nom podera mayor fazer. E trouueram-no a Portugall, e hij foy soterrado.

although without giving the impression that they were abandoning the war that they had initiated. For this reason, the King did not want to travel by the way they had come, but by another route, so as to demonstrate their intention of going on through Castile. So they came to Villalpando.

While Ruy Mendes de Vasconcelos with some others was raiding and skirmishing near Castroverde, he received a slight wound from a crossbow bolt just above the arm—brace near the shoulder. The bolt penetrated so slightly that he continued with it hanging from him making light of the injury. When he reached his tent and his armour was taken off, he said to those present, "Surely I have been wounded with a poisoned bolt?" The others denied it, while he insisted that it was so; and when the King was told he was very worried and came immediately to try and drive away such thoughts from his mind. As the King endeavoured to convince him that it was nothing, he replied saying, "Sire, I have always heard that anyone wounded with a poisoned weapon feels as if his lips were crawling with ants. It seems to me as if I have all the ants in the world crawling on mine." "In that case", said the King, "drink some urine immediately, for it is very beneficial in such cases." He said that he would not drink it, not for anything in the world. The King went on insisting, and he went on refusing; and at last, like a loving lord wanting him to recover and in order to convince him that no harm would come of it, the King himself tasted the urine and then said to him, "So now why cannot you drink what I drink?" But he would not do so, no matter how hard they tried to make him. The King came to see him two or three times every day. On the third day, as the King was talking to him, using many forceful arguments, he replied, "Sire, I am most grateful to you for your kind words and your visits. But I know that there is nothing in me but death. I know this because whereas your conversation and your encouragement ought to be putting me in good heart, in fact, I feel as low as I would if you were someone whom I disliked."

When he heard this, the King turned his back and left the tent, his eyes brimming with tears, saying to the others that what he had been told was a bad sign. Indeed, that same day the knight passed away. Because he was a fine knight, so full of strength and courage, and because he died in such an unfortunate way from so trifling an injury, his death caused the King, the Duke and the whole camp great pain and sorrow. Gonçalo Vasques mourned him as deeply as he would have done had he been his very own brother or son. They brought him to Portugal and there he was laid to rest.

Como el-Rey partio com sua hoste, e foy presso Diogo Lopeȝ dAngul

Dally partio el-Rey com sua hoste e veo pousar a çima de Çamora duas legoas, jumto com o ryo em dereito de Santa Maria do Viso; e el-Rey mandou buscar o ryo, que era em amcho huum gram tiro de beesta, se poderia auer vaao [5] pera passar. E amtre aquelles que o buscar forom foy huum escudeiro que deziam Aluaro Vaasquez, alcayde dAlcanede; e buscamdo o vaao, cayo o cauallo com elle e morreo ally; e outros acharom depois logar per hu pasassem a seu saluo. Em outro dia, que eram quimze de mayo, partio el-Rey, e passou toda a hoste aquell vaao, assy de pee come de cauallo, que nenhuuma pessoa nem besta pereçeo; e poserom logo seu arreall da parte aallem, nom queremdo mais amdar por o camsaço da passagem.

Desy no seguimte dia mouerom dally, e forom pousar a huum logar que chamam Curalles, preto de Çamora, na quall estaua dom Lourenço Soarez, Mestre de Samtiago, com muyta gemte darmas; porem nom prouou descaramuçar nem fez remetida nenhuuma.

Dally partyo el-Rey outro dia caminho de Çidade Rodrigo peramtre Sallamanca e Ledesma. E himdo a hoste per aquell logar, sayo de Sallamanca, homde estaua o jffante dom Joham com outros fronteiros comsigo, Diogo Lopez dAngull, gemrro de Pero Lopez dAyalla que fora presso em Portugall, com ginetes amtre seus e doutros ataa huuns iij[c]. E porque emtam chegara nouamente, quis prouar fazer alguuma cousa per que tirasse dally nomeada. A hoste vijnha bem hordenada com sua avanguarda e allas e a cariagem em meo e el-Rey e o Duque na reguarda. Diogo Lopez, deseiamdo de lhe fazer nojo, chegou-sse tamto aa gemte da reguarda que eram açerca de os poder remesar. El-Rey, quamdo vyo que tal fouteza mostrauom comtra elle, mouido com sanha pasou pella cariagem e chegou a avanguarda e allas, e disse ao Comde que se alguuma gemte leuaua bem emcaualgada, que a escolhese (e) el jsso mesmo mandarya da sua, e que fossem aaquellas gemtes que tal desprezamento mostrauom comtra elle.

O Comde disse que tam bem emcaualgada gemte nom tragia e que tal escolha faria gram detemça, mas que passasse a cariagem e el çom a reguarda, e el hiria a elles com esses que o seguir podessem. Emtom passou a carriagem e desy el-Rey, cuydando os emmjgos que o faziam

How the King departed with his army and how Diego López de Angul was captured.

The King left there with his army and camped beside the river some two leagues above Zamora, and opposite Santa María del Viso. [1] The King ordered a reconnaissance of the river which in that place was as wide as a good crossbow shot, in order to ascertain whether or not it might be possible to ford it. Among those who went on this expedition was a squire called Álvaro Vasques, castellan of Alcanede. While searching for the ford, horse and rider fell, and there he died. Subsequently, some others found a spot where it was possible to cross safely.

On the next day which was 15 May, the King set out, and the whole army, both cavalry and foot, crossed by that ford. Not one single person or animal perished. They set up camp immediately on the other side because they did not wish to travel any further, exhausted as they were after the crossing.

Then on the following day, they moved from there and camped at a place called Corrales near Zamora. The Master of Santiago, Don Lorenzo Suárez, [2] was in Zamora with a large force of men—at—arms, but he did not venture to engage them nor did he make any sally whatever.

From there the King moved on the next day in the direction of Ciudad Rodrigo, passing between Ledesma and the city of Salamanca where Prince João was stationed with other commanders. As the army went along, Diego López de Angul, Pedro López de Ayala's son—in—law, who had been a prisoner in Portugal, came out of Salamanca with some three thousand troops, including his own men and some of other commanders. Because he had only recently arrived he was eager to undertake something that might bring him some renown.

The army advanced in good order with its vanguard and wings as well as the baggage—train in the centre, while the King and the Duke brought up the rearguard. Wishing to harry the army, Diego López came so close to the rearguard that his force was nearly able to strike at them. When he saw their determination to attack, the King in a high state of indignation moved through the baggage—train to reach the vanguard and wings. There he told the Count that if he had some well—horsed men, he should single them out and he himself would send over others from his own company. These could then engage the enemy force that was showing such hostility towards him.

The Count replied that he had none with him as well horsed as that, and picking out a detail in this manner would in any case cause considerable delay; but if the King would move forward with the baggage—train and rearguard, then, he would attack the enemy with whatever men were in a position to follow him. Then the baggage—train passed on and the King with it, and the enemies

com medo. Em esto sayo o Comde rijamente a elles e alguuns del-Rey em sua companha, e tam de uomtade toparom em elles que todo o ardil que tragiam perderom, voltamdo cada huum per hu melhor podia. E como tragiam os cauallos folgados e de boom pemsso, sayam-sse muy ligeiramente logo no começo. A pouco despaço, amte que mea legoa coressem, começaram-lhe a estancar os cauallos; e os portuguesses que os encalçauom premdendo e matando em elles, saltou aquell Diogo Lopez em terra com sua darga e espada na maão, e assy foy tomado sem defe(n)ssam que prouasse de fazer, ca lhe nom compria a tal tempo. Dos outros forom pressos quorenta e oyto e mortos huuns quimze.

E tragido Diogo Lopez amte el-Rey, preguntou-lhe estomçe, dizemdo: *Que he jsso, Diogo Lopez? Como fostes assy tomado, ca boom cauallo tragiees vos? — Boom, senhor? disse elle, que mas olliuas o matem! Mas por recolher huuns poucos damigos e criados que eram comigo, hia-me detemdo, e por jsso fuy assy tomado.*

O Duque, quando vio esto que os portuguesses assy fezerom, mostraua gram lediçe e prazer, dizemdo altas vozes comtra os seus: *O, que boom Portugall!*

CXII
Dalguuns que corressem pomtas em aquell logar.

Tornou-sse o Comde a avamguarda e a hoste aa hordenança em que amte vinha, e poussarom naquelle camjnho damtre Sallamanca e Ledesma.

Omde sabee que dos estrangeiros que pellas fromtarias estauom da parte del-Rey de Castella, que taaes hij avia que conheçiam alguuns do Duque, comendo e beuendo com elles quamdo se açertaua de corerem pomtas, de que elles amdauom muyto perçebidos (d)e boons coregimentos pera tal jogo; e tragiam caretas, quamdo vinham a elle, caregadas de pam e de vinho e carneiros e doutras viamdas, de que os jmgreses ledamente tomauom comuite.

Hora assy foy que monsse Joham dOllamda, condestabre do Duque, e monsse Arnao de Roy, caualleiro del-Rey de Framça, se desafiarom pera corer pontas çertas careiras a cauallo. Monsse Joham se fez prestes e coregido pera o atemder. Veo monse Arnaao bem fremosso caualleiro, mais comprido que monsse Joham, coberto el e o cauallo de uelludo rasso vermelho e huum moto de leteras de chaparia dourada em seu pequeno escudo aa guissa de tallabarte, que deziam: *Belle*. E pareçia naquell jogo mais çerto e desemuolto que monsse Joham. E himdo a primeira careira, foy emcomtrado monsse Joham, e cayo huuma gram queda limpo fora do cauallo; e leuamtou-sse rijo com tal queixume que pareçia que jugara as punhadas com o framçes, se o ally teuera. Emtom

thought that they did so out of fear; whereupon the Count broke out of the army and came at them fiercely, accompanied by some of the King's own men. They fell upon the Castilians with such a will that the latter lost all their courage and each and every one fled as best he could. Given that their horses were fresh and well fed, they easily escaped at first; but after a short while, before they had gone half a league, the Castilians' horses began to tire. Thus the Portuguese caught them up, capturing and killing them. Diego López himself leapt from his horse, shield and sword in hand, and thus was taken but without making any resistance whatever, for resistance would have been of little avail in the circumstances. Of the rest, some forty—eight were captured and some fifteen killed.

When Diego López was brought before the King, the King put the question to him thus: "What is all this, Diego López? How did you come to be captured in this fashion, for you had a good horse?"

"Good, my lord?" he riposted. "May bad olives kill him. The fact is that I slowed down in order to gather up a few friends and servants in my retinue, and that is why I was captured thus."

When the Duke saw just what the Portuguese had done, he was clearly overjoyed, shouting to his men: "Well done, good Portugal!"

CXII
Of some of those who jousted in that place.

The Count returned to the vanguard and the army reverted to its original formation. They camped on the route between Salamanca and Ledesma.[1]

Now you need to know that in many of these frontier strongholds there were foreigners campaigning in the service of the King of Castile, some of whom knew some of the Duke's men. These were in the habit of eating and drinking together. At such times they were wont to joust together, extremely well accoutred for such a pastime. When these foreigners came to the camp they would bring with them carts laden with bread, wine, mutton and other victuals. The English gladly welcomed such invitations to eat and drink with them.

So it was that Sir John Holland, the Duke's Constable, and Sir Renaud de Roye,[2] one of the knights of the King of France, challenged one another to a contest in the lists on horseback. Sir Renaud came up, a very handsome knight and more accomplished than Sir John. He and his horse were both dressed in smooth red velvet; and on his small shield there was a device in letters of gold plate as if written on a sword belt, saying: *Belle*. He appeared more confident and relaxed in this activity than did Sir John. In the first encounter, Sir John was caught and took a straight and heavy fall from the saddle; but he leapt up shouting so fiercely that he looked for all the world as if he would be at daggers drawn with the Frenchman if given the opportunity. Once he was remounted, they

caualgou, e forom outra vez. E emcontrou monsse Joham tam baixo ho outro, nom leuando bem a llamça na reste, que lhe ferio o cauallo no pescoço de guissa que moreo; e por este aazo nom forom aa terçeira careira.

Outro bom jogo aconteçeo hij dhuum françes com huum jngres, corendo pontas a pee, de facha, que himdo o framçes contra elle, alçamdo a facha pera lhe dar, cuydamdo que o tinha de ssy preto, ficou tamto aaquem delle que camanho golpe pemsou que lhe daua, tamanho deu comsigo e com a facha no chaão, caymdo ante os pees do jmgres estemdido; o quall, vemdo-o assy jazer, descaregou huuma tall fachada neelle, de que o framçes deu huum gramde gimido; e porque nom auya de seer mais dhuum golpe de cada careira, alçou-sse, e nom forom outra.

Outros muytos corerom pomtas pee terra com os jmgresses, assy fframçesses come castellaãos, despadas e fachas e doutras maneiras, que por nom alomgar leixamos de dizer.

Em este caminho era a hoste tam mynguada de carnes que parte della o sentia muyto; porem de uaca nunca el-Rey eraua tres jguarias, desfeito e assado e cozido. Outros passauom como podiam, emtanto que, achamdo huum dia ninhos de coruaãs per aqueçimento, acudio ally tamta gemte que pareçia que se queriam matar sobrellas; e quem podia auer escussada huma que a el-Rey em presemte mandasse, cuydaua que lhe fazia gram serujço.

CXIII

Como el-Rey passou per Çidade Rodrigo, e chegou a Portugall.

Leuamdo el-Rey com sua hoste aquell caminho de Çidade Rodrigo, o jffamte dom Joham e Martynannes, Mestre dAlcantara, e Garçia Gonçalluez de Grijalua e outros capitaães amtre castellaãos e françesses, dos que estauom pellas fromtarias, que seriam huumas quatro mjll lamças, ouueram nouas como muytos do areal hiam enfermos; e jumtaram-se com suas gemtes, e veerom de noite per caminhos desuairados todos aaquella çidade com emtençom de pelleiar com el-Rey.

A manhaã vimda e elles todos fora, poseram-sse pee terra aredados da çidade quamto seriam dous tiros de beesta, aguardamdo a hoste, que vinha dally huuma gramde legoa. O Comdestabre tragia a auanguarda e as allas corregidas em sua hordenança; e os castellaãos, quamdo os virom daquel geito vijr, cuydamdo que nom eram mais, porque a reguarda nom pareçia ajmda, acordarom de pellejar com elles. O Comde

278

went at it again; and Sir John caught his adversary so low, for his lance was not properly couched in the rest, that he wounded the horse's neck in such a way that it died. For this reason they dispensed with the third encounter.

Another good bout took place there between a Frenchman and an Englishman who jousted on foot using axes. The Frenchman charged and lifted his axe to strike the Englishman thinking that he was sufficiently close; but in fact he was far short of him, so that although he intended to strike him a particularly mighty blow, such was the impetus of it when he missed, that both he and his axe came to earth and he ended up flat on the ground at the Englishman's feet. Seeing him lying there, the latter delivered him such a blow with his axe that the Frenchman let out a loud groan. Because each man was supposed to deliver only one blow at each encounter, this particular one was terminated and they did not face one another again.

Many more Frenchmen and Castilians jousted on foot with the English, with swords, axes and other weapons; but in order not to prolong the episode overmuch, we shall refrain from describing these bouts.

On this stretch of the journey the army was so short of meat that a part of it suffered greatly; but the King never failed to have every day three dishes of beef, chopped up, roasted or boiled. Others managed as best they could, so that, chancing one day upon a nest of young crows, so many converged on it that it looked as if they might kill one another over it. Anyone who could get anything extra to send to the King as a present considered that he was doing him a great service.

CXIII
How the King passed by Ciudad Rodrigo and reached Portugal.

As the King travelled with his army along the road to Ciudad Rodrigo, Prince João, the Master of Alcántara,[1] Martim Eanes, García González de Grijalba and other Castilian and French captains, among those garrisonning the frontier strongholds, and numbering some four thousand lances, received news that there was much sickness in the camp of their enemies. So they all assembled their forces and came to that city by night along out—of—the—way roads with the intention of doing battle with the King.

By daybreak they had drawn up their battle—lines at a distance of about two crossbow—shots from the city, and awaited the army which was still a good league away. The Constable had the vanguard and the wings drawn up in battle order. When the Castilians saw them approaching in this fashion, they thought that the enemy forces amounted to no more than this, for the rearguard had not yet come

auya de passar huum pequeno rio, que hia per hij, per huuma pomte estreita; a quall era ja guardada dos emmjgos, assy homeens darmas come de pee e beesteiros, por embargar aquel passo. Martym Gomçalluez, comendador moor de Christos , com as (gentes) do Mestre e suas altas prumas em uez de bandera, e outros com elle, chegou ally, e pee terra maao seu grado fez aos emmjgos leixar aquell porto. E o Comde passou aquel pequeno ryo, e pose-sse em batalha hordenada porque nom sabya que os castellaãos queriam fazer. Em esto asomou el·Rey com sua rreguarda e foy visto dos emmigos. Emtam diserom huuns contra os outros: *Mais gemte he esta da que cuidamos. Nom compre de nos embaraçar com elles.* Disse estomçe Garçia Gonçalluez ao jffamte dom Joham que era bem de se colherem aa çidade, pois aquellas gemtes eram tamtas. E o jffamte respomdeo, dizemdo: *Firmae, firmae bem os pees nos estribos se os nom trazees bem firmes, ca ajmda me pareçe çedo pera nos tornarmos.*

El-Rey, quamdo os deuisou e vio assy daquell geito, nom temdo ajmda passado o rio que o Comde passara, pedio outro cauallo e o baçinete, e pose-o e emcamjnhaua ja pera homde os castellaãos estauom. E jmdo pera la, chegarom Aluaro Coitado e Joham Afomsso Pimente(l), ambos a cauallo com lamças nas maãos a guissa de coredores; e diserom: *Senhor, hu uos hijs? Nom vaades per este caminho, ca ally vay huum alto passo dhuum rregato cauado muy maao de passar per huuma ponte estreita, e pode·sse ajmda embargar.* El-Rey ouuyndo esto, deteue-sse estomçe, e começou de fazer tornar os que hiam com elle, que nom leuassem aquell camjnho. Os castellaãos, vemdo que el-Rey tinha ajmda de passar o rio que o Comde ja tinha passado e que auya de deçer a elle per huuma ladeira afumdo, poseram-sse muytos a cauallo pera os remesar aa de çima, ca o podiam bem fazer a seu saluo.

El-Rey, quamdo vio aquello e emtemdeo o que fazer queriam, mandou chamar todollos beesteiros que vinham na reguarda, que ficassem ally aa passagem pera tirarem aos de cauallo, e deu carego a Gonçallo Vaasquez Coutinho que os acaudellasse; o quall, come ardido caualleiro, emcima dhuum cauallo murzello sem outro homeem darmas comsigo os acaudellaua, temdo esta maneira: em quamto huuns tirauom, armauom os outros. E como alguuns castellaãos se queriam adeamtar, poinha Gomçallo Vaasquez huuma espada darmas soo o braço, e hia a elles, e os beesteiros seguiam-no tiramdo. E assy os faziam afastar de ssy, de gujssa que toda a gemte da reguarda passou, que nunca nenhuum teue geito de poder remesar lamça com temor da beestaria.

Como a ribeira foy passada, jumtou-sse o Comdestabre com el-Rey, e apousentou-sse o arreall açerca de mea legoa açima da çidade. E el-Rey

into view; so the Castilians decided to engage them. Now the Count was obliged to cross a stream that flowed through that place, by means of a narrow bridge which was guarded by hostile men—at—arms, foot soldiers and bowmen whose task it was to bar the route. Martim Gonçalves, Grand Commander of the Order of Christ, with the Master's forces and their tall plumes instead of a standard, along with some others, reached the spot and forced the enemy to abandon that crossing against their will. The Count crossed the stream and then put his force in battle—order because he did not know what the Castilians might be planning to do. At this point the King appeared with his rearguard and was seen by the enemy, who said to one another, "There are more men than we thought. It is too risky to engage them." Then García González said to Prince João that it would be prudent to retire to the city seeing that the enemy was so numerous; but the Prince replied saying, "Hold hard, hold hard your feet in your stirrups if they are not firm already, for it seems to me that to turn back at this stage is somewhat premature."

When he caught sight of them and saw how they were situated, the King, not having yet crossed the stream that the Count had crossed, asked for another horse and bacinet which he put on, and then made his way towards the place where the Castilians were. As he was going there, Álvaro Coitado and João Afonso Pimentel came up, both on horseback with lance in hand like jousters. They said to him: "Where are you going, my lord? Don't go this way, for it leads to a crossing high above a deep stream which is difficult to cross because the bridge is narrow and it could hold you up."

When he heard this, the King stopped and began turning round the men who were with him, telling them not to proceed by that way. When they saw that the King had still to cross the stream that the Count had already crossed and that he would have to go down to it by descending a steep slope, the Castilians mounted horses in large numbers in order to charge down on them from above, for they were in a position to do so without any risk to themselves.

When he saw that and realized what they were hoping to do, the King ordered all the bowmen of the rearguard to be summoned and positioned at the ford so as to fire at the horsemen, under the command of Gonçalo Vasques Coutinho. Intrepid knight that he was, Coutinho, mounted on a dark—bay horse without any men—at—arms, took charge of the bowmen and proceeded in the following manner. While some were firing, the rest were reloading. As some Castilians were trying to break through, Gonçalo Vasques went at them with a ceremonial sword under his arm. The bowmen followed him, shooting as they went. In this way they drove off the enemy so that the whole rearguard succeeded in crossing. No one else was able to throw a lance at them for fear of the crossbow fire.

When they had crossed the stream, the Constable joined up with the King and set up camp almost half a league above the city. Until

e o Comde andarom sempre a cauallo ataa que a hoste foy asessegada e suas guardas postas, por serem tam preto de seus emmigos; porem que em passamdo esto que dizemos, foram feitas alguumas escaramuças em que nom compre fazer detemça.

Em outro dia partimdo el-Rey dally, monse Johann dOllanda se espedio del-Rey e do Duque, e com alguuns caualleiros e outros jmgresses da companha do Duque, que passauom de çimquoenta de cauallo, e sua espossa com outras molheres de casa da Duquessa se partirom dally e forom pera os emmigos com cartas de saluo comduto que ja tinham del-Rey de Castella pera passarem per seu regno e se hirem a Gasconha, senhorio dImgraterra. El-Rey foy marauilhado quamdo vio tall partida, e o Duque e sua molher nom mostrauom que faziam desso comta.

Dally partio el-Rey caminho de Portugall, e veeo a hoste pousar a Val de lla Mulla ; e em outro dia chegou a Almeida, que era o primeiro logar de seu regno per aquell camjnho.

CXIV
Como veerom a el-Rey de Castella as duas mjll lamças que lhe el-Rey de França prometera em ajuda.

El-Rey e o Duque em Portugall postos, amte que mais ouçaaes desto que fallamos, conuem que se diga das duas mjll lamças que el·Rey de Castella aguardaua em ajuda; nom por nom termos que comtar e fazer daquisto estorya, mas, porque a Framça leuamos recado e trouuemos a reposta que vistes, a rrezam requere que dessegees saber que comprimento ouue tal promessa.

Omde assy foy que el·Rey e o Duque partidos da conquista e tornados a Portugal, ouue el-Rey de Castella nouas como o duque de Borbom, tyo del-Rey de Framça, jrmaão de sua madre, vinha em sua ajuda por capitam das duas mjll lamças por que el esperaua, e que eram ja nos termos do Gronho , andamdo quanto podiam por chegar a sseu regno. Em esto chegou o duque primeiro, e el-Rey o reçebeo muy bem. E auemdo com el comselho que maneira se teria em fazerem todos guerra, alguuns capitaães framçesses e muytos dos castellaãos diziam que era bem que el-Rey emtrasse em Portugall, e que fosse pellejar com o Duque e com o Mestre que se chamaua Rey. Outros a que nom prazia poynham gram duujda em acharem vyamdas que abastassem pera tamta gemte.

the whole army had settled down and guards had been posted for the night, the King and the Count patrolled on horseback, for their enemies were so near. Nevertheless, while all that we related was happening, there was some skirmishing on which it is not worthwhile to dwell at this point.

On the following day as the King was setting out again, Sir John Holland took his leave of the King and the Duke. With some knights and other Englishmen of the Duke's company, some fifty horse, and his wife together with other women of the Duchess's train, he left there in the direction of enemy territory. They bore letters of safe—conduct that they had already received from the King of Castile enabling them to pass through his kingdom and repair to Gascony, which was an English possession. The King was astonished at such a departure, but neither the Duke nor his wife showed the slightest concern about it.

The King set out in the direction of Portugal. The army camped at Vale de la Mula and the next day reached Almeida, which was the first Portuguese town along that road.

CXIV
Of the two thousand lances that the King of France had promised the King of Castile by way of assistance and of how they reached him.

Before you hear more of what happened once the King and the Duke reached Portugal, it is important to speak of the two thousand lances whose assistance the King of Castile was waiting for. Not because we have nothing more to say about the former subject, but because we described how the request was sent to France and how the reply came back as you saw, so it is only reasonable that you should wish to know in what manner the promise was kept.

With the King and the Duke already having abandoned their expedition and returned to Portugal, the King of Castile received news that the Duke of Bourbon, uncle of the King of France as brother of his mother, was coming to his assistance at the head of the two thousand lances for which the King of Castile had been waiting. They were already on the outskirts of Logroño and were travelling as fast as they could in order to reach his kingdom.

At this juncture the Duke arrived ahead of his force and was well received by the King of Castile. In the course of a council with the King concerning the best way for them all to prosecute that war, some French commanders and many of the Castilian commanders said that the King should enter Portugal and that he should fight the Duke and the Master who called himself King. Others who were less happy with this idea cast grave doubts on the possibility of finding victuals to supply the needs of so many men.

Hora posto que alguumas estorias nom façam disto tam larga mençom, a uerdade dello se passou desta guissa:

El-Rey era muy gastado da paga do soldo que ao(s) seus e aaquellas gemtes suas e estrangeiras fazia; em tamto que alguuns , nom sabemdo remedio que poer, — assy como ao comde de Lomgavilla, que estaua em Vilhalpamdo e nom tinha per hu lhe pagar, mandou que tomasse os mantimentos aa ssua vomtade, sem fazer delles pagamento; e el assy o fazia, e roubauom o logar todo. E por tamto disse el-Rey aaquelles capitaães que eram hij de Framça, que *el lhe gardeçia muyto o afam e trabalho que por seu seruiço auyam soffrido, de vijr (de) tam lomga terra pera o seruyr; e que pois a Deus graças os emmigos ja eram fora de seus regnos e el entendia trautar com o Duque de virem ambos a boa avença, que el achaua em seu conselho que era bem de se tornarem pera sua terra; e que el lhe mandaria pagar todo o que auyam dauer, de gujssa que fossem contentos.*

E elles respomderom que *eram ally vimdos per mandado del-Rey, seu senhor, pera o seruir e fazer todo o que lhe mandasse; e que muyto lhe prouguera* [3] *de virem amtes por acharem seus comtrairos e pellejar com elles; e que se sua merçee fosse demtrarem em Portugall a buscar batalha, que prestes eram de o fazer, e todos tal mandado tragiam.* E el-Rey disse que lho gardeçia, e nom fallarom mais em esto.

Emtom hordenou que dom Joham Manrique, arçebispo de Santiago, com aquelles capitaães fossem a Burgos, e ally fezessem conta do soldo e gajas que auyam dauer, e lhe fezesem de todo pagamento. E tomada leçemça, espedidos del-Rey, foram-sse aaquella çidade; hu foy feita conta de quanto lhe montaua. E delle lhe pagarom logo, e parte lhe ficou por pagar que lhe el-Rey depois pagou, e jsso mesmo seu filho depois de sa morte.

CXV

Como os mesegeiros del-Rey de Castella veerom fallar ao Duque, e se acordarom em çertas auemças.

Visto o tempo que o Duque com el-Rey amdou em Castella e quamto lhe aveeo ata a presemte sazom, hora conuem que digamos que fim ouue tamanho negoçio e como se quitou delle de todo, pois que ficamos pera o dizer. Mas porque coussas alguumas amtreueeram em meo deste tempo que nom som pera esqueçer, razom he que as contemos ataa que el parta do regno pera Imgraterra.

Omde sabee que el-Rey, como foy em seu regno, mandou o Condestabre que se fosse a Allemtejo por gar da da terra e cousas que lhe compriam. E el, segumdo o uoto que prometido tinha ante que emtrasse em Castella, partio logo de pee pera Santa Maria dOliueira, que era dally huumas xxx. legoas na villa de Guimaraaes, por comprir sua romaria.

Now although some histories make little mention of the matter, the truth is that it happened in the following manner.

The King had emptied his coffers in paying the wages of his own soldiers and the foreign troops; so that some, like the Count of Longueville who was in Villalpando and whom he was unable to pay, were given permission by the King to take what provisions they needed, without paying for them; and Longueville did so, pillaging the whole town. Therefore, the King said to those commanders that had come from France, that he deeply appreciated the dedication and effort that they had expended, travelling so far in order to do him service; but now that, thanks be to God, the enemy was out of his kingdom, he intended to negotiate with the Duke and reach an understanding with him. Therefore, he thought it best for them to return to their own land. For his part, he would order that they be paid what was due to them so that they might be satisfied.

They replied that they had come on the orders of their lord and king in order to serve him and do whatever he commanded. They would have liked to have come earlier so as to find their enemies and fight them; and if it was his will that they should enter Portugal in order to do battle, they were ready to do so, for they had come on this understanding. The King said he was grateful to them for this, and they spoke no further on the matter.

Then he ordered Don Juan Manrique, Archbishop of Santiago, to accompany those commanders to Burgos, where he would calculate the pay and the wages due to them, and pay them in full. After taking leave of the King, they went to that city, where the entire amount owing was calculated. They were paid some of it there and then, while a part was left outstanding, which was actually paid later by the King and, after his death, by his son.

CXV
How the messengers of the King of Castile came to speak with the Duke, and came to an agreement over certain matters.

We have looked at the period that the Duke spent with the King in Castile and at what befell him there. It is now fitting that we should relate the outcome of such a great enterprise and how he emerged from it in the end, since we are bound to do so. However, because in between times some other happenings intruded that ought not to be forgotten, it is only right that we should relate them up to the moment he left the kingdom for England.

Now you must understand that when he was back in his kingdom, the King commanded the Constable to go to the Alentejo to guard the region and perform certain necessary duties. The King himself at once set out for Santa Maria de Oliveira, some thirty leagues away in the town of Guimarães, in order to fulfil the vow of a pilgrimage which he had made before entering Castile.

285

E o Duque hordenou em tamto dhir a Cojmbra veer sua filha. E el na villa de Tranquoso, que eram dally noue legoas, chegarom mesegeiros del-Rey de Castella por trautar com o Duque alguumas auemças per que se partissem desta comtenda; porque o comuum soom que as gentes fallauom, todo era que el hia por jumtar mais gemtes pera vijr outra vez a Espanha; da quall cousa a el-Rey muyto desprazia, moormente por teer el-Rey de Portugal em ajuda. E por em lhe mandou requerir o que ja damte cometido tinha, que se lhe prouguesse casar sua filha dona Catellina com dom Emrique, seu filho, herdeiro dos regnos de Castella, que el daria a el e a sua molher e aa jffante, assy em villas come em denheiro, aquello que rezoado fosse.

E fallando sobrestas cousas, no casamento bem se acordauom; mas nas cousas que o Duque pedia eram em gram desauemça.

Finalmente veerom comcordar que *o casamento fosse feito; e que el-Rey de Castella desse em dote a sua nora que auya de seer a çidade de Soria e a villa dAlmaçam e a villa dAtemça e Deça e a villa de Mollyna, e que desse aa Duquessa sua madre em sa vida Guadalfajara e Medina del Campo e Olmedo; e que el-Rey de Castella desse mais ao Duque em denheiro, por as despessas que feytas auya, seisçemtos mjll framcos douro pagados em çertos tempos, e mais cadano em sua vida e de sua molher, quall delles mais viuesse, quoremta mjll framcos pagados em tempo assynado; e que o Duque e sua molher se partissem de toda demanda e comtenda que comtra os regnos de Castella auer podiam. E porque o trauto destas cousas melhor e mais compridamente se fazer podesse, que o Duque se partisse de Portugall e se fosse pera Bayona, que he no senhorio de Ingraterra açerca da comarca de Castella; e que ally mandaria el-Rey seus procuradores pera se desto fazer scpritura naquella firmeza que compridoiro fosse.*

Semdo acordados, tornaram-se os mesegeiros com esta reposta; e o Duque se ueo a Cojmbra, xxvj. legoas, dhu a Rainha sua filha estaua.

CXVI

Como el-Rey partio camjnho de Cojmbra, e adoeçeo no Curuall.

Partio el-Rey de Guimaraaes pera o Porto, e dhij caminho de Cojmbra homde estaua a Raynha sua molher, que eram dezoito legoas dhuuma çidade a outra. E elle nos paaços de Curuall, que som em meyo do camjnho, adoeçeo de grande door de quentura a que nom podiam poer cobro; e era esto na fim de junho. A Raynha, como taaes nouas ouuyo do seu muyto amado marido que ella tamto preçaua, trigosamente partio

As for the Duke, he decided meanwhile to go to Coimbra to see his daughter. While he was at Trancoso, some nine leagues from there, messengers arrived from the King of Castile in order to negotiate accords with the Duke with a view to a mutual cessation of their dispute. For it was widely rumoured that the Duke was going away to recruit more troops in order to return again to Spain. This prospect made the King most uneasy, especially considering that the Duke had at his disposal the assistance of the King of Portugal. Therefore, he ordered his messengers to propose to the Duke the offer that he had originally made: namely, that the Duke might look kindly on a marriage between his daughter, Lady Catherine, and the King's son, Don Enrique, heir to the kingdoms of Castile; and in return, the King would give to the Duke, his wife and the Princess whatever might be considered reasonable in towns as well as money.

After discussion of these matters, they easily reached an agreement over the marriage; but with regard to those things the Duke asked for, they were in considerable disagreement.

Finally, they agreed that the marriage would take place. The King of Castile would give to his future daughter—in—law, as her dowry, the city of Soria and the towns of Almazán, Atienza, Deza and Molina. Her mother, the Duchess, would receive, to hold for as long as she lived, Guadalajara, Medina del Campo and Olmedo. The King of Castile would give the Duke for the expenses he had already incurred, the sum of six hundred thousand gold francs to be paid within a certain time; and in addition, as long as either of them might live, he and his wife would receive yearly forty thousand francs to be paid at stipulated times. The Duke and his wife would give up all possible claim to the kingdoms of Castile. In order that the treaty might be drawn up the better and the more thoroughly, the Duke was to leave Portugal and go to Bayonne, an English lordship close to Castilian territory. The King would send his procurators there so that the documents might be drawn up in a firm and binding fashion.

These matters having been agreed, the messengers returned with this reply. The Duke, meanwhile, went to Coimbra, twenty—six leagues distant, where his daughter the Queen was staying.

CXVI
How the King set out in the direction of Coimbra and fell ill at Curval.[1]

The King went from Guimarães to Oporto, and from there he set out on the road to Coimbra, some eighteen leagues away, where his wife the Queen was staying. When he got to the palace of Curval, which is about halfway along the road, he fell very ill of a fever which seemed incurable. This was at the end of June. The Queen loved him very much, and when she heard this news of her beloved husband, she set out in haste for that place accompanied by

pera aquelle logar, e o Duque seu padre com ella. E quando chegarom e o virom tam fraco e sem esforço que adur lhe pode fallar, ficaram tam nojos(os) e tristes, espeçialmente a Rainha, quanto se dizer nom pode, de guissa que logo moueo huuma criamça, e nom sem razom, ca se uia em terra estranha casada de pouco, posta em tam gramde homra, e falleçer-lhe logo assy çedo, bem se tinha por malaventuirada amtre as molheres do mundo. E cuidamdo esto em sua alma e spritu, nom çessaua de chorar, pedimdo aa morte que a leuasse.

El-Rey mandara chamar o Comdestabre e jsso mesmo alguuns fidalgos. E feito seu testamento e repartidas suas cousas, era o desmanho [3] tam gramde em todos que, atemdendo por sua saude, tal esperamça emtendiam seer vaã; e nom fallauom em nenhuum cobro que ao regno poer podessem, saluo nos camjnhos claros e abertos, como Portugal per sua morte de todo ponto era perdido.

A muyto nojossa Rainha chegaua-se a el-Rey por o comsollar, nom tiramdo os olhos delle, e nom sabia como reteer as lagrimas que embargauom a sua doçe falla. E atemdendo por sua saude, via-o cada vez mais fraco; e oolhamdo como se todos apuridauom huuns com outros, esto a poinha em mayor desperaçam, assy que a seu nojo sobre gujssa nom sabia comselho que poer, senom tornaua-se ao muy alto Deus e aa sua preçiosa Madre, rogamdo-a ameude em suas deuotas oraçoões que se qujsesse amerçear do seu desemparo, e assy como Mestra de Mysericordia [4] prouese de saude ao seu desejado marido; aa quall prougue por sua merçe empetrar tamta graça do seu bemto filho que el-Rey começou de conualesçer e melhorar pera saude, cousa que nom foy em menos conta theuda como se resuçitara da morte aa vida.

E aproueitando el-Rey em sua boa melhoramça, chegou-se huum dia o Duque aa cama, e disse que lhe pedia por merçee que perdoasse ao comde dom Gomçallo e a Ayras Gonçalluez de Figueiredo alguum erro se lho feito tinham, e os mandasse soltar e seu filho com elles. *Em verdade,* disse el-Rey, *eu nunca os mandey premder por cousa que emtendesse que comtra mym obrassem; mas fize-o por me nom fazerem desseruiço, que me pareçeo que queriam fazer, e por em os retiue ataa ora; amte mandaua dar mantimento a elles e a suas molheres, como saberes por verdade. Mas pois a uos, senhor, praz, eu som ledo que os soltem logo.* E assy era de feito como el-Rey disse; ca o comde auya por mes quinhentas liuras, que eram vimte dobras, e Ayras Gonçalluez auya seis. O Duque mostrou que lho gardeçia muyto, e fez geito de lhe beixar a mão segumdo costume de Portugall; mas el-Rey nom lho qujs comsentir.

her father the Duke.   When they arrived there and saw the King so weak and helpless that he could barely speak, they were so terribly upset, especially the Queen, that she had a miscarriage.   This was hardly surprising because there she was, in a foreign land, recently married and in a position of such great honour, and if her husband were to die so soon she could consider herself the most unfortunate woman in the world.   Turning all this over and over in her heart made her weep continually, begging Death to carry her off.

The King summoned the Constable, who in turn sent for some nobles.   Once the King had made his last will and testament and shared out his property, everyone was so dismayed that although they hoped he would recover, they considered their hope an empty one; and they could see no future for the kingdom except the clear and obvious one that through his death Portugal would be totally destroyed.

The Queen went in great distress to the King's side to comfort him, not taking her eyes off him; and she did not know how to hold back the tearful sobs which choked her gentle words.   With regard to his condition, she could see him growing continually weaker; and seeing everyone speaking in such low tones to each other made her even more desperate, so that she did not know how to relieve her sorrow at all, other than by turning to God Most High, as well as His precious Mother whom she begged constantly and devoutly in her prayers to have pity on her own forsaken state and, as Mistress of Mercy, to restore her beloved husband to health.   Out of compassion, the Mother of God was pleased to ask her Blessed Son for such a great favour, so that the King began to get better and to improve in health.   This caused as much astonishment as if he had risen from the dead.

Whilst the King was convalescing, the Duke came one day to his bedside and said that he begged him as a favour to pardon Count Gonçalo and Airas Gonçalves de Figueiredo for any harm they had done him and to order their release together with his son.

"The truth is", said the King, "that I never ordered them to be arrested for anything I thought they had done against me.   I did so in order to prevent them doing me the harm which I thought they wanted to do, and it is for this reason that I have kept them captive until now.   Indeed, I even ordered them and their wives to be maintained at my expense, as you will know to be true.   But since it pleases you, my lord, I am happy for them to be set free straightaway."

Indeed, what the King said was true; for every month the Count received five hundred pounds, that is, twenty *dobras*, and Airas Gonçalves received six.   The Duke showed that he was very grateful to the King, and tried to kiss his hand according to the Portuguese custom; but this the King would not allow.

CXVII
Como dous do Duque emtrarom em campo, e a raȝom por que.

Prougue ao Senhor Deus (d)e dar saude a el-Rey. E partirom daquel logar e veeram-se todos a Cojmbra; omde estamdo per alguuns dias, foy descuberta huuma treiçam que hordenada fora contra o Duque, a quall por renembramça das cousas passadas e aujssamento das que som por vijr queremos aquy comtar, e foy daquesta gujssa:

Amdando el-Rey e o Duque na conqujsta que ouujstes, vimdo huum dia aa tornada antre Çamora e Touro pera huuma aldea, que chamam Curralles, juntarom-sse huuma vez gemtes de cauallo, assy de Portugall come de Castella, pera hirem huuns comtra os outros como se costuma de fazer. E damtre os castellaãos sayo huum homem de cauallo , coremdo quanto podia por se lamçar com os portugueses, com cruz vermelha de Sam Jorge que com braados vinha mostrando, dizemdo que lhe acorresem, por quamto tras el vinham alguuns fimgimdo que o queriam premder; e el que tragia o cauallo ligeiro, desy os outros sem vomtade de o filhar, say(o)-sse delles quanto queria. Os portuguesses, vemdo aquesto, sayrom a elle por o defemder, e colheram-no amtre ssy, preguntamdo-lhe que era aquello. E el respomdia a todos, dizemdo: *Leuay-me a el-Rey de Castella meu senhor, duque dAllamcastro, e aa Raynha sua molher, e eu direy esto porque he.* E leuarom-no antelle, assy como pedia. E depois que lhe foy apresentado, disse que elle vinha a elle como seus senhores que eram, herdeiros do regno de Castella per bem del-Rey dom Pedro seu padre, que criara el e sua linhagem e lhe dera huuma comenda e terra que tinha, e que todo leixaua por os vijr seruir e ser em ajuda de vimgar a morte de seu senhor el-Rey dom Pedro.

O Duque e sua molher, quando esto virom, contaron-lho por gram bomdade, damdo-lhe dessy boom acolhimento, e prometendo-lhe de fazer merçee; e traziam-no em booa conta, segundo seus jguaes, e el vinha por lhe dar peçonha. E amd(amd)o el assy, nom cuydamdo nenguem tal cousa, per sua maa descriçom e pouco avissamento veo-sse a dessavijr com huum seu homeem que desta maldade sabia parte; o quall o descobrio a el-Rey e ao Duque, que desto ficarom muy spantados. E preso por esto e negando que nom, e ho outro afirmando que sy, foy-lhe dado campo a seu requirimento. E emtrando em elle o seruidor lho fez conheçer. E comfessado per elle, foy mandado que o queimassem, e assy fez maa fym de sa vida, guardando Deus o Duque de tamanho cajom.

CXVII
How and why two of the Duke's men fought a judicial combat.

The Lord God was pleased to restore the King to health, and they all left that place and came to Coimbra, where they stayed for some days. Then a treacherous plot against the Duke was discovered, which we shall describe here in order that past events may be recorded and may provide a warning for the future. It happened like this:

When the King and the Duke were engaged on the expedition to conquer Castile, about which you have already heard, they came one day on their return journey to a village between Zamora and Toro called Corrales; and there there took place the usual skirmishing between knights of Portugal and knights of Castile. Then one knight shot out from among the Castilians and rushed as fast as he could to join the Portuguese, showing the red cross of St. George and shouting out for help, while others came after him pretending that they wanted to capture him. Since they really had no desire to take him, and he was riding a light horse, he was easily able to out—distance them. When the Portuguese saw this, they went out to protect him and, surrounding him, they asked him what this was all about. He answered them all saying: "Take me to my lord the King of Castile, Duke of Lancaster, and his wife the Queen, and I shall explain all this." They took him there just as he asked. When he was presented to the Duke, he said that he came to them as his lord and lady, heirs of the kingdom of Castile by virtue of their father, King Pedro, who had brought him and his family up and had given him a commandery[1] and the land which he held, and that he had left all this in order to come to serve them and help them to avenge the death of his lord, King Pedro.

When the Duke and his wife saw this, they considered it a great piece of good fortune, and made him very welcome and promised to reward him; and they treated him well according to his status, when in fact he had come in order to poison the Duke. Nobody realized this, and things were in this state when, because of his own bad character and foolishness, he quarrelled with one of his servants who knew part of his wicked plan and revealed it to the King and the Duke, who were horrified. The man was arrested and denied the charge, but his servant affirmed that it was true. So they were given a field for a judicial combat, and the servant made his master confess. Once he had confessed his crime, he was sentenced to be burnt; and so he made a bad end, and God preserved the Duke from such a great danger.

CXVIII

Reposta a alguumas raҫoões que huum estoriador pos em sua cronica.

Estamdo o Duque com el-Rey naquella ҫidade per espaço dalguuns dias, hordenou partir de Portugall e se hir aaquella comarca homde ficara com os embaxadores de Castella. El-Rey, que parte sabia de todo seu feito, tinha ja mandado armar seis gallees na ҫidade de Lixboa, as quaaes eram partidas pera o Porto por se juntarem com outras que hij estauom; de guissa que eram per todas quatorze, de que Afomsso Furtado leuaua gouernamça, que era capitam do mar. O Duque partio com sua molher e famillya pera aquella ҫidade hu auya dembarcar, e el-Rey e a Rainha em sua companha; homde folgarom huum pouco despaço, nom [1] por as gallees nom estarem prestes, ca o eram muy compridamente de todallas cousas que em mester auyam, mas por sollaçar com a Rainha, sa filha, que nom sabia quamdo a auya de uer

Hora ante que o Duque parta, porque auemos dhir com elle pera uos dar comta do que lhe aueer sobreste negoçio, queremos primeiro respomder aalgmas nom bem ditas razoões que huum auctor em este passo, mais por defamar que por fazer estorya, e(n)xertou em seu volume; das quaaes huuma , que el-Rey de Portugall em esta ҫidade, amte que o Duque partisse, lhe pedira que dotasse sua filha, com que casara, o que era razom de fazer; a outra, — que lhe pagasse o soldo que auya dauer el e as gemtes que com el emtrarom em Castella e as despessas que naquella jda fezera. Das quaaes razoões, diz, que se o Duque queixou, dizemdo comtra el-Rey que fiamdo el delle sua filha e leixamdo-lha em arafeens por o que el e sua companha auyam dauer de seu soldo, pera despois casar com ella tamto que despemsaçom ouuesse, que el a tomara por molher, dormyndo com ella amte que as leteras de Roma veessem, por as quaaes el mandara o bispo dEuora e Gomçallo Gomez da Silua; e que a nom poderom auer do papa Vrbano, que emtom era; e que por estas razoões forom per dias nom bem acordados. E que estomçe el-Rey ficara de mandar por a despemsaçam; e que o Duque, vemdo que nom podia ja mais fazer, catara a melhor maneira que podera, a quall fora que por dotar sua filha e paga do soldo que el-Rey e os seus auyam dauer e despessa que na jda gastara, que o Duque lhe fezera doaçam dos logares todos que em Galliza auja ganhados. E feitas scprituras disto quaees compria, que o Duque par tira do Porto, e se fora pera Bayona dImgraterra. E aquy acabou seu maao razoado.

O quall, posto que de reposta mereçedor nom seja, a clara verdade

CXVIII
The answer to some remarks which a historian put in his chronicle.

When the Duke had been with the King in that city for some days, he arranged to leave Portugal and go to that district where he had agreed to meet the ambassadors of Castile. The King, who knew part of all his affairs, had already ordered six galleys to be fitted out in the city of Lisbon, and they had set out for Oporto to join others which were already there, so that there were fourteen galleys altogether, under the command of Afonso Furtado, who was a sea—captain. The Duke went with his wife and family to that city where he was due to embark, and the King and Queen went with him. There they spent a certain time relaxing together, not because the galleys were not ready, for they were fully equipped with everything that they needed, but so that the Duke could enjoy the company of his daughter the Queen, for he did not know when he might see her again.

We must accompany the Duke on his journey in order to explain to you what happened to him in this business; but before his departure, we would first like to refute some mis—statements on the part of an author at this point in his book, and which were made more in order to defame the King than in order to write history. [1] One of these was that in this city of Oporto before the Duke left, the King of Portugal asked him to provide a dowry for his daughter whom the King had married, as was only right; and the other was that he asked the Duke to pay him the salary due to him and to the men who had gone with him into Castile, as well as the expenses which he had incurred in that expedition. According to the aforementioned author, the Duke answered these requests by complaining that he had confided his daughter to the King and left her as a hostage to guarantee that he and his men would eventually receive their pay, and as the King's future bride as soon as they could get a dispensation to marry, but that the King had already taken her as his wife and slept with her before the letter of dispensation came from Rome, which he had sent the Bishop of Evora and Gonçalo Gomes da Silva for, but which they were unable to get from Pope Urban, who was the Pope at the time. According to our author, for these reasons the King and the Duke were for some days in considerable disagreement; then the King stopped asking for the dispensation; and seeing that he could do no more, the Duke looked for the best solution, which was that in order to provide his daughter with a dowry and pay the salary of the King and his men and the expenses he had incurred, he should give him all the places which he had won in Galicia; and documents were drawn up stating these conditions, after which the Duke left Oporto and went to Bayonne. This was the end of the mis—statements of our author.

Even though he does not deserve an answer, the clear truth

breuemente o jmpuna desta gujssa: Vos achares no quarto capitollo do trauto que el-Rey com o Duque fez, quamdo se primeiro ambos virom, que el com hoste de duas mjll lamças e mjll beesteiros e dous mjll homeens de pee em sua propria pessoa e aa sua custa e despessa fosse theudo de o ajudar aquel tempo que emtom deujssarom; e por em nom tinha razom de lhe requerer tal paga, como de feito nom requerio. E posto que a conuença tal fora e lho el-Rey estomçe requerira, nom era eror que em el desfezesse; ca se nom tinha por menos de senhor e estado o Primçepe de Gallez, filho del-Rey de Imgraterra, que veo ajudar el-Rey dom Pedro quamdo foy a batalha de Najara, e a ssoldado vinha el e todollos que eram com elle, como veeres hu fallamos desses feitos; e pero se muyto trabalhasse dauer (de todo pagamento, e o não podesse auer,) de nenhuum lhe foy emtom comtado por myngua, como este autor cuidou que prasmaua, posto que acomteçera como erramdo scpriueo.

Que o Duque dotasse sua filha, esto nom auya por que lho pedir. Ca em huuma clausulla desse mesmo trauto diz que por bem daquell matrimonio e ajuda que o Duque del-Rey auya dauer, lhe dauam a el e sua molher aquellas villas e logares que no trauto som nomeadas, de que se el-Rey assaz contemtou, posto que tal esperamça duuidosa fosse; e nom auya por que lhe mais pedir outro dote, pois de todo o que o Duque trautaua el-Rey de Portugall era sabedor.

A doaçam que lhe fez das villas e logares que em Galliza auya cobrado, — a razom jsto nom quer comsentir. Ca el era posto dacordo com el-Rey de Castella per seus mesageiros como dissemos, e nom auja por que fazer doaçam do que a outrem ja tinha leixado, nem el-Rey nom açeptara, que de seus feitos bem sabia parte.

Que alguum outro queira que lhe el requeria dote de dinheiros, — esto mais pouco lhe pederia el-Rey. Ca o Duque estaua emtom assy mesteiroso que era escusado tal requirimento; moormente que sua gramdiossa liberallidade era assy comtenta do linhagem e uirtuossas comdiçóões da Rainha sa molher, que esto era a el abastamte dote pera comtentar sua profumda gramdeza; a quall emprestou ao Duque assaz de prata que mester ouue e dous mjll e duzemtos nobres, amte que se fosse, e nom lhe requerio dello pagamento. E mais pouco lhe requereria esto que por mall dizer foy asacado!

A lleixada que diz de sua filha em poder del-Rey e a tomada que comta, como a ouue, e desacordo em que por estas cousas per alguuns dias esteuerom, — jsto nom soomente he falsso e de todo comtra a uerdade, mas ajmda he clara mentira; hora seja tomada estreitamente, saber, por maliçia do que a diz, hora seia per largo modo, quamdo se

294

easily refutes him in the following way: in the fourth chapter of the treaty which the King made with the Duke when they first met, you will find it set down that he was bound to help the Duke at the time which they then agreed, with his own person and with an army of two thousand lances, one thousand cross—bowmen and two thousand foot—soldiers, and at his own expense; so that he had no reason to ask the Duke for payment and did not in fact ask him for any. Even if the treaty had stipulated such a payment and even if the King had asked for it, that would not have been any defect or stain on his character; for the Prince of Wales, son of the King of England, was not considered any the less in lordship and status when he came to help King Pedro in the battle of Nájera, though he and all his companions came for pay, as you will see in the place where we spoke of these deeds; and though he strove hard to recover the pay owed to him, and could not get it, nobody thought any the less of him, as this author considered that they would have done had things occurred as he erroneously claimed.

There was no reason for the Duke to be asked to provide a dowry for his daughter. For in one clause of that same treaty it says that for the benefit of that marriage and for the help which the Duke was to receive from the King, the Duke gave him and his wife those towns and places which are named in the treaty; and the King was quite content with this even though the outcome of his expectation was uncertain; and there was no reason to ask for a bigger dowry, since the King of Portugal was privy to everything the Duke was doing.

Reason rejects the idea of the concession allegedly made to the King of the towns and places which the Duke had taken in Galicia, for the latter had made an agreement with the King of Castile through his envoys, as we have said, and he could not now concede something which he had already abandoned to someone else. Nor would the King have accepted it, for he was well informed of the Duke's affairs.

Much less was the King likely to ask him for a dowry in cash, as someone else claims. For the Duke was then so short of money that any such request would have been in vain, especially since the King's magnanimity was so content with the ancestry and virtues of his wife the Queen that this was sufficient dowry to satisfy his generosity of spirit. Indeed, this generosity caused him to lend the Duke all the silver he needed and 2,200 nobles before he went away, without asking him for repayment; and so, much less was he likely to ask him for the other cash as calumny has claimed.

The leaving of his daughter in the King's power and the story of her bedding as you have heard it, together with the disagreement which these things caused between the King and the Duke during several days, all this is not only false and completely untrue, but an obvious lie, whether in the narrow sense, that is to say, of something said through malice, or else in the broader sense, that is, of

afirma per jnoramçia do que a razoa. Porque el-Rey sempre foy dacordo com elle e muyto obediente no que lhe podia comprazer; e a seu requirimento fez voda com sua filha, de que o Duque foy muyto comtento, como se largamente podia mostrar. Mas esto que se segue por breue enformaçam abaste, saber, que o Duque no começo destes feitos estamdo açerca de Chaues em huuma aldeea que chamam Carrazedo, chegou a el huum leterado do comselho del-Rey por cousas alguumas que lhe per el mandaua dizer, das quaees o Duque lhe emuyou reposta per huuma carta, cujo ditado era este:

Muy nobre e muy homrado e poderosso nosso paremte e amjgo:

Nos, el-Rey de Castella e de Leom, duque dAllamcastro, vos enuiamos muyto saudar como a rey que muyto amamos e prezamos e de que muyto fiamos e pera quem queriamos muyta homra e booa vemtura e tamta vida e saude como pera nos mesmo. Fazemos-uos saber, etc. E depois de muytas cousas que na carta eram contheudas, huuma verba dizia assy: *Outrossy uos agardeçemos muyto e teemos em mesura a cortessya e nobreza que contra nossa filha mostraaes, e de uossos rricos dooes que uos prougue de lhe dar e da booa hordenamça que auees feita pera mantimento della e de seu estado e dos que com ella estom; por o quall nos somos muyto theudo a fazer por homra vossa e de uossas cousas assy como per nosas mesmas, e fyamos em Deus que nos ponha em tal estado que vollo possamos conheçer como compre a nossa homra e vossa. Muy nobre e muyto homrado e poderoso Rey, nosso paremte e amygo, nosso Senhor Deus uos aja todo tempo em sua guarda, etc^{ra}.*

E assy pareçe muyto o comtrairo do que aquel autor por mal dizer scpreueo açerca de taaes feitos.

Aa despemsaçam, em que pos boca, respomderemos tanto que veermos, porque de presente teemos muyto de fallar em outras cousas.

CXIX
Como o Duque partio do Porto, e do trauto que foy firmado amtrelle e el-Rey de Castella.

Depois que o Duque folgou alguuns dias com el-Rey e sua filha, embarcou por fazer viagem el e os seus, que eram muyto poucos; ca todos hiam em seis gallees bem folgadamente, e as outras por homra em sua companha. E era esto na fym de setembro. Ellas saydas de foz em fora e postas em-no mar, deu-lhe Deus tam booa viagem que em breues dias chegarom a Gasconha a huuma çidade que chamam Bayona, do senhorio de Imgraterra.

Como el-Rey de Castella soube que o Duque era em aquell logar, hordenou demuyar a el seus embaxadores por firmarem aquel trauto de que ja fezemos mençom. E os que el-Rey nomeou pera hirem la, forom

something being affirmed through the ignorance of the speaker. For the King was always on good terms with the Duke and very obedient to him in any way he could in order to please him. He married his daughter at the Duke's request, which pleased the Duke very much, as could be shown at length. May the following suffice as a brief demonstration of this truth: that is, that when the Duke was in a village called Carrazedo[2] near Chaves at the beginning of these affairs, there came to him a lawyer of the King's Council with certain messages from the King, and the Duke replied with a letter which read as follows: "Our very noble and very honourable and powerful relative and friend: We, the King of Castile and León and Duke of Lancaster, send you many greetings as to a King whom we greatly love, admire and trust, and for whom we desire great honour, good fortune and as much life and health as for ourselves. We inform you, etcetera." And after many other things contained in the letter, it said as follows: "Moreover we are most grateful and thankful for the courtesy and noble conduct which you are showing our daughter, as well as for the rich presents which you have been pleased to give her, and for the good arrangements which you have made for the maintenance of her and her status and her companions. For this reason we are absolutely bound to promote your honour and your interests just as much as our own, and we rely on God to place us in such a position as will allow us to observe this as befits your honour and our own. Very noble, very honourable and powerful King, our relative and friend, may Our Lord God have you always in his keeping, etcetera."

Thus it appears to be very much the opposite of what that libellous author wrote about those events.

Moreover, as far as the dispensation is concerned, which he spoke about, we shall answer him as we shall see fit, for at present we have much to say about other matters.

CXIX
How the Duke left Oporto, and of the treaty which he and the King of Castile signed.

After enjoying several days in the company of his daughter and the King, the Duke and his companions went on board. As they were very few in number, they all went very comfortably in six galleys, so that the other galleys merely accompanied them to do them honour. This was at the end of September. They went out of the estuary and on to the high seas. God gave them such a good voyage that in a few days they arrived at a city of Gascony called Bayonne, which belonged to England.

When the King of Castile learned that the Duke was at that place, he ordered his ambassadors to go there to sign that treaty which we have already mentioned. The men whom the King

frey Fernam dIlhescas da ordem de sam Framçisco, que era seu comfessor, e Pero Samches de Castilha, doutor em lex, e o doutor Aluaro Martijnz, que da primeira com os outros mesegeiros veerom fallar ao Duque. E porque nas auemças que comcordadas forom na villa de Tranquoso fora razoado açerca desto quanto mester fazia, nom foy compridoira mais lomga tardança, senom hordenar o trauto de guissa que fosse valiosso. E leixadas muytas clausulas que em elle forom postas, soomente das que pertemçem aa sua requesta diremos aquy, e mais nom; saber:

Que el-Rey de Castella e o Duque dAllancastro e a Duquesa sua molher feζessem todo seu poder que casasse per pallauras de presente o jffante dom Emrique, primogenito del-Rey de Castella, com dona Catellina, filha do dito Duque; e que do dia que este trauto jurado e afirmado fosse ataa dous meses seguimtes se feζesse este casamento pubricamente em faςe da¹ Igreja, e se acabasse per matrimonio quamto bem ςedo ser podesse.

Outrosy, que o jffamte dom Fernamdo, segundo filho del-Rey de Castella, nom esposasse nem tomasse molher nenhuuma ataa que o dito jffamte seu jrmaão fosse de jdade de quatorζe annos; ca el era entom de noue, e esto pera poder com dereito outorgar seus esposoyros e comprir o casamento; e que desto esse jffante dom Fernamdo feζesse juramento; e que acomteςemdo, o que Deus nom quisesse, que amte da jdade dos quatorζe annos, nom temdo comsumado seu matrimonjo esse jffamte dom Emrique, el viesse a morer, que entam a dita dona Catellina casasse com o jffamte dom Fernamdo, seu jrmaão.

E que o dito Rey de Castella desse logo ao jffante dom Emrique, seu filho, e a dona Catellina, sua espossa que auja de ser, a ςidade de Soria e as villas dAlmaςam e de Ateença e de Deςa e de Molina, com seus termos e todos seus dereitos:

E mais, que ataa dous meses seguimtes depois da firmeζa deste trauto, el-Rey ordenasse suas cortes, nas quaaes feζesse jurar aos poboos dauerem o dito jffante e dona Catellina, sua molher, por herdeiros e senhores de Castella:

E emtregue dona Catellina a el-Rey pera seer molher do jffamte dom Emrique seu filho, que el-Rey fosse theudo de dar e pagar ao Duque e a sua molher seisςentos mjll framcos douro de justo pesso da moeda de França; e que o Duque e a Duquesa renunçiase(m) e leixassem de ssy todo dereito que auer podiam nos regnos de Castella e de Leom, e o posessem em el-Rey e em seus herdeiros; e que estes seisςentos ·mjll framcos se pagassem em ςertos termos que amtre sy deuisarom: e mais que el-Rey de Castella e seus sobςesores desem ao Duque e sua molher em vida dambos e do que postumeiro moresse quorenta mjll framcos daquella mesma moeda, postos e pagados naquelle logar de Bayona: e per se comprir esta paga daquelles seisςemtos mjll framcos, que el-Rey de Castella desse ao Duque arefeens de ςertas pessoas de quallquer estado e comdiςom que fossem, que teueram a parte do Duque e lhe derom villas e castellos, reςebemdo-o por senhor:

298

nominated to go there were Fray Fernando de Illescas of the Order of St. Francis,[1] who was his confessor, Pedro Sánchez de Castilla, doctor of laws, and Dr. Alvaro Martínez, who had come to speak with the Duke together with the other messengers on the very first occasion. Now because all that was necessary had already been worked out in the agreements made in the village of Trancoso, it was not now necessary to have a long delay but only to arrange the treaty in such a way that it would be valid. So, leaving aside many clauses which were put in the treaty, we shall mention now only those which related to his request, that is to say:

"That the King of Castile and the Duke of Lancaster and his wife the Duchess shall do all in their power to marry Prince Enrique, eldest son of the King of Castile, to Lady Catherine, daughter of the said Duke; and that the wedding shall be celebrated publicly in the eyes of the Church within two months of this treaty being agreed and sworn to; and that the marriage shall be consummated as soon as possible thereafter.

Moreover, that Prince Fernando, the second son of the King of Castile, shall not marry or take a wife until his brother, the said Prince, is fourteen years old" (for he was then nine years old, and this was so that he could validly agree to the wedding and consummate the marriage); "and that Prince Fernando should swear to do this; and that if, God forbid, the Prince were to die before he reached the age of fourteen, without consummating this marriage, then the said Lady Catherine should marry his brother, Prince Fernando.

The said King of Castile shall give to his son Prince Enrique and to Lady Catherine his future wife, the city of Soria, and the towns of Almazán, Atienza, Deza and Molina, with their territories and all their rights.

Moreover, that within two months after the signing of this treaty, the King shall hold a meeting of his Cortes, and make his people swear to accept the Prince and his wife Lady Catherine as heirs and lords of Castile.

Once Lady Catherine is handed over to the King to be the wife of his son Prince Enrique, the King is obliged to give and pay to the Duke and his wife 600,000 gold francs, of full weight, of French money. Then the Duke and Duchess will renounce and abandon any rights they may have in the kingdoms of Castile and León, in favour of the King and his heirs. These 600,000 francs shall be paid within a certain time — limit on which they agreed. Moreover, the King of Castile and his successors shall give the Duke and his wife, and whichever of the two survived the other, throughout their lives, 40,000 francs of the same money, to be paid in that place of Bayonne. As a guarantee that he will pay those 600,000 francs, the King of Castile shall give the Duke as hostages certain persons of whatever status and social class they may be, who will hold some towns and castles on behalf of the Duke and give them to him and receive him as their lord.

*E que esta transauçam e renunciaçom se emtendesse assy: que el-Rey
dom Joham de Castella, e o jffante dom Emrique depois delle, possuyssem
os regnos e senhorios que o Duque demandaua, e os netos e bisnetos deste
jffante e de sua molher ligitimamente desçendentes; e se esta dona Catellina e seu marido nom ouuessem filho nem filha que herdasse os regnos de
Castella, que esta mesma comdiçam pasasse (a)o jffante dom Fernamdo;
e morendo o jffante dom Fernamdo sem filho nenhuum legitimo nado, que
em este caso tal heramça e suçessom trespasassem a quaaesquer filhos ou
netos lidimos do dito Rey dom Joham; e nom ficamdo herdeiro ligitimo
do dito Rey nem dos jffantes dom Emrique e dom Fernamdo, seus filhos,
que estomçe o dereito e senhorio dos regnos de Castella pasasse ao Duque
e sua molher e filha e a quaaesquer outros legitimos desçendentes delles e
de cada huum delles:*

*Outrosy, da paga dos quorenta mjll framcos que el-Rey e seus her-
deiros auyam cada anno de dar ao Duque, que esto fosse per esta gujsa:
que nom pagamdo emteiramente per tres annos, huum depos autro, que o
Duque podesse tornar a demandar o dereito que ante demandaua; e que
nenhuum outro caso nom ouuesse logar de britar esta transauçom saluo
este:*

E pera guarda destas cousas e comprimento de cada huuma paga
como se auia de fazer, deu el-Rey çertas [3] arrefeens ataa huum dia çerto,
saber: dom Fadrique, duque de Benauente, seu jrmaão, ata a primeira
paga; e assy outras arrefeens ataa çertas pagas, assy como dom Pero
Pomçe de Leom, senhor de Marchena, e Joham de Vallasco, filho de
Pero Fernandez, e Karllos dArelhano e Joham de Padilha e Rodrigo de
Rrojas e Lopo Ortiz dEstunhega e Joham Rodriguez de Çisneiros e Rodrigo de Castanheda e alguumas outras de çertas çidades. E como faziam
alguuma paga dos seis(centos) mjll framcos ao termo deuissado, assy
tirauom çertas arrefeens; e acabadas as pagas, assy forom todos liures:

*E mais, que el-Rey desse a dona Costamça, molher do Duque, em sa
vida Guadalfajara e Medina del Campo e Olmedo, com todas suas
remdas e senhorio.*

Outras liamças damizades e capitollos de desuairadas cousas forom
postos naquel trauto, que por esquiuar prolixidade leixamos aquy de
dizer.

CXX
*Como dona Cateluna foy tragida a Castella, e a ssua madre veo veer
el-Rey, seu primo.*

Feito este trauto que breuemente contamos, hordenarom mais em
aquel logar que o jffante dom Emrique se chamasse Prinçepe das Esturas e sua molher dona Catellina Prinçesa, e que a dias çertos fosse
tragida a Castella e emtregue em esse regno. E el-Rey hordenou logo

This agreement and renunciation shall be understood as follows: the kingdoms and lordships claimed by the Duke shall be possessed by King Juan of Castile, and after him by Prince Enrique, and then by the grandchildren and great–grandchildren who were the legitimate descendants of this Prince and his wife. If this Lady Catherine and her husband do not have any son or daughter to inherit the kingdoms of Castile, then this same condition shall apply to Prince Fernando. If Prince Fernando dies without any legitimate son, in this case then the inheritance and succession shall pass to any legitimate children or grandchildren of the said King Juan. If there is no legitimate heir either to this King or to his sons, the Princes Enrique and Fernando, then the right to, and lordship over, the kingdoms of Castile will pass to the Duke and his wife and daughter, and to any other legitimate descendant of both, or either of them.

Moreover, the 40,000 francs which the King and his heirs are bound to pay annually to the Duke shall be paid on the following condition: that if full payment is not made for three successive years, then the Duke can again claim the rights which he had formerly claimed; and that under no other conditions may this agreement be broken."

As a guarantee of these terms and of each of the payments which had to be made, the King provided certain hostages for specific lengths of time; that is Fadrique, Duke of Benavente, his brother, until the first payment; and similarly other hostages until other payments had been made, such as Pedro Ponce de León, Lord of Marchena; Juan de Velasco, son of Pedro Fernández; Carlos de Arellano; Juan de Padilla; Rodrigo de Rojas; Lope Ortiz de Estúñiga; Juan Rodríguez de Cisneros; Rodrigo de Castañeda; and some hostages from certain cities. As each payment is made of some of the 600,000 francs total, on the dates agreed, then certain hostages were released, and when all the payments had been made, all of them were freed.

"And moreover, the King should give the Duke's wife, Lady Constanza, Guadalajara, Medina del Campo and Olmedo, with all their rents and lordship, to hold for her life–time."

Other bonds of friendship and chapters concerning disparate matters were included in that treaty, but we shall omit to mention them here in order to avoid prolixity. [2]

CXX
How Lady Catherine was brought to Castile, and how her mother came to see her cousin the King.

Once the treaty had been made which we have summarized, they also agreed in that place that Prince Enrique should be entitled Prince of Asturias and his wife Lady Catherine, Princess; and that within a certain time she should be brought to Castile and handed over in this

como enuiasse por ella; e mandou alla senhores e prellados e donas e caualleiros, quaaes compria a ssua homra. E chegarom a huum logar que chamaam Fonterabya, que he em Gipuzca, terra de Bizcaya; e ally trouuerom a primçesa cáualleiros do Duque dAllamcastro, entregando-a aaquellas homradas pessoas que el-Rey por ella mandou. E reçeberom logo çerta soma douro, e as arrafeens que auyam de ser postas; e espe-diram-sse huuns dos outros.

El-Rey atendeo sua nora na çidade de Pallemça, que era moça de quatorze annos, por se fazer ally sollempnemente a festa dos sposoiros; e quamdo chegou, reçebeo-a el-Rey com muy gramde homra. E a poucos dias na jgreja cathedrall dessa çidade esposarom como he costume, com gramdes (prazeres)² de justas e torneos e doutras allegrias. E deu el-Rey suas joyas aalguns do Duque que ally chegarom; e foram-sse.

Dally partio el-Rey e veeo-se a Outerdesilhas; e ally foy hordenado como dona Costança, sua prima, molher do Duque, veesse a Castella veer el-Rey; o quall a mandou reçeber per gramdes (senhores) e prel-lados, fazemdo-lhe muyto seruiço e homra per homde quer que vinha. E quamdo chegou, rreçebeo-a el-Rey muy homradamente, e esteue hij alguuns dias, damdo-lhe el-Rey de suas joyas; e mais, (a villa) de Huete que a ouuesse em sa vida, a quall lha logo mandou entregar. E emuyou o Duque a el-Rey per ella huuma coroa douro muy rica, (e fermoosa, dizendo que aquella tinha elle feyta) pera se coroar nos regnos de Castella, mas que ja (que) eram conuyndos e dasessego, que a el compria de a trager. E mais lhe mandou huuma çimta douro muy rica. E el-Rey enujou a elle cauallos e genetes e mullas bem fremosas e outras cousas.

CXXI

Como el-Rey de Castella se mandou escusar ao Duque que o nom podia ver por sua doemça.

Passou este anno de iiijᵉ.xxvj e veo a era de xxvij, na quall el-Rey partio de Medina del Campo pera hir a terra de Tolledo, que era comarca mais quente; e ally se trautou que el-Rey se uisse com o Duque amtre Bayona e Fomterabia. E partio el-Rey dAlcalla de Fenares e a Duquesa sa prima com elle, e veeram-sse ambos aa çidade de Burgos pera fazerem prestes as cousas que compriam pera taaes vistas. E estamdo el-Rey em Burgos na quaresma, adoeçeo; e depois que se semtio melhor, partio dally pera Vitoria, por emcaminhar pera Fomterabia. E dally — de Burgos — se partio a Duquesa, sua prima, pera Bayona de Imgraterra, homde estaua o Duque seu marido. E el-Rey chegamdo a Vitoria, tornou-lhe a door que ouuera em Burgos; e os fissicos lhe dise-rom que nom partisse dally, porque a terra que auya damdar era traba-lhosa de maaos caminhos.

kingdom. The King then ordered that she should be sent for; and he sent lords, prelates, ladies and knights for her, as befitted her honour. They came to a place called Fuenterrabia, in Guipúzcoa, in the land of Vizcaya; and there knights of the Duke of Lancaster found the Princess and handed her over to those honourable persons whom the King had sent for her. They then received a certain sum of gold, together with the hostages who were to be handed over; and the two parties took leave of each other.

The King awaited his daughter—in—law, who was a girl of fourteen years, in the city of Palencia, in order to solemnize the wedding there. When she arrived, the King received her with very great honour. Within a few days they were wedded in the cathedral of that city, according to custom with great rejoicings, jousts, tournaments and other festivities.[1] The King gave his jewels to some of the Duke's men who had come there; and they went away.

The King left there and came to Tordesillas; and there it was arranged that his cousin, Lady Constanza, the Duke's wife, should come to Castile to see the King; and he ordered her to be received by great lords and prelates, doing her great honour and service wherever she went. When she arrived, the King received her with great honour, and she was there for several days.[2] The King gave her jewels and, in addition, the town of Huete, to hold for her lifetime, which he ordered to be handed over to her straightaway. The Duke sent to the King, by his wife, a very costly and beautiful gold crown, saying that he had had it made in order to be crowned King of Castile, but that now that they were both in agreement and at peace, it was more fitting for King Juan to wear it. In addition, he sent him a very rich belt of gold; while the King sent to him horses, jennets, very fine mules and other things.

CXXI
How the King sent his excuses to the Duke for not being able to meet him on account of his illness.

The year 1388 ended, and 1389 began. The King left Medina del Campo and went to the land of Toledo, which was a warmer region; and there it was agreed that the King should meet the Duke between Bayonne and Fuenterrabia. The King set out from Alcalá de Henares with his cousin the Duchess, and they both came to the city of Burgos to prepare the things which would be necessary for such a meeting. Now whilst the King was at Burgos during Lent, he fell ill; but when he felt better, he went from there to Vitoria, with the intention of going on to Fuenterrabia. The Duchess, his cousin, left Burgos for Bayonne, where her husband the Duke was. However, when the King reached Vitoria, the pain he had felt in Burgos returned; and so the physicians told him not to go on, because the region he would have to traverse was difficult and had poor roads.

Estomçe emuyou el-Rey ao Duque o bispo dOsma e Pero Lopez dAyalla e frey Fernam dIlhescas, seu comfessor; per os quaaes lhe fez saber como chegara a Vitoria, xxiiij.° legoas de Bayona, por ho hir veer, como tinham acordado; e que como ally fora, que se nom semtira bem, em tanto que lhe conselhauom os fissicos que se nom posesse em trabalho de tall caminho, e que lhe rogaua que o quisesse auer por escusado.

Os embaxadores chegarom a el e comtaram-lhe sua neçesidade quall era; e o Duque nom se contentou das razóes que lhe deziam, nem queria crer as escussaçoões que lhe fallauom, e razoou com elles muytas cousas, as quaaes emtendera de fallar com el-Rey; speçialmente dizemdo que *pois el-Rey de Castella e el-Rey de Imgraterra nom auyam guerra, saluo por aquella demanda que ja era fimda, em que se el chamaua Rey de Castella por raҙom da Duquesa sua molher, filha del-Rey dom Pedro, que lhe pareçia que deuya seer amygo com el-Rey de Imgraterra, e que se lhe desto prouuesse, que el tinha poder abastamte del-Rey de Imgraterra, (seu ssobrynho e senhor, peraa o faҙer conpridamente).*

(Hos enbaixadores diseerão a jsto que o começo da guerra) que amtre estes rex ouuera fora per aaҙo da ajuda que el-Rey dom Eduarte, seu padre, e o Primçepe de Galleҙ, seu jrmaão, feҙerom a el-Rey dom (Pedro contra el-Rey dom Anrryque, padre del-Rey dom)[3] Joham, seu senhor; por a quall a el-Rey dom Emrique conuehera de faҙer liga muy abastante com dom Karllos, Rey de Framça, que de presemte reynaua; e que depois desto el casara com a jffamte dona Costamça e se chamara Rey de Castella, tragendo armas dereitas do regno: e como quer que este debate ja era çessado, que a amiҙade e liga de Framça ficaua em sua força e vertude, em tanto que el-Rey seu senhor o nom poderia ajudar comtra ella, saluo guardada aquella amiҙade, assy como deҙiam; moormente que naquella emtrada, que el feҙera com el-Rey de Portugall em sua terra, el-Rey de Framça lhe emuyara o duque de Borbom, seu tio, com duas mjll lamças de muy boõa gemte, afora outros senhores e capitaães que se de seu grado veherom ao seruir naquella guerra ; assy que per nenhuuma gujssa el nom se parteria daquella amiҙade.

O Duque disse que *lhe prouguera muyto se podera seer; mas pois que assy era, que feҙessem outra cousa que seria seruiço de Deus e proueito dos regnos, saber: que os mercadores e os romeus de Castella e de Imgraterra fossem seguros per mar e per terra, espeçialmente os que quisessem vijr a Santiago.*

Os mesegeiros diserom que *a raҙom era booa, mas que pemsauom que el-Rey seu senhor o nom podese faҙer, segumdo o trauto antre el e el-Rey de Framça posto; ca gramdes senhores com muytas gentes podiam seer taaes romeiros que era duuidosa cousa; porem, que elles o deriam a el-Rey seu senhor, e el lhe emuyaria depois a reposta.*

Then the King sent the Bishop of Osma,[1] Pedro López de Ayala and Fray Fernando de Illescas, his confessor, to the Duke, to tell him that on the way to see him as they had agreed, he had arrived at Vitoria, twenty—four leagues from Bayonne, but when he got there, he felt so ill that the physicians advised him not to expose himself to the hardship of such a journey. Therefore he begged the Duke to hold him excused.

The ambassadors came to the Duke[2] and explained their King's straits to him; but the Duke was not satisfied by what they told him nor was he inclined to believe the excuses which they made to him. Furthermore, he communicated to them many things that he wished to say to the King himself. In particular, he said that since the King of Castile and the King of England were not at war, except for his own claim, which was now finished with, namely to be King of Castile by right of his wife the Duchess, daughter of King Pedro, it seemed to him that the King ought to be the friend of the King of England, and that if he were agreeable, the Duke had sufficient authority, in the name of his nephew and lord, the King of England, to arrange this to the satisfaction of everyone.

To this the ambassadors replied that the war between the kings had begun because of the help given by King Edward, his father, and the Prince of Wales, his brother, to King Pedro against King Enrique, the father of their lord King Juan; and because of that help King Enrique had had to make a very close alliance with Charles who was King of France at that time.[3] After that the Duke had married Princess Constanza and entitled himself King of Castile, and bore the coat—of—arms of the Kingdom; and although that dispute was now ended, the friendship and alliance with France were still strong and valid, so that their lord the King could not help the Duke against France, especially since in that invasion of their land which he had made in conjunction with the King of Portugal, the King of France had sent his uncle, the Duke of Bourbon, with two thousand good lances, as well as other lords and captains who came of their own free will to serve King Juan in that war; so that he would not abandon that French alliance in any way whatsoever.

The Duke said that he would have been delighted had the King been able to do so; but since that was the case, they should do something else which would be to the service of God and benefit of their kingdoms; that is, that the merchants and pilgrims of Castile and England should be safe from attack on land and sea, especially those who wanted to go to Santiago.

The envoys said that the idea was good, but they thought that their lord the King would not be able to carry it out, due to his treaty with the King of France; for such pilgrims might include great lords with their retinues, and this would be a doubtful business. However, they would suggest it to their lord the King and he would send him his answer later.

Esteuerom emtom alguuns dias com o Duque amte que partise; e espedidos delle, tornarom-se pera homde el-Rey estaua.

CXXII
Como el-Rey juntou aquel ouro que auya de pagar ao Duque.

Rezam tem de duujdar quallquer avisado que per esta estorea leer, pois el-Rey de Castella nom tinha donde pagar soldo aas gemtes estramgeiras que pellas fromtarias posera nem aas duas mjll lamças que lhe el-Rey de Framça mandou em ajuda, domde aueria seisçemtos mjll francos que ao Duque auya de dar. E o que sobresto acomteçeo aueo desta gujssa :

Tamto que el-Rey soube que o Duque dAllamcastro era naquel logar de Bayona e que auya la demuyar seus embaxadores, sabemdo bem que firmariam o trauto, fez logo cortes na villa de Briuesca, homde veerom os procuradores das villas e çidades do regno; nas quaaes foy fallado que maneira se auya de teer em juntar tam gramde conthia como aquella que o Duque auya dauer. E como quer que alguuns comtradisessem, em fim acordarom que el-Rey lançase peita per todo o regno, de que nom fosse escussado clerigo nem leigo nem fidalgo nem outra pessoa de quallquer estado e condiçam que fosse. E os que jsto comselhauom, deziam que pois el-Rey liuraua o regno de tam gram demanda e sogeiçam, que todos deuyam ajudar a pagar em tal peita. E per tal hordenamça fezerom cartas, e emuyam per todo o regno; da quall cousa forom muy queixosos os fidalgos e donas e domzellas, e feito gramde mouymento amtrelles, de guissa que se nom cobraua dinheiro.

E el-Rey vemdo aquello, ouue de buscar outra maneira; que foy esta :

El-Rey dom Emrique, quamdo comprou de mosse Beltram a çidade de Soria e as villas dAlmaçam e (A)teença e Deça e outros logares que lhe auya dados, lamçou huuma peita que chamou emprestido, dizemdo em suas cartas que lho mandaria descomtar nas remdas que delles auya dauer. E foy feito repartimento desto per todollos logares, a cada huum çerta conthia, de guissa que juntou emtom xv. comtos de marauidijs e mais, de que fez pagamento da compra daquelles logares. E estomçe fez el-Rey outra tal maneira de pedido, em que nom pagarom donas nem fidalgos nem outra clerzçia; e per tal emprestido jumtou el-Rey tamta contya per que pagou os seisçemtos mjll framcos aos tempos que theudo era, e quitou suas arefeens.

They then spent several days with the Duke before departing; and once they had taken their leave of him, they returned to where the King was.

CXXII
How the King got together the gold which he had to pay to the Duke.

Any intelligent reader of this history may reasonably ask himself where the King of Castile was going to get the 600,000 francs which he had to pay the Duke, since he had no money with which to pay either the foreign troops which he had posted along the frontiers, or the two thousand lances which the King of France had sent to his aid. What happened was this:

As soon as the King learnt that the Duke of Lancaster was in that place called Bayonne, and that he had to send his ambassadors there, in the full knowledge that they would sign the treaty, he summoned the Cortes to the town of Briviesca.[1] The representatives of the towns and cities of the kingdom arrived and discussed what method might be adopted to collect such a great sum of money as was to be given to the Duke. Although some of them spoke against this, at last they agreed that the King should levy a poll—tax on all his kingdom, with no exemption for clerics or laymen or nobles or anyone else, no matter what his social status or rank. Those who advised this policy said that since the King had freed the kingdom from such a great claim and from subjugation, everyone ought to help to pay for such a tax. For this law they issued royal writs and sent them throughout the kingdom; but this caused the nobles, ladies and damsels to complain bitterly. They were greatly stirred up by this, to such an extent that the money was not collected.

When the King saw this, he had to look for another method, which was the following:

When King Enrique bought from Sir Bertrand the city of Soria and the towns of Almazán, Atienza, Deza and other places which he had given to him, he levied a poll—tax which he called a loan, saying in his letters that he would order it to be discounted from the rents which he was due to receive from them. Every place was assessed at a certain amount for the purposes of this poll—tax, so that the King collected at that time 15,000,000 maravedís and more, with which he paid the purchase—price of those places. And now King Juan levied another tax of the same sort, from which nobles, ladies and clerics were exempt; and with it he collected such a large sum of money that he was able to pay the 600,000 francs on the date agreed, and thus free his hostages.

Começo de reposta aa despemsaçam em que disemos que aquel estoriador fallara.

Pois que ja tornamos de Bayona de Ingraterra acabados os feitos do Duque, conuem que respondamos ante que contemos outra cousa aaquella mal fallada razom em que pos boca aquell estoriador que dissemos, notando por maldizer que o Papa nom despensara com el-Rey que casar podesse, nem lhe fora tragida tal letera, e que ficara ao Duque de mandar por ella.

Hora fundamento desta razom seia: que se poucos homeens som que nom tenham emmjgos e comtrairos ou a que todos bem queiram, bem se pode esto dizer del-Rey dom Joham, que nom soomente dos castellaãos a elle vizinhos, mas de seus naturaaes portugueses tantos emmjgos e contrairos tinha; os quaaes nom com zello de bomdade, mas prenhes de mal fallar parirom, dizemdo duas falssas razões: a primeira, que o Papa Vrbano nom quisera despemssar com elle; a segumda, que Bonjfaçio, que depois vehera, despemsara con çertas condiçõoes; assy que nom forom ligeiros os erros que de taaes estorias naçerom. Mas porque a breue scpritura nom pode declarar as lomgas duuidas nem em poucas pallauras muyto comcludir, em soma, a nos conuem por reposta desto per meudo contar duas prinçipaes cousas: a huuma, cuja foy a despemsaçam e com que condiçõoes; a outra, quall foy a causa de sua tardamça.

Omde ja ouujstes como os poboos e prellados do regno, tanto que o Mestre foy alçado por Rey, suplicarom ao Papa Vrbano que os demouera a emlegerem prinçepe e senhor e poer naquell real estado, e que por quanto pera auer o regno e liçitamente poder casar conujnha seer despemsado com elle, que pediam, aa Ssua Santidade que o quisesse fazer e auer por bem feito quamto em ello auyam obrado; e como despois o bispo dEuora e Gomçallo Gomez da Silua que auya mais dhuum anno que com esta supricaçom em duas gallees pera em corte partirom, e mandarom recado a el-Rey quando trautaua seus feitos com o Duque, dizemdo como chegarom a Genoa homde acharom o Padre Santo, e que apresentada amtelle a ssuplicaçom que de seus feitos leuauom, que el em to dallas cousas por sua parte pedidas beninamente despemsara, e que o rol era ja assynado, e trabalhariam de tirar as leteras. E andando elles em este cuidado por o dar a execuçom, forom embargados per huum mestre Amrique, jmgres, que estomçe estaua em corte; o quall, fingendo-sse grande serujdor do Duque, sem sabemdo el nem sua molher desto parte, falsamente enformou o Papa, dizemdo que o regno de Portugall pertençia aa Duquesa dAllamcastro dona Costamça, e desy ao Duque dAllamcastro por seer seu marido.

O Papa, ouuyndo estas razões, porque el-Rey de Imgraterra, sobrinho deste Duque, era huum dos notauees senhores que lhe estomçe obe-

CXXIII
The beginning of our answer to the question of the dispensation which we said that that historian had spoken about.

Since we have now finished with the deeds of the Duke and are leaving Bayonne, it is appropriate that before recounting anything else, we should answer the mis—statements made by the historian whom we mentioned earlier, when he wrote the libel that the Pope had not given the King a dispensation to marry, that no letter of dispensation had been brought, and that the Duke had had to send for one.

Now, the basis of the argument may be that if there are few men who lack enemies and adversaries and are beloved by everyone, this is even more true of King João, who had so many enemies and adversaries not only among the Castilians who were his neighbours but also among his own Portuguese countrymen. Now these, not out of zeal for good but out of calumnious intent said two false things: firstly, that Pope Urban did not want to grant him a dispensation; and secondly, that Boniface, the next Pope, granted him one on certain conditions. Thus, out of such stories, great errors have arisen. However, since such large questions cannot be summarized briefly nor resolved in a few words, we shall have to give an answer by recounting two principal matters in detail: firstly, who granted the dispensation and on what conditions; and secondly, what was the reason for the delay in granting it.

You have already heard how, as soon as the Master was proclaimed king, the people and prelates of the kingdom petitioned Pope Urban to allow them to elect a prince and lord and place him on the throne, and that, since he needed a dispensation in order to have the kingdom and contract a legitimate marriage, they begged His Holiness to grant this and to authorize all that they had done in this matter. One year after the Bishop of Évora and Gonçalo Gomes da Silva set out for the Curia with this petition in two galleys, they sent a message to the King when he was negotiating with the Duke, saying that they had arrived at Genoa, where they found the Holy Father. They had handed him the petition which they had taken with them, and he had benignly granted all the requests which they had made to him. The roll of petitions had already been signed, and they were now working to get the letters issued. However, whilst they were thus engaged to get the matter completed, they were hindered by a certain Englishman, Master Henry, who was then in the Curia. Pretending to be a great servant of the Duke, but without the latter or his wife knowing anything of it, this man falsely informed the Pope that the kingdom of Portugal belonged to Lady Constanza, Duchess of Lancaster, and so to the Duke of Lancaster because he was her husband.

When the Pope heard this, because the Duke's nephew, the King of England, was one of the notable lords who at that time were in his obedience, and because some claimed insistently that the King

deçiam, desy porque alguuns afirmauom muyto que el-Rey de Imgraterra queria trautar que el-Rey de Castella se deçesse da temçom que tinha e veesse a obediençia da Igreja, mandou as leteras estar assy quedas, ataa que fosse sabudo em çerto como era o que lhe fallara aquel mestre Amrique.

Soube el-Rey esto a que o mandarom dizer e teue dello gram queixume e sentido , cuydando que por parte do Duque lhe fora posto tal embargo, nom sabemdo em ello que cuidar; e emuyou a el sobresto recado per huum doutor de seu comselho, mostramdo-lhe huuma carta de crença. O quall lhe respomdeo per outra, de que leixamdo o ditado porque o ja temdes ouuydo, dizia desta guissa:

Fazemos-uos saber que Gill dOsem do uosso comselho veo a nos e deu-nos huuma vossa carta de creença, e disse-nos da uossa parte alguumas cousas, espeçialmente em como vossos embaxadores, que emuyarades a corte de Roma, forom embargados de vossos negoçios, que emuyarades deliurar com o Papa, per huum mestre Amrique, jmgres; dizemdo que o dereito do regno de Portugal pertemçia a mjnha molher, e a nos em seu nome. E emtendemos todo o que sobresto nos emuyastes dizer.

Muy nobre e poderoso Rey, uos sede çerto que esto nunca foy fallado per nos nem per nosso mandado nem da dita Rainha, nem nos prougue nem praz dello. Amte sabee que assy per alguuns vossos que mandauees, como per outras pessoas que hiam a corte, emuyamos demandar afficadamente ao Papa que por amor de nos deliurasse logo uossos negoçios assy como se fossem nossos, ca temos que os nossos feitos e os vossos, que todos eram huuns, segundo as maneiras que amtre nos e vos eram, que esto lhe teeriamos em graça espeçiall. E por esto nom deuees de cuydar que por nos nem por a dita Rainha fosse mandado nem consentido cousa per que a vosos negoçios veesse embargo; e deuel-lo auer por çerto por alguumas razoões, espeçialmente se nos ouuessemos fallado em ello, como trautariamos nos casamento de nosa muyto amada filha Philipa com uosco; ca a nos compria, segundo nosso estado, que ella ouuesse homra e estado, segundo (a) linhagem domde he.

Outrossy, porque vos emtendaaes que nos auemos em nosso coraçam vossos negoçios, assy como nossos mesmos, (hordenamos) denuiar a corte de Roma o nosso bem amado mestre Guilhelm, doutor em lex, chamçeller do nosso sello da puridade, pera que em nosso nome enforme o Papa da nossa vomtade nos feitos que tangem a vossa homra e deliuramento de uossos negoçios. Dat.

Assy que este foy o começo da tardamça por que as leteras logo nom veerom.

of England wanted to persuade the King of Castile to abandon his present intention and return to the obedience of the Church, the Pope ordered the letters not to be issued until he could discover for certain whether what Master Henry had said to him was true.

The King learned what his envoys wrote to him and was very grieved and sorry at it, thinking that this hindrance had been placed in his way by the Duke's orders. Not knowing what to think of it, he sent a message to the Duke by a doctor of his Council, who was furnished with a letter of credence. The Duke answered with another letter, which read as follows, (omitting the heading because you have already heard it):

"We inform you that Gil do Sem of your Council came to us and gave us your letter of credence, and he told us various things, especially how your ambassadors whom you sent to the Roman Curia were hindered in the negotiations which you had sent them to have with the Pope by a certain Englishman, Master Henry, who said that the kingdom of Portugal belonged by right to my wife and to me in my wife's name. We heard everything which you sent to tell us about this matter.

Very noble and powerful King, you may be certain that this matter was never spoken of by me, nor by my command, nor by that of the said Queen, and we are not at all pleased with it. Instead, you should know that both by some of your men whom you sent, as well as by other persons who were going to the Curia, we sent to ask the Pope very pressingly that, for love of us, he should expedite your affairs as if they were our own, for we consider that your affairs and ours are all one, according to the agreements between you and us, and that we would be especially grateful to him for this. So you ought not to believe that we or the said Queen would have ordered or agreed to anything which might hinder your negotiations. You should consider this certain, for several reasons; especially, that if we had spoken of this, how would we have arranged for the marriage with you of our beloved daughter Philippa; for it was to our benefit, according to our status, that she should have honour and status, according to her ancestry.

Moreover, so that you should understand that we have your business at heart, just as much as our own, we order that our well—beloved Master William, doctor—in—laws and Chancellor of our Secret Seal, be sent to the Roman Curia so that in our name he should inform the Pope of what we want in the matters which touch upon your honour and the successful conclusion of your business. Dated, etc."

So this was the beginning of the delay in the coming of the letters.

Como moreo o Papa Vrbano, e el-Rey mandou seus embaxadores a Bonyfaçio.

Vemdo os embaxadores tam abertos aazos pera este negoçio se perlomgar muyto, partiram-se de corte e chegarom a Portugall, contando todo o que se pasara e como leixauom o rol assynado e çertas razoões da sua detemça.

El-Rey hordenou, sem poer mais tardamça, de mandar logo la outra vez; e tornarom a corte aquel dom Joham, bispo dEuora, e em vez de Gomçallo Gomez foy Joham Afomsso, priol da alcaçeua de Santarem, bacharel em dereito, filho do homrado caualleiro Afonso Steuez da Azambuja. Forom estes mesegeiros ao Papa, e rrequerimdo-lhe per vezes que mandasse fazer as leteras como no rol era contheudo, ja per elle assynado, el daua a ello suas colloradas escusas, leuamdo-os de dia em dia, de que elles nom eram contentos; em tanto que, fallamdo-lhe huuma vez açerca desto, presemte alguuns cardeaaes, e vemdo como se hia perlomgamdo muyto aallem do rezoado, disse aquel Joham Afomso que hia com o bispo que pois aa Ssua Santidade nom era praziuell de lhe logo mandar fazer taaes leteras, e poinha em ello tam lomgo trespasso, que a elles compria mais tornarem-sse sem reposta, que estarem ally perdemdo seu tempo. O Papa disse que nom auyam por que se agrauar, ca elle auya el-Rey de Portugall por asolto e com elle despemsado compridamente em todallas cousas que lhe mandara pedir, posto que as leteras tam çedo feitas nom fossem. Joham Afomsso respomdeo a esto alguumas razoões de que o Papa desprougue; e assy como queixoso fallou comtra elle, dizemdo: *Tu te podes hir quando quiseres. Mas se te fores, tu hiras e tornaras.*

Acordarom elles, vemdo sua vomtade, de se partirem sem mais tardamça. E vijndo seu camjnho pera embarcar em Framdes, forom presos em Allemanha e retheudos sem por que, saluo por os espeitarem. Ouuerom-se de render per dous mjll florijns da camara. Fezeram-no saber a el-Rey, que sem mais perlomga mandou fazer delles caimbo , e emtregue em Medyoburgo, forom soltos e tornados ao regno.

E hordenamdo el-Rey mandar la outra uez por dar fym a esto que lhe tanto conuinha, este Papa Vrbano moreo, auendo ja doze annos que regia a Igreja, e passaua de dous que assinara o rol daquesta despemssaçam. E des quimze dias dOutubro, que se el finou em Roma, ataa os dezoito seguyntes forom os cardeaaes ocupados em sua sepultura e estar no comclauy pera emleger; e aos dous dias do mes de nouembro foy emleyto em papa outro que chamarom Boniffaçio nono, que soçedeo em seu logar.

El-Rey, como disto soube çertas nouas, nom embargando a ssuplicaçom que pellos embaxadores primeiros mandara e o assynamento do Papa Vrbano que de sua despemsaçom leixara feito, hordenou logo de

How Pope Urban died and the King sent his ambassadors to Boniface.

Seeing such obvious reasons for this business to be long drawn out, the ambassadors left the Curia and came to Portugal, explaining everything which had happened, and how they had left the roll signed and certain reasons for their delay.

Without more delay, the King ordered another embassy to be sent at once; and that Dom João, Bishop of Évora, returned to the Curia, and instead of Gonçalo Gomes, there went the Prior of the citadel church of Santarém, João Afonso, who was a graduate in law, and son of the honourable knight Afonso Esteves de Azambuja.[1] These messengers went to the Pope, and asked him many times to have bulls drawn up in accordance with what was contained in the roll and had already been signed by him. He kept putting them off, from one day to the next, with merely rhetorical excuses. They were discontented, to such an extent that when they were speaking to him one day about this matter in the presence of some cardinals, and could see how he was procrastinating much more than was reasonable, that João Afonso said that he was going off with the Bishop, for since His Holiness had no wish to order such bulls to be written for him at that time, and was delaying it for such a long time, they themselves were wasting their time there and had better go back home without any answer. The Pope said that they had no reason to feel aggrieved, for he had absolved the King of Portugal and dispensed him fully in all the petitions which he had sent him, even though the bulls were not yet written. João Afonso answered this with some remarks which offended the Pope; and the Pope responded, as if complaining of them, saying, "You can go when you like; but if you go, you will go away and then you will have to come back again."

Seeing his attitude, they decided to leave without delay. On their journey to embark in Flanders, they were captured in Germany and imprisoned without cause, except for the ransom money. Their ransom was fixed at two thousand florins of the Chamber. They informed the King, who without delay ordered the money to be changed and handed over in Middleburg. They were then released and returned to Portugal.

Then, when the King was arranging for an embassy to be sent once more to complete the task which meant so much to him, this Pope Urban died after ruling the Church for twelve years. It was now over two years since he had signed the roll approving this dispensation. From 15 October when he died in Rome, for the following eighteen days, the cardinals were busy with his burial and in the conclave to elect his successor. On 2 November another pope was elected to succeed him, who was called Boniface IX.[2]

As soon as the King heard this news for certain, notwithstanding the petition which he had sent with his first ambassadors and the signature of Pope Urban granting him his dispensation, he at once

313

mandar em corte com outra suplicaçom de nouo feita, assy como a primeira. Os do comselho que eram leterados diserom que tal cousa era escusada; ca pois o Papa Vrbano com el despemsara, e ho rol era ja assynado per que as leteras fossem feitas, que nom auya mester mais saluo requerir que as fezessem, e que jsto era regra geeral na camçellaria do Papa, e cousa mandada e posta em husso per todollos sumpmos pontificos, que a graça feita pello Santo Padre, posto que nom fosse scprita em sua forma, ou fosse feita e nom bullada, que nom expiraua porem per morte delle, mas ficaua em sua força des aquel tempo que a el outorgara, e nom do tempo que fosse feita ou lhe possessem o ssello; assy que a graça era do Papa finado, e a bulla do que soçedia, e por em nom auya por que mais supplicar outra uez.

El-Rey, nom embargamdo jsto e outras cousas que lhe razoaram, por moor cautella e auomdamento mandou fazer huuma tall como a primeira, em que el e os poboos supplicauom aquello que ouujstes que na outra hia, pedimdo aa Sua Santidade que em todo mjsericordiosamente quisesse despemssar. E emuyou la por embaxadores aquel Joham Afomsso, que era ja bispo de Silues, e huum homrado fidalgo Joham Rodriguez de Saa, que ante desto per vezes nomeamos; os quaaes partirom em duas gallees, e segujndo seu camjnho, chegarom a corte. E dada ao Papa a supplicaçom que assy leuauom, elle a ouue por sobeja; e benignamente respomdendo, disse que pois seu amteçessor auya outorgado tall graça e o rol assynado, segumdo el sabia que era de presente estomçe, que escussado era supplicar mais sobrello, senom soomente requerir as leteras. E temdo-lhe elles em gramde merçee, na melhor maneira que o dizer souberom, pedirom mais aa Ssua Santidade que de como o Papa Vr bano auya despemsado com elle tamto que sua supplicaçom lhe fora mostrada, posto que dalguuns jmpedimentos ouuessem torua per que as leteras nom forom tiradas, que desse dello testemunho em sua bulla, pera remouer das gemtes alguuma errada temçom que muytos comtra esto tinham. O Papa disse que lhe prazia muyto, e que todo o que se perantel passara, notifficaria aos poboos do regno, e mais outra letera em que abastosamente se conteuesse todo aquello que elles desejauom.

As leteras feitas, partiram-se da corte e chegarom a Portugall, e ujstas per el-Rey e os do seu conselho, por quanto que a pubrica voz e fama nom dereitamente contada muytas vezes empeeçe aa verdade, e por çessar de todo quallquer razom que a esto fosse comtraira, mandou el-Rey que as pubricassem na jgreja cathedrall de Lixboa, por tirar de sospeita o que alguuns jnorantes fallauom, dizemdo que pois seus embaxadores tamtas vezes hiam e vinham, que o Papa Vrbano nom qujsera despemssar com elle. A esta çidade, que he cabeça do regno, forom as leteras enuiadas e feito geerall chamamento de todollos çidadaãos e ajmda donas e muyto outro poboo pera ouuir esto. Eram presemtes os

arranged to send another embassy to the Curia with another petition like the first one, but written anew. The graduate members of his Council said that such a thing was unnecessary, for since Pope Urban had granted him a dispensation and the roll had already been signed for the bulls to be drawn up, there was no further need for anything other than to request that they be, in fact, drawn up. This, they said, was the general rule in the papal chancery, ordered and practised by all the popes, that any favour granted by the Holy Father, even if it were not formally written down, or were written but not sealed, would not be invalidated by his death but would remain valid from the time that he granted it, and not from the time when it was written down or sealed. Thus, the favour belonged to the late Pope, and the seal to his successor; and therefore there was no need to petition for it all over again.

Despite this and other arguments which were presented to him, for greater security and out of meticulousness, the King ordered another petition to be made just like the first one in which he and the people made the same request as you have heard was in the first one, begging His Holiness kindly to grant all the dispensation. He sent there as his ambassadors that João Afonso, who was now Bishop of Silves, and an honourable nobleman, João Rodrigues da Sá, whom we have occasionally mentioned before. They left in two galleys and, after a voyage, arrived at the Curia. Once they had given the Pope the petition which they took with them, he approved it and answered benignly that since his predecessor had granted that favour and signed the roll, as he himself knew because he had been present at the time, it was unnecessary to present any further petition about the matter and only necessary to ask for the bulls. They were most grateful and, speaking as politely as they could, they explained to His Holiness that Pope Urban had granted the King his dispensation as soon as the petition had been shown to him, although certain impediments had then caused an obstruction so that the bulls were not immediately issued. They therefore made the extra request that the Pope should bear witness to this fact. The Pope said that he would be very pleased to do so, and that he would explain to the people of Portugal everything which had happened in his presence, and would issue another letter which would contain a full account of everything which they wanted.

Once the letters had been issued, they left the Curia and came to Portugal. The King and his Council saw the letters, and since public gossip and false rumours often distort the truth, and in order to cut short any untrue version of what had happened, the King ordered the letters to be published in Lisbon cathedral, in order to remove the suspicion which some ignorant people were voicing that since his ambassadors were coming and going so many times, Pope Urban did not want to grant him a dispensation. The papal letters were sent to Lisbon, which is the capital of the kingdom, and all the citizens and even the women and many other people were summoned

gramdes padres e senhores dom Joham, bispo dessa çidade, e dom Joham, bispo do Porto, e os homrados dayam e cabydo dessa jgreja. Isso mesmo de pessoas leigas estauom hij os prudentes e discretos baroões Louremçeannes Fogaça, chamçeller moor del-Rey, e Martym Afomsso Vallamte e Louremço Esteuenz da Azambuja e outros caualleiros, e muytas pessoas, assy eclessiasticas come secullares, que nom faz mingua serem nomeadas. E huum domingo, que eram noue dias de julho, perçebido pera esto huum gramde leterado, mestre em theologia, muy famoso pregador da hordem de sam Framçisquo, chamado frey Rodrigo de Simtra, todos atemtos com manso sillençio pera o ouuir, foy per elle feito huum sermom assaz de sollemne, a tal auto pertemçente; e acabada sua pregaçam, forom vistas huumas leteras apostolicas de toda sospeiçom careçemtes; as quaaes em alta e emtendida voz de çima do pulpito pubricadas, a primeira continha este theor:

CXXV
Teor de primeira letera que na See foy pobricada.

Bonifaçio, bispo, seruo dos seruos de Deus, a todos aquelles que estas leteras virem e esguardar qujserem saude e apostollicall bemçom.

Porque de boa raxom pertençe e aa honestidade conuem que as graças procedidas do romano Pontifico, posto que as leteras sobre taaes cousas aconteçesse nom seerem feitas, que consigam seu effectu e venham em pubrico conheçimento; por em a todos geeralmente notificamos e (a) vossa notiçia per estas presemtes faxemos çertos, que nos passados dias por parte dos amados filhos prellados e nobres baroões e poboos dos regnos de Portugall e do Alguarue a Vrbano sexto, da boõa memoria, nosso predeçesor, — pello homrado jrmaão, bispo dEuora, e per alguuns outros seus embaxadores — fosse signifficado que elles por çertas raxoões e avidentes causas, — moormente porque Joham Amrriquez, ocupador dos regnos de Castella e de Leom, esses regnos de Portugall e do Alguarue se esforçaua (a) sojugar e destruir, seendo careçemtes de rey que os defender podesse, — que elles saudauellmente proueendo aa homra e estado dos ditos regnos e comtrariar aos maaos deseios dese Joham Amriquez, esforçado perseguidor delles e da santa Egreja, espossa de Jhesu Christo, o muyto amado nosso filho Joane, filho naturall de Pedro da boa memoria, aaquel tempo Meestre da cauallaria da hordem dAujs, todos dhuum coraçam e vomtade o pediram e tomarom em Rey e senhor dos ditos (reynos), assentando-o na seeda reall e vestimdo-o de rreaaes vestiduras, guardamdo em ello todallas homras e solemnjdades deuidas e acostumadas.

O quall Johane, per este modo Rey, o reçebimento e assumpçom delle feita e as outras cousas como dito he, por gramde neçessidade e claro

generally to hear the news. There were present the great fathers and lords, Dom João, Bishop of this city, and Dom João, Bishop of Oporto, and the honourable dean and chapter of this church.[3] Moreover, among the lay people there were the prudent and discreet barons Lourenço Eanes Fogaça, Grand Chancellor of the King, Martim Afonso Valente, and Lourenço Esteves de Azambuja together with other knights, as well as many ecclesiastical and secular persons who do not need to be named individually. A great scholar and master in theology was appointed for this task, a very famous preacher of the Order of St. Francis called Fray Rodrigo de Sintra. On Sunday 9 July, when all were silent and paying attention to hear him, he delivered a very solemn sermon appropriate to the occasion. Once he had finished the sermon, the papal letters were shown, free from any suspicion, and were published from the pulpit in a loud and clear voice which everyone could understand.

The first of them was as follows:

CXXV
The meaning of the first letter which was published in the cathedral.

Boniface, Bishop, Servant of the Servants of God, to all those who see this letter and wish to keep it, health and apostolic benediction.[1]

Because it is reasonable and honourable that favours granted by the Pope of Rome should be carried into effect and be of public knowledge, even if the letters about them have by chance not been issued, we hereby therefore notify and certify to everyone that recently our predecessor, Urban VI, of happy memory, was informed by our beloved sons, the prelates, noble barons and peoples of the kingdoms of Portugal and the Algarve, through the honourable brother, the Bishop of Évora, and some other ambassadors of theirs, that Juan Enríquez, usurper of the kingdoms of Castile and León, was striving to subjugate and destroy these kingdoms of Portugal and the Algarve, which lacked any king able to defend them. Therefore, for this and other obvious reasons, they made healthy provision for the honour and status of these kingdoms and for the frustration of the evil desires of that Juan Enríquez, who was a determined persecutor of them and of the Holy Church, the Bride of Jesus Christ. So they all unanimously sought our well−beloved son João, natural son of Pedro of happy memory, at that time Master of the knights of the Order of Avis, and took him as king and lord of these said kingdoms, seating him on the royal throne and dressing him in royal robes, and treating him with all due and customary honour and solemnity.

Once this João had been accepted and raised to be king in this way and the other things had been done as I have said, because of the great necessity of and clear benefit to these kingdoms which had

proueito desses regnos pello dito Joham Amrique͚ destroidos e ocupados, aceptara [6] e comsentira, leixamdo o aveto da dita ordem, e vesteduras reaaes tragemdo, como de feito tragia; e por defemssam desses regnos em autos darmas se mesturara, nos quaees ençendidos e homeçidios de pessoas, assy eclessiasticas come seculares, e outros muytos danos se seguirom. E por tamto per esses prellados e nobres do poboo a esse Vrbano, predeçessor nosso, per seus embaxadores humjldosamente foy suplicado que, pemsadas estas cousas per jmtrimseca caridade, este Joane, Rey aaquell tempo, Mestre da dita hordem, per apostolicall autoridade teuesse por bem assoluer do laço da culpa e excomunham que per ocassyom de quallquer dellas lhe acomteçesse emcorer.

Desy porque em outro tempo, quamdo Fernamdo, Rey desses regnos, jrmaão deste dom Joam, Rrey, se jumtara a Rroberto, filho de perdiçom, que per escumungado atreuimento se chamou, come presume de chamar, Clemente septimo, nom curamdo dos proçessos comtra elle e o dito Joham Amrique͚ feitos, fora presemte nas vodas desse Joham Amrique͚ e dhuuma filha do dito Fernamdo, Rey, quamdo ambos casarom, fauoriçamdo esse Antipapa e Joham Anrique͚, tragendo pubricamente vestiduras de sirgo teçidas com ouro, e outras vaãs e desonestas cousas, em que se mestu ramdo apostatasse sua hordem, e de toda ma͚ella de jffamya e hinabelidade em que per quallquer modo emcoresse teuesse por bem de o remouer.

E ajmda com esse Joane, Rey, nom embargando as cousas ja ditas e o defectu de sua naçemça, — semdo geerado daquell Pedro, Rey, e dhuuma molher nom sua, posto que fossem ambos casados, — e posto que o dito Rey fosse professo da hordem da cauallaria dAujs, da quall os professos em seus estados aa obseruamça regullar dos monges de Cistell deuem ser comformes e per nenhuma guissa casar, que el podesse auer esta dignidade de nome e homra de rey, e reteer e possuir e casar liçitamente... e se per uentura com a muyto amada em Christo nossa filha Filipa, Rainha desses regnos, ouuesse casado como hordenara de casar, e se Johane Rey e Fillipa Rainha, sem embargo dempedimento quallquer de parentesco ou das cousas susso ditas, liçitamente podessem ficar no dito casamento, e a geraçam ja conçebida, ou que de tal matrimonio naçesse, per autoridade apostollica declarasse seer legitima; a quall coussa esse Vrbano, nosso predeçessor, em presemça dalguuns cardeaaes seus jrmaãos, do numero dos quaaes nos aaquell tempo eramos presente, a esse Joane obispo, como em çima he contheudo, humjldosamente suplicante respomdeo e em pubrico disse e afirmou que elle, consiradas todallas coussas susso ditas e outras çertas e ra͚oaues causas a esto mouentes seu coraçam, esse Joane Rey, aaquell tempo Mestre da dita ordem, absoluera e habillitara, e ajmda com elle e com a dita Filipa despemssara, e o exemptara e absoluera da obligaçom da dita (hordem) [1], e todallas outras cousas a cadahuuma dellas como lhe suplicado fora, assy como cousa neçesaria comçedera e outorgara.

E ajmda huum outro dia a esse Joane bispo supplicante, nos e os

been occupied and destroyed by the said Juan Enríquez, João accepted and consented to his own accession, leaving off the habit of the said Order and wearing royal robes, as indeed he wore them. For the defence of these realms he was involved in feats of arms, in which there occurred burnings and killings of people both clerical and secular, and many other acts of violence. Therefore these prelates and nobles of the people, through their ambassadors, humbly begged our predecessor, Pope Urban, to consider these matters with inward charity and with his apostolic authority to deign to absolve this João, Master of the said Order and King at that time, from the bond of guilt and excommunication which he might by chance have incurred through any of them.

Then, because at another time, when Fernando, King of these kingdoms and brother of this Dom João, joined Robert, the son of perdition who with an effrontery which earned him excommunication, was calling himself, as he still presumes to call himself, "Clement VII", and taking no heed of the trials against him and the said Juan Enríquez, our Dom João was present at the wedding of that Juan Enríquez to a daughter of the said King Fernando, favouring that Antipope and Juan Enríquez, and publicly wearing silk robes woven with gold and other vain and dishonest things, with which he apostatized from his Order, he now asks to be forgiven for this, and also that all stain of infamy and disqualification which he may in any way have incurred, be removed.

Moreover, notwithstanding the above–mentioned matters and also the defect of his birth — since his father, King Pedro, and his mother, were both married, but not to each other — although he was professed in the Order of the knights of Avis, the professed friars of which ought to follow the regular observance of the Cistercian monks and not get married at all, it is requested that he be allowed to have the name, dignity and honour of King, and retain and possess and marry legally.....and if by chance he has married our beloved daughter in Christ, Philippa, Queen of these kingdoms, as he had intended, that King João and Queen Philippa, despite any impediment of family relationship or of the above–mentioned matters, may legitimately remain in the said marriage, and the children already conceived or to be born of this marriage may be declared legitimate by apostolic authority. Our predecessor Urban, in the fraternal presence of some cardinals, including ourselves, answered the humble petition of that Bishop João in this matter as is contained above, and publicly said and affirmed that, having considered all the aforementioned matters and certain other reasonable causes which motivated his heart to this, he absolved that King João, at that time Master of the said Order, removed his disqualifications, gave a dispensation to him and to the said Philippa, exempted and absolved him from the obligations of the said Order, and conceded and granted all other things and every one of them that his petition contained, as a necessary thing.

Moreover on another day, in the presence of us and of the

outros cardeaaes presemtes, publicamente respondeo e afirmou que elle auya esse Johane Rey sobre as cousas amte ditas por absolto e com elle despemsado, como ja dito he.

Hora como he uerdade que (so)bresto veo a morte ao dito Vrbano, nosso prodeçessor, e as leteras apostollicas sobre taaes cousas nom forom feitas, por em nos, querentes prouer aa homra desses Joane Rey e Filipa Rainha, sua molher, e todos moradores desses regnos, posto que taaes leteras sobrestas cousas nom fossem feitas viuendo nosso prodeçesor, esses Rey e Rainha e os suplicantes ja ditos nom careçam de seu effectu, pois que se todo assy passou, aa uossa notiçia por renembrança pera sempre per estas presentes o faҁemos çerto.

Porem nos, por moor cautella e segurança e ajmda moor firmeҁa, esse Joane Rey de nouo asoluemos, e toda magoa dinfamya e jnabilli dade de todo lhe tiramos, e com elle sobre as cousas assy ditas e com a dita Filipa, Rainha, despensamos que liçitamente fiquem no casamento feito amtrelles, e a geraçam conçebida do dito matrimonio e a que se comçeber declaramos ser legitima, e todallas cousas susso ditas, a nosso prodeçessor suplicadas, auer feito e comprido e outorgado, assy como dito he. E se per uentura em estas presemtes alguuma cousa desfalleçe, nos todo deffecto e myngua suplimos, como se mais compridamente contem em outras nossas leteras que sobresto mandamos faҁer.

A nenhuum, ergo, homem de todo em todo conuenhà esta letera de nosso demostramento, reduçom e asoluymento, habillitaçom e despemsaçom, comçedimento e suppleiçom da nossa vomtade quebrar, ou per samdeu atreuymento fallar o contrairo. E se per uentura alguum esto presumjsse temtar, saiba que na jra e maldiçam de Todopoderosso Deus e dos bem-auenturados apostolos Pedro e Paulo emcorera. Data, etcetera.

CXVI
Pubricaçam da segunda letera que os mesegeiros trouuerom de corte.

Acabada de leer esta letera e ouujda com muyta lediçe, fezerom callar todo aquell poboo por bem escuitar, como da primera. Emtom pubricarom outra desse mesmo Boniffaçio Papa, cujo trellado se segue:

Boniffaçio, bispo, seruo dos seruos de Deus, ao muyto amado em Christo filho, esclareçido Rey, dom Joham de Portugall e do Alguarue, ҁaude e apostollicall bemçom.

Per desposiçom da diuinall clemença per que os reis reinam e os prinçepes se asenhoram sem nosso mereçimento somos posto assy como huum claro lume sobre as gemtes dos Christaãos. E por em aas veҁes he

other cardinals, Pope Urban publicly answered the petition of that Bishop João and affirmed that he considered that King João absolved and dispensed about the aforesaid matters, as has already been said.

Now, as it is true that death then came to the said Urban, our predecessor, and the apostolic letters about these matters were not written, therefore, wishing to provide for the honour of that King João and Queen Philippa his wife and all the inhabitants of those kingdoms, although these letters about these matters had not been written in the lifetime of our predecessor, that King and Queen and the petitioners aforementioned did not lack for their effect, since everything happened thus, we hereby certify the fact for you as a permanent record.

Therefore, for greater security and safety and even greater confirmation, we absolve this King João anew, and remove from him every stain of infamy and disqualification, and we grant a dispensation to him about the aforesaid matters and to the said Queen Philippa, that they can legitimately remain in the marriage effected between them. We declare that any children conceived already or in the future from the said marriage are legitimate, and that we have dealt with, concluded and granted in the manner already stated all the aforesaid matters requested of our predecessor. And if by chance anything is lacking in this letter, we supply every defect and lack, as is more fully contained in our other letters which we order to be written about this.

Let nobody, therefore, break or through insane rashness contradict this letter of our demonstration, reduction and absolution, dispensation, removal of disqualification, concession and petition of our will. And if by chance anyone presumes to attempt this, let him know that he will incur the wrath and curse of Almighty God and of the blessed apostles Peter and Paul.

Dated, etcetera.

CXXVI
Publication of the second letter which the messengers brought from the Curia.

When this letter had been read and heard with great joy, they made all that crowd keep silence in order to listen carefully, as for the first. Then they read out another letter of that same Pope Boniface, of which the meaning was as follows:

Boniface, Bishop, servant of the servants of God, to the well beloved son in Christ, the illustrious King Dom João of Portugal and of the Algarve, health and apostolic beneiction.

By the disposition of divine clemency through which kings rule and princes govern, and without any merit of our own, we are placed as a clear light above the Christian peoples. Therefore, it is

neçesario dalguuns regnos e senhorios despoer por paz e justiça dos poboos, e exalçar os que conheçemos que som dignos e pertençentes pera reger e gouernar as gentes, delles moradores; e postos em tall dignidade, os deuemos nella conseruar e fazer fortes, por tal que julguem os poboos em jgualleza e emcamjnhem as naçoões delles, como pertemçe ao senhorio que tomarom e poderio que lhes do çeo he dado pera castigo dos maaos e gloria e louuor dos boons, de guissa que sua vomtade seia sempre em execuçom da justiça, e seu pensamento na dereita ley e guarda da sancta paz.

Assy he que na fillial petiçom, que o homrado bispo de Silues e amado Johan Rodriguez de Saa, embaxadores (teus) e dos prellados e poboos desses regnos, a nos sobresto enuiados, certamente se continha que, semdo esses regnos nos dias pasados per morte del-Rey dom Fernamdo orphaãos e vagos da real dignidade, çarramdo seu postumeiro dia sem filho legitimo que os derdar ouuesse, os ditos prellados e poboos delles, veendo como Johan Amriquez, teedor dos regnos de Castella e de Leom, seu jniusto perseguidor, emmjgo de Deus e da sua Espossa de Roma e de Vrbano da boa memoria, nosso prodeçessor, Papa, sexto; o quall como scismatico herege per semtença condenou ser punido, porque ao filho de perdiçam Ruberte, cardeal emtom chamado dos Doze Apostolos e agora per sacrilega ousadia Clemente septimo presumio de se nomear e presume, sem curando dos proçessos per nosso predeçesor contra el e seus çaquazes feitos, e como emadendo mal a malles, esse dito Johan Anriquez constrangeo de lhe obedeçer as gentes a el sogeitas, e de todo em todo esses regnos de Portugall e do Alguarue se esforçaua ocupar e possuir; a cujos peruersos cometimentos e esforços os ditos poboos e prellados proueitosamente resistir nom eram abastantes, pois de Rey defemssor perteençente resistir de todo careçiam: e reçeamdo que elles e os ditos regnos ao depois veessem a poder e tirania do dito Ioam Amriquez e obediencia desse Antipapa, em perjuizo gramde de suas almas e pessoas: que por tamto, queremdo elles proueer assy mesmos e honra e saluaçam·dos ditos regnos e contrariar a taaes danos e perigos, lhe conueo e foy forçado enleger tal homeem por seu Rey e senhor, que soubesse e podesse saudauelmente os ditos regnos reger e gouernar e com gramde ardideza emparar e defemder das forçosas maãos do dito Johan Anriquez, e recobrar os logares que ja eram de todo perdidos: e que estomçe, aderençamdo os olhos do seu entemdimento e suas çertas consiraçoões a ty, nom legitimo filho de Pedro, Rey da boa memoria de Portugall e do Alguarue, jrmaão do dito Rey dom Fernando, postumeiro Rey desses regnos, professo que emtom eras (da hordem de Callatraua no bispado d'Euora,) da ordem e regra de Cistell, Mestre da casa d'Avijs, por singular deuaçam e especial amor que em ty viam açerca de nosso prodeçessor e da santa Egreja de

sometimes necessary to dispose of some kingdoms and lordships for the peace and justice of the peoples, and to exalt those whom we know to be worthy and fit to rule and govern the nations dwelling there; and once they are placed in such a position of dignity, we ought to preserve them and strengthen them in it, so that they may judge the peoples in justice and lead their nations along the right way, as is the function of the lordship which they took and the power which has been given them from heaven for the punishment of the wicked and the glory and praise of the good, so that their will may be ever fixed in the execution of justice and their thought in the right law and the keeping of the holy peace.

It is thus that in the filial petition which the honourable Bishop of Silves and the beloved João Rodrigues de Sá sent to us as ambassadors of you and of the prelates and peoples of those kingdoms about this, it was certainly contained that, when those kingdoms were recently orphaned and lacking royal dignity through the death of King Fernando, who ended his days without any legitimate son who might inherit them, the said prelates and peoples of those kingdoms saw how Juan Enríquez, usurper of the kingdoms of Castile and León, their unjust persecutor, and the enemy of God and of his Bride of Rome and of Pope Urban VI, of happy memory, our predecessor, who passed a sentence condemning him to be punished as a schismatical heretic, this said Juan Enríquez forced all his subjects to obey the son of perdition, Robert, then Cardinal of the Twelve Apostles and now with sacrilegious boldness and presumption entitled Clement VII, without caring about the legal processes carried out against him and his followers by our predecessor, and added insult to injury, striving to occupy and possess entirely these kingdoms of Portugal and the Algarve. The said peoples and prelates were not sufficient to resist successfully his perverse attacks and assaults, because they totally lacked a king fit to resist and defend them. So, fearing that they and the said kingdoms might later fall under the dominion and tyranny of the said Juan Enríquez and be forced to obey this Antipope, to the great harm of their souls and bodies, and wishing to care for themselves and for the honour and salvation of the said kingdoms and avoid such great harm and dangers, they found it fitting and necessary to elect as their king and lord such a man as was capable of ruling and governing the said kingdoms in safety, and could with great boldness protect and defend them from the violent hands of the said Juan Enríquez, and recover the places which had already been entirely lost. Then, concentrating the gaze of their understanding and their secure consideration on you, the illegitimate son of Pedro, King of Portugal and the Algarve of happy memory, brother of the said King Fernando, last King of these realms, and professed friar as you then were of the Order of Calatrava in the bishopric of Évora, of the Order and Rule of Cîteaux and Master of the House of Avis, because of the particular devotion and special love which they saw in you towards our predecessor and the holy Church

Roma, dessy pureza de ffee e bondade darmas, pella (quall) tu e teu christianjssimo linhagem com muyto louuor auerdes esclareçido, conheçerom e conheçem per deliberado comselho e madura concordança, todos dhuum coraçam, nenhuum desto desuyando, per deuinall jnspiraçom como se piadosamente cree, guardadas as çerimonias e devidas solemnidades, canonicamente te enlegerom e tomarom por Rey dos ditos regnos, assentando-te em rreal asentamento, vestido de reaaes vestiduras, guardando todallas outras cousas em semelhante auto costumadas.

E tu, comsiramdo as ditas cousas, por paz e saude e bem desses regnos cobiçando daproueitar mais que asenhorar , na dita emliçam consentiste, açeptando estado e nome de real dignidade, leixamdo o regullar auito, — nom em desprezamento da dita hordem nem do poderio das nossas claues, mas esperamdo na benignidade da see apostollica que auerias sobresto despemssaçom; — e des entom teueste e posoisti, como ajnda tee(n)s e gouernas, esses regnos como Rey; e com a muyto amada em Christo Filipa, filha do nobre baram Johane, duque d'Allancastro, ennobreçida Rainha desses regnos, per pallauras de presente e acabado matrimonio casaste, auendo della geraçam.

E se agora leixases a dignidade, nome e homra de Rey e desemparases os ditos regnos, semdo quite e apartado della, poder-se-hiam segujr desto gramdes danos e escandallos, por em por tua parte e desses prellados e poboos ja ditos humjldosamente nos foy suplicado que de benignidade apostollicall teuessemos por bem a ty sobresto prouer de benefiçio dasolujmento e de conueniente graça de despemsaçam.

E nos, que de todollos fiees christaãos, segundo obrigado somos, paz das almas e corpos desejamos, cobiçando saudauelmente aa homra de teu estado e deses regnos prouer, e aos ditos scandallos, quanto com Deus podemos, resistir, e querendo temperar o rigor dos santos canones per huuma piadosa despensaçom, assy como os Papas, nossos prodeçessores, per diuinall poder dotados, virtuosamente acostumarom, mouendo-os a ello justas e euidentes causas, moyormente açerca das pessoas esplandeçentes per linhagem e alteza dhomroso estado; desy consirando que tu, com a ajuda do muy alto Deus, per tua prudençia e vallentia darmas, liuraste os ditos regnos das maãos desse Joham Anriquez, teendo-(o)s pella mayor parte ocupados, cobrando os logares que em seu poder tinha, os quaaes se allegram por serem tornados a sua antiga liberdade, e delle, perseguidor de Deus e nosso e da sua sancta Egreja, vitoria e trihumpho per diuinall graça perpetraste; auendo sobresto com nossos jrmaãos assaz de fallamento per sollempne deliberaçam, aas tuas supplicações enclinados, e sguardando a gram deuaçam que a nos e aa dita Egreja sempre ouueste, de conselho delles todos a tua pessoas e teu preclaro e real linhagem e os herdeiros de ty lidimamente descemdentes determynamos dhomrar, e per speçiaaes graças e fauores quaaes a ty conuenham proseguir.

324

of Rome, as well as purity of faith and goodness in arms, whereby you and they know through careful consultation and mature agreement, unanimously, with no dissenting voices, and by divine inspiration as is piously believed, and fulfilling the ceremonies and due solemnities, they elected you canonically and took you as King of these realms, seating you on the royal throne, garbed in royal robes, and observing all the details customary in such a ceremony.

Considering these matters and desiring to benefit these kingdoms through peace and health and goodness rather than to lord it over them, you consented to this election, accepting the status and name of the royal dignity, renouncing the habit of your religious Order. You did not do this out of contempt for that Order nor for the power of our keys, but hoping in the benignity of the Apostolic See that you might obtain a dispensation for this. Thenceforward you held and possessed these kingdoms as their king, as you still hold and govern them; you married our well beloved daughter in Christ, Philippa, the daughter of the noble baron John Duke of Lancaster, and Queen of those kingdoms, with a real wedding; and you consummated the marriage and had children from it.

If now you were to renounce the dignity, name and honour of king and remove your protection from the said kingdoms, and were to be quite set apart from all that, great harm and scandals could follow from this; and therefore you and these prelates and peoples already mentioned have humbly petitioned us that with apostolic benignity we should deign to provide you with the benefit of absolution and of the appropriate favour of a dispensation.

We are obliged to desire the peace of souls and bodies of all faithful Christians, and we do wish rightly to provide for the honour of your own status and that of those kingdoms, and to resist the aforementioned scandals, as far as we can do so without disobeying God. We also wish to temper the rigour of the holy canons through a compassionate dispensation, just as our predecessors the Popes endowed with divine power were virtuously accustomed to do, under the stimulus of just and obvious reasons, especially concerning persons distinguished by their lineage and their high and honourable social status. So, considering that with the help of the Most High God and through your own prudence and military courage, you freed the aforesaid kingdoms from the hands of that Juan Enríquez, who had occupied most of them; and that you recovered the places which he had in his power and which rejoice in having returned to their old freedom; and that by God's grace you achieved victory and triumph over that persecutor of God, of us, and of His Holy Church, we discussed this with our brothers in a solemn deliberation. Being inclined to your petitions and remembering the great devotion which you always showed toward us and the said Church, on the advice of all of them we decided to honour your person, and your illustrious and royal lineage and your heir legitimately descended from you, and to grant the special graces and favours which are appropriate for you.

E por tamto a louuor do poderoso Deus Padre e Filho e Spritu Sancto e da sempre Virgem gloriosa Maria e dos bemauenturados apostolos Pedro e Paulo, e homra e boom estado da sancta sagrada Egreja, nossa espossa, semdo em esta parte emclinados aas tuas petiçoões e dos nobres e prellados e poboos deses regnos, per nossa apostollicall autoridade e theor destas presentes te absoluemos de todas semtenças descomunhoões e doutras quaaesquer penas per homem ou per dereito pronunçiadas, posto que taaes semtenças seiam per apostollicos s(c)pritos decernydas, se per uentura por as ditas razoões em algumas dellas emcoreste; as quaaes queremos aquy auer por soffiçientemente expressas.

E ajmda te absoluemos e liuramos de toda obrigaçom e legamento de uoto dobedieuçia, castidade e pobreza, e profissam e obseruamça regullar, em que aa dita hordem per quallquer modo theudo e obrigado fosses, posto que de guardar todos ou cada huum delles juramento fezesses; e jsso mesmo de todo perjuizo e magoa dinfamya e jnhabilidade que por as ditas razoões ou outras alguumas teuesses.

E mais te legitimamos e restituimos a llegitimo naçimento e te habilitamos, despemsamdo contigo que, nom embargando as ditas cousas e o ffally-mento de tua naçemça, semdo geerado do dito Rey dom Pedro e dhuma molher que per matrimonio nom era a el com junta, posto que esse teu padre e madre cada huum fosse casado no tempo do comçebimento e naçemça.

E posto ajmda que no tempo da tua emliçom e aceptaçom e comsentimento fosses professo desa hordem e Mestre da dita casa, e legado per semtenças e pennas, e jnhabillitado per magoa dinfamia, e depois casasses com essa Rainha Fillipa; e posto outrossy que em alguuma maneira obedeçesses e desses conselho, ajuda ou fauor a Roberte Antipapa e Joham Amriquez sobreditos, e nom embargando quaaesquer constituçoões, assy apostolicas como lex jmperiaaes, estatutos e costumes, per alguum modo esto comtradizentes, outorgamos que a enliçom, assumpçom, açeptaçom, consentimento, e todallas cousas que se desto seguirom, compridamente valham e sejam firmes pera sempre; e tu possas teer e posuir os ditos regnos e dignidade e nome e homras de Rey, e de nouo possas seer enlegido a quaaesquer outros regnos, dignidades, homras e senhorios, e os posas açeptar e em elles consentir tomar e posoir e trespasar a teus herdeiros lidemos desçendentes, assy nados como por naçer, e outros collateraaes e quaaesquer estranhos per testamento ou ab intestado, e que possas viuer e estar no dito casamento feito com essa Rainha Phillipa.

E se aconteçesse fazer Deus outra cousa da sua pessoa, que possas liçitamente, cada uez que tal caso aueer, com quaaesquer outras molheres, nom temdo embargo de lidemos jmpedimentos, casar e em tal casamento liuremente viuer como homem de todo jssento e liure e limpo de quallquer

Therefore, in praise of the powerful God the Father and the Son and the Holy Spirit, and of the glorious Mary, ever Virgin, and of the blessed apostles Peter and Paul, and of the honour and good status of the Holy and Sacred Church, our Bride, and being in this matter inclined to your petitions and those of the nobles and prelates and peoples of those kingdoms, by our apostolic authority and the substance of the present letters, we absolve you from all sentences of excommunication and any other punishments pronounced by man or by the law, even though such sentences may be decreed in apostolic documents, should you by chance have incurred any of them for the aforesaid reasons; and we wish this mention here to be sufficient mention of them.

Moreover we absolve you and free you from all obligation and constraint of your vows of poverty, chastity and obedience, and of regular profession and observance, by which you were held to the said Order in any way, even if you swore an oath to keep all, or any one, of them; and we similarly free you from all prejudice and stain of infamy and disqualification which you may bear for the aforesaid, or any other, reasons.

Moreover we legitimize you and restore your birth to legitimate status and remove your disqualifications, granting you a dispensation, despite these matters and the defect of your birth, that is, that you are the son of King Pedro and of a woman who was not married to him, even though your father and mother were each married to someone else at the time of your conception and birth.

Moreover, although at the time of your election and your acceptance and agreement you were a professed friar of that Order and Master of the said House in it, and subject to sentences and punishments, and disqualified by the stain of infamy, and afterwards you married that Queen Philippa, and although you obeyed and advised, helped and favoured to a certain extent the Antipope Robert and Juan Enríquez the aforementioned, despite certain apostolic constitutions, imperial laws, and statutes and customs which forbade this, to a certain extent, nevertheless we grant that the election, accession, acceptance, consent and all their other consequences shall all be fully valid and confirmed forever. You can keep and possess the said kingdoms and the royal title, dignity and honours, and can be furthermore elected to any other kingdoms, dignities, honours and lordships. You may accept, take and possess them and leave them to your legitimate descendants as your heirs, whether already born or to be born in the future, and to other collateral heirs or even outsiders through your testament or even if you die intestate; and you can live and continue in this marriage which you have contracted with that Queen Philippa.

And if God should choose to do something else with her person, you can licitly marry any other woman, unless there are legitimate impediments, whenever such an eventuality may arise, and live in such a marriage freely, as a man totally exempt and free and clean of any

magoa; soplimdo per nossa pastorall autoridade e apostolico poderio todo fallimento, se alguum per uentuira antreueo , assy da tua parte como dos prellados e clereȝia e fidalgos e poboos em todo o que dito he. E por tanto *nom se atreua nenhuum per alguum modo esta carta de nossa absolluçom, exempçom, liuredom, restituiçom, abillitaçom, despensaçom, conçessom, supplimento quebrantar, ou per sandia ousamça comtradiȝer. E se alguum esto presumir tentar, saiba que na jra do Todopoderoso Deus e dos bemauenturados apostollos Pedro e Paulo emcorera. Dat. etcetera.*

As leteras pubricadas no modo que dizemos, foy feito huum gramde rumor amtre a multidom daquell poboo, fallamdo naquella errada oppiniom que ante desto muytos afirmauom; e çessada sua falla de todo, aquel Louremçeannes Fogaça, para el-Rey seu senhor, e o homrado Joham Domynguez, thesoureiro dessa egreja, por parte do cabido della, e Fernamdauluarez, procurador da çidade, em nome de todollos moradores, pedirom a Joham Rodriguez, pubrico notairo que presente estaua, que lhe desse o trellado da guissa que o dereito quer; e assy lhe foram dados.

Hora esguardem vossas ensinanças per esto que temdes ouujdo, como aquell estoriador depois de tamtos annos foy ousado dizer taaes razões por fortifficar sua defamaçom; as quaaes por serem de todo nenhuumas careçem dauer ffee; porque homde a uerdade he çerta e clara, quallquer coussa que se em contrairo diz bem proçede de famtastico sisso ou peruersa e maliçiosa vomtade.

With Gaunt's departure from the Peninsula, many Portuguese return home from Castile, where they have either been prisoners or have fought on the Trastamaran side. Among them is Inês de Castro's younger son, Prince Dinis, who is at once sent by João I as an envoy to England. Fernão Lopes describes his journey there so inaccurately as to discredit him and present João I in a favourable light (CXXVII–CXXX).

Meanwhile, despite the agreement of Bayonne, hostilities continue between Portugal and Castile, with Nun'Alvares skirmishing successfully against Juan I's Gascon auxiliaries in Extremadura. João campaigns in the Minho valley in the winter of 1387–88, and captures Melgaço; then he goes south to the Extremaduran frontier, where he accepts the surrender of Castilian–held Campo Maior in December 1388; and in the following summer he besieges and captures Tuy (CXXXI–CXL).

On 29 December 1389, Castile and Portugal sign a truce whereby João I relinquishes Tuy and Salvaterra, in return for

stain. With our pastoral and apostolic authority we compensate for any defect should any such by chance arise, either on your part or on that of the prelates, clerics, nobles and peoples in all that has been said. Therefore let no one dare to break or through insane rashness in any way contradict this letter of our absolution, exemption, liberation, restitution, removal of disqualification, dispensation, concession, and petition. And if anyone should presume to attempt this, let him know that he will incur the wrath of Almighty God and of the blessed apostles Peter and Paul.

Dated, etcetera.

When the letters had been read out in the way we have explained, there went up a great noise among that multitude of people, as they spoke of that mistaken opinion which many had affirmed before this. When their talking had quite ceased, that Lourenço Eanes Fogaça, on behalf of his lord the King, the honourable João Domingues, treasurer of that church, on behalf of its chapter, and Fernando Alvares, proctor of the city, in the name of all its inhabitants, begged João Rodrigues, the public notary who was present, to give them an authorized copy of the sort that is valid in law; and so these were given.

Now take a lesson from what you have just heard, how that historian, after many years, dared to state such arguments in order to support his calumnies, arguments which are totally null and void and therefore undeserving of credence. For where the truth is certain and clear, anything that may be said to contradict it surely derives either from a fanciful imagination or from some perverse and spiteful motive.

Mértola and so many other towns that in the Cortes of Guadalajara (1390) Juan I is criticized for conceding too much to Portugal. Still determined on revenge for Aljubarrota, he explains how he plans to become King of Portugal by renouncing the Castilian throne in favour of his son Enrique; but his Cortes advises against this, pointing out that the plan involves a partition of his kingdom, a device which has always been fatal in Castile, and that if he renounces the Castilian throne he cannot expect support from his vassals in Vizcaya and elsewhere. Moreover, Enrique is barely eleven years of age and a regency at this time is inopportune. The Cortes also advises King Juan to abandon plans to gather funds for a fresh invasion of Portugal. In fact, all his ambitions are ended when he is killed, falling from a horse.

On receiving news of Juan I's death, João I is advised to take advantage of the minority of the new king of Castile, Enrique III, to invade his kingdom; but he is determined to honour the truce which he made with the latter's father (CXLI−CXLVII).

Fernão Lopes now describes João I's children, beginning with those he had by his mistress, Dona Inês: Afonso, later Count of Barcelos and Duke of Bragança, who was to be a leader in the civil war of the 1430s and 1440s; and Beatriz, who would marry the Earl of Arundel. Next are listed João's children by Queen Philippa: Princess Branca, who died at eight months; Prince Afonso, who lived only twelve years; the future King Duarte; Prince Pedro, later Duke of Coimbra and another leader in the civil wars; Prince Henrique, 'the Navigator'; Princess Isabel, who later became Duchess of Burgundy as wife of Duke Philip the Good; Prince João, a future Master of the Order of São Tiago; and finally, Prince Fernando, a future Master of Avis, whom Fernão Lopes served for so many years as private secretary, and who finally died in Africa. Lopes's description of all these princes is, naturally, a panegyric, especially of their exemplary behaviour towards their father; and he presents them all as paragons of filial love and duty (CXLVIII–CXLIX).

He now describes a new truce between Portugal and Castile, signed on 15 May 1393 and intended to last for fifteen years. However, the non–fulfilment of its clauses soon provokes further hostilities, in which the Portuguese capture Badajoz through the treachery of a gate–keeper (CLII–CLVII). João I then tries to use Badajoz as a bargaining–counter, but Castilian forces continue to raid central Portugal, burning Viseu and other places. The Constable replies with two sorties into the districts of Cáceres and Badajoz, during the second of which the Castilians consistently refuse to meet him in open battle (CLVIII–CLXVII).

In May of 1398 João I assembles an army in Ponte de Lima, besieges Tuy and captures it in July. Prince Dinis now returns to Portugal, calling himself King (since his brother Prince João has died), but his support melts away at the news of the Comdestabre's approach and he is forced to return to Castile (CLXVIII–CLXXIV).

After some more skirmishing and another abortive attempt at an agreement, Enrique III of Castile, mindful of the fact that the wars have deprived him of Badajoz and Tuy, persuades King João to try to make peace through their joint establishment of a five–man council, including Nun'Álvares and the Bishop of Coimbra. This council meets at Olivenza in February 1399, but the Portuguese reject the Castilian proposals as too excessive (CLXXV–CLXXXII). Hostilities are resumed, Dom João besieges Alcántara (1401) without success and the Constable ravages Western Extremadura. Meanwhile, in 1402 Portuguese ambassadors travel to Segovia in a further attempt at peace, but find that Enrique III is demanding a very high price: the return of Badajoz; an indemnity of 700 gold francs and 40,000 dobras every year during the lifetimes of Enrique III and of his daughter, María; the use of ten armed galleys for six months in every year and one thousand men–at–arms under the same conditions; and the obligation on the King of Portugal in person to join Castile whenever it fights against the Muslims. Moreover, the

King of Castile will renounce his claim to the Portuguese throne as King Fernando's closest relative only if Dom João pays him a sum of money similar to that which his father, Juan I, had paid to the Duke and Duchess of Lancaster. To this last, the Portuguese ambassadors reply that the two cases are not comparable, for whereas the Duke had a legitimate claim to the throne of Castile through his wife Constanza, daughter of Pedro I, the King of Castile has no such claim to the Portuguese throne and therefore his arguments are outrageous. So the talks on a permanent peace break down. They eventually settle for a truce to date from 1402 to 1413 (CLXXXIII–CLXXXVII).

Fernão Lopes relates the background to the permanent peace that is being prepared. He notes how Queen Catherine, John of Gaunt's daughter, tries to persuade her husband, Enrique III, to make a permanent peace with Portugal; and how on Enrique's death Catherine, as joint regent with Enrique's brother Fernando, is able to arrange a peace conference near San Felices de los Gallegos in 1407, though the conference breaks up after mutual recriminations (CLXXXVIII–CXC).

Queen Catherine now takes an active role, offering a peace on certain conditions. At first, João I refuses to have anything to do with it but, as a sign of goodwill and friendship, eventually consents to send ambassadors again to Castile. During this visit, the Castilians continue to insist on a peace with conditions and the Portuguese ambassadors on an unconditional peace. At this juncture, having spoken with the Portuguese ambassadors, Queen Catherine again intervenes crucially, persuading the Castilian Council and her brother–in–law, Prince Fernando, to accept an unconditional peace. Fernão Lopes describes briefly what he calls this boa e simplez paz por sempre (good and unconditional peace forever) in which the only real conditions are that the King of Portugal shall make restitution to and pardon all Portuguese living in Castile who have sided with Queen Beatriz in the civil war, and the Castilian King shall do likewise for all those in Portugal who have goods in Castile. All Portuguese and Castilians who were in one another's countries when the war began will have their goods returned to them or be indemnified for their loss (CXCI–CXCV). The treaty is signed on 31 October 1411, although there are fears that when the young King of Castile reaches fourteen years of age, he may object to certain parts of the peace agreement. This in fact is what happens, for Juan II refuses to sign (1420), and only three years later does the peace finally satisfy him enough for him to approve it entirely; and even then, not forever. Not until 1431 does this happen, at which time, Lopes declares that "thus did the war entirely come to an end" (CXCVI).

The concluding chapters tell of various happenings occurring in the early years of the fifteenth century before and after the peace of 1411 but which are related by Fernão Lopes with no clear

chronology: campaigns against the Muslims of Granada; more importantly an abortive attempt by Queen Catherine to marry her daughter Princess Catalina to Prince Duarte, the heir to the Portuguese throne, in order, as Lopes sees it, to secure a permanent peace thereby; an equally abortive attempt by Dom João to marry his daughter Isabel (afterwards Duchess of Burgundy) to Juan II of Castile; certain doings of Nun'Álvares during these later Castilian wars at a time when the years, Fernão Lopes observes, have given him wisdom as they did, so it is related, "to Diego López Pacheco and others like him that one could name"; and similar doings in time of peace and how he and Dom João worked together to ensure peace and justice in the kingdom.

Finally, Fernão Lopes records the marriages of João I's two illegitimate children, that of his son Dom Afonso to the Constable's daughter Beatriz, and that of his daughter Beatriz to Thomas Fitzalan, Earl of Arundel, in 1405 (CXCVII—CCII).

NOTES

334

NOTES TO THE INTRODUCTION

1.　　All the works mentioned in this paragraph were published by A. Herculano in *Portugaliae Monumenta Historica*. *Scriptores* (Lisbon, 1856), with the exception of the *Crónica Geral de Espanha de 1344*, edited by L.F. Lindley Cintra, 3 vols (Lisbon, 1951—61).

2.　　For a discussion of this vexed question, see Nathan Adams, *Fernão Lopes, Late Medieval Portuguese Chronicler* (Michigan: University Microfilms International, 1955), pp. 96—115. To this book we also owe our quotations from documents relating to the career of Fernão Lopes.

3.　　*Dom João*, II, XIV. Henceforth, when quoting from the Chronicle in this introduction, we shall refer to the three chronicles in the main as *Dom Pedro*, *Dom Fernando* and *Dom João*, I and II.

4.　　P.E. Russell, *As fontes de Fernão Lopes* (Coimbra, 1941), pp. 16—43. For an excellent study and a more critical analysis of these last two sources, see Adams, pp. 349—58. For Ayala, see also Michel Garcia, *Obra y personalidad del Canciller Ayala* (Madrid, 1983).

5.　　M. McKisack, *The Fourteenth Century, 1307—1399* (Oxford, 1959), chapters 4, 5 and 9, and especially pp. 245—50; C.T. Allmand, ed. *Society at War* (Edinburgh, 1973), especially chapter 3.

6.　　A. MacKay, *Spain in the Middle Ages. From Frontier to Empire, 1000—1500* (London, 1977) especially chapter 6; J.F. O'Callaghan, *A History of Medieval Spain* (Ithaca—London, 1975), especially pp. 330—486, 523—34; R. Menéndez Pidal, ed. *Historia de España. Tomo XIV* (Madrid, 1966), pp. 3—285; J.B. Sitges, *Las mujeres del rey don Pedro* (Madrid, 1910), *passim*; P.E. Russell, *The English Intervention in Spain and Portugal in the Reigns of Edward III and Richard II* (Oxford, 1955), *passim*.

7.　　MacKay, p. 121.

8.　　J. Valdeón Baruque, *Enrique II de Castilla: la guerra civil y la consolidación del régimen* (Valladolid, 1966), *passim*.

9.　　L. Suárez Fernández, *Navegación y comercio en el golfo de Vizcaya* (Madrid, 1959), pp. 9—71.

10.　　Russell, *The English Intervention, passim*; S. Armitage—Smith, *John of Gaunt* (Westminster, 1904), especially pp. 92—102.

11.　　L. Suárez Fernández, *Castilla, el Cisma y la crisis conciliar (1378—1440)* (Madrid, 1960), especially, pp. 3—23.

12.　　Russell, *The English Intervention, passim.*; L. Suárez Fernández, *Historia del reinado de Juan I de Castilla, Tomo I* (Madrid, 1977), especially pp. 93—308; A.H. de Oliveira Marques, *History of Portugal*, Vol. I (New York & London, 1972), chapter 2; H. Livermore, *History of Portugal* (Cambridge, 1947), pp. 161—83; Jaime Cortesão, *Os factores democráticos na formação de Portugal*

(Lisbon, 1964), especially pp. 111–117; A.J. Saraiva, *A cultura em Portugal: Teoria e História*, 2 vols (Lisbon, 1981), especially volume I.

13.   F. de Rades y Andrada, *Crónica de las tres órdenes de Santiago, Calatrava y Alcántara* (Toledo, 1572; reprinted Barcelona, 1980), *passim*.

14.   McKisack, *op.cit.*, pp. 397–498.

15.   Beryl Smalley, *Historians in the Middle Ages* (London, 1974), p. 67.

16.   William J. Brandt, *The Shape of Medieval History: Studies in Modes of Perception* (New Haven and London, 1966), p. 51.

17.   *Ibid.*, p. 88.

18.   Maria Lúcia Perrone de Faro Passos, *O héroi na Crónica de D. João I, de Fernão Lopes* (Lisbon, 1974), pp. 177–86.

19.   A.J. Saraiva, *Fernão Lopes* (Lisbon, n.d.), p. 47.

20.   P.E. Russell, *The English Intervention*, pp. 466–67.

21.   Nicholas G. Round, 'The Revolution of 1383–84 in the Portuguese Provinces: Causality and Style in Fernão Lopes', *Dispositio*, 10 (Nr. 27), 70.

22.   João Mendes, *Literatura Portuguesa*, 4 vols (Lisbon, 1974), I, 88–90.

23.   J.H. Saraiva, introduction to Fernão Lopes, *História de uma revolução: Primeira Parte da "Crónica de El–Rei D. João de Boa Memória"* (Lisbon, 1977), p. 9.

24.   *Ibid.*, p. 12.

25.   Round, pp. 81–82.   This article is a close reading, one of the very few ever attempted, of five chapters of *Dom João, Part I* (XLII–XLVI) in which Lopes describes provincial risings in 1383.

26.   Luís de Sousa Rebelo, *A Concepção do Poder em Fernão Lopes* (Lisbon, 1983), especially pp. 57–89; see also his fine article, 'The Idea of Kingship in the chronicles of Fernão Lopes', in *Medieval and Renaissance Studies on Spain and Portugal in Honour of P.E. Russell*, edited by F.W. Hodcroft et al. (Oxford, 1981), pp. 167–79, which complements this profound study of messianism and millenarianism in the *Crónica*.

27.   Rebelo, *O poder*, p. 23.

28.   J.H. Saraiva, pp. 12–25.

29.   A.J. Saraiva, *Fernão Lopes*, p. 33.

30.   Adams, p. 91.

31.   *Fernão Lopes*, p. 16.

32.   Joaquim Veríssimo Serrão, 'Fernão Lopes', in his *A Historiografia Portuguesa: Doutrina e Crítica*, 3 vols (Lisbon, 1972), I, 62–64.

33.   A. Borges Coelho, introduction to *Crónica de Dom Pedro* (Lisbon, 1967), pp. 28–38.

34.   Mendes, pp. 93–117.   See also Rebelo, 'The Idea of Kingship', for a more detailed analysis of the role of Justice as well

as a survey of the other ethical, moral and political themes that structure the Chronicle.

35. Ricardo Arias y Arias, *El concepto del destino en la literatura medieval española* (Madrid, 1970), pp. 202–3.

36. *Ibid.*, pp. 43–44.

37. As demonstrated by Anthony Goodman, 'England and Portugal 1386–1986: John of Gaunt – Portugal's Kingmaker', *History Today* (June, 1986), pp. 17–21.

38. Benoît Lacroix, *L'Historien au Moyen Âge* (Paris, 1971), pp. 133–46.

39. *Ibid.*, pp. 160–67.

NOTES
THE CHRONICLE OF DOM FERNANDO

Chapter III: 1.   On 1 August 1366.

2.   Joan of Kent, Princess of Wales, wife of the Black Prince.

3.   A Derbyshire knight who fought at Sluys, Crécy, Poitiers and other battles against the French, was Constable of Aquitaine, and died (1370) after being mortally wounded at the battle of Lussac.

4.   King Pedro's three daughters by María de Padilla were Beatriz, who died in late 1366 or early 1367, Constanza and Isabel.

5.   Carlos II, 'the Bad', King of Navarre (1349—87) constantly played off the English against the French in the Hundred Years' War.

Chapter IV: 1.   Martín   Enríquez   de   Lacarra   was   the standard—bearer and leader of the Navarrese army.

2.   Sir Olivier de Mauny was a Breton knight, companion and nephew or cousin of Bertrand du Guesclin, and lord of Lesnons.

3.   Sir Bertrand du Guesclin (c.1320—1380), a Breton knighted in 1357, who served the kings of France against Edward III, and was rewarded with the County of Longueville (c.1364). He led the Great Companies which placed Enrique de Trastámara on the Castilian throne in 1366, and again in 1369; then he returned to become Constable of France (1370) and to defend the Valois against the English until his death. The surname Claquin mentioned in this chapter was claimed to be derived from a mythical Moslem ancestor.

4.   Gavray, near Coutances in Normandy, belonged, like many northern French towns, to the Evreux dynasty which ruled Navarre from 1328 to 1512.

5.   Pedro, Count of Mortain, was a baby, born in 1366.

Chapter V: 1.   Alfonso de Villena, Count of Ribagorza and of Denia, was the son of Prince Pedro, the son of King Jaime II of Aragon (1291—1327).

2.   Juan Martínez de Luna.

3.   Pedro Jordán de Urriés was an important financial official (*mayordomo*) of King Pedro IV of Aragon (1336—87).

4.   Arnoul d'Audrehem (c.1300—71) was the son of the lord of Audrehem village, and du Guesclin's friend and protector. He fought against the English in France, Scotland and Spain, and was Marshal of France from 1351. Though captured at Poitiers (1356) and released on promise of a ransom, he had not paid it, though he had been able to help finance the expedition which placed Enrique de Trastámara on the Castilian throne in 1366. This led to the quarrel with the Black Prince described below in Chapter X.

5.   Pierre de Vilaines, nicknamed 'the Stutterer', came from Beauce and fought in many battles against the English. He helped make Enrique II King of Castile (1366), and to defeat and kill King

Pedro (1369), and he was rewarded with the County of Ribadeo. In France he was Chamberlain of the Duke of Normandy (1362) and of King Charles VI (1380), and ambassador to Castile (1390), before being disgraced and imprisoned in the coup d'état of 1392.

6.   Gonzalo Mejía, Enrique II's appointee as Master of Santiago (1366–70), had been left to guard Seville with Juan Alfonso de Guzmán, a distant cousin of Enrique's mother.

7.   The Order of the Sash was an order of chivalry founded by Alfonso XI, in an attempt to use Arthurian traditions and those of the military orders to inspire the Castilian nobles and unite them under his leadership.

8.   The Castilian chronicler, whose writings Fernão Lopes here follows closely.

9.   Sancho, Count of Albuquerque, was, like his brother Enrique II, a son of Alfonso XI and Leonor de Guzmán.

10.   Pedro Manrique had been *adelantado mayor de Castilla*, that is, head of the royal administration in Old Castile since 1363, under Pedro I; and like many others had changed sides without losing his post.

11.   Juan Rodríguez Sarmiento.

12.   Tello, Count of Vizcaya and Lord of Lara, was another son of Alfonso XI and Leonor de Guzmán.

13.   The head of the military order of St John, or Hospitallers, in Castile was the Grand Prior of Castile. The post was nominally held in 1355–69 by the Aragonese Juan Fernández de Heredia but, distrusting him, King Pedro appointed Gómez Pérez de Porras instead. Porras, left behind by Pedro in 1366, defended Galicia for two months against Enrique, and then changed sides and helped the latter besiege Zamora.

14.   Pedro Muñiz de Godoy was Enrique II's nominee as Master of Calatrava and was recognized in Aragon, whereas Diego García de Padilla was Pedro's nominee, accepted in Castile (1354–68). Padilla joined Enrique in 1366, rejoined Pedro in 1367, and died in 1368. Godoy survived as Master of Calatrava until 1383, when he became Master of Santiago, dying at Aljubarrota (1385).

15.   Fernando Osórez was the Grand Commander of Leon in the Order of Santiago until 1370, when he succeeded his uncle, Gonzalo Mejía, as Master of Santiago (1370–83).

16.   Pedro Rodríguez de Sandoval was Grand Commander of Castile in the Order of Santiago.

17.   Alfonso Enríquez, Count of Noreña (c.1355–c.1400) was Enrique II's illegitimate son by Elvira Iñiguez de la Vega. On his career, see J. Uría, 'El conde Don Alfonso', *Asturiensia Medievalia* 2 (1975), 177–237.

18.   Iñigo López de Orozco had been the steward of Pedro I's household in 1351; and in 1366, as governor of Alfaro, he had surrendered this town to Enrique, thus not merely changing sides but giving the rebel his first foothold in Castile. Presumably this explains

Pedro's particular desire for vengeance on him.

19.   Ambrogio Boccanegra was a member of the Genoese family which Alfonso XI had persuaded to settle in Castile and reorganize his navy.   He was to defeat the English at La Rochelle (1372), and blockade Lisbon (1373) before dying, probably later in 1373.

Chapter VI: 1.   Sir Robert Knollys was a Cheshire knight who fought in Britanny (1346), and alongside Duke Henry of Lancaster (1357).   He died in Norfolk in 1407.

2.   Sir Hugh Calveley, from Lea in Cheshire, and possibly Knollys's half−brother, fought in the French wars from 1351 onwards as one of the leaders of the Free Companies, before retiring and dying in 1393.

3.   Olivier IV, Lord of Clisson, near Nantes (1336−1407), was another of the Breton knights fighting against the English at the side of du Guesclin, whom he succeeded as Constable of France in 1380.

4.   Jean I, Count of Armagnac (1311−73), fought in Italy (1333−34) and then in the Hundred Years' War, mainly for the Valois, then (c.1363−68) for the Plantagenets.   Eventually he became a loyal ally of Charles V.

5.   Armand Armanieu succeeded his father as Lord of Albret (1358) and fought alternately for the Valois and the Plantagenets until 1368 when he definitively joined Charles V.

6.   Guillaume Amanieu de Maduilhan, Lord of Rauzan, near Libourne, fought under the Black Prince at Poitiers and Nájera, and remained loyal to the English side in the subsequent wars.

7.   The 'King of Naples' was Jaume 'IV' of Majorca, son and heir of King Jaume III, whose kingdom of Majorca had been annexed by Pedro IV of Aragon in 1343.   In 1362 his son Jaume 'IV' escaped from captivity in Barcelona and married Queen Giovanna I of Naples (1343−82), thus acquiring the title of 'King of Naples'.   He spent the rest of his life until his death (1375) in adventures aimed at defeating his enemy Pedro IV and recovering his father's kingdom.

8.   As the map shows, there were two roads from Pamplona to Burgos, the southern one through Logroño, traditionally followed by pilgrims to Santiago, and the northern one, more mountainous, through Vitoria.   When King Enrique camped at Santo Domingo de la Calzada to block the southern road (in February 1367), the Black Prince marched from Pamplona along the northern road, as far as Ariñez.   Enrique dashed north to confront him, and took up an impregnable position near Añastro.   With the northern road blocked, the Black Prince decided to rejoin the southern road by marching south, probably via Santa Cruz de Campezo.   He reached Logroño by 1 April, only to discover that Enrique had also dashed south and was now trying to block the southern road at Nájera.

9.   The hill was near Ariñez, and the Englishmen led by Sir William Felton.

10.   The hill of San Román is about two miles west of

Logroño.

Chapter VIII: 1.   This letter is a standard piece of Trastamaran propaganda portraying Pedro I as a cruel tyrant.   Popular versions of the same can be seen in the anti–Pedro songs of the period, some of which are published by Roger Wright, *Spanish Ballads* (Warminster, 1987), nos. 54–58; and such ballads are discussed by W.J. Entwistle, 'The *Romancero del Rey Don Pedro* in Ayala and the *Cuarta Crónica General*', *Modern Language Review*, 23(1930), 306–26.

Chapter IX: 1.   Santisteban del Puerto in the province of Jaén.
2.   Fernão Lopes's Orozco is a misreading of Ayala, who gives the name as Sancho Sánchez de Moscoso, Grand Commander of Santiago.
3.   The true date of the battle was 3 April 1367, which was the Saturday before Passion Sunday.   Fernão Lopes has misread López de Ayala's words 'La batalla fue sabado antes del domingo de Lazaro en tres dias de abril', conceivably using a manuscript in which 'tres' was written 'III' and misreading it as 'VI'.

Chapter XII: 1.   The great Cistercian nunnery and royal pantheon, two kilometers west of Burgos, founded by Alfonso VIII (c.1186), and still flourishing today.
2.   The cathedral of Burgos.

Chapter XIII: 1.   A Genoese sailor and brother of the famous Doge of Genoa Simone Boccanegra, Egidio defeated the Moors at the River Salado (1340), became Grand Admiral of Castile, helped Alfonso XI besiege and capture Algeciras (1344) and served him and Pedro I until he joined Enrique de Trastámara in 1366.
2.   Martín López de Córdoba was perhaps Pedro I's most loyal vassal, and served him as Master of Alcántara and of Calatrava. After Pedro's death he held Carmona against Enrique II until captured and killed by treachery.
3.   Mohammed V (1354–59, 1362–91), an ally of King Pedro.
4.   Her real name was Urraca.
5.   Martín Yáñez de Aponte was Pedro's treasurer (1360–66).
6.   Mateo Fernández de Cáceres was Pedro's Chancellor of the Privy Seal from 1361 to at least 1368.
7.   There seems no other evidence of these embassies.

Chapter LXVII: 1.   Juan Fernández Andeiro was a Galician knight who married well; and after Pedro I's death at Montiel (1369), he fled, like many other *petristas* to Portugal and then (1371) to England, where be became a dependant of John of Gaunt.   He arranged the Anglo–Portuguese treaties of alliance of 1373 and 1380, and returned to Portugal in 1380 as Queen Leonor's lover, King Fernando's adviser and effective controller of Portuguese foreign

policy. He now directed this towards friendship with Castile and arranged for Juan I of Castile to marry Fernando's daughter Beatriz and to rule Portugal after Fernando's death (See the summary of the final chapters of the *Chronicle of Dom Fernando*). When Fernando did die, however, a popular rebellion overthrew the pro−Castilian government and Andeiro, now Count of Ourém, was assassinated by João of Avis (See the summary of the opening chapters of the *Chronicle of Dom João, Part I*).

2. Gaunt appointed his squire Roger Hore and Andeiro as his proctors in a document dated Hertford, 1 March 1372, and published by Russell, pp. 559−61.

3. The treaty, agreed in the church of São Salvador de Tagilde, near Guimarães, on 10 July 1372, is published by Russell, pp. 557−61. Obviously the copy kept by King Fernando and read by Lopes was the one signed by Gaunt in the Savoy Palace. In Gaunt's royal title the kingdom after *Córdoba* should be *Murcia*, instead of Lopes's mis−read *Molina*.

4. According to Russell, p. 196, his letter of proxy was issued by Fernando on 21 November 1372; he remained constantly on the Anglophile, and later Urbanist, side in Portuguese politics.

Chapter LXVIII: 1. Diego López Pacheco (1304−?) was a Galician nobleman who began his long and adventurous career as counsellor at the court of Afonso IV of Portugal. He rose to become Chancellor like his father, Lope Fernández Pacheco before him. Suspected of having had a hand in the death of Inés de Castro, he fled the Court when Dom Pedro came to the throne. Historians have more recently exonerated him from all blame. Unfortunately, the poor man remains lumped together with the real assassins in the most famous account of the death of Inés in *The Lusiads* of Camões (Canto III) as a black−hearted villain. Fernão Lopes records King Pedro's 'rancura' against Diego López Pacheco in Chapter XXX of the *Chronicle of Dom Pedro*. As a consequence of the Castro affair, Pacheco fled to Spain, and his goods were confiscated and only restor_d to him after the death of Pedro I. He subsequently entered the service of Enrique of Trastámara when the latter returned from France after the battle of Nájera. This is how he came to be in Lisbon in 1372 as one of Enrique II's ambassadors negotiating a peace with Fernando I. King Fernando returned him as his ambassador in Castile, but he again exiled himself because he disapproved of Fernando's marriage to Leonor Teles. Thus he reverted to serving Enrique II and his role in the latter's invasion is described by Fernão Lopes. After Fernando's death he entered the service of João I and, despite his advanced years, lived to fight at the battle of Aljubarrota.

2. Juan García Manrique, as a loyal supporter of the Trastámaras, held successively the sees of Orense (1371−75), Sigüenza (1375−81), Burgos (1381−82) and Santiago (1382−98); but he then quarrelled with King Enrique III, fled to Portugal and died as Bishop

of Coimbra (1403−07). It is unclear whether the ambassador here mentioned, in late 1372, is Juan García Manrique or the then Bishop of Sigüenza, Juan, ex−abbot of Salas.

3.   João Afonso Telo de Meneses, brother of Queen Leonor, became Admiral of the Portuguese fleet in 1380 with disastrous results. He succeeded his uncle, also called João Afonso Telo de Meneses, as Count of Barcelos in 1382. After the Lisbon rising he was rewarded by Juan I for his adhesion to the Castilian cause with the County of Mayorga (1384). He was killed at Aljubarrota fighting on the Castilian side. There is an obvious irony in the fact that after the great battle, none other than Nun' Álvares Pereira himself succeeded to the now vacant Countship of Barcelos (8 October 1385).

4.   The Treaty of Alcoutim, of 31 March 1371, was published by the Visconde de Santarém, *Corpo Diplomático Português*, (Paris 1846) vol I, pp. 336−347.

Chapter LXIX: 1.   Fernán Alfonso de Zamora seized Viana del Bollo in Galicia, and used it as a base for raiding the neighbouring countryside, according to Ayala, p. 14.

Chapter LXX: 1.   It was traditionally believed that Judas was red−haired, and that red−haired men were likely to be traitors.

Chapter LXXXII: 1.   Guy de Boulogne (c.1313−74) was the son of Count Robert VII of Boulogne, and with his family connections and personal talent rapidly became a canon of Reims (1328), Archbishop of Lyon (1340), Cardinal−priest of Santa Cecilia (1342) and Cardinal−Bishop of Porto (1350). He carried out difficult diplomatic tasks for the papacy in Hungary (1349−50), France (1353−54), Castile (1359−61), and Castile and Portugal (1372), adopting policies which varied between neutrality and covert support for the Valois and their allies, including Aragon and the Trastámaras.

2.   1 March 1373 was in fact Shrove Tuesday.

3.   Afonso Correia was Bishop of Guarda from 1364 until 1384, when as a supporter of the claims of Clement VII and Juan I, he fled to Castile where he was compensated with the bishopric of Segovia (1394) until his death (1398).

4.   For the Treaty of Santarém, of 19 March 1373, see P.E. Russell, 'Fernão Lopes e o tratado de Santarém', *Revista Portuguesa de História* 5(1951), 455−73.

5.   Ayala, p. 16, says five galleys, though he does not specify that they were to be paid by Fernando.

6.   Ayala, p. 16, says that these Castilian exiles numbered up to five hundred.

7.   Ayala, p. 17, mentions as part of the agreement proposed marriages between Enrique II's bastard, Fadrique, and Fernando I's legitimate daughter Beatriz; and between Enrique's bastard Count Alfonso of Noreña and Fernando's illegitimate daughter Isabel, who

was to bring with her as her dowry the towns of Viseu, Celorico de Beira and Linhares.

8.   Lançarote Pessanha was the son of the Genoese sailor Emanuele Pessagno whom King Dinis appointed Grand Admiral of Portugal in 1307, and whose descendants normally held the post until the seventeenth century.   Lançarote refused to attack the Castilian fleet in the Tagus estuary in 1373; and in consequence, King Fernando dismissed him and appointed his brother—in—law, João Afonso Telo as Admiral instead.

Chapter CXV: 1.   Edmund of Langley (1341—1402), leader of the English expedition described in detail by Fernão Lopes in chapters CXXVIII to CLVI, was the fifth son of Edward III, Earl of Cambridge (1362) and Duke of York (1385).

2.   In mid—June 1380, according to Russell, p. 298.

3.   Leonor Teles de Meneses, Queen of Portugal, was born in Trás—os—Montes (c.1350)).   Her father was Martim Afonso Telo de Meneses and her uncle, João Afonso, first Count of Barcelos. Married at a very young age to a noble from Beira, she became a lady—in—waiting in the train of Princess Beatriz.   This brought her to court in 1370.   The story of how Dona Leonor's first marriage was annulled so that Fernando could marry her in the teeth of considerable opposition is, of course, narrated vividly by Fernão Lopes. By the time of her liaison with Juan Fernández Andeiro, her ascendancy over the King appears to have been total.   After Fernando's death she ruled Portugal as Regent; but faced with the rising power of João de Avis, she invited the Castilians into Portugal and paid the penalty by being made King Juan's captive.   She died at the nunnery of Santa Clara in Tordesillas on 27 April 1386.

4.   Fernando renewed his alliance with England on 15 July 1380 (Russell, p. 298; Rymer VII, pp.262—65).

Chapter CXXVIII: 1.   Edward, future Earl of Rutland (1390—1415), and Duke of Aumale (1397—99).

2.   On 17 June 1380 a Castilian fleet under Fernán Sánchez de Tovar routed a Portuguese galley—fleet under João Afonso Telo at Saltes in the estuary of the River Odiel.   The action is described in chapter CXXIV.

3.   A small port near Figueira da Foz.

4.   Sir John de Southeray (c.1364—c.1383), bastard son of Edward III and Alice Perrers, was knighted and married (1377), and received a £100 annuity from the Exchequer.   In the summer of 1382 he led a mutiny of English troops at Vila Viçosa which Cambridge could not suppress, and Fernando had to buy off; but he was not among the mutineers arrested on their return to England.

5.   The youngest son of Thomas Beauchamp, Earl of Warwick, he fought at Nájera, Limoges and elsewhere, became lord of Abergavenny and died in 1411.

6.   Sir Mathew Gournay (c.1310−1406) fought on the English side at Sluys, Crécy, Poitiers and Nájera, defended Bayonne against Enrique II (1378) served as Constable in Gaunt's expedition to Castile (1386−87) and eventually became a member of the House of Lords.

7.   Elie de Latrau, nicknamed 'the Sultan' (*soudan*), came from Latrau, in the Gironde, and fought under the Black Prince at Nájera and elsewhere.

8.   Sir Thomas Symond was one of the many knights receiving an annuity at this time from John of Gaunt.

9.   Juan Gutiérrez, Dean of Segovia, was the most important cleric loyal to the *petrista* cause.   He went into exile with Pedro the Cruel, and remained attached to the latter's daughter Constanza and to Gaunt whom he served as Castilian secretary.   He was rewarded with the Gascon bishopric of Dax (1380−93).

10.   Thierry de Robersart, nicknamed 'the Canon', was a knight from Hainault who came to England with Edward III's queen, Philippa of Hainault, and fought thenceforward on the English side in many battles in France and Spain.

11.   A knight of Gaunt's retinue receiving an annuity from him at this time.

12.   Possibly the Sir John Hastings (c.1328−93) whose brother Sir Hugh Hastings took part in the Nájera campaign, and whose nephew, also Sir Hugh Hastings, fought in Gaunt's invasion of Castile in 1386.   Clearly the family had a tradition of fighting in Spain.

13.   Chico Novell, like Garro and Botareos, has eluded identification.

14.   A Poitevin knight of Gaunt's retinue, who was killed in the 1386 invasion of León.

15.   Raymond−Bernard, lord of the Gascon village of Castelnau−'Tursan, near Saint−Sever.

Chapter CXXIX: 1. Santa Maria de Escada was a statue of Our Lady in a chapel which, although next to the high altar of the Dominican conventual church, was approached by a separate entrance and a long staircase, whence its name, since *escada* means 'staircase' in Portuguese.

Chapter CXXX: 1.   Urban VI (1378−89) was elected Pope on 8 April 1378; but on 20 September 1378 some dissident cardinals elected Cardinal Robert of Geneva as Pope Clement VII (1378−94), thus beginning the Great Western Schism.   Clement, based in Avignon, was supported by France and its allies, while Urban, in Rome, was supported by England and most other countries.   The Iberian kingdoms began as neutrals, but then recognized Clement: Portugal in January 1380, Castile on 19 May 1381, and Aragon and Navarre in 1387.   The latter three kingdoms remained loyal to Clement, but Portugal, as explained here, changed its allegiance on 29 August 1380 in conformity with its English allies.

2.   The feast of the decapitation of St. John the Baptist is celebrated on 29, not 19, of August. Has Fernão Lopes mis—read 'XXIX' in his source as 'XIX'?

3.   Lourenço Vicente (1374—97).

4.   Martín was a Castilian cleric who had become Bishop of Silves (1373—79) and then Lisbon (1379—83), to which he had been appointed by Clement VII. He naturally supported Clement in the Schism, and the pro—Castilian party at the Portuguese court, and he was murdered by a nationalistic Lisbon mob on 6 December 1383, seventeen days before Clement VII, not knowing of his death, appointed him a cardinal.

Chapter CXXXI: 1.   Dom João was the son of Pedro I of Portugal and his mistress Inés de Castro, and although of doubtful legitimacy, a possible threat to his half—brother King Fernando. He fled to Castile in 1380 and remained there thenceforward, serving the Trastámaras. When Fernando died (1383), João was at once imprisoned by Juan I of Castile who rightly considered him a more popular candidate for the Portuguese throne; but it was another half—brother João, the Master of Avis, who in fact became King in Lisbon, and Prince João settled down as a magnate in Castile. For his biography, see Arnaut, *passim*.

2.   Diego Martínez was Master of the Military Order of Alcántara from c.1375 to 1383.

3.   Ayala, pp. 75—76.

4.   Almeida.

Chapter CXXXII: 1.   Vila Viçosa, Borba, Monsaraz, Redondo and the other towns mentioned in this paragraph lie within Portugal but near to the River Guadiana which formed the frontier with Castile.

Chapter CXXXIII: 1.   Fernán Sánchez de Tovar appears in Castilian royal documents as Grand Admiral (*almirante mayor del mar*) c.1379—c.1383. See Chapter CXXVIII, note 2.

Chapter CXXXVI: 1.   Matt. XXV, 14—30.

2.   Pedro Álvares was one of the thirty—two illegitimate children of Álvaro Gonçalves Pereira, whom he succeeded as Prior of the Portuguese Hospitallers. Like most Portuguese nobles he served Fernando I loyally until the latter's death, and then transferred his loyalties to Juan I, although this meant losing his priorate.   In compensation, Don Juan made him Master of Calatrava (1384—85), but he died at Aljubarrota fighting on the opposite side to Nun'Álvares, his brother, the great Constable of João I.

3.   Nun'Álvares Pereira (1360—1431), João I's great Constable, called *O Santo Comdestabre* (The Saintly Constable), was born in Bonjardim, near Sertã.   He was an illegitimate son of Álvaro Gonçalves Pereira, head (Prior) of the Portuguese branch of the

military Order of the Hospitallers of St. John. As Fernão Lopes tells us, he rose to prominence as a forceful and effective captain when still a very young man and was Constable of the kingdom at the age of twenty—four. He adhered to the cause of João of Avis from the first; and despite a number of differences of opinion with his master, remained his faithful lieutenant long after the great victories of Trancoso, Os Atoleiros, Aljubarrota and Valverde in the years 1384—85. To the *Comdestabre* is attributed the introduction into the Portuguese army of the 'new' battle—field tactics that had been perfected by the English armies in the Hundred Years' War and of which we make mention in our Introduction. The great Constable continued to campaign through the nineties when the Castilian threat was renewed; and he supported the Ceuta Expedition (1415). Dom João showered him with honours and lands. He became Count of Ourém, Barcelos and Arraiolos. His line married into the Royal House of Avis when his daughter Beatriz married Dom Afonso, illegitimate son of João I. In his old age the *Comdestabre* founded a Carmelite House in Lisbon and entered the Order himself in 1423. Nun'Álvares Pereira, Constable of Portugal, died on 1 April 1431, and was beatified in 1918.

Chapter CXXXVII: 1.   Santos was the chief nunnery of the Portuguese military Order of São Tiago.

Chapter CXXXIX: 1. After Inês de Castro's murder, Pedro I never re—married but had several mistresses only one of whom, the Galician Teresa Lorenzo, bore him a son. The latter, João (1358—1433) was educated by a Lisbon citizen and by Nuno Freire de Andrade, Master of the military Order of Christ (as Fernão Lopes explains in *Dom Pedro*, chapter XLIII). At the age of seven, his father had him appointed Master of the Order of Avis; and later had him educated at Court with his half—brothers, Princes João and Dinis, of whom he became a close friend.

2.   Gonçalo Vasques de Azevedo had been private secretary to Pedro I, and became lord of Torres Vedras and Governor of Santarém. He married Inês Afonso, a lady—in—waiting to Queen Leonor, which is how he first enters the *Chronicle of Dom Fernando*. He is a not inconsiderable figure in the Chronicle of Fernão Lopes, but little is known about him. Although he appears in these tense chapters of *Dom Fernando* as a persecuted comrade—in—arms of the Master of Avis, later, as *The Chronicle of Dom João I, Part I* makes clear, his behaviour will prove more equivocal politically. During the crisis of 1383—85, he vacillated, inclining towards the Queen and Castile. Fernão Lopes depicts the weakness and lack of commitment in this man with a 'womanish heart' (*Dom João, I*, chapter CLV). Once in Castile, King Juan showed him favour, bestowing upon him the office of *adelantado—mayor* (head of the local administration) of Old Castile. He died at Aljubarrota, fighting on

the Castilian side.

3.   Aristotle, *Posterior Analytics*, Book II, chapter 11.

4.   Afonso IV of Portugal (1325–57) fought alongside Alfonso XI of Castile at the battle of the River Salado (1340), in which they decisively defeated the Moslem Kingdoms of Morocco and Granada. This was the only notable Portuguese battle on land against the Moslems between 1250 and 1415, and therefore sufficient to identify Afonso IV by the phrase in the text.

Chapter CXLVI: 1. As in the case of Gonçalo Vasques de Azevedo, here is a man who figures prominently in the Chronicle, especially in *Dom João*, but about whom virtually nothing is known outside the pages of Fernão Lopes. He was, in effect, second in command in the Order of Avis, and consequently, very close to Dom João; but as Fernão Lopes indicates here in *Dom Fernando*, Porcalho was no supporter of the Master even when he was only the Master. His name appears far more frequently in *Dom João* where, in the face of the Master's confidence in him, he proves to be not only hostile but also a traitor within the Avis camp. Having finally gone over to the Castilian cause, he fled to Castile after King Juan's defeat.

Chapter CXLVII: 1. João's gratitude may well have encouraged him later to look to England for refuge and support. His determination to flee to England in particular is stressed by Fernão Lopes at the beginning of the *Chronicle of Dom João I, Part I*.

Chapter CXLVIII: 1. A shrine some six kilometers from Avis.

Chapter CXLIX: 1. For Edward III's bastard and the other commanders, see the notes to Chapter CXXVIII.

2.   Sir John Falconer was one of Gaunt's leading retainers who fought in his expeditions to Scotland (1384) and Castile (1387). In contrast, Sir Roger Othiquiniente remains unidentified.

Chapter CLII: 1. Ayala, who is the main source for this chapter, states on p. 77 that Juan I appointed two marshals, Fernán Alvárez de Toledo and also Pedro Rodríguez Sarmiento.

Chapter CLIII: 1. Caia is a hamlet, now the frontier–post, halfway between Elvas and Badajoz.

2.   Note that the English show themselves to be sticklers for the rules of chivalry, and that the Portuguese defer to them.

3.   Presumably Sir Thomas Symond.

Chapter CLIV: 1. Lopes's summary of this Treaty of Badajoz is largely translated from Ayala, p. 78, though Ayala does not include the promise that Castile would hand back Almeida and Miranda do Douro. Lopes may have taken this clause from the treaty itself, of

which no copy seems to have survived, though the revised versions of 1382−83 are published by Arnaut, *docs.* 23,26.

Chapter CLVI: 1. Pedro de Luna (1328−1423) was an Aragonese noble who, after fighting at Nájera on the Trastamaran side, became a cleric and Cardinal of Santa Maria in Cosmedin. As Clement VII's main agent in Spain he won the support of Castile, Aragon and Navarre; and he was elected Clement's successor as Pope Benedict XIII (1394−1423).

2.   Dr Gil do Sem was a doctor of laws and counsellor to both King Fernando and King João I.

3.   Rui Lourenço was a licentiate in canon law and bachelor in civil law, and also counsellor to the Kings, Fernando I and João I.

4.   João das Regras (c.1340−1404) was a married cleric whose real name was João de Aregas. Born into a noble family whose line can be traced back to the reign of Afonso II, he studied at Bologna where he obtained a doctorate in civil law. He is considered responsible for introducing Roman Law into Portugal. On his return from Italy in 1382, he became Rector of Lisbon University and it is at this point that he enters the Chronicle of Fernão Lopes. He failed to prevent Dom Fernando from swearing loyalty to the Avignonese Pope, Clement VII; and on the death of Dom Fernando sided with the pro−Avis faction in 1383. He became Dom João's Grand Chancellor soon after and had his finest hour at the Cortes of Coimbra in April of 1385 where his clever arguments in favour of the Master of Avis prevailed over the opinions of the anti−Avis nobles there present. All this is described in the closing chapters of the *Chronicle of Dom João I, Part I*. He remained Grand Chancellor until his death. His mother was married twice; the second time to none other than Álvaro Pais, the most celebrated and arguably most important leader of the Lisbon rising of 1383. It was in this man's house that João das Regras received his early education.

CHRONICLE OF DOM JOÃO: PART I

Prologue 1.   Cicero, *De finibus bonorum et malorum*, edited by
H. Rackham,
(London, 1971), Book II, chapter 14.

Chapter XXI   1.   Atouguia, or to give it its full name, Atouguia
da Baleia (Atouguia of the Whale), is a small town some four miles
from Peniche.   Of scant importance today, its appearance in *Dom
João I, Part I* where it is clearly being used to designate a
considerable length of the Portuguese coastline above Sintra, gives
some indication of its significance in the later Middle Ages.   Precisely
during the reigns of Pedro I and Fernando I it was a port of
considerable importance.

Chapter XLVII   1.   Thomas Daniel was a Bristol merchant who
exported cloth and other merchandise to Portugal and elsewhere in the
Iberian Peninsula in the years 1378–82.   João I's lack of upper–class
support in 1383 is indicated by his need to employ as ambassadors a
mere squire, Lourenço Martins, and a foreign merchant like Daniel.
2.   Fernando Afonso de Albuquerque, bastard son of Juan
Alfonso de Albuquerque, had become Master of the Portuguese
Military Order of São Tiago and, as a protégé of Queen Leonor, had
followed her in her flight from Lisbon to Alenquer at the end of
1383.   He then retired to his Order's chief fortress at Palmela,
decided to change sides and appeared in Lisbon to become the vassal
of João of Avis, bringing with him, of course, the support of the rest
of his Order, its troops, castles and revenues.   This was a big
reinforcement for the Avis cause; but Albuquerque was clearly
mistrusted and was packed off to London.   There he ran up great
debts with London merchants, dabbled in smuggling and kept an
English mistress, Laura; but he also achieved the primary goal of
negotiating the Treaty of Windsor, an achievement great enough to
cover all his peccadilloes.
3.   Lourenço Eanes Fogaça had been the Grand Chancellor of
Portugal under Fernando I; and, as an Anglophile who could speak
Norman–French, he went on several embassies to the English court.
As a loyal bureaucrat he supported Queen Leonor after Fernando I's
death, but he was alienated by Juan I, and in March 1384 he joined
João of Avis, who re–appointed him Grand Chancellor and
immediately sent him to England where he negotiated the Treaty of
Windsor, returning to Portugal in July 1386.
4.   Parliament met in Salisbury on 29 April 1384.   Meanwhile,
Gaunt had been in Calais negotiating the truce of Leulinghen with the
French (26 January), and in Scotland fighting the Scots for most of
April.   He returned to Salisbury in May, when the Portuguese
ambassadors laid their proposals before Richard II's council.
5.   For these men, see Russell, p. 373.

6.   These names seem to refer to Nicholas Brembre, Lord Mayor of London from 1383, and Sir Henry Green. On loans and recruitment, see Russell, pp. 364–73.

CHRONICLE OF DOM JOÃO: PART II

Chapter LXXIX 1.   A copyist's error, no doubt, for 31 March 1384.

2.   P.R.O. Exchequer. Diplomatic Documents, no. E30/307, dated Coimbra 15 April 1385.

3.   João III Eanes, Bishop of Evora (1384–1404), had been one of the bishops present at the Cortes of Coimbra which elected João of Avis as king.

4.   This is a loose and abbreviated translation of the Latin original, which is published by A. Domingues de Sousa Costa, O.F.M. in *Monumenta Portugaliae Vaticana*, Vol.II (Braga, 1970), pp. cv–cvii.

Chapter LXXX 1.   João I routed Juan I of Castile at Aljubarrota on 14 August 1385, so the news of his victory probably reached Richard II about ten days later.

Chapter LXXXI 1.   Parliament opened in October 1385, and discussed Iberian affairs in November.

2.   Sir John Clanvow, a knight of the King's Chamber and royal diplomat, and Sir Richard Abberbury, one of Gaunt's retinue who was included in the committee presumably in order to watch over the Duke's interests.

3.   Master Richard Ronhale.

4.   Sir William Par took the message, leaving England in mid–January 1386 and presumably arriving at Chaves half–way through the siege, which lasted from late December until the end of March.

Chapter LXXXII 1.   The Treaty was made at Windsor on 9 May 1386, approved at Westminster on 17 May 1386 and confirmed by João I at Coimbra on 12 August 1387. It is published by Rymer, Vol. III, pp.200–203.

2.   Edmund of Langley, q.v. above, *Chronicle of Dom Fernando, passim.*

3.   Richard II's brother–in–law, Wenceslas of Luxemburg, who though elected King of the Romans (1378–1400) was never crowned Holy Roman Emperor and was eventually deposed.

Chapter LXXXIII   1.   On the preparations and voyage, see Russell, pp. 406–20.

2.   Sir John Holland (c.1352–1400) was a son of Joan, Countess

of Kent (1328—85) by her first husband, Sir Thomas Holland.   After the latter's death (1360) she married the Black Prince (1361) to whom she bore the future Richard II.   Sir John was a violent man, but his status as the King's half—brother allowed him to escape punishment for his crimes, and he became Earl of Huntingdon (1387—1400) and Duke of Exeter (1397—99) before being beheaded for plotting against Henry IV.

3.   Elizabeth (1364—1426) was one of Gaunt's daughters by his first wife, Blanche.   Though betrothed in 1380 to the eight year—old John Hastings, Earl of Pembroke, she was seduced, made pregnant and quickly married in early 1386 by Sir John Holland.

4.   Roger de Scales (c.1350—86) inherited the lands and title of Lord Scales from his father Robert de Scales, when the latter died in 1369.   He himself died of disease in Spain on 25 December 1386 and was succeeded by his own son, Robert.

5.   Richard, Lord Poynings (c.1355—87) was the son of Sir Michael de Poynings, a Sussex knight, and brother and heir of Thomas, Lord Poynings (1349—75).   Knighted in 1377, he followed Gaunt only to die of disease at Villalpando on 25 May 1387.

6.   Sir Hugh Hastings, son and heir of the Sir Hugh Hastings (c.1335—69) who had fought at Nájera, served on the Breton expeditions and followed Gaunt only to die of disease on 6 November 1386.

7.   Could this be Henry, Lord Ferrers of Groby (1356—88)? It is clearly not Sir John Ferrers of Chartley (1331—67) who was slain at Nájera.

8.   Sir Richard Burley was a knight of Gaunt's retinue, receiving annuities from him at least since 1372 and serving as constable for life of Gaunt's castle of Kidwelly.

9.   Sir Thomas Percy the Younger (c.1365—87) was the younger son of Henry Percy, first Earl of Northumberland (1342—1408) and his first wife Elizabeth Neville.   He married Elizabeth, daughter of David, Earl of Atholl, and died in Spain in March 1387, leaving a son and heir, Henry.

10.   Sir Baldwin de Frevill was a leading Warwickshire knight in the 1380's.

Chapter LXXXIV   1.   Juan Serrano was the Chancellor of the Privy Seal of Juan I, prior of the monastery of Guadalupe (c.1382—88), and Bishop of Segovia (1388—89) and Sigüenza (1389—1402).   He died in 1402, apparently poisoned by a rival candidate for the archbishopric of Seville.

Chapter LXXXV 1.   Alfonso X (1252—84).
2.   Fernando III (1217—52).
3.   Fernando de la Cerda (1255—75).
4.   Sancho IV (1284—95).
5.   Fernando IV (1295—1312).

6.   Alfonso XI (1312—50).

7.   Enrique II's wife, Juana Manuel, was the daughter of the great magnate and writer, Juan Manuel (see *Conde Lucanor* in this series), by his wife Blanca Núñez de la Cerda, who in her turn was the daughter of Fernando, younger son of Prince Fernando de la Cerda.

Chapter LXXXVI   1.   Juan Gutiérrez, Bishop of Dax (1380—93). See the *Chronicle of Dom Fernando*, chapter cxxviii, note 9.

Chapter LXXXVII   1.   The summary which follows of Castilian history in the period 1252—1369 is accurate, as can be seen from a comparison with, say, J.F. O'Callaghan, *A History of Medieval Spain* (Ithaca—London, 1975), Part IV, though it shares the bias against Alfonso X already shown by the official chronicle of his reign.

2.   Prince Alfonso, Pedro I's son and heir by María de Padilla, was born in 1359 and died in 1362.

3.   Ayala, p.114.

Chapter LXXXVIII   1.   Clearly Edward III by modern reckoning. Either this is a copyist's mistake or, possibly, Fernão Lopes is counting from Edward the Confessor (1042—66).   Edward III's wife was, of course, called Philippa, not Isabel.

2.   In 1359 Gaunt married Blanche, the younger of the two daughters and co—heiresses of Henry, Duke of Lancaster.   Henry died in 1361, and his elder daughter soon afterwards, so that Blanche and Gaunt inherited everything.

3.   i.e. Henry IV (1399—1413), Henry V (1413—22) and Henry VI (1422—61, 1470—71).

Chapter LXXXIX   1.   Gaunt, born in 1340, was only forty—six years old in 1386.

2.   Possibly Juan Gutiérrez, Gaunt's loyal Castilian cleric.

Chapter XCI   1.   One of Fernando I's trusted officers, he took Princess Beatriz to Castile to marry Juan I, but refused to proclaim the latter as King of Portugal when Fernando died.   When Leonor quarrelled with Juan I, Melo joined João of Avis, as did his son, of the same name, who died at Aljubarrota.

Chapter XCII   1.   The river to which Fernão Lopes refers in this passage is, of course, the Minho.

2.   Aljubarrota.

Chapter XCIII   1.   The terms of the Treaty of Ponte de Mouro seem to be known only from this summary.   The surrender of so much Castilian territory to Portugal would in theory make it easier to defend Lisbon; it would certainly discourage Castilians from supporting

the Lancastrian claim to the throne.

2.   The Order of Santiago owned at least Alcuéscar, Medina de las Torres, Cañaveral and Fuente del Maestre; and the Order of Alcántara owned at least Alcántara and Valencia de Alcántara.

Chapter XCIV   1.   There were two main stages in the obtaining of favours from the papal chancery.   Firstly, the petitioner would present a written request or list of requests (*rotulus supplicationum*) to the Pope, who would indicate which ones he was willing to grant by writing the word *fiat* in the margin.   Secondly, the petitioner had to get the papal chancery clerks to issue a formal document, a papal bull, legally granting the requests which the Pope had approved. João I's ambassadors easily achieved the first stage, under Urban VI, but then had considerable difficulty in the second, until the election of a new pope, Boniface IX (1389—1404).   Surviving Portuguese petitions of this period are being published by A. Domingues de Sousa Costa, *Monumenta Portugaliae Vaticana*, (Braga, in several volumes beginning in 1968).

2.   Lourenço Vicente, Archbishop of Braga (1373—98?), supported the Roman side in the papal schism, as well as João of Avis and the English alliance.

3.   i.e. Nun'Álvares Pereira.

Chapter XCV   1.   In the later middle ages, Christians normally got married in two successive ceremonies, the betrothal and the wedding, which might be separated by weeks or even years, but both of which ought normally to have been celebrated publicly in church. Since neither was normally allowed during Lent, a time of sorrow and penance, João I tried to hold both ceremonies as quickly as possible before Lent began on Wednesday 20 February 1387.

Chapter XCVI   1.   Although most of the diocese of Ciudad Rodrigo was in Castile, accepted Clement VII as pope and had a Clementist bishop, the western part of the diocese was in Portugal, accepted Urban VI as pope and had Fray Rodrigo as its bishop.   He was present at the Cortes of Coimbra which elected João of Avis as king, presided at his wedding and was later rewarded with the commendatory abbacy of São Vicente de Fora, in Lisbon.   It is, nevertheless, a little odd that he presided at the wedding rather than João III, Bishop of Oporto (1373—89).

Chapter XCVIII   1.   The Use of Sarum was a local modification of the Roman liturgy used in Salisbury, compiled there in the early thirteenth century and gradually adopted in the next two centuries by most churches in England, Wales and Ireland; in content, arrangement and music it followed the basic Gregorian model, but with post—1066 French accretions.

Chapter XCIX   1.   Possibly São Julião.

Chapter C   1.   Possibly Peso de Regoa, or Rego da Barca.

2.   Gonçalo Vasques, son of Vasco Martins de Melo, had been governor of Évora, Olivenza and Campo Maior, had fought at Aljubarrota and would eventually (1415) participate in the conquest of Ceuta.

3.   Among them, of course, Lord Scales, who had died on Christmas Day.

4.   Palm Sunday was on 31 March in 1387.

5.   Álvaro Gonçalves Camelo.

6.   Lopo Dias de Sousa.

Chapter CI   1.   Villalpando is twenty—six kilometers to the south—east of Benavente, Valencia de Don Juan thirty—five to the north, and Castroverde thirty to the east.

2.   Sir Robert de Bracquemont was a Norman knight who commanded some of the French troops sent to defend Galicia in 1386. In 1387 he withdrew to the Leonese region, where he helped defend Benavente and Valderas and also jousted with Mauburney.   Later he was among the witnesses of the Franco—Castilian treaty of 1390; he served Charles VI of France as ambassador to Castile (1408), and as Chamberlain and Admiral; and in 1419 he commanded a Franco—Castilian fleet in naval operations against the English.   His family settled in Castile and gave their name to the town of Peñaranda de Bracamonte, near Salamanca.

Chapter CII   1.   7 April 1387.

Chapter CV   1.   San Millán de los Caballeros.

2.   Alfonso Enríquez, Admiral of Castile (1354—1429) was the bastard son of Enrique II's brother, Fadrique.

Chapter CVI   1.   This is probably not the whole story. Despite the surrender by Sancho de Velasco, the three hundred and eighty—seven citizens of Valderas rejected the conditions, burnt their grain and other foodstuffs, poured their wine stocks away and fled, leaving practically nothing for the victors.   The story is told in a charter issued by Juan I on 3 June 1387; and it demonstrates how little support Gaunt could hope for in the heartland of Castile.   See L. Suárez Fernández, *Historia del reinado de Juan I de Castilla*, Vol I (Madrid, 1977), p. 266.

Chapter CVIII   1.   The River Cea.

2.   Martim Gonçalves de Ataíde had been a loyal vassal of Juan Fernández Andeiro, and after the latter had been assassinated by João of Avis, he supported Juan I's claim to the Portuguese throne, defending Chaves as long as he could against Avis's siege, and then

continuing to serve Juan I in Castile.

Chapter CIX   1.   Olivier du Guesclin, brother of Bertrand du Guesclin.

Chapter CXI   1.   Santa María del Viso was a sanctuary containing a life−size statue of Our Lady, on the Viso hill, near to Madridanos on the south bank of the River Douro.
    2.   Lorenzo Suárez de Figueroa, Master of the Order of Santiago (1387−1409).

Chapter CXII   1.   Possibly near Golpejas, according to Russell, p. 482.
    2.   A son of Mathieu de Roye, probably from Roye near Montdidier. Gaunt granted him and his fellow knights a safe−conduct for jousting, valid from Monday to Saturday; the date is not stated, but Russell, p. 483, suggests 20 to 25 May 1387. See E.C. Lodge & R. Somerville, *John of Gaunt's Register, 1379−1383*, 2 vols (London, 1937), II, no. 1233.

Chapter CXIII   1.   Martim Eanes de Barbuda had been a commander in the Order of Avis, under João's Mastership, but had abandoned him to support Juan I, fighting for the latter in the battles of Os Atoleiros and Aljubarrota. Juan rewarded him with the rather empty title of Master of Avis, and then (1385−94) with the more solid position of Master of the Military Order of Alcántara.

Chapter CXVI   1.   Near Oliveira de Azemeis.

Chapter CXVII   1.   Clearly a middle−aged member of a military order, who may well have been inspired by the story of the owls and the crows, written by Juan I's grandfather, Juan Manuel (see *Conde Lucanor* in this series).

Chapter CXVIII   1.   Ayala, p. 117.
    2.   Possibly Carrazedo de Monte Negro, twenty−eight kilometers south of Chaves.

Chapter CXIX   1.   A Franciscan friar, and Master in Theology, he was Juan I's confessor, and acted as his ambassador to Avignon, Rome, Naples, Navarre and Portugal.
    2.   The texts of the Treaty of Bayonne, concluded in July 1388, and of the preliminary agreements at Trancoso in June−July 1387, have hitherto been known only from the summaries in Lopes and Ayala; however their full texts have now been discovered and published in the series of Exeter hispanic Texts, *The Treaty of Bayonne (1388) with the Preliminary Treaties of Trancoso*, (Exeter, 1988) by Dr John Palmer and Dr Brian Powell, to whom we are

sincerely grateful for allowing us to see their work in typescript. It is clear that Ayala and Lopes give accurate summaries of the negotiations and final agreement.

Chapter CXX 1. In St. Antolín's cathedral, probably on 14 September 1388, by Pedro Alvárez de Albornoz, Archbishop of Seville (1379—90).
2. In November 1388.

Chapter CXXI 1. Pedro Fernández de Frías, Bishop of Osma (1379—94).
2. Presumably early in 1389.
3. Clearly this is untrue: the Black Prince's support for Pedro I was the result, not the cause, of Charles V's support for Enrique II. The whole of the Castilian response to Gaunt's requests shows how clearly Ayala understood the importance of the Franco—Castilian alliance, and how little Gaunt's expedition had done to weaken it.

Chapter CXXII 1. This was in early December 1388.

Chapter CXXIV 1. João Afonso de Azambuja went on to a most successful clerical career: Bishop of Silves (1389—91), Oporto (1391—98) and Coimbra (1398—1402), Archbishop of Lisbon (1402—11) and Cardinal (1411—15).
2. Urban VI died on 15 October 1389; Boniface IX was elected on 2 November 1389 and died on 1 October 1404.
3. João Eanes, Bishop of Lisbon (1383—1402) and João, Bishop of Oporto (1373—89).

Chapter CXXV 1. This papal bull and the following one were dated in St. Peter's, Rome, on 28 and 27 January 1391, respectively, and published by A. Domingues de Sousa Costa, *Monumenta Portugaliae Vaticana*, Vol II (Braga, 1970), cxii—cxv, cviii—cxi. A comparison with these originals shows Lopes to have translated their gist quite accurately, although with certain omissions, mainly of redundant phrases.

INDEX OF NAMES

360

261−73, 287, 291, 293, 299−305, 317, 323, 338−42, 344−48, 354, 355
Castrocalbón, 247
Castro de Avelãs, 239
Castro Urdiales, 3, 17−31
Castroverde, 245, 273, 354
Catalina, daughter of Enrique III, 332
Catalonia, xxiii
Catherine, daughter of John of Gaunt, 187, 209, 219, 271, 287, 299−303, 328, 331, 332
Cea, River, 354
Celanova, 219, 227
Celorico de Beira, 55, 343
Ceuta, ix, xxix, 346, 354
Chandos Herald, xxv
Channel Isles, xvi
Charles IV, King of France, x
Charles V, King of France, xv, xvi, 9, 305, 339, 356
Charles VI, King of France, 71, 171, 181, 269, 277, 283, 338, 354
Chaves, 181, 189, 193, 297, 350, 354, 355
Cheshire, 339
Chester, 13, 15
Chico Novell, 67, 344
Christ, xxx, 177, 317; Order of, xxiii; Master of, see Lopo Dias de Sousa
Christopherus, Dr, viii
Chronica Gothorum, vii
Chronicon Conimbricense, vi
Cicero, 157, 349
Ciudad Rodrigo, 36, 51, 179, 275, 279, 353
Claquin, 337
Clement VII, Pope, xviii, xix, 58, 69, 71, 151, 161, 213, 319, 323, 327, 342, 344, 345, 348, 353
Clisson, 339
Coelho, A. Borges, xxix
Coimbra, vi, 33, 48, 151, 176, 178, 181, 183, 185, 241, 287, 291, 330, 344, 348, 350, 353; Bishop of, see João Afonso Esteves de Azambuja
Constanza, daughter of Pedro I of Castile, xiii, xvii, 37, 75, 139, 185−89, 197−203, 207−13, 225, 227, 233, 239, 241, 243, 283, 287, 291, 299−305, 309, 311, 331, 337, 344
Constanza Manuel, xix
Córdoba, xii, 31−34, 39, 341
Coria, 215, 241
Cornwall, 13, 15, 193
Coroniqua de como Dom Payo Corea Mestre de Santiago de Castela tomou este reino do Algarve aos moros, vii
Corrales, 275, 291
Cortijo, 125,127
Corunna, 59, 81, 195, 199, 213, 215, 241, 245
Couna, River, 85,
Coutances, 337

Crato, xxiii, 175
Crécy, xii, 337, 344
Cressyngham, 171
Crónica da Tomada de Ceuta, ix
Crónica do Comdestabre or *Condestável*, viii
Crónica dos Cinco Reis, viii
Crónica dos Sete Reis, viii
Crónica Geral de Espanha, vii
Curval, 287

Damião de Góis, ix, x
Dartmouth, xvi
David, Earl of Atholl, 351
Dax, Bishop of, See Juan Gutiérrez
Denia, Count of, see Alfonso
Derby, Earl of, see Henry IV
Derbyshire, 337
Deza, 287, 299, 307
Diego Alfonso de Carvajal, 53
Diego Fernández, 33
Diego Fernández de Aguilar, 149
Diego García de Padilla, xxiii, 338
Diego Hurtado de Mendoza, 149
Diego López de Angul, 275, 277
Diego López Medrano, 197, 199, 203
Diego López Pacheco, 37, 39, 49, 55, 176, 241, 332, 341
Diego Martínez, Master of Alcántara, 73, 345
Diego Sánchez de Torres, 53
Dinis, King of Portugal, vii, viii, xxiii, 207, 343
Dinis, Prince, son of Pedro I of Portugal and Inés de Castro, xix, 37, 55, 178, 328, 330, 346
Diogo Álvares, 87, 95
Diogo Peres de Avelar, 263
Douro, River, 227, 241, 275, 355
Duarte I, King of Portugal, vi, xxix, xxx, 330, 332
Duarte Galvão, viii
Dublin, xx

Ebro, River, 7, 13
Edmund of Langley, Earl of Cambridge and Duke of York, xvii, xviii, xxvi, xxx, 59−71, 81, 83, 107, 113, 119−123, 129, 135−143, 147−151, 180, 191, 211, 343, 350
Edward the Confessor, 352
Edward II, King of England, xii
Edward III, King of England, x, xi, xiii−xv, xvii, xxiv, 3, 5, 13, 25, 37, 65, 125, 139, 180, 209, 211, 305, 337, 343, 344, 347, 352
Edward, Prince of Wales, 'the Black Prince', xi, xiv−xvi, 3−31, 35, 180, 209, 211, 295, 305, 337, 339, 344, 351, 356
Edward, Earl of Rutland and Duke of Aumale, 65, 71, 141, 343
Egidio Boccanegra, 33, 340
Elias Blyth, 171

363

368

Roger Wright *(Liverpool)*
SPANISH BALLADS WITH ENGLISH VERSE TRANSLATION
The Spanish ballad tradition is one of the largest and most colourful in Europe, as reflected in this collection of seventy one of the best examples. Dr Wright's brilliantly performable verse translations closely recapture the style of the originals and make the meaning and spirit of the medieval ballad tradition come alive. His careful transcriptions of the Spanish texts and his detailed historical and linguistic notes provide a valuable insight into this splendid tradition.

TEXTS FROM ARABIC LITERATURE
THE ADVENTURES OF ANTAR An early Arabic Epic, edited by
H.T.Norris *(S.O.A.S.)*
This epic, almost unknown in Europe, is comparable with the great epics of European literature and deserves to stand beside them in esteem.

Al Jahiz
EPISTLE ON SINGING GIRLS translated and edited by A.F.L.Beeston
This epistle purports to be a defence of the practices of singing girls and their masters in 9th century Arab society. 'lucid and erudite' *J.R.A.S.*

Ibn al—Marzuban
THE SUPERIORITY OF DOGS OVER MANY OF THOSE WHO WEAR CLOTHES edited and translated by G.R.Smith & M.A.S.
Abdel Haleem
A fascinating collection of stories and poems from 10th century Baghdad. 'a rewarding work of literature' *J.R.A.S.*

MEDIEVAL LATIN TEXTS
JOSEPH OF EXETER
The Trojan War I—III edited by A.K.Bate *(Reading)*
'this accesible edition should act both as an entreé and inducement to the exploration of later Latin' *JACT Review*

THE RUODLIEB edited by C.W.Grocock
An anonymous 11th century narrative poem from Germany telling of the wanderings of a young man in search of a fortune.

WILLIAM OF NEWBURGH
The History of English Affairs I, edited by P.G.Walsh & M.Kennedy
(Glasgow)
William's *History* exemplifies the best historical writing during the High Middle Ages. This volume covers the years 1066—1154, the reign of Stephen.

Jorge de Alarcão *(Coimbra)*

ROMAN PORTUGAL

The heart of this magnificent work is the Gazetteer in which nearly 3,000 Roman sites are plotted and briefly described with their bibliography. This is the first time that any such comprehensive survey has been attempted for the country that was the heart of ancient Lusitania and spilled over into Baetica as well. Much new and often unpublished information has come to light in the course of the detailed research for this which has enabled Professor Alarcão to write a new Introduction to Roman Portugal. He begins with the history as it is recorded in the Latin and Greek sources and from the numerous archaeological finds, particularly the inscriptions. He then looks in some detail at the administration, the roads, the villas, the economy, religion and art to create a rounded picture. Appendixes list native deities, the administrative towns, pottery kilns etc.

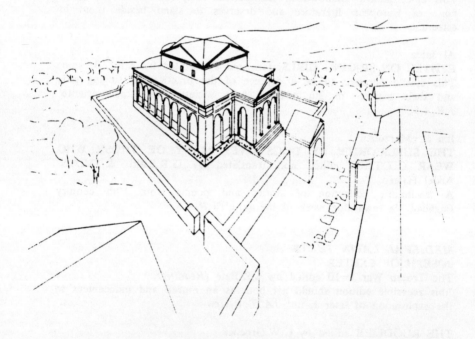

Vol I AN INTRODUCTION TO ROMAN PORTUGAL
Vol II GAZETTEER OF ROMAN PORTUGAL
Fascicle 1 Porto, Bragança & Viseu
Fascicle 2 Coimbra & Lisbon
Fascicle 3 Evora, Faro & Lagos